MICHAEL JACKSON

Also by J. Randy Taraborrelli

Call Her Miss Ross

Sinatra
The Man Behind the Myth

Jackie, Ethel, Joan
The Women of Camelot

Madonna
An Intimate Biography

Once Upon a Time
The Story of Princess Grace, Prince Rainier and Their Family

Elizabeth

Diana Ross
An Unauthorized Biography

MICHAEL JACKSON
The Magic and the Madness

J. RANDY TARABORRELLI

PAN BOOKS

First published 1991 by Birch Lane Press, New York

First published in Great Britain 1992 by Headline, London

A revised, expanded and updated hardback edition published 2003 by Sidgwick & Jackson

This updated edition published 2004 by Pan Books
an imprint of Pan Macmillan Ltd
Pan Macmillan, 20 New Wharf Road, London N1 9RR
Basingstoke and Oxford
Associated companies throughout the world
www.panmacmillan.com

ISBN 978 0 330 42005 1

A CIP catalogue record for this book is available from
the British Library.

Typeset by SX Composing DTP, Rayleigh, Essex
Printed and bound in the UK by
CPI Mackays, Chatham ME5 8TD

Visit **www.panmacmillan.com** to read more about all our books and to buy
them. You will also find features, author interviews and news of any author
events, and you can sign up for e-newsletters so that you're always first to hear
about our new releases.

This book is dedicated to all those readers of mine who have kept faith with me over the years. I thank you.

JRT

E

Why not just tell people I'm an alien from Mars. Tell them I eat live chickens and do a voodoo dance at midnight. They'll believe anything you say, because you're a reporter. But if I, Michael Jackson, were to say, 'I'm an alien from Mars and I eat live chickens and do a voodoo dance at midnight,' people would say, 'Oh, man, that Michael Jackson is *nuts*. He's cracked up. You can't believe a damn word that comes out of his mouth.'

Michael Jackson to J. Randy Taraborrelli, September 1995

J

Contents

ix

PART FIVE

PART SIX

PART SEVEN

PART EIGHT

PART NINE

PART TEN

PART ELEVEN

Prologue

I first met Michael Jackson when we were both children. The Jackson 5 had just appeared at the Philadelphia Convention Center on Saturday evening, 2 May 1970, their first performance subsequent to signing with Motown Records. It was a heady time for the boys; Michael was a very young eleven-year-old trying to come to terms with it all. I remember him then being happy, so full of life. Something happened along the way, though . . . we both grew up, but in very different ways.

When I moved to Los Angeles at the age of eighteen to begin my career as a writer, I regularly interviewed Michael for magazine features. I clearly remember the day I wrote 'Michael Jackson Turns 21.' Then, there was 'Michael Jackson Turns 25.' 'Michael Jackson Turns 30,' and so many other articles about him in celebration of milestones along the way, and those of his talented family members. As he grew older, I watched with mounting concern and confusion as Michael transformed himself from a cute little black kid to . . . what he is, today. As a journalist and frequent chronicler of Michael's life, I had somehow to make sense of what was happening, putting the pieces of the puzzle together to see how they fit in with the Michael I had known of yesteryear. Thanks to my many encounters with him, I am able to quote at first hand his intimate reactions to so much of what has taken place during his life and career.

In 1977, when I was at the Jackson home in Encino, California, to interview the family, Michael wandered into the room with bandages on his face; he was nineteen at the time. I remember being dismayed. I thought then that rumours his father, Joseph, was beating him might be true, and that bothered me for many years.

Actually, as I later learned, he had just had the second of many plastic surgeries.

In another interview, conducted after Michael had just returned from making *The Wiz* in New York in 1978, he mentioned to me that he had certain 'secrets' he didn't wish to reveal to me, adding that '*everybody* has deep, dark secrets'. I never forgot his words, especially as the years went by and he became stranger, his behaviour more opaque and incomprehensible to many people.

Why are we still so fascinated by Michael Jackson after all of this time? Is it because of his awe-inspiring talent? Of course, that's part of it. The voice is instantly recognizable, and the dance moves are his and his alone. Just as he had been influenced by trailblazers before him, such as Jackie Wilson and James Brown, he has influenced a generation of entertainers. When you watch Justin Timberlake perform, does he remind you of anyone else?

Michael is also an important touchstone for many of us, personally. Since he's been famous for more than thirty years, some of us can mark moments in our lives by certain achievements in his. Many of us are old enough to remember how impossibly adorable and prodigious he was as lead singer of The Jackson 5, and we can remember where we were at when the brothers first became famous. We may recall the first time we saw him glide across a stage or screen doing the magical 'Moonwalk'; we remember the day we first saw the 'We are the World' video, in which he led an all-star cast in the first charitable effort of its kind in the United States; we remember his amazing concert appearances and groundbreaking videos.

To say that Michael has succeeded spectacularly in his career is to state the obvious. However, as record-breaking and historical as his artistry has been, it is his private life that has kept many of us on tenterhooks.

We probably also remember the first time we saw each of his new physical 'looks', and wondered what on earth that boy was doing to his face.

Did you ever wonder if he was straight? Or gay? Or asexual?

What did you think when you first heard that he had been accused of being a paedophile?

Do you remember seeing the emotional speech from Neverland, during which he spoke of the police having photographed 'my body, including my penis, my buttocks, my lower torso, thighs and any other areas they wanted'?

And what of Lisa Marie Presley and Debbie Rowe, his mysterious ex-wives? Have you ever speculated about the true nature of their relationships with him?

Now, he has children and makes them wear masks in public.

'How does it feel when you're alone, and you're cold inside?' Michael asked in his song 'Stranger in Moscow'. Indeed, how in the world, we wonder, did he turn out as he has?

Of course, fame twists everything. It's a strange phenomenon that no one but the famous can truly understand. However, ask yourself: if your entire life had been played out under heavy and unyielding scrutiny, made even more torturous by an abusive father, what would you be like? What if you were infantilized by an adoring public who celebrated you primarily as a talented youngster? Do you think you might, over time, be compelled to infantilize yourself? Out of frustration and desperation, might you revolt and begin to do whatever you wished without considering the logic of your decisions, the common sense of your choices, or the propriety of your behaviour?

What if you also had an inordinate amount of wealth, giving you the power to redress your deepest insecurities and desires by any means at your disposal, no matter how extreme, and with no one around daring to challenge you? Don't like the colour of your skin? Fade it away. Never had a real childhood? Say hello to Neverland. Want to sleep in the same bed with boys? No problem, there. Don't like how you look? Change your face. Still don't like it? Change it to another face, and another and another.

Why can't he see what's happening to himself? we ask about Michael. Why doesn't he *understand*? How does he see himself, anyway? As the King of Pop, a trailblazing, misunderstood musical genius whose career spans an entire lifetime? Or an insecure, basically unhappy adult with enough money and power to do whatever he likes and get away with it? Perhaps only one thing is certain: if you were an unfettered combination of both, chances are you would be like . . . Michael Jackson.

PART ONE

Introduction

The bucolic town of Los Olivos in Santa Barbara County is a little more than a hundred years old. If a visitor wants a sense of the local history, Mattei's Tavern, built in 1886, is the place to go. One of many monuments to a by-gone era, it was a stagecoach stop where guests stayed overnight during their journeys, back when the only mode of transportation was horse-drawn carriage. It also became a stop-off point for the Pacific Coast Railway narrow gauge line, constructed in the 1880s when travel by land along the coast ranged from difficult to impossible. At its zenith, it stretched over seventy-five miles from what was once called Harford Wharf on San Luis Bay, south to Los Olivos. Passengers spent the night at Mattei's before taking the stagecoach to Santa Barbara, the next day. Today, the Carriage Museum is on this site, providing a visual history of the region. The original watering hole is now a charming eatery called Brothers Restaurant at Mattei's Tavern.

One recent day, a strange-looking man came through the Museum with a boy, a girl and an infant. He was accompanied by two women, senior citizens who tended to the youngsters, maybe nursemaids, one cradling the baby in a blanket. Also present was a male assistant who appeared to be in his early twenties. His eyes darted about, as if he was on high alert, vigilantly aware of his surroundings, of what others were doing in his presence.

The older man, wearing a deep-purple, silk surgical mask, a fedora over ink-jet black hair and over-sized sunglasses, stood before one of the photographic displays. 'Prince! Paris!' he called out. 'Come here. Look at this.' The tots ran to his side. He pointed to the picture with one chalky, spindly finger – at the tip of which was wrapped a band-aid – and read the accompanying description, his high-pitched voice sounding instructive. In the middle of his reading, he admonished the boy to pay closer attention, insisting that 'this is important'. The group moved from one display to the next, the masked man reading each narrative, beseeching the children to listen, carefully.

After the day's lesson, the small group enjoyed a bite to eat in the restaurant. While there, they laughed among themselves, sharing private jokes, yet seeming closed off from their environment, never acknowledging the existence of anyone outside their miniature world. The masked man fed himself by lifting his disguise just a tad, rather than take it off. The locals tried to ignore the odd contingent. However, it was difficult not to stare, particularly since the children had been wearing masks, too – not surgical, though . . . just Halloween. They took them off to eat, and then put them back on, once again hiding their faces.

In the early 1900s, a major new rail line was built thirty miles closer to the Pacific coast. Because Los Olivos had been bypassed by it, the population of the once-thriving town dwindled. However, it has since been rediscovered, thanks to an influx of tourists in the last twenty years. Now, there is an Indian reservation and gambling casino, as well as a number of spas and New Age healing centres. Small and locally owned art galleries, antique stores, gift shops, boutiques and wineries flourish in restored western-themed buildings.

One afternoon, the masked man visited one of the art galleries. 'Now, *this* one would be just perfect in the bedroom, wouldn't it?' he said to his young assistant. He held up a small oil painting of two angels floating ethereally above a sleeping child. The assistant nodded. 'Yoo-hoo,' called out the masked man. 'How much for this one?' He and the curator conferred, privately. Then the man in the disguise walked over to his assistant and whispered into his ear. 'Okay, very good,' he finally said to the store-owner. 'I'll take it.'

The proprietor scribbled on a piece of paper and handed it to the younger man, who then extracted a wad of bills from his wallet. He counted them off to pay for the purchase.

'No, wait! That's too much,' said the masked man who had been watching, carefully. 'I thought you said it was a hundred dollars. Not a hundred and six dollars, and change.' There was a quick, urgent conference. 'What? *Tax?* Really? On *this?*' He made a show of thinking hard. 'Well, okay, then,' he decided. 'Thanks, anyway.' He put the painting down.

More negotiation.

'Really? Okay, good, then. A hundred dollars it is.'

The covered man regarded the painting, again. 'My God, it's so beautiful, isn't it?' he remarked, picking it up. 'The way those children are so . . . *protected*. How sweet.' As he and his assistant walked out of the gallery, he turned and hollered back to the proprietor, 'I just want you to know that I think you're a wonderful person, and I wish you all the luck in the world with your store! I'll be back soon.'

Los Olivos is the home of about five hundred horse ranch estates, Victorian-style homes and about two dozen businesses. A thousand people, maybe less, call this remote and slumbering place home (fewer than a dozen of them, black), including one unlikely resident, the only man in town who wears a mask: Michael Joseph Jackson.

Figueroa Mountain Road winds upward through the lush and rolling Santa Ynez Valley of Los Olivos. A man sells apples under a leafy old shade tree on the side of the road; he's been doing so for years. Every day, he sits with nothing to do but sell his fruit, enjoy his day and bake in the sun. It's just that kind of place.

A half mile back from the road, behind an imposing oak gate, is 5225 Figueroa Mountain Road, a massive Danish-style split-level farmhouse, its brick and masonry walls crisscrossed with wooden beams. This is where Michael Jackson lives.

This 2700-acre property, originally a ranch for farming dry oats and running cattle, was once known as Sycamore Ranch. It came on the market at $35 million; Michael purchased it for $17 million in May 1988. He then changed the name to Neverland Valley Ranch – Neverland, for short – an *homage* to Peter Pan's Never-Never Land. The first order of business for Michael was to build his own amusement park own the acreage, including a merry-go-round, giant sliding board, railway with its own train and even a Ferris wheel. With his kind of money, he could pretty much do anything he wanted to do . . . and he would do it all at Neverland.

Michael's corner of the world is verdantly green as far as the eye can see. Old-fashioned windmills dot the landscape. There is an elegant softness to the grandeur; thousands of trees gently shade superbly manicured grounds which include a five-acre man-made, ice-blue lake with a soothing, never pummelling, five-foot waterfall and a graceful, inviting stone bridge. It is here, amidst the infinite silence of unfarmed, rolling and gentle countryside, that Michael Jackson has created his own environment, a safe haven for him from an ever-pressing, ever-difficult world.

Two thousand miles east, in the grimy industrial city of Gary, Indiana, there is a small, two-bedroom, one-bath, brick-and-aluminum-sided home on a corner lot. The property, at 2300 Jackson Street, is about a hundred feet deep and fifty feet wide. There is no garage, no landscaping and no green grass. Thick smoke plumes upward from nearby factories; it envelopes the atmosphere in a way that makes a person breathing such air feel just a little . . . sick. Joseph and Katherine Jackson, Michael's parents, purchased the home in 1950 for $8,500, with a $500 down-payment.

This place, primarily a black neighbourhood, is where Michael Jackson first lived as a child, with his parents and siblings Maureen, Jackie, Tito, Jermaine, LaToya, Marlon, Janet and Randy.

Like most parents, Joseph and Katherine wanted their children to succeed. In the early fifties the best they could do was two bedrooms and one bath for eleven people; clothes and shoes bought in second-hand stores. They hoped that when the youngsters graduated from high school, they would find steady work, perhaps in the mills . . . unless they could do better than that.

However, when the Jackson parents discovered that some of their kids had musical talent, their dreams expanded: the boys with the surprising musical and dance abilities would win contests, they decided, and be 'discovered'.

After their sons cut their first records, the imaginings of the parents grew more grandiose: a sprawling estate in California; servants at their beck and call; expensive luxury cars for everyone; three-piece suits, diamond rings and great power for Joseph; mink coats, jewels and a better social life for Katherine. They fantasized about flipping on their television and seeing their celebrated children perform their number-one hit songs for an appreciative world. As a result of the boys' fame, they figured, the entire family would be recognized, sought-after, asked to pose for pictures, sign autographs. They would *all* be stars. What a great world it would be, for each of them. No more worries; everything taken care of, handled by their good fortune.

Was it too much to ask? It certainly seemed like a good idea, at the time. However, as proverbial wisdom has it, be careful what you wish for. You just might get it.

Joseph and Katherine

Joseph Walter Jackson was born on 26 July 1929, to Samuel and Chrystal Jackson in Fountain Hill, Arkansas. He is the eldest of five children; a sister, Verna, died when she was seven. Samuel, a high school teacher, was a strict, unyielding man who raised his children with an iron fist. They were not allowed to socialize with friends outside the home. 'The Bible says that bad associations spoil youthful habits,' Chrystal explained to them.

'Samuel Jackson loved his family, but he was distant and hard to reach,' remembered a relative. 'He rarely showed his family any affection, so he was misunderstood. People thought he had no feelings, but he did. He was sensitive but didn't know what to do with his sensitivities. Joseph would take after his father in so many ways.'

Samuel and Chrystal divorced when Joseph was a teenager. Sam moved to Oakland, taking Joseph with him, while Chrystal took Joseph's brother and sisters to East Chicago. When Samuel married a third time, Joseph decided to join his mother and siblings in Indiana. He dropped out of school in the eleventh grade and became a boxer in the Golden Gloves. Shortly thereafter, he met Katherine Esther Scruse at a neighbourhood party. She was a pretty and petite woman, and Joseph was attracted to her affable personality and warm smile.

Katherine was born on 4 May 1930, and christened Kattie B.

Scruse, after an aunt on her father's side. (She was called Kate or Katie as a child, and those closest to her today still call her that.) Kattie was born to Prince Albert Screws and Martha Upshaw in Barbour County, a few miles from Russell County, Alabama, a rural farming area that had been home to her family for generations. Her parents had been married for a year. They would have another child, Hattie, in 1931.

Prince Scruse worked for the Seminole Railroad and also as a tenant cotton farmer, as did Katherine's grandfather and great-grandfather, Kendall Brown. Brown, who sang every Sunday in a Russell County church and was renowned for his voice, had once been a slave for an Alabama family named Scruse, whose name he eventually adopted as his own.

'People told me that when the church windows were opened, you could hear my great-grandfather's voice ringing out all over the valley,' Katherine would recall. 'It would just ring out over everybody else's. And when I heard this, I said to myself, "Well, maybe it is in the blood."'

At the age of eighteen months, Katherine was stricken with polio, at the time often called infantile paralysis because it struck so many children. There was no vaccine in those days, and many children – like Joseph's sister Verna – either died from it or were severely crippled.

In 1934, Prince Scruse moved his family to East Chicago, Indiana, in search of a steady job. He was employed in the steel mills before finding work as a Pullman porter with the Illinois Central Railroad. In less than a year, Prince and Martha divorced; Martha remained in East Chicago with her young daughters.

Because of her polio, Katherine became a shy, introverted child who was often taunted by her schoolmates. She was always in and out of hospitals. Unable to graduate from high school, she would take equivalency courses as an adult and get her diploma in that way. Until she was sixteen, she wore a brace, or used crutches. Today, she walks with a limp.

Her positive childhood memories have always been about music. She and her sister, Hattie, grew up listening to country-western radio programmes and admiring such stars as Hank Williams and Ernest Tubbs. They were members of the high school orchestra, the church junior band and the school choir. Katherine, who also sang in the local Baptist church, dreamed of a career in show business, first as an actress and then as a vocalist.

When she met Joseph, Katherine fell for him, immediately. Though he had married someone else, it lasted only about a year. After his divorce, Katherine began dating Joseph, and the couple soon became engaged. She was under his spell, gripped by his charisma, seduced by his charm, his looks, his power. He was a commanding man who took control, and she sensed she would always feel safe with him. She found herself enjoying his stories, laughing at his jokes. His eyes were large, set wide apart and a colour of hazel she had never before seen, almost emerald. Whenever she looked into them, as she would tell it, she knew she was being swept away, and it was what she wanted for herself. Or, as she put it, 'I fell crazy in love.'

They were opposites in many ways. She was soft. Joseph was hard. She was reasonable. Joseph was explosive. She was romantic. Joseph was pragmatic. However, the chemistry was there for them.

Both were musical: he was a bluesman who played guitar; she was a country-western fan who played clarinet and piano. When they were courting, the two would snuggle up together on cold winter nights and sing Christmas carols. Sometimes they would harmonize, and the blend was a good one, thanks to Katherine's beautiful soprano voice. Michael Jackson feels he inherited his singing ability from his mother. He has recalled that in his earliest memory of Katherine, she is holding him in her arms and singing songs such as 'You Are My Sunshine' and 'Cotton Fields'.

Joseph, twenty, and Katherine, nineteen, were married by a justice of the peace on 5 November 1949, in Crown Point, Indiana, after a six-month engagement.

Katherine has said that she was so affected by her parents' divorce, and the fact that she was raised in a broken home, she promised herself once she found a husband, she would stay married to him, no matter what circumstances may come their way. It didn't seem that she had much to worry about with Joseph, though. He treated her respectfully and showed her every consideration. She enjoyed his company; he made her laugh like no one ever had in the past. Importantly, there was a tremendous sexual bonding between them. Joseph was a passionate man; Katherine, less so a woman.

However, they were in love; they were compatible and they made it work.

The newlyweds settled in Gary, Indiana. Their first child, Maureen, nicknamed Rebbie (pronounced Reebie), was born on 29 May 1950. The rest of the brood followed in quick succession. On 4 May 1951, Katherine's twenty-first birthday, she gave birth to Sigmund Esco, nicknamed Jackie. Two years later, on 15 October 1953, Tariano Adaryl was born; he was called Tito. Jermaine LaJuane followed on 11 December 1954; LaToya Yvonne on 29 May 1956; Marlon David on 12 March 1957 (one of a set of premature twins; the other, Brandon, died within twenty-four hours of birth); Michael Joseph on 29 August 1958 ('with a funny-looking head, big brown eyes, and long hands,' said his mother); Steven Randall on 29 October 1961, and then Janet Dameta on 16 May 1966.

Early Days

Talk about cramped quarters . . . once upon a God-forsaken time, all eleven members of the Jackson family lived at 2300 Jackson Street. 'You could take five steps from the front door and you'd be out the back,' Michael said of the house. 'It was really no bigger than a garage.'

Katherine and Joseph shared one bedroom with a double bed. The boys slept in the only other bedroom in a triple bunk bed; Tito and Jermaine sharing a bed on top, Marlon and Michael in the middle, and Jackie alone on the bottom. The three girls slept on a convertible sofa in the living room; when Randy was born, he slept on a second couch. In the bitter-cold winter months, the family would huddle together in the kitchen in front of the open oven.

'We all had chores,' Jermaine remembered. 'There was always something to do – scrubbing the floors, washing the windows, doing whatever gardening there was to do,' he said with a smile. 'Tito did the dishes after dinner. I'd dry them. The four oldest did the ironing – Rebbie, Jackie, Tito, and me – and we weren't allowed out of the house until we finished. My parents believed in work values. We learned early the rewards of feeling good about work.'

Joseph worked a four o'clock-to-midnight shift as a crane operator at Inland Steel in East Chicago. In Michael's earliest memory of his father, he is coming home from work with a big bag of glazed doughnuts for everyone. 'The work was hard but steady, and for that I couldn't complain,' Joseph said. There was never enough money, though; Joseph seldom made more than sixty-five dollars a week, even though he often put in extra hours as a welder. The family learned to live with it. Katherine made the children's clothes herself, or shopped at a Salvation Army store. They ate simple foods: bacon and eggs for breakfast; egg-and-bologna sandwiches and sometimes tomato soup for lunch; fish and rice for dinner. Katherine enjoyed baking peach cobblers and apple pies for dessert.

There are few school pictures of the Jackson children today, because they could not afford to purchase them after posing for them. For the first five years that they lived on Jackson Street, the family had no telephone. When Jermaine contracted nephritis, a kidney disease, at the age of four and had to be hospitalized for three weeks, it hit Katherine and Joseph hard, financially, as well as emotionally.

Whenever Joseph was laid off, he found work harvesting potatoes, and during these periods the family would fill up on potatoes, boiled, fried or baked.

'I was dissatisfied,' Joseph Jackson remembered. 'Something inside of me told me there was more to life than this. What I really wanted more than anything was to find a way into the music business.' He, his brother Luther and three other men formed The Falcons, a rhythm and blues band that provided extra income for all of their families by performing in small clubs and bars. Joseph's three oldest sons – Jackie, Tito and Jermaine – were fascinated with their father's music and would sit in on rehearsals at home. (Michael has no recollection of The Falcons.)

In the end, The Falcons was not commercially successful; when they disbanded, Joseph stashed his guitar in the bedroom closet. That string instrument was his one vestige of a dream deferred, and he didn't want any of the children to get their hands on it. Michael referred to the closet as 'a sacred place'. Occasionally Katherine would take the guitar down from the shelf and play it for the children.

They would all gather around in the living room and sing together, country songs like 'Wabash Cannonball' and 'The Great Speckled Bird'.

With his group disbanded, Joseph didn't know what to do with himself. Now working the swing shift at Inland Steel and the day shift at American Foundries, all he knew was that he wanted much more for himself and his family. It was the early sixties and 'everybody we knew was in a singing group', Jackie recalled. 'That was the thing to do, go join a group. There were gangs, and there were singing groups. I wanted to be in a singing group, but we weren't allowed to hang out with the other kids. So we started singing together 'round the house. Our TV broke down and Mother started having us sing together. And then what happened was that our father would go to work, and we would sneak into his bedroom and get that guitar down.'

'And I would play it,' Tito continued. 'It would be me, Jackie and Jermaine, and we'd sing, learn new songs, and I would play. Our mother came in one day and we all froze, like "Uh-oh, we're busted," but she didn't say anything. She just let us play.'

'I didn't want to stop it because I saw a lot of talent there,' Katherine would explain later.

This went on for a few months until one day Tito broke a string on the guitar. 'I knew I was in trouble,' Tito recalled. 'We were *all* in trouble. Our father was strict and we were scared of him. So I put the guitar back in the closet and hoped he wouldn't figure out what had happened. But he did, and he *whooped* me. Even though my mother lied and said she had given me permission to play the guitar, he tore me up.' When Tito tells the story, his words tumble out and he gets tongue-tied. So many years later, one can still sense his anxiety about it. 'She just didn't want to see me get whipped,' he said, sadly. 'Not again.

'Afterwards, when Joseph cooled off, he came into the room. I was still crying on the bed. I said, "You know, I can play that thing. I really can." He looked at me and said, "Okay, lemme see what you can do, smart guy." So I played it. And Jermaine and Jackie sang a little. Joseph was amazed. He had no idea, because this was the big secret we had been keeping from him because we were so scared of him.'

Joseph later said that when his sons revealed their talent to him, he felt a surge of excitement about it. 'I decided I would leave the music to my sons,' he told me, many years later. 'I had a dream for them,' he said. 'I envisioned these kids making audiences happy by sharing their talent, talent that they'd maybe inherited from me.' He seemed touched by his own words as he looked back on the past. 'I just wanted them to make something of themselves. That's all I wanted,' he added.

Joseph went off to work the next day and, that night, returned home holding something behind his back. He called out to Tito and handed him the package. It was a red electric guitar. 'Now, let's rehearse, boys,' Joseph said with a wide smile. He gathered his three sons together – Jackie, nine, Tito, seven, and Jermaine, six – and they practised. 'We'd never been so close,' Tito would recall. 'It was as if we had finally found something in common. Marlon and Mike, they would sit in the corner and watch. Our mother would give us some tips. I noticed our mother and father were happy. We were all happy. We had found something special.'

In the sixties, Gary was a tough, urban city, and the Jacksons' neighbourhood was sometimes a dangerous place for youngsters. Katherine and Joseph lived in constant fear that one of their children would be hurt in the streets. 'We were always protected by our parents,' Jackie recalled. 'We were never really allowed to have fun in the streets like other kids. We had a strict curfew. The only time we could actually play with people our own age was in school. We liked the social aspect of school.'

Katherine Jackson, a strong force in the lives of her children, passed on to them a deep and abiding respect for certain religious convictions. She had been a Baptist and then a Lutheran but turned from both faiths for the same reason: she discovered that the ministers were having extramarital affairs. When Michael was five years old Katherine became a Jehovah's Witness, converted by a door-to-door worker. She was baptized in 1963 in the swimming pool at Roosevelt High in Gary. From then on, she asked that the rest of the family get dressed in their best clothes every Sunday and walk with her to Kingdom Hall, their place of worship. Joseph, who had been raised a

Lutheran, accompanied his wife a couple of times to placate her, but stopped going when the children were still young because, as Marlon put it, 'it was so boring.' As time went on, Michael, LaToya, and Rebbie would become the most devout about their religion.

Had that religion been any but the Jehovah's Witnesses, Michael Jackson would probably have evolved in a completely different way. So removed are Jehovah's Witnesses from mainstream Protestantism, they were sometimes considered a cult, especially in the fifties and sixties. No matter where they live, no Jehovah's Witness will salute a flag (they believe it is idolatrous to do so) or serve in any armed forces (each Witness is considered an ordained minister and, therefore, exempt). They don't celebrate Christmas or Easter or birthdays. They usually will not contribute money to any group outside their own church because they consider preaching the gospel the most worthwhile, charitable deed. Jehovah's Witnesses periodically make news because they refuse to receive blood transfusions for themselves or their children, no matter how gravely ill the patient may be.

In the strictest sense of the teachings, Jehovah's Witnesses considered themselves the sheep; everybody else is a goat. When the great battle of Armageddon is fought – it was expected in 1972 and then in 1975 – all the goats will be destroyed at once and the sheep will be spared. The sheep will then be resurrected to a life on earth as subjects of the Kingdom of God. They will be ruled by Christ and a select group of 144,000 Witnesses who will reside in heaven by Christ's side. At the end of a thousand years, Satan will come forth to tempt those on earth. Those who succumb to his wiles will be immediately destroyed. The rest will live, idyllically. Of course, as with those who adhere to religious beliefs, some Witnesses are more adamant about those teachings than others.

Estimates are that 20 to 30 per cent of its members are black. Witnesses are judged solely by their good deeds – their witnessing, or door-to-door proselytizing – and not on new cars, large homes, expensive clothes and other status symbols. Because of her devotion to the Jehovah's Witnesses, Katherine was mostly satisfied with what she had in Gary, Indiana. She enjoyed her life, and had little issue with it other than her concern that the city didn't offer much promise for her children's future, other than work in factories for the boys and domestic life for the girls. Would that be so bad? Yes, Joseph would tell her, absolutely, yes. Sometimes, she agreed. Sometimes, she wasn't so sure what to think about any of it.

Every day, for at least three hours, the boys would rehearse, whether they wanted to do so or not, with Joseph's only thought being to get his family out of Gary.

'When I found out that my kids were interested in becoming entertainers, I really went to work with them,' Joseph Jackson would tell *Time*. 'When the other kids would be out on the street playing games, my boys were in the house working, trying to learn how to be something in life, *do* something with their lives.'

Though the Jacksons' music may have brought them closer together as a family unit, it also served to further alienate them from everyone else in the neighbourhood. 'Already, people thought we were strange because of our religion,' Jackie would remember. 'Now they were sure of it. They'd say, "Yeah, look at those Jacksons. They think they're something special." Everyone else used to hang out on the corners and sing with their groups. But we weren't allowed to. We had to practise at home. So the other kids thought we thought we were too good to sing with on the corner.'

Rehearsals were still held twice a day, before school and after, even though their peers in the neighbourhood thought the Jacksons were wasting their time. As they practised, voices from outside would taunt them through open windows, 'You ain't *nothin'*, you Jacksons!' Rocks would be hurled into the living room. It didn't matter to the Jacksons; they ignored the taunts and focused on their practice sessions.

By 1962, five-year-old Marlon had joined the group, playing bongos and singing, mostly off-key. (Marlon couldn't sing or dance, but he was allowed in the group anyway because Katherine would not have it any other way.) One day when the boys were practising while Joseph was at work, Katherine watched as Michael, who was four years old, began imitating Jermaine as he sang a James Brown song. When Michael sang, his voice was so strong and pure, Katherine was surprised. As soon as Joseph got home, she met him at the door with some good news: 'I think we have another lead singer.'

Joseph Hits Michael

Today, Michael Jackson often speaks about the abuse he suffered at the hands of his father. When he gave his controversial 2003 interview to Martin Bashir, quick tears came to his eyes when he remembered the way his dad treated him. 'It was bad,' he said of the beatings. 'Real bad.' Watching Michael as he took himself back to the days in Gary when his father hit him was truly painful. Clearly, all these years later, he is still traumatized by that part of his childhood.

Little Michael was a fascinating child. 'Ever since Michael was very young, he seemed different to me from the rest of the children,' Katherine said. 'I don't believe in reincarnation, but you know how babies move so uncoordinated? Michael never moved that way. When he danced, it was as if he were an older person.'

Michael was always precocious. His mother has recalled that at the age of a year and a half he would hold his bottle and dance to the rhythm of the washing machine. His grandmother, Chrystal Johnson (her later married name), has recalled that he began singing when he was about three. 'And what a beautiful voice he had,' she enthused. 'Even back then, he was a joy to listen to.'

Michael was too sensitive a boy to be manhandled the way he was by his father. He was also quick on his feet, and determined to avoid an altercation with Joseph. Tito remembered that Michael was 'so quick that if my mother or father used to swing at him, he'd be out of their way. They'd be swinging at air.'

Joseph believed in the value and impact of brute force as a disciplinary tool. 'Either you're a winner in this life, or a loser,' he liked to say. 'And none of my kids are gonna be losers.' To be sure of that, he would smack his kids without giving it a second thought in order to keep them on the right track to being 'winners'. Shoving them into walls was not unusual behaviour for him, especially the boys. Michael, however, was the one boy in the family who would attempt to fight back when provoked by his father. Once, when he was just three, Joseph spanked him for something he had done. Crying, Michael then took off one of his shoes and hurled it at his father. Joseph ducked; the shoe missed him.

'Are you crazy?' Joseph screamed at him. 'Boy, you just signed your own death warrant. Get over here.'

Infuriated, Joseph grabbed Michael and, according to Marlon, held him upside down by one leg and pummelled him over and over again with his hand, hitting him on his back and buttocks. Soon, Michael was crying and screaming so loudly it seemed as if he was trying to summon the entire neighbourhood to his aid.

'Put him down, Joseph,' Katherine hollered. 'You're gonna kill him! You're gonna kill him.'

When Joseph released the boy, he ran to his room, sobbing, 'I hate you.' Those were fighting words for Joseph. He followed Michael into the bedroom, slammed the door and then let him have it.

'Joseph once locked Michael in a closet for hours,' said a friend of the Jackson family's. '*That* was traumatizing, horrible for him.'

Katherine didn't know how to reconcile herself to her husband's treatment of their children. How could a man so gentle at times that he would kiss her fingertips in a romantic moment, turn around and beat her children? His behaviour simply wasn't in the sphere of her understanding, as a God-fearing woman. However, she didn't know what to do about it. As much as she loved him, she feared him. She would speak up at times, but reluctantly.

In truth, Katherine had also been the target of Joseph's fury. When Rebbie was a baby, Joseph was on edge because of sleep deprivation and a heavy work schedule. One day, he returned home to a crying baby, only to find Katherine outside talking to one of the neighbours. He ran out to get her. 'The kid is screaming her head off,' he shouted. Katherine immediately returned to the baby's side. 'I'm sorry, Joseph,' she said, according to her memory. 'I didn't know she had awakened.' Suddenly, Joseph turned around and smacked his wife across the face. 'My cheek went numb,' Katherine recalled. Her reaction was swift and immediate fury. She took a ceramic bottle warmer and threw it at him with everything she had in her. It struck him on his forearm and shattered, cutting him deeply. Blood gushed from the wound as the two argued. 'Don't you ever hit me again,' Katherine warned him, 'or I'll leave you so fast your head will spin.' Katherine says that the violent episode marked the first and last time Joseph ever struck her – but, apparently, he turned his violent temper on her children.

When Michael was five, he toddled into a room and had his breath taken away when Joseph tripped him and he fell to the ground, bloodied. 'That's for whatcha' did yesterday,' Joseph said. 'And tomorrow, I'm gonna get you for what you'll do today.'

Michael began to cry. 'But I didn't even do nothin' yet,' he said through his tears.

'Oh, you will, boy,' Joseph said. 'You will.'

From that point onward, whenever young Michael walked into a room he looked left, then right, as if crossing the street. He was hoping to avoid his father. How does a young boy deal with such fear? 'I began to be so scared of that man,' Michael later recalled. 'In fact, I guess it's safe to say that I hated him.'

Michael recalled that his father 'was always a mystery to me, and he knows it. One of the things I regret most is never being able to have a real closeness with him.' In truth, none of the Jackson children ever developed 'a real closeness' with Joseph, who was not affectionate toward them. Sometimes he took his boys camping and fishing on weekends or taught them how to box to defend themselves, but he never paid much attention to the girls. (As a toddler, Janet liked to crawl into bed with her mother and father, but she had to wait until Joseph was asleep.)

Aspects of Joseph's parenting were unconventional, to say the least. Whenever the boys left their bedroom window open at night, he would go outside and climb into their room and then scream at them at the top of his lungs . . . while wearing a fright mask. The youngsters would begin crying and hyperventilating, frightened half to death. Why would a father cause his children such trauma? Joseph explains that he was trying to demonstrate why they should not leave the windows open at night. After all, what if a burglar were to enter the house? Michael and Marlon would, for many years afterwards, suffer from vivid nightmares of being kidnapped from the safety of their bedrooms.

Suffice it to say that as he grew older Michael pulled about as far away from Joseph as he could, clinging to his mother, whom he adored, as if his very life depended on it (and maybe it did). 'Even with nine children, she treated each of us like an only child,' he would remember to this writer in 1991. 'Because of Katherine's gentleness, warmth and attention, I can't imagine what it must be like to grow up without a mother's love. [What an ironic statement, considering that both of his children are, today, being raised without their mother, Debbie Rowe.] The lessons she taught us were invaluable. Kindness, love and consideration for other people headed her list.'

And, as for Joseph? 'I used to throw up whenever I thought of him,' Michael recalled, succinctly. In his 2003 Martin Bashir interview, he noted that Joseph has blue eyes. Clearly, he hasn't looked into his father's eyes in some time; they're hazel, almost green.

Climbing Mountains

In 1963, at the age of five, Michael Jackson began attending Garnett Elementary School. Katherine has said that he was generous to a fault, so much so that he used to take jewellery from her dresser and give it to his teachers as tokens of his affection for them. A stubborn child, he continued to do so even after his mother chastised him for giving away her possessions.

One of Michael's first memories concerns performing at the age of five, when he sang 'Climb Ev'ry Mountain' from *The Sound of Music* a cappella for his class. The other children were impressed as much by his self-confidence as by his talent; he received a standing ovation. The teacher started to sob. Katherine attended the performance with Joseph's father, Samuel, who was not a sentimental man, yet even he was moved to tears by Michael's mellifluous performance. 'I don't know where he got it from,' Katherine said of Michael's prowess as a singer. 'He was just so good, so young. Some kids are special. Michael was special.'

Five-year-old Michael had so much energy and charisma that Jackie, who was twelve at the time, decided his younger brother would become 'the lead guy'. That was perfectly fine with Michael; he enjoyed being the centre of attention. However, Jermaine's feelings were hurt. He had been the lead singer of the group, and now suddenly he wasn't good enough. Some family members have theorized that one of the reasons he stuttered as a child was a lack of confidence. Still, Jermaine would support the family's decision because Michael was so obviously a natural entertainer. However, it must be said that it always seemed that Jermaine competed with Michael, especially as an adult, often trying to best him.

'He became this great little imitator,' Jermaine would remember of Michael. 'He'd see something – another kid dance, or maybe James Brown on TV – and next thing you knew, Michael had it memorized and knew just what to do with it. He loved to dance too. Marlon was a good dancer, maybe better than Mike. But Mike loved it more. He was always dancin' 'round the house. You'd always catch him dancin' for himself in the mirror. He'd go off alone and practise and then come back and show us this new step. We'd incorporate it into the act. Michael began choreographing our show.'

'Finally it was time for us to enter a talent contest,' Michael recalled. 'This is something I remember like it was just yesterday.

'Everyone on the block wanted to be in the talent show and win the trophy. I was about six years old but I had figured out then that nobody gives you nothin'. You got to win it. Or, like Smokey Robinson said in one of his songs, "You got to earn it". We did this talent contest at Roosevelt High School in Gary. We sang The Temptations' "My Girl" and won first prize.'

The boys also performed their rendition of the Robert Parker hit song, 'Barefootin''. During a musical break in the middle of the song, little Michael kicked off his shoes and started doing the barefoot dance all over the stage, much to the crowd's delight.

'After that, we started winning every talent show we entered,' Michael said. 'It was just going from one thing to another, up, up, up. The whole house was full of trophies, and my father was so proud. Probably, the happiest I ever saw my mother and father was back there in Gary when we were winning those talent shows. That's when we were closest, I think, back in the beginning when we didn't have anything but our talent.'

By 1965, Joseph was making only about eight thousand dollars a year working full-time at the mill. Katherine worked part-time as a saleswoman at Sears. When Joseph wanted to start spending more money on the group – musical equipment, amplifiers, microphones – Katherine became concerned.

'I was afraid we were getting in over our heads,' she would recall.

She and Joseph had vociferous disagreements about finances. 'I saw this great potential in my sons,' Joseph once told me, in his defence. 'So yes, I did go overboard. I invested a lot of money in instruments, and this was money we did not have. My wife and I would have heated arguments about this "waste of money", as she would call it. She'd yell at me that the money should have been put into food, not into guitars and drums. But I was the head of the household and what I said was the final word. I overran her opinion.

'Black people were used to struggling and making ends meet. This was nothing new for me or any of us. I came up struggling, so my kids knew how to economize. They had no choice. We made a penny stretch by eating foods like chitterlings and collard greens. I used to tell them we were eating soul food in order to be able to play soul. We were trying to move upward, trying to get ahead. I wasn't going to let anything stop us.'

In the end, he and Katherine always got past the fights. After the shouting, Joseph would lean in and kiss her lightly on the lips. He could be surprisingly gentle. She later said she would tremble whenever he took a romantic approach; he could always reason with her in that way. 'Joseph convinced me that the boys were worth it,' she recalled. 'No one ever believed in his sons more than my husband believed in those boys. He used to tell me, "I'd spend my last dime on those boys if that's what it took".'

Soon Joseph was driving his children to Chicago to compete in talent contests there. Chicago was a city bustling with sensational sixties' soul music and teeming with talent like Curtis Mayfield, The Impressions, Jerry Butler and Major Lance. Joseph may not have been a showman, but he certainly knew about performing. He taught his boys everything he knew – by experience, observation and instinct – about how to handle and win over an audience. 'It's incredible how he could have been so right about things. He was the best teacher we ever had,' Michael would say.

'He wouldn't make it fun, though,' Michael said. ' "You're doing it wrong; you gotta do it like *this*," he'd say. Then he would hit me. He made it hard for me. He would say, "Do it like Michael," and make me the example. I hated that.

'I didn't want to be the example, I didn't want to be singled out. My brothers would look at me with resentment because they couldn't do it like me. It was awful that Joseph did that to me. But he was brilliant, too. He told me how to work the stage and work the mike and make gestures and everything. I was always torn. On one hand he was this horrible man, then on the other he was this amazing manager.'

When the group played its first paying performance at a Gary nightclub called Mr Lucky's, they made roughly seven dollars for the engagement. The boys then began playing in other clubs and the patrons would throw coins and bills on to the stage. 'My pockets would just be bustin' with money,' Michael once told me. 'My pants couldn't even stay up. Then I would go and buy candy, loads and loads of candy for me and for everyone.'

Many neighbourhood boys would accompany the Jacksons as musicians from time to time, and by 1966, Johnny Porter Jackson (no relation) was added to the group as a permanent drummer. Johnny's family was friendly with the Jacksons, who, in time, would consider Johnny a 'cousin'. Ronny Rancifer, a keyboardist, was also added to the band. The boys played clubs in Gary and as far away as Chicago; Michael was eight years old and singing lead. Tito was on guitar, Jermaine on bass guitar; Jackie played shakers and Johnny Jackson was on drums. Marlon sang harmony and danced, though he wasn't a very good dancer. (He worked at it, though, and was so persistent at wanting to be good at it he, eventually, would rival Michael!)

The Jacksons would pull up in their Volkswagen bus to 2300 Jackson Street at five in the morning on Monday, after an exhausting weekend of performing. Joseph would kiss Katherine on the nose upon their arrival, giving her a boyish grin. 'How ya' doing, Katie?' he would ask. For Katherine, there was nothing better than the expression on her husband's face when everything had gone well for the boys on the road. It was one of sheer joy. Each of her sons would embrace her. Then, they would all sleep for a couple of hours while Katherine unpacked their bags, and cooked a tremendous breakfast for them before Joseph went off to work, and the boys and their siblings to school.

Though thrilled about her sons' growing success, Katherine was uneasy about the family's shifting priorities. Suddenly, the emphasis was not only on making music for fun, but also to make a living. It was as if earning money made it all right to want *more* money. However, as a Jehovah's Witness Katherine valued good works over money. Therefore, she was concerned about how jubilant the boys were when they'd come home from a concert date with their pockets full of change. 'Remember, that's not the important thing,' she would tell them. But what kid would believe her, especially when she herself was encouraging them to win more talent shows – and, as a consequence, make more money?

It was in the inauspicious surroundings of a shopping mall in Gary, Indiana, that The Jackson Five got their name. 'I got to talking with a lady, a model named Evelyn Leahy,' Joseph once told me. 'The boys were performing in a department store, and she said to me after the show, "Joseph, I think The Jackson Brothers sounds old-fashioned, like The Mills Brothers. Why don't you just call them The Jackson Five?" Well, that sounded like a good name to me, The Jackson Five. So that's what we called them from then on. The Jackson Five.'

The group soon found themselves doing more club dates out of town on weekends. Joseph put a luggage rack on top of the family's Volkswagen bus for their equipment before hitting the so-called 'chitlin' (as in chitterling) circuit: two-thousand-seat theatres in downtown, inner-city areas like Cleveland, Ohio; Baltimore, Maryland and Washington, DC. There would always be many other acts on the bill, all diligently vying for the audience's favour. Sometimes these entertainers would be established artists – like The Four Tops – but often they would be unknowns, like The Jackson Five. This arrangement gave the upstarts an opportunity to learn from the experienced players. After their act, Michael's brothers would go off on their own, but Michael would stay behind and observe the other performers on the bill. Whenever anyone wanted to find eight-year-old Michael, they always knew where to look: he'd be in the wings, watching, studying and, as he remembered, 'really taking note of every step, every move, every twist, every turn, every grind, every emotion. It was the best education for me.'

It wasn't long began Michael began to appropriate routines and *shtick* from the best of the acts on the same bill with the brothers, like James Brown, whom Michael would watch, repeatedly. (Diana Ross used to do the same thing before The Supremes were famous. She stole from everyone on the Motown Revue!)

'James Brown taught me a few things he does on stage,' Michael remembered back in 1970. 'It was a couple years ago. He taught me how to drop the mike and then catch it before it hits the stage floor. It only took me about thirty minutes to learn. It looks hard, but it's easy. All I want now is a pair of patent leather shoes like James Brown's. But they don't make them in kids' sizes.'

The Jackson Five won the amateur talent show at the Regal, a theatre in Chicago, for three consecutive weeks, a major coup for the family. The Jackson boys were becoming more experienced and polished, their lead singer, Michael, more poised and professional. They played St Louis, Kansas City, Boston, Milwaukee and Philadelphia. Not only did they open for The Temptations, The Emotions, The O'Jays, Jackie Wilson, Sam and Dave, and Bobby Taylor and the Vancouvers, but they formed friendships with these artists and learned first-hand from many of them what to expect of the entertainment world.

Before one talent show, one performer remarked to another that they'd better watch out for The Jackson Five, 'because they got this midget they're using as a lead singer'. Jackie overheard and couldn't stop laughing.

When Michael heard about it, he was hurt. 'I can't help it if I'm the smallest,' he said, crying.

Joseph pulled his young son aside. 'Listen here, Michael,' he said, kneeling down to eye-to-eye level with him. 'You need to be proud that you're being talked about by the competition,' he said, his tone gentle. 'That means you're on your way. This is a good thing.'

'Well, I don't like it,' Michael recalls saying. 'They're talking bad about me.'

Joseph kissed his son on the top of the head, a rare moment of gentleness from him. 'This is only the beginning, Mike,' he said, smiling, 'so, get used to it.'

In August 1967, The Jackson Five performed at the famed Apollo Theater in Harlem, as contestants in its world-renowned amateur show. Working at the Apollo was the dream of most young black entertainers at the time. In his book *Showtime at the Apollo*, writer Ted Fox observed, '[The Apollo was] not just the greatest black theatre but a special place to come of age emotionally, professionally, socially and politically.' Joseph and Jack Richardson, a close friend of his, drove the boys to New York in the family's Volkswagen. At this time, Jackie was sixteen; Tito, thirteen; Jermaine, twelve; Marlon, ten; and Michael had just turned nine. The brothers entered the so-called Superdog Contest, the winning of which was the most prestigious achievement in any of the categories.

Michael once told me, 'The Apollo was the toughest place of all to play. If they liked you there, they really *liked* you. And if they hated you, they'd throw things at you, food and stuff. But, you know what? We weren't scared. We knew we were good. We had so much self-confidence at that time. At the other gigs we'd played, we had 'em in the palms of our hands. I'd be on stage singing and I'd look over at Jermaine and we'd wink at one another because we always knew we had it. I mean, you have to feel that way just to get up on that stage and take the chance, you know? Plus, Joseph would not have had it any other way. We wanted to please him. I mean, that was as important as winning any contest.'

Backstage at the Apollo, The Jackson Five found a small log that had been mounted on a pedestal, which supposedly came from the fabled Tree of Hope.

According to legend, The Tree of Hope had stood in front of Connie's Inn, where Louis Armstrong performed in the famous Harlem version of Fats Waller's *Hot Chocolates*. Over the years, hundreds of performers would stand under that tree and touch it for good luck. It became tradition. When Seventh Avenue was widened during New York City road construction, the tree was uprooted. However, Bill 'Bojangles' Robinson arranged for the Tree of Hope – he was the one who named it – to be moved to a street island, at Seventh Avenue, south of 132nd Street. Eventually, the tree was cut down; no one remembers the reason, and a plaque is all that remains at its final location. However, a small log from the Tree of Hope was mounted on a pedestal backstage at the Apollo. It then became tradition that the first-timer who touched the tree before he went out on to the stage would be destined for good luck: he would join the ranks of those black performers who had struggled to make their dreams a reality, who had fought for respect, who had paid their dues and eventually triumphed, shaping American popular culture in the image of their race and heritage.

The pedestal was placed off to the side of the stage so that the crowd could watch as the performers touched it. It was a Wednesday night and The Jackson Five were on the bill with The Impressions, one of the most popular vocal groups of the day. One of its founding members, Fred Cash, once told me that he went to nine-year-old Michael before the brothers hit the stage and told him the legend about the tree. 'No kiddin'?' Michael asked Fred, his eyes wide as saucers. 'Wow. That is so great. I love that. I'll bet it works, too.'

'Hey, guys, did you know 'bout this tree thing?' Michael then asked his brothers. 'Touch this tree and we'll have good luck.'

'Nah. I don't believe in luck,' Tito deadpanned.

'Well, I sure do,' Michael countered. 'Wish I could take that log home with me. Then I'd *always* have good luck.'

'Ladies and gentlemen,' the announcer said as the boys pulled themselves together backstage, 'here they are, The Jackson Five.'

The lights went up. It was time for The Jackson Five to take their rightful place in history. Joseph watched proudly as each of his sons touched the plaque of the Tree of Hope: First, Jackie; then Tito; Jermaine; Marlon; Michael; then, 'cousin' Johnny. The group ran out on to the stage as the audience offered its applause. Michael, though, was the last one at the footlights. He ran back to touch the Tree of Hope one more time . . . just to be on the safe side. It must have worked; the boys won the contest, an enthusiastic audience response sealing their victory.

'My poor, poor family'

Ever since Michael Jackson was a teenager, the public has speculated about his personal life. Straight, gay or even asexual, it is fascinating that the sexual proclivity of a performer with as much on-stage sexual appeal as Michael has always been such a mystery.

At an early age, Michael received mixed signals about sex. The message from Katherine was loud and clear; with her strong faith as a Jehovah's Witness, lust in thought or in deed was considered sinful.

According to 1 Corinthians 6:9, none of the unrighteous – 'neither fornicators, nor idolaters, nor adulterers, nor effeminate men, nor abusers of themselves with mankind' – would inherit the Kingdom of God. Therefore, physical intimacy was reserved for marriage.

However, from Joseph, who shunned the religion Katherine had embraced, the boys received a message that came more from his actions than from his words. In the group's early days, Joseph booked the boys into dives and strip joints. Ordinarily strict, he apparently gave his sons free rein at those times, allowing nine-year-old Michael to stand in the wings and watch as the male audience leered and whistled at voluptuous women who stripped until naked on stage. Once, Michael watched in fascination as a well-endowed stripper took off everything but her underwear. Then, at just the 'right' moment, she pulled two large oranges from her bra and took off a wig to reveal that 'she' was actually a he.

When the boys played the Peppermint Lounge in Chicago, there was a peephole in their dressing room through which they had a clear view into the ladies' bathroom. They would each take turns peering into it. 'We learned everything there was to know about ladies,' Marlon recalled. (Some years later, the group was performing in London when Michael, thirteen, and Marlon, fourteen, discovered a peephole that looked directly into an adjoining dressing room occupied by theatre star Carol Channing. 'Look, she's naked!' Marlon said excitedly as he peered through the hole. 'I can't look,' Michael protested. 'But she's naked,' Marlon enthused. 'Carol Channing is *naked*.' Michael took a quick look. 'Ugh,' he groaned. 'She *is* naked.')

It's safe to say that these kinds of experiences would impact on Michael for the rest of his life. At nine, Michael was not psychologically equipped to fully understand any sexual stimulation he may have received from what he had witnessed, such as the strip teases. He *must* have been conflicted: he had an overly rigid view of the world from his mother and an overly promiscuous view of the world from his father.

One of The Jackson Five's early performance numbers was their rendition of soul singer Joe Tex's raucous 'Skinny Legs and All'. As part of the act, Joseph encouraged young Michael to go into the audience, crawl under tables, lift up women's skirts, and peek at their panties. No matter how embarrassed Michael was by this gimmick, he embellished each performance by rolling his eyes and smiling wickedly. He knew that the audience members loved the bit enough to throw money on to the stage afterwards. The boys would then scramble for the loose change. After a show like this one, the boys would go home to their religious mother, who would then tuck them into bed and remind them of the virtues of being a good Jehovah's Witness. She truly never knew anything about the nightclub act until many years later.

Of course, when the Jackson boys were on the road, Katherine remained at home with the younger children. Her absence gave Joseph carte blanche to date other women – mostly groupies. The boys were well aware that he was exploiting their talent for the purposes of having sex. Marlon has recalled his father coming into his sons' hotel rooms with shapely beauties on both of his arms. 'G'night, fellows,' he would say. The boys, in bed in their pyjamas, would watch silently as their father and his lady friends closed the door behind them. They could then hear laughter and other sounds from Joseph's room, next door. It was as if he *wanted* them to know what he was doing behind Katherine's back. What was he thinking? Who knew? He'd become an enigma, just as much a mystery then, in his thirties, as his son, Michael, would be at the same age.

However, a few things about Joseph seemed clear: he was an insecure man with crippled judgement. Also, he never felt fully appreciated by his family. No matter how successful and popular Joseph would make his sons, or how much he gave to his wife and daughters, he always felt a lack of gratitude and respect from them. They rarely showed him affection. Tender moments between any of them were uncommon. Perhaps it was because he had stopped being a demonstrative person once his focus in life completely shifted to the success of his sons (and he had never been that effusive, anyway). His family did not know how to relate to him, and he couldn't understand them either. Therefore, Joseph wandered outside the household for appreciation, for validation.

'He used to do the meanest things to us,' Michael once told me of his father. He said he was revolted by the thought of whatever was occurring in Joseph's room with his girlfriends. (The lyrics to his song 'Scream', come to mind: 'Oh, father, please, have mercy 'cause

I just can't take it/Stop fucking with me!'.) At such a young age, Michael was forced to wonder how Joseph could repeatedly betray Katherine and, apparently, not be the least bit ashamed of his actions. Decades later, he is still conflicted by his father's actions. 'I loved Joseph,' he said during a break from his 2003 interview with Martin Bashir. Unexpectedly, tears welled in his eyes. 'At the same time, I hated him for what he did to my mother.' He swallowed hard, trying to push back the emotion. 'My poor mother,' he said. 'My poor family,' he added, sadly. 'My poor, poor family.'

None of her sons would ever hurt Katherine by revealing to her what her husband was doing while they were on the road, and they certainly didn't dare betray Joseph in that way, either. Having to lie to their mother was an additional burden. 'Katherine, of course, has never had a lover. She's always been faithful to Joseph,' recalled Susie Jackson, who was married to Johnny Jackson, the group's drummer. 'This only made them love their mother even more. The kids just had to learn to lie to heir mother, be hypocritical, and be very good at it. She would ask, "Well, what does Joseph do while you guys are out there working?" And they would say, "Nothing. He just lays around." It was true, but not by himself.'

Dr Carole Lieberman, a Los Angeles-based psychologist, who has not treated Michael, speculated, 'The father's infidelity would certainly have hit the youngest child exposed to it the hardest. [In this case, that would have been Michael, since he was the youngest member of the group privy to Joseph's indiscretions. It would be years before his younger brother and sister, Randy and Janet, would know about their father's philandering.] He would have thought that by not telling the mother he had betrayed her the most. Of course, this would have impacted him in many ways, and lying about it at such an early age obviously just taught him, simply, that it was okay to lie.'

'I may be young,' little Michael used to say while introducing the Smokey Robinson song 'Who's Lovin' You' in the group's act, 'but I do know what the blues are all about.' Though the line was just a part of the group's stage patter, the truth of it was more accurate, and more painful, than anyone in the audience ever could have guessed.

*

The Jackson family was ecstatic over the boys' tremendous success at the Apollo Theater, and with good reason: this success marked a defining moment for them in terms of their future. 'I'm so damn happy, I could fly to Gary without an airplane,' Joseph said afterward, his grin wide. Elated at their performance and proud of their determination to be the best, Joseph was determined to continue doing whatever was necessary to ensure his family's fortune in a tough, competitive business. To that end, he decided to work only part-time at Inland Steel so that he could devote more time to his sons' careers.

In 1968, Joseph would earn only fifty-one hundred dollars rather than his usual eight to ten thousand. He would give up relative financial security in order to gamble on his family's future. However, the gamble quickly paid off; the boys started making six hundred dollars per engagement. With the influx of money, Katherine and Joseph were able to redecorate their home and buy their first colour television.

Now flushed with success, the Jacksons continued to work on their performance in daily rehearsals that would often become emotional. Once, when Joseph tried to convince Michael to execute a dance step a certain way, Michael refused. According to Johnny Jackson, Joseph smacked Michael across the face. Michael fell backwards.

'Now, you do it the way I told you to, you hear me?' Joseph hollered at the nine-year-old.

Michael began to cry, his right cheek red and sore. 'I ain't doin' it that way,' he said.

Joseph glared at him and took one step forward, his hand raised to strike again.

Michael scrambled up off the floor. 'Don't hit me,' he warned his father. ''Cause if you ever hit me again, it'll be the last time I ever sing, and I mean it.' Father and son exchanged angry stares. However, Michael must have said the magic words because Joseph turned and walked away, muttering something about his 'ungrateful' son.

Michael has recalled that as Joseph got older, he became more violent. It became a running theme in his young life: his father was a bully, and he would have to live with it. 'If you messed up during rehearsal, you got hit,' Michael would remember, 'sometimes with a belt, a switch. Once, he ripped the wire cord off the refrigerator and whooped me with it, that's how mad he was at me.' It was a vicious cycle: the more his father beat him, the angrier Michael became at him. The angrier he became, the more he antagonized him . . . and the more he got beaten by his father. The beatings were fierce, recurring and traumatizing. 'I'd try to fight back,' Michael would recall, 'just swinging my fists. That's why I got it more than all my brothers combined. I would fight back and my father would kill me, just tear me up.'

Once, Michael was late arriving at rehearsal, and when he walked in, Joseph came up from behind and shoved him into a stack of musical instruments. Michael fell into the drums and was badly bruised. 'That'll teach you to be late,' Joseph said.

Rebbie Marries

At about this time, 1968, when Michael was almost ten, the Jacksons faced a family crisis. Eighteen-year-old Maureen had fallen in love with Nathaniel Brown, a devout Jehovah's Witness. She announced that she wanted to marry him and move to Kentucky. Katherine, happy for her daughter, encouraged her. In Katherine's view, there was no more important role for any of her daughters to play than that of being a wife and mother.

However, Joseph was against the marriage. 'It was all cooked up by Maureen and her mother,' he would later explain. 'I wasn't happy about it at all.'

Because Maureen – Rebbie, as she was known in the family – had a powerful singing voice, her father had hoped she would consider a career in show business. He felt that if she married and raised a family, she would never be able to devote her attention to the entertainment field. However, though Maureen had taken dance and piano lessons as a child, she was not interested in a musical career. She preferred the comfort and security of a happy home life to the instability of show business.

Also, of course, Rebbie wanted to get out of that house. There was always so much drama occurring within the walls of that small home on Jackson Street; from the exuberant high when the boys would win a talent show, to the crashing low when they were chased and bullied by Joseph. Rebbie wanted out. Who could blame her? As it would happen, her defection from the ranks would be just the first of such crises in the family, as several of the children chose to marry at an early age against their father's wishes in order to get away from him.

The arguments went on for weeks until, finally, Joseph relented. Fine, Rebbie could get married. However, he would have the final word: he would not give her away.

The First Record Deal

After winning another talent contest, this one at Beckman Junior High in Gary, the boys were brought to the attention of a man named Gordon Keith, who owned a small local label called Steeltown Records. Keith immediately signed the brothers to a limited record deal.

On a Saturday morning filled with great promise, Joseph took his brood to Steeltown's recording studio. The boys were led into a small glass booth. Michael was given a large set of metal headphones which came halfway down his neck. His brothers plugged their instruments into amplifiers. There were backup singers and a horn section. This was the record business – at last! The Jackson youngsters were thrilled, as anyone could see by looking at their young, bright faces. Of course, this was a big day for Joseph, too. It took a few hours to record that first song. After that, they would return every Saturday for the next few weeks for more recordings. One song was an instrumental; Michael sang lead vocals on the other six. It was obvious that he was to be the centrepiece of the group, he was so obviously unique with such a true 'sound' and amazing self-assurance at an early age.

Two singles were eventually released on Steeltown in 1968: 'Big Boy', backed with 'You've Changed', and 'We Don't Have to Be Over 21 (to Fall in Love)', backed with 'Jam Session'. Both were mediocre numbers that don't really hint at Michael Jackson's potential as a vocalist, but the boys were thrilled with them just the same. After all, these were their first records. From here, it seemed, anything might be possible. What a memorable moment it must have been for them, then, when the family gathered around the radio to hear the broadcast of that first recording. Michael recalled that as it played, they sat in the living room, stunned. 'Then, when it was over, we all laughed and hugged one another. We felt we had arrived. This was an amazing time for us as a family. I can still feel the excitement when I think back on it.'

Ben Brown, then a high-level executive at Steeltown, remembered the day the Jackson boys posed for publicity photographs, in March 1968. 'After the photographer positioned the boys, Michael left the lineup and stood off to the side, pouting,' Brown said. ' "This isn't gonna look like a publicity portrait," Michael complained. "It's gonna look like a family portrait." "Well, fix it," Joseph said. Then, Michael went and rearranged the whole group, put himself in front on one knee, and said, "Go ahead, take the picture now." We took it, and you know what? That was a great shot. How did he know how to do that, how to take a publicity photo? He was such an old soul, as if he had been a superstar in another life.'

In May 1968, the group was invited back to the Apollo to perform and, this time, be paid for their appearance. They were on a bill with Etta James, Joseph Simon and another family group, The Five Stairsteps and Cubie – a singer who was just two years old. 'Michael was a hard worker,' rhythm-and-blues singer Joseph Simon said in an interview, adding in an echo of the memories of practically everyone who ever worked on the same stage as the young Jackson star, 'there was a part of me that thought he was a midget. His father was a slick businessman, I had heard. It would've been just like him to pass a midget off as a child, I heard. I remember going up to Michael and looking at him real close, thinking, Okay now, is this kid a midget or not?

' "Hey man, stop starin' at me, okay?" he told me.'

'I remember him being talented, yes,' Etta James said of Michael, 'but polite and very interested too. I was working my show, doing my thing on stage, and as I'm singing "Tell Mama", I see this little black kid watching me from the wings. And I'm thinking, Who is this kid? He's distracting me. So I go over to him in between songs, while the people are clapping, and I whisper, "Scat, kid! Get lost. You're buggin' me. Go watch from the audience." I scared the hell out of him. He had these big ol' brown eyes, and he opened them real wide and ran away.

'About ten minutes later, there's this kid again. Now he's standing in front of the stage, off to the side. And he's watching me as I work.'

After the show, when Etta was in her dressing room taking off her makeup, there was a knock on the door.

'Who is it?' she asked.

'It's me.'

'Who's me?'

'Michael,' the young voice said. 'Michael Jackson.'

'I don't know no Michael Jackson,' Etta said.

'Yes, you do. I'm that little kid you told to scat.'

Etta, a robust black woman with dyed blond hair and a big, booming voice, cracked the door open and looked down to find a nine-year-old gazing up at her with large, wondering eyes. 'Whatchu want, boy?' she asked.

In a manner that wasn't the least bit timid, Michael said, 'Miss James, my father told me to come on back here and 'pologize to you. I'm sorry, ma'am, but I was just watchin' you 'cause you're so good. You're just so *good*. How do you do that? I never seen people clap like that.'

Etta, now flattered, smiled and patted the boy on the head. 'Come on in here and sit with me,' she said. 'I can teach you a few tricks.'

'I don't remember what I told him,' Etta recalled, 'but I remember thinking as he was leaving, Now, there's a boy who wants to learn from the best, so one day he's gonna *be* the best.'

While Joseph was at the American Federation of Musicians' hall in New York filling out certain forms for the Apollo engagement, he met a young, white lawyer by the name of Richard Arons. After talking to him for just a few moments, Joseph asked Arons to help him manage his sons. Joseph relished the idea of having white assistance – a preference that would cause problems for him in years to come. Arons, as a co-manager, began seeking concert bookings for the group while Joseph tried to interest the record industry in them. At one point, he tried to contact Berry Gordy, president of Motown, by sending him an audiotape of some of the Jacksons' songs; there was no reaction from Gordy, or from anyone else at Motown.

In 1968, when The Jackson Five played The Regal Theater in Chicago, Motown recording artist Gladys Knight arranged for some of Motown's executives – but not Berry – to attend the show. There was some interest in the group at that time; word got back to Berry that the Jacksons were an up-and-coming act, but still, there was no interest from him in terms of signing them to the label.

In July 1968 – when Jackie was seventeen; Tito, fourteen; Jermaine, thirteen; Marlon, ten; and Michael, nine – the group performed at Chicago's High Chaparral Club as an opening act for a group called Bobby Taylor and the Vancouvers. After he saw the Jackson boys in action, Taylor telephoned Ralph Seltzer, head of Motown's creative department and also head of the company's legal division, to suggest that the group be allowed to audition for Motown.

'I had some doubts,' Ralph Seltzer would recall. 'Creative considerations aside, I had concerns about their age and the way they would change when they grew older, in terms of their appearance and their voices. But there was so much excitement about them from Bobby, I finally told him to bring them on to Detroit.'

Though the Jacksons were scheduled to leave Chicago for a local television programme in New York, Bobby Taylor convinced Joseph that he should, instead, take the boys to Detroit for an audition. Taylor arranged to film their performance. If the boys were impressive, he said, Ralph Seltzer would then forward the film to Berry Gordy, who was in Los Angeles, for his approval.

Later that day, Katherine called the High Chaparral Club to talk to her husband. She was told that he and the boys had gone to the Motor City. 'Detroit?' she asked, puzzled. 'You mean to tell me they gave up that television show to go to Detroit? What in the world for?'

'Motown,' said the voice on the other end. 'They've gone to Motown.'

The Jacksons Sign with Motown

It was quarter to ten in the morning on 23 July 1968 when the Jackson family's Volkswagen minibus eased into a parking space in front of a cluster of small white bungalows at 2648 West Grand Boulevard, Detroit. The sign above one of the structures said it all: Hitsville U.S.A. This was Motown Records, the place from which had sprung forth so many memorable, chart-topping hit records. By 1968, Berry Gordy, Jr., had made an indelible impression on the entertainment world with this company. Gordy was a maverick in the record business in every way, a visionary who had plucked young, black hopefuls from urban street corners to then transform them into international superstars, with names such as The Supremes, The Temptations, The Miracles, The Vandellas and The Marvelettes. His success with those kinds of groups and solo artists, like Stevie Wonder, Marvin Gaye and Tammi Terrell, was largely the result of his brilliance at surrounding the singers with the most talented writers, producers and arrangers Detroit had to offer: Smokey Robinson, Brian Holland, Lamont Dozier and Eddie Holland, Norman Whitfield, and Barrett Strong, to name just a few. Using the notion of team work as their foundation, they and the artists formulated an original, contagious style of music that sold millions of records. It was called the Motown Sound.

A muscular rhythm section, engaging hook lines and choruses, and witty lyrics were all standard elements of songs like 'Where Did Our Love Go?' and 'I Can't Help Myself'. 'Dancing in the Streets', 'Please Mr Postman', 'Stop! In the Name of Love', 'The Tracks of My Tears' and seemingly countless others became not only anthems of an entire generation, but also emblems of the period in American history in which they were recorded.

Berry Gordy was a tough taskmaster who encouraged intense competition among his groups, writers and producers. The biggest criticism levelled at Gordy – by outsiders at first and then, later, by the artists themselves – had to do with the complete control he exercised over his dominion. Practically none of the artists had a clue as to how much money they generated for the company, and they were usually discouraged from asking questions about it. They sang and performed, and that was all that was expected of them. 'I never saw a tax return until 1979,' Diana Ross, who signed with Gordy in 1960, once said. 'Berry was such a mentor and strong personality, you found yourself relying on that. You didn't grow.'

Joseph had heard some rumours about Motown – nonsense about it being linked to the mob, for instance – and had also heard that some artists had trouble being paid for their work. However, none of that was on his mind when he took his boys there that day in 1968 for their audition.

Joseph and Jack Richardson, a close family friend who travelled with them and acted as a road manager, were in the front seat of the van as they drove up to Hitsville. Crammed in the back were the Jackson boys with a plethora of instruments, amplifiers and microphones.

'Get out and in line for inspection,' Joseph ordered.

The youngsters clambered out on to the already-warm Detroit street, where, as if a military troop, they lined up according to age: seventeen-year-old Jackie; fourteen-year-old Tito; thirteen-year-old Jermaine; ten-year-old Marlon, and nine-year-old Michael. Seventeen-year-old Johnny Jackson joined the group. Though they were not related, Joseph treated him just like he treated his own sons, and Johnny obeyed just as quickly. 'All right,' Joseph growled. 'It's ten o'clock. Let's go. Remember everything I taught you and, except when you're singing or being spoken to, keep your mouths shut. And remember what I always say . . .' He looked at Jermaine.

'Either you're a winner in this life, or a loser,' Jermaine said. 'And none of my kids are losers.'

'Thata' boy,' Joseph said, patting him on the back.

Inside the main building, the first person to greet the gang was a sharply dressed, black man. When he asked how he could assist them, Joseph explained that they were the Jackson family from Gary and that they had an appointment for an audition. The man said that he'd been expecting them. 'You must be Michael,' he said, looking at the smallest. Then, pointing to the boys in turn, he correctly called each one by his name. 'And you, sir, you must be Joseph,' he announced as he and the family patriarch shook hands. The boys looked at each other, amazed.

The family was then led into a small studio. As they walked in, they noticed a person setting up a film camera on a tripod. There were ten folding chairs in front of the small, elevated wooden platform which would serve as a stage.

Suzanne dePasse, creative assistant to president Berry Gordy, entered the studio wearing a blue miniskirt and a yellow blouse with ruffles. Her high heels clicked as she approached the group to introduce herself. She was an attractive, young black woman with shoulder-length, soft hair and a bright, friendly smile. The boys liked her immediately.

Ralph Seltzer was the next to appear. A tall white man wearing a dark suit and conservative tie, Seltzer seemed more intimidating than dePasse. He shook the hand of each boy, and then Joseph's and Jack's.

'We've heard a lot about your group,' he said to Joseph. 'Mr Gordy couldn't be here, but—'

'You mean Mr Gordy's not here?' Joseph asked, unable to hide his disappointment.

When Seltzer explained that Gordy was in Los Angeles, Joseph said that they should reschedule the audition when he was back in Detroit. He wanted his sons to audition for the boss, not his flunkies. However, Seltzer explained that they intended to film the audition, and then have it sent to Gordy on the West Coast. 'Mr Gordy will render a decision at that time,' he said.

'He'll render a decision,' Joseph repeated, more to himself than to Seltzer.

'Yes, he will,' Seltzer said, nodding his head. 'Mr Gordy will render a decision at that time.'

'Mr Gordy's gonna render a decision,' Michael repeated to Marlon. 'What's that mean?' Marlon whispered.

Michael shrugged his shoulders.

After all of the boys' equipment was lugged in from the van and set up, eight more staffers who did not introduce themselves filed into the studio, each with a notepad. Michael was ready to speak into the microphone when he heard someone in the corner snicker and say, 'Yeah, the Jackson Jive.' ('The Jackson Jive' is an old slang expression.) It sounded like an insult. Ralph Seltzer cleared his throat and glared at the person who made the remark.

'First song we'd like to do is James Brown's "I Got the Feeling",' Michael announced. 'Okay? Here we go.' He counted off – 'A-one, a-two, a-three' – and then Tito on guitar, Jermaine on bass, and Johnny Jackson on drums began to play.

'Baby, baby, baa-ba. Baby, baby, baa-ba. Baby, baby, baa-ba,' Michael sang. He grimaced and grunted, imitating James Brown. 'I got the fe-e-e-lin' now. Good *Gawwd* almighty!' He skated sideways across the floor, like Brown. 'I feel *goooood*,' he screamed into the microphone, a wicked expression playing on his little face.

Suzanne dePasse and Ralph Seltzer smiled at each other and nodded their heads. The other Motown executives kept time to the music. Joseph, standing in a corner with his arms folded across his chest, looked on approvingly.

After the boys finished, no one in the audience applauded. Instead, everyone feverishly wrote on their notepads.

Confused, the youngsters looked at each other and then at their father for a hint as to what they should do. Joseph motioned with his hand that they should continue with the next number.

'Thank you. Thank you very much,' Michael said, as though acknowledging an ovation. 'We 'preciate it.'

Michael then introduced the group, as he did in their live show, after which they sang the bluesy 'Tobacco Road'.

Again, no applause, just note-taking.

'Next song we'd like to do is a Motown song,' Michael announced. He paused, waiting for smiles of acknowledgement that never materialized. 'It's Smokey Robinson's "Who's Loving You" Okay? Here we go. A-one, a-two, a-three . . .'

They closed the song with a big finish and waited for a reaction from the Motown staffers. Again, everyone was writing. 'Jackson Jive, huh?' someone in the room said. 'These boys ain't jivin'. I think they're great.'

Michael beamed, his eyes dancing.

Ralph Seltzer cleared his throat and stood up. 'I'd like to thank you boys for coming,' he said. His voice gave no hint of how he felt the audition had gone. He shook each of their hands before walking over to Joseph and explaining to him that the company would put them all up at a nearby hotel. 'I'll be in touch with you,' Seltzer concluded, 'in two days . . .'

'When Mr Gordy renders a decision,' Joseph said, finishing Seltzer's sentence. He didn't sound happy. The boys were also clearly disappointed. As they filed out, no one said a word.

Two days later, Berry Gordy saw the sixteen-millimetre black-and-white film. He made a quick decision. 'Yes, absolutely, sign these kids up,' he told Ralph Seltzer. 'They're amazing. Don't waste a second. Sign 'em!'

On 26 July 968, Ralph Seltzer summoned Joseph into his Motown office for a meeting. During the two-hour conference – while the boys waited in the lobby – he explained that Berry Gordy was interested in signing The Jackson Five to the label, and then outlined the kind of relationship he hoped the company would develop with the Jackson youngsters. He spoke of 'the genius of Berry Gordy' and Gordy's hopes that The Jackson Five would become major recording stars. 'These kids are gonna be big, big, *big*,' Seltzer enthused, his manner much more cordial than it had been on their first visit. 'Believe me, if Mr Gordy says they're gonna be big, they're gonna be big.' Joseph must have felt like he was dreaming.

Then Seltzer presented Joseph with Motown's standard, nine-page contract. It never occurred to Joseph that he should probably have shown up with independent legal counsel for such an important discussion, and Seltzer hadn't suggested it.

'Berry did not want outside lawyers looking over any of our contracts,' Ralph Seltzer would explain in an interview long after he and Gordy had parted ways. 'Quite simply, he did not want outsiders influencing the artists. I thought it was more than fair for an artist to be able to take the contract home and read it, think it over. Berry told me that if I ever allowed an artist to take a contract home, that artist would not sign the contract. I tried once, and he was right: the artist did not sign. It was best, Berry decided, that potential contractees read over the agreement in my office and then just sign. If they had a problem with that, they did not become Motown artists. It was that simple.'

Seltzer began with clause number one, which stated that the agreement was for a term of seven years.

'Hold it right there,' Joseph interrupted. 'That's too long.'

Joseph felt that they should be committed for only one year. That brief length of time was unheard of at Motown, where the minimum arrangement was five years. Gordy felt it took that long to fully develop an artist, and then see a return on the company's investment.

Ralph Seltzer picked up the telephone and called Berry Gordy in Los Angeles. He explained the problem and handed the phone to Joseph, whom Berry had never met. After a brief conversation, Joseph hung up.

'He said he was gonna think about it,' Joseph told Seltzer, who smiled knowingly. Two minutes later, the phone rang again. It was Gordy wanting to talk to Joseph. He explained to Joseph that, as far as he was concerned, the real issue was a basic matter of trust. If Joseph really believed in Gordy and Motown, he wouldn't mind having his children obligated to the company for seven years. After all, Gordy was willing to pay for their accommodation, recording sessions, rehearsal time, and so forth. However, if Joseph *insisted* on changing the clause, then it would be changed, 'because, after all, I just want what's best for the kids,' Gordy explained.

Joseph smiled and gave Richardson the thumbs-up signal. He handed the phone to Seltzer who got back on the line and spoke to Berry for a moment. Then Seltzer put Gordy on hold and summoned an assistant into his office who took some quick dictation from Gordy. About five minutes later, the assistant returned with a new clause, which stated that the group was obligated to Motown for only one year. Joseph beamed; he had won a strategic battle against Berry Gordy.

Ralph Seltzer quickly explained the rest of the contract. Joseph nodded his head, then called his boys into the office.

'We got it, boys,' he announced.

'Oh, man, that's too much!'

'We're on Motown!'

'We got us a contract!'

They all began jumping up and down and hugging one another.

Ralph Seltzer gave each boy a contract. 'Just sign right there on that line, fellas.'

They looked at their father.

'Go ahead. It's okay. Sign it.'

Though Joseph had not even read the contract – he just had it explained to him – and neither had any of his sons, each boy signed.

'And here's an agreement for you, Mr Jackson,' Ralph Seltzer said, handing Joseph a paper. 'This is a parental approval agreement and it says, quite simply, that you will make certain that the boys comply with the terms of the contract they just signed.'*

Joseph signed the agreement.

'Well, congratulations,' Ralph Seltzer said with a smile and a firm handshake for Joseph. 'And let me be the first to welcome you to Motown.'

In years to come, many would wonder why Joseph Jackson allowed his sons to sign Motown contracts – and why he himself would sign an accompanying agreement – without first reading the documents? In litigation against Motown, years later, Joseph would explain, 'I did not read these agreements nor did my sons read these agreements because they were presented to us on a take-it-or-leave-it basis. Since my sons were just starting out in the entertainment field, we accepted these contracts based on the representations of Ralph Seltzer that they were good contracts.'

Ralph Seltzer would disagree, and in a way that was a bit unsettling. 'I have no recollection of ever saying to Joseph Jackson or The Jackson 5 that the agreement being offered by Motown was a good agreement.'

Later, after leaving Ralph Seltzer's office, Joseph telephoned Richard Arons, the man he had hired as his lawyer and the group's unofficial co-manager. Arons would recall, 'Joseph called me up and said he had signed with Motown. There wasn't much I could offer at that point.'

It's easy to understand why Joseph would just sign the deal. It *was* Motown, after all. However, there were significant problems with the contract, many of which would cause trouble for the family later on down the road.

Clause Five, for instance, stated that The Jackson 5 would be unable to record for any other label 'at any time prior to the expiration

---

*Katherine Jackson would also sign a similar parental approval agreement on 17 October 1969. It appears that she did not actually read the agreement, for in it she and Joseph are referred to as the parents of John Porter Jackson – Johnny Jackson, the group's drummer, to whom they are not related.

of five years from the expiration or termination of this agreement'. This was a standard Motown clause that applied whether an act was signed for seven years, five years, or, as in the case of The Jackson 5, one. So Berry Gordy's concession to Joseph Jackson proved meaningless; The Jackson 5 were still tied up for at least six years.

Furthermore, the third clause stated that Motown was under no obligation to record the group or promote its music for five years, even though this was purportedly a one-year contract! Some other contractual stipulations that Joseph might have questioned had he read the agreement: Motown would choose all of the songs that the group would record, and the group would record each song until 'they have been recorded to our [Motown's] satisfaction'. However, Motown 'shall not be obligated to release any recording', meaning that just because a song was recorded, it would not necessarily be issued to the public. The group was paid $12.50 per 'master', which is a completed recording of a song. But in order for the recording to be considered a master, the song had to be released. Otherwise, they were paid nothing. In other words, they could record dozens of songs and see only one issued from that session, and that would be the one for which they'd be paid. As for the rest, well, they would just be a waste of time.

It's been written that the Jacksons received a 2.7 per cent royalty rate, based on wholesale price, a standard Motown royalty of the 1960s. Actually, according to their contract, the boys would receive 6 per cent of 90 per cent of the wholesale price (less all taxes and packaging) of any single or album released. It was the same rate as Marvin Gaye, and also The Supremes, got. Marvin, as a solo artist, did not have to split his percentage, though. The Supremes had to divide it three ways. And this amount had to be split five ways among the Jackson brothers. In other words, Michael would receive one-fifth of 6 per cent of 90 per cent of the wholesale price – or a little under one-half of a penny for any single and $0.0216, about two cents, per album released (based on an assumed wholesale price of $0.375 a single and $2.00 an album).

Also, as per the terms of the contract, Motown was obligated to pay the cost of arrangements, copying and accompaniment and all other costs related to each recording session, whether the song was released or not – but these expenses and others would have to be recouped by the company from the royalties generated by sales of the records that were released. This arrangement would lead to many complaints by Motown artists, and it would be a big problem for The

Jackson 5. But Joseph never imagined that the group would record so many songs that would not be issued – and they did, perhaps as many as a hundred! Later, it would be virtually impossible for the group to make any money on the ones that *were* released, because the boys would still have to pay for all the ones that weren't.

Also, if Michael or any of his brothers were to leave the group, he would have no right ever to say that he was a member of The Jackson 5, 'and shall have no further right to use the group name for any purpose whatsoever'. Joseph may not have realized it, but this could be a big problem. For instance, when Florence Ballard was fired from The Supremes in 1967, she was not able to promote herself as having been a member of the group. Her press biography for ABC, when she signed to that label as a solo artist in 1968, could state only that she was 'a member of a popular female singing group'.

Also Motown could, at any time, replace any member of the group with any person the company chose. In other words, if Tito acted up, for instance, he could be bounced from the act and replaced by someone else selected by Motown, and not by Joseph.

An even more limiting clause – number sixteen – stated that 'Motown owns all rights, title and interest in the names Jackson 5 *and* Jackson Five.' In other words, they may have gone to the company as The Jackson Five, but they sure weren't going to be leaving that way. When The Supremes wanted to leave the label in 1972, they were welcome to go – but they'd have to change the group's name to something else. They stayed.

The contract with Motown could have also stated that Joseph would be obligated to hand Randy and Janet over to the company to raise as Gordy saw fit, and he might have agreed to it. The important thing was that the boys were with Motown, on any terms.

Thus, on 26 July 1968, in tiny, barely legible handwriting, Michael signed the deal: 'Michael Joseph Jackson'.*

---

*Michael's signature meant nothing since, at nine years of age, he was a minor. Having him and his brothers sign contracts was only intended to make them feel part of the Motown family. Underneath Michael's signature, Joseph W. Jackson signed as guardian.

'Hollywood Livin''

On 27 September 1968, Motown Records booked The Jackson 5 to appear in a benefit concert at Gilroy Stadium in Gary, Indiana, the purpose of which was to defray the costs of Richard Hatcher's mayoral campaign. On the bill that day were Motown recording artists Gladys Knight and the Pips, Shorty Long, and Bobby Taylor and the Vancouvers. The Jackson 5 opened the show. In years to come, the official Motown story would be that *this* was where Diana Ross saw the boys for the first time, 'discovered' them, and brought them to Gordy's attention. In truth, The Jackson 5 were already signed to the label. Moreover, Diana Ross was nowhere near Gary at the time. She was in Los Angeles, rehearsing with The Supremes.

Around Christmastime, Berry Gordy hosted a party at the Detroit estate he had purchased in 1967 for a million dollars. (Though he had moved to the West Coast, he still maintained his Michigan residence.) The Jackson 5 were asked to perform at the party for the Motown artists and other friends of Gordy's. *This* was a big deal.

Gordy's three-storey mansion boasted a ballroom with marble floors and columns, an Olympic-sized swimming pool, a billiard room, a two-lane bowling alley, a private theatre linked to the main house by a tunnel, and a pub whose furnishings were imported from England. All of the rooms were decorated with gold leaf, frescoed ceilings and elaborate crystal chandeliers. Expensive oil portraits of Gordy's friends and family decorated the entryway.

If the Jacksons had ever seen a home like this before, it was only in movies where the occupants usually were royalty – white royalty. 'Black people actually live like this?' Joseph recalled asking himself as he wandered throughout the mansion, shaking his head. 'I just can't believe that this kind of thing is possible.' When Gordy happened to overhear the comment, he put his hand on Joseph's shoulder and whispered something in his ear that made Joseph smile. The two men shook hands in agreement and Gordy led Joseph into the living room.

'So tell me, man, what do you think about this?' Gordy asked, stopping before an enormous painting of Gordy dressed as Napoleon Bonaparte. It had been commissioned by his sister, Esther.

'Jesus. What can I say?' Joseph asked. 'That's *you*? Man, it's too much to believe.'

'Well, do you like it?' Gordy pressed.

'I, uh . . . You, uh . . .' All Joseph could do was stammer. Just at that moment, his son Michael came running up to him. 'Hey, who's that funny-lookin' guy in the picture?' he asked.

Joseph cringed and shot his son a look. Gordy smiled.

'I'll never forget that night,' Michael would say. 'There were maids and butlers, and everyone was real polite. There were Motown stars everywhere. Smokey Robinson was there. That's when I met him for the first time. The Temptations were there, and we were singing some of their songs, so we were real nervous. And I looked out into the audience, and there was Diana Ross. That's when I almost lost it.'

After the boys' performance, Berry introduced them to Diana for the first time. Diana looked regal in a white, draped silk gown and her hair pulled back in a chignon.

'I just want to tell you how much I enjoyed you guys,' she said as she shook their hands. 'Mr Gordy tells me that we're going to be working together.'

'We are?' Michael asked.

'Yes, we are,' Diana said. Her smile was almost as overwhelming as the diamonds she wore at her ears and around her neck. 'Whatever I can do to assist you,' she said, 'that's what I'm going to do.'

'Well, Miss Ross, we really appreciate it,' Joseph Jackson managed to say. Usually a smooth talker, Joseph was not having an easy time that night.

Diana's smile was warm and sincere. She turned to Michael. 'And you, you're just so cute.' When she pinched his cheek, Michael blushed.

Immediately after signing to the label, the Jacksons began to record at the Motown studios under the direction of producer Bobby Taylor, the man who had really discovered them in Chicago. For the next few months, they would spend their weeks in Gary attending school and their weekends – and many of their weeks as well – in Detroit, sleeping on the floor of Taylor's apartment. They recorded fifteen songs, most of which would surface later on their albums. Taylor would say later that he was not paid for those sessions. 'Sure, I would have liked the recognition for having discovered The Jackson 5,' he said. 'But recognition don't pay the bills.'

(One day, Berry Gordy and Bobby Taylor were talking about the boys, and Bobby was saying how thrilled he was to be in on the ground floor of something as exciting as The Jackson 5. 'Taylor, let me tell you something,' Gordy said, according to Bobby's memory. 'As soon as they get rich, they're gonna forget who you are.')

The next eight months would prove to be difficult. Berry did not feel The Jackson 5 were ready to have a single release yet; he wasn't satisfied with any of the songs they had thus far recorded. Everyone in the family was becoming impatient, especially since conditions in Gary were getting worse with street gangs terrorizing the neighbourhood. Joseph was mugged and, later, a punk pulled a knife on Tito. Every day, the family would wait for that call from someone — *anyone* — at Motown, telling them what the next step in their lives would be.

On 11 March 1969, the Motown contract was finally fully executed. The delay had been caused when Ralph Seltzer discovered The Jackson 5 were still committed to Steeltown Records, despite Richard Aron's previous efforts to extricate them from that deal. Motown had to make a settlement with Steeltown, much to Gordy's chagrin. By this time, according to Ralph Seltzer, Motown had spent in excess of thirty thousand dollars on The Jackson 5, and this sum did not include any settlement made to Steeltown. Gordy was anxious to begin recouping his investment.

In August 1969, more than a year since their audition, the call came from Motown: Gordy wanted Joseph, his five sons and Johnny Jackson and Ronny Rancifer to move to Los Angeles. They would attend school on the West Coast while recording at Motown's new Hollywood facilities. Though Gordy wasn't enthused by any of the Jacksons' songs, he was impressed with young Michael. 'Michael was a born star,' he would later say in an interview. 'He was a classic example of understanding everything. I recognized that he had a depth that was so vast, it was just incredible. The first time I saw him, I saw this little kid as something real special.'

Joseph, Tito, Jack Richardson, drummer Johnny Jackson, and keyboardist Ronny Rancifer drove to Los Angeles in the family's new Dodge Maxivan. Motown paid for Jackie, Jermaine, Marlon and Michael to fly out a few days later. It was Joseph's decision not to move the entire family from Gary to Los Angeles until he was certain that their future there would be secure. It was possible, after all, that Berry could be wrong, that the group would be a failure, and that they would have to start all over again. So Janet, Randy and LaToya stayed behind with Katherine in Gary.

Berry registered the family at one of the seediest motels in Hollywood, the Tropicana, on Santa Monica Boulevard. Michael, Marlon and Jermaine shared one room while Tito and Jackie were in another. Joseph was down the hall. The family saw little of their rooms. Since it was still school vacation, they spent most of their waking hours at Motown's Hollywood studios rehearsing and recording.

Eventually, Gordy pulled the family out of the Tropicana and moved them to the Hollywood Motel, across the street from Hollywood High and closer to Motown headquarters. This was an even more dreadful residence for young boys; prostitutes and pimps used it as a place to conduct business. However, none of that mattered to the Jacksons. Why would it? They were living in California. Even if they didn't see movie stars on every corner as they had dreamed, Los Angeles was heaven compared to Gary.

To the Jacksons' young eyes, everything seemed new. Michael had never seen a real palm tree before he got to California. 'And here were whole streets lined with them,' he once recalled. There were expensive, luxury automobiles everywhere they looked, and everyone driving them seemed to wear sunglasses, even on those overcast mornings when the sun didn't emerge until noon. In fact, as the young Jacksons would soon learn, many people wore their sunglasses at night too. 'Now *that's* Hollywood livin',' Joseph said.

One afternoon, Berry called a meeting of the gang at Diana Ross's home. This was the first time the boys had seen her since the show they gave at Berry's home in Detroit the previous winter. Diana's house may not have been spectacular by Hollywood standards – she was a single woman, at the time, living in a three-bedroom temporary residence in Hollywood Hills while in the process of purchasing a new, more opulent home in Beverly Hills – but when the five Jackson boys and their father compared her digs to their garage-sized house in Gary, it was hard for them to act cool.

Michael has recalled that Gordy sat the boys down in Diana's living room and had a talk with them. 'I'm gonna make you kids the biggest thing in the world,' he told them. 'You're gonna have three number-one hits in a row. They're gonna write about you kids in history books. So get ready, 'cause it's coming.'

That was exactly what the Jacksons wanted to hear. Joseph had wanted nothing more for his sons than to be successful, and it seemed a sure-thing, now. He told them that they were to do whatever 'Mr Gordy' asked of them, with no questions. Simply put, Joseph was in awe of Berry. However, he was also intimidated by him. 'Here's a black man who has made millions of dollars in show business,' Joseph had said. 'If I can just learn a few things from this guy, then I'll have it made too.'

As the meeting was about to conclude, Diana swept into the room looking like . . . well, *Diana Ross* . . . in a black satin hot pants outfit, huge natural hairstyle and gold hoop earrings. 'She always looked like a goddess,' Jermaine recalled. 'I remember that when she walked into the living room that day, all of our mouths dropped open.' Although the boys had met her before, they were still awed. Joseph fell all over himself to make an impression.

'I just want to tell you boys once again that I'm here for you,' she said. 'If there's anything I can do for you, I hope you'll let me know.'

She seemed sincere, Jermaine would remember. 'It was hard to believe that she was saying those words to us,' he said. 'I mean, what did we do to deserve her assistance? Talk about luck.'

What Jermaine remembers most about the day is the telegram that Diana showed them. 'This is from me to lots and lots of people,' she explained. It read: 'Please join me in welcoming a brilliant musical group, The Jackson 5, on Monday, 11 August 6:30 to 9:30 p.m. at the Daisy, North Rodeo Drive, Beverly Hills. The Jackson 5, featuring sensational eight-year-old Michael Jackson, will perform live at the party. [signed] Diana Ross.'

'I think you made a mistake,' Michael told her. 'I'm not eight. I'm ten.'

'Not any more you're not,' Berry said with a grin.

Berry explained that the discrepancy was a matter of public relations. What ensued was a brief discussion with Michael about the art of PR; he was reminded that, as far as the media were concerned, Diana Ross was the one who had brought him and his brothers to Motown. He should always remember that because, as Diana explained to him, 'It's all for your image.'

'Got it,' Michael said. 'I'm eight. And we were discovered by the great Miss Diana Ross.'

'You got it, all right,' Diana said with a grin. She hugged him tightly. 'You are just so cute,' she said, again.

Michael would later recall, 'I figured out at an early age that if someone said something about me that wasn't true, it was a lie. But if someone said something about my *image* that wasn't true, then it was okay. Because then it wasn't a lie, it was public relations.'

On 11 August 1968, Diana Ross introduced her new protégés, The Jackson 5, with the kind of pomp and pageantry usually accorded major Hollywood debuts. Three hundred of Gordy's and Diana's 'closest' friends and business associates crammed into the chic Beverly Hills private club, the Daisy, all having been personally invited via Diana Ross's telegram. They stood and cheered as Michael Jackson and The Jackson 5 – as they were introduced by Diana – performed Motown songs such as Smokey Robinson's 'Who's Loving You' and even Disney classics like 'Zip-a-dee-do-dah'. The boys wore identical lime green vest suits with gold shirts and matching green boots. Every move had been carefully choreographed for them, and rehearsed in the professional Motown tradition. They were a hit. Afterwards, a Motown press release was distributed to everyone in attendance, with two years shaved off the age of each boy.

Beaming with pride at their reception, Berry announced that The Jackson 5 would next appear in concert with Diana Ross and The Supremes at the Forum five days later, and then later in October when Diana would play hostess on *The Hollywood Palace* television show.

Each Jackson boy met the press in a receiving line, with Diana

Ross making the introductions: 'This one's Michael. Isn't he *cute?* And that one's Jermaine. Isn't he *adorable?* And over there's Jackie. Look how *tall* he is,' and so forth.

Soul reporter Judy Spiegelman recalled, 'I remember being impressed with the courteous, outgoing attitude of the youngsters. After all, they were just kids but yet not at all affected by the attention.'

Pauline Dunn, a reporter from the *Sentinel*, a Los Angeles black newspaper, approached Michael.

'How's it feel to be a star, Michael?' she wanted to know.

'Well, to tell you the truth, I had just about given up hope,' Michael said with a grin. He was wearing a black bowler hat over his Afro-style hair. 'I thought I was gonna be an old man before being discovered.' Then, in a hushed, dramatic tone he concluded, 'But then along came Miss Diana Ross to save my career. She *discovered* me.'

'And just how old are you, Michael?' she asked.

Michael looked up at Diana, who was standing proudly behind him, her hand on his shoulder. Berry Gordy stood nearby.

'Eight,' Michael said.

'But I thought you were older. Going on eleven, maybe,' the suspicious journalist pressed.

'Well, I'm not,' Michael insisted. 'I'm eight.'

'But I heard—'

'Look, the kid's eight, all right?' Berry broke in. 'Next question.'

'Next question, *please*,' Michael corrected him. He smiled and winked at Pauline Dunn as if to say, This is how we play the game.

Creating The Jackson 5's First Hit

The early 1970s were the most significant transitional years Motown Records had undergone since shoring itself up as a major musical force. By that time, although the company was still producing superb pop and rhythm-and-blues music, some of its biggest stars had begun grumbling about Motown's conveyor-belt method of creating hit records.

The seventies was a period of change, both socially and politically, and the production of pop music did not go unaffected. To keep pace with the times, many labels eventually dismantled their songwriting/production staffs and signed prolific singer-songwriters and self-contained bands who wrote and performed their own music. Berry Gordy was not thrilled about this trend. He had always discouraged his acts from writing and producing their own material because, it was said, he did not wish for them to share in the music's publishing, which was the inevitable next request. He preferred having his own stable of writers and producers, all of whom were signed to his own publishing company, Jobete. In the end, much of the money stayed in Motown's coffers.

However, some of Motown's acts craved more artistic freedom. For instance, Stevie Wonder and Marvin Gaye both felt that they'd outgrown manufacturing music the Motown way – singing songs supplied to them by staff writers and producers. They must have finally realized that staff producers and writers like Smokey Robinson and Norman Whitfield were earning large sums from songwriting royalties without having to sweat through gruelling forty-city tours and public appearances. Wonder and Gaye were now asking Berry for the opportunity to express themselves musically through songwriting and, by extension, share in the publishing of their songs.

The fact is that music wasn't at the forefront of founder Berry Gordy's reasoning when he decided to relocate Motown from Detroit to Los Angeles. Berry picked up and moved two decades' worth of Michigan roots for the same reason optimistic high school graduates and pretty young runaways swarm to the City of Angels every day from all over the world: the Silver Screen. Berry wanted to get into films, and his protégée Diana Ross was to be his ticket. In masterminding the westward move, Gordy was his usual methodical self. He used the occasion to clean house: employees and artists considered deadweight would be left behind in the Motor City, while desired staffers could keep their jobs, but only if they were willing to relocate to Los Angeles.

When Berry Gordy saw the film of The Jackson Five's Detroit audition, he realized that these youngsters had arrived at a precipitous time. Not only would this group usher in a new musical era for Motown, but they would do so with a hit single supplied by Motown's own production staff. These kids didn't want to write and produce their own songs, they just wanted to be stars. For Berry, this must have been déjà vu. How he longed for a time not so long ago when Stevie and Marvin cared only about singing and not about publishing. Signing a group that would be exclusively reliant on Motown for its material would validate the tried-and-true Motown process for at least a few more years. (Even Gordy couldn't have predicted, though, how much Jobete would prosper as a result of his signing of The Jackson 5.)

In 1969, Motown's West Coast Division was operated under the direction of one of the company's top staff writer-producers. As an integral part of a writing-producing team at Motown called the Clan, Deke Richards was responsible for some terrific songs (such as The Supremes' 'Love Child'). He and Berry enjoyed a close relationship; Deke even had a phone line exclusively for Berry's use, and Berry would call him at all hours of the early morning, brimming with ideas.

Integral to Deke's job as Creative Director of Talent for Motown's West Coast Division was an on-going search for promising new writers and artists to bolster the company's roster. That year, he was introduced to two talented young writers, Freddie Perren and Fonce Mizell. He thought both had amazing ability and couldn't wait to bring them into the Motown family.

For the next three months, Deke Richards, Freddie Perren and Fonce Mizell collaborated on a song entitled 'I Want to Be Free', which was intended for Gladys Knight and the Pips. The team went into the Motown studios with a talented corps of musicians to cut the instrumental track for 'I Want to Be Free', remembered fondly by Perren as 'one of Motown's greatest instrumental performances'.

Meanwhile, Berry invited Deke to the show The Jackson 5 gave at the Daisy, presented by Diana Ross. Deke was impressed.

He had heard through the Motown grapevine that Bobby Taylor was presently recording material with the brothers in Detroit. Though Taylor was producing some good songs, everyone knew that there wasn't a hit record to be found in the bunch. When Deke played the track of 'I Want to Be Free' for Berry, he liked it so much he thought it might be ideal for the Jackson boys. 'Give the song a Frankie Lymon treatment,' he told Deke, 'and we'll see what happens.'

Deke recalled, 'Berry lived with the track for a while and had a couple of ideas which were good. He was starting to get excited. I *wanted* Berry to get involved. This was starting to become a very exciting proposition for all of us.'

Deke decided to call the team of Fonce Mizell, Freddie Perren, himself and Gordy the Corporation, which would reinforce the democratic premise that there would be no overblown egos involved in the work and that everyone would be treated fairly. He remembered, 'After the basic instrumental track was finished, it was time to begin rehearsing the kids' vocals to record over it. The boys came over to Berry's house, and that's when we started talking about the song with them and developing a rapport. For the next few weeks, those kids worked a tremendous number of hours on this one song. It was hard work. Eventually, the song was retitled "I Want You Back".'

'The biggest problem with The Jackson 5 was not the willingness to work,' said Deke. 'The problem was that you not only had to be a producer, you had to be a phonetics and English teacher. It was draining, teaching them the pronunciation of words. We had to go over and over words one at a time, which was tough.

'If Michael had any problems other than phonetics, they had to do with attacking and sustaining words and notes. Like any kid, he tended to throw away words, he would slur a note rather than hold on to it. He'd be thinking about dancing or whatever and not concentrate on getting the lyrics out. I'd have to tell him, "I need those notes, Michael, every last one of them."

'As a singer, though, he was great. As far as tone and all, he was terrific. We put a lot of pressure on him, because whenever you find a little kid who can sing like that, the feeling is, "Yeah, he's so great I want him to be even greater." I felt that if he could be that good in the raw, imagine how amazing he could be if you really polished him up.'

'I remember that Deke Richards was one of my first teachers,' Michael Jackson said. 'God, we spent so much time on "I Want You Back". He was really patient with me, all of us. I think I must have recorded that thing two dozen times. I had no idea that recording could be such work. I remember falling asleep at the mike. I wondered if it would ever be finished. Just when I thought we were through, we'd have to go back and do it again.'

The final recording session for 'I Want You Back' lasted until two in the morning. 'This had to be the most expensive single in Motown history, up to that point,' Deke Richards added. 'It cost about ten thousand dollars. At that time the cost of a Motown single was about two thousand. We kept adding and subtracting music until the very end. In fact, the original song started off with just a guitar, but at the last minute I wanted a piano glissando at the top. I had Freddie and Fonce go in there and run their fingers down the piano to kick the song off.'

On 2 October 1969, after the final mixing of 'I Want You Back', Berry asked Deke how he thought the group's name should appear on the record's label. 'Jackson Five'? 'Jackson Five featuring Michael Jackson'? Deke said he thought the group should be called simply The Jackson 5, with the numeral 5. Berry agreed. Joseph Jackson wasn't even consulted. Imagine what kind of tension might have resulted in the family if Deke had suggested 'Jackson Five featuring Michael Jackson'?

Michael Moves in with Diana

On 1 October 1969, as his father and brothers were being shuffled from one hotel to another by the Motown brass, it was decided that Michael Jackson would move in with Diana Ross in her Hollywood Hills home. 'It was a calculated thing. I wanted him to be around her,' Berry Gordy explained. 'People think it was an accident that he stayed there. It wasn't. I wanted Diana to teach him whatever she could. Diana's a very influential person. I knew that Michael would pick up *something* just by being around her. Diana had said that he sort of reminded her of herself at age eleven. Michael was anxious and interested, as well as talented, like Diana was when I first met her. She was sixteen, then.

'I asked her if she minded and she didn't. She wanted him around.

It was good for her to have someone else besides herself to think about. It was just for four weeks, the month of October.'

As much as she may have wanted to help, Diana was so consumed by the demands of her own career, she probably wasn't prepared for the role of surrogate mother. Still, she gave it everything she had, treated Michael like a son and became attached to him. However, Michael's lifestyle in the Ross household must have seemed to be everything he had been brought up by his mother to shun as wicked. Nothing else really mattered in these surroundings, it seemed, but show business. 'You are going to be a great, great star,' Diana would remind him over breakfast. 'Now, eat your cereal.'

Though Diana remained at home during the month of October, she was extremely busy. She was about to leave The Supremes and embark on a solo career. Meanwhile, she and Berry were having a tumultuous romance. Michael, no doubt, heard many arguments between the couple, and then probably watched as they smiled and cooed at one another for the sake of reporters. He was learning a lot about show business public relations, but only time would tell how he would be affected by it.

Michael attended school during the day and recorded in the studio until late at night, but had noted that during the time he lived with Diana Ross, she found time to teach him about art. 'We'd go out, just the two of us, and buy pencils and paint,' Michael wrote of his time with Diana in his autobiography. 'When we weren't drawing or painting, we'd go to museums.'

Michael's fascination with Diana – some would later see it as an obsession – would last for many years. As well as a mother figure when his own was thousands of miles away, she was an accomplished performer; he studied her constantly. 'I remember I used to just sit in the corner and watch the way she moved,' he recalled of Diana. 'She was art in motion. Have you ever seen the way she works her hands? I was,' he struggled for the right word, '*enthralled* by her. All day long when I wasn't rehearsing my songs, I'd be listening to hers. I watched her rehearse one day in the mirror. She didn't know I was watching. I studied her, the way she moved, the way she sang, just the way she was. Afterwards, I told her, "I want to be just like you, Diana." And she said, "You just be yourself and you'll be a great star." '

Michael, at age eleven, did have some lonely moments living in the Ross home while she was away at work; he missed his mother and talked to her on the telephone constantly, running up Diana's phone bill.

Katherine was troubled by Michael's life during that time, according to one family friend, a woman who asked for anonymity because she is someone in whom Katherine still confides. 'Katie truly was concerned about Diana Ross's lifestyle and how it might influence her son,' said the friend. 'She didn't want her son to be corrupted by Diana or her show-business circle of friends. Also, she knew very little about Diana. She knew her as a star with a reputation for being egotistical and self-involved. The whole time Michael was away from her, Katie could only imagine what was going on in the Ross household and how Michael was coping with it. Her imagination ran wild. It was a time of great concern, wondering what kinds of values Diana Ross was passing on to her son.'

Perhaps making matters more difficult for Katherine, Diana seemed reluctant to talk to her directly. When Katherine would telephone to check in on Michael, she would have to talk to one of the household staff if Michael wasn't available. Diana would usually not come to the phone.

If Katherine was distressed about the possibilities of wild parties at the Diana Ross residence, she need not have been. Diana was a serious person, not a party girl. She would go to bed early in order to be up on time for her many appointments. If anything, she passed on to Michael a work ethic that would serve him well as a youngster. She wanted to be an example to him, and she was sure to not allow him to see anything but her best side.

'I got to know her well,' Michael would say many years later, 'and she taught me so much by example. I remember she would be in the recording studio until all hours of the morning, get home, have a costume fitting, a rehearsal, lunch, a TV show, and then she would crash for maybe two hours. Then back in the studio. I remember thinking, I don't have it bad at all. Look at *her*. And she's Diana Ross!'

Success!

Stardom for The Jackson 5 was just around the corner, but with a detour or two along the way. When 'I Want You Back' was released in October 1969, it wasn't an immediate hit. The song entered *Billboard*'s Top 100 at number 90. Motown's promotion and sales department had to continually encourage disc jockeys to play it and record stores to stock it. Then, finally, ten weeks later, on 31 January it shot to number one, displacing B. J. Thomas's 'Raindrops Keep Falling on My Head'.

With 'I Want You Back', Berry Gordy, Deke Richards, Fonce Mizell and Freddie Perren managed to launch Motown's latest find with a blast, and the record label into a new and exciting decade. A precocious yet completely adorable and endearing Michael led his older brothers into the hearts, homes and stereos of middle-class white America. The rousing single also found success on the black or rhythm-and-blues charts.

As with the successful Supremes' formula of the sixties, The Jackson 5 sound presented a wholesome, non-threatening soul music, easily digested and readily accepted by all races of record buyers. Though the record was only number one for a week in America, it went on to sell an amazing 2,060,711 copies in the United States, and another four million abroad. In the UK, the song peaked at number two and remained on the chart for thirteen weeks, selling 250,000 copies.

'The pros have told us that no group has ever had a better start than we did,' Michael Jackson has remembered. 'Ever.'

Once 'I Want You Back' was released, The Jackson 5 had an image makeover. Motown's famous charm school – the artist development classes held in Detroit to turn street kids like The Temptations into savvy show people – was no longer in business now that the company had relocated to Los Angeles. All of the image-changing work now had to be done by whomever Gordy could coax into helping the cause. Suzanne dePasse – now president of Motown Productions – became responsible for repackaging the youngsters. Stylists with Colourform models worked with them to come up with the best haircuts and stage outfits for each group member. Suzanne and the boys went shopping for the most outrageous outfits they could find – and some of them were truly atrocious, with wild colours and designs. Yet, oddly, it all worked. It was the seventies, after all.

18 October 1969, marked another major milestone for The Jackson 5: their first appearance on national television, on *The Hollywood Palace*, hosted by Diana Ross. (The Supremes were there, too, though Mary Wilson and Cindy Birdsong didn't get much air time that night.) Backstage, Joseph kept peppering his boys with last-minute advice, the way he always did before they performed. Michael once recalled that it was usually easy to tune Joseph out; he'd said the same things a hundred times before. This evening, Joseph was even more intense, according to Jack Lewis, a set designer on the ABC programme.

'Joe paced back and forth backstage like a lion,' he remembered. 'There's no doubt in my mind he was more nervous than his kids. The boys were excited about the break. Diana Ross kept going backstage and having private conversations with Michael. She patted him on the head a lot, which I noticed annoyed Joe.'

Diana wore a white midriff-baring halter and white slacks which emphasized her reed-thin figure. Her hair was pulled into an elaborate topknot; her shoulder-length silver earrings flew to and fro when she danced with Michael backstage before the show. 'Come on, get down!' she said, beckoning him. 'You're the man! You're the man!' Michael did a quick James Brown spin and collapsed to the floor on his knees, then back up again in a flash. 'I'm the man,' he said, laughing. 'You got that right.'

Berry Gordy was backstage too. Right before they went on, Gordy pulled all of them together in a huddle and had an impromptu conference. Then when he finished, Joe – not to be outdone – did the same thing.

From behind the curtain, they heard Diana's introduction: 'Tonight, I have the pleasure of introducing a young star who has been in the business all of his life. He's worked with his family, and when he sings and dances, he lights up the stage.'

At that moment, Sammy Davis, Jr., came bounding out on to the stage for a comic bit. He supposedly thought Diana was introducing him, but she explained that she was actually referring to – and then she made the introduction – 'Michael Jackson and The Jackson 5.'

At that, the curtain opened and The Jackson 5 bounded out, singing the Sly Stone composition, 'Sing a Simple Song'. The fellows were dressed alike in the costumes they had worn for their debut appearance at the Daisy: pale, lime-green, double-breasted, wide-lapelled, sleeveless jackets with matching bell-bottom slacks and suede boots in exactly the same shade. Their shirts, with the full-gathered sleeves, were gold. (While many observers assumed that these outfits were paid for by Motown, actually they were purchased off the rack by Joseph and Katherine back in Gary.)

As they sang, according to set designer Jack Lewis, Joseph Jackson and Berry Gordy became embroiled in a heated argument, backstage.

'What's this "Michael Jackson and the Jackson 5" stuff?' Joseph demanded. 'No one told me about that. No one cleared that with me.'

Berry shrugged his shoulders. 'It wasn't written that way on the cue card,' he explained. 'Diana just blurted it out. She's that way. She does what she wants to do. Been trying to tell her what to do for years,' he said with an easy smile. 'It ain't gonna happen.'

'Well, I don't like it,' Joseph fumed. 'All the boys are equal. We're not singling Michael out from the rest. It'll just cause problems.'

'But, look, Joe, he's obviously the star.' Berry said, not taking his eyes off the performance. 'Come on! Look at him. You gotta be kidding me?'

'No, they're *all* stars,' Joseph countered.

'Well, it's too late now,' Berry said, shrugging his shoulders, again. Then the two of them watched the rest of the performance, Berry with a big smile and Joseph with a sour frown.

When the brothers finished their next two songs – 'Can You Remember?' and 'I Want You Back' – the applause, led by Diana, was generous. They made a solid impression, there was no doubt about it.

After the show, there was pandemonium backstage, with the boys whooping and hollering, slapping one another on the back, jumping up and down and hugging each other. Joseph was in the middle of it all, enjoying a sweet moment of victory with his sons.

Diana walked into the backstage area and went right to Michael. 'I am so proud of you,' she enthused. 'You are the best! Just the greatest. You're gonna be a big, *big* star.' She took such pride in Michael's achievement; one might have thought she was his actual mother, not just a figure-head in his life. Then, she turned from her 'son'.

'Will someone please get me a towel?' Diana asked no one in particular. She raised her voice. 'There should have been a towel back here waiting for me. *I want a towel*. Now, where is it? *Somebody?*'

'I'll get you one, Miss Ross' Michael offered. He disappeared for a moment and came back with a fluffy white towel.

Diana smiled and took it. 'Thanks, Michael,' she said, patting him on the head.

He beamed and ran off.

Berry walked over to Diana and, as Jack Lewis listened, he asked, 'What was with that introduction, "Michael Jackson and The Jackson 5"?'

Towelling off her bare shoulders, Diana looked at Berry with a proud expression. 'Oh, I threw that in myself,' she said. 'Pretty good, huh?'

'I figured. But the father was really pissed off about it,' Berry said.

Diana looked at Berry as if he were daft for caring what 'the father' thought . . . 'So what?' she asked. 'Here, take this,' she said, handing him the towel as if he was her assistant instead of the president of her record company. 'Michael! Oh, Michael,' she called out as she walked away. 'Now, where is that boy?'

Not since Sammy Davis, Jr., had the world seen a child performer with as innate a command of himself on stage as Michael Jackson. Both as a singer and dancer, young Michael exuded a presence that was simply uncanny. After this youngster was heard recording Smokey Robinson's plaintive, bluesy 'Who's Loving You?' the question among Motown's staffers was 'Where did he learn that kind of emotion?' The answer is that he didn't have to learn it, it just seemed to be there for him.

Producers were always astonished at how Michael would, in between recording sessions, play games that pre-teen children enjoy such as cards and hide-and-seek, and then step behind a microphone and belt out a song with the emotional agility and presence of an old soul who's seen his share of heartache. Equally amazing was the fact that, aside from listening to demonstration tapes of the songs sung by a session singer to give him direction on the lead melody and Deke Richards' constant prodding to clean up his diction, Michael was pretty much left to his own devices in the studio. When he was told to sound like a rejected suitor, no one in the studio actually expected him to do it, to understand the emotion involved in heartbreak. How could they? After all, he was eleven.

'I'll tell you the honest-to-God truth. I never knew what I was doing in the early days,' Michael confessed to me once. 'I just did it. I never knew how to sing, really. I didn't control it. It just formed itself. I don't know where it came from . . . it just came. Half the time, I didn't even know what I was singing about, but I still felt the emotion behind it.'

Producer Deke Richards used to have to sit Michael on top of a trash can in order for him to sing into the boom mike above him. Jermaine and Jackie would stand on either side of Michael – Marlon and Tito rarely recorded backing vocals in the early days since neither had a knack for harmony – and sheet music would be positioned in front of Michael's face on a music stand. From the control booth, all Richards could see in the studio were Jermaine and Jackie standing on either side of two sneakers dangling at the sides of a trash can.

When Michael and his brothers became professional performers, there were probably a million youngsters with as much raw dancing talent. What set Michael apart from the schoolyard hoofers was his execution, undoubtedly gleaned from years of observing headliners in the rhythm-and-blues revues in which he and his brothers used to appear. The kid had an eye for what worked.

From legendary soul singer Jackie Wilson, Michael mastered the importance of onstage drama. He learned early on that dropping dramatically to one knee, an old Wilson tactic, usually made an audience whoop and holler. However, for the most part, watching young Michael at work was like observing an honour student of 'James Brown 101'. Michael appropriated everything he could from the self-proclaimed 'hardest-working man in show business'. Not only did he employ Brown's splits and the one-foot slides, he worked a microphone bold-soul style just like Brown – passionately jerking the stand around like a drunk might handle his girlfriend at the corner pool hall on a Saturday night.

Michael also pilfered James Brown's famous spin. However, back then, the spin didn't go over nearly as well with a crowd as Michael's version of another dance of the day that Brown popularized, the Camel Walk. When Michael strode across the floor of *American Bandstand* during The Jackson 5's first appearance on that programme, even the audience of pretty white teenagers got caught up in the frenzy of excitement.

From Diana Ross, Michael got not only a sense of style, but an appreciation of power. Diana had a *quiet* authority, the power of presence. He'd observed how people reacted to her when she walked into a room. She was revered. She was given deferential treatment. She had a special power. He liked that.

There was one other thing Michael got from Diana: his early *ooohs*. Michael's early vocal ad-libs were almost always punctuated with an *oooh* here or there; not a long-drawn-out *oooh*, but rather a stab, an exclamation mark. Diana used this effect on many of The Supremes' recordings. Michael delighted in it and put it in his grab bag of influences. Indeed, for little Michael Jackson, every little *oooh* helped.

At the beginning of November 1969, Berry Gordy leased a house for the Jackson family at 1601 Queens Road in Los Angeles. Michael moved out of Diana Ross's home and in with his father and brothers. A month later, Katherine, LaToya, Janet and Randy joined the rest of the family. Motown paid for their flights, their first plane ride.

As they arrived at the house, the boys were waiting on the front lawn. Michael was the first to throw himself into his mother's arms. 'But you got so big,' she exclaimed. Tears streamed down her face as she hugged each of her boys in turn. Jackie, ever the tease, lifted Marlon up and tossed him in the air. 'Me next, me next,' three-year-old Janet squealed.

Katherine would recall that, once inside the house, she took a long look around the living room. It was so large – twice the size of the entire house in Gary – that she was dumbstruck. 'It ain't Gary, that's for sure,' Joseph told her with a proud smile. Then Joseph had

Katherine close her eyes. He led his wife out to the backyard patio. 'Okay, you can open them now,' he told her.

A panorama of dusk-time Los Angeles lay stretched below the hillside home, thousands of lights twinkling like earthbound stars. A dark-blue sky above, clear and cloudless, was full of stars. 'This must be what heaven looks like,' Katherine said, when she could speak. 'I've never seen anything so beautiful.'

'Well, it's here for you every night,' Joseph told her. He was happy to see her, his wife and partner. Sometimes, Katherine's sadness was so acute, it bordered on depression. Joseph knew he was responsible; he tried not to think about what he was doing to her, focusing instead on what he was doing *for* her – such as being able to present her with such a new and exciting lifestyle. Though Joseph had his dalliances, he had always insisted that Katherine Jackson was the only woman he had ever truly loved and the rest were . . . diversions. Joseph could be cruel and unconscionable, at times. He could be selfish. Over the years, he would watch as Katherine's love for him foundered on the rocks of his blatant infidelity and dogged ambition. However, when he was alone with her, what they shared in those quiet moments was real and powerful, and it lasts to this day. They have been married for fifty-three years.

Katherine recalled that she asked to be left alone for a moment in the outdoors of her new home. There she stood, among the orange trees and flower beds, all illuminated in a spectacular way. Joseph had turned on the outdoor sound-system so that romantic music could be heard playing softly in the background. The air smelled of jasmine. It was magical.

'Lovely, isn't it?'

Katherine whirled around at the sound of the woman's unfamiliar voice, but before either of them could say anything, Michael was at Katherine's side. 'Momma, this is *her*. This is Diana Ross,' he said, excited. 'Isn't she beautiful? Isn't she just beautiful?'

Later, telling a friend about the incident, Katherine would remember that Diana was as slim, young and attractive as she appeared on the television screen. Katherine, who was short and rounded, became painfully aware of how plain she herself may have looked to the glamorous singer. She walked towards her with a limp. Diana glided, as if on air. She was warm and friendly. Her large, dark eyes dancing, she took Katherine's hand. 'Mrs Jackson, I am so happy to meet you,' she said. 'Your kids have talked about you so much. They are just the best.'

As pleased as she was to hear her children praised, Katherine could not help wondering why Diana was at the house, and when she had arrived. Diana must have sensed her unspoken questions. 'Oh, I was just visiting,' she said by way of explanation. She hugged Katherine warmly and kissed her on the cheek.

Katherine told Diana that she was grateful for all she had done for her boys, especially Michael, and that she was happy to be able now to raise him herself. 'He needs his mother,' she said, firmly. 'I have been gone too long,' she added pointedly. At that, Diana seemed to become uncomfortable; her attitude changed. 'I'm happy for you,' she said, softly. She seemed crestfallen by the subtle reminder that she might no longer be as influential in young Michael's life. She loved being his 'mother', even for just such a short time. She would miss it. Her life had been lonely, one devoted to career pursuits since she was about fifteen. However, it wouldn't be long before she would have children of her own – three girls and then later two boys – and devote as much of herself to them as she would to her career. 'I'd love to chat,' she told Katherine, 'but I can't because I'm very busy.'

'Can't you at least stay for a cup of coffee?' Katherine offered.

'No, not really. I must run now. I'm sure you understand.'

'Oh . . . sure,' Katherine said.

Without another word, Diana turned and walked into the night.

'Bye,' Michael called out after her, but Diana didn't answer.

Katherine hugged Michael. Then, without a backward glance at the breathtaking view, mother and son walked hand in hand into the house to begin their new life.

PART TWO

'ABC' and 'The Love You Save'

By the end of 1969, Michael Jackson, now eleven years old and reunited with his mother, was a bubbly, energetic and happy youngster. 'All I want now is to see how far we can go as a family,' he told *Soul* magazine reporter Judy Spiegelman. 'I like show business, Hollywood, and all that stuff, the things people like Berry Gordy do to make you look good. I'm real excited about things.'

In December, Motown Records released the brothers' first album, *Diana Ross Presents The Jackson 5*. It would go on to sell 629,363 copies, an amazing number for a debut album. In Britain, it peaked at number sixteen and remained in the Top 100 for four weeks. 'Honesty has always been a very special word for me – a special idea,' Diana Ross wrote in the liner notes. 'But when I think of my own personal idea of honesty, I think of something being straight out, all there, on the table – the way it is . . . That's how I feel about The Jackson 5 – five brothers by the name of Jackson whom I discovered in Gary, Indiana. They've got great talent,' Diana Ross concluded. 'And above all, they're honest.'

Michael read an advance proof of the album jacket in one of the Motown offices as his brothers and a promotion man looked on.

'Wouldn't even let us play our own instruments on the album,' Tito grumbled. 'But here we are in the picture holdin' 'em like we played 'em. Don't seem right to me.' In truth, Tito and Jermaine were not permitted to play their bass and guitar in the Motown sessions because Berry didn't think they were ready for studio work. All of the instrumental music was recorded by Motown's top team of musicians before the Jacksons even got to the studio. The boys would then have to learn to duplicate the sound as best they could for live performances.

'I think we should be playin' on this record album, here,' Tito decided.

Michael rolled his eyes. 'So?' he asked.

'So, it's not true,' Tito said. 'It's not honest, like Miss Ross said on the jacket.'

'And what about this part?' Jermaine asked, still looking over Michael's shoulder. He pointed to Diana's line about discovering the group. 'That ain't honest, either. Bobby Taylor was the one.'

Michael shrugged his shoulders. 'It's called *public relations*,' he said, matter-of-factly. 'C'mon, guys. Get with it.'

'He was really into this image thing at a pretty early age,' said Stan Sherman, the independent promotion man who witnessed the exchange. 'The other boys were sort of befuddled about all the lies, but not Michael. Once you explained it to him, he not only agreed with it but, I think, he even started to believe it. To me, that was frightening. He seemed willing and even eager to adjust to the fantasy of it all.'

Later in the month, on 14 December 1969, The Jackson 5 appeared on *The Ed Sullivan Show*. Although they had already made one national television appearance on *The Hollywood Palace*, in October, being asked to perform on *The Ed Sullivan Show* was an important milestone in their career.

The programme couldn't credit its success to its host. Stiff and usually unsmiling, Sullivan, a columnist for the *New York Daily News*, did little more than introduce his guests, whose names he routinely mispronounced or forgot. Once, when Smokey Robinson and the Miracles appeared, he introduced them as 'Smokey and his little Smokeys'. The lure of the show was its roster of guests, though. Newcomers knew they had the brass ring in their reach when they were asked to perform; those already established were assured they were still on top. Ed Sullivan never bothered with has-beens or wanna-be's.

As soon as Sullivan introduced this 'sensational group', Marlon, Jackie and Michael, flanked by Tito and Jermaine on guitar, started their set with their rendition of the Sly Stone song 'Stand'. They were dressed in a variety of mod clothes purchased off the rack in Greenwich Village by Suzanne dePasse.

Michael, again, was the star. When he sang, his eyes sparkled. He looked adorable in his magenta cowboy hat. Anyone who saw the performance would remember how impossibly cute this little kid was while on that stage. No diamond in the rough, he already seemed a polished, seasoned performer. When he sang 'Can You Remember?' his voice had a purity and range of tone that belied his years. By the time The Jackson 5 finished the set with a rousing 'I Want You Back', the audience had been completely won over. Just to appear with Ed Sullivan was an accomplishment, but to receive such rousing applause seemed a clear prophecy for success.

As was his tradition, Sullivan engaged in some minimal banter with his guests, but he soon turned his attention to a member of the audience: 'The person who discovered The Jackson 5, Diana Ross.' Diana, clad in what can only be described as a grown-up version of a little girl's pink organdy party dress, stood and modestly took a bow.

The difficult task at hand for Motown was to follow The Jackson 5's first number-one record with another chart-topper. Since it was his policy to allow the writers and producers of a hit song the opportunity to come up with another one just as successful, Berry Gordy gave the chore to Deke Richards and the Corporation. 'One night I was at Fonce's [Mizell] and Freddie's [Perren] apartment and we were fooling around on their electric piano,' recalled Deke Richards, 'and I started thinking about Holland, Dozier and Holland and how they often did the same types of records over and over again, using the same progressions. Theirs was a proven hit formula. So I took a section of "I Want You Back" – the part where the group sings the chorus – and decided to make those exact same chords the foundation of their next single.

'I was sitting at the piano, playing chords and I came up with the lyric, "A, B, C". Fonce and Freddie looked at me like I was crazy.

'"So, now what?" I asked myself. "I know, how about, one, two, three." By now the guys thought I was nuts. And then I came up with the next line, "Do, re, mi." And I finished with a big bang: "You and me."'

'That's it,' Deke told his partners, laughing. 'That's a hit.'

In a short time, the three men were in the studio recording the song 'ABC', with Michael and his brothers.

'I loved "ABC" from the first moment I heard it,' Michael said. 'I had more enthusiasm for that than I did for "I Want You Back". It was just such a hot song, such a great idea with a hot track. I couldn't wait to record it. I remember when Deke and the other guys were coming up with the middle of the song right there on the spot. "*Siddown* girl, I think I love you." Then it was "Shake it, shake it, baby", you know, like The Contours and old groups like that. I didn't know you could do that in the studio, just come up with parts like that at the last minute.'

In February 1970, Motown released 'ABC' as the second Jackson 5 single. It went straight to the top of the *Billboard* charts in just six weeks, supplanting 'Let It Be' by The Beatles. The song, which sold 2,214,790 copies – even more copies than 'I Want You Back' – seemed to poke fun at, and also make acceptable, a new and growing trend in popular music, the predominantly white 'bubble gum' style. In the UK, the song peaked at number eight and remained on the charts for almost three months. With 'ABC''s buzzing bass, sprightly keyboard and charming chorus, The Jackson 5 were on a roll.

Freddie Perren recalled, 'After those two hits, Berry kept asking, "What about the follow-up? What about the follow-up?" He really wanted to bring that third one home. We were cutting the track for that third song at the Sound Factory in Hollywood. Berry never came to tracking sessions, but he came to this one. He listened for about fifteen minutes and said, "I'm not worried. You guys got another hit." And he left. That's when we knew we had the third hit.'

The song was 'The Love You Save', which was released in May 1970, another terrific teenybopper song with a breathless lead by Michael. For 'The Love You Save', a cute verse and a pleading chorus was the bait, the infectious combination of guitars and percussion the hook. Just as Deke Richards predicted, the Corporation had developed a successful hit formula for The Jackson 5 in much the same way that Holland-Dozier-Holland had done for The Supremes. Diana and the girls' first three number one hits, 'Where Did Our Love Go?' 'Baby Love' and 'Come See about Me', were basically the same song with the chord structures cleverly changed in the right spots. Deke and company applied the same magical twist to 'I Want You Back', 'ABC' and 'The Love You Save' – songs that sound so much alike, it's easy for the uninitiated to confuse them. Berry had wanted three number-one songs for The Jackson 5, and, as usual, he got what he wanted.

At 1,948,761 copies sold, 'The Love You Save' came up a bit short in comparison to the sales of the preceding two singles but was still considered a huge hit. In England, it reached number seven and was in the charts for almost two months. The song also gave The Jackson 5 the distinction of being the first group of the rock and roll era to have their first three songs go to the top of the charts. Again, they knocked The Beatles ('The Long and Winding Road') out of the number-one spot.

'It just kept gettin' better . . .'

The Jackson 5 made their first concert appearance as a Motown attraction at the Philadelphia Convention Center on Saturday evening, 2 May 1970. Despite their terrific record sales, no one could have guessed how popular they had become in barely five months. More than thirty-five hundred screaming fans mobbed Philadelphia International Airport hoping to catch a glimpse of the young brothers. Only a huge force of Philadelphia's finest and airport security officers protected the Jacksons from being completely over-whelmed.

The scene was repeated the following evening at the concert, with one hundred police officers forcing the audience back from the stage time and time again. Three motorcycle-escorted limousines managed to get The Jackson 5 back to their hotel after the concert. Once Michael got into his room, he broke down and started crying.

'Michael [who was eleven years old] was scared to death,' Jermaine said. 'The rest of us were more amazed than scared, but Mike was genuinely frightened. "I don't know if I can do this forever," he said. "Maybe for a little while, but not forever."'

The pandemonium served as a warning to Motown that the next time the brothers made a concert appearance, the company should be better prepared.

That same month, The Jackson 5's second album, *ABC*, was released. It would go on to be even more successful than the debut album, selling 867,756 copies. After the second album was shipped, Berry arranged for the family to move from the home on Queens Road to a bigger one on Bowmont Drive above Trousdale Estates. Liberace lived nearby, as did Davy Jones of The Monkees. 'They [the Jacksons] were kicked out of several houses,' Berry Gordy explained to Michael Goldberg in an interview in *Rolling Stone*. 'You see, they would make too much noise. They had their band, and we would put them in a house, and then they would get kicked out. We'd lease another place, and they would make too much noise, and they would get kicked out.'

In July 1970, The Jackson 5 broke attendance records at the Los Angeles Forum, raking up 18,675 paid admissions. The concert grossed $105,000.

'I was at that concert at the Forum with Berry and Diana,' said the group's producer Deke Richards. 'We almost got trampled to death. Before they started 'The Love You Save', Michael said something like, "Here it is, the tune that knocked The Beatles out of number one", and that caused sheer pandemonium. We were in the third row, and in the middle of the concert we heard this tumultuous sound and the rows were folding one at a time, people falling over themselves. Someone ran on to the stage and got the kids off. They didn't even finish the song. Berry, Diana and I got out of our row just in time before it was toppled over by kids trying to get to the stage.'

A month later, the company issued The Jackson 5's first ballad, 'I'll Be There'. Switching gears to a ballad seemed to Gordy to be the obvious next step, yet it would have to be the right song in order to be accepted by fans accustomed to an upbeat sound. 'I'll Be There' was a tender blend of soulful pleading and sweetly delivered inspiration. To the strains of harpsichords and keyboards, Michael's performance was flawless. The song is considered to be the one record that solidified The Jackson 5's success as versatile recording stars. It was number one for five weeks in America, selling more than two and half million copies worldwide (250,000 of these in the UK alone). Its top positioning in the UK was number four, and it remained on the British charts for more than four months!

'I'll Be There' pushed Neil Diamond's 'Cracklin' Rosé' out of the number-one position on *Billboard*'s pop charts and became Motown's biggest-selling record; the company claimed that over four million copies were eventually sold, but actually the figure totalled some 800,000 copies less than that, at 3,178,523 copies. In the end, The Jackson 5 became the first act in pop music history whose first four singles each became number-one hits on the *Billboard* chart. Or, as Michael put it, 'It just kept gettin' better and better.'

In October 1970, the group took their act on the road again for additional dates on the East Coast. Three dates in Texas were placed in jeopardy, though, when the concerts were opposed by members of the Southern Christian Leadership Council's Operation Breadbasket, an organization dedicated to improving economic conditions in the black community. Dick Clark was promoting the tour and Breadbasket representatives felt that someone black should have been hired by Motown. 'That's absolutely ridiculous,' Berry Gordy said. 'Black, white. What the hell's the difference as long as we all make money?'

Still, the protestors had leaflets printed up and were preparing to picket at the concert sites. The press was waiting for a scandal. 'Just what we need,' Berry told a Motown promoter working with Dick Clark. 'Cancel. Tell Clark to cancel the whole goddamn state. They'll see The Jackson 5 when they get some sense.' The dates were cancelled.

'The Jackson 5 are bigger than any race issue,' Berry Gordy said later. 'No one can tell me how to run these boys' careers. Black or white, I make the decisions. This is *my* group.'

No doubt, Berry's declaration would have been news to Joseph.

By January 1971, twelve-year-old Michael Jackson understood that entertainment was a difficult business. He had witnessed as much for the last couple of years, but still managed to take in his stride the pressures of recording, touring and making television appearances. His success was still too new to be anything but a constant thrill. 'This is the best thing that ever happened to us,' Michael said of his family's accomplishments. 'Miss Ross has told me that people in show business can get hurt. I don't see how.'

At this time, Motown issued The Jackson 5's fifth single, 'Mama's Pearl'. On a stylistic par with their previous upbeat singles, this one featured Michael in the lead again, of course, surrounded by his brothers offering an occasional lead line through the verses. There were buzzing guitars on the choruses, and the Corporation's swirling production throughout.

From the beginning, there had been some hesitation about 'Mama's Pearl'. Deke Richards had decided to have Fonce Mizell and Freddie Perren work on it without him to see what they would create. Deke walked into the studio to find Michael singing the lyric, 'He said what's mine is his and his is all mine . . .' What they had come up with for Michael was a song called 'Guess Who's Making Whoopie (With Your Girlfriend)', which was about girl swapping, certainly not the right image for the youngster. Deke had Fonce and Freddie rework the lyrics – not the track – and, in a short time, they came up with 'Mama's Pearl'.

Even though the record 'only' went to the number two on *Billboard*'s chart, it was number one on *Cash Box*'s, so Berry was satisfied. In the UK though, it only peaked at number 25.

The year had been off to a sentimental start when, on 31 January, The Jackson 5 returned to Gary, Indiana, their hometown. At this time, Jackie was nineteen; Tito, seventeen; Jermaine, sixteen; Marlon, thirteen; and Michael, twelve. On behalf of Mayor Richard Gordon Hatcher's re-election campaign, the group was asked to perform two concerts at Westside High School. The distance between Gary and Los Angeles can be measured in miles, but the distance between Gary and stardom can only be measured in light years. Going home as stars, the Jackson brothers arrived in grand style, in a helicopter that landed in Westside High's parking lot where two thousand students had gathered in subzero weather to greet them.

Both concerts were sell-outs. Fifteen thousand lucky ticket holders came to pay homage to five homeboys. Two years ago, many of these same neighbourhood kids had thrown stones at the Jackson house to taunt the group as they rehearsed; now they were sharing in their success, proud to know that they'd all come from the same streets. As the spotlights revealed the Jacksons in their rainbow-hued regalia, the group's fans could not be contained. The gym was packed to the rafters with what was probably the noisiest audience the boys had so far encountered. There were so many flashbulbs popping at once, it looked as though flocks of fireflies had come to swarm.

After the first concert, Mayor Hatcher escorted the Jackson family back to their former residence on Jackson Street, which had, for the day, been renamed Jackson 5 Boulevard in their honour. A sign was placed on the lawn in front of the old homestead at 2300 Jackson Street: WELCOME HOME JACKSON FIVE. KEEPERS OF THE DREAM. Afterwards, as the limo pulled away, fans hurled themselves at its tightly closed windows. Inside, the boys smiled and waved, amazed at the frenzy. Their next stop was city hall, where the group was presented with individual keys to the city. The boys had returned home as heroes, symbols of hope. In his speech that day, Mayor Hatcher said he was honoured that 'The Jackson 5 has carried the name of Gary throughout the country and the world, and made it a name to be proud of.' Joseph could not have been more proud of his boys. He stood at the podium and said, 'One thing I have always told my boys is that you're either a winner in this life or a loser, and none of my kids were ever gonna be losers. I'm proud to say that they proved me right.'

The Jackson 5's next single, 'Never Can Say Goodbye', would be released in March 1971, and peak at number two a month later, selling almost two million copies. It only managed a number thirty-three positioning in the UK though, so Gordy was becoming a little concerned about the group's international appeal. Still, it was a memorable record. The song's writer, actor Clifton Davis, recalled, 'This was an emotional song that meant a lot to me when I wrote it. I was worried that Michael might not understand the lyrics of pain and heartbreak. I recall him asking about one of the lines. "What's this word mean? *Anguish*," he asked me. I explained it. He shrugged his shoulders and just sang the line. "There's that anguish, there's that doubt," he sang. And I believed him.'

Joseph and Katherine Buy an Estate

On 5 May 1971, after the boys returned from another national tour, the Jacksons moved into their large estate at 4641 Hayvenhurst in

Encino, California, the one in which Joseph, Katherine and miscellaneous other Jacksons (who aren't Michael and Janet) still live today.

Joseph and Katherine purchased the property for $250,000; they moved in a day after Katherine's forty-first birthday. Katherine had asked Joseph not to sell the two-bedroom home in Gary, 'just in case the family fortunes took a turn for the worse and they all had to move back to Indiana.' Although Joseph didn't think that such a reversal of fortunes was likely, he decided to rent, rather than sell, the house, at 2300 Jackson Street. (Today, the property is worth roughly $100,000, and still owned by the family.)

Joseph and Katherine had never made as large a purchase as the Encino estate and were naive as to how to go about it. Joseph wanted to pay cash for the estate ('At least, then we own it and no one can kick us out.'), but he didn't have that much capital. Anyway, Berry Gordy convinced him that the family needed as much of a tax write-off on the property as possible, since their income was increasing monthly, and that the interest on a loan could be written off their taxes. Although Joseph decided to put down as little as possible on the Encino property, because his credit profile was not a good one he had to raise nearly 40 per cent in order to qualify for a mortgage. That was a lot of money for a down-payment: $100,000. Berry offered to lend Joseph and Katherine the funds, but Joseph declined. 'If we're going to live in that house, it's gotta be ours,' he told Berry. Motown already had too much control over his kids; Joseph didn't want Berry also to have a vested interest in the family home.

In the end, Joseph did manage to get the $100,000, but he had to secure a large advance on his sons' future earnings. Of course, that advance came from Motown . . . which was, Berry.

Encino, which is a thirty-five-minute drive from downtown Los Angeles, is one of the wealthiest communities in Southern California and home to many celebrities. The two-acre Jackson estate, resplendent with eighteen citrus trees and countless exotic plants, was guarded by an electronic gate and flanked by a guest house, playhouse and servants' quarters.

Johnny Jackson and Ronny Rancifer, The Jackson 5's drummer and organist, moved into the household with the rest of the family. This arrangement occurred because Joseph and Katherine were concerned about the influence both boys – but particularly Johnny – were having on their sons. Both youngsters liked to spend what little money they were given, rather than save it. They were also smoking cigarettes and drinking liquor. Joseph had considered letting them both go, but decided that it wouldn't be fair since the boys had been a part of the band since the early days in Gary.

'The house had five bathrooms and six bedrooms,' recalled Susie Jackson, Johnny's former wife. 'Jackie and Ronny shared a room. Tito was with Johnny, Jermaine with Marlon, Michael with Randy, and LaToya with Janet. And then there was one left for Joseph and Katherine, so there were a lot of people living there'.

The family room had a recessed floor surrounded by a wrap-around couch. The walls were lined with numerous plaques, gold and platinum records signifying million-selling singles and albums. One reporter noted that the room resembled 'a cross between a motel lobby and the foyer of a Sunset Boulevard record company.'

The grounds contained an Olympic-size swimming pool, a basketball half-court, a badminton court and an archery range. The tranquil surroundings promised limitless peace for such a famous family. Hopefully, here they could be soothed and refreshed in their time away from the invasive eye of the public.

Plans were made to add a hundred-thousand-dollar recording studio and a twenty-five-thousand-dollar darkroom.

Jackie Jackson's Datsun 240 Z was usually parked in the drive-way, along with Katherine's new Audi, Joseph's gold Mercedes 300 SE convertible, and the family's huge van.

'We had fun up the Big House,' said Susie Jackson. (In time, many of the family's relatives referred to the Jackson estate as the Big House because they felt it had become as much a prison to the Jackson sons and daughters as it had been a home.) 'It wasn't all drama and backstabbing. There were parties and, in the beginning, we had a special closeness. I remember a lot of fun times when they first moved in. Every time you were in that house, they were roasting peanuts.'

Though Katherine enjoyed the opulent estate and other aspects of her new life, she missed Gary. Simply put, she was not as happy as she thought she might be in Los Angeles. She missed her old friends and relatives.

If Southern California had to be her new home, Katherine would not allow the glamorous surroundings to influence her or her family to act in a pretentious manner. She was determined to maintain a sense of normality around the household.

Also, the Jackson family did not hesitate to show their appreciation to people who had helped them in their careers. Instead of small, intimate gatherings, they preferred large, ostentatious affairs where quantity was the most important consideration. Katherine looked at these parties as come-on-overs. Only instead of root beer and pretzels on the back porch, she put out a lavish spread at the family estate. Always a gracious hostess, she made everyone feel welcome. Joseph's pride in the house was obvious. He would give tours to anyone who seemed interested. In August 1972, after The Jackson 5 finished their engagement at the Forum in Los Angeles, Katherine and Joseph held just such a party at the family home for about fifty press and show-business friends.

Katherine and Joseph did not disappoint their guests. The twelve-foot-long buffet offered hamburgers, roast beef, chilli, shish kebabs, fresh chilled fruit and seafood. Pastries were heaped on a cart decorated with red and yellow roses. In the middle of the family's oval swimming pool, Joseph floated a huge J-5 logo made of roses and tinted carnations. For entertainment, The Jackson 5 challenged The Temptations to a basketball game. The Jacksons won.

(This writer was a guest at many of the Jackson family's 'come-on-overs' between the years 1976 and 1981 at the Jacksons' estate in Encino.)

The Jacksons' phone number would be routinely changed by the phone company every month to guard against outsiders having it. Nevertheless, the number always got out. Once, a girl from Newark called to talk to Michael at two in the morning – just one day after the new number was assigned.

As always, Joseph limited phone calls to five minutes and would not hesitate to use a strap on any junior family member who broke that rule, pop star or no pop star. To say the least, the children were well disciplined. In fact, the boys were known in Hollywood circles as the best-behaved youngsters in show business. 'You sometimes thought they were too nice,' said one reporter. 'It was as if something was wrong somewhere. They were sort of spooky.'

Jermaine has recalled that when the family moved into the Encino home their familial closeness began to dissipate, simply because there was so much space. 'We were real close when we had the other homes, before Encino,' he remembered. 'In Gary, we had two bedrooms, one for our parents and one for all of us. You *had* to be close. You felt that closeness as a family. But in Encino, the place was so big we had to make plans in advance to see each other. I think that Michael, in particular, was unhappy there. He felt, as I did, that we were all losing touch with each other.'

In June 1971, The Jackson 5 released another single for Motown, 'Maybe Tomorrow', which went on to sell 830,794 copies, not as many as previous efforts but still respectable. A month later, the group taped its first television special, *Goin' Back to Indiana*, for ABC-TV. (It would air in September.) Later, they would even have their own cartoon series, that's how popular they'd become in such a short time. (The Jacksons' actual voices were heard in musical numbers, but their dialogue was provided by young black actors.) That summer, The Jackson 5 performed fifty shows on tour, the longest series of one-night performances ever attempted by the boys. 'I wish for once we could finish a show and not have to leave before the end because of the crowds rushing the stage,' Michael complained. 'We have a real good ending, but we never get the chance to do it.'

At Madison Square Garden in August of that year, the show had to be stopped after only two minutes when the audience stormed the stage. 'Return to your seats, please,' a frightened Michael begged. Ultimately, though, the group had to be extracted from the crowd and rushed away from the premises. The show resumed after the audience calmed down. Sixty minutes later, when the concert was over, the Jacksons sprinted to waiting limousines, without finishing their last number, in order to get away as quickly as possible. The audience went berserk. Once the fans realized that the group was gone, they surged on to the stage like an angry mob, sweeping away police and security men, and swarming the dressing room looking for their idols.

This was a heady time for the boys from Gary, and they were never again to be as close as they were during these early days – nor would they have as much fun. Insulated from outsiders by the

Motown representatives and their father, they had only each other for company. To occupy their free time, they enjoyed dropping water balloons and paper bags filled with water from hotel-room windows, having pillow fights with one another, and playing Scrabble, Monopoly and card games. (They gave Jermaine the nickname 'Las Vegas' because he became such a skilled card shark.) Michael has fond memories of tag-team wrestling matches and shaving-cream wars with his brothers while they were cooped up in hotels, 'or fast-walk races down hotel hallways once our chaperone was asleep,' he said. Michael, who was twelve at this time, was quite a prankster. He liked to phone room service, order huge meals, and then have them sent to the rooms of strangers in the hotel; and he especially enjoyed setting up a bucket of water as a booby trap above the doorway to his and Jermaine's room (they always shared quarters), drenching whoever happened to walk into the room.

'Mike always blamed me,' Jermaine recalled with a grin. 'He loved practical jokes, locking us out of our rooms in our underwear, squirting us with water pistols. They were almost always his idea. We had so much fun. It was all fun, all the time.'

Indeed, success was sweet and innocent for The Jackson 5. 'We don't have no gold records,' Michael once told me during this time, a sad expression on his face. Then, after a beat, he explained, 'They're all *platinum*! Ha-ha!'

Occasionally one of the Jackson brothers would show some interest in the opposite sex. Backstage at the Hollywood Bowl, when the group performed there, Berry Gordy's sixteen-year-old daughter Hazel had her arm around Jermaine, also sixteen, and seemed to be nibbling on his ear. Joseph watched with great interest and pulled Jermaine aside.

'What's the deal with her?' he demanded to know.

'I don't know,' Jermaine said, shrugging his shoulders. 'She likes me, I guess.'

At first, Joseph was annoyed. Then, he became thoughtful and nodded his approval. 'Berry's kid,' he muttered to himself. 'Hmmm. Not bad. Not bad at all.'

During the concert, Jermaine decided to dedicate his solo of 'Bridge Over Troubled Water' to 'Hazel, for her birthday'. The audience's reaction was lukewarm. Whereas he usually got a standing ovation for the number, this evening it seemed that the female fans in the crowd did not appreciate Jermaine's honesty about his friendship with Hazel.

Jermaine recalled, 'My father pulled me aside, I remember, and he said, "You'd better not do that again." And I said, "You know, you're right. I'd better not." And I didn't.'

Michael's First Solo Record

Joseph Jackson always had his eye on the competition, namely the Osmond Brothers, a family group from Salt Lake City, Utah. In June 1971, MGM Records released 'Sweet and Innocent' by the youngest member of the group, Donny Osmond, as a solo act. That record's success all but guaranteed him teen-star status in the predominantly white teenybopper magazines. Because of their colour, The Jackson 5 could never be perceived as teen idols in those magazines, despite all of their success and good looks. Though the Jacksons would make occasional appearances in magazines like *16* and *Fave*, the Osmonds and other white stars like them dominated the pages of such publications. This practice chagrined Joseph, who viewed it as racism.

After Donny Osmond's hit, Joseph decided that Michael should also record a song on his own. He and Berry Gordy decided to release a song called 'Got to Be There', as Michael's first solo, instead of as a group effort as originally planned. Michael would still be a part of the group, just as Donny was a part of The Osmonds, but he would now also be a solo Motown artist. 'Then we can all make more money,' Joseph reasoned. Joseph never dreamed that he had just put into motion a plan that would one day separate Michael not only from his brothers, but from him as well.

'Got to Be There' was issued in October. Although it would not reach the top of the charts, it was a reality check of sorts for the

Jackson brothers when they saw that Michael could crack the Top Five on his own. In England it was a number five hit, and stayed in the Top 50 for almost three months. Globally, 'Got to be There' sold 1,583,850 copies.

This lushly produced and orchestrated, mid-tempo love song was the perfect vehicle for launching Michael's solo career; it's surely one of the most beautiful songs in Motown's publishing catalogue. At the time, it was the envy of many artists whose flagging careers could have been salvaged by such a versatile, well-tailored number. Instead, it served to bolster the enormously popular lead singer of The Jackson 5.

Immediately after Christmas in 1971, The Jackson 5 embarked on a concert tour of the South. In Dallas, a reporter arranged an interview in their hotel room. It wasn't long before fans had congregated outside the door, chanting, 'Michael! Michael! Michael!' Tito went out in the hallway hoping to quieten them down. When he opened the door, a group of girls burst into the room and began kissing and hugging Michael, totally ignoring the others. The brothers did not appear to be jealous and, rather, treated the incident as a chance to tease Michael. 'Just wait till I get my solo song released,' Jermaine said. 'Then *I'll* be the ladies' man 'round here.'

'Well, right now Michael's the real ladies' man,' Jackie said after the girls were escorted out of the room by security guards.

'Aw, c'mon, you guys,' Michael said, bashfully.

'You *are*, Mike,' Jermaine agreed. 'But not for long . . .'

Then all four brothers jumped on Michael, tickling him good naturedly and wrestling him to the ground. One could hear their laughter echo through the halls.

Growing Up in the Public Eye

It's always tempting, when dissecting a person's life, to go back in time and assign blame for the way things turned out, but it's not always fair. Certainly, Joseph and Katherine had the best intentions when they were raising their family, and didn't intend to harm their children. It's the rare parent, one would hope, who purposely sets out to completely screw up his kids' lives. If Joseph had told his brood to forget about show business, and focus on lives out of the public eye, such a demand would not have gone over well, at all. Try as they might have, the value system the Jackson parents passed on to their children was, at best, warped. Whatever it takes to get to the top, that's what they were told they had to do – *that* was their value system. Katherine tried to fight it and hoped to instill other ideals along the way – especially having to do with her religion – but none of them really seemed to matter when applied to the world in which her children were being raised, the world of show business. They were all caught up in the powerful illusion that if they became rich and famous, their lives would be better. Fate and circumstance, along with an obvious inadequacy in parental skills, set into motion a chain of events that would do irreparable harm to all of the Jackson children, and especially, to Michael. At least the older brothers had had a few years to act like children. Michael never did; he was barely five years old when thrust into show business.

Of course, the boys loved to perform and even *wanted* to perform. They excelled in that arena. The look of satisfaction on Michael's face when he was onstage made it clear that he was doing what he wanted to do, and that if someone had given him the choice between playing basketball with his friends and entertaining them on a stage, he would have chosen the later. However, a fine line exists between what children may want, and what may be in their best interests. It's not likely that Joseph understood as much, or was able to gauge the difference between what might be in the best interest of his children, and what his own agenda was for them.

It is not only the vast sums of money child stars earn which set them apart. Most child performers are shortchanged on their education, as well. Few have ever attended public school regularly. In the film industry, they are often tutored on the set. MGM even had a school for the youngsters who worked in their movies. Although the children were supposed to study a certain number of hours each day, filming often took precedence over education. They gleaned from their studies what they were able to, and then went back to their work in front of the cameras.

What's more, child performers are often cheated out of learning social skills – the all-important art of getting along with people. The other boys and girls with whom they associate are usually working children like themselves. Some of Judy Garland's happiest memories were of the short time during her teens when her career seemed to be going nowhere. She left the studio school, enrolled in Hollywood High – hiding her background from her fellow students – and enjoyed herself, immensely. (That happy period came to an abrupt end when a vice-principal told her she shouldn't be enrolled in school with 'normal people'.)

The couple of years that the younger Jackson boys spent in public schools are romanticized by Michael and Marlon as highlights of their lives but, in truth, they weren't very happy. Michael attended sixth grade at Gardner Street Elementary in Los Angeles, though not consistently because of his work schedule. In truth, he was just a guest there, making cameo appearances in the classroom as he might on a television variety show. His sixth grade teacher, Laura Gerson, remembered, 'Once I was teaching the kids a song with a three-part harmony, and I hit a flat note that made my hair stand on end. Michael's eyes popped wide open. Nobody but him noticed. He never talked about himself. Occasionally, he would disappear and turn up on television . . .'*

In the seventh grade, Michael joined Marlon at Emerson Junior High. But by this time, The Jackson 5's accomplishments at Motown had robbed them of their privacy. They only had two weeks at Emerson, obviously no time to integrate into the population or get to know anyone, before they were forced to leave. There had been a death threat against them, and that was the end of that: Joseph pulled them out of public school. His decision was fine with the boys; they wanted to leave, anyway. 'There were mobs of people standing in the hallways just looking into the classrooms,' Marlon recalled. 'It was

*On 11 October 1989, school officials at Gardner Street Elementary School dedicated the 'Michael Jackson Auditorium' in Jackson's honour. Michael attended the ceremony.

embarrassing, and frightening.' From that time onward, the two were either enrolled in private schools or tutored at home.

California law requires that minors have a minimum of three hours of schooling a day when they are working. Mrs Rose Fine, accredited by the state as a 'children's welfare supervisor', became the tutor for all of the younger Jacksons. Much of their travelling time was spent studying for tests that they would take as soon as they checked into their hotel rooms. Between their studies, rehearsals, sound checks and concerts, and the usual goofing off, the Jacksons were kept busy.

When in private school, which occurred from time to time in between touring, Michael was bored by his studies, refused to do his homework, and was a terrible student. During class, he would draw pictures of animals and monsters when he should have been paying attention to his lessons. When called upon for an answer, Michael didn't have a clue as to what was going on, and he didn't care.

Jackie and Tito have unpleasant memories of their time at Fairfax High School, a public school in Los Angeles. The demands of their careers made normal routines almost impossible; they couldn't join any of the sports teams – a crushing disappointment for Jackie, who loved baseball – because they were the focus of attention. When they were singled out by classmates who had previously ignored them, the two brothers became suspicious of everyone. Who was legitimate in their intentions, and who had ulterior motives in wanting to know them?

Jackie and Tito would graduate from Fairfax when they were eighteen. At least they can reflect on a small period of time when they were exposed to people who weren't in show business, even if they did not enjoy that time. Michael, Marlon and Jermaine can not do as much; they were granted high school equivalency diplomas by Rose Fine, who was empowered to award them. Though technically graduated, the three younger Jacksons certainly did not obtain a good grounding in basic subjects, no slight to Rose Fine who probably did the best she could with them. To this day, each has problems with penmanship, grammar and (Michael in particular) spelling. They also lack a sense of history, except that which they managed to pick up during their travels.

As early as 1972, when Michael was about fourteen, he began exhibiting behaviour unlike that of his brothers. While they took the pressures of success in their stride, Michael seemed more affected by it. 'He's just more sensitive than the others,' Katherine would explain. If anyone in show-business history could ever be said to be lacking in 'people skills', it would be Michael Jackson. To this day, he doesn't really understand people, or even *try* to understand them, because when he was a youngster he was surrounded, for the most part, by either showbiz kids or wealthy students who, like himself, were never exposed to the 'normal' masses.

By the time Michael was fourteen, Bill Bray (The Jackson 5's security man, who still works for Michael) would arrange for him to have access to freight elevators in hotels, rather than take public lifts along with 'normal people', as Michael called them.

A year earlier Michael had told Judy Spiegelman of *Soul* magazine, 'I'm just like other kids.' However, he soon realized he was not like them at all. The other group members didn't seem to mind 'normal people' – as long as they weren't in the form of a pack of rioting fans – even if they had nothing to do with them. Michael, though, was always the one who attracted the most attention. If he entered a room with any of his other brothers, he was the one to whom the fans would flock. Being singled out, being made to feel different, knowing all eyes were on him, had a deep impact on Michael. He began to show signs of a deep insecurity, and even inadequacy. It was as if he knew he didn't fit in. If he could spend his life on stage, he felt he would be happy. Unfortunately, the world was not his stage. He had to deal with the public, and he wasn't able to do so in a way that made him feel comfortable in his own skin.

'He became a loner,' Katherine Jackson would remember. 'I was worried about him, but I hoped he would grow out of it, that it was a phase. He didn't get along with other people his age. He was better with adults. I don't know that he had friends his own age. I think, probably not. As always, his brothers were his friends. As long as we all had each other, I figured we would be okay. I prayed we would be okay.'

Tito Marries

Along with their incredible success in the music industry came, for the Jacksons, the inevitable lure of available women. Women of all shapes, sizes and colours began to proposition them, appearing backstage after concerts and offering to do all sorts of 'favours' for them. Though Michael and Marlon were too young, Jermaine and Jackie saw no reason not to take advantage of their young fans' overworked libidos. Tito wasn't really interested in groupies, though. He just wanted to settle down – and also get out of the household and put some distance between him and Joseph.

In 1972, Tito announced that he wanted to marry seventeen-year-old Delores (Dee Dee) Martes, whom he had met at Fairfax High School a few months before the group became famous. Joseph and Katherine were extremely upset, concerned that Dee Dee might be a gold-digger and Tito too inexperienced to see it. The least he could do, they argued, was insist that his fiancée sign a pre-nuptial agreement. He did, and she agreed.

Michael felt strongly that Tito was letting their fans down by marrying, and attempted to convince him to change his mind. 'Think about all of those girls out there who love us,' he said, trying to reason with his brother one day in the Motown offices.

'They don't even know us, Mike,' Tito said. 'We can't live our lives for perfect strangers.'

'But they *do* know us,' Michael argued, according to a witness, 'and we owe them, Tito. We owe them.'

'So what are we supposed to do?' Tito wanted to know. 'Put up with Joseph for the rest of our lives? If that's the case, I don't even want to be in the group, then.'

Michael stopped arguing with Tito at that point, perhaps fearing Tito's next step might be to just quit the act.

Joseph and Katherine had hoped that Berry Gordy would insist that Tito, as a Motown recording artist, remain single. When Joseph presented the situation to Berry, however, he wanted no part of it. 'Keep me out of it,' he said. 'As long as Michael isn't getting married, I'm cool.'

Joseph's face darkened. 'Michael ain't the only one in the group, Berry,' he said, according to his recollection. 'Thanks for nothing.'

The wedding took place in June 1972 in a small, unpretentious chapel in Inglewood, California. Joseph spent most of the evening glaring at Dee Dee and her family. Katherine was nicer, though one suspected she was just trying to get through the day. (Their first baby, a son named after Tito, was born about a year later. Tito was on tour, so LaToya acted as Dee Dee's Lamaze labour coach.)

Groupies

Young Tito Jackson may have been off the open market, but Jackie and Jermaine were young, single and ready to explore whatever fame might bring their way in terms of female companionship. Joseph had been a terrible example to them in the past, and he didn't improve with time. In fact, when the boys became famous, he starting having liaisons with their fans! With him as their guide, was there any reason to think the brothers would act in a responsible manner? By 1972, the older Jacksons had left a long trail of broken hearts as they toured the country, city by city. Then, they rented an apartment near their house in Encino, where they could hang out with their female conquests away from Katherine's scrutiny.

Rhonda Phillips was one of 'those' girls. Today, she is a forty-nine-year-old divorcée who lives with her three children in Long Beach, California. Back in August 1972, she was eighteen when she met her idol, Jackie, who was twenty-one. She had been selected from the audience by one of the group's road managers when the brothers were on stage at the Forum in Inglewood, California. Backstage, Jackie gave Rhonda a slip of paper with an address on it and told her to meet him at that location in an hour. As she mulled over his offer, she sensed someone behind her, and turned around. It was Michael. 'He was just a cute little guy,' she said. 'He had big teeth, a flat, wide nose, a perfectly combed natural; he looked like any pretty fourteen-year-old black boy you'd find in the neighbourhood.

He noticed the slip of paper in my hand.'

'Did Jermaine give you that?' he asked.

'No, Jackie.'

'He wants you to meet him, doesn't he?' he asked.

'Yes,' Rhonda said. 'I don't know if I should—'

Michael cut her off. 'Don't,' he said. 'I don't think you should meet him.'

Rhonda asked Michael why she shouldn't go. She remembered his answer: 'My brothers don't treat girls too good. They can be mean. Please, don't go.'

Rhonda remembered thinking that Michael was only fourteen; what could he know? She changed the subject and asked him for his autograph. She thrust forward the piece of paper Jackie had given her, he scribbled on it and handed it back to her.

The group's representative had arranged the cab fare for Rhonda to meet Jackie. She was taken to the Jacksons' apartment in Encino. As the car pulled up to the curb, she happened to turn over the slip of paper in her hand and realized that Michael had written more than just his name on the back of it. There was a message: 'I hope you don't go.' It was signed 'Michael Jackson'.

She went inside the apartment complex, found the Jacksons' and had sex with Jackie. 'I won't be able to see you after this,' he told her when they were finished. She began to cry.

'Suddenly, I was ashamed,' she recalled many years later. 'He held me for a little while and then told me that someone from Motown would be waiting outside to take me home. He kissed me, and I left. The whole thing took less than half an hour.'

As Rhonda was walking down to the street, a white Rolls-Royce pulled up. Michael and Marlon were sitting in the back seat. The car pulled up to the curb. The boys got out and Marlon ran past Rhonda up to the apartment. Michael came over to her.

'What are you doing here?' he asked, his tone accusatory. 'Were you up there with Jackie?'

'Yeah, I was,' she answered.

'Did you have sex?' Michael wanted to know.

Rhonda began to cry.

Michael shook his head sadly. 'I'm sorry,' he said. 'Did he make you do it?'

'No, of course not. I wanted to.'

'You *wanted* to?' Michael asked, seeming astonished. 'But why would you *want* to?'

Rhonda got into the car. She rolled down the window. Michael was still standing at the curb. 'Are you gonna be all right?' he asked.

'Yeah, I will be,' she answered.

'By now, I was sobbing,' Rhonda recalled. 'I rolled up the window and the car pulled off. I looked out the back window and the last thing I saw was Michael Jackson standing there waving goodbye to me.'

During these salad days, Michael, fourteen, often shared a room with his brother, Marlon, fifteen and Jermaine, seventeen. Jermaine would wait for their security man, Bill Bray, to go to sleep before sneaking down to the lobby to pick up girls. Often, he would bring them back to the room and then instruct Michael and Marlon to, as Marlon recalled it, 'play sleep'.

Yolanda Lewis is, today, forty-six, married, and living in St Louis. In an interview, she recalled an experience she had with Jermaine Jackson in 1972 when she was sixteen. 'I was a real groupie,' she remembered, 'and the boys did a concert in Cleveland, where I was living at the time. Afterwards, a group of us girls went to the hotel where we knew they were staying. We had our J-5 buttons and posters, just wanting autographs, hoping to see the guys, maybe get a picture with them. Jermaine came down and struck up a conversation with a few of us. He was sweet, shy. He pulled me off to the side and asked me if I would like to come up to his room. Of course, I said yes. He was so handsome, with his big natural and white teeth.

'We got up to the room, and I walked in behind Jermaine. It was pitch-black, with just a night light on in a corner.

' "Michael and Marlon are sleeping," he whispered to me. "So we have to be quiet. Take off your clothes. Quick." He wasn't exactly romantic. I jumped into bed with him and he climbed on top of me. As he climaxed, he shuddered so loudly I was afraid he would wake up Michael and Marlon, who were sleeping three feet away in the next bed. Or at least I thought they were sleeping. As I was slipping out of the room, I heard Michael say to Jermaine, "Nice job. Now, can we *please* get some sleep?" '

It would be a couple of years before Marlon began playing around with groupies. However, Michael was never a player; he simply wasn't interested, and thought his brothers' behaviour towards their female fans was deplorable. After years of traumatizing overexposure, it was as if the very idea of sex had become abhorrent to him.

A person who has known Michael since 1974, once told me, 'I was having a conversation with Rebbie when she said, "Michael doesn't have time for girls." I asked, "What kind of guy doesn't have time for girls?" She said that there were special circumstances with Michael. When I asked her what she was talking about, she told me a horrible story.

'She said that when Michael was fifteen years old, a certain member of his family, someone he trusted – I won't say who, even though Rebbie did – decided he was old enough to have sex, and that he *had* to have it. This person then arranged the services of two hookers for Michael. He told them to work him over, and then locked Michael up in a room with them. Rebbie said that this incident absolutely traumatized her brother. I don't know whether or not Michael actually had sex with the hookers. Rebbie didn't say.'

Certainly, if this story is true, such a scenario must have had a deep psychological impact on Michael, as it would on any youngster going through puberty. After that happened, it's been said, Michael turned to prostitutes, not for sex – but for conversation. It was as if Michael had retaliated against his brothers' actions with groupies by trying to reassure himself that women were good for more than just fun times in bed. James McField, the group's former pianist and band director, recalled, 'Sometimes – maybe once, maybe twice – Michael just needed to have someone to talk to and – maybe once, maybe twice – a woman would be introduced to him as someone very nice that he could be with, to have the company of a female. But he wouldn't have sex with her, to my knowledge. As far as I know, nothing intimate would ever happen. He liked nice girls, pure girls who appeared to have no street background.'

One such 'date' remembered meeting Michael after a concert in New York. 'I was hanging around backstage, working Madison Square Garden's dressing area,' said Lillias Harris, 'when someone who introduced himself as an employee of the Jacksons came over to me and asked me if I wanted to spend an evening with Michael. "Hell, yeah," I said. He asked me how much, and I told him I would do it for free. I wanted to have sex with Michael Jackson. Who wouldn't?

'He brought me back to the dressing room. Michael was there, alone. I walked in, and he told me to close the door. The first thing out of his mouth was, "Why are you a prostitute?" I answered, "Because I need the money." He said to me, "Would you like to have sex with me?" and I said, "Yes, of course I would." He asked me how much it would cost. I told him, "No charge." He seemed interested. So, I undid my blouse and showed him my breasts. He then turned his head, repulsed. "Stop. I can't have sex with you," he said. "Please put them back," he added, referring to my breasts.

'When I asked him why, he told me, "Because I just can't." I thought he meant he couldn't get an erection, he looked so sad. Then, he said, "Can we talk about you and your life?" I didn't want to talk, that's not why I went there. So I gave him my telephone number.

' "Anytime you want to get off, you call me," I said. Michael looked at me and asked, "What does that mean, *get off*?" He was totally sincere. "It means screw, Michael," I told him. "Anytime you want to screw, call me. Get it?"

'He said, "Oh, okay. Maybe I'll call you someday. I doubt it, though." And then I left.

'He struck me as lonely and naive,' Lillias Harris concluded. 'He was a nice, mixed-up, good-looking guy who wanted female companionship. No way was he about to have sex that night, though. He was scared to death. I wondered if he would ever call me. He never did.'

'Rockin' Robin' and 'Ben'

By winter of 1972, Motown had released two more solo singles by Michael Jackson, the first being 'Rockin' Robin'. While Michael twitters his way through the song, the session player bangs out the easy ditty on the piano to create a song that was irresistible. 'Rockin' Robin' became an even bigger success than 'Got to Be There'. The song peaked in the same position for Michael as the original did for the late Bobby Day, at number two.

One early record of Michael's that still brings snickers today is 'Ben'. The words of the song extol friendship, though there is no clue in the lyrics that the song is actually about a rodent. (In the film, *Ben*, a young boy befriends a rat named . . . Ben. A little-known fact is that Bing Crosby was one of the movie's producers.) Michael's voice complements the delicately orchestrated piece, with its solo guitar accompaniment; the recording is layered at all the emotional peaks with a precise string arrangement. The song obviously stood on its own, independent from the film. It became Michael's first number-one solo record, selling an amazing 1,701,475 copies. It was also nominated for an Oscar.

Michael saw the movie *Ben* many times, sitting in the back of the theatre just waiting to hear his song and then see his credit on the screen. As a child, Michael loved rats. At one point, Katherine was horrified to find that Michael had thirty rats in a cage in his bedroom. He was passionate about the rodents until the day he discovered that they were eating each other – as rats will do. Sickened by the sight, Michael put the rat cage outdoors.

In addition to his solo records, Michael started recording the group's songs separately from his brothers, putting the lead vocal on tape alone in the studio. Later, the brothers would come in and record their background vocals. Often, additional – anonymous – singers would be added to the mix. This was a decision made by Motown to make the recording process more expedient. All it did for Michael, though, was make him feel more singled out, and not a part of the group. He didn't like it.

In November 1972, The Jackson 5 embarked on a twelve-day European tour, which would begin with a royal command performance before Queen Elizabeth. There was actually some concern at Motown that the tour would not be a success, based on the group's flagging record sales in Europe. Unlike the situation in America, sales were down for The Jackson 5 in Europe, and especially in Britain. The group's *Maybe Tomorrow* album, for instance, didn't even make the UK Top 50. Their single 'Sugar Daddy' also flopped in the UK.

However, as a solo recording artist Michael was faring well. 'Got to Be There' and 'Rockin' Robin' sailed to the British number five and three positions, respectively. Later in the month, 'Ben' would peak at number seven and sell more than a quarter of a million copies, just in the UK. So even if the group was falling short in record sales with a British audience, it was hoped that thanks to Michael's popularity the tour would draw audiences. It did, and in a big way. As British teenagers swarmed London's Heathrow Airport to welcome the group, the ensuing mob scene was reminiscent of Beatlemania.

'Large plugs of hair were jerked from the scalp underneath Jermaine's giant Afro by souvenir hunters,' reads Motown's 22 November press release. 'Noise so intense that it drowned out the whine of jet engines drove tears to Michael's and Marlon's eyes. Tito was bruised and shaken by the stampede of the thundering herd. Randy nearly panicked when frenzied females devoured him with bear hugs and wet kisses. Jackie was cool but more than a little bit worried. It was sheer pandemonium. It was near chaos. It was frightening. It was JACKSONMANIA.'

Besides losing a shoe, Michael was almost choked to death. 'He was really frightened,' recalled Jermaine. 'They were pulling on both ends of his scarf, actually choking him. He had to put his hand up under his scarf and start screaming so that it wouldn't tighten up on his neck.'

Michael loathed such mob scenes. He recalls having to run through crowds of screaming girls with eyes covered by his hands for fear that their nails would scratch him. He remembers hiding in broom closets, hoping the throng would rush by and miss him. 'They grab your hair and pull hard and it hurts like fire,' he recalled. 'You feel as if you're going to suffocate or be dismembered.'

Fans barricaded the entrance to the Churchill Hotel where the group stayed in London, preventing them from leaving the scene after their royal variety performance. Joseph called the police, who arrived with water hoses, which they unleashed on the fans. The next day, a nine-year-old girl threatened to use a knife on a hotel doorman unless he allowed her access to Michael's room. She was detained by the police. A Rolls-Royce limousine carrying the group sustained twelve thousand dollars' worth of damage when it was dented and scratched by young girls clawing to get to their idols. Later, as the Jacksons performed at the Talk of the Town nightclub, souvenir hunters stripped their limousine of its cushions, radio, lights, tyres . . .

It was this way wherever the brothers travelled on the rest of their tour, whether in Amsterdam, Brussels, Munich, Frankfurt or Paris.

Katherine Files for Divorce

Katherine Jackson had tolerated many years of unfaithfulness from Joseph. She knew he was cheating on her. Everyone knew. Joseph had been on the road with the boys for years and having brief encounters with their groupies. Not only had her friends told her, several of Joseph's more audacious girlfriends had telephoned the house over the years to brag about their encounters with him. 'I don't want those women calling the house,' she would scream at Joseph, sometimes in front of the children. 'I'm sick of it, Joseph. Enough is enough.' The reasons for Joseph's actions didn't matter to Katherine. She wasn't even sure she wanted him to stop his philandering, as she told one friend. She simply wanted him to be more discreet. 'Do you have to play me for a fool?' she would ask him, tearfully. A terrible rage began to fulminate in her. 'Don't you dare treat me like I'm stupid,' she screamed at him. 'There's nothing worse than being made to feel this way.'

In truth, Joseph treated Katherine just as she had allowed him to treat her for as long as they'd been husband and wife. There was little reason for him to stop, as far as he was concerned. In his view, he worked hard for the Jacksons, he supported his family, he gave them a good life, so what he did on his free time was none of their concern, as long as he was present when they needed him.

In January 1973, Katherine learned that one of Joseph's girl-friends had become pregnant and had a miscarriage. At first, she couldn't believe it; it was more than she could bear. However, when she confirmed that it was true, she decided that she had no choice but to end the marriage. 'It's over,' she announced. 'My marriage is over.'

Immediately, the children sided with her; oldest daughter Rebbie, who was twenty-three, couldn't bear to be in the same room with her father. 'I don't know how my mother hung in there all those years,' she later said. 'She didn't need that heartache with everything she had to deal with, being a mother, supporting the children's performance, getting involved in the business end of things. It was too much. I encouraged her to leave him. I knew that he was damaging her spirit, that she couldn't possibly have peace of mind.'

The Jackson offspring had seen Joseph mistreat Katherine for so many years, they were happy to see her finally take a stand against him. 'I hate Joseph,' Michael said to one of the Motown staffers. 'I hate him so much for what he has done to my mother. I hate him more than I can even say.'

'But, Michael,' the Motown employee said, 'you shouldn't feel that way. After all, he's your father.'

'I wish he wasn't my father, sometimes,' said fourteen-year-old Michael. 'I wish it with all of my heart. He's the loser here,' Michael said. 'His whole thing is always about winners and losers and who wins and who loses. With this thing, he loses. Big time.'

Katherine filed for divorce in Los Angeles on 9 March 1973.

Joseph was stunned. He had been controlling and manipulating Katherine for so many years, he couldn't fathom her fighting back in this manner. He also knew that he could not live without her. Plus, they had a family, growing children. He had to change her mind. Who was going to raise all of those kids?

Katherine was faced with a dilemma when she and her attorneys began filling out the required forms. She didn't have a clue as to the value or extent of her community property with Joseph. She had no idea how much her husband – or her children – earned annually, or what the extent was of their now vast business enterprises. She didn't even know Joseph's social security number. Therefore, she had to leave two pages of questions regarding this personal information unanswered. Her lawyer, Neil C. Newson, typed on the form, 'The information required in this declaration is currently being compiled. A separate amended financial declaration will be filed.' Katherine paid her attorney $150 and then went back to the house on Hayven-hurst. She did not move out of the house, and neither did Joseph. They just didn't speak to each other.

'When Motown heard that Katherine had filed for divorce, all hell broke loose,' remembered one family friend. 'This could have ruined everything in terms of their family image. All of those stories about how close they were, what a loving family they were . . . It had the potential to be a public relations disaster. It was decided by Gordy that no one was to know that Katherine and Joseph were splitting up. It would be a closely guarded secret by the press department. Today, you couldn't keep something like that out of the press, especially with a court filing. In the early seventies, the press wasn't as intrusive as they are today. The news was never leaked. However, Katherine was badgered constantly by company officials who tried to convince her to reconcile with Joseph for the sake of her family's image.'

'I'm finished with Joseph,' Katherine told one Motown official at a meeting to discuss the possible consequences of her decision. She looked bone-tired, recalled the lawyer. She wore a simple yet elegant black dress, pearls at her neck, a fine, diamond pin on her shoulder. Her hair was a jet black coif around her head. 'It should have nothing to do with the boys' career,' she said, firmly. They can still make records and be famous, and their parents can be divorced, and that will just have to be the end of it, I'm afraid.'

Though the Motown adviser was not convinced, her son, Michael, had made up his mind about his parents' marriage. 'As far as I'm concerned, it's over,' he told Diana Ross, according to a later recollection. 'My father has hurt my mother, and that's all I need to know. That, to me, is the end of it.'

'But people are so complicated,' Diana told Michael, hinting at the complexity of Joseph's problems. 'Who knows why they do the things they do.'

'I know why,' Michael insisted. 'It's because Joseph is a bad man, that's why. My brothers are going down the same road,' he concluded. 'I can see it, already.'

After a couple of months, Katherine withdrew her divorce papers. Joseph promised her that he would try to change, and that she should not break up the family over his past behaviour. Much to the dismay of her children, Katherine and Joseph were reconciled.

The Downslide

Despite The Jackson 5's world-wide popularity with concert-goers, trouble was brewing where their record sales were concerned. In Europe, sales had always been uneven. However, record store performance in America had always been strong. By April 1972 though, whether from overexposure or lack of promotion, the group was losing steam. The April release of 'Little Bitty Pretty One', was a huge disappointment. Except for a seasonal release of 'Santa Claus is Coming to Town', it became the poorest-selling Jackson 5 single to date, netting only 590,629 copies, globally. Its follow-up, 'Lookin' Through the Windows', fared even worse: 581,426 copies. This was a terrible showing. (It is interesting, though, that this song marked a sudden sales resurgence in Britain – a Top 10 hit that was no doubt a consequence of their recent tour.) When 'Corner of the Sky', from the Broadway musical *Pippin* (which Gordy had financed), sold only a disappointing 381,426 copies worldwide, Joseph became irate.

'What the hell is going on?' he fumed. He began showing up at Motown, harassing the sales staff and badgering the promotion executives. The problem was that Berry Gordy was no longer personally involved in what was going on with the record company. Instead, he put in charge a man named Ewart Abner, a seasoned executive in the recording industry by the time he got to Motown. For his part, Berry now devoted most of his time to Diana Ross's film career, and to establishing Motown Productions in the movie business. Although still Motown's chairman of the board, he was interested only in filmmaking, not in record production. A star vehicle for Diana Ross called *Mahogany* was in the works, a venture that would monopolize most of Berry's time.

At the time, Motown was capitalizing on a more socially conscious sound with Marvin Gaye and Stevie Wonder. Perhaps The Jackson 5's audience had become hungry for a hipper sound than what they got with the group's next release, 'Hallelujah Day'. It sold less than a quarter of a million discs; too bad, it was a terrific little record with leads shared by Michael, Marlon and Jackie.

In truth, Ewart Abner didn't care about The Jackson 5. He wasn't involved in signing them to the company, and he felt their best days were behind them. 'They already had their own cartoon, for Christ's sake,' he argued. 'Why spend any more money on them?' If sales figures were low and the group was losing its audience, it was the group's fault, not Motown's, he decided. With that point of view, it wasn't surprising that Joseph disliked Ewart Abner, and in an intense, passionate way.

When an album, *Skywriter*, was released in March and sold only 115,045 copies, it became the group's poorest-selling album. (It didn't even reach the Top 50 in Britain.) Joseph believed that all of the records which had been failures could have been more successful if Motown had simply promoted them properly.

There was a reprieve in the downward slide when producer Hal Davis put together a terrific track for the Jackson boys called 'Get It Together'. The production was tight; the music, background vocals and Michael's maturing lead all blended nicely on this performance, a departure from the sweeter, pop music styles previously associated with the group. Released in August 1973, it sold over 700,000 copies. Though not a million-seller, it encouraged Joseph in his belief that his sons still had an audience. To his way of thinking, The Jackson 5 was not finished. If anything, *he* was finished . . . with Motown.

Jermaine Falls for the Boss's Daughter

In early 1973, while Katherine and Joseph were distracted by the discord in their marriage, their son Jermaine was falling in love . . . with Berry Gordy's daughter. He had been dating Hazel Gordy for several months and, at just eighteen, seemed about to follow Rebbie's and Tito's lead by using matrimony to extricate himself from the Jackson homestead.

It was clear to the brothers that Hazel had become an important and influential presence in his life. For example, at a rehearsal in March, the group had been attempting to solve a problem in choreography with Suzanne dePasse. After a decision had been made about how best to handle the situation, the brothers were in agreement. However Hazel, who had begun attending all practice sessions, pulled Jermaine aside and whispered something in his ear. Jermaine listened, nodded absently, and walked back to his brothers. 'I think we oughta change this step,' he announced, dutifully.

'But why?' Michael protested, according to a witness's memory. 'It's perfect as it is.'

'Because Hazel has a better idea. Look, Mike, you stand here,' he said positioning his brother. 'And Tito here, Marlon there, and Jackie over there.' Jermaine then demonstrated Hazel's 'great idea' which, upon execution, made Jermaine more prominent in the presentation. When Suzanne realized what had happened, she shot Hazel a look. Hazel smiled innocently. Since Hazel was Berry's daughter, Suzanne had no choice but to agree with her suggestion. 'Looks fine, guys,' she said. 'Let's keep it.'

'Well, I hate it,' Michael announced, looking at Jermaine. 'C'mon, Jermaine,' he said, 'I thought we agreed.'

Jermaine looked away.

The other brothers tried to ignore what had happened. 'It ain't that important,' Tito decided.

'Well, I think it *is* important,' Michael concluded. 'But you guys can do whatever you want.' He then looked over to Jermaine, who now was in another conference with Hazel, shook his head and rolled his eyes.

Jermaine had been attracted to Hazel when they first met in 1969, but not in the same way in which she fancied him. After a short time, Hazel told Jermaine she was in love with him; he made it clear that he was not sure he could return her affection. He was a teenage idol, a star, and could have his pick of dozens of willing young women. This kind of idolatry was heady stuff for a young man like Jermaine. It made the idea of settling down with one woman seem confining, no matter who she might be.

'Jermaine likes girls too much to get married,' Michael had said. 'I think he'll be in his thirties before he does anything like that.'

However, Hazel was a young, idealistic girl who wanted more than anything to marry and have a family. Not only had her father been divorced three times, she had witnessed his tumultuous, heart-wrenching affair with Diana Ross. Though young, Hazel believed that true love was elusive, she remained a romantic. 'I can truthfully say that since I fell in love with Jermaine I have never even thought about any other man,' she said.

Delores Robertson, who was a friend of Hazel's at the time, recalled, 'Berry Gordy had been lavishing Hazel, his only daughter, with gifts for as long as she could remember. She told him that she was in love with one of The Jackson 5 and she wanted him for her own. Her feelings for Jermaine were so strong, she was afraid to let him slip through her fingers for fear that no one like him would ever come along again. She was jealous when she would see Jermaine with female fans. "Michael can have fans, but you can't," she used to tell him. Berry made sure she usually got what she wanted. Now she wanted Jermaine. Berry got to know Jermaine and, even though he felt there might be a problem with Joseph, believed that Jermaine was right for Hazel. When Jermaine asked Berry for her hand, he said, yes.'

Though Berry thought Joseph might be a stumbling block to any union between his daughter and Jermaine, that wasn't the case, at least not at first. Hazel actually found an unexpected ally in Joseph, who might not have insisted on a pre-nuptial agreement anyway (as he had with Tito's wife). He was certain that marriage between his son and the boss's daughter would ensure job security for the Jackson clan at Motown, especially since he was having a difficult time of late in even getting Berry on the telephone. He did all he could to help the youngsters, even referring to her as 'my Hazel' and saying that he loved her.

Had Joseph given the matter more thought, he might have been more concerned about the recent turn of events. When Berry's sister, Anna, was married to Motown singer Marvin Gaye, the alliance never gave Marvin special privileges at the company. In fact, according to Marvin, it only served to complicate his life and career because Anna acted as a spy for her brother during times of conflict. Marvin was rarely able to make a move that Berry didn't know about in advance. Also, Marvin said that he always felt a strong conflict of interest whenever he and Berry battled, which was often.

Many other Motown artists felt as Marvin did, that Jermaine was about to be groomed by Berry to become a major star just as Diana Ross had been lifted from The Supremes to superstar status; that

Jermaine's two solo releases for the company, 'That's How Love Goes' and 'Daddy's Home', had been successful, and he did have the potential to be one of the company's biggest stars. Actually, some critics cited strong similarities between Jermaine's vocal style and Marvin Gaye's. The truth is that Jermaine had his own sound, and it was a good one, too, full-bodied and always an interesting contrast to Michael's high-pitch on the many songs the two shared at Motown. (Actually, the reason Jermaine started singing leads at the company was that the group's producer, Deke Richards, was hospitalized with a slipped disk. He didn't want Fonce Mizell and Freddie Perren, to work with Michael without him, so he told them to write something for Jermaine. That song was 'I Found That Girl', the flip side of 'The Love You Save'.)

PART THREE

Jermaine's and Hazel's Wedding

In November 1973, Katherine and Joseph had another serious argument; distraught, she left town, leaving her family in a state of confusion and bewilderment. 'The children were devastated, Michael in particular,' recalled Joyce Jillson, a friend of Katherine's at the time. 'He wanted to go with her. "If you're leaving, so am I," he told her. "I'm not going to let you go without me." Michael didn't want to find himself in that house with his brothers and sisters and father, unless Katherine was present as a buffer. To Michael, she was his only link to sanity. But now even she had become unpredictable. It was unlike her to disrupt the family, but she just couldn't take it another second. She told Michael to stay behind and assured him that she would return. He cried. "Why can't Joseph go?" he kept asking. "*He's* the one who should be going."'

When Katherine heard through friends that the press had become aware of problems in her marriage, she became concerned. She wanted Jermaine's upcoming wedding, not her separation from Joseph, to be the focus of media attention. Therefore, she returned home just days before the wedding. Sensing in Joseph injured pride rather than true contrition, she wasn't sure how long she would stay with him now, but she knew she'd have to be at his side at Jermaine's wedding. She felt an obligation to her son, to her family.

Jermaine's wedding to Hazel Gordy on 15 December 1973 was an expensive, ostentatious affair. 'If my kid is going to get married,' Berry had said, 'she's going to marry in style. Sky's the limit,' he insisted. The wedding would cost him about a quarter of a million dollars, a lot for the times. Berry's money would create a winter wonderland at the exclusive Beverly Hills Hotel for the festivities. Artificial snow-covered pine trees, 175 white doves in white cages, and thousands of white camellias, chrysanthemums and carnations decorated the rooms in which the wedding, reception and luncheon took place. One hundred guests were invited to the ceremony; five hundred-plus to the after-gatherings.

Ebony called it 'the wedding of the century'. Guests were overheard comparing it to the royal wedding in London when Princess Anne had married Captain Mark Phillips a little more than a month earlier. Abe Lastfogel, a William Morris founder, called it 'the most lavish merger I've ever seen'. To ensure that the media would report the details correctly, Motown handed out publicity releases to the invited reporters.

Sixteen-year-old Marlon was the best man. Fifteen-year-old Michael, along with brothers Jackie (twenty-two), Tito (twenty), and Randy (eleven), were ushers. Michael's duties that day were not complicated: escort the guests to their seats before the ceremony, and escort one of the bridesmaids out of the chapel after it. However, people close to the Jackson family have indicated that Michael felt preoccupied on this day. Jermaine, who had always been his favourite big brother, was getting married and, in his view, it was going to make a difference in the way things were run.

'At first Michael had thought it wouldn't matter,' said one close family friend. 'Tito was married and The Jackson 5 had continued as before. His wife never had anything to do with group business or politics. But Jermaine was marrying Hazel, the boss's daughter, a lady who had strong opinions and got her own way. As the wedding day got closer and closer, Michael noticed that Jermaine was looking at things differently – through Hazel's eyes. He was becoming less Michael's best friend and more Hazel's man. Michael would feel the loss keenly. He and Jermaine were so close, he felt he was losing his best friend.'

In truth, Joseph had also become disenchanted with Hazel when he realized how much influence she had on Jermaine. He felt that she could be manipulative and, therefore, might interfere with group dynamics. Also, she had her dad's ear. There was no telling how things would work out, and Joseph couldn't help but be concerned.

At the reception, in the hotel's Lanai Room, show-business

luminaries such as Smokey Robinson, Diana Ross, Lola Falana, Diahann Carroll and Billy Dee Williams mingled with other notables such as Coretta Scott King, widow of Martin Luther. Katherine forced herself to act as if nothing was wrong, even though she was so unhappy. No matter how hard she tried to conceal it, her sadness was apparent. As soon as the photographers finished taking pictures of her and Joseph, she would pull away from him. At one point a concerned Michael asked her if she would like a glass of punch. Katherine shook her head absentmindedly as she gazed over her son's head at Joseph. 'I don't feel like dancing, honey,' she said. Michael watched, his eyes full of warmth for her, as Katherine turned away and walked into the crowd. To even the most casual observer, she seemed very alone.

It wasn't long before Diana Ross became the centre of attention, posing and preening for photographers as only she can. 'I brought him to Mr Gordy's attention,' she said, pulling Michael into the frame, 'and now look where he is today. *Everybody* wants to have their picture taken with this cutie,' she said. 'It's amazing.' Diana squeezed Michael tightly, as if he were a trophy. A mixture of love and pride illuminated her face. 'And just look at his little suit,' she said, tugging at Michael's lapel. A flicker of annoyance crossed his face.

'You're awfully grateful to Miss Ross, aren't you, kid,' a reporter asked Michael, 'for discovering you?'

'Uh . . . yeah,' Michael said. He must have wondered how long he was going to have to live with the fabrication that Diana Ross had 'discovered' him.

'Oh, isn't he sweet?' Diana cooed. 'You see, how it happened was, I was in Gary, Indiana, and I saw this group perform, and I said to myself . . .'

Las Vegas

Joseph Jackson was always competitive. However, he seemed even more so after Jermaine's wedding, as if his son's new alliance with Berry Gordy had caused Joseph to consider himself a 'David' determined to slug it out with Motown's 'Goliath'. To make more of an impression on the entertainment industry, Joseph formed his own record company, Ivory Tower International Records, and signed a female quartet from Ashtabula, Ohio, called M.D.L.T. Willis. The company and the group would not go far, which only served to reaffirm Berry's feeling that Joseph was well-meaning, but inept.

However, one goal Joseph had that seemed to not occur to Berry, or to his right-hand man at Motown, Ewart Abner, was to break his sons out of the teen-idol mould and into a more secure niche. He realized that the careers of most teen idols last about two years before newer stars come along to replace them. Joseph wanted to change The Jackson 5's public image before it was too late.

Joseph and Berry disagreed about the state of The Jackson 5's career. Joseph thought it was in trouble, citing the recent string of poorly selling records. However, Berry felt that the group was still popular, and he cited their latest record 'Dancing Machine', a rhythmic production by Hal Davis.

As the onslaught of disco began to homogenize the pop-R&B scene, The Jackson 5 managed, with 'Dancing Machine', to maintain their originality while capitalizing on the new trend. A high-spirited Michael bantered the lyrics above his brothers' strong choral chants, all to an infectious beat. In the pop-music world, the Jackson brothers were clearly holding their own alongside the likes of The Temptations, The Spinners and The Four Tops, who were no longer idols, but peers. The Jackson 5 were many years ahead of their time and on to the electric sound of the eighties – the style of 'Dancing Machine' is similar to a sound that, a dozen years later, would be known as 'techno-pop'.

As puberty set in, Michael's voice changed. Gone was the pubescent shrill popularized on 'I Want You Back', 'ABC', and 'The Love You Save'. It was replaced by a clearer, more refined tone, as heard on 'Dancing Machine'.

'Dancing Machine' would eventually hit number two on the *Billboard* charts and sell 2,170,327 copies, the most single sales for the group since 'Never Can Say Goodbye'. Therefore, as far as Berry was concerned, all was well in the Jackson 5's world. Most of those sales, though, were in America. In Europe, the song was not as successful, and in Britain it didn't even make the Top 50! (Future single and album releases in the UK would have such poor sales that they're not even worth mentioning further.) But Joseph didn't like such spotty sales; it was becoming impossible to predict when Motown would get behind the group and when it would not be supportive of the act. Joseph wasn't happy about any of it.

In the winter of 1974 during a family meeting, Joseph made the announcement, 'Boys, we're gonna play Las Vegas.'

'But Vegas is the thing you do when you don't have hits,' Jackie said, 'when you don't have a choice.'

'The brothers thought hangin' out in the hotels with white people would be no fun,' Michael recalled later. 'But I wanted to play Las Vegas. To me, Las Vegas was part of show-business tradition. At that meeting, our father told us two things: first, he said he was trying to show the world that we were every bit as good as The Osmonds; then he told us about Sammy Davis and what he went through so that guys like us could play Las Vegas.'

Joseph explained to his sons that in 1945 when Sammy Davis, Jr., his father, Sammy, and his uncle, Will Mastin, were booked into the El Rancho Vegas hotel in Las Vegas for five hundred dollars a week. At the time, Las Vegas was the new show-business Mecca. However, even though the Davis act was invited to appear in the El Rancho showroom, they were not permitted to stay at that hotel because they were black. Rather, they had to check into a boarding house with the black porters and dishwashers who worked at the hotels. This was not unusual. Even a major star like Billy Eckstine, who was also working in Las Vegas at the same time, could not stay at the hotel at which he appeared. The showrooms and casinos were also off-limits to black patrons; blacks could entertain but not gamble or socialize with whites.

In years to come, Sammy Davis, Jr., would break through these barriers by virtue of his talent and persistence – and, also, a little help from Frank Sinatra, who used his influence to open certain doors for his pal, Sammy. Sammy went from being a member of the Will Mastin Trio to being a solo star, paid over $175,000 a week in Las Vegas. By using his celebrity power and refusing to take no for an answer, 'Mr Show Business' was instrumental in de-segregating the town so that blacks could not only appear but also vacation and have fun there. By attending city hotel board meetings and working *within* the political system instead of against it, Davis also made it possible in the late fifties for more blacks to be hired at the Sands, where he performed. When Sammy died in May 1990, the Las Vegas strip went dark for ten minutes in his memory.

'I wanted more than anything to be a part of that great tradition,' Michael said years later when recalling his first Las Vegas engagement. He had been a Sammy Davis admirer since the age of ten. 'To me, it was important. It was a giant step.'

When it was finally confirmed that the Jackson 5 would open in Las Vegas in April at the MGM Grand, the newest and most prestigious hotel in the city, the Motown brass was unimpressed. 'If you decide to do this thing, you'll be doing it on your own,' Ewart Abner told Joseph. 'Motown won't be involved. These kids aren't ready for Las Vegas.' Later, Berry telephoned Joseph, personally, 'You're makin' the biggest mistake of their career,' he said.

'Butt out!' was Joseph's response. 'These are *my* goddamn kids. Las Vegas has a good tradition, and I want them to know about it. It's time for them to grow.'

'Hey, man, that's my son-in-law's career, too. I'm worried about him, about all of them.'

Joseph hung up on him.

Certainly, Berry understood the value and prestige of a successful engagement in Las Vegas for any performer. After all, he was the one who had championed the Las Vegas breakthrough of The Supremes in 1966. However, that engagement occurred only after years of carefully honing the trio's act to sophistication. Berry wanted his Motown performers to appeal to adults, especially to white adults, but he was certain that the Jacksons would fail miserably because of their lack of experience with the kind of material necessary to please a middle-of-the-road, predominantly white audience.

'Fine, then, let 'em go into Las Vegas if they want,' Berry reasoned to one of his aides. He was still stung by Joseph's reaction to him; few people ever hung up on him. 'I'm afraid that they'll fail there,' he added, 'but maybe it'll teach Joseph a lesson. Too bad the boys have to suffer on his account, especially Jermaine.'

Joseph was anxious to teach Berry a lesson of his own. At his urging, the entire family rallied together to prove Berry mistaken. 'We knew that Motown didn't believe in what we were doing,' Jermaine recalled. 'My father was out to prove them wrong, and the brothers were behind him one hundred per cent. I was torn. I had a suspicion that Berry was right.'

To make his family's show unique for Las Vegas, Joseph followed an example set by The Osmonds. That group had brought in younger brother, Jimmy, and sister, Marie, for their Caesars' engagement, and to great acclaim. Not to be outdone, Joseph recruited LaToya, seventeen, as well as Randy, twelve, and Janet, seven. (Rebbie was also expected to perform. However, when she sprained her ankle, her debut with the act was postponed a few months, until June.)

None of the new additions to The Jackson 5 show was over-whelmingly talented, but their marginal ability did help gloss up the overall show. It was Katherine's idea to have Randy and Janet do impressions of Sonny and Cher, rhythm-and-blues stars Mickey and Sylvia, and even Jeanette MacDonald and Nelson Eddy. Janet also did a cute Mae West in a backless, pink satin gown and feather boa, which *Variety* would call 'hilarious'.

LaToya joined the tap dancing routine to 'Forty-second Street'. There was a bit of a problem with LaToya, though. She wanted to sing a solo in the act, but had limited vocal talent. 'She wanted the spotlight' remembered a friend of hers. 'She would rant and rave, cry and throw fits. Joseph told her that all she would be allowed to do was mouth the words of songs on stage in group numbers, acting as if she were singing but not really singing at all. She didn't like that, but she had no choice.'

On stage, the MGM Grand orchestra loomed large behind the Jackson family on opening night, 7 April 1974. It was the kind of oversized orchestra that could never fit on most stages. A small group of musicians – Motown's rhythm section – was added to the mix to help re-create the sound of the familiar Jackson 5 hit records. Bright and colourful firework patterns burst across a pale blue backdrop as the Jacksons appeared on stage, much to the excitement of their audience.

Although The Jackson 5 had, for the most part, built their reputa-tion on rhythmic music, for their Las Vegas show they showcased a variety of song styles, as typified by a centre-piece medley which they introduced on opening night. The presentation was different, for them. Instead of dancing, the brothers sat on tall stools side by side, with mikes in front of them. Their outfits could best be described as 'mariachi-band mod'. The waist-length jackets worn over ruffled, white, open-neck shirts were reminiscent of those that draped strolling Mexican musicians, but the resemblance ended there. These costumes had sequin-scrolled lapels and were in untraditional colours: olive, green, pumpkin, pink, purple and gold. The bell-bottom trousers were light olive green, pale orange, maroon, lavender and brown. White patent shoes had clunky two-inch heels.

The medley began with Tito strumming on guitar, he played his solo instead of singing it, followed by Michael with a fluid rendition of Roberta Flack's 'Killing Me Softly'. On the last line, Michael turned to Jermaine, who sang a gentle version of Glen Campbell's 'By the Time I Get to Phoenix'. Midway through that number, Michael and Jermaine harmonized the chorus. It seemed so effortless, their voices blending together to create a sound so natural, so right. They turned to Jackie. The music then segued into the classic, 'Danny Boy', an excellent choice for Jackie's falsetto voice. As Marlon joined in, the two sang as one. Though there was none of the vocal interplay shared by Michael and Jermaine a moment earlier; still, the two voices – sounding like one – created a full-bodied, clear-as-a-bell tone. The set ended with the three-song selections being interwoven – a line here, a line there, each one joining the other. It was obvious the brothers had devoted themselves to perfecting such an intricate, beautiful arrangement, one that did not just feature Michael. The audience could feel the closeness between them as brothers, much more than just fellow performers. The standing ovation was loud and long.

When Michael had his turn in the spotlight, though, it was clear that he was the star. Spinning like a human top in his sparkling suit and flanked by his siblings, Michael churned effortlessly through each number – 'I Want You Back', 'ABC,' 'The Love you Save' and all the rest – changing pace again and again but always maintaining the mesmerizing grip on his audience so essential for a performer. 'When we started out, I used to be little, cute, and charming,' Michael said in the act. 'Now I'm *big*, cute and charming.' After each song, he would walk to the footlights and accept the plaudits of his fans.

For their Las Vegas debut, the Jackson family had pulled out all the stops, coming together as a family for a stellar performance. As all of them joined hands and raised their arms triumphantly, the audience erupted into a standing ovation. Katherine was front and centre, leading the applause.

In the wings, stage right, Joseph rocked back and forth on his heels, hands jammed in his tux pockets, a grin spread across his face. With the exception of the absent Rebbie, this night was the realization of his greatest dream: all of his children on stage, performing together. 'They did it,' he said to no one in particular. 'They did it.'

When Berry learned that The Jacksons had enjoyed a successful opening night in Las Vegas, he sent a contingent of Motown executives to the city in order to present an image of corporate solidarity behind the family. 'We were always certain that the boys had what it took,' he then noted in a prepared statement sent to the press. 'This is just the tip of the iceberg where The Jacksons' talent is concerned . . .'

Backstage, after the fourth night's performance, Joseph read the press release article to his family. The family felt betrayed, except for Jermaine who had no comment to make about it. The triumph in Las Vegas was Joseph's to claim, not Berry's. After he finished reading the article, Joseph crumpled the newspaper in his hands and flung it into a trash can.

In August 1974, the Jackson family was again booked into the MGM Grand in Las Vegas, but behind the scenes things were no less tense. Album releases were becoming less frequent. Whereas they used to have at least three a year, in 1974 there was only one, the *Dancing Machine* album. Two singles that were released at the end of the year, 'Whatever You Got I Want' and 'I Am Love', were not successful. Motown then cancelled the release of a Michael Jackson single called 'Doggin' Around'. A string of unsuccessful records usually put a disgruntled artist in his place when he was going up against a major label like Motown, and the Jackson family was having quite a losing streak on the charts.

As if all of the business problems were not enough of a distraction for the young performers, their mother discovered that Joseph had been having an affair with a Jackson 5 fan from Kansas. She was a twenty-six-year-old black woman who had, at first, been attracted to Jackie. When he expressed no interest, she turned to his father.

It was rumoured that the woman was pregnant. The issue was not discussed openly; the boys whispered about it among themselves. The question was obvious: was Joseph the father of her child? The thought that Joseph was having a child with another woman was so upsetting to Michael, he could barely perform. It was, as far as he was concerned, the ultimate betrayal of his mother.

After one of the shows in Las Vegas, Joseph called a group meeting to discuss glitches he saw in the boys' performances. As far as he was concerned, the show had to go on, despite any personal problems the family might be experiencing. However, Michael decided to boycott the meeting.

Later, Joseph caught up with Michael as he was wandering through the casino of the MGM Grand. He tapped Michael on the shoulder. Michael glanced back, saw who it was, and continued walking. Joseph roared, '*What the hell?*' He shouldered aside patrons in an effort to reach his son.

'I remember it like it was yesterday,' recalled Steven Huck, a Jackson 5 fan who had gone to Las Vegas to see the show. 'Michael was dodging his father all over the casino, hopping around like a jackrabbit, trying to outrun Joseph. "You listen to me," Joseph demanded. Then he grabbed Michael by the arm. I had no idea what was happening, what the problem was, but I couldn't help but watch.'

Huck recalled that Joseph spoke softly, rapidly into Michael's ear. Michael listened, his face a blank. Then, in mid-sentence, it seemed, he shook himself free of Joseph and pushed him away. "Don't you ever touch me again. Do you hear me?" Michael's voice could be heard above the din of the slot machines. People in the vicinity turned to stare and, upon recognizing him, began to whisper among themselves. No one came forward.

'I never dreamed that Michael Jackson could raise his voice to his father, or to anyone else,' Huck said. 'I was shocked. He sounded hurt. When he shouted, it was an odd sound, like a wounded animal.'

Joseph seemed shaken. Father and son glared at each other for a moment before Joseph raised his right hand as if he were about to strike. It wouldn't have been the first time, but the expression on Michael's face indicated that it would have been the last. Joseph's jaw sagged; he backed up two steps. Michael then ran off into the bustling casino.

It would be years before he would learn the truth about his father's affair – and about his half-sister, Joseph's secret daughter.

Jackie Marries

In the winter of 1974, Michael Jackson's twenty-three-year-old brother, Jackie, made newspaper headlines when he suddenly married Enid Spann. Jackie had met her at a birthday party for Hazel Gordy five years earlier. Enid attended Beverly Hills High (as did Hazel) and was just fifteen when she and Jackie, three years her senior, became attracted to each other.

She got the news about a pre-nuptial agreement early on. She and Jackie had barely started dating, but the Jackson attorney, Richard Arons, heard through the family grapevine that she was interested. He decided to take preventive measures and meet with her, telling her that if she married Jackie, she would have to sign a pre-nuptial agreement.

'Let me tell you something,' the teenager said to the lawyer. 'When I marry Jackie Jackson – which I now think will never happen – if signing that marriage licence isn't good enough for him, then I don't need him and I don't want him.'

Arons was surprised by her audacity.

'And another thing,' she added, 'I wouldn't talk, if I were you, because *you're* the one who's living off of their gravy.'

Enid recalled that she was then 'totally turned off' the Jackson family. 'And when I told my mother what had happened, she was upset. It was a mean thing to do to a fifteen-year-old. After that, me and Jackie didn't hit it off. I thought he had something to do with my conversation with Richard. However, when I finally told him what Richard and I discussed, he got angry and told him, "How dare you say that to her!" '

Jackie and twenty-year-old Enid were married in a small private ceremony in Jackie's room at the MGM Grand in Las Vegas during another of the family's engagements there. Joseph suspected that Enid had ulterior motives for marrying his son, especially since, unlike Tito's wife Dee Dee, she would not sign a pre-nuptial agreement. He also felt that Enid was too outspoken and independent, and would be a problem. That Joseph forbade Jackie to marry Enid Spann only served to motivate his eldest son towards the altar. For Jackie, the fact that he was uniting himself with a woman with whom he presumably would spend the rest of his life seemed less important than the fact that he was defying his father.

As a manager, Joseph did his best. As a parent he was making a mistake with his children by holding on so tightly, and it was one he would pay dearly for in the future. In a way, it's the same mistake Berry Gordy had made with many of his Motown performers, but Joseph was a parent as well as a manager, and he was unable to distinguish between where one role began and the other ended. He treated his children the same way he did his business associates: he negotiated by pounding his fist on the table and yelling louder than anyone else in the room. His behaviour was frightening to his wife and daughters, and emasculating to his sons. 'Michael said that they used to run down the hall and slam their bedroom doors closed when they heard that Joseph was coming home,' Jane Fonda recalls.

Michael's Private Meeting with Berry

In January 1975, Motown released Michael Jackson's fourth solo album, *Forever Michael*. It was not a success, peaking at only 101 on the charts, eight notches lower than Michael's poorly selling *Music and Me* album. Neither album would even make the Top 50 in the UK, and the rest of Europe also showed dismal sales. 'That's it!'

Joseph decided. 'He's not recording any more solo albums for Gordy. That man's gonna ruin Michael!'

Joseph had become increasingly agitated by Motown's lack of promotion and Berry's contention that the group had no potential to write or produce their own music. Joseph realized that his sons would never make big money unless they owned the publishing rights to their own songs. If an artist writes his own material, he makes not only an artist's royalty, but an additional royalty, since songwriters are paid a royalty on every record that is sold. At this time, the rate was an additional two cents per copy sold, split fifty-fifty with the song's publisher. Therefore, the B-side of a million-selling song, the side that rarely if ever gets radio airplay, could be worth up to twenty thousand dollars. At least, Joseph reasoned, the boys should be able to write their own B-sides. Was that too much to ask?

Most of Berry's songwriters were signed to Jobete, his publishing company. Therefore, they had to split their two cents with Berry. Joseph wanted his boys to establish their *own* publishing company so that they could keep the money in the family. The more he pressed the idea forward, the more Berry resisted it.

In the past, Berry had always been reluctant to share the money generated from publishing rights to Motown songs. At this same time, Smokey Robinson, Berry's closest friend, was negotiating with Berry to allow him to publish his own songs, as well. Jobete owned all of Smokey's songs, too, and Smokey, like Joseph Jackson, wanted a bigger piece of the pie. Eventually, Berry did allow Smokey to share that money, so he could be swayed. However, persistence was always the key when it came to getting Berry Gordy to do something about which he was reluctant. Smokey and Berry were friends, yet Smokey had to endure a fair amount of tough negotiation. What could Joseph – certainly no friend – expect from Berry? It seemed that he and his sons would have little chance of controlling publishing rights to their material as long he and Berry had such a contentious relationship. Ewart Abner was now practically running the record division of Motown, anyway . . . someone else Joseph disliked.

Joseph's mind was made up: The Jackson 5 would have to leave Motown.

Was it even possible? If not for Berry and Motown, where would The Jackson 5 be? Perhaps, still in Gary, Indiana, was the answer.

Still, if the circumstances didn't soon change at Motown, it was clear that the group's commercial future would be in jeopardy.

Though the group hadn't yet voted on the decision – and it's likely that Joseph's vote would sway his sons – Michael said later that he knew the brothers would agree with his father. Michael was as unhappy as the rest of the family about what was going on at Motown, yet he still felt a loyalty to Berry. After all, it was largely due to Berry's confidence in The Jackson 5 that the family now found itself in a position to be able to pick and choose among other record companies. This was a major decision for young Michael, and he didn't want his father, a man he didn't trust, or even like, making it for him.

The other Jacksons thought of Michael as being bashful and reserved, which was certainly true in most cases. However, there was another dimension to Michael, a side he did not often show but which was there just the same: his resolve. Where his future at Motown was concerned, sixteen-year-old Michael Jackson was prepared to take matters into his own hands. He picked up the phone in his bedroom and dialled. 'Mr Gordy,' he said, 'you and I need to talk.'

None of the Jackson brothers had ever had a private meeting with Berry Gordy. Until now, there had never been a reason for one. It's unlikely that Berry would have consented to meet with Jackie, Marlon, Randy or Tito. None of them possessed Michael's commercial voice or magical showmanship. And Berry felt he owed it to the teenager to hear him out. Though he liked Michael, he considered him shy and meek, hardly the person to be blunt and forthright. Therefore, he was probably intrigued by the notion of a private conference with him.

Michael didn't care how his father felt about his decision to meet with Berry. In fact, he didn't discuss it with him. Still angry at Joseph for all he had done to Katherine, not to mention the abuse he had heaped upon his sons, Michael made up his own mind. Also, Michael would say later that his intuition told him the difficult situation with Motown could have been resolved sooner if only Joseph hadn't been so ill-tempered and possessive.

Others at the label agreed. Smokey Robinson said, in retrospect,

'Joe never got used to Berry being the one to tell his kids what to do. He believed that since he was their father, he was their boss, and that was the end of that. But Joe wasn't a businessman. He kept screwing things up and pissing people off. No one wanted to do business with him, and that was a poor reflection not only on the Jacksons but also on Berry and Motown. Without Joe's involvement, Berry would have worked things out with the Jacksons the way he did with me, Stevie Wonder, and anyone else who was unhappy at Motown, but ultimately stayed on.'

Nor did Michael tell his brothers of his plan to meet with Berry, since he felt certain that they would try to talk him out of it. The Jacksons prided themselves on one vote each, even though Joseph's vote usually trumped everyone else's. Most certainly, Michael's siblings would have felt that by meeting with Berry he was seizing more power than he was entitled to have as part of the group.

Michael and Berry arranged to meet at the Gordy estate in Bel Air on 14 May 1975. 'It was one of the most difficult things I've ever done,' Michael would recall. Mustering up his courage, he laid his cards on the table.

'We're all unhappy, Mr Gordy,' he said, according to his memory. 'Do you really want us to leave Motown?'

'Well, Michael, someone as smart as you,' Berry began, 'should know that without Motown, The Jackson 5 would still be in Gary, Indiana, today.'

Michael wasn't cowed by the fact that Berry had apparently decided to play the guilt card. 'That doesn't answer my question,' he told him.

Michael would later recall that he complained to Berry about the fact that Motown would not allow the brothers to write or produce their own music or control publishing rights. He was unhappy because he hadn't been allowed to contribute to The Jackson 5's most recent album, *Dancing Machine*, despite the fact that he thought he had some strong songs he could have added to the package. If he could have had just one song on the album, Michael said, it would have shown that Gordy had confidence in him as a songwriter.

Berry remained calm. 'I've been hearing this from my artists for years,' he said. 'However, we can work it out, Michael. Look, I worked it out with Stevie [Wonder], and Marvin [Gaye], didn't I?'

He was clear. He said he did not want the group to leave Motown. However, he added, 'If you think you can get a better deal somewhere else, then you have to go somewhere else, I guess. But it just won't be right . . . or fair.'

In Michael's eyes, Berry Gordy was a hero. He respected him and admired the tenacity with which he had transformed The Jackson 5 of Gary, Indiana, from local homeboys to international superstars. He thought of Berry as one of the smartest men he had ever known, and was amazed by the way he had made Motown such an international success story. Berry was an inspiration to Michael. To hear him now say that the Jackson family was being unfair to him – after he had brought the group to Los Angeles, made arrangements for their living conditions, paid for their educations, and made them stars – was difficult for Michael.

'What makes you think you can write or produce your own hit?' Berry asked Michael.

'I just know it,' was Michael's quick answer.

Berry looked at him sceptically. 'I don't know that that's good enough.'

'Well, what made *you* think you could build Motown into what it is today?'

Berry didn't answer.

'You just *knew* it, right?' Michael challenged.

Berry flashed a tolerant grin. 'He nodded at me as if to say, "You're going places, kid," ' Michael recalled. It ended with Berry emphasizing that he thought of himself as a father-figure to Michael, yet also stressing that it was important for the teenager to honour his natural father. 'He said he believed I would do what was best,' Michael told me later, when remembering the meeting. Michael added that he 'felt a little sick about the whole thing', especially when Berry hugged him as he was leaving because, in his gut, he knew that no matter what he expressed to Joseph and the brothers about it, the cards were stacked against the Jacksons staying with Motown.

'I can promise you this,' Berry concluded, 'I won't do anything to hurt you or your family.'

Michael's meeting with Berry Gordy showed surprising initiative, as well as no small measure of courage for a teenager. It was the first hint to many at the time that he was more than just a child prodigy. He had moxie. He seemed to understand what his father didn't: that there are times when it makes sense to sit down with your opponent and try to reason with him. In his own uncomplicated way, Michael was able to cut through some of the rhetoric that had lately been so prevalent in the communication between Berry and the Jackson family. He was able to extract from Berry a promise that he would not do anything to hurt the family, which was quite a statement for him to make, and seemed genuine.

Joseph had heard from an associate at Motown that Michael had seen Berry in private. Imagine his fury. When Michael got back to Encino, he was pacing in the living room like a caged animal waiting for dinner. Michael would not discuss with me the details of the argument that ensued between him and his father, but it isn't difficult to imagine that Joseph made it clear that, in his view, Michael was out of his league in trying to negotiate with someone like Berry Gordy. Once he calmed down, he had to admire his son's nerve, though. At least, one would hope so. The brothers, however, were annoyed.

'Michael had no right to meet with Berry Gordy,' Jackie said, years later. 'It was unfair of him to go behind our backs. We were all mad at him. And really, what did he accomplish?'

Perhaps Michael didn't accomplish much in terms of The Jackson 5's future at Motown, but his meeting with Berry was an important personal milestone. He had obtained Berry's attention, which was something even his father, as well as his brothers (with the exception of Jermaine), had not been able to do. However, it did set him apart from the brothers and, from this time onward, none of the brothers would be warm to any suggestion that Michael be further individualized from the group. 'Michael always had his own idea of how things should be done,' Marlon Jackson once said. 'But The Jackson 5 was a group, not his special project, and his was just one vote.' In other words, Marlon saw the writing on the wall.

The night after Michael's meeting with Berry, Joseph called a group meeting in the living room of their Encino home. All of the brothers were expected to appear, except for Randy and Jermaine. Young Randy had no say in any group matters, at this time. Jermaine was on holiday with Hazel, but he probably would have been excluded, anyway, since the family felt he had lost his objectivity about Motown. Jermaine later said, 'Because of me being married to Hazel, they thought they couldn't trust me so they kept me in the dark.'

Jackie, Tito, Marlon, Michael and Joseph voted unanimously to leave Motown. Michael was ambivalent, but he knew it wasn't smart to be the one dissenting vote. What good would it do him, anyway?

'I just want it to be done fairly, and something about this doesn't seem fair to me,' Michael said. 'Berry made us stars. Don't forget that.'

'Look, Berry's fine, but it's over,' one of the brothers said. 'It's time for us to be making the big bucks.'

'I agree,' said another one. 'It's time to go. We're dying at Motown.'

'He said he wouldn't hurt us,' Michael said, trying to stick up for Berry.

'Yeah, right,' Joseph said, sarcastically. 'Look, it's settled,' he concluded.

'But what about Jermaine?' Michael wanted to know.

'I'll take care of Jermaine,' Joseph said. 'What do I always tell you kids?'

'There are winners in this life, and losers,' Michael said, parroting his father's credo. 'And none of my kids are ever gonna be losers.'

Joseph smiled. 'If we stay at Motown,' he concluded, 'we lose. And we're not losing.'

CBS Offers the Jacksons a 'Sweet Deal'

After the die was cast, Joseph Jackson and his attorney, Richard Arons, quietly began scouting for a new record deal, meeting first with Atlantic Records, which had a long experience with rhythm-and-blues music. Surprisingly, Atlantic's chairman, Ahmet Ertegun, was unenthusiastic about The Jackson 5, he said, because of their inconsistent record sales at Motown in recent years. Joseph was not interested in trying to convince anyone of his sons' popularity. He'd had enough of that at Motown. If anything Ahmet's view helped to underscore Joseph's opinion that Motown truly had damaged his sons' reputation in the music industry.

Joseph was more interested in the CBS Records Group anyway, at which most of the black acts were contracted to the Epic subsidiary. CBS was renowned for its excellent record distribution and promotion network. 'They make Motown look sick,' is how Joseph put it.

Ron Alexenberg, president of Epic, and, ironically enough, a former protégé of Motown's Ewart Abner, was interested in signing The Jackson 5. Joseph respected Alexenberg – under his guidance, Epic had increased its annual billing from less than $10 million to over $100 million. A competitive leader with his finger on the pulse of the record industry, he suspected that Berry Gordy had tapped only a small percentage of the Jacksons' fullest potential. He wanted to find out what else was there.

Joseph was also attracted by the company's profitable relation-ship with Kenny Gamble and Leon Huff, producers of the so-called Philly Sound that had generated millions with hit records by black groups like The O'Jays and Three Degrees. Gamble and Huff had their own label at CBS, which they called Philadelphia International. Though Joseph felt that Philadelphia International was too small a subsidiary for The Jackson 5, he admired CBS's commitment to black music. Perhaps the company would one day award him his own label, as well, he thought. He saw a future at CBS, not just for his sons but for himself.

Ron Alexenburg told Walter Yetnikoff, president of CBS Records, that he wanted to sign The Jackson 5 immediately. Walter was sceptical. 'They haven't been hot in a long time,' he said. 'And now look at them. They're into this kitschy, Vegas thing.'

'Trust me,' Ron told him, according to his memory. 'This group isn't finished. It hasn't even begun yet.'

After quick and easy negotiations, an agreement was struck, one that Joseph called 'a sweet deal'. The Jackson 5 would receive an advance – known in the record industry as a 'signing bonus' – of $750,000. They would also receive an additional $500,000 from a 'recording fund' – money meant specifically to produce the group's albums. They were guaranteed to be paid $350,000 per album, far more than they had ever received at Motown (but many millions less than Michael Jackson would be paid for his services a scant five years down the road).

All of the advance money from CBS was to be recouped from royalties, but the royalty rate the new label offered was 27 per cent of the wholesale price for records released in the United States. At Motown The Jackson 5 had been paid 2.7 per cent, and before they saw that they knew they would have to pay back the costs of expenses – including studio time, over which they had little to no control – from royalties.

At this time, 1975, an album retailed for approximately $6.98, $3.50 wholesale. So at Epic the Jacksons would make approximately 94.5 cents per album sold in the United States, and 84 cents abroad. At Motown, they made roughly 11 cents per album sold in the United States, with no difference in the European rate.

As outlined in the Epic deal, after each Jackson 5 album topped $500,000 in sales, the group's royalty rate would jump to 30 per cent, about $1.05 a disc. In terms of income, this new deal was worth about *five hundred times* more than the one the group had at Motown.

A snag in negotiations occurred when Walter Yetnikoff refused to allow the Jacksons to write and produce, or even choose, all of their own material. He simply did not have confidence in their abilities as writers or producers since none of them had any experience in that arena. Ron Alexenberg assured Walter that 'demos' – roughly recorded samples – of songs penned and produced by the Jacksons, which Joseph had submitted, showed great promise. Still, Walter was not swayed. Therefore, the best Joseph could negotiate was that his sons would be able to choose at least three songs on each album, written by them or someone else. Also, there was an understanding that if the group came up with three good songs of their own, those tunes would receive fair consideration for use on an album. This, too, was more than they had ever gotten at Motown. However, the concession was not to be in the contract. It was verbal, and anyone knows that in the world of business a verbal agreement is tough to enforce. Still, at least there was some dialogue about the notion of the group having artistic freedom. Joseph was confident that his boys would only have to prove themselves one time . . . and after that they'd never look back.

Michael was amazed by the contract CBS had offered the family. He had no idea that the group was worth so much and that this was the kind of contract other superstar acts were accustomed to in the record business. He had to admire his father's tenacity. After all, had it not been for Joseph, The Jackson 5 might have slid into obscurity at Motown. 'I had to admit it,' Michael later noted, 'this was one incredible record deal. My father did an amazing job for us.'

Still, Michael was torn between the notion of loyalty to Berry and that of good business sense. He decided to discuss the matter with Diana Ross. Her reaction was predictable. She said that she had no influence over Berry where business matters were concerned – and she wasn't lying, she didn't – but that Michael should listen to him because, as always, he knew what was best for all of his artists. 'I just believed that the boys should stay at Motown,' she recalled in a 1981 interview. 'I was loyal to Berry at that time, and I felt that they should be as well. I told Michael that loyalty is the most important thing, not money.'

In six years Diana Ross would change her mind about being loyal to Berry Gordy and Motown. When she was having her own disagreements with him and decided to check on her value at other companies, RCA offered her $20 million, much more than what Berry could offer her. She turned to Smokey Robinson for advice. Smokey gave her the same advice she had given Michael about loyalty to Berry. However, she felt she had no choice. It didn't make sense to turn down that much money: she signed with RCA.

Joseph to Jermaine: 'Sign It!'

The CBS contracts were drawn up in a couple of days. Each of the four brothers eagerly signed them.

The problem then became how to break the news to Jermaine, and convince him to sign the deal. Jermaine's father-in-law, Berry Gordy, was now considered to be the enemy, but Joseph realized that Berry had a powerful influence over his son. Berry had recently promised Jermaine an exciting and lucrative future at Motown; he suspected that the group would try to leave and he wanted to assure Jermaine of his future at the company. He had trusted him enough to give him his only daughter in marriage. It would be Joseph's challenge to convince his son that his wishes should prevail over Berry's. He waited three days before summoning Jermaine, trying to determine a strategy. He soon realized there was no easy way to coax Jermaine away from Berry. It shouldn't be that difficult a decision for Jermaine, anyway, he decided. After all, *he* was Jermaine's father, not Berry. He was certain that Jermaine would make the 'right' decision. 'After all,' he said, 'Jermaine's not stupid. I hope.'

'Come to the house tonight,' he told Jermaine on the telephone. 'Come alone. Don't bring that wife of yours.'

'That's when I knew something was wrong,' Jermaine recalled, years later. 'Hazel is a very strong person and asks a lot of questions. I'm sure my father thought he could get me to do anything if Hazel wasn't there. I was afraid to go, afraid of what I'd find.'

When Jermaine arrived at the Encino estate, Joseph escorted him into the bedroom and closed the door. The contracts were spread out on a bureau, signatures on four of them. A fifth contract was unsigned. Joseph picked up Jermaine's contract and handed it to him. 'Sign it,' he ordered. He didn't attempt to reason with him, or even explain anything to him . . . he just told him to 'sign it'. How Joseph could be so obtuse remains a mystery. He may have been able to get Jermaine's signature if only he had used a modicum of common sense in his approach. Of course, Jermaine refused.

'I said, sign it.'

'No, Joseph,' Jermaine said. 'I'm not signing.'

'You sign this damned contract, Jermaine.'

'I ain't signin''

'Think about the money,' Joseph shouted at him. 'Real money. You think Motown's gonna come close to this deal? Look at this money.' He flipped through the pages, trying to find the clause that outlined terms.

'I don't care,' Jermaine said. 'It's not about money for me.'

'You don't care? You're crazy. That's what you are,' Joseph said, angrily. By now he was shaking his fist at his son. 'You sign this goddamn contract, Jermaine, or you'll be sorry. CBS says The

Jackson 5 will be the next Beatles, and you know that's what we've been working for.'

'Hell no. I don't want to be no Beatle,' Jermaine said. 'I'm not signing it, Joseph. Forget it.'

With that, as Jermaine recalled it to me in an interview years later, he ran from the bedroom and out of the house. He told me that he knew he had to tell Berry what had happened – and that the Jacksons were actually leaving Motown – and the news couldn't wait until he got home. He pulled over to a pay telephone and called his father-in-law.

'The brothers, they signed with CBS, Berry,' he blurted out as soon as Berry picked up. 'I can't believe it. But they did it. They left Motown.'

Jermaine recalled that there was silence on the other end of the connection. Finally, in a soft and calm voice, Berry spoke. 'Are you absolutely sure, Jermaine?'

'They already signed the contracts,' Jermaine answered, his tone frantic. 'I saw them with my own eyes.'

'Well, what about you? Did you sign?' Berry asked.

'The brothers are leaving because there are problems at Motown,' Jermaine said, 'but I want to stay, Berry. I want to help work out the problems.'

Jermaine later recalled, 'I told him I didn't sign and that I wasn't going to. He told me to come by his house, which I did. We talked it out. That night, he became like a second father to me, a sensible father. "You're on your way to the top," he told me. "You could be running Motown one day." That's what I wanted. I wanted to be the president of Motown. I knew I could do it. I knew I had it in me, even if Joseph never believed I did. Berry gave me the confidence to know that I could go places if I stayed with him and with Motown. I believed him. I didn't believe anything my father had to say about anything. I believed in Berry Gordy, not in Joseph Jackson.'

Despite the fact that there was such turmoil in the family, the group still had work to do on the road. When Jermaine came back to the house a few days later to rehearse for the show, he and Katherine had a loud discussion about his decision not to sign the CBS contract.

Katherine was angry with him, and she let him know it. Jermaine reminded her that Berry Gordy had been the one 'who put steaks on our table and teeth in our mouths'. Katherine couldn't believe her ears. 'We were *already* eating steaks in Gary,' she told her son heatedly. 'And as for the teeth he put in Jackie's and Tito's mouths, he's recouped that money hundreds of times over, you can be sure of that.' (However, it doesn't seem likely that the Jacksons *were* 'eating steaks in Gary'.)

The next stop for the group was the Westbury Music Fair on New York's Long Island. On the way, Michael attempted to act as referee between Jermaine and Jackie, who argued loudly about the question of Motown versus CBS. In the end, the brothers, with the exception of Michael, had completely turned on Jermaine. 'They couldn't understand how they could go one way and I the other,' Jermaine remembered. 'It was tense. It was bad.'

Michael adopted a more even-handed position than his brothers. 'I thought he would see things our way, eventually,' he later recalled. 'I never had a doubt things would work out.'

In some ways, the familial pressure manifested itself in predictable ways. Hazel, who almost always travelled with the group, had become protective of her husband, not allowing him out of her sight. One of the group's road managers recalled, 'After we checked into the hotel in Long Island, we were all down in the lobby having fun, the other brothers and their friends. I went up to Hazel and Jermaine's suite to see where Jermaine was, but Hazel said that Jermaine couldn't "come out and play". I thought that odd, and pushed her on it. She got upset, "I said, he needs his rest. Now, please go. Leave him alone." Jermaine didn't have a performance until the next evening, with the group. Why did he suddenly need more rest than the others? Hazel continued, "I said he can't come out, so he can't come out. And that's final." It seemed that her whole thing at that time was to separate Jermaine from his family.'

Jermaine has said that, prior to the group's leaving for New York, Berry Gordy sat down with him and Hazel 'and told us that the first loyalty of a husband and wife must be to *themselves*, not to *anyone* else, not to anything else in the world.' According to Jermaine, Berry said, 'Whether it's me and Motown or the Jackson family and CBS, *everything* comes second to yourselves as man and wife, because you are the two people who are going to have to live with each other and with whatever decisions you make.'

Berry's diplomacy aside, he most certainly recognized the truth: Jermaine would not be able to leave Motown, not if he wanted to stay married to the boss's daughter.

After The Jackson 5's first performance at the Westbury Music Fair, the telephone rang in the dressing room. It was Berry calling for Jermaine.

As his family watched Jermaine's face for a hint as to what the conversation was about, Jermaine clutched the telephone tightly. He didn't say much, other than goodbye. He exhaled deeply, and he hung up.

'Okay, I guess I gotta go,' Jermaine announced.

'Now? We go on in thirty minutes!'

'How're we gonna work around you?' Jackie gasped, incredulously.

'I can't believe you're doing this to us,' Tito added.

Everybody was talking at once, Joseph's voice being loudest of the din. 'Are you crazy?' he stormed. '*We're* your family. Not the Gordys. What's wrong with you, Jermaine? You ain't going *nowhere*, boy.'

Berry had demanded that twenty-year-old Jermaine make the most important decision in his life, and make it right then, right there: Motown or CBS? The Jacksons or the Gordys. His birth family or his family by marriage?

Whether Jermaine acted on impulse or understood the ramifications of what he was about to do, he rushed out of the dressing quarters with tears in his eyes. 'I'm outta' here,' he said. He took a car to his hotel room, where he packed his suitcase in about five minutes. 'What's goin' on? What's goin' on?' Hazel wanted to know. Jermaine could not speak through his racking sobs. 'We're leaving,' was all he could say. A black Motown stretch limousine waited to whisk the couple to the airport, and then back to Los Angeles.

'We were surprised, really in shock, absolutely stunned,' Marlon later remembered. 'It was like a dream, Jermaine getting that call and then walking out on us like that. We were about an hour from show time. The place was already packed. We had a show to do. We couldn't dwell on any of it. Michael was crying, and I said, "Not now, Mike. We have fans out there. We have to buck up." Wiping his eyes, he said, "I can do it, Marlon. But, later, we gotta deal with this. We gotta get Jermaine back."'

That night, The Jackson 5 exploded on to the stage of the Westbury Music Fair with such elation, no one in the audience would ever have guessed the backstage drama that had just unfolded. Michael's first responsibility was to his audience. He was just sixteen, but he knew what he had to do. During 'Dancing Machine', he whiplashed the mike stand into a wobble, did a motorized shuffle across the stage as if he were a robot, and then executed a split at the precise moment the stand crashed down upon his shoulder. He then looked at the instrument with a disdain that implied mortal insult. The crowd roared its approval.

This journalist – a teenager at the time – was present for this show, a Jacksons' performance still recalled with vivid clarity. Though Jermaine was missed – Michael announced that he had the flu – it was still a dizzying performance.

During an ironic tribute to the Motown Sound, Michael prowled the stage like a fierce, balletic wolf – 'I Want You Back', 'ABC', 'The Love You Save', 'Never Can Say Goodbye', all the Motown hits and more were performed with graceful and often demanding choreography. Whatever it took to please his fans, that's what Michael did, transforming, as always, personal frustrations into sheer energy. While accepting his audience's approval, he seemed purged of all anxiety. Once again, he was with the only people he knew he could completely trust: his fans.

The plaintive riff from The Jackson 5 hit 'I'll Be There' rang even more bittersweet as Michael performed it during this evening's show. Without any rehearsal, Marlon stepped in and took Jermaine's ironic lines. 'I'll be your strength,' he sang, 'I'll keep holding on.' Marlon had always been underrated as a singer, never having had a chance to truly shine in his brothers' shadow. Tonight, he held his own, and against great odds. Still, Jermaine belonged on that stage, in his rightful place next to Michael. It just wasn't right.

By the time the youngsters were finished, members of the audience were bouncing out of their seats; there were three encores. But afterwards, backstage, there was no music, no partying, no laughing as usual after a stellar performance. Everyone returned to his own dark mood. 'Why does the show have to end?' Michael asked his brother Jackie. He seemed disheartened. Though he tried and tried to hide his feelings, they always seemed to show. 'I wish it could just go on for ever.'

I walked over to Michael. 'Hey, man, what happened to Jermaine?' I asked. 'But, what a great show, anyway,' I added. 'Wow, man. Wow.' If it was possible for a teenage admirer to be too fawning, I wasn't aware of it at the time. 'What a great show that was,' I went on. 'My God. The whole thing was just so . . . *cool*.'

Michael accepted my compliments with a soft, sad smile. 'Thanks. Jermaine will be back,' he said. 'He's . . . sick.'

Joseph sat in a corner silently. It appeared that the act – his family – was breaking up, and that there was nothing he could do about it. Anyone looking at him would have been heartbroken by his forlorn expression. He seemed uncharacteristically vulnerable as he sat slumped in a chair, shaking his head as if to say, I just don't understand it. How in the world could this have happened?

Michael went over to his father and studied him. He put his hand on Joseph's shoulder. There was a moment between them, a genuine . . . *moment*.

Suddenly, Joseph stood up. In a matter of seconds, he went from sadness to fury. 'It's my blood that flows through Jermaine's veins,' Joseph bellowed. 'Not Berry Gordy's. *Not Berry Gordy's*.' Then, he stormed out of the dressing room and slammed the door behind him.

What's in a Name?

It seemed, at first, that leaving Motown would be easier than Joseph thought it would be. Berry Gordy had done nothing to prevent their departure; he was preoccupied with Motown's film business, anyway, and didn't seem too dismayed by the fact that The Jackson 5 was leaving the company. As long as he had Jermaine in his corner, and had won that particular battle, Berry seemed satisfied. Because he did not want to deal with Joseph anyway, Ewart Abner was the one handling most matters concerning The Jackson 5, during their final days at Motown.

But few acts have ever left Motown without at least a little melodrama. Unbeknownst to Joseph, Berry Gordy had one more surprise in store for him.

In the last week in June 1975, Berry Gordy's vice-chairman of Motown telephoned Joseph Jackson with a bombshell: Motown owned the name The Jackson 5. The group could leave Motown, Joseph was told, but they would have to leave the name. 'Jackson 5' would stay behind with the company.

'What are you talking about?' Joseph demanded, according to his memory. 'We came to Motown as The Jackson 5. That's my family name.'

'I don't know if you came here as The Jackson 5, or not,' Michael Roshkind told him, 'but you're sure not leaving as The Jackson 5, I can tell you that much.'

'What the hell do you mean?' Joseph asked.

'The fact is that there are probably forty thousand people named Jackson running around this world,' Roshkind said. 'We made five of them stars. We can find five more if we have to, and we can make them stars, too,' Roshkind said.

'Why, you *son of a bitch*,' Joseph exclaimed. He slammed the phone down.

As it happened, clause sixteen of the Motown recording contract, which Joseph had never read but had signed in 1968, stated, 'It is agreed that we [Motown] own all rights, title and interest to the name "The Jackson 5".'

Furthermore, to insure the company's ownership of the name, on 30 March 1972, after The Jackson 5's first string of hit records, Motown applied to the United States Patent Office to register the logo 'Jackson 5'. The name 'Jackson Five' and 'Jackson 5' were also exclusively owned by the Motown Record Corporation.

Of course, Joseph could have registered the names 'Jackson Five', 'Jackson 5', and any other name he wanted to hold on to – had he only thought to do it. It simply had not crossed his mind. However, it had been common practice for Motown to register the name of its acts, whenever possible. The company had done so with The Supremes, the Temptations . . . and with many of its acts over the years.

With this latest salvo, the group's departure from Motown had become bigger than the record business, it was now a battle between two families: the Jacksons and the Gordys. It seemed to some observers that anything Berry could do to demonstrate his power to an ever-scrutinizing record industry and press, he would do, even if that meant preventing the boys from using their name. 'That was hardball, of course,' Michael told me, later.

Michael was actually intrigued by Berry's tactic regarding the group's name. 'I never even *thought* of that,' he said. It was as if he was as much a student of Berry's as he was an adversary. While the other brothers watched, waited and fumed, Michael learned. 'I want to know how he did it,' Michael said of Berry's having registered the name. 'I'll have to remember all of this,' he added, as if stockpiling information for future use.

There was another family meeting. What do we do now?

'If Berry owns the name, he owns the name,' Michael said, according to his memory. 'We don't have to be The Jackson 5, do we? I mean, can't we just be The Jackson Family? Or The Jacksons?'

'We might not have a choice,' Joseph said. 'It makes me sick to lose that name. All the work we put into it.'

'And you know damn well that they ain't gonna use it,' grumbled Tito. 'It'll just be wasted.'

Tito was correct. Once Motown claimed the name, there wasn't much they could do with it, other than to market old products by the group.

The Jacksons Leave Motown

On Monday 30 June 1975, Joseph Jackson arranged a press conference to announce the family's new affiliation with CBS. With over eight months still to run on the Motown contracts, Joseph seemed more eager than ever to leave Motown. Even though he was extremely busy at this time dealing with Diana Ross and post-production on her film *Mahogany*, Berry fought back. On the morning of Joseph's announcement, Michael Roshkind told the press that if CBS expected to get all of the members of The Jackson 5, they would be disappointed – meaning that Jermaine would never leave Berry's side. Furthermore, Roshkind said, 'There is no way the group will ever sing under that name for anyone else. They'll never get all five members of the group, and they won't be getting The Jackson 5.'

Earlier that morning, Berry had one of his lawyers send a telegram to Arthur Taylor, president of CBS Records, warning him that his company had better not host a press conference relating to The Jackson 5 since Gordy had exclusive rights to 'issue authorized publicity'. When Berry learned that Taylor planned to ignore the warning, he sent him another telegram warning him that he'd better not refer to the group as The Jackson 5 at the media summit since Motown owned exclusive rights to that name.

The press conference took place at the Rainbow Grill atop the Rockefeller Center in Manhattan. As a room full of reporters and photographers recorded the event, eleven members of the Jackson family were solemnly ushered into the room single-file by a CBS publicist. There were no smiles. Each Jackson took his seat on the dais, where ten high-backed black chairs were arranged behind a long, narrow table. All of the family members, with Jermaine conspicuously absent, put forth a united front to announce the group's signing with CBS, effective 10 March 1976, the day their Motown contracts expired. Katherine, Maureen (Rebbie), LaToya, Janet and Randy had been told by Joseph to be present in order to demonstrate family solidarity.

The atmosphere was sombre, such as one might find at a meeting at the United Nations. Joseph – stage right, at the end of the dais – in a dark pin-striped suit, announced that the Jacksons had signed with CBS Records; he then turned the floor over to members of the family.

Jackie explained that the group – referred to that afternoon as 'The Jackson Family' – was signing with Columbia, 'because Columbia is an album-selling company, and albums is what really makes you known.' When asked if the group had tried to renegotiate with Motown, he answered, 'Yes, but the figures, they was just Mickey Mouse.'

Michael, in a black velvet jacket and matching vest, didn't have much to say. 'I think the promotion will probably be stronger,' he observed, meekly. He seemed awkward and uncomfortable, especially when contrasted with his confident brothers. It was painfully obvious that Michael wished he were somewhere else. 'I think Motown did a great job for us,' he said, tentatively. Joseph shot him a hot look. Michael caught the current and quickly added, 'But, now, things will be even better.'

'How will all of this affect your relationship with Berry Gordy?' asked one writer.

Everyone on the dais looked to Joseph for an answer. He shrugged his shoulders and forced a thin smile. 'You take it as it comes,' he said. 'Next question.'

'Will Jermaine be joining the group?'

Again, Joseph answered. 'Yes. But it'll take a while. Next question.'

'Why isn't Jermaine here?'

'Next question.'

After the press conference, Berry Gordy filed a lawsuit against Joseph Jackson, The Jackson 5 and CBS, seeking five million dollars in damages for signing with CBS before the Motown contract had expired. Joseph countersued, claiming Motown owed the family royalties, unpaid advances, and expenses. Joseph thought Motown owed them money. Wrong. He owed *Motown* money. For by the terms of their contract, The Jackson 5 were liable for the costs of all of the songs they recorded for Motown, including the ones that were not released.

To say that Motown had kept the boys busy would be an understatement. Michael Jackson and The Jackson 5 recorded 469 songs for Motown in the six years from 1969 to 1975. That's about seventy-five songs a year, which is astonishing considering that this isn't *all* the boys did for a living. Besides having to learn those songs before they could record them, they also rehearsed their ever-changing stage show, toured the world with their act, appeared on many television programmes – including their own specials – sat through countless interviews, posed for innumerable photos (there are thousands of photos of the boys the public has never seen), and also tried to have the semblance of a personal life outside of show business.

Of those 469 songs recorded by The Jackson 5, only 174 were

actually released, or 37 per cent. The other 295, it was decided by company producers and Berry Gordy, were not up to Motown's standards. Therefore, much to the group's chagrin, the Jacksons owed Motown over $500,000 for songs that the public had never even heard. 'That sucked,' Joseph later said. 'They really got us good.'

Michael Jackson, who was about to turn seventeen in August 1975, was sceptical. He had begun to have serious doubts about Joseph's ability as an entertainment manager. To his way of thinking, his father had made some major mistakes: he gave away Jermaine, he gave away their group name, and now he had to give away a lot of money, paying for songs that had never been released. 'Maybe we shoulda' read that contract,' Michael said, bitterly.

However, taking the boys away from Motown and to Epic would not later be catalogued as one of Joseph's mistakes. If not for Joseph's decision, Michael would probably have ended up an obscure showbiz act, relegated to Las Vegas lounges – and not major showrooms, either. There is little doubt in the minds of most music historians that, after *Moving Violation*, The Jackson 5 would have stagnated at Motown in much the same way other groups who had stayed after their heyday did, such as The Supremes after Diana Ross left for happier trails.

If Joseph hadn't had his way when he did, Michael would probably be performing on 'oldies-but-goodies' revues today with one authentic Temptation, a couple of Four Tops, and Mary Wilson of the original Supremes. He would have aged into his forties singing 'I Want You Back' and 'ABC', to make a buck, much like the great Martha Reeves, still out there singing 'Love is like a Heatwave', maybe not so much because she wants to as much as because she must. It's a tough life for Motown survivors like Martha, and not one for the faint of heart. It would have been Michael's life, too, had he never had the freedom to write and produce his own songs. No matter what some may think of Joseph Jackson as a personal manager, in the final analysis, that man saved Michael Jackson's career.

Jackson Family Values

It would be eight months before the Jacksons would be able to record for CBS. They had signed with the new label before their Motown agreement expired and would have to wait until the contract ran out before they could go into the studio. To fill the lag-time, Joseph signed them to CBS-TV for a summer variety series to begin airing in June 1976.

At this time, Michael was often asked about Jermaine in interviews, and he tried to stress that 'business is business and family is family. He still comes over.' He went on to say, 'We talk to one another. We go different places together. That's very important, because that's the basis of our whole organization: good friendship and a strong family. The show-business part is important, but even more important is that the family stick together at all times.'

All of it was wishful thinking on Michael's part. The family members were drifting apart, even though Michael may have wished it was not the case. Jermaine did visit now and then, but only when Joseph was not around. 'I just couldn't stand to be around him any more,' Jermaine explained. 'He had hurt me so deeply. Even my mother was asking me what was wrong with me and how could I betray the family as I did. It was tearing me apart.'

The other brothers still harboured resentment against Jermaine for his decision. 'They were hanging up on me. One of them told me I was no longer a brother. How could they hurt me like that? No matter what, I thought we were family. After all, that's what we were always preaching. But when it came time to act on it, I didn't see that happening. I was an outsider.'

Jermaine may have at least found some shelter in the arms of his wife, but other members of the Jackson family seemed to be growing more antisocial, shunning exposure to people outside the gated Jackson estate (by Joseph's orders) and burying themselves in their Jehovah's Witness faith (by Katherine's). None of the siblings who were still living at home – LaToya, Marlon, Michael, Janet and Randy – seemed to have any strong relationships outside of their own family.

'I don't date,' LaToya told me at this time. 'I don't trust people. To be honest with you, I have no friends. It doesn't bother me. When I get lonely, I read the Bible.' I thought to myself, what a shame she has to be so leery of others. She also said that she rarely went out in public unless she was with other family members. She expressed no interest in marriage or raising a family of her own. 'I would never bring a child into a society like this one.'

It was as if the Jackson siblings were being raised to mistrust all outsiders. When Jackie started having marital problems, Joseph was able to point to such discord as evidence that outsiders can't be trusted. Enid Jackson filed for divorce in September 1975, nine months after she and Jackie married. 'You see that?' Joseph told his sons. 'After just nine months, look at the problem Jackie's got on his hands.' (The couple reconciled and would remain married for eleven more years.)

Then Marlon dropped a bomb in January 1976: he had secretly run off and married someone – four months earlier! While the group appeared in Las Vegas, Marlon married an eighteen-year-old fan from New Orleans, Carol Parker. The ceremony took place on 16 August 1975. He hadn't trusted any of his brothers with the news because he was sure they would tell Joseph. He didn't want to go through what Rebbie, Tito and Jackie had gone through with parental opposition to marriages, and he also didn't want Joseph and Katherine to know that Carol did not sign a pre-nuptial agreement.

Michael was hurt by Marlon's secret union; he thought he and his brother were closer than that. 'We share all the bad times, but never the good ones,' he complained. 'I don't understand my family at all, and I don't like some of the things my brothers do to their wives. I'm never going to marry,' Michael added. 'Marriage is awful. I don't trust anyone enough to do it.'

At a time when he should have had enthusiasm for his life and career, Michael Jackson was on the verge of hopelessness and despair. 'People hurt each other over and over and over again,' he said bleakly. 'I spend a lot of time being sad. I feel like I'm in a well,' he concluded. 'And no one can reach me.'

Michael Jackson's vote was just one of six when it came to group decisions: the five brothers, plus Joseph. (When Jermaine left the group, young Randy took his place in the line-up, though he would rarely sing leads. Marlon took most of Jermaine's parts in the songs, and Jermaine's solo hits were, of course, never performed by the group.)

Though it was obvious that Michael was probably the most important member of the group, the family did not want to allow him any special consideration. It was feared that if he was bolstered too much, Michael might one day have the confidence to separate himself from the group – which was the last thing they wanted to happen. Michael recognized their fear. 'They don't listen to me because they're afraid to,' he said to one associate. 'I guess I can understand it. They don't want to lose me. They don't want me to have too much power. But it makes me mad.'

When Joseph signed the boys to CBS-TV to do a television series in 1976, Michael made it clear that he did not want to participate. However, he was outvoted. *The Jacksons* was a thirty-minute programme that ran for four weeks featuring the family, with celebrity guest-stars. The first episode, aired 16 June 1976. As in the family's Las Vegas act, LaToya, Janet and Rebbie participated in the series, too.

It was the first time a black family had ever starred in a television series, and if the show received decent ratings, there was a chance CBS might pick it up in January as a mid-season replacement. Michael was miserable. Because of a gruelling production schedule, there was no time for him to polish any of the routines and he loathed going on stage feeling unprepared. He hoped that the show would not be renewed. Unfortunately for him, the ratings were solid enough for CBS to order more episodes, to begin airing in January 1977. Michael cringed . . . and then he signed on the dotted line. Today, he refers to the venture as 'that stupid TV series. It was a dumb move to agree to do it,' he says, 'and I hated every minute of it.'

In the end, Michael's instincts about the programme were

inadvertently on target; *The Jacksons* proved to be more trouble than it was worth. Apparently, someone at CBS-TV, probably a hapless assistant in the art department, accidentally used a picture of the old Jackson 5 with Jermaine in a *TV Guide* advertisement for *The Jacksons* series. As soon as Joseph alerted CBS to the mistake, the network pulled the ad and sent a letter to Motown apologizing for it and promising that it would never happen again. Too late. Motown used the goof as an opportunity to amend its original lawsuit against the group, raising the damages sought from five million to twenty million dollars. Michael Roshkind said the mistake 'had a severely damaging effect on our credibility' and 'caused us real dollar damage'. The allegation was extreme. The ad was one-half of a page, its artwork so blurry no one could even recognize Jermaine in the picture. It was obvious that Joseph was not the only one holding a grudge.

Joseph tried to prove that he had been treated unfairly by Motown, even going so far as to forsake his pride. He admitted in his deposition that on that fateful day in Detroit (26 July 1968) when he sat with Berry's attorney, Ralph Seltzer, and was presented with the contract, he didn't read it before allowing his children to sign it. Ralph even backed Joseph up, admitting in his deposition: 'I do not recall that any of them [The Jackson 5 or Joseph Jackson] read it through in its entirety prior to signing it.'

Why not? Joseph explained, 'Because the extent of my formal education is through the eleventh year of high school. The 1968 contract with Motown was the first recording contract that I was ever presented with or ever looked at.' (Joseph's statement didn't seem likely since his sons were signed to Steeltown Records before they were signed to Motown . . . unless he hadn't read that contract, either.)

Joseph had to admit that he also didn't read the 'Parental Agreement' before he signed *it* – which said that he would make certain his sons abided by the provisions of the Motown recording contract. In truth, Joseph hadn't read anything. He'd just signed the contract where instructed to sign it. He wanted his kids to make it. He would have done anything for them. Of course, he signed a contract.

In the end, Berry would be awarded $600,000 in damages, including un-repaid advances and some compensation for the group having signed with CBS before the Motown contract had officially expired. He was also paid compensation for 'damages' suffered when Joseph would not allow the boys to record new songs for Motown (this, after he figured out that the group owed $500,000 for all the other ones they'd recorded that hadn't been released). In all, the Jacksons paid Gordy and company about two million to leave Motown.

More importantly, and maybe surprisingly to some, the Jacksons agreed to surrender royalties due them on recordings they made before 1 December 1979 and on future releases of recordings made before 11 March 1976 – in other words, *on all of their hits*. In exchange, Motown agreed to accurately account for, and pay, royalties on any 'new product', which included pre-1976 recordings that had been recorded but not yet released and on any 'best of' albums they may put out in the future.

It actually wasn't unusual for a Motown act to abandon their royalties in order to settle things with Motown. However, in retrospect, it often proved to be a bad decision for them – which may be one of the reasons there are so many former Supremes, Marvellettes, Vandellas, Temptations and Miracles who, today, find themselves in dire financial straits.

When the judge ruled in Motown's favour, Motown's vice-president Michael Roshkind said, 'This is a gratifying day, not because of our winning but because it was a matter of principle.'

It was enough to make some observers sick to their stomachs.

The first Jacksons album for CBS, *The Jacksons*, was released in the spring of 1977, on the Epic label. The album had a lot going for it. 'Blues Away', one of the first songs Michael had ever written, and 'Style of Life', written by the brothers, were both included. Those two songs were co-produced by The Jacksons, so they were actually doing that for which they had left Motown. For the rest of the album, executive producers Gamble and Huff recruited their staff producers (Dexter Wansel, Gene McFadden and John Whitehead) to assist them in compiling a strong, if not innovative, collection. Michael says he learned a great deal from working with Gamble, Huff and company, in terms of structuring a melody and what he calls 'the anatomy of a song'.

The Jacksons spawned one major hit for the group, 'Enjoy Yourself', their first single for Epic. A rollicking dance number, it went on to become their most successful record since 'Dancing Machine', three years earlier. The single went to number six on the pop charts, but because it was the only hit from the album, *The Jacksons* peaked at only number thirty-six on the American charts. Not great. In the UK, 'Enjoy Yourself' didn't even chart, when first released. Then it was reissued, but still didn't crack the Top 400. The international record-buying public seemed confused, maybe because Motown issued its own Jacksons album, *Joyful Jukebox Music* (compiled from some of those previously unreleased songs for which the group had been charged), in what seemed like a crass attempt to cash in on CBS's promotion of the group. The Motown album was the first Jackson 5 album not to enter the Top 200 in America, and did even worse in the UK. It also served to dilute the impact of the new CBS product. As Michael would put it, 'Berry Gordy was playing hardball, of course.'

The Jacksons' showing on the pop charts proved disappointing, but not as upsetting as the showing of Jermaine's record. After all the public and private angst about whether he should go with his father and brothers, or stay with Gordy, *My Name Is Jermaine*, peaked at just 164 on the Top 200. The single 'Let's Be Young Tonight' only went to number fifty-five. In the UK, Jermaine didn't matter at all to record-buying audiences. This was a terrible shame; Jermaine deserved better from Motown in terms of promotion. One now had to wonder what Motown's intentions were where Jermaine's career was concerned. (As it would turn out, he only had a few hits at the company, never really fulfilling his potential, there. He should have been a much bigger star for Motown; he had everything going for him.)

The Jacksons continued to tour without Jermaine. It was business as usual. They performed in Memphis, Tennessee, in May 1977. During that engagement, Michael had to escape to the roof of a Woolco department store when ten thousand people caused a near riot as they waited in line for hours hoping to jam into the store's record department, where Michael had promised to autograph copies of *The Jacksons*.

That same night, backstage before the show, John Seaver, who worked for the firm that promoted the Memphis engagement, later recalled, 'I showed a *Billboard* article to Michael that said Jermaine's Motown album was a big bomb. It made unfair comparisons to The Jacksons' album, saying that that one was a smash. Michael didn't say anything at first. Then he commented, 'Oh, he'll bounce back. I know it. Jermaine won't let this get to him.' He seemed genuinely sorry for his brother.

'The article was passed along to the other brothers, who scanned it. Marlon said something about "too bad". Tito said that the album wasn't any good, but that Jermaine would probably come up with something stronger next time out. "No matter what, he's our brother," Tito said, "and I don't like seeing him do anything that's not a success. Just proves, I think, that Berry doesn't know what he's doing." They all agreed with Tito.'

Then Joseph came into the dressing room.

'What are you boys reading?'

Jackie handed him the article. 'Read this, about Jermaine,' he said.

Joseph read the feature quickly. 'Well, you know, I think it serves Jermaine right,' he said as he smacked the magazine on a table. He then walked away. The brothers looked at each other with raised eyebrows. There was silence. It must have been difficult for them to recognize Joseph's pain, the betrayal he felt – not to mention the way he felt taken advantage of by the Motown machinery. Of course, Joseph never revealed himself to his family in a way that might bring about any kind of understanding for him. Therefore, he never got it. As he walked out the door, Michael gave him a cool, appraising glance. 'Some father,' he muttered.

PART FOUR

Tatum

By the time Michael Jackson turned nineteen in August 1977, he was one of the best-known entertainers of recent years, the idol of many young women. While his brothers often availed themselves of the sexual opportunities presented to them on the road, Michael never followed suit. Though much of Michael's music has had a sensual edge over the years, and his dancing has often been suggestive, he was not sexually adventurous as a young man.

'I think it's fun that girls think I'm sexy,' Michael told me in 1977. 'But I don't think that about myself. It's all just fantasy, really. I like to make my fans happy so I might pose or dance in a way that makes them think I'm romantic. But really I guess I'm not that way.'

Most people who were close to Michael when he was a teenager agree that he never had a serious romantic life at that time. Michael did not trust anyone enough to allow them to penetrate the shell he had built around himself. Perhaps he felt he had been betrayed too often by people he had loved or admired – his father, his brothers, maybe even Berry Gordy – to permit himself to be vulnerable to a relationship. Still, Michael understood the value of public relations and show-business hype. Therefore, he did parade a few 'relationships' for public consumption.

As recently as the Martin Bashir interview in 2003, Michael said that actress Tatum O'Neal, who was thirteen in the summer of 1977, was his first girlfriend. Michael and Tatum first met two years before at a party hosted by Paul McCartney aboard the Queen Mary in Long Beach, California. They had no contact with each other again until the spring of 1977, when Michael spotted Tatum with her father, Ryan O'Neal, at a club in Los Angeles. Michael was socializing with two publicists from Epic, Susan Blond and Steve Manning when, as he recalled it, 'all of a sudden I felt this soft hand reach over and grab mine. It was Tatum.' The fact that Tatum had deigned to hold Michael's hand was, for him, a colossal event. 'It was serious stuff to me. *She touched me*,' he said.

The next day, Tatum invited Michael to a dinner party at *Playboy* publisher Hugh Hefner's rambling Holmby Hills estate. There they watched *Roots*, the highly rated Alex Haley television mini-series, on videotape. When Tatum became bored, she asked Michael to get into the hot tub with her. 'But I don't have a bathing suit,' he said.

'Who needs bathing suits?' Tatum responded.

When Michael began to blush, Tatum asked one of Hefner's assistants for two swimsuits, then handed one to Michael.

Tatum's hair was soft, blond and flowed just below her shoulders. Her skin was baby pink and her figure quite ample for a girl who wouldn't turn fourteen until close to the end of the year. She was almost plump. 'She's like a sacred doll,' Michael observed of her to a friend. He said that while soaking in the water and watching for shooting stars, the two shared secrets with one another.

Years later, rumour would have it that they were nude together in the hot tub. 'Oh, we weren't naked,' Michael firmly pointed out to me in an interview. 'We had on bathing suits. Why do people have to always find something dirty in everything?'

Tatum O'Neal had won an Oscar at the age of nine for her role as the chain-smoking, swearing companion to a Bible-belt swindler (played by her father) in the film *Paper Moon*. Her own childhood was difficult.

Born to actress Joanna Moore and Ryan O'Neal, Tatum saw her parents split up when she was three. For a while, she lived on a ramshackle ranch with a dying horse, some dead chickens, and a mother who was addicted to drugs. At seven, Tatum grew flowers in a wrecked car in the yard and cooked breakfast and lunch for herself and her younger brother, Griffin. Her father was permitted to visit on weekends.

'When she was living with her mother, I could always tell what shape Tatum was in by the look of her hair,' Ryan said. 'I knew if it was healthy, she was at peace with herself. If things were bad, there were clumps missing from her hair. She'd sometimes take a scissors to herself.'

Joanna, anguished and on the verge of defeat by 1972, decided to seek help from her ex-husband, who had been giving her thirty thousand dollars a year in alimony. Ryan paid for her rehabilitation and she, in turn, surrendered eight-year-old Tatum to him. Tatum hated Joanna. When the little girl went to visit her in the hospital, Tatum became so disgusted with her mother that she spat in her face. When she told Michael about her life, he said he had never heard a story so tragic.

'My mother is a saint,' Michael said in 1977. 'When I hear about Tatum's mother and what she went through with her, it makes me thank God for Katherine. People think I have had a hard life. But look at Tatum's. That's why I like her, because she's a survivor.'

Unlike Michael, whose goal it was to be an entertainer, Tatum became an actress by accident. Ryan helped her get her first solo mostly as a way to keep an eye on her while he worked on *Paper Moon*. When Tatum became a working actress, Ryan O'Neal took over her career much the same way Joseph Jackson had commandeered Michael's. 'I chose *International Velvet* for her,' Ryan said. 'She didn't even read the script. I just said, "This is the one you're doing," because I knew it was good.'

When Tatum complained about the way her father ruled her life, Michael empathized with her. 'I know exactly what you're talking about,' he told her.

However, Tatum did make some of her own decisions. She once told Michael the story of how she turned down the role of the young hooker in *Taxi Driver*, a part that eventually went to Jodie Foster. At the audition, Tatum said she wanted to play the part of the taxi driver; she was twelve. The producer ignored Tatum's suggestion and kept talking up the role of the hooker. Finally Tatum said, 'Frankly, I think the part's too small. I did win an Academy Award, you know.'

'I can't believe you said that. I don't think I would ever have the nerve,' Michael told her when he heard that story. 'I want to be like that. I want people to think of me as having a lot of nerve.'

In his autobiography Michael wrote that Tatum was his first love 'after Diana'. Tatum has indicated, however, that her relationship with Michael was strictly platonic.

It's telling of the fantasy Michael has created around his childhood and teen years that the women he claims to have had romances with – including Diana Ross and Brooke Shields ('We were romantically serious for a while,' he wrote of Shields in his book) – have all denied ever having been intimate with him. After Michael talked about Tatum on his 2003 Martin Bashir interview, saying she came on to him, she issued a statement saying he had 'a vivid imagination'. Says actress Sarah Jackson (no relation to Michael), who was a friend of Tatum's at this time, 'Tatum told me that Michael was a nice guy, but so shy. "How can any girl have a relationship with him? When we're together, he hardly says two words. I know he's a virgin. Someone needs to have a talk with him about it. I wonder if he's afraid to have sex. He doesn't seem very interested."'

'Why do people think I'm gay?'

Michael Jackson's sexuality has been the subject of speculation since he was a teenager. Perhaps it was his high-pitched speaking voice; or maybe it was his bashfulness, or the fact that he tended to avoid eye contact and seemed so uncomfortable in his own skin that caused some to think that he was either concealing something about himself or had not yet come to terms with it.

Michael has been dealing with the tabloid press for many years and feels he is misunderstood because of unfair and dishonest media coverage of his life. However, it was when he was nineteen that he first became upset about a story that was not true. Like a lot of untruths, it was silly: supposedly, he was going to have a sex-change operation and marry a handsome actor named Clifton Davis, writer of 'Never Can Say Goodbye'. The story spread quickly across the country; numerous music publications rushed to the presses with it.

Michael once told me that he was in the music department of a store in the South when he first heard about the rumour. He said, 'This girl came up to me and said, "Please tell me it isn't true! Please tell me!" She was crying. I asked, "What? What isn't true?" She said, "Tell me you're not going to become a girl. *Tell me*." '

'Where in the world did you read that?' Michael asked. '*Jet* magazine,' she responded. 'It was in *Jet* that you were going to have a sex change.'

'I felt I didn't know who I was at that moment,' Michael recalled. 'I told her to tell all her friends that it was just a stupid rumour.'

'Stupid' as it was, it seemed to Michael that everywhere he went, he heard the story. At the time, nothing could be worse for him than the notion that there were people who thought he might be homosexual. Michael was raised in a family where homosexuality was sinful.

After the rumour had been circulating for months, Michael was at Caesars Palace to see Diana Ross perform when he ran into Clifton Davis. Clifton was backstage with performer, Leslie Uggams. 'I was with Diana, holding her hand,' Michael remembered. 'Clifton was standing next to me, and he was holding Leslie's hand. As I was standing there posing for the photographers, I thought to myself, Oh no, this is a perfect setup for some magazine to doctor up a picture so that it looks like Clifton and I are holding hands. That's how paranoid I was getting about that story,' Michael confessed.

After the photographers departed, Clifton went over to Michael and joked, 'Hey, look at you. You're not a girl after all, are you?' Michael didn't think Clifton's question was very funny. He would never get used to the stories that he leads a secret gay life, and is still upset when confronted with questions about his sexuality.

'Just for the record, are you or are you not gay?' I asked him during an interview in 1979.

'No, I am not gay,' Michael snapped. 'I am not a homo. People make up stories about me being gay because they have nothing else to do. I'm not going to let it get to me,' he continued. 'I'm not going to have a nervous breakdown because people think I like having sex with men. I don't and that's that,' he said, his sentences pouring out. 'If I let this get to me, it will only show how cheap I am. I'm sure I must have a lot of fans who are gay, and I don't mind that,' he continued, speaking faster. 'That's their life and this is mine. You can print that,' he said, thrusting his index finger at me. 'What is it about me that makes people think I'm gay? Why do people think I'm gay?'

I didn't think I should answer his question. He was already upset.

'Is it my voice?' he continued. 'Is it because I have this soft voice? All of us in the family have soft voices. Or is it because I don't have a lot of girlfriends? I just don't understand it.'

The truth is that Michael would never have allowed himself to have homosexual relationships, even if he did have feelings for other men. He was too puritanical as a result of his religious background. The Jehovah's Witnesses firmly believe that world destruction is imminent and that only a few of God's servants will survive the horrible holocaust. One question had hung over Michael's head for his entire youth; would he win salvation or burn in hellfire? If he wanted to be saved – if he wanted to be with his mother through all eternity – he would have to live up to all of the church's rigid teachings, which sure meant he couldn't be gay. Indulgence is not part of the Jehovah's Witnesses' creed. Any congregant who does not adhere to the rules and dogma is shunned or 'disfellowshipped'. By the time Michael was a teenager, he had been trained to live his life a certain way. He would not be able to break that conformity.

Also, if Michael had any homosexual leanings he would have been too fearful to act on them. He knew that with any relationship he ever had – be it with a man or a woman – he ran the risk of the other person reporting the details to a newspaper or magazine, one that would pay astronomical sums for the story, especially if it were a sensational one. Although some public figures who are homosexual have come out of the closet in recent years – not many, though – back in the 1970s it just didn't happen at all.

Still today, many entertainers hide their true sexual identities from their fans and peers because they fear rejection, and the loss of income. Ever practical where his work is concerned, Michael is aware that being gay would damage not only his career, but his relationships with his family, as well. How would Katherine and Joseph handle it if he were to announce that he is, as he put it so many years ago, 'a homo'? 'When I first heard the rumours that he was gay, I thought I'd go crazy,' Katherine once said. 'He's my son and I know the truth. He knows the truth too. We both talked about it and cried about it. Michael was very hurt by the rumours. He is not gay. It's against our religion.' They cried about it; tears shed over the fact that people they didn't even know had whispered such things.

How would his brothers react if Michael said he was gay? Back in the seventies, they would have been upset because it might have projected a controversial image for the group. Today? Publicly, they might offer their support. However, privately, they would probably be thrown. Like their mother, they are not progressive-minded. Indeed, if Michael were a gay man today – and no one is saying he is – and suddenly made the decision to bolt from the closet after all of these years, the only Jackson who would probably be able to come to terms with it would be Janet, a woman who has been around enough and seen enough to know that there are gay people in all walks of life.

Besides dealing with upsetting questions about his sexuality, Michael had other problems in the late seventies. Of course, most people have a difficult time with certain stages of adolescence, but Michael was much more sensitive than most people his age about the common challenges of puberty, perhaps because he was the subject of such intense public scrutiny. For instance, his face had broken out severely with acne in the mid-seventies; he was so ashamed of the way he looked that it was extremely difficult for him to go out into public. 'I seemed to have a pimple for every oil gland,' he recalled. Onstage, his condition was difficult to notice because of carefully applied makeup and the benefit of lighting. However, offstage it was obvious that Michael had complexion problems. Reporters would comment to each other about his skin. Fans would be shocked by his appearance. Michael could barely stand the humiliation.

'I became subconsciously scarred by this,' he has confessed. 'I got very shy and became embarrassed to meet people. The effect on me was so bad that it messed up my whole personality.'

Michael couldn't look at people when he talked to them. Rather, he would look down or away. He wouldn't even look at his mother when he spoke to her. 'He didn't want to leave the house,' Katherine would recall. 'When he did, he kept his head down.' He would never really recover from the psychological effects of the acne. 'The changes that it wrought in him became permanent,' Katherine said. 'He was no longer a carefree, outgoing, devilish boy. He was quieter, more serious and more of a loner.'

Complicating matters was Michael's belief that, acne aside, he was not good-looking. His skin was too dark, he decided, and his nose too wide. Even though his family was aware of Michael's

sensitivities, Joseph and the brothers did not afford him any special treatment. They were a rowdy, boisterous bunch offstage and teased each other, playfully. Either a brother took it well, or he didn't.

At nineteen, Michael was nothing if not a study in contrasts. He was a young man who could muster enough courage to meet with the president of Motown, yet was afraid of the kinds of propositions most teenagers found exciting, such as the opportunity to drive an automobile. Whereas many youngsters are eager to get behind the wheel of a car by the age of sixteen, Michael was still petrified of the notion three years later. 'I just don't want to,' he said, when pushed. 'I just don't have the desire. Whenever you do something, you have to want to do it. And even though there are some things you just have to do, I don't have to drive. And I simply don't want to. There's nothing special about it for me.' Michael would usually have a limousine take him wherever he wanted to go, though often one of his brothers would drive him.

Besides the fact that he was frightened of driving, Michael also didn't want to go to the Department of Motor Vehicles to take the driver's test. He was afraid he'd be recognized and then be humiliated because he still didn't have a licence at his age. The thought of this kind of embarrassment was stressful for him. At one point, when he thought he might at least try to drive, he tried to obtain special consideration so that he wouldn't have to go to the Department of Motor Vehicles for the testing. However, the Encino division of the D.M.V. is accustomed to dealing with celebrities; officials there don't consider any of them special. It was all just too much to bear for Michael. He couldn't do it. 'But suppose you're someplace and your chauffeur gets sick,' Katherine argued with him. 'You need to be able to drive.' Michael would be twenty-three before he'd finally obtain his driver's licence, and only at Katherine's insistence.

Michael and Joseph Meet with CBS

Michael Jackson's teenage melancholy intensified when The Jacksons' second album for CBS, *Goin' Places*, released in the winter of 1977, was a major disappointment. Despite the fact that the first album for the new label had received mixed reviews and had only gone gold when everyone was hoping for platinum sales, CBS sent the group back to Philadelphia to work once again with Kenny Gamble and Leon Huff. The title track of *Goin' Places* only went to number 52 on *Billboard*'s top 100; the album peaked at 63 on the Top 200. In the UK, it peaked at number forty-five and only stayed on the charts for a week! However, despite such sporadic sales, The Jacksons at Epic were still faring better than Jermaine Jackson was at Motown. His *Feel the Fire* album, released at the same time, peaked at number 174 in America and did even worse in the UK and the rest of Europe. Most industry observers now believed that Motown was mysteriously intent on wasting Jermaine's career even if he was married to the boss's daughter.

On *Goin' Places*, Michael wrote a rhythm number called 'Different Kind of Lady', which became a successful club hit but was seldom played on the radio. It was not issued as a single. Another song penned by the group, 'Do What You Wanna', also went unreleased as a single. By this time, The Jacksons hadn't had a number-one record since 'Mama's Pearl' in 1971. Joseph was concerned. It was painfully clear that the new relationship with CBS wasn't working out as he had hoped it would for his sons.

Joseph decided to meet with Ron Alexenberg, the man who had originally signed The Jacksons to Epic, to try to convince him once and for all that the group should be able to write and produce its own material. Perhaps Joseph remembered the way Michael used his own initiative to meet with Berry Gordy when the chips were down, because he asked his son to accompany him.

Michael was astonished that his father would ask for his assistance and couldn't help but be suspicious of his motives. Still, he agreed to go along. Michael considered the group's future so important, he was willing to overcome – at least temporarily – his aversion to his

father and cooperate with him on this matter. Just as Joseph put on his public facade as father, Michael would put on his public facade as son.

'He was still the soft, tender Michael Jackson everyone thought he was, but something was definitely different about him by this time,' said James Situp, the Jacksons' pianist and band director. 'Everyone who dealt with him closely, family included, began to tread softly when dealing with Michael. The quiet power he was gaining was amazing to me. I'd never seen anyone have that much influence over people without having a stern attitude. I noticed that when he spoke, people were starting to listen. He was still outvoted on things, but now it was a bit more reluctantly. Joseph and the brothers were beginning to give him space. I began to notice that if they saw one iota of displeasure in his face, they began to get worried. For sure, things were changing as Michael was growing up.'

Still, it is not difficult to imagine that his brothers resented Michael's power. Even if it did benefit them, it didn't feel good to them that Michael was the one who always ended up meeting with their record company bosses.

During the meeting with Ron Alexenberg, Michael and Joseph explained that they were unhappy with the way the Jacksons' careers had thus far evolved at CBS, and that the time had come for the company to finally allow them control over an album. 'If you can't do it,' Michael said, 'then we need to move on. Why waste more of your money on records that aren't going to sell? Let us work on our own record. Then, you'll have a hit. Otherwise, you won't.'

Ironically, and unbeknownst to Michael and Joseph, the new CBS Records president Walter Yetnikoff had already decided to drop The Jacksons from the label. In his view, The Jacksons were no longer commercially viable. With that thinking, he was on the same page as Ewart Abner at Motown!

The two CBS albums were not successful enough to warrant a third, said Walter Yetnikoff. Bobby Colomby, then head of Epic's West Coast artist relations, recalled, 'The people I was working with at CBS really wanted me to get them out of the deal with The Jacksons. They wanted me to try to buy them [The Jacksons] out. But I felt so bad for these guys. I liked them. I said to myself, "My God, if I give these people a hundred thousand dollars to go away,

they're going to take it, pay their bills and then be out of the music business for ever." '

Imagine the humiliation Joseph and his sons would have suffered if, after all they had gone through to sever their ties with Berry Gordy, the new label's president were to them drop them from his roster. Bobby Colomby was right; the setback probably would have finished The Jacksons for good, and Joseph would have been blamed for the act's demise.

Luckily for all concerned, Bobby Colomby managed to convince his bosses to give The Jacksons one more chance at Epic. This time, the brothers would have more involvement in their work. If they failed, they would have no one to blame but themselves. So, when Michael put forth just that proposition at the meeting, Ron Alexenberg agreed to it. It was a done deal, anyway, before Joseph and Michael even got to the meeting. However, father and son apparently needed to show the label executives that they had the incentive and drive to take on a project of their own before they would be guaranteed the company's full support.

'That went pretty well, didn't it, son?' Joseph said in the elevator after the meeting. He emphasized the word 'son'. They were descending in a car full of CBS executives and employees during lunch hour. Michael was observed smiling bitterly at his father. He later recalled that the subsequent ride back to the hotel was 'a silent one'. When they got back to the hotel, as Michael recalled it, Joseph put his arm around Michael's shoulder as they walked through the lobby. 'You're a winner, Michael,' he told him. 'All my boys are winners. Every single one of 'em. You got that?'

'I got it, Joseph,' Michael said. 'I got it.'

The Wiz

By 1977, nineteen-year-old Michael Jackson happened to find himself on the same career path as his mentor, Diana Ross. He wanted to begin making decisions regarding his own future, just as Diana, who had been dominated by Berry Gordy for seventeen years, was beginning to break his hold on her. Determined to be a film actress, she was anxious to find a property in which to star, and one she could claim responsibility for finding – unlike her previous two opuses, *Lady Sings the Blues* and *Mahogany*, both Motown discoveries.

At the same time, through a production deal with Universal, Berry Gordy's Motown Productions had acquired *The Wiz*, a musical based on L. Frank Baum's classic, *The Wonderful World of Oz*. *The Wiz*, an all-black production, had opened on Broadway in January 1975 and gone on to win seven Tony awards.

By 1977, Rob Cohen, a twenty-four-year-old white wunderkind who headed Motown Productions, had been trying to launch *The Wiz* for some time. He recalled that the project was intended to be a low-budget film featuring Stephanie Mills, who had starred in the Broadway play. Stephanie had also been a Motown artist, though her experience at the company was less than satisfying for her; her one album for the label, *For the First Time* (produced by Burt Bacharach and Hal Davis), was a commercial disaster when issued in 1975, despite the fact that it was an excellent recording. Appearing in the motion picture version of *The Wiz* would have been a coup for her. However, when Diana Ross decided that *she* wanted to play Dorothy, it was all over for Stephanie Mills. 'I absolutely believed in Dorothy and in her search to find who she is,' recalled Diana. 'It seemed so very parallel to who I am.'

To Diana, this film presented an opportunity to demonstrate to Berry that she had not only talent but creative vision, as well. Berry disagreed. He thought casting her in *The Wiz* was a dreadful idea – which only encouraged Diana to want the role even more. A tug-of-war ensued between Svengali and protégé. Eventually Diana prevailed.

Practically everybody at Motown agreed that, at thirty-three, Diana was too old to, as Berry put it, 'play anybody's damn Dorothy'. Still, Berry and Rob Cohen secured a million-dollar contract with Universal for her. 'I wanted to do this project, and I honestly didn't care what I was going to be paid,' Diana said at the time. 'I was very happy, though, to be paid what, at this point in my life, I *should* be getting paid.'

After the Ross casting, Berry decided to give full responsibility for *The Wiz* to Rob Cohen. Rob then recruited director Sidney Lumet, whose film credits included *Serpico*, and *Dog Day Afternoon* and *Equus*. He'd never before directed a musical.

Sidney Lumet's concept was to make the film a modern-day Manhattan fantasy using actual New York locations. Diana would play a twenty-four-year-old school teacher – Dorothy – who is whisked into Oz by a blizzard. The late Ted Ross and Nipsey Russell were hired to play the Lion and Tin Man, respectively. Richard Pryor and Lena Horne were also featured players. It was also Sidney's idea to cast comic Jimmie Walker, best remembered for his overblown portrayal of the loud-mouthed J.J. on television's black sitcom *Good Times*, as the Scarecrow. However, Rob Cohen wanted Michael Jackson for the role.

'I was always impressed by Michael,' Rob recalled. 'He struck me as being so polished, yet still pure. Plus, he could sing – which Jimmie could not do – and this *was* a musical.'

When Rob suggested to Diana that Michael might be right for the part, she agreed, whole-heartedly. It was she, then, who suggested it to Michael. Though he'd seen the Broadway play a half-dozen times and, obviously, loved it, Michael was reluctant. He felt that Berry Gordy might use his influence to have him rejected because of the bad blood that still existed between Motown and the Jackson family. Diana reassured him that he would be given a fair chance. A few days after Michael auditioned, Sidney Lumet telephoned him at the Encino estate to tell him that he had the job.

Joseph did not want Michael to have the kind of solo attention a major movie would generate for him. Since family prosperity through unity had always been Joseph's goal, he was never one to encourage individuality within the group. When Michael recorded solo albums at Motown, it was with the understanding that Jermaine and Jackie have the same opportunity. (Tito and Marlon also worked on solo album projects for Motown, though the records were never released.)

Of course, Joseph knew that without Michael's voice, personality and charisma, The Jacksons would be a completely different kind of act, and maybe not a good one, either – especially now that Jermaine was gone. Working with his brothers had never been a problem for Michael in the past; he was always group-minded. However, now that he was older, he was beginning to feel constricted by the group's democratic mentality. And, the fact that they were all so unsupportive of his solo dreams made him feel that, at the core, they were just being selfish.

Though Joseph had been trying for years to find a property that would star *all* of The Jacksons, the brothers didn't really care about making movies as much as Michael. 'I watch movies constantly and envision how it would have been if I could have been the star,' he recalled. 'I wanted nothing more than to be a movie star.' As much as he wanted the role of the Scarecrow, accepting it was not easy for him. In order to do so, Michael had to defy Joseph and risk the disapproval of his entire family. Also, he was going to have to perform in a strange medium. A weekly TV variety show that he loathed doing was insufficient preparation for a major movie role. Michael, always the perfectionist, wondered if he would be up to the challenge. Though he agonized over what to do, in the end he decided to follow his heart. 'I'm doing the movie,' he told Joseph. 'I hope you'll support me.'

'Well, if I can't talk you out of it, then go ahead and do it,' Joseph said. 'But don't say I didn't warn you. It's a big mistake.'

Michael became upset. 'You're the one always telling us about winners and losers,' he said, according to his later recollection. 'Now you're telling me not to do this thing when I *know* I can be a winner at it.'

Joseph had to think about that comment for a moment. 'It's a gamble, Michael.'

'Sure,' Michael said. 'Just like all the gambles you took, Joseph. Just like the one when you brought us out here.'

'You're right,' Joseph said with a smile. 'Do the movie, Michael. Take a shot. You're the man. But always remember one thing?'

'Winners and losers?' Michael asked, referring to his father's credo.

'No,' Joseph said. 'Remember that you are a member of this family, and a part of a singing group with your brothers, no matter what you do. Family, Michael, that's everything.'

The two men smiled at each other. If things had been different between them, perhaps they would have embraced but that wasn't how their relationship worked. Michael gave his father a thumbs-up and dashed off.

The brothers did not share Joseph's benevolence where Michael and *The Wiz* was concerned.

'To tell you the truth, we thought he was biting off more than he could chew,' recalled Jackie. 'We didn't think it was right for him, or good for the group. So, yeah, we kinda wished he wouldn't have done it.'

However, Michael refused to deny his dream simply because his brothers did not share it. He's a born gambler, though few thought of him in that way at the time. Exhilarated by his imagination, he wanted to take chances. ' "I have to make this film for personal reasons," he told me,' Rob Cohen recalled. ' "There are things I have to prove to myself, and to a few others." '

The Wiz offered Michael a temporary avenue of escape from the negativity of his male siblings and father. When he moved to New York in July 1977 to begin the film, he asked LaToya to accompany him. The two resided in an exclusive two-thousand-dollars-per-month, thirty-seventh-floor apartment located in Manhattan's expensive Sutton Place. These few months would be the first time the two Jacksons had ever been away from the rest of the family. Katherine was nervous about her children being off on their own, but she decided that it would be best if someone could be with Michael, 'and LaToya's being there was as close to me being there as possible. She and I were so much alike back then.'

Because LaToya was anxious about her time away, she turned to chocolate for comfort. 'She ate chocolate the whole time she was in New York,' Susie Jackson said. 'She became addicted. She told me that it got so bad, she had such chocolate fits, that she would take Hershey's cocoa and just mix water with it and drink it, that's how addicted she was to it. By the time she came back, she had gained twenty pounds.'

Though LaToya was apprehensive about being away from home, Michael basked in his new independence. 'He was nothing like the odd Michael Jackson you hear about nowadays,' Rob Cohen remembered. 'Back then, he was great fun; we had the best time. He, LaToya, me and some of the others involved with the project would go to clubs every night to dance. He was not fearful of going out in public, then. He was excited, like a little kid in a playground. The only thing on his mind was work during the day – and I've seldom seen anyone work as hard other than, perhaps, Diana Ross – and play at night.'

Filming the $24-million movie – at the time one of the most expensive films ever produced – took place from 3 October through 30 December 1977, at Astoria Studios. It was hard work, six days a week. Michael would awake at four in the morning in order to leave for the studio by 5:30. Following her mother's instructions, LaToya would prepare an early breakfast for her brother, usually consisting of orange juice, bacon, buttered toast, herb tea and oatmeal. Michael's makeup for his role as Scarecrow took cosmetologist Stan Wilson five hours to apply.

'I loved it,' Michael told me after the film was done. 'I was the Scarecrow from the time the makeup was put on until the time it came off, which I hated.' Sometimes, he said, he would even go home at night wearing the makeup. It was a welcome cover for his acne, he said. Once it was applied, and his phony nose and fright wig of steel-wool pads were in place, Michael could walk around and not be recognized – though, of course, he drew more attention in that get-up than he would have without it.

'Manhattan was full of excitement for Michael,' Rob Cohen recalled. 'He met Jacqueline Onassis at the Rainbow Grill. He talked about her for days afterwards, how glamorous and sophisticated she was, how he hoped one day to know her better. He met Caroline and John Kennedy at the Robert Kennedy Tennis Tournament. He did more socializing then than he does today, sometimes with Diana.'

There was actually a bit of tension between Michael and Diana during production. In July, the cast began rehearsing their musical numbers at the St George Hotel in Brooklyn. Michael was an accomplished dancer; however, Diana had to work at it. Whereas, Michael could remember the choreographer's direction immediately and execute the step with precision, Diana would have to rehearse for hours and would still have some trouble with it. During one particularly trying session, she pulled Michael aside. 'You're embarrassing me,' she said, urgently.

'What do you mean?' Michael asked. His surprise was genuine.

'You're learning the dances too quickly.'

'I was sort of shocked,' Michael told me. 'I didn't mean to

embarrass her, that's for sure. So I tried to act like I didn't always know what I was doing, so I could make her feel better.'

Michael had only happy memories to share with the press where Diana and *The Wiz* are concerned. 'She would come into my dressing room every day and ask what she could do to make things more comfortable,' he said. 'She was like a mother to me. I love her very much.'

At this time, a nineteen-year-old friend of Michael's, Theresa Gonsalves (whom he first met in November 1974 when she went to Las Vegas to see the group for her sixteenth birthday), telephoned him to say she was going to New York for a visit. They made plans to see each other in New York.

'When I got to the apartment building, he told the doorman to send me up,' Theresa recalled. "Toya answered the door. She was irritated. "Michael didn't tell *me* that the two of you made plans," she said. It was as if he was supposed to check with her before he made plans, and he hadn't.

'So I asked 'Toya where he was, and she said that he was in the kitchen baking chocolate chip cookies. After Michael and I talked and ate the cookies, I took a look around. The suite had a balcony. Michael used to like to hang over it like he was going to jump. He loved acting like a fool to upset his sister. 'Toya had the most wonderful room, a real showplace with a huge bed and a mirror above it, a penthouse bedroom befitting a star. Michael had a small, simple bedroom with a twin-sized bed in it and a desk. I asked myself, Why does she have such a great room and he's stuck with *this*?'

One day, Michael returned from the studio very excited about a new structure that had been built for his character at the studio. 'Follow me,' he told Theresa. She followed him into his modest bedroom. As the two of them stood at his desk, he started showing her a scrapbook of photographs of the movie set.

'So what do you think? Great, huh?' Michael asked.

'Yes, you're so lucky,' Theresa enthused.

Michael closed the book and looked into Theresa's eyes, thoughtfully. He tilted his head and leaned over to her, awkwardly.

At that moment, LaToya walked into the room. 'What's going on in here?' she wanted to know. Michael pulled back nervously.

'So anyway, I uh . . .' he stammered.

Years later, Theresa would recall, 'I wanted him to kiss me so badly. And I know he would have if 'Toya hadn't surprised us.'

A Rendezvous with Destiny

After *The Wiz* was filmed and before the movie was released, it was back to business as usual for The Jacksons. However, Michael now felt differently about his family and his career. Satisfied with his work in New York, and having been praised by people whose opinions mattered to him, he was filled with a new confidence in himself as an individual artist. He wanted to begin work on the solo album he had been promised by Epic as soon as possible, even though the rest of the family wanted to concentrate on the third Jacksons group album for the label. The family won again.

The group went into the studio to record *Destiny*, the first Jacksons album said to be written and produced by the group itself. Although the Jacksons did, indeed, write all but one of the songs, executive producer Bobby Colomby and Mike Atkinson did most of the production work. When there was some disagreement as to what credit they should receive, Michael was the only one of the brothers who felt that Colomby and Atkinson should be credited as executive producers.

Destiny was, by far, the most exciting Jacksons album to date, including all of those recorded at Motown. For the first time, the group put together a cohesively structured album. There were no filler songs; all eight songs were noteworthy.

What's more Michael had never sounded better than he did on this album. His performance on the dreamy ballad 'Push Me Away', with its orchestral sweep and rapturous melody, is carefree and effortless. Yet upon closer inspection, it becomes obvious that Michael's delivery is tightly measured and precise. He knows exactly how to settle his mind on the heart and story of a song in order to create the proper mood. As a result of years in the studio and in front of audiences, and a genuine love for singing, he had become an intuitively brilliant stylist.

Though off to a bad start with the high-flash pop of 'Blame It on the Boogie' (a single that didn't even make the Top 40 in the US, but sailed into the Top 10 in Britain), *Destiny* would fare much better than *Goin' Places*. The real showcase was the mesmerizing 'Shake Your Body (Down to the Ground)', written by Michael and Randy. Released in February 1979, it was the biggest hit of the album, peaking at number seven on the pop charts and selling two million copies globally. 'Shake Your Body' personified the contemporary disco trend with its crackling lead vocal by Michael, whip-snapping chorus from the brothers and insistent, persistent backbeat. It is still regarded by many music critics as the perfect dance record and one of The Jacksons' strongest efforts.

The Jacksons did many interviews with the press to discuss their new album, often emphasizing that they had been writing songs for years, but *Destiny* marked the first time they'd been able to dominate an album with their own compositions. They had left Motown to do just this and had good reason to feel triumphant. They certainly could not be criticized in terms of their ability to write songs; they proved themselves with *Destiny*. However, what was striking about the brothers at this time is how they were still unable to discuss their music with authority. Rather, the brothers – Jackie, twenty-seven; Tito, twenty-five; Marlon, twenty-one; Michael, twenty, and Randy, sixteen – were ambiguous in their comments, merely serving up heaps of platitudes about how 'wonderful' it was to write and produce their own music. Because of their early training at Motown to say only what they were told to say, now that The Jacksons could express themselves freely to the press, they didn't know how to do it.

I was one of the reporters the Jacksons spoke to when they were promoting *Destiny*. Since I had interviewed them so many times in the past, I knew to stay clear of in-depth musical discussions. Still, my time with them that August day in 1978 was memorable, not so much as for what they said about their work as for what I observed about their relationships with one another.

When I pulled up to the Jacksons' Encino estate with my

photographer, the ominous, black wrought-iron gate was open so we were able to drive right through, into the circular driveway, upon which was parked a cache of Cadillacs, Rolls-Royces and Mercedes-Benzes. Three sentry dogs, penned up at the end of the drive, hurled themselves against the chain-link fence, their ferocious barks in stark contrast to the high-pitched cries of three large peacocks also caged, nearby.

Looking around, I noticed the custom-made street sign, Jackson 5 Boulevard, on a nearby tree trunk. I remembered the barbecue I had attended a year earlier during which Michael and Jermaine proudly nailed the sign, made for them as part of 'Jackson 5 Day' in Gary, to the tree. To my left was the court where I and a few other weakling reporters stood on the sidelines with Michael, Janet and LaToya while the brothers and members of the Temptations played ball. When I glanced up at the two-storey house, I noticed four people looking down at me: Michael, LaToya, Randy and Katherine had their solemn faces pressed against the glass panes, almost as if prisoners in a compound.

Twenty-two-year-old LaToya, looking fresh and young in a white tennis outfit, answered the front door to us. When Michael approached seconds later, she excused herself, dashed out into the driveway, got into a sporty red Mercedes convertible, and sped off, the brakes screeching.

'Glad you could make it,' Michael said as we shook hands. 'Good to see you, again.' He was wearing a yellow *Jaws* T-shirt, black jeans and a safari hat, around which his Afro billowed. His feet were bare. He spoke in an odd falsetto whisper, which seemed even softer than it had the last time we talked. In exactly a week, he would turn twenty.

Michael led us through the house towards the living room. A huge yellow and green parrot sat perched on a ledge outside the window, shucking peanuts. A red, blue and yellow cockatoo eyed us warily through another window. It let out an ear-piercing screech as we sat down.

'How come you're not getting your guests lemonade?' Katherine asked Michael when she came into the room. Though she had a limp, she walked into the room with total self-assurance and a bearing that could only be described as regal. She was forty-nine.

'Oh, sorry,' Michael murmured. He dashed off to the kitchen, giving me an opportunity to catch up with Katherine while the photographer set up his equipment.

The living room's decor was a mixture of pale yellows, soft greens and stark white splashed with pink. It was a bit on the garish side. Katherine told me that she had designed the motif herself, an assignment for a home-decorating class. She was getting ready to redecorate their kitchen, she said. She then mentioned that Michael's favourite foods at that time were hot apple turnovers and sweet-potato pies. 'Lately, I can't get him to eat *anything*. I try and try,' she said, dismayed. 'I keep thinking he'll eat when he gets hungry, but the boy never gets hungry. Have you noticed how skinny he is? It worries me.'

I looked around. 'These last few years have sure been good ones,' I observed. 'Maybe the best of your life?'

'Not really,' she answered. 'The best years were back in Gary,' she said, her eyes now reflective. 'We had one bedroom for the boys and they all slept together in triple bunk beds. Before going to sleep, I'd sing folk songs to them. I'd always wanted to be a country star,' she said, 'but who'd ever heard of a black country star, back then?'

Katherine rose and walked to a small, antique writing desk in a corner. She opened a drawer and pulled out a photograph. 'We were so happy, then,' she said, showing me the dog-eared picture. It was of the entire family in Gary, posing in front of the house on Jackson Street. 'I'd give up all that we have now for just one of those days back in Gary when it simpler. When we first came to California, I don't know how many times I said, "I wish things were the way they used to be in Gary." But things have never been the same,' she added, fingering the picture. 'It's all changed now.'

Michael came back into the room with two glasses of lemonade. After handing one to me and the other to the photographer, he sat in a chair in a lotus position. Katherine excused herself.

During our two-hour interview, Michael shared his thoughts on a wide range of subjects. 'I don't know much about politics,' he admitted at one point. 'Someone told me recently that Gerald Ford was President.' He chuckled; he was in good spirits, not at all the shy, reclusive superstar he would become in a few years. I laughed with him, thinking we were sharing a joke, but we weren't. He was serious. 'I remember when he was Vice-President,' Michael continued thoughtfully. '*That* I remember. But, President?' He shrugged his shoulders helplessly. 'That I missed.'

Surprised by his uninformed nature, I asked, 'How do you keep up with current events? Do you read newspapers? Watch TV?'

'I watch cartoons,' he told me, his eyes lighting up. 'I *love* cartoons. I love Disney. The Magic Kingdom. Disneyland. It's such a magical place. Walt Disney was a dreamer, like me. And he made his dreams come true, like me. I hope.'

'What about current events?'

Michael looked at me blankly. 'Current events?'

'Do you read the newspaper?' I asked.

He shook his head. 'See, I like show business. I listen to music all the time. I watch old movies. Fred Astaire movies. Gene Kelly, I love. And Sammy [Davis]. I can watch these guys all day, twenty-four hours a day. That's what I love the most.'

We talked about old movies for a while, and about his involvement in *The Wiz*. I then asked what he saw as his biggest professional challenge.

'To live up to what Joseph expects of me.'

'Living up to what your father expects of you is a *professional* challenge?' I asked.

Michael mulled over my question. 'Yes,' he decided. 'A professional challenge.'

'What about the personal challenges?'

'My professional challenges and personal challenges are the same thing,' he said uneasily. 'I just want to entertain. See, when I was in the second grade, the teacher asked me what I wished for. I asked for a mansion, peace in the world, and to be able to entertain . . . Can we talk about something else?'

'Do you have any friends that you can really confide in?'

Michael squirmed. 'No, not really. I'm pretty lonely.'

'How about Tatum?' I wondered.

Michael considered the question. 'She's nice,' he said. 'She was happy for me when I got the part in *The Wiz*. She and Ryan were on my side, helping me with my lines. Tatum understands me. She's gonna teach me to drive a car. She introduces me to people, famous, *famous* people.'

'Any other friends?'

'Well, I do have one friend,' he said. 'A very dear, close friend that I can tell my deepest, darkest secrets to because I know she won't tell anyone else. Her name is . . .' He paused for dramatic effect. 'Miss Diana Ross.'

'You have deep, dark secrets, Michael?'

He laughed. '*Everybody* has deep, dark secrets.'

At this point, Michael was joined by Jackie, Tito, Marlon and Randy. We talked about the group's success at Motown and about the fanatical hysteria generated by their fame.

'Once at a record store in San Francisco, over a thousand kids showed up,' Michael said in a hushed tone. 'They pushed forward and broke a window. A big piece of glass fell on top of this girl. And the girl's throat was *slit*.' Michael swiftly ran his index finger across his neck.

'Michael, don't do that. That's gross,' Randy, said.

Michael ignored his youngest brother and continued with his story. 'She just got *slit*. And I remember there was blood everywhere. Oh God, so much blood. And she grabbed her throat and was bleeding and everyone just ignored her. Why? Because *I* was there and they wanted to grab at *me* and get *my* autograph.' Michael sighed. 'I wonder whatever happened to that girl.'

'Probably dead,' Tito muttered, deadpan.

Fans were as much a curse as a blessing. 'We got these three guard dogs. One is named Heavy, one is Black Girl, and the other one don't got no name,' Michael said. 'We *have* to have them,' he insisted. 'Once, a lady jumped over the gate and into the house and sat down in the den. We came home, and she looked at us and what did she say?' He turned to Marlon for help. 'What'd that lady say?'

'She said, "I'm here 'cause God sent me,"' Marlon recalled.

'God sent her,' Michael repeated.

Jackie laughed. 'Yeah, God sent her to sit in The Jackson 5's den and wait for them to get home so she can get their autograph, and maybe her picture with them, too. She was on a divine mission.'

'And then once, a whole family managed to get into the estate somehow, and they toured the house,' Michael continued. 'Lookin' at all our stuff. Findin' all our most *private* things. And Janet was here all by herself. It was scary. And sometimes, fans ask weird questions.

They don't think you're real. Once a fan asked me the most embarrassing question and in front of everyone. She said, "Do you go to the bathroom?" I was so embarrassed.'

In the middle of the interview, good-natured ribbing among the brothers turned nasty when someone brought up the subject of nicknames.

'Mike has a nickname,' Jackie mentioned, his eyes teasing. 'It's a good one.'

Michael's smiling face turned serious. 'Don't, Jackie,' he warned. He looked away.

'We call him—'

'Please, you guys!' Michael pleaded.

'Big Nose,' Jackie finished.

The brothers laughed among themselves. Michael shifted in his chair.

'Yeah, Big Nose,' Marlon repeated, grinning. He reached over and punched Michael on his arm, playfully. 'What's happenin', Big Nose?' Michael threw Marlon a scathing look. His mouth parted, but no words came out. He would say little more as long as his brothers were present.

After the interview, we walked outside to take photographs in the warm California sunlight. Joseph, a hulking six-footer with a mole on his face, a pencil-thin moustache, and a diamond pinky ring the size of a marble, approached me. 'You see, I have a philosophy about raising children,' he said, engaging me. 'My father was strict. He was a schoolteacher, and he treated me like I was one of his students, not like I was his son. I never got any special treatment. I'm glad that happened. I got a strict raising when I was young, and I've been able to accomplish a lot because of that. And my kids have gotten a strict raising, and look at what *they've* accomplished. I think children *should* fear their parents. It's good when they fear you. It's good for them, and it's good for the parents too. I did my best with those boys,' he said, pointing to them as they posed for pictures.

'Have they ever disappointed you?' I asked.

A sober expression crossed his face. 'Lots of times,' he answered. 'Jermaine's with Berry at Motown, instead of with us. He chose Berry over me. Do you know how that makes me feel? It hurts right here.' Joseph thumped the left side of his chest with his fist. 'I've been disappointed other times too,' he continued. 'But I don't think I have ever once let my boys down. If I did, too bad for them. You do the best you can do, raising kids,' he said, smiling. 'It helped that they had something to look forward to. They always had entertainment, and me to rehearse them. And they also play character-building sports like football and baseball.

'Jackie could have been a baseball player if he wanted to, in the majors with the Chicago White Sox. They're all good at sports, except for Michael who never picked up a bat in his whole life.' Joseph smiled. It was an unexpected moment of gentleness from him. 'Wouldn't know what to do with a baseball bat, I think. We tease him about it, but he doesn't like it. Michael has always been sensitive,' he observed.

'One thing about Michael, though,' Joseph added, 'is that ever since he was four, he wanted to be an entertainer. And he always wanted to be number one. That's why sports upset him, because his brothers can whip him and outdo him at sports and he can't be number one at it. But in music, Michael *knows* he's number one.'

'And speakin' of Michael, Marlon told me about what happened. You're not gonna write that part about Michael's nickname, are you?' he asked. 'That boy is so sensitive about his nose,' Joseph added. 'Do you see anything wrong with his nose? That's all he ever talks about, his damn nose. He threatened to have it fixed, but what can he do with it? I told him I'd break his face if he ever had it fixed.' Joseph's green eyes twinkled. He threw back his head and roared with laughter. 'You don't fix something that isn't broken,' he added. 'He's got a great nose. It looks like mine.'

Afterwards, Michael returned to the living room for some final thoughts about his life and career. As the photographer and I watched, he crossed his left leg over his right knee and began absent-mindedly picking at his toenails. 'When I'm not onstage, I'm not the same. I'm different,' he observed. 'I'm addicted to the stage. When I can't get on to a stage for a long time, I have fits and get crazy. I start crying, and I act weird and freaked out. No kiddin', I do. I start dancin' 'round the house.'

He began to talk rapidly. 'It's like a part of me is missin' and I gotta get it back, 'cause if I don't, I won't be complete. So I gotta dance and I gotta sing, you know? I have this craving. Onstage is the only place I'm comfortable. I'm not comfortable around . . .' he paused, searching for the right word, '*normal* people. But when I get out onstage, I open up and I have no problems.' He seemed flustered, unnerved. 'Whatever is happening in my life doesn't matter. I'm up there and cuttin' loose and I say to myself, 'This is it. *This* is home. This is exactly where I'm supposed to be, where God meant for me to be.' I am *unlimited* when I'm onstage. I'm number one. But when I'm off the stage,' he shrugged his shoulders, 'I'm not really . . .' Again, he paused, trying to find the right word. 'Happy.'

Earlier in the day, I had conducted an interview with Sidney Lumet, director of *The Wiz*. 'Michael Jackson is the most gifted entertainer to come down the pike since James Dean,' Lumet told me. 'He's a brilliant actor and dancer, probably one of the rarest entertainers I have ever worked with.'

I shared Sidney's observation with Michael. He seemed embarrassed for a moment. Then, he asked, 'Who's James Dean?'

Later, he began talking about his role as the Scarecrow in *The Wiz*. 'What I like about my character,' he observed, 'is his confusion. He knows that he has problems, I guess you could call them. But he doesn't know why he has them or how he got that way. And he understands that he sees things differently from the way everyone else does, but he can't put his finger on why. He's not like other people. No one understands him. So he goes through his whole life with this, uh . . .' he paused, 'confusion.'

Michael looked off into the distance, now seeming lost in his thought process. 'Everybody thinks he's very special, but, really, he's very sad. He's so, so sad. Do you understand?' He fixed his thoughtful gaze on me and asked, again. 'Do you understand his sadness?'

The *Wiz* is a Flop

When *The Wiz* was released in October 1978, it became a critical failure and a box-office disappointment. The finished film was an overblown spectacle, one that most people who were involved with would just as soon take off their résumés. Even the commercial release of 'Ease On Down the Road', teaming Michael with Diana Ross – a coupling that seemed destined for the Top Ten, in theory – didn't even crack the Top Forty. Berry Gordy, who had nothing to do with the actual production of the film and didn't believe Diana should have been cast in it, has never discussed *The Wiz*, publicly.

'It was a big dream that got away,' said producer Rob Cohen, in retrospect. 'A brilliant idea gone wrong. The knowledge that two years of my life, twenty-three million dollars of Universal's money, thousands of man hours of labour, and all of the hopes and dreams of everyone involved went into a movie that didn't stand a chance makes me sick.'

Despite its failure, the making of *The Wiz* marked a personal victory for Michael Jackson. Identifying himself with the role of the Scarecrow gave him the opportunity to look within and discover a new sense of strength and self-confidence. 'Working in the movie showed me what makes kings of the world and what makes giants,' he said. 'It showed me how I can believe in myself in a way I never could before.' He also expanded his professional horizons and, in the process, won the respect of fellow workers, and even some critics who had panned the movie.

Still, Michael could not ignore the fact that *The Wiz* was a failure at the box office. He was shattered by it; he had never suffered such a high-profile failure. 'Did I make a mistake?' he asked Rob Cohen a few weeks after the movie was released. 'Maybe I shouldn't have done the film? Maybe I should have listened to my family. What will it mean to my career?'

'Look, you followed your instincts,' Rob told him. 'We all did. Don't second-guess yourself now. We have nothing to be ashamed of. We did the best job we could.'

'But—'

'But nothing,' Rob said. 'Go on with your life and career. Be a star. You've only just begun.'

Joseph also supported Michael during this disappointing time. When one of the brothers said something disparaging about the movie, Joseph gave him a sharp punch on the shoulder. 'Ouch! Joseph,' said the brother. 'That hurt.'

'Ouch, my ass,' Joseph countered. 'You don't criticize your brother. At least he tried. How many movies have *you* made, big shot?'

Transition

At the end of 1978, Joseph Jackson severed his ties with Richard Arons. In Richard's wake, Joseph recruited Ron Weisner and Freddy DeMann as managers. Both were experienced in the entertainment field, Weisner as a business manager and DeMann as a promoter. Joseph felt that he needed the assistance of these men, both white, in order to insure that CBS would promote The Jacksons as the company did its white artists. He believed that the company considered his sons a 'black act' and was, therefore, restricting the way it promoted and marketed them. Joseph's concern is a common, and often justified, complaint of black acts signed to record companies, like CBS, which are manned predominantly by white executives. Like Joseph, many black managers maintain that white executives don't know how to market black entertainment 'across the board', meaning to white record buyers, as well as to black. Of course, Richard Arons is also white, so it was clear that Joseph felt the new managers were more experienced as well, and had more clout in the music business.

Joseph's strategy worked in America. *Destiny* sold over a million copies and reached number eleven on *Billboard*'s album chart, not bad for a group that hadn't had a major record in some time.

Destiny didn't do as well in the UK, however. It took six months for it to be released there, and the highest it hit was number thirty-three. But it was now accepted that the Jacksons had sporadic sales in the UK; there was little anyone could do about it. They simply weren't as hot in England as in the States. That was fine with Joseph; the focus at this time was on US sales anyway, not European.

However, Michael was still unhappy. Despite what his brothers tried to promote, he knew in his heart that he and they were not fully responsible for the success of *Destiny*. CBS had whipped up quite a publicity frenzy about how terrific the brothers were as producers, yet it was not true. They hadn't actually produced that album on their own; Michael hated living the lie. He was too old for such nonsense, he felt. Gone were the days when it was acceptable to promote such untruths.

Michael had never been dismayed about his life and career as he was when he finished the 1979 Destiny tour. While on the road, he had lost his voice making it necessary for Marlon to sing his higher-register parts while Michael just moved his mouth. He found the process humiliating. Eventually, two weeks of performances had to just be cancelled because of Michael's throat problems.

Throughout the tour, Michael was tired and discouraged and couldn't seem to find the unlimited supply of energy he had always relied upon in the past. As enthusiastic as the audiences were to the show, Michael felt that something was missing from it. Barely twenty-one, he felt he'd stopped growing professionally; he was frustrated by being in a group. 'It was the same thing over and over,' he told me in an interview after the tour. 'It was all for one and one for all, but I was starting to think that maybe I should be doing some things on my own. I was getting antsy.'

To make matters worse, Michael loathed having to answer to Joseph and was getting to the point where he didn't even want to be around him.

Though many industry observers believed that, based on the success of *Destiny*, Joseph Jackson had become a brilliant entertainment manager, Michael was not one of them. In Michael's view, his father used a shotgun approach to his work: 'If you shoot enough bullets, one will hit the target, eventually,' Michael explained. 'But you can also waste a lot of ammunition and maybe hit some targets you would rather not,' Michael explained. 'Look at the way Joseph alienated Berry and everyone else at Motown.' Some people, Michael argued, determine their target, stalk it as long as necessary, and then get it cleanly with one shot. 'That's the way to go,' Michael reasoned.

In truth, Joseph would never be able to win with Michael, no matter how many bull's-eyes he scored. Getting the group away from Motown was the best thing he'd ever done, but Michael could not see it that way. His perception of Joseph was understandably clouded by his personal views about him, and his judgement of his father as a child abuser and philanderer. There was no way Michael would be able to credit Joseph Jackson . . . with anything . . . ever.

Michael didn't feel that the group had made an impact after leaving Motown and signing with CBS, even though they had a hit with 'Shake Your Body'. It wasn't enough. He was tired of The

Jackson 5 image. He knew what he wanted to do: record another solo album, one for CBS that would fulfil his ambition, expand his artistry and ease the restlessness that had plagued him since the Destiny tour ended. Day after day, Michael stayed alone in his bedroom pondering, as Marlon would later say, 'who knows what, he's very secretive.'

His brothers soon realized that something was different about Michael, and it scared them. 'Mike was acting strangely,' Tito would remember. 'It was as if something had snapped in him. He stopped showing up at family meetings, and when we discussed our future plans, he had nothing to offer. Maybe he was plotting to go out on his own, I don't know. He never did say much. You never really knew what he was thinking.'

'I just didn't think it was fair that I had stopped recording solo albums,' Michael would say years later when looking back on this time. 'Part of our contract with CBS was that I would get to record on my own. When that wasn't happening because we hadn't been able to find the time, I started getting nervous and upset.'

When Michael told his father that he wanted to record a solo album, Joseph's reaction was predictable – supportive but with qualification. 'Why not?' he remarked. 'You know how I feel about it, Michael. Do what you want as long as it doesn't interfere with group business.'

'What does that mean?' Michael wanted to know.

'You know what it means,' his father warned him. 'Family is the most important thing.'

Perhaps Joseph wasn't overly concerned about Michael doing a solo album because, in truth, his albums never amounted to much: his first two for Motown, *Got to Be There* and *Ben* (1971 and 1972 respectively), each sold a little over 350,000 copies, which wasn't bad. However, his third album, *Music and Me* (1973), sold only 80,286 copies, a dismal showing. His last solo album for the company, *Forever Michael* (1975), did a little better (99,311 copies). Albums featuring all of the Jacksons always sold better than solo albums; let's not even get into the statistics for sales of Jackie's solo album which, incidentally, was terrific. Joseph always felt it was in everybody's best interest to keep the act together.

Therefore, if Michael felt the need to record a solo album in order to 'get it out of his system', it was fine with Joseph – as long as the Boy Wonder remembered that his first allegiance was to his family and to the group, not to himself.

Off the Wall

When Michael Jackson set out to make his new solo album, he didn't know what he wanted to be the final result. However, he knew what he *didn't* want, and that was to make a record that sounded like a Jacksons' album. From the start of his professional career, someone had decided the sound of Michael's music. First, it had been Motown's crack production staff and then the artist and repertoire executives at CBS/Epic. Though the family was given the freedom to write and 'produce' the *Destiny* album, Epic insisted that they record a song they didn't write, 'Blame It on the Boogie'. Other concessions and compromises were made along the way with the three albums for that label, and Michael never felt totally responsible for the results. While *Destiny*'s hit single, 'Shake Your Body', re-established The Jacksons in the marketplace, many observers in the music business felt as Michael did, that the brothers had left their magic at Motown.

Now, Michael wanted more creative freedom. He wanted to do his next album totally outside the family, even though the brothers tried desperately to make his solo album a group production as soon as they heard about it. They were hurt that Michael wanted to exclude them from the project, but he stood firm. 'I'm doing this on my own,' he said. 'They're just going to have to understand. For once.'

Uncertain as to how to proceed, Michael called Quincy Jones, who had offered a helping hand during production of *The Wiz*. The two had their first exchange one day on the set as Michael rehearsed a scene in which, as the Scarecrow, he pulled a slip of paper from his stuffing and read a quote by Socrates. He attributed the statement to *Soh-crates*, as if it rhymed with 'no rates'. 'That's the way I had always assumed it was pronounced,' Michael said later. When he heard the crew giggling, he knew he had it wrong.

'*Sock-ra-tease*,' someone whispered in his ear. 'It's *Sock-ra-tease*.'

He turned and saw Quincy, the film's musical director.*

The older man extended his hand. 'I'm Quincy Jones,' he said with a warm smile. 'Anything I can do to help . . .'

Michael would remember the offer. A little more than a year later, he called Quincy and asked him to suggest possible producers for his solo endeavour. Quincy suggested himself.

Quincy seemed an unlikely choice of producer for Michael. He had found success in the pop-R&B arena with his own albums, which were virtual music workshops of musicians, writers and arrangers with Jones overseeing the entire programme. Quincy had also found mainstream success with the Brothers Johnson, a sibling duo out of Los Angeles, whose platinum albums he produced. Still, most industry observers privately felt that Quincy was too musically rigid to make a great pop record; many of these people believed that his records with the Brothers Johnson, for instance, though successful, sounded too homogenized.

However, Quincy had a long and varied show-business career, starting as a fifteen-year-old trumpet player and arranger for Lionel Hampton. Over the years, he immersed himself in studio work, arranging, composing, and producing for Dinah Washington, Duke Ellington, Big Maybelle, Tommy Dorsey and Count Basie. In the early sixties, he was a vice-president of Mercury Records, the first black Executive at a major label. In 1963, he began a second career in Hollywood, where he became the first black to reach the top rank of film composers, with thirty-eight pictures to his credit, including *The Wiz*.

'I didn't even want to do *The Wiz*,' Quincy has said. 'I thought, There's no way the public is going to accept a black version of *The Wizard of Oz*. I kept telling Sidney Lumet I didn't want to do it, but because he's a great director and because he hired me to do my first movie soundtrack [*The Pawnbroker*, 1965], I did it. Out of that mess came my association with Michael Jackson.'

When Quincy and Michael came together in a recording studio in

*The Socrates quote was ultimately edited from the final cut of *The Wiz*. Michael had actually met Quincy Jones when he was twelve, at Sammy Davis, Jr.'s home. Michael doesn't remember the meeting, though Quincy does.

Los Angeles to start laying rhythm tracks together in 1979, the artist and producer turned out to be a perfect match. Quincy's in-studio work method was to surround the artist with superior songs and fine musicians and then let that artist have free reign. Michael had been so accustomed to being on a short creative leash, he was ecstatic when Quincy began taking his ideas seriously. Quincy recalled that, at first, he found Michael 'very, very introverted, shy, and non-assertive. He wasn't at all sure that he could make a name for himself on his own. Neither was I.'

Quincy, on the other hand, hadn't worked with unharnessed brilliance like Michael's since his days with some of the jazz greats. In Michael, he'd finally found what he'd been looking for in a talent. As he would tell me, 'Michael is the essence of what a performer and an artist are all about. He's got all you need emotionally, and he backs it up with discipline and pacing. He'll never burn himself out. Now I'm a pretty strong drill sergeant when it comes to steering a project, but in Michael's case it's hardly necessary.'

Quincy was also amazed at Michael's versatility. 'He can come to a session and put down two lead vocals and three background parts in one day,' he said at the time. 'He does his homework, rehearses and works hard at home. Most singers want to do everything in the studio – write words and music, figure out harmonies, try different approaches to a song. That makes me crazy. All I can see is dollar signs going up. Studio time is expensive, and that's why someone like Michael is a producer's dream artist. He walks in, prepared. We accomplish so much in a single session, it stuns me. In my opinion, Michael Jackson is going to be *the* star of the eighties and nineties.'

The two developed a close rapport outside the studio as well, and over the years, Michael would think of Quincy as a hip father figure. Michael would confide in Quincy and take direction from him in a way that reminded many observers of the kind of relationship the public *thought* Michael had with Joseph. However, Quincy was the antithesis of the natural father who used to hit Michael to get him to perform up to expectations.

'When I'm in the studio, I don't believe in creating an atmosphere of tension or hostility,' Quincy once told Oprah Winfrey in an interview. 'That serves no purpose. I believe in creating an atmosphere of love.'

Finally, after listening to hundreds of songs, Michael and Quincy decided on a batch to record. Among them were three Michael Jackson compositions: the funky 'Don't Stop 'Til You Get Enough', the dance-floor scorcher 'Working Day and Night', and the prowling, urgent 'Get on the Floor' (co-written with Louis Johnson, bassist of the Brothers Johnson).

Quincy sought to balance the mixture of songs with melodic pop ballads like the emotional and symphonic 'She's Out of My Life', contributed by songwriter-arranger Tom Bahler; the bright, melancholy 'It's the Falling in Love', written by David Foster and Carole Bayer Sager; the cute, sugary Paul McCartney song 'Girlfriend'; and most significantly, the romantic, mid-tempoed 'Rock with You', the driving 'Burn This Disco Out', and the mighty 'Off the Wall', (which would end up as the title of the album), all written by Rod Temperton, chief songwriter and keyboardist for the Britain-based pop-R&B band, Heatwave.

With the songs selected, Quincy Jones then summoned a handful of crack session players – keyboardists Greg Phillinganes, George Duke and Michael Boddicker; guitarists David Williams and Larry Carlton; bassist Louis Johnson; percussionist Paulinho DaCosta; and the Seawind Horns, led by Jerry Hey – and they all went to work.

During 'Don't Stop 'Til You Get Enough' (which would become *Off the Wall*'s first single), Michael unveiled a playful, sexy falsetto no one had ever heard from him before. All of the right elements were in place on this song: an unstoppable beat, a meticulous, well-balanced delivery of lyrics and melody and a driving energy. Michael explained that he couldn't shake the song's melody when it came to him one day. He walked throughout the house humming and singing it to himself. Finally, he went into the family's twenty-four-track studio and had Randy put the melody down on the piano (Michael can't play). When he played it for Quincy, it was a done deal: it had to be on the album.

'Don't Stop' was released on 28 July 1979. In less than three months, it was top of the charts, Michael's first solo number-one record in seven years. It soared to number three in the UK, a huge hit for him. It was also the subject of his first solo video. When compared to the kind of musical videos Michael would do in just a few years, 'Don't Stop 'Til You Get Enough' comes across as primitive. In the only attempt at innovation, Michael appears briefly dancing in triplicate. Still, it's fun and memorable because, after all, it's the first one.

The album that resulted from all of Michael's work with Quincy, *Off the Wall*, was released in August 1979. Almost as much attention had been lavished on the album jacket as on the record itself. The cover photograph showed Michael smiling broadly and wearing a natty tuxedo – and glittering white socks. 'The tuxedo was the overall game plan for the *Off the Wall* album and package,' said Michael's manager at the time, Ron Weisner. 'Michael had an image before that as a young kid, and all of a sudden, here was a hot album and somebody very clean-looking. The tuxedo was our idea as managers,' Ron concluded. 'The socks were Michael's.'

Fans and industry peers alike were left with their mouths agape when *Off the Wall* was issued to the public. Engineer Bruce Swedien had made sure Quincy Jones's tracks and Michael Jackson's voice showed to their best advantage. Michael's fans proclaimed that they hadn't heard him sing with such joy and abandon since the early Jackson 5 days. The album showcased an adult Michael Jackson, for the first time a real artist, not just someone's vocal stylist.

Michael Jackson had officially arrived. The performances revealed sides of him never before heard by record buyers. For instance, no one knew Michael could be as smooth and sophisticated as he was on the album's outstanding track, Stevie Wonder's 'I Can't Help It'. The song was important to the project because its luscious chord changes were the closest Michael had ever come to singing jazz on record.

Even more revealing was an emotional Michael crying real tears on the tail end of 'She's Out of My Life'. (Jones would later comment that Michael cried every time they cut the vocals. After several attempts with the same results, the decision was made to leave the tears on the track.) The understated arrangement of this song, also a crowd-pleaser with its sparse keyboard accompaniment, allowed Michael to soulfully plead his regret of lost love in a touching, sometimes searing, delivery.

When 'Rock with You' also made number one, and then 'Off the Wall' and 'She's Out of My Life' both went to number ten, Michael became the first solo artist to have four Top Ten singles from one album in America. In Britain, *Off the Wall* also made recording history with five hits released from a single album. Although it would sell six million copies worldwide, it never went beyond number three in the US and number five in the UK. Michael was excited but cautious. 'It's a start,' he said.

Joseph was a bit concerned. 'This thing with Michael, it's good,' he said to one of the family's attorneys. 'I'm proud of the kid, but I'm worried.'

'About what?' asked the lawyer.

'Too much independence,' Joseph said. 'It's not good.'

'You know, throughout history, stars have left groups,' said the attorney. 'Sammy Davis left his family. Diana left The Supremes. Smokey left The Miracles. It happens. You can't keep a good star down.'

Joseph shook his head. 'Not in this family, it doesn't happen,' he said. 'Michael knows. He *knows*.'

When *Off the Wall* won only one Grammy (in an R&B category), Michael was crushed. 'It bothered me,' he said. 'I cried a lot. My family thought I was going crazy, because I was weeping so much about it.'

'He was so disappointed,' Janet concurred. 'I felt bad for him. But he finally said, "You watch. The next album I do, you just . . . I'll show them."'

For his part, though, Joseph wasn't so disappointed. 'I think it's good to keep things in perspective,' he said, privately. 'The boy doesn't need more success, he needs to get into the studio with his brothers. *That*'s what he needs.'

Michael Turns Twenty-one . . . and Gets His Own Lawyer

On 29 August 1979, Michael Jackson turned twenty-one. Even though he, as a Jehovah's Witness, did not celebrate his birthdays, we in the media did, especially the important ones. I had interviewed Michael for magazine articles to mark important age milestones – 'Michael Turns 16', 'Michael Turns 18' and even 'Michael Turns 20' – so I was happy to meet with him once again for, yes, 'Michael Turns 21'. It was a turning point in his life, and he felt it in a keen way. He had come of age, was about to take his life and career into his own hands. 'I really feel that being a man is doing exactly what you want to do in this life and to do it successfully and to conquer a goal,' he told me. 'Age is just a number, I know. I'm no more a man now than I was yesterday. But, still, it means something to me to be twenty-one. I've seen a lot, done a lot. However, now I think things will be different for me, better.

'To me, Walt Disney is a real man,' he observed. 'Charlie Chaplin, a real man. Fred Astaire, a real man. Bill Robinson, a real man. Not only did they achieve goals, but look at how much joy they gave other people. People looked up to them. I want people to look up to me, too. They made paths. I want to make one, too. That's what being a man means to me.'

Just days after I interviewed Michael, he and Joseph had an argument, one more bitter than any in recent memory. Michael decided that the time had come to make it clear to his father that he wanted more control over his career. Joseph didn't like being criticized by Michael, but he asked for it. When he inquired as to the problems Michael had with the way things had gone in the past, Michael gave him a list of grievances. In part, he didn't like the way the situation with Jermaine had been handled, wasn't satisfied with the way the group had left Motown, and was also unhappy with the recent CBS product, with the exception of *Off the Wall*. Wisely, Michael kept it all about business; he left out personal complaints and certainly didn't address the subject of Joseph's blatant unfaithfulness to Katherine.

'I let you make that movie, didn't I?' Joseph shot back at him. 'This is how you repay me?'

'You didn't *let* me make that movie,' Michael answered, his eyes blazing. 'I'm a grown-up now, Joseph. I'm *Michael Jackson*. I make my own decisions.'

'Why, you little . . .' Joseph lifted his hand and was about to smack his son, just like old times. However, he changed his mind. Michael gave him a defiant look and walked away.

Joseph was as hurt as he was angry. He thought Michael was being far too critical of him as a manager, and couldn't imagine how he had ended up with a son who was such an ingrate. When Michael said he was going to meet with an attorney to investigate his 'options', Joseph was crushed. Prior to this time, Michael and his siblings only used Joseph's attorneys and accountants. Now that Michael wanted his own representation, Joseph felt as if his son didn't trust him. *Of course*, Michael didn't trust him. Michael had more than a million dollars in his own bank account now, as a result of *Off the Wall*, and he wanted to hang on to it. He realized that money was power, and if he wished to break away from the family it was his bank account that would best support that effort – not Joseph, and not his brothers. All of this information was a rude awakening for Joseph. 'All right, fine. If that's what you want,' he said, defeated. Wisely, he didn't want to further antagonize his son. He hoped that Michael would not follow through with the idea, that this particular storm would blow over. He was wrong.

Michael's accountant, Michael Mesnick – who also represented the Beach Boys – arranged for Michael to meet with three entertainment lawyers and choose the one he liked best. First on the list was John Branca, a thirty-one-year-old native New Yorker with a background in corporate tax law and music industry negotiations for performers such as the Beach Boys, Neil Diamond and Bob Dylan. Bright, young, aggressive and determined, John was eager to make a name for himself in the entertainment industry.

Because he was more a rock and roll fan, John was only vaguely familiar with Michael's music and career. However, when he checked with his colleagues he was told that Michael was perceived by the music industry as someone with the potential to be a superstar. John was intrigued. He thought that Michael might be an artist he could take to the next level. At the same time, he felt that an association with Michael could establish his own career as an attorney.

John recalled that his meeting with Michael was a bit unusual. Michael took his sunglasses off only once, at the beginning when he eyed John and asked if the two had previously met. When they established that they hadn't, Michael smiled and put his sunglasses back on. Michael Mesnick asked John a list of questions, and Michael listened to the answers. At first, he seemed shy and uncomfortable.

Finally, when he began to relax, he told John that the reason he needed representation was that he wanted independence from his family, 'once and for all,' and especially from his father. At that time, The Jacksons had a group contract with Epic; Michael said he wanted one for himself as a solo artist, as well as a member of The Jacksons. Also, he wanted all of his business affairs reviewed, including his publishing deal and his record sales.

John was enthusiastic, full of valuable information and eager to assist in any way possible. He was also, as far as Michael was concerned, the right man for the job. After the meeting, Michael cancelled the other two interviews, and hired John Branca. John was impressed with Michael's total belief in himself, he said, later. It was infectious; John could not wait to get started working for him.

Early in their relationship Michael confided in John his two principal goals: first of all, he said, he wanted to be 'the biggest star in show business'. Secondly, he wanted to be 'the wealthiest'. He told John that he was angry that *Off the Wall* had only garnered one Grammy nomination. 'I sold five million in the US, six million foreign. That's a big record,' he told him. 'It was totally unfair that it didn't get Record of the Year, and it can never happen again.'

Michael was frustrated by what he saw as a lack of respect from the entertainment industry. For instance, he felt he deserved to be on the cover of *Rolling Stone* and asked his publicist, Norman Winter, to try to arrange it. 'We would very much like to do a major piece on Michael Jackson but feel it is not a cover story,' was publisher Jann Wenner's response in a letter to Winter (dated 27 November 1979).

When Michael saw that letter, he became exasperated. 'I've been told over and over again that black people on the covers of magazines don't sell copies,' he complained. 'Just wait. Someday those magazines are going to be *begging* me for an interview. Maybe I'll give them one. And maybe I won't.'

For the next twenty-odd years, John Branca would, unarguably, be the single most important figure in Michael Jackson's career. He would negotiate every business deal for him, become a trusted friend and adviser, and see to it that this talented kid from Gary realized both of his goals.

John's first course of action was to renegotiate Michael's CBS contract with the company's president, Walter Yetnikoff. John managed to secure for Michael the highest royalty rate in the business at that time: thirty-seven per cent of a hundred per cent of wholesale, which was the same rate given to Neil Diamond and Bob Dylan. He also made a deal with Walter and with The Jacksons' legal representation, John Mason, that Michael could leave The Jacksons at any time in the future. John Branca worked it out that if Michael did leave the group, CBS would still be obligated to record The Jacksons without him. It was a nice gesture and one that placated Joseph. He fully believed that without Michael the group could continue because, as he had been putting it for years, 'It's not all about Michael.' Of course, Joseph must have known better, but his focus was always on family.

From this point on, legally and thanks to John Branca, Michael Jackson would never have to record another song with his brothers, unless he truly wanted to do it. Obviously, the Jackson brothers weren't happy with Michael's new independence, but the full ramifications of the deal would not hit them for a while. They were accustomed to Michael doing solo albums, and still felt secure that he would remain with the group. (Of course, in structuring Michael's freedom, he and John Branca had not considered the 'Katherine factor', soon to come into play: if the brothers would want Michael to do something he didn't want to do, they would learn to ask their mother to intervene.)

Michael's new deal was impressive, so much so that his brother, Randy, who suddenly had solo aspirations, decided that he wanted to hire John Branca. During a lunch meeting with him, John asked Michael what he thought of the idea. 'I think it stinks,' Michael told him, according to the attorney's memory. 'I can't believe it. I do this one thing for myself, hiring you, and now they're all gonna try to weasel in on it. You wait, first Randy. Next, you'll be hearing from Jackie. Probably Tito wants to do a record, too.'

'Are you saying you don't want me to represent Randy?' John asked with a smile. He couldn't help but be bemused by Michael's adamant reaction (not to mention the notion of Tito Jackson making a record).

'What I'm saying,' Michael told him, his voice crisp and cool, 'is that I don't want you representing Randy, Jackie, Tito or anyone else with the last name Jackson, ever. If you do, then we'll be finished, you and I.'

'You got it,' John agreed.

'Oh, and another thing,' Michael added. 'I don't want Randy to know that this is my decision,' Michael added. 'I want you to make it look like it's yours.'

'Cool,' John said. The two shook hands. They were developing trust in one another, and nothing could come of such faith but the very best that the record business had to offer – for both of them.

Joseph's Secret

Many people today think of Michael Jackson as an enigma. It's ironic that, twenty-some years ago, his father, Joseph, was thought of in exactly the same way – if not by the public, most certainly by his family and friends. 'Sometimes, I think he leads a double life,' Michael said of his father back then. 'He is a very mysterious person.' Of course, Joseph's other life involved the women with whom he had assignations outside of his marriage. But was there more? In 1980, office employees at Joseph Jackson Productions began to suspect that their boss was trying to hide more than just infidelity.

By early 1980, a nineteen-year-old employee named Gina Sprague had become particularly close to Joseph. Gina is of Mexican-English-Irish descent. At five feet five, one hundred pounds, with shoulder-length brown hair, she was vivacious, intelligent and gorgeous. Joseph was taken by her. However, she insists that she and Joseph were not having an affair, though many Jackson intimates do not believe her. They were, she says, just close friends. 'He needed a friend,' she said. 'He was so estranged from his family. Sometimes, he would need to talk. I was there for him. I knew he had a reputation of being a womanizer, but that is not what our relationship was about.

'If he believed in you, he gave you enough strength and courage to try and attain your goal, even if you didn't think you could do it.

Once I knew him, I could understand why the family had become superstars. I had to remind Joseph that he should be proud. I used to tell him, "Sure, Michael and the rest get all of the attention, but look at where they came from."

' "The kid hates my guts," he said of Michael. I said, "Joseph, that's not true." He said, "You haven't seen the way he looks at me." There were tears in his eyes. "The kid hates me, Gina. Hates my guts. They all do."

'One thing that struck me very strange is that Michael and his brothers and sisters called him Joseph,' she recalled. 'The first time Janet came into my office she was about thirteen. She walked in and, in a very flip manner, said, "Hello. Where's Joseph?" Or Michael would call. "Hello, Gina, this is Michael. Is Joseph there?" And I would say, "Your *father* is in a meeting at the moment." '

One day Gina, concerned about Joseph's recent mercurial behaviour and mysterious disappearances, asked him what was going on in his life. 'I'm not gonna tell you,' he said with some hesitation. 'Instead, I'll show you.'

Joseph then drove Gina to a building in a suburban Los Angeles neighbourhood where he introduced Gina to Cheryl Terrell. Then, a small African-American child of about six years of age came bounding into the living room. 'Daddy! Daddy!' she exclaimed.

'There she is,' Joseph said with a big smile. 'My little girl.' He scooped the child up in his arms and hugged her tightly.

As he later explained it, Joe and Cheryl Terrell had an affair in 1973. The result of that relationship was a daughter, Joh'Vonnie, born in Los Angeles on 30 August 1974, the day after Michael's sixteenth birthday. Joseph Walter Jackson's name appears on the birth certificate. His occupation is listed as 'entertainment manager'. His age was recorded as forty-six at the time of the baby's birth; the mother's age, twenty-six.

Joseph kept the secret for many years but by 1980 he had decided to tell his family about his daughter. He wanted to become more involved in her upbringing and wanted her to be recognized as a member of the family.

After breaking the ice with Gina, Joseph gathered his sons together in a dressing room after a performance to tell them that they had a half-sister. One can only wonder what he thought their reaction to such news might be – and why he decided to tell them the news *before* telling Katherine? Of course, they were all upset. The sons then told the daughters, who were also hurt and angry. The children then wrestled with the question of how to tell Katherine, or, if they even *should* tell her. What a burden it was for them to have this information. In the end, according to LaToya, one of the brothers – it's not known which one – told Katherine. Of course, she was overcome with understandable emotions.

After she and Joseph had it out, there was nothing to do but deal with the situation as it existed. As a practical woman committed to family values, Katherine put her feelings aside and agreed that Joseph had a responsibility to Joh'Vonnie and to her mother. As a way of providing for them, she and Joseph purchased a three-bedroom home in Van Nuys, a suburb of Los Angeles, for $169,000. As a trustee of his daughter's estate, Joseph then signed the property over to Joh'Vonnie. She and her mother then moved into the home. Katherine could do no more than that. Her nephew, Tim Whitehead (Tim's mother was Katherine's sister, Hattie, and his father is Joseph's stepbrother, Vernon), said, 'Joseph wanted the child to be accepted into the family, but there was no way that was going to happen, I'm afraid. It was too painful for my aunt, and for the children. This was difficult, heartbreaking.'

According to Jerome Howard, Joseph's and Katherine's former finances manager, 'Katherine told me she went into the grocery store one day and saw Joseph's girlfriend and the daughter. She said she just stood there, frozen. "Jerome, the girl looks *exactly* like Joseph," she said.'

Though Katherine seemed to be acting in a logical and sensible manner, she was not as unfazed by the news of Joh'Vonnie's existence as she may have wanted people to believe. Michael would indicate later that it was at this time that he sensed an emotional transformation in his mother. She rarely smiled during these days. Her temper would flare over unimportant matters. She ever swore from time to time, which was unusual, and had called Joh'Vonnie a 'bastard'. When Michael protested, she suggested that if he looked up the word in the dictionary, he would find that she was using it properly. Apparently, Joseph's indiscretions had worn her down, chipped away at her self-esteem, her pride. She now sometimes seemed bitter and angry.

Even though Katherine was going through an ordeal, and the family was being torn apart by the recent turn of events, the Jacksons had no choice but to continue to express a strong sense of unity to the media. Public relations was an important consideration. The family had been turning away from reality and toward image-making ever since they arrived in Los Angeles from Gary. However, for Michael, nothing would ever be the same. Joseph's actions had resulted in the ultimate betrayal of his mother, indeed his entire family, and Michael would have a difficult time dealing with his father on any level, for many years. Despite what people may have thought, Michael somehow expected more from his father.

Though Katherine was clearly angry, and had good reason to be, she was a religious woman who desperately wanted to be a forgiving Jehovah's Witness. She would not confide in anyone about her fury, would not discuss her hurt over what had happened with Cheryl Terrell and Joh'Vonnie. It was just a matter of time before her suppressed rage would erupt, especially when she heard rumours in the summer of 1980 that Joseph was having an affair with Gina Sprague, the woman in whom he had first confided about Joh'Vonnie. Some of her friends felt that Katherine Jackson was much like a time bomb, ticking, ticking, ticking . . . about to explode.

Katherine is Pushed Too Far

As time passed, Gina Sprague began to 'cover' for Joseph Jackson whenever he wanted to visit his daughter. 'Even though the family knew about her, he didn't want to flaunt her,' says Gina. 'Sometimes, they would call and ask for him and, even though I knew he was with Joh'Vonnie and maybe even Cheryl, I would lie and say he was in a meeting, or otherwise unavailable. This went on for months.'

Because Joseph and Gina seemed to share so many secrets, the word was out in his production company that they were having an affair. According to Gina, someone in the office began feeding misinformation to Katherine, who was already suspicious of all of Joseph's female friends and still reeling from the shock of Cheryl and Joh'Vonnie.

One day, the phone rang. Gina picked it up. 'Good afternoon, Joseph Jackson Productions.'

'I want you to quit your job,' said a female voice. 'Do you hear me? Quit, or we're coming to get you.'

'What? Who is this?' Gina asked, panicked.

The caller hung up.

Gina was upset. She went straight to Joseph and told him about the mysterious call.

'Oh, that's just nonsense,' Joseph told her, barely glancing up from his paperwork. 'No one is coming after you, Gina,' said. 'I promise you. You'll be fine.'

The next day, 16 October 1980, at three o'clock in the afternoon, Gina was behind her desk in the reception area of Joseph Jackson Productions, 6255 Sunset Boulevard, Suite 1001 (the same building in which Motown Records was housed), when Randy Jackson, then eighteen, entered. He asked two other employees to leave the office so that he and Gina could be alone. The two employees did as they were told. Randy then also left for a moment, and returned with Janet, fourteen, and with Katherine. A bitter argument about Gina's relationship with Joseph ensued.

Then, according to what Gina told police, matters got out of control and Katherine, Randy and Janet pulled her into a stairwell and assaulted her. When Jim Krieg, an office security guard, heard screams, he ran to investigate and later said he observed Randy holding Gina against the wall while Katherine pummelled her with her purse. Upon seeing the guard, Janet hissed at him, 'Leave, mister. This is a family affair.' He left, as instructed by the fourteen-year-old. Katherine grabbed a gold medallion from Gina's neck. 'This belongs to me,' she said. 'Not you.' When one of Diana Ross's brothers happened by, he asked 'Mother, what are you doing?' [Many of her friends called Katherine 'Mother'.] 'Go about your business, this is a family matter,' she told him, according to what he later recalled. He ran off, stunned. The rest of the police report is graphic in its account of the violence Gina says took place that afternoon.

Joseph was in a meeting with his door closed. When Gina came stumbling back into the office suite, she was crying. He ran out of his private office. 'My God, what happened to you?' he asked her.

Too upset to speak, Gina collapsed on to the floor. Police officers and an ambulance, summoned by Jim Krieg, arrived on the scene. When medics lifted Gina to put her on a stretcher, she let out a piercing scream. Joseph leaned over and whispered urgently in Gina's ear, 'Tell me, who did this to you? Was it some crazy fan?'

'It was Katherine,' Gina said through her tears, her voice lowered so as not to be heard by anyone by Joseph.

Joseph's eyes widened. 'But that can't be true,' he whispered.

'It is true, Joseph,' Gina insisted.

Gina Sprague was taken to Hollywood Presbyterian Medical Center, where she was treated for multiple cuts, bruises, and a minor head injury. Joseph did not visit her there. She was released the next day. Exhausted, she went to bed as soon as she got home. Just as she was about to doze off, she heard loud voices, as her friend refused to allow Joseph into the house. Gina got up and went to the door. 'You can let him in,' she said.

Joseph looked worn out from lack of sleep, sapped of his usual vitality. With some hesitation, Gina's friend left them alone.

'Why, Joseph?' Gina asked him, according to her memory.

'I just can't believe she would do that,' Joseph said, putting his head in his hands. Gina had never seen him this way before; it was a shock. Still, she was furious with him.

'You called the cops, didn't you? Now what's gonna happen?' Joseph asked. 'And you, of all people in my life, know how much I love my family. They're everything to me.'

Gina shook her head in astonishment. 'I was trying to cover up for you so you could visit Joh'Vonnie, and this is what happened to me because of it,' she said, angrily. 'Don't you even care about that?'

'What I care about is my family,' Joseph repeated. He wiped his eyes with the back of his hand. 'I have worked so hard,' he said, reaching into the breast pocket of his jacket. Then, with a shaking hand, he pulled out an envelope and handed it to Gina. Inside, as Gina recalled it, there was a cheque for a large sum of money.

'Take it,' Joseph instructed. 'It's yours.'

She gave him an incredulous look. 'I don't want your money, Joseph,' she said. She crumpled the cheque and threw it at him. 'Leave my house,' she demanded. '*How dare you?*'

Floundering, Joseph walked out of the room, his head drooping. Gina slammed the door behind him.

Michael was stunned by the way his mother, sister and brother had supposedly attacked Gina. He could not reconcile such a violent act with the image of his beloved and gentle mother. He refused to believe it, and insists to this day that it never happened. Most of the family, though, knows that Katherine had reached her limit. 'Basically, Joseph was in love with that girl Gina,' recalled Tim Whitehead. 'And my aunt didn't like it and wanted it to stop. She became extremely upset, and went to the office to see Gina. After so many years, Kate had just reached her breaking point. You can only push a person so far.'

Gina decided not to press charges against the Jacksons. She says that her attorney told her not to bother, 'because those rich people will never be going to jail, and you'll be wasting your time trying to put them there.' Instead, she filed a twenty-one-million-dollar civil lawsuit against Katherine, Janet and Randy.

Katherine, Randy and Janet denied that the incident ever happened. They claimed in their answer to the suit that Gina would never have been injured if she had exercised 'ordinary care on her behalf', which seemed . . . odd.

In the end, Gina and Joseph negotiated an out-of-court settlement, the details of which she is not at liberty to disclose. 'I felt sorry for them,' she concludes. 'I loved that family. I know that I was the proverbial straw that broke the camel's back, but like I told Katherine in court, next time, kick *his* ass. Not mine.'

At this time, the autumn of 1980, Michael supervised a music video of the Jacksons' song 'Can You Feel It?'. Ironically, considering what was going on at home with Gina Sprague, the song, written by Michael and Randy, is an anthem to loving human relations. In the video, the brothers appear as superhuman behemoths hoisting a colourful rainbow to light the heavens. They sprinkle stardust upon the earth, which causes small children of all races and colours to beam at them with appreciation. Bathed in rainbow hues, the youngsters gaze up in wonder at Michael and his brothers. In return, the Jacksons smile down upon the children benevolently; Michael with the biggest smile of all.

'It's a nice place Michael comes from,' Steven Spielberg has observed. 'I wish we could all spend some time in his world.'

Michael also became close to actress Jane Fonda, at this time forty-two, about twenty years Michael's senior, who would try to encourage him to see his mother in a more human light. He and Jane met in 1980 at a press function in Los Angeles. The two discussed their lives, both having come from show-business families, and quickly became close. Some people in Michael's world have speculated that the reason he gravitated towards powerful women who seem self-sufficient, such as Diana Ross and, later, Elizabeth Taylor, was because he had felt so helpless while watching his mother being abused by Joseph. He viewed Katherine as weak and victimized, therefore he searched for a substitute mother, a strong woman he could emulate and respect. It's as good a theory as any other; who knows? Maybe he just likes to hang out with divas.

Jane's Fonda's father, legendary actor Henry Fonda, had been an emotionally distant, difficult man, much like Michael's father, Joseph. She understood Michael's anger at the way Joseph treated his wife, Katherine, had similarly heated emotions about her own parents, and had worked for years to resolve them. She invited Michael to stay with her in her cabin on a New England lake as she and her father, along with veteran actress, Katharine Hepburn, filmed *On Golden Pond*. 'In some ways,' Jane Fonda recalled, 'Michael reminded me of the walking wounded, an extremely fragile person.'

As Michael sat with Katharine Hepburn with a tape-recorder, she shared anecdotes about her life. 'Every one included some kind of message for Michael,' said Jane, 'about the way he might want to handle fame, about the way he might want to deal with his life. They became good friends. He just thought she was fascinating.'

While in New England, Michael also befriended Henry Fonda.

He and Jane, though, were the closest. As he told me, 'We would go out on the water together in a row boat and just talk, talk and talk . . . you name it: politics, philosophers, racism, Vietnam, acting, all kinds of things.'

Once, Michael and Jane were taking a drive – Jane was behind the wheel – and they were discussing possible film projects for him. 'God, Michael, I wish I could find a movie I could produce for you,' she said, wistfully. Suddenly, an idea occurred to her. 'I know what you've got to do,' she said. '*Peter Pan*! That's it!'

Tears began to well in Michael's eyes. He wanted to know why she would suggest that character. She told him that, in her mind's eye, he really was Peter Pan, the symbol of youth, joy and freedom.

Michael began to weep. 'You know all over the walls of my room are pictures of Peter Pan. I totally identify with Peter Pan,' he said, wiping his eyes, 'the lost boy of Never-Never Land.'

When the subject of Katherine came up between them during one conversation, Michael confided in Jane about the Gina Sprague incident. According to Bernice Littman, who was a Beverly Hills friend of Jane Fonda's and worked for her as a personal assistant at this time, 'Jane thought the whole [Katherine vs. Gina.] thing was tragic, and that Michael was too fragile to handle it. She also felt badly for Michael's mother and wondered just how far a woman has to be pushed before she reacts in such a way. She spent a lot of time trying connect with him, really worked at it, took it on as a true concern in her life. "I feel a responsibility to him," she told me, "just from one human being to another. He so needs love." "You have to stop trying to find strength in other people," she told him one day during one of their talks. He was at her home in the library with her; I was in the outer office. "Your mother has flaws, Michael, just as we all do. But you're an adult, now," she said. "Why not let your mother be who she is, and find your own strength, within?" I don't think Michael could understand what she was saying. "Can you help me?" he asked her. "I'm so miserable. I'm having a terrible life." They embraced. "You're having a wonderful life, Michael," she said. "These are just hard years, but it'll get better. I promise."

'Michael sobbed like a baby,' said Bernice. 'So did I. I stood outside of the library and just cried. It was so sad. He was so sad. It was as if he was an alien, just visiting, from another world.'

Meanwhile, in the real world, a CBS Records executive telephoned Michael to ask him how he should handle the press, who had begun asking questions about his mother.

'What do you mean? Michael wondered.

'The Gina Sprague incident.'

'Who's she?' Michael asked, snappishly.

'The woman who got into the disagreement with your mother, Randy and Janet.'

'That never happened,' Michael said, quickly.

'But—'

'I'm sorry,' Michael concluded, 'but I have to go, now.'

With that, he hung up the phone. Michael was withdrawing deeper into his fantasy world, a place where such things as his mother possibly assaulting his father's girlfriend would never occur. He was becoming more distant, harder to reach. How long would it be before no one, not even someone like Jane Fonda, would be able to connect with him? It would simply be too painful for him to allow anyone to get that close.

PART FIVE

The First 'Nose Job' . . . and Other Freedoms

Despite the inroads he had made towards independence from his family, by 1981, Michael Jackson still felt that his life was spinning out of control. When he was onstage, performing, he could transform himself into the desirable person of his dreams: a sexy, outgoing, confident person who exerted total control over himself and his audience. But offstage was another story. When he looked in the mirror, he saw a person he didn't like very much, a person who still allowed himself to be controlled by other people, whose talent was respected but whose opinions didn't matter. He'd begun to work on some of that with John Branca, but what could he do about the physical appearance of the man in the mirror? He'd never felt handsome, that's for certain, and by 1981 he had a litany of personal complaints, all adding to his deep insecurity.

Michael considered rhinoplasty surgery, popularly known as 'a nose job', as a possibility to thin out his wide nose. Since about the age of thirteen, he'd always been fixated on the size of his nose, and his brothers had only made matters worse with their nickname for him: Big Nose. Wide, flat noses were a Jackson family trait, inherited from Joseph. Michael had been threatening to have the surgery for years, but he was too afraid actually to go through with it. However, in the spring of 1979, he tripped during a complicated dance routine, fell onstage . . . and broke his nose. Fate had intervened; he had no choice. He flew back to Los Angeles and had his first rhinoplasty.

Gina Sprague recalled, 'Joseph told me he doubted that Michael would ever have had the nose job if he didn't have to do it. That was the first. No one ever dreamed what it would lead to in the future. After the bandages came off, Michael liked what he saw.'

The result of that first surgery is the nose seen on the cover of Michael's *Off the Wall* album, one just a bit smaller than the one with which he was born. Indeed, Michael's face had been surgically transformed, confirming the notion for him that his appearance was one thing over which he could absolutely exert control if he wanted to do so. However, afterwards Michael complained of some breathing problems, and trouble singing. He was then referred to Dr Steven Hoefflin, who would suggest a second surgery. Hoefflin would perform that surgery, and others that Michael would eventually have on his face.

His friend, Jane Fonda was sufficiently distressed enough about Michael's new plastic surgery to approach him about it. She was perceptive enough to speculate that the real reason for the operations on his nose was not so that he could look like Diana Ross – as rumoured – but, so that he would *not* end up looking like his father, Joseph. She was a different kind of friend for Michael, a person with more on her mind than just show business. Thoughtful and direct, she was the only person in his life who actually confronted Michael about his surgeries. 'I want you to stop now,' she told Michael, according to a later recollection. 'No more. Promise me you won't go too far with this thing. Love yourself the way you are, for who you are.'

'I'll try,' Michael promised.

'And stand up straight,' she told him, as if his school teacher. 'You must look like you are somebody important, and that you understand what you're doing and why you are here. If you at least *look* self-confident, maybe you won't be so shy.'

'Yes, Jane.'

But Michael obviously was *not* self-confident. By 1980, he had his new nose, but he was still desperately unhappy. 'Even at home, I'm lonely,' he said. 'I sit in my room sometimes and cry. It's so hard to make friends, and there are some things you can't talk to your parents or family about. I sometimes walk around the neighbour-hood at night, just hoping to find someone to talk to. But I just end up coming home.' The notion of Michael Jackson – a world-renowned superstar – walking around his Encino neighbourhood in search of someone to talk to is startling. Imagine the depth of his despair, his loneliness.

The fact that his face was still broken out with acne did not help matters. Michael had read that the types of greasy foods he enjoyed contributed to the problem. Jermaine, who also had acne, became a vegetarian in order to solve the problem. It worked. Michael decided that he would do the same. One unexpected consequence of the diet was that he lost weight. Michael was certainly not fat, obviously, but he still had 'baby fat' around his waist, and his face was full. He longed to be slimmer, to have what he called 'a dancer's body'. In time, his figure would become more streamlined and the roundness in his face would disappear. His acne would also clear up. Many people would think that Michael had 'cheek implant' surgery in 1980, but the new, clearly defined lines of his face were actually brought about by the gradual weight loss he had experienced after becoming a vegetarian, and also by the natural aging process.

It was John Branca's suggestion that, if Michael wanted to forge some independence he might want to consider purchasing his own real estate. He was twenty-two. Why did he have to live at home? The idea of moving away from Joseph was exhilarating for Michael, even though he didn't want to leave Katherine. Still, he thought he might try it. Therefore, in February of 1981, Michael bought a three-bedroom, three-bathroom condominium at 5420 Lindley Avenue in Encino for $210,000. He paid $175,000 in cash. The balance – $35,000 – came from Katherine. In exchange, Michael gave her equity in the condominium as sole and separate property, meaning she did not have to share it with Joseph as community property. It was his way of giving her a bit of freedom, as well. Certainly, Michael didn't need her to contribute $35,000. No doubt, she wanted to pay for the possibility of having her own freedom, just like her son. 'Now, if you can't stand him for another second,' Michael said, speaking of Joseph, 'you can move here. It will be great. We could live here together, imagine that! And without *him*.'

In the end, Michael could not go through with it; he couldn't move out, especially since Katherine didn't want to go, either. 'I just don't feel it's time for me to move away from home yet,' he said. 'If I moved out now, I'd die of loneliness. Most people who move out go to discos every night. They party every night. They invite friends over, and I don't do any of those things.' (In a couple of years, Michael would move into the condominium temporarily, along with other family members, when the Encino home was remodelled. He still owns the condominium today; it has been used as a haven for his brothers when they have had marital difficulties.)

In the spring of 1981, plans were being finalized for The Jacksons to embark on a thirty-nine-city concert tour of the United States to support their new album, called *Triumph*. Michael didn't want to go. One problem he had with touring concerned the enormous amount of preparation and work involved. Then when it was over, it was over – unlike a movie or a video, which is timeless and lasting. 'What's so sad about the whole thing is that you don't capture the moment,' he told me of live performances. 'Look at how many great actors or entertainers have been lost to the world because they did a performance one night and that was it. With film, you capture it, it's shown all over the world, and it's there for ever. Spencer Tracy will always be young in *Captains Courageous*, and I can learn and be stimulated by his performance.

'So much is lost in live theatre. Or vaudeville. Do you know how much I could have learned by watching all of those entertainers? When I perform, I feel like I'm giving a whole lot but for nothing. I like to capture things and hold them and share them with the world.'

He really had no choice, however. His family wanted him to go on the road with them – the tour was projected to gross millions of dollars for them – the record label had also insisted upon a tour . . . so there would be a tour. Michael just hoped that it would, in some way, unite the family after such difficult times at home. He was frustrated and upset, but he would force himself along. Still, some would notice a cold implacability on his face when with the family at rehearsals. He seemed removed from the proceedings, not involved, not interested.

Before embarking on the Triumph tour, Michael underwent the second rhinoplasty surgery recommended by Dr Steven Hoefflin. 'He didn't tell his family he was doing it,' said Marcus Phillips. 'He just did it. He came home all black and blue and bandaged, and Katherine said, "Michael, what in the world happened to you?" She must have thought he'd been beaten up. "Did you break your nose again?" she asked. He told her he hadn't, that his doctor recommended a second operation. Then, he went to his bedroom and stayed there for a week, coming down to the kitchen every now and then for some vegetables.

'One thing I know to be true is that Michael was elated about the fact that with the second nose job he looked less like his father,' Marcus Phillips said. 'That appealed to him very much. If he couldn't erase Joseph from his life, at least he could erase him from the reflection in the mirror. Already, he was talking about having a third nose job.'

Even though Michael never discussed his surgery with anyone, he was crying out for help, becoming obsessed by the appearance of the man in the mirror, and a dangerous pattern was beginning to emerge.

In June 1981, Michael and Quincy Jones began work on a story-telling record book of Steven Spielberg's film, *E.T.* Michael would also be featured as vocalist on one song, 'Someone in the Dark', written by Alan and Marilyn Bergman. Michael was so enchanted by the story of *E.T.* that he couldn't wait to meet the animated extra-terrestrial 'actor' when a publicity photo session was arranged. 'He grabbed me, he put his arms around me,' Michael said of the animatronic robot, his face filled with child-like wonder. 'He was so real that I was talking to him. I kissed him before I left. The next day, I missed him.'

Later in the month, Michael went into the studio with Diana Ross to produce a song for her called 'Muscles' – named after his pet snake. Michael was ecstatic about the opportunity to produce a record for his idol. Some claimed that the reason Michael had his plastic surgery was in order to look more like Miss Ross. However, as one Jackson confidant put it, 'If Michael Jackson wanted to look like Diana Ross, believe me, he had the millions to look *exactly* like Diana Ross. That was never his intention. However, that's not to say that he wasn't tickled that people thought he resembled her. "Do you really think I do?" he would ask, tilting his head in a pose. "Because if I do, wow! How amazing would *that* be." '

At this time, Diana had left Motown and was recording her second album for RCA, *Silk Electric*. The album was shaping up to be a disaster and she needed something outstanding on the collection, which is why she contacted Michael. 'I was coming back from England, working on Paul McCartney's album, zooming along on the Concorde, and this song popped into my head,' Michael recalled.

'I said, "Hey, that's perfect for Diana." I didn't have a tape recorder or anything, so I had to suffer for like three hours. Soon as I got home, I whipped that baby on tape.'

Diana has said that Michael seemed intimidated by her while the two of them worked together in the studio. He couldn't bring himself to direct her.

'You're the man,' Diana insisted, an admiring look in her eyes. 'You're the boss on this one.' Diana wanted Michael to take control of the recording session, but it was difficult for him. 'In the end, the song just sort of produced itself,' said a friend of Diana's. The kinky lyrics of 'Muscles' extol the joys of a man's muscles 'all over your body'. 'I don't know whether it's supposed to be Michael's fantasy or mine,' Diana said when it was finally released.

Either way, it was a Top Ten record for Diana Ross.

The Triumph tour began in Memphis, Tennessee, on 9 July 1981, and ended with a record-breaking, sell-out, four-night engagement at the Los Angeles Forum. The biggest numbers of the show were always Michael's solo songs from the *Off the Wall* album. There were also special effects arranged by magician Doug Henning: Michael seemed to disappear into a puff of smoke after performing 'Don't Stop 'Til You Get Enough'. Offstage, Michael also seemed to want to disappear, rarely socializing with his brothers or the rest of the entourage. 'This is my last tour,' he promised anyone who asked. 'I will *never* do this again. Ever.'

Being on the road with him made the Jackson brothers realize how far Michael had distanced himself from them. He started talking to the press about the possibility of a solo career. 'I think that will happen gracefully in the future,' he told Paul Grein of *Billboard*. 'I think the public will ask for it. That's definitely going to happen.'

It was not what his brothers wanted to hear. It didn't help them feel any more secure when Michael began involving himself more in the business end of the show. For instance, one day he was scheduled to rehearse with the group when someone handed him a copy of the contract for the trucks that were to carry equipment for the tour. Michael glanced at it and said, 'Wait, I need to check something with my lawyer.'

'That can wait, Michael,' Jackie said, bristling with anger. 'This rehearsal is important.'

Michael ignored his older brother's remark, left the stage area and found a telephone. He called John Branca. 'He wanted me to explain a paragraph that dealt with what happened if the truck broke down, if it had a flat tyre, or the road washed out,' John recalled. 'I explained the paragraph. He asked a couple of questions and said, "Okay, I understand." He was all about details, always with the details, wanting to know everything. He used to say, "It's important that I *know*."'

Michael then returned to the stage, signed the contract, and went back to work.

Around this time Michael finally learned to drive so he could leave the estate when it became too difficult for him there. Singer Mickey Free (formerly of the group Shalamar) remembered his first meeting with Michael in the fall of 1981. 'I was signed to Diana Ross's management company at that time. She was staying at the Beverly Hills Hotel and asked me if I wanted to come down to her bungalow and meet Michael. Well, who wouldn't?' he recalled. 'So I had dinner with Michael, Diana and Gene [Simmons of Kiss, Diana's boyfriend at the time]. I was freaking out because I always wanted to meet Michael, and he was so nice. So it came time for me to go home. Diana's car had brought me there, and she said, Okay, I'll call the driver to come and get you.' Michael very softly said, "Oh, that's okay, I'll take Mickey home."'

Diana and Gene were astonished. 'Are you sure you want to do this, Michael?' Diana asked him. 'Are you sure you can handle it?'

'Yeah, I can do it, Diana,' Michael said, confidently.

Mickey got into Michael's Silver Shadow Rolls-Royce, and the two sped off down the driveway in front of the Beverly Hills Hotel. 'Be careful,' Diana hollered after them. 'Don't drive too fast, Michael.'

When they got to Mickey's apartment building about fifteen minutes later, Michael drove around the block a few times before sheepishly confessing, 'You know what? I can drive this thing, but I don't know how to parallel park it. Can you park for me?' Michael stopped the car in the middle of the road and the two traded seats.

'I rode around the block ten times to find a parking place so people could see me driving Michael Jackson around in his fabulous car,' Mickey recalled.

An Indirect Conversation

By the fall of 1981, despite CBS Records' best efforts to keep the Jackson family's domestic turmoil a secret, most industry insiders were aware of what had happened between Katherine and Gina because of the public filings of the lawsuit litigation. Michael had made it clear that he did not want to have to face any reporters, because he was afraid that he might be asked to comment on the matter. However, the press grind to promote *Triumph* would continue, Michael's wishes notwithstanding.

Michael Jackson, who had just turned twenty-three, was a contradictory figure. He was decisive and determined, as he had proved a few times along the way, but he was also vulnerable and confused. Though he was beginning to seize control of his career, he was still reluctant to sever ties with his family. 'I'd die if I were alone,' he told me in a telephone interview on his birthday. He was unable to leave the womb, to move out of the house. 'No way,' he said. 'I could never leave here.'

Instead of growing up, Michael actually seemed to be regressing – buying toys, playing childlike games and, for the first time, actually surrounding himself with children. Young fans who gathered at the gates of the estate to catch a glimpse of a Jackson coming or going were now being invited to spend time in the inner-sanctum with Michael. It was odd behaviour. Jackie now called him a 'Man-Child', explaining, 'He's a man, but still a kid, a wonderful combination.' When asked about the possibility of having his own children, Michael shook his head, no. He'd like to raise a child, he said, but it would be one whom he would adopt, 'in the far future'. He would not procreate, he said. 'I don't have to bring my own into the world,' he said uneasily. 'It's not necessary for me to do that.'

He continued, 'One of my favourite pastimes is being with children – talking to them, playing with them in the grass. They're one of the main reasons I do what I do. They know everything that people are trying to find out, they know so many secrets, but it's hard for them to get it out. I can recognize that and learn from it. They say things that astound you. They go through a brilliant, genius stage. But then, when they become a certain age . . .' Michael paused. 'When they get to a certain age, they lose it.'

I was scheduled to interview this extraordinary 'Man-Child' on 3 October 1981, an encounter that was arranged by a publicist at Epic. In advance, I was warned not to mention Gina Sprague or ask questions about 'the incident' or the state of Michael's parents' marriage.

I was at my desk compiling a list of questions when the telephone rang. It was Michael. He got to the point, quickly. 'There's a certain way I want to do this interview,' he told me.

'Sure thing, Michael. Whatever you like.'

'Well,' he began slowly. 'I'd like for Janet to help.'

'Help?'

'Yes. See, Janet is going to sit in on our interview,' he told me. 'You'll ask *her* the questions, and then *she'll* ask *me*. Then, see, I'll give *her* the answers, and then she'll give them to *you*. How does that sound?'

'It sounds strange, Michael. I don't even think I understand it. Could you explain that to me, again?'

He repeated the scenario and said that it was the only way he would consent to the interview. 'So, I hope you understand,' he said, briskly. 'Okay, bye.'

'Wait,' I said. 'I don't get it, Michael. You're giving me an interview, but you're not talking to me? What kind of madness is that?'

'It might seem like madness to you,' he said. 'But there are reasons for the things I do. You just have to try to understand. If you're willing to do it my way, I'll see you tomorrow. Okay? Bye, now.'

I wondered if I could conduct an interview in that manner. Did it make any sense? Of course, I had to try. How could I turn down the opportunity to engage in, no doubt, the strangest interview I'd ever had with Michael, or with anyone else, for that matter.

The next day, I arrived at the Encino home in time for the interview. 'Sure glad you could make it,' Michael said as we shook hands. He was wearing a black T-shirt and matching jeans. His feet were bare. I noticed that his nose was thinner and more defined than it had been the last time I saw him, which was about six months earlier backstage at a Patti Labelle concert in Hollywood. His falsetto whisper of a voice seemed even softer than it had been at that time.

After Michael and I exchanged pleasantries in the living room, Janet, age fifteen, walked in wearing a red leather miniskirt, black boots, and a plaid sweater. She did not greet me. Rather, she sat at Michael's side in a robotic fashion, not even acknowledging his presence.

Michael introduced me to her, as if we had never met. (Of course, we had.) We shook hands, but she never made eye contact with me. I sat opposite them.

'Now, you'll do the interview the way you promised, won't you?' he asked.

When I said that I hadn't 'promised' anything, he rose from his chair. 'Well, then, we can't do the interview,' he said, his words clipped.

'Wait,' I told him, motioning for him to be seated. 'Let's try it. Let's start with the new album, *Triumph*. How do you feel about it?'

Michael pinned me with his dark eyes and nodded toward his sister. I redirected my question. 'Janet, would you please ask him how he feels about the album.'

Janet turned to Michael. 'He wants to know how you feel about the album,' she said.

'Tell him I'm very happy with it,' Michael said, his tone relaxed. 'Working with my brothers again was an incredible experience for me. It was,' he stopped, searching for the word, 'magical,' he concluded.

Janet nodded her head and turned to me. 'He told me to tell you that he's very happy with the album,' she repeated. 'And that working with his brothers was an incredible experience for him.'

There was a pause.

'You forgot the part about it being magical,' Michael said to her, seeming peeved at her for not doing her job properly.

'Oh, yes.' Janet looked at me with apologetic, brown eyes. 'He said it was magical.'

'Magical?' I asked.

'Yes. *Magical.*'

As I tried to think of another question for Janet to ask him, I scrutinized Michael carefully for the first time that day. It suddenly struck me that he was wearing makeup; his brows and lashes were darkened with mascara, his eyelids coated with soft pink shadow. Rouge emphasized his cheekbones and . . . was that lipstick? Yes, I decided, scarlet lipstick. Today, the notion of Michael Jackson wearing makeup in day-to-day living (as opposed to onstage or on camera, where practically all men in show business wear it) is certainly not novel. Back in 1981, though, it would never have occurred to anyone that Michael would wear makeup in his home for an interview. It was applied subtly and with great care. He looked exotic.

The 'interview' went on for about thirty more awkward minutes. Occasionally, Janet would inject a comment of her own, in an effort, it seemed to me, to keep the conversation alive. 'Michael, remember when that girl got upset because she had heard you had a sex change?' she said to him. 'Do you remember what happened to her? She got so upset, she jumped right out a window. I think she died,' Janet said. 'Poor thing.'

Michael looked into space, blankly.

Finally I decided that I'd had enough of the odd exchange and said I'd rather not continue with the interview. 'But why not?' Michael wanted to know. 'Wait. Janet will tell you what happened when I visited Katharine Hepburn last month,' he offered. 'It's a good story.'

'I'd rather *you* tell me, Michael,' I pressed.

'Well, I can't . . .'

There was a small silence between us.

'Then, look, just forget it,' I said. 'Let's just forget the whole thing. Michael.'

'Okay, cool,' he said. Smiling somewhat ruefully, he rose. 'Nice to see you again,' he remarked, not connecting with my frustration. 'Let's do this again, sometime.' Then, he left the room. Janet threw me a look and extended her hands at me, palms up, as if to exclaim, Now, look what you've done.

Once alone in the Jacksons' living room, I tried to figure out what had just occurred. As I was putting my tape recorder and notes in my brief case, Katherine walked in. She looked disheartened. 'Did you just interview Michael,' she asked. 'Please be nice to him. The press is so mean these days.' She shook her head, at a loss. 'I don't know what to tell you,' she said. She slumped into the chair opposite me, practically speechless with fatigue. It was disconcerting. In the past, she always had such dignity and poise.

'I'm worried about him,' she said, finally looking at me. Her eyes were full of warmth and concern. 'There's so much pressure, things are so . . . difficult.' When she realized she was, perhaps, saying too much, she stopped herself. 'Would you let yourself out?' she asked me, abruptly.

I had a sinking feeling in my stomach as I walked out the front door. What is going on in this household? I wondered. While walking down the driveway, I looked up at the mansion and saw a face peering out from one of the upstairs windows. It was Michael. When he realized that I had spotted him, he ducked out of sight.

The next morning, I received a telephone call from Joseph. Just before I had pulled out of the Jackson estate's gates, I had seen him in the driveway. I stopped to tell him what had happened. His cocoa-coloured, weather-beaten face broke into a wide grin. He shrugged his shoulders, 'Well, that's my boy,' he said. Now, on the telephone, he could not have been more apologetic. 'I'm sorry about that, man,' he told me. 'I was thinking about it, and I wanted to explain.'

According to Joseph, Michael had told his record company that he no longer sought direct contact with the media for fear of questions about 'that girl, you know, the one we got that problem with.' I knew he was referring to Gina Sprague. 'Plus some other stuff that's going on,' Joseph continued. 'But when he said he didn't want to do no interviews, the label [Epic executives] forced him to. Me, too. I told him he needs to talk to you and the other guys in the press. It's the right thing to do,' Joseph said. 'So, what can I say? He did it his way. Sorry. Guess he wanted some control in his life, huh?'

'Guess so, Mr Jackson,' I said. We spoke for about fifteen

minutes. He seemed fine, as if nothing unusual was going on in his life. 'Come on by sometime and do a story on LaToya,' he told me. 'We got some plans for her. Just wait till you see what we're going to do. Girl's gonna be a big star. Huge, I'm tellin' ya. *Huge*.'

When I hung up, I thought about Joseph's explanation. Michael's tactic might have been ludicrous, I thought, but it's true that desperate people take desperate measures to make a point . . . especially when nobody will listen. I felt a grudging admiration for the way Michael had gotten what he wanted. He had manipulated the situation in order to make a mockery of the promised interview. I never wrote about the episode. Instead, I cancelled the feature. Michael got what he wanted: no story.

Katherine Tells Joseph to 'Get Out!'

By the summer of 1982, Katherine Jackson simply couldn't take any more of Joseph's unkind behaviour. Whatever had happened with Gina Sprague, it had certainly been a nasty bit of business. Joseph wouldn't learn, however; either his appetite for women was insatiable or he simply couldn't fill whatever emptiness he felt in his heart. Looking back on it now, it seems he may have been inflicting his own pain on Katherine to make her identify with him, so lonely and marginalized did he feel in the family. Whatever his hidden motivation – and maybe even he didn't understand it – Katherine suspected he was having another affair.

One day, after a series of 'hang-ups' – when she answered the phone there would be no one on the other end – Katherine walked into the kitchen to tell Joseph that she was leaving the estate to go shopping. He kissed her goodbye, on the top of the head. As she walked down the driveway, the telephone rang again, just as she suspected it might. She calmly walked into the guest house and, once there, took a deep breath and picked up the extension. She listened in as Joseph spoke to the woman with whom he was apparently having a romantic relationship. He sounded sweet, happy. Katherine later recalled her heart tightening in her chest. She felt unsteady and breathless, as if she'd been punched in the stomach.

Once the conversation was over, Katherine's steps carried her down the driveway and back into the front door of her home. She found Joseph in the living room, his feet up on the couch, as if he hadn't a care in the world. Holding him with her eyes for a moment, she couldn't believe, as she would later tell it, that he would do this to her . . . again. She cleared her throat, loudly.

'Oh. Hi, Kate. I thought you were gone,' he said, springing to his feet.

'I'll just bet you did,' she responded. 'I heard your conversation with your little *girlfriend*,' she remarked, spitting out the words. 'You bastard, you.'

Then, she let him have it. She pummelled him with her fists. She pulled his hair. She threw a vase at him. When he ducked, she lunged for him, again. There was no stopping her. 'I don't want you any more, Joseph,' she screamed at him. 'I don't *need you*, any more. I want you out of this house. You're nothing to me, now.'

Joseph was floored, at least for a moment. 'Okay, okay,' he said, his hands up in defence. 'Not even going to give me a chance to explain, huh?' he asked. Now, his tone was even, well-controlled. It seemed as if he was trying to act unconcerned. How upsetting, Katherine would later say, for him to act as if he didn't have enough invested in the moment to even be troubled by it.

'Doesn't anything ever get to you?' she asked, angrily.

'Of course,' he said, sadly. 'You did, Katie. When I first fell in love with you.'

'*Get out!*'

As he turned to walk out of the room, a shaking Katherine Jackson grabbed a silver-framed photograph of the two of them from a table and hurled it to the floor with everything she had in her. She was filled with such contempt for Joseph, she didn't even know what she was doing. The glass smashed to smithereens, a fitting metaphor for her life.

The next day, 19 August 1982, Katherine quietly filed for divorce. Her action got practically no press coverage. She was discreet, not wanting to jeopardize the family's image with a public and volatile divorce. In her petition, she said:

'Approximately one year ago, Joseph told me that we were running short of money. I asked him questions about the business and he told me to "stay out of the business". I am informed and believe that within the last year, Joseph has spent in excess of $50,000 on a young woman and has purchased for her parcels of real property from our community funds. I am fearful that unless restrained by an order of this court, Joseph will continue to dissipate community funds and transfer community funds in jeopardy of my community property rights.'

Though Katherine had only a vague idea of exactly how much community property existed, she wanted to keep Joseph from transferring or otherwise disposing of any of it. The property she was aware of included her interest in the Encino home, furniture, furnishings, and other personal property, her interest in Joseph Jackson Productions and in various bank accounts. She made a list of the rest of the community assets: a 1979 Mercedes-Benz (colour not indicated in legal documents), a 1971 blue-grey Mercedes-Benz, a 1971 white Rolls-Royce, a 1978 brown Mercedes-Benz, a 1971 blue Rolls-Royce, a 1974 G.M.C. motor home, a 1981 Toyota truck, a 1980 white Cadillac limousine, a 1978 Ford van, two boats (day cruisers) with trailers, and a Keogh financial plan.

There was only one snag in Katherine's declaration of independence. Jerome Howard, who would become her business manager in 1988, recalled, 'She told me that after she filed for divorce, she naturally expected Joseph to move out of the house. However, he refused to leave. So what could she do?'

'This is my house, too,' Joseph told Katherine, defiantly. 'You're my wife, I love you, and it's going to stay that way.'

Michael could not remain neutral and uninvolved. 'You have to kick him out,' he told his mother. 'Or call the police. Or get a restraining order. But he can't stay here just because he wants to.'

Katherine would not discuss the matter with Michael, or any of her children. This was her cross to bear, not theirs.

'This is killing me,' Michael told his oldest sister, Rebbie, according to her memory. 'I will never get married. I will never trust a person in that way. I couldn't bear to go through this again.'

'But, Michael, this is their life, not yours,' she said in her most compassionate voice. 'You will live your life differently. Trust me.'

'But how do you know that?' Michael asked, his eyes red from crying. 'Mother never planned any of this for herself, did she?'

'No, I'm sure she didn't,' Rebbie said, embracing him. 'I'm sure she didn't.'

Did Michael Get His Way?

In August 1982, Michael began work with Quincy Jones on a new album at Westlake Studios in Los Angeles. The album would be entitled *Thriller* with a budget of about $750,000 to produce, and nine songs carefully selected by Michael and Quincy from about three hundred. The sessions went well; Michael was satisfied with the work. However, once they played back the album – the 'master pressing', as the final mix was called – it didn't sound as good as Michael thought it should. In fact, to his ears, it sounded terrible. He was crushed. Never one to shy away from a good old-fashioned 'scene', Michael ran from the studio, sobbing.

To solve the problem, each song had to be remixed, bringing up the level of some orchestration and voices and toning down others. It was time-consuming, tedious work at the rate of two songs a week, but in the end it proved to be worth the effort. Quincy Jones along with one of Michael's managers, Ron Weisner, and his attorney, John Branca, sat with Michael in the Westlake Studio as he listened to a playback of the album. To Michael the music now sounded terrific. He was optimistic, bobbing his head to the rhythm and smiling broadly as each cut played.

'Mike, you know, the record market is off right now,' Ron Weisner told him as the title track, 'Thriller', blared from the speakers. He had to almost shout to be heard above it.

'Yeah, Mike,' Quincy agreed. 'You can't expect to do with this one what you did with *Off the Wall*.'

'These days, two million is a hot album,' Ron added.

'Yeah, it's a tough market. Nobody's having hits,' Quincy said.

'Turn it down,' Michael shouted out at the engineer. 'I said, *turn it down.*' His smile was now gone. 'What's the matter with you guys?' he wanted to know. 'How can you say that to me? You're wrong. You are dead wrong.'

'But, Michael—' Quincy began.

'Look, don't even talk to me,' Michael said, turning away from Quincy. 'I've had it with you, Quincy. Don't ever tell me anything like that again,' he added, angrily. 'What kind of attitude is *that* to have?'

John Branca sat in a corner and watched the scene. A wry smile touched his mouth; he'd been around Michael enough to know how this scene would climax.

'Goodbye,' Michael announced as he stormed out of the studio.

By the next day, Michael had worked himself into a fully fledged fury. He telephoned John Branca and told him how angry he had been at Ron and Quincy for predicting that *Thriller* would 'only' sell two million copies.

'I know,' John recalls saying. 'Don't listen to those guys, Mike. You're the one who knows. They don't know.'

'But Quincy should know,' Michael said.

'Well, maybe not this time,' John told him. 'You're the man. Call Walter [Yetnikoff] and he'll tell you the same thing.'

'No, you call him,' Michael said. 'And tell him this. Tell him the record is *cancelled*, John. It's over. I ain't even submitting it to CBS.'

'But Mike—'

'No, John. If Quincy and Ron don't have faith in it, then forget it,' Michael said. 'I'm not even going to let the album come out. *Thriller* is gonna be shelved for ever,' he said. 'I'd rather it go unheard than see it not get the attention it deserves.'

'But, Mike—'

'Let me tell you something,' Michael said, cutting him off. 'There are winners in this life, Branca, and there are losers.' Before John had a chance to respond, Michael hung up.

Ten minutes later, John telephoned Michael to tell him that he had passed on the message to Walter Yetnikoff and – no big surprise – Walter wanted to talk to Michael. He wanted Michael to call him. 'What? No way,' Michael said. 'Tell him to call me.'

'But, Mike—'

'*Tell him to call me.*' Michael hung up.

Whereas most of the CBS artists were intimidated by Walter Yetnikoff, Michael was not at all cowed by him. After all, he'd dealt with Berry Gordy, one on one. Walter called, as instructed.

According to Walter's memory, when Michael told him what had occurred at the studio, he tried to calm him down. 'What the hell do they know?' he said of Quincy and Ron. '*You're* the superstar, not them. Jesus, Michael. We trust *you*. Not Quincy, all due respect to the guy. And certainly not one of your managers. You're the superstar.'

'You think?' Michael asked, coyly,

'Absolutely.'

'So you agree?'

'Of course.'

'Okay,' Michael decided. 'Then it can come out.'

Michael Jackson had created a melodrama surrounding the completion of *Thriller*, there was little doubt of that. Would he really have cancelled the release of the album simply because Quincy had predicted it would only sell two million copies? Perhaps. However, the more likely scenario is that Michael was just trying to, as they might have said in the Jackson family, 'get his way'. The manner in which he handled the situation couldn't exactly be described as 'artful' or 'strategic'. It was more like the dynamics of a family flare-up – one party has a tantrum, just as people in big families often do with one another . . . then pushes and pushes and pushes until he gets his way, and until he feels validated. Such tactics would work for Michael many times in the future. Obviously, there is no road map to success. Few entertainers ever reach a goal of stardom at all, and if one finds a way to go about it, he has to be given credit. It would seem that Michael Jackson had certainly found a way that worked for him.

Thriller is a . . . Thriller

On 1 December 1982, *Thriller* was released to a market of seasonal shoppers. It seems ironic, considering the impact *Thriller* would have on the record industry, that when CBS released the album's first single (in October, a little over a month before the issuance of the album) many observers thought *Thriller* would be a disappointment. The auspicious pairing of Michael Jackson and Paul McCartney for the mid-tempo 'The Girl is Mine' (which the singers co-wrote while watching cartoons) appeared to be of greater interest than the song itself which, while cute, was lacking in substance. Many in both the black and white music communities felt that Michael and Quincy Jones had gone too far in consciously tailoring a record for a white, pop audience. If this first single was an indication of what else would be found on *Thriller*, Michael seemed to be in big trouble.

And then came 'Billie Jean'.

Dark and sparse by Quincy Jones production standards, 'Billie Jean' prowled in rhythm like a predatory animal. It's a disturbing song Michael wrote about a girl accusing him of fathering her child. Joseph Jackson's extramarital affairs and his daughter, Joh'Vonnie, must have come to mind when Michael wrote the lyrics. However, there was another experience Michael had, which was the catalyst for 'Billie Jean'.

In 1981 a female fan wrote Michael a letter to inform him that he was the father of her baby. She enclosed photographs of herself – a young, attractive, black woman in her late teens whom he had never met – and of the infant. Michael, who often received letters of this nature, ignored it as he does the others. This teenager, however, was more persistent than the rest. She loved Michael, she claimed, and longed to be with him. She wrote that she could not stop thinking about him, and about how happy they would be as they raised their child, together. She was obviously disturbed.

In months to come, Michael would receive dozens more letters from this woman. In one, she claimed that the baby and Michael had similar eyes and wondered how he could ignore his flesh and blood. It wasn't long before Michael began having nightmares about the situation. He fixated on her, wondering where she was, when she would show up at his front gate, and what he would do then. It seemed to some in the family that he had become as obsessed with her as she was with him.

One day, Michael received a package from her. When he opened it, he discovered another photograph: her high school graduation picture. In it, she smiled with girlish innocence. Also in the box was a gun. In a note, the fan asked that Michael kill himself on a certain day, at a certain time. She wrote that she would do the same – right after she killed the baby. She had decided, she wrote, that if the three of them could not be together in this life, perhaps they could in the next. Michael was horrified. He took the photograph, had it framed, and displayed it in the dining room on a coffee table, much to Katherine's dismay. 'God, what if she shows up?' he fretted. 'What will I do? I have to remember this face. Just in case. I must never forget this face.'

She never showed up at Michael's gate. In fact, he later learned that the poor young woman ended up in an insane asylum.

After 'Billie Jean' came out, Michael said that he wrote the song with his obsessed fan in mind. Ironically, Quincy Jones did not want to include it on the *Thriller* album; he did not think it was a strong enough song to be a part of the collection. Michael so believed in the song, he and Quincy had strong disagreements about its merit. When Michael came up with the title of the song, he asked LaToya, 'You don't think people will believe I'm talking about that tennis player, do you?' He was referring to Billie Jean King; LaToya didn't think so. Quincy Jones did, however, and wanted to change the title of the song to 'Not My Lover'. Of course, Michael vetoed that.

In truth, the relationship between Michael and Quincy rapidly deteriorated during the recording of *Thriller*, especially when Quincy would not give Michael a co-producing credit on 'Billie Jean' and 'Beat It'. The demonstration tapes Michael had recorded of both songs – before Quincy worked on them – sounded almost exactly like the final product. Michael felt it was only fair that he be given co-producing credit, and additional royalties as well. Quincy disagreed, much to Michael's chagrin.

Closer inspection of *Thriller* as a whole revealed an ambitiously crafted work that moved in a number of directions. The suburban, middle-of-the-road calm of 'The Girl is Mine' was the antithesis of the rambunctious 'Beat It', another highly charged Jackson composition in which Michael augmented his crossover rhythm-and-blues style by employing a harder-edged rock-and-roll sound. Some reviewers felt 'Beat It' was a shameless quest to attract hard-rock fans; the track featured Eddie Van Halen, whose band Van Halen was a preeminent rock group, on searing guitar bridges. While the tune was more of a marketing concoction – in the past, Michael had never shown any particular fondness for straight-out rock and roll – 'Beat It' would still find acceptance among rock fans.

On the other hand, if the funky 'Wanna Be Startin' Somethin'' sounds like a distant relative of *Off the Wall*'s songs 'Don't Stop 'Til You Get Enough' and 'Working Day and Night', the similarity occurred because Michael wrote them all during the same period. In 'Startin' Somethin'', Michael pointedly revealed his feelings on gossips and unwanted babies, and all to a bulleting bass and shuffling percussion. The tune's centrepiece, a climaxing Swahili-like chant, gave the song an international flavour. It was difficult to listen to Michael as he spat out angry lyrics about hate and feeling like a vegetable and not wonder about his state of mind at the time.

There were other stand-outs: the moody and introspective 'Human Nature', written by Steve Porcaro and John Bettis, was an expansive pop ballad whose sheer musicality kept it from being mushy. The funky 'PYT' (standing for 'Pretty Young Thing'), credited to James Ingram and Quincy Jones, and the sultry ballad 'Lady in My Life', by Rod Temperton, were both efforts to beef up *Thriller*'s R&B direction. 'Lady in My Life' was, by the same token, as close as Michael had come to crooning a sexy, soulful ballad since his Motown years. Perhaps that was why it required so many takes before the lead vocal was to Quincy Jones's liking.

The title track, 'Thriller', was its own animal. The song said much about Michael's fascination with the supernatural and the lurid. 'Thriller' is a typical Rod Temperton song – melodic, with a fluid bass line and big, mind-imprinting hook. The lyrics had excitement and intrigue, and the song concluded with a stately rap by the master of the macabre, Vincent Price. 'Thriller' would have been even more compelling as the title track of a concept album, but *Thriller*, the album, had no actual focus. It was just a bunch of great songs. Even the album's cover art, a photograph of a casually posed Michael uncharacteristically dressed in white jacket and pants, seemed incongruous. However, it's the picture many people refer to when discussing his plastic surgery, saying, 'If he had just stopped there, he would have been fine!'

With *Thriller*, Michael and Quincy had successfully engineered glossy, authentic versions of pop, soul and funk that appealed to just about everyone. However, no one in the music business expected the public to take that appeal so literally. At some point, *Thriller* stopped selling like a leisure item – like a magazine, a toy, tickets to a hit movie – and started selling like a household staple. At its sales peak, CBS would report that the album was selling an astounding 500,000 copies a week.

To the press, Quincy acted as if he knew *Thriller* was going to be huge. 'I knew from the first time I heard it in the studio, because the hair stood straight up on my arms,' he said. 'That's a sure sign, and it's never once been wrong. All the brilliance that had been building inside Michael for twenty-four years just erupted. I was electrified, and so was everyone else involved in the project. That energy was contagious, and we had it cranked so high one night that the speakers in the studio actually overloaded and burst into flames. First time I ever saw anything like that in forty years in the business.' What in the world was he talking about, speakers bursting into flames? Quincy is nothing if not a good showman. In truth, of course, he had predicted two million in sales, a moderate hit, for Michael, and much to Michael's dismay.

'What did I tell you?' Michael crowed to John Branca when it was clear that *Thriller* had taken off in an astronomical way. 'I *knew* it. I just knew it.' John could only smile.

By the end of 1983, *Thriller* would sell a staggering thirteen million copies in the United States and nearly twenty-two million worldwide. At the time, the all-time best-selling album was the original soundtrack to *Saturday Night Fever*, with worldwide sales of twenty-five million since its 1977 release. It wouldn't be long before Michael toppled that record; he had already achieved one milestone: until now, no other solo album had sold more than twelve million copies.

In addition to his personal achievements, Michael had single-handedly revived a moribund recording industry. When people flocked to the record stores to buy *Thriller*, they purchased other records too. As a result, the business had its best year since 1978. As Gil Friesen, then-president of A&M Records said at the time, 'The whole industry has a stake in *Thriller*'s success.' Michael's success also generated new interest in black music in general.

Ultimately, Thriller would go on to sell more than fifty million copies wordwide; it would spend thirty-seven weeks at number one

Michael Jackson
at the age of
twelve in 1970.
(© 1970 *Soul*
magazine. All
Rights Reserved.)

The Jacksons posed for a family photo in June 1970. Top row: Jermaine, fifteen; LaToya, fourteen; Tito, sixteen; Jackie, nineteen. Bottom row: Michael, eleven; Randy, seven; Katherine; Joe; Janet, four; and Marlon, thirteen. (© 1970, *Soul* magazine. All Rights Reserved.)

Michael in 1971. (J. Randy Taraborrelli Collection)

An early publicity photo of The Jackson 5 (1969). Top Row: Tito, sixteen; Jackie, eighteen; Jermaine, fifteen. Bottom Row: Marlon, twelve; and Michael, eleven.
(Retro Photo)

By the time The Jackson 5 played the Los Angeles Forum in 1970 'Jackson-Mania' was in full bloom. Michael seems to be doing his best James Brown impression here.
(Retro Photo)

By the end of 1972, the family was enjoying tremendous success. Top row: Jackie, twenty-one; Katherine (with newly frosted hair); Joe; Janet, six; Jermaine, eighteen; Michael, fourteen. Bottom row: Marlon, fifteen; Randy, ten; Tito, nineteen; and LaToya, sixteen. (J. Randy Taraborrelli Collection)

Diana Ross was credited with discovering The Jackson 5. Here, she seems to be telling Michael and Marlon, 'Now here's what I want you to say . . .' (J. Randy Taraborrelli Collection)

Twelve-year-old Michael doing his slick Frank Sinatra impression on Diana Ross's *Diana!* special, April 1971. (J. Randy Taraborrelli Collection)

Thirteen-year-old Michael in his bedroom, posing with one of his many pet rats. The bedroom walls were always covered with cartoon figures and publicity photos of entertainers (note the pictures of The Jackson 5 and The Supremes). (J. Randy Taraborrelli Collection)

Tito was the first brother to marry. Dee Dee Martes was told to sign a prenuptial agreement before the wedding on 17 June 1972. (Retro Photo)

When Jermaine Jackson married Berry Gordy's daughter, Hazel, the ceremony made the worldwide news. (J. Randy Taraborrelli Collection)

Jackie married Enid Spann on 24 November 1974. Theirs was a sometimes difficult union and Enid held on as long as she could. (J. Randy Taraborrelli Collection)

When Marlon married Carol Parker on 16 August 1975, the couple kept their union a secret . . . rather than risk the wrath of Marlon's father, Joe. (Retro Photo)

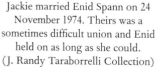

Michael Jackson and J. Randy Taraborrelli
as youngsters in the late 1970s,
before the madness set in . . .

Michael in 1977, at the age
of nineteen, before plastic surgery.
(© 1977 *Soul* magazine.
All Rights Reserved.)

Michael turned twenty-one in August 1979.
Here, he poses for a photo wearing a rebel cap –
perhaps signifying a newfound independence.
From this time on, Michael would have a
hand in all of his business matters.
(© 1979 *Soul* magazine. All Rights Reserved.)

An extremely rare photograph of Michael Jackson's half-sister, the lovely Joh'Vonnie Jackson, sixteen when this picture was taken in February 1991. Ms Jackson hopes to follow in the footsteps of her famous half-brothers and -sisters, and become an entertainer. (J. Randy Taraborrelli Collection)

In 1977, the Jackson daughters hoped to start their own singing group. However, since LaToya and Rebbie couldn't see eye-to-eye on the group's direction, and Janet wanted to be an actress, the act never got off the ground. Left to right: LaToya, twenty-one; Janet, eleven; and Rebbie, twenty-seven. (© 1977, *Soul* magazine. All Rights Reserved.)

on the *Billboard* charts, which was amazing. In the UK, it also hit number one and stayed on the charts there for an incredible 168 weeks! (The release of *Thriller* marked the first time an album was number one in the USA and the UK at the same time.) Also, prior to *Thriller*, no other album had ever spawned seven Top Ten singles: 'Billie Jean', 'Beat It', 'The Girl is Mine', 'Human Nature', 'Wanna Be Startin' Somethin'', 'PYT' and 'Thriller'. All of the songs sold hugely, right around the world.

CBS made at least sixty million dollars just on *Thriller*. Michael fared well too. According to, John Branca, Michael had 'the highest royalty rate in the record business'. That rate escalated along with the sales, but averaged 42 per cent in the wholesale price of each record sold, or about $2.10 for every album sold in the United States – thirty-two million dollars on *Thriller*'s domestic sales alone. Roughly fifteen million dollars more was made in foreign sales. Those figures, of course, did not include the royalties for the four songs he penned on the album.

Michael Jackson was, at twenty-five, a very wealthy young man. He had certainly come a long way from that 0.2 per cent royalty rate Motown once offered him.

The more *Thriller* was heard – and it was possibly the most played record of all time, both privately and on the radio – the better it sounded. Michael and Quincy had achieved their goal: to many listeners – whites, blacks, highbrows, heavy metal fans, teeny-boppers, parents – *Thriller* was the perfect album, every song an exercise in pop music production, every arrangement, every note in perfect place. This achievement made Michael more than a hero; the music industry promoted him to higher ground, almost sainthood. Of course, in entertainment circles these days, even the most untalented artist who sells huge amounts of product becomes a 'visionary'. However, Michael's phenomenal sales, along with his astounding talent, established a precedent of excellence with *Thriller* – and one that he would secretly attempt to surpass for the rest of his career.

Joseph Jackson is known among his friends and associates as a man given to overextending himself by investing in unsteady business ventures outside of the careers of his children. Of course, some of the investments have been profitable. For instance, a limousine company he owned did manage to turn a profit. More often, though, Joseph would lose his investment and then some. For instance, he once started his own record company, which cost him a small fortune. He had also invested a great deal of money in producing and managing singing groups, perhaps to prove that he could do for others what he had done for his sons. However, none of his acts ever amounted to much, if anything. And who in his circle would ever forget 'Joe-Cola', his own soft drink – which also failed in the marketplace? One had to give him credit for trying, though. He was never afraid to take a chance, invest in what he thought might be a good idea and take it all the way to fruition. After all, that's how he got The Jackson 5 to Los Angeles, and to Motown, wasn't it?

By the beginning of 1981, however, Joseph was having financial problems serious enough to warrant his wanting to sell the Encino estate. It's a tribute to him that he never attempted to siphon money from his children's income to solve his own financial problems. 'I'd say we were among a fortunate few artists who walked away from a childhood in the business with anything substantial – money, real estate, other investments,' Michael would say. 'My father set all these up for us. To this day I'm thankful he didn't try to take all our money for himself, the way so many parents of child stars have. Imagine stealing from your own children. My father never did anything like that.'

Joseph may have been a lot of things, but he wasn't was a thief. He took care of his children's investments, and if they lost money – and all of them did, except for Michael and Janet – it may be because they have inherited Joseph's penchant for bad investments. It wasn't because they didn't receive money that was owed to them.

Joseph found the perfect buyer for his Encino estate: his own son, Michael.

One might wonder if Joseph first examined the ramifications of his offer to Michael before he made it. No doubt, once he changed roles from owner to tenant, his relationship with Michael would change as well. Barring unusual circumstances, in most familial situations, the heads of the family provides the lodgings; when the children become adults, they move on to their own homes. Changing roles in a basic way can often contribute to family dysfunction. Joseph had always held fast to the theory that a father should be able to control his children – no matter what their ages, their desires, their expertise. Being so determined to be in charge, it's surprising that Joseph never realized how threatened he would eventually feel by having to live in his son's house – especially when it had once been his own. Of course, Joseph was dealing with Michael, and he knew and understood Michael's gentleness towards Katherine, if not towards him. He knew that Michael wouldn't kick them out of the house. In the end, Michael paid about $500,000 for his equity in the estate. Katherine and Joseph owned the other half. Eventually, Joseph would sell his quarter to Michael, leaving 25 per cent to Katherine. One might also wonder if he had considered that the next time Katherine wanted to evict him, it might be a lot more likely that he would have to leave since she and Michael owned the estate, not him.

Once he took over part-ownership, Michael decided to completely demolish and rebuilt the house. The address may have remained the same, but the new estate – Michael's estate, which took two years to finish – became palatial in scope. What sweet and poetic justice it was that Michael was able to destroy the house in which he had so many bad memories and, from its ashes, raise a new one, perhaps fresh with possibilities for the future. While on tour in England a few years earlier, he had become enchanted by the Tudor-style mansions he saw in the countryside. When finished, the estate was – and still is, today – indeed, special.

The brick-laid drive opened to an ornate three-tiered white fountain in front of a Tudor-style home. All of the windows of the house were made of leaded stained glass with bevelled panes. When Michael was in residence, the Rolls-Royce that Tatum O'Neal helped him select sat parked in front of the four-car Tudor-style garage opposite the home. (Michael was still uneasy about driving; he would much rather take an hour-long detour than have to drive on the freeway in Los Angeles. 'I can't get on them,' he complained, 'and I can't get off them, either.')

A large 'Welcome' sign appeared above the garage doors. In the centre of the garage structure stood an oversized clock with Roman numerals. Upstairs, on the second floor of the garage, a visitor entered a three-room picture gallery with hundreds of photographs of the Jackson family on the walls and even the ceilings.

Outside, graceful black and white swans could be found languishing in backyard ponds. A pair of peacocks; two llamas; two deer, a giraffe and a ram were also in residence. The animals, kept in stables at night, were allowed to roam freely during the day. Muscles, the eight-foot boa constrictor, was, he told me, 'trained to eat interviewers'. Once, Katherine was straightening out the living room when she discovered Muscles under one of the couch cushions. She let out a scream that might have been heard all over Encino.

Next to the garage, Michael constructed a mini-version of Disneyland's Main Street U.S.A., including the candy store. There was a replica of a robotic Abraham Lincoln, which spoke, just as the Lincoln attraction did at Disneyland. Whenever Michael went to Disneyland, his 'favourite place on earth', there would be total chaos because of his fame. Therefore, he preferred the Disney employees to lead him through the back doors and tunnels of the attractions. In Encino, he built his own little world of Disney, a precursor to the expansive amusement park he would one day build at Neverland. Other puppet characters were added to the private amusement park. 'These are just like real people,' Michael explained to the writer who looked at them askance. 'Except they don't grab at you or ask you for favours. I feel comfortable with these figures. They are my personal friends.'

Winding brick paths decorated with exotic flowers and neatly cut shrubs led to secluded corners of the large estate where Michael would often wander alone to meditate. The swimming pool was huge and inviting. Water spouted from four fountainheads carved like bearded Neptunes on a retaining wall. A waterfall spilt in front of two lovebirds, the ceramic fashioned in elaborate, colourful tile work. Cool-looking water cascaded down into the main pool, and then flowed into a bubbling Jacuzzi.

On the ground floor of the main house was a thirty-two-seat theatre with plush red velvet seats and equipped with 16-millimetre and 35-millimetre projectors. The walls and the curtain in front of the screen were teal blue. Michael spent countless hours in the theatre; there were always Fred Astaire movies ready to be screened, as well as Three Stooges films. 'I put all this stuff in here,' he observed, 'so I will never have to go out *there*,' he said, indicating to the outside world.

There was also a wood-panelled trophy room where many of Michael's trophies were displayed in mahogany cases. All of the Jacksons' gold and platinum albums cover the walls. The family joked that if LaToya ever managed to get a gold album, there will be no place to hang it. (So far, that has not been a problem.)

Amid the magazine covers and other memorabilia, there was a six-foot-long diorama of Snow White and the Seven Dwarfs. 'One day I got a call from Mike,' recalled Steve Howell, who was employed by Michael as a video historian. ' "Come by with the video equipment, you'll never guess who's comin' over." "Who?" I asked. "Snow White and the Seven Dwarfs!" He'd hired Disney's costumed actors. I said, "Oh, okay, cool." Nothing was unusual when you worked for Michael.'

Steve's video of that day shows a childlike Michael, twenty-six years old at the time, playing with the dwarfs in the trophy room and being serenaded by Snow White. From the expression on his face, one might think it was one of the happiest days of his life.

A circular white marble staircase with a green carpeted runner led to the upstairs quarters: a gym, and four bedroom suites, each with its own bathroom. Michael's bedroom was large and cluttered. 'I just want room to dance and have my books,' he said. He had no bed; he slept next to the fireplace on the floor, which was covered with a plush green rug. Some of the walls were covered with fabric. Pictures of Peter Pan hung on others. There were wooden shutters over the windows, which he usually kept closed. The room was always a mess, not slobbish, just messy – books and records were everywhere, videotapes and music tapes piled high. Fan mail was stacked in the corners.

Also in the bedroom were five female mannequins of different ethnic groups – Caucasian, Oriental, Indian and two blacks. They were posed, looking with blank eyes at visitors. Well dressed and life-sized, they looked like high-fashion models, wearing expensive clothing. Michael said that he originally planned to have one room in the house specifically for the mannequins, but he changed his mind and decided to keep his plastic friends in his room. Katherine must have been relieved.

'I guess I want to bring them to life,' Michael explained. 'I like to imagine talking to them. You know what I think it is? Yeah, I think I'll say it. I think I'm accompanying myself with friends I never had. I probably have two friends. And I just got them. Being an entertainer, you just can't tell who is your friend. So, I surround myself with people I want to be my friends. And I can do that with mannequins. I'll talk to them.'

Dr Paul Gabriel, a professor of clinical psychiatry at New York University Medical Center, has a theory about Michael's penchant for mannequins – which he still has today, as seen on Martin Bashir's 2003 documentary about him: 'That's a special eccentricity, in the category of narcissism. We like to think we're beautiful. We make images of ourselves. Children are very narcissistic. They see themselves in their dolls, and that's what this is about for Michael Jackson. After age five or six, they begin to give some of that up, but he apparently never did that.'

Later, there would be a crib in the corner of the bedroom, which was where Michael's chimpanzee, Bubbles – who became a celebrity himself – slept.

Michael's bathroom was impressive, all black marble and gold. The sinks had brass swans for faucets.

A winding stairway led from the bedroom up to a private balcony on which Michael had an outdoor Jacuzzi for his own use.

LaToya's bedroom was down the hall from Michael's. 'He makes so much noise,' she once complained. 'You hear music in his room when he's trying to create. Or you hear the Three Stooges on TV, and he's up all night, laughing. The light is always on; Michael is forever reading books. You can't get in his room for the books and junk. I feel sorry for the housekeeper.' Ever the practical jokester, Michael enjoyed hiding bugs and spiders under LaToya's sheets so that she would scream upon finding them. Also, said LaToya, Michael wouldn't think twice about going into anybody's bedroom, opening drawers, and looking inside. He would frequently exasperate his family members by poking his nose into their personal businesses, but he would become extremely upset if anyone ever did such a thing to him.

Hayvenhurst – unofficially named after the Encino street on which it was located – was the perfect retreat for Michael Jackson. It was certainly a far cry from the modest home in which he had been raised as a small child, and even from the traditional home that had previously been on the property. From the roof of the house, Michael would watch the sunset and the glow of the twinkly white lights that decorated all of the property's trees and outlined the framework of the house.

Michael Meets with Berry, Again

On 12 March 1983, the co-management contract Michael Jackson and his brothers had with their father, Joseph Jackson, and with the team of Ron Weisner and Freddy DeMann expired. It was expected that Michael would renegotiate and sign a new deal. However, he was not eager to do it. 'Let's just wait and see what happens,' he kept saying when the subject was broached. Michael, now twenty-four years old, had experienced great solo success with *Thriller* and, as a result, was more confident in his decision-making processes. He had just been presented with a double-platinum award for *Thriller* at a press conference held at CBS's West Coast offices; he knew how powerful he had become in the record industry. He no longer felt compelled to follow the lead of his brothers, who had said they wanted to continue with Joseph. From this point on, Ron Weisner, Freddy and Joseph would work without a contract while Michael made up his mind how to handle them.

Certainly, if Joseph wanted to continue managing Michael's career, he was not scoring any points by mistreating Katherine. Michael had witnessed a great deal of domestic heartbreak in recent years and found it impossible to separate the man he held responsible for it from the one who managed him. He was beginning to contemplate his options. 'Why does Joseph have to be in the picture at all?' he wondered. 'Is it because he's my father? Well, that's not good enough.'

Michael was also still troubled by a letter Joseph had written to Ron and Freddy back in 1980. In it, he assailed the managers for spending too much time on Michael's career and not enough on that of his other sons. Joseph probably did not expect the letter to get into Michael's hands. If it was up to Joseph, Michael wouldn't even have a successful solo career. Of course, Michael's success with *Thriller* could actually bode well for the brothers, in terms of work opportunities – as long as Michael remained a part of the group, which was beginning to seem an unlikely proposition, especially after his next television appearance.

In March – the same month Michael had a number-one hit with 'Billie Jean' – Suzanne dePasse was in the final stages of mounting an NBC special 25 called *Motown 25: Yesterday, Today and Forever* to celebrate Motown's twenty-fifth anniversary. Suzanne, president of Motown Productions at this time and Berry Gordy's respected right-hand woman, expected all of the former Motown stars, some of whom had left the company acrimoniously, to reunite for this one evening to pay tribute to fifty-four-year-old Berry, and acknowledge his impact on their lives and careers.

Suzanne did not find it easy obtaining commitments from the artists. For instance, it had been her idea to reunite Diana Ross and The Supremes, thirteen years after that group disbanded. But Diana, now an RCA recording artist, hadn't seen Berry since she left Motown, wasn't sure how she felt about him, and decided not to cooperate. Her decision put a proposed Supremes reunion segment in jeopardy. It was decided that there would, instead, be a reunion of Michael Jackson and The Jackson 5, including brother Jermaine, who had not performed with the group since 1975. All of the brothers agreed that it would be an excellent idea to have a reunion for *Motown 25* – all, that is, except for Michael.

First of all, Michael did not want to appear on a television programme. The reason he so enjoyed making music videos was because, in that format, he could have complete control over the final product. Every aspect of his performance could be perfected – either by multiple takes or by careful editing. Performing 'live' for a studio audience on a programme that would be taped for later television broadcast was a risky proposition. He would not have as much control as he felt he needed in order to duplicate the quality of his video work. No matter how he did it on television, there was no way it would be as . . . *magical*.

Also playing a large part in Michael's lack of interest in *Motown 25* was that working with his brothers again, even if for a national, prime-time audience, wasn't as appealing to him as it was to the rest of the family. For years he had depended on the Jacksons for love, support and even professional status. However, recently he had begun to break away — first, emotionally by distancing himself from them and then, pro-fessionally, by out-scaling their success with his own. He never actually made an announcement that he was leaving the group, but Michael definitely no longer wanted to be perceived as one of The Jacksons.

Beyond that, Michael had ambivalent feelings about Berry. He hadn't forgotten the meeting they had had in 1975. Berry had promised that he would do nothing to hurt the Jackson family. However, he then seemed to encourage Michael's favourite brother, Jermaine, to leave the group. It was a bit more complicated, but that's the way Michael chose to remember it. He also felt that Motown had, as he put it, played 'hard ball' by preventing him and his brothers from using the name 'Jackson 5' at CBS. In a sense, Michael had unfinished business with Berry and, like Diana Ross, was unsure about participating in a tribute to him.

It was no surprise that Joseph thought the idea of a reunion was a good one. For him, it wasn't that he cared to pay tribute to Berry Gordy (not likely!) but that he saw an opportunity to present the family singing group in the way he always believed they should be presented: as a united front, brothers till the end. Joseph also saw an opportunity to parlay the group's reunion into a major, money-making tour. The idea was sure to make Michael shudder, however Joseph was considering it, just the same. 'He'll do what I tell him to do,' Joseph said, confidentially. As usual, though, he had underestimated his son. Disregarding Joseph's wishes, Michael discussed the matter with his other managers, Ron Weisner and Freddy DeMann and, also, his attorney, John Branca. He then decided that he wasn't going to appear on the programme.

Berry was fairly blasé about the reluctance of some former Motown stars to pay homage to him. Even Marvin Gaye, his former brother-in-law, had said he would not appear. 'It's gonna be a great special anyway,' Berry said. 'Oh yeah?' Suzanne dePasse argued. 'Without Diana Ross and Michael Jackson, what kind of special do we have? We got DeBarge. We got High Inergy. [Both were minor Motown acts.] You have got to talk to these people.'

Berry telephoned Diana; after their discussion, she agreed that she would appear on the programme. Marvin Gaye eventually made the same commitment. However, Michael was still a hold-out.

One night, while Michael was editing a special mix of 'Billie Jean' in a Motown recording studio (which he had leased for the session), Berry decided to show up at the session, unannounced. At first, Michael was flabbergasted to see Berry, but he quickly regained his composure. Berry meant a lot to Michael, despite whatever had happened in the past. At one point, he actually wished that Berry was his father instead of Joseph. The truth is, business complications aside, Berry was always personally kind to Michael, which couldn't always be said about Joseph. Berry also had great respect for Michael, which, again, couldn't always be said about Joseph. Seeing Berry once again felt good to Michael, his smiling face a reminder of some good times at the beginning, at Motown.

Sitting next to him at the control board, Berry asked Michael why he would not appear on the *Motown 25* broadcast. Michael explained why he disliked performing on television, but he did not offer his reservations regarding his brothers, or even Motown. Finally, the two began discussing old times at the company, and it was clear that Michael still felt a kinship to his past there. Still, he really didn't want to perform – unless he could get something out of it for himself. Why not? Everyone else was getting something out of it: Berry was getting a tribute; the brothers, a reunion; Joseph, his way; the network, big ratings . . . why not something for Michael? 'Listen, if I do this thing, I want to have a solo spot,' Michael told Berry.

'Hey, man, that's cool,' Berry said eagerly. 'I *want* you to have that, too.'

Berry assumed that Michael was talking about singing one of his Motown solo recordings, such as 'Got to be There' or 'Ben'. Berry began rattling off a list of the solo songs. He even mentioned 'Never

Can Say Goodbye', which, of course, was not a solo recording. However, to Berry, who was never much for the details of Motown history, they were all the same: hits.

Michael shook his head. 'No, Berry,' he said, firmly, 'I want to do "Billie Jean".'

Berry started chewing on his tongue, as he always does when he's deep in thought. He explained that the special was a celebration of Motown and since 'Billie Jean' had been recorded for CBS, it made no sense to have him perform it on the programme.

Michael told Berry that if he couldn't do 'Billie Jean', he would simply not appear on the show. He wanted to prove that, as good as the classic Motown hits were, he had been able to come up with a song that was, arguably, even better. Though he'd never been sure it was a good career move for the Jacksons to leave the company that had made them world-famous, it turned out that it was the best thing that could have happened to him and to his brothers. Now, he wanted the public to see his growth. He also wanted to promote 'Billie Jean', which was in the Top Ten and didn't really need it, but why not? Of course, he also wanted 'his way'.

'I don't know about "Billie Jean",' Berry said, stalling. 'It doesn't seem right to me.'

'Well, then, Berry, I'm sorry . . .'

There was a moment of silence.

'Okay,' Berry agreed with a grin. 'It's "Billie Jean". Hey, what the hell, I love that song.'

'Oh, and I want to have final edit on the videotape of the song before it's broadcast,' Michael added.

No other artist had made this particular request; most would not have bothered since it was so highly unusual; Berry wasn't sure what to think about it. Motown always liked to have control over final product; it's just the way it had always been. However, things had to change if he wanted Michael aboard.

'Okay,' Berry concluded with a firm handshake. 'And you'll do The Jackson 5 reunion, right? 'Cause Jermaine's lookin' forward to it.'

Michael rolled his eyes and sighed. 'Yeah, sure. Why not?'

The two smiled at one another as they rose from their chairs. Michael embraced Berry and whispered something in his ear. Berry left the studio beaming.

Yesterday, Today and Forever

It had been years since his last television performance and on 25 March 1983, at the taping of *Motown 25: Yesterday, Today and Forever*, Michael Jackson looked different: slimmer, almost fragile. His nose was now streamlined and sculpted, a tribute to a twentieth-century Michelangelo – his plastic surgeon. The new face had been skilfully enhanced: almond-shaped eyes outlined in black and lightly shadowed, high cheekbones emphasized by the merest hint of rouge, lips glossed to a subtle sheen. His former Afro hairstyle had been replaced by soft curls which framed his face; two wisps adorned his brow.

The Jackson 5 reunion went well. By the time they took the stage at the Pasadena Civic Center, the audience had already seen Marvin Gaye, Smokey Robinson and Mary Wells perform. They erupted in applause at the sight of the reunited brothers. For 'I Want You Back', Jermaine was back, smiling broadly and standing right next to Michael, in his old position. By the time the Jacksons swung into 'The Love You Save', and Randy trotted on stage to join them, the crowd – men in tuxedos, women in evening gowns – were standing and applauding. During 'I'll Be There', when Michael and Jermaine shared the spotlight and microphone, the two seemed choked up. Jermaine's eyes welled with tears. Michael draped an arm over his brother's shoulder and the two looked at one another with great warmth. It was an emotion-packed, memorable moment.

After hugs all around, the other Jacksons left the stage.

Then, the spotlight found *him*. It caught the glint of his black sequined jacket with cuffs that matched the silver sequined shirt, the white glitter socks that peeped from beneath the just-above-the-ankle black trousers, the shiny black penny loafers. And of course, there was the single left-handed white glove with its hand-sewn rhine-stones.

Michael thanked the audience. He hesitated, speaking haltingly. 'I have to say those were the good old days. I love those songs,' he said of the medley. 'Those were magic moments with all my brothers – including Jermaine.' Michael began pacing the stage, his hand in his pocket, talking as though he were just voicing some thoughts that happened to pop into his head, as though he were alone, as though the audience was not there. Actually, he was walking to the side of the stage to sneak the fedora into his hand. 'But, uh, you know,' he continued, 'those were the good songs. I like those songs a lot. But especially, I like' – he was centre stage by this time, facing the audience – 'the *new* songs.' The audience knew what was coming. They began calling out for 'Billie Jean'.

As the funk-infused guitar riff of 'Billie Jean' began, Michael went into his routine. He was going to be lip-synching – that was obvious from the first note – but no one watching cared. As the music pulsated, he jammed a black fedora over his eyes and struck a pose – his right hand on his hat, his left leg bent and poised for action. The stance may have been a tribute to Bob Fosse or Sammy Davis, Jr., but Michael imprinted it with his own magic. While most entertainers perform for their audiences, Michael seemed to be performing for himself, tonight. Maybe it was catharsis, his way of dealing with his personal pain, exorcising the demons in his life, coming to terms with the disappointments of the past just as others around him had celebrated it.

He threw the hat aside with a graceful flourish, the audience went wild.

He moved constantly. Even when he was standing still, he seemed to be moving.

Michael's brothers stood in the wings, their mouths open. His parents and sisters sat in the audience, spellbound. 'He just stole the show,' Joseph exclaimed to Katherine. '*That boy just stole the show.*' Berry was also seen standing and applauding, one of the biggest fans in the house.

'Billie Jean is not my lover,' Michael sang, a pained expression playing on his face. It was a deeply personal song about fathers and sons, about denial, entrapment, and hypocrisy, about coming close to the outer edges of madness.

The whole of Michael's performance was spellbinding, but during a brief instrumental interlude, he executed a combination of moves that would seal his reputation as a dance legend. He commenced with a series of split-second locking moves and poses before gliding across the stage via his now-famous sleek and graceful moonwalk – a reversed syncopated glide, heading forwards and sliding backwards at the same time. The moonwalk gave way to that equally renowned spin – now refined, after years of practice, to tornado speed – and then, immediately, he was up on his toes. Nobody but Michael Jackson could dance like that, and the audience went wild.

Michael hadn't invented any of these moves; the poses were modified versions of 'locking', a street dance from the 1970s. The moonwalk was a move TV's *Soul Train* dancers had discarded almost three years earlier. Sammy Davis, Jr., James Brown and Jackie Wilson all used to execute that same spin, and going up on the toes is a touch Michael saw Fred Astaire use in his classic films of the 1930s. To combine all those moves, from all of those eras – to take different styles and make them his own – *that's* Michael Jackson's genius as a dancer and creator.

Since he was a child and lead singer of The Jackson 5, Michael had possessed a magical ability to move an audience with his singing and dancing. However, somehow tonight, something was different. Tonight, his audience was just as exhilarated by the force of his personality as they were by his voice and footwork. Videotapes of Michael's performance do not begin to capture the pandemonium his act generated that evening. The few minutes Michael spent onstage alone at the Pasadena Civic Center would add up to *the* performance of his career. After this evening, his life – both personally and professionally – would never again be the same.

When it was over, Michael appeared surprised; he took one more step before he realized that the music had stopped – or, perhaps, it was just his own momentum carrying him. A standing ovation rocked the hall. Michael bowed, then straightened and raised his arm. His doe eyes looked straight ahead, his body motionless. He didn't smile or acknowledge the moment which, of course, was part of the act.

He would later remember that he was disappointed in the performance. He had planned to execute a spin and stop on his toes, suspended. The spin worked, but he didn't stay on his toes as long as he had planned to when he rehearsed in the privacy of his kitchen. Always the perfectionist, he wished he could do it over again. And if this had been a video – not television – he could have. It wasn't such a hot performance, he would remember thinking to himself, despite the crowd's approval.

Backstage, his brothers awaited him. All five – Jackie, Tito, Jermaine, Marlon and Randy – embraced him as he exited the stage.

'What a job, Mike,' Jackie exclaimed.

'I've never seen anything like it,' Jermaine added.

They were all talking at once. They had had no idea what Michael was going to do during his solo spot; he had decided not to tell them.

Jermaine kissed him on the cheek. Then Jackie, then the others. It was an unusual display; the brothers, following Joseph's example, were usually not affectionate or effusive with one another. However, Michael had shown them what he was capable of, they respected him for it and couldn't contain themselves. Maybe it really was a good performance, after all.

However, it wasn't long before the moment was shattered. The brothers were soon talking about what Michael's glory might mean for *them* – the possibility of taking the group back out on the road and making more money than ever before. 'The Jackson 5 are back,' Jackie kept repeating, and the others agreed, enthusiastically. 'This is gonna be great.'

Michael didn't want any part of that idea. He turned and began walking away from them. 'Hey, man, we're family,' one of his brothers reminded him. Michael, an inscrutable expression on his face, just shook his head and kept walking.

As Michael continued down the hall, a young boy in a tuxedo followed him. 'Hey, Michael,' the youngster called out. 'Wait up.'

Michael stopped.

'Man, who ever taught you to dance like that?' The kid looked up at his idol with adoring eyes.

'Practice, I guess,' Michael said.

'You were amazing,' the fan told him.

'Thanks, I needed that,' Michael responded.

The youngster turned and walked away.

Michael nodded to himself, and as he walked down the hall alone, he began to smile. *Now*, he felt good.

The atmosphere at the Jacksons' house on Hayvenhurst was holiday-like, with people telephoning from across the country to rave about Michael. The house swarmed with people – relatives, CBS and Motown executives, neighbours and even fans – as members of the family repeatedly ran the videotape of Michael's exciting performance. 'You gotta see this one more time,' Joseph, the proud father, told everyone who came by. 'I've never seen anything like it. Just look at this kid.'

Joseph may not have realized it, but video players all over the country were in overdrive, as well. With his appearance on *Motown 25*, Michael accomplished two things: he reconfirmed for lifelong fans that, yes, he is the amazing talent they had always revered. Also, through the might of television, he reached millions of viewers who had never experienced him as a performer. Only on two other occasions – the first national television appearances of Elvis Presley and The Beatles, both on *The Ed Sullivan Show* – has television so handily delivered pop music superstardom. However, Michael Jackson's was quite possibly *the* single most captivating pop music performance in television history – the singing *and* the dancing. 'Beat It' had just hit number one two weeks earlier; it was Michael Jackson's world, and all of the other Jacksons were just living in it.

Even the dance greats, such as Fred Astaire, were impressed by Michael's prowess. The day after the special aired, Fred telephoned Hermes Pan, the legendary choreographer and Oscar winner who taught Fred and Ginger Rogers their most memorable dance steps (and who was his neighbour in Beverly Hills). He told him to come by as soon as possible.

When Hermes arrived, Fred put in a videotape of the performance. 'Just wait till you see this.' Then the two old pros watched in awe as the new kid on the block wowed America. Fred, never one to give light praise to other male dancers, was knocked out by Michael.

'We agreed that we must call Michael, immediately,' Hermes Pan told me. 'Somehow, Fred tracked him down. He told him that he was one hell of a dancer. "A great mover." He said, "You really put them on their asses last night. You're an angry dancer. I'm the same way." I got on the line to say hello, and this whisper of a voice answered me. I was surprised, actually, that a person who dances with such anger would have such a soft voice. I told him how much I enjoyed his work, and he was very gracious, very excited to hear from us. For a moment, I believed he thought it was a practical joke. I liked him right away because he seemed so unaffected by show business, and also star struck. He really could not believe that Fred Astaire had called him.'

Michael would say later that Fred's compliment meant more to him than any he had ever received. Michael's voice teacher, Seth Riggs, recalled that, 'Michael was eating breakfast when Astaire called, and he became so excited he actually got sick and couldn't finish his meal.' Later, Fred invited Michael to his home so that he could teach him and Hermes how to moonwalk.

Soon after that, Gene Kelly visited Michael in Encino to talk shop. 'He knows when to stop and then flash out like a bolt of lightning,' Gene would say of Michael, who had, it seemed, joined a new brotherhood of dance. 'He's clean, neat, fast, with a sensuality that comes through,' Bob Fosse would say of Michael after *Motown 25* was broadcast. 'It's never the steps that are important. It's the style.'

The moonwalk dance movement was taught to Michael by one of the former dancers on the popular American television programme called *Soul Train*. The steps had been around for about three years. When he saw the routine for the first time while watching the show, Michael simply had to learn it. Ron Weisner put him in touch with sixteen-year-old Geron Candidate, who went by the stage name of 'Casper', the kid who actually invented the move.

'I saw something you guys did on *Soul Train*,' Michael told Casper, 'where it looks like you're going backward and forward at the same time.'

'It's called the backslide,' Casper exclaimed.

'That's amazing!' Michael exclaimed. 'Can you teach me to do that?'

Casper was so stunned, he could barely answer yes. The next day Casper and his dance partner, Cooley Jackson, met Michael at a rehearsal studio in Los Angeles. To the music of 'The Pop-Along

Kid', by the group Shalamar, Cooley proceeded to demonstrate a version of the backslide which was more like pushing in place rather than walking backwards. It wasn't what Michael wanted. Then, Casper demonstrated the slide where it appears the dancer is walking backwards and forwards at the same time. Michael leaped into the air. 'Yes! *That's* it. That's the one I want to learn.'

When Casper sat down, Michael grabbed at his shoes to examine their soles. 'What do you have on the bottom of your shoes?' Michael wanted to know. 'You got wheels under there, don't you? That's how you do that step, isn't it?'

Casper explained that there were no special shoes or wheels involved; it was just a cleverly executed dance step. With the help of a chair, Casper began to teach it to Michael. For this practice session, Michael grabbed on to the chair back and executed the step in place repeatedly, in an effort to become accustomed to the foot movement. 'He learned the basic concept in about an hour,' Casper remembered. 'He wasn't comfortable with it, but he had it down.'

A couple of days later, Casper had another session with Michael. 'He still wasn't at ease with it,' Casper recalled. 'Whereas I made it look so natural, like I was walking on air, he was stiff. It bugged him. "I can't do this in front of people unless I can do it right," he kept saying.'

After those rehearsals, Michael went on tour with his brothers. 'I went to see the show in Los Angeles, and he didn't do the step,' Casper said. 'I was surprised. When I went backstage and asked him about it, he said he just didn't feel ready yet. He didn't feel he knew it.'

Casper was home watching *Motown 25*, like millions of others, when he saw Michael do the step for the first time in front of an audience. 'I couldn't believe it,' he remembered. 'My heart started pounding. I flew right out of my chair and screamed out, "Yeah! He did it. He finally did it. And I'm the guy who taught it to him." It's not the moonwalk though,' he explained. 'It's the backslide. The moonwalk is when you do the step in a complete circle. But, some-how, the step Michael did on TV became known as the moonwalk, instead of the backslide.'

Indeed, the moonwalk – or backslide – soon became Michael's signature dance step. His *Motown 25* performance was nominated for an Emmy (and the programme itself won one). For teaching it to him, Casper was paid just a thousand dollars. 'That's how much I asked for,' he said, laughing. 'I was sixteen. To me, that was good money. I would have done it for free, to tell you the truth. How was I supposed to know it would become Michael Jackson's trademark?'

♣

'Billie Jean' and 'Beat It' Videos

In March 1983, Michael hit number one again with 'Billie Jean'. It would stay atop the charts for seven weeks, primarily because of the impact of the *Motown 25* appearance, but also as a result of the video Michael made for the song. 'When his people approached us about doing the video for "Billie Jean", they didn't have any ideas at all,' recalled Simon Fields, who produced the 'Billie Jean' video. Fields said that the concept came from its director, Steve Barron. 'Basically, Michael was just following our direction,' he said. 'But the guy is a genius, so you can count on him to do wonderful things.'

'Billie Jean,' the first video from the *Thriller* album – and Michael's first major music clip – is ultimately too artsy for its own good. In a series of abstract shots, Michael plays high-tech hide-and-seek with a stalking, probing photographer – the only other major character – clearly suggesting Michael's paranoia about the press. However 'Billie Jean' the song – about a girl who haunts Michael, insisting that he is the father of her son – boasts too strong and visual a storyline to have been so overlooked in its video. In the end, the video is largely a series of odd scenes strung together.

Michael Jackson's biggest advance with this video was in showing viewers a new side of himself. Here Michael was cool, mysterious and evasive. The most compelling moment in 'Billie Jean' comes, as usual with Jackson, when he dances. With each step he takes, the sidewalk underneath his feet lights up as if infused by, as Michael would say, 'magic'.

Michael demonstrated more of his deft dancing abilities in his excellent 'Beat It' video. While he had begun with only a vague concept for the 'Billie Jean' clip, he knew precisely what he wanted for 'Beat It'. Veteran commercial director Bob Giraldi and Broadway choreographer Michael Peters collaborated with Michael on what would be one of the most dynamic, and expensive, videos to date. The choreographed ensemble-dancing in 'Beat It' would be often imitated in years to come, and is still a staple in the videos of many pop artists.

Perhaps of all the numbers Michael had presented his fans during his career, the 'Beat It' video marked the biggest departure. As a song, the track was unadulterated rock and roll, something Michael's core fans, especially the majority of his black ones, initially rejected. Beyond that, the video depicted a Jackson never before seen: Michael as urban dweller, a kid living on the wrong side of the tracks – a *human* Michael.

Some of Michael's public, particularly those living in urban neighbourhoods, found the storyline patronizing. In 'Beat It', which Michael has said was written with youngsters in mind, he is the good guy who ultimately stops two powerful gangs from warring with each other. Those viewers unable to separate Michael Jackson the musical enigma from Michael Jackson the actor missed the point when they asked angrily, 'What does *he* know about gangs?' and 'Does he really think dancing through the problems we're having down here – muggings, killings, drug addiction – is the answer to our woes?'

'The point is no one has to be the tough guy,' Michael would explain. 'You can walk away from a fight and still be a man. You don't have to die to prove you're a man.'

Visually, Michael's video was convincing enough. Shot on location on the mean streets of Los Angeles, it looked dark and grimy. In a quest for authenticity, one hundred members of two real-life, rival Los Angeles street gangs were hired as extras and atmosphere people. (They were each fed and paid one hundred dollars for two nights' work.)

'The gangs were sort of on the periphery of the location,' choreographer Michael Peters once said, 'so Michael really didn't have to deal with them. But he was a little nervous, as we all were at the beginning. However, he was wonderful with them. I think the turning point was when the gangs saw us dance. They had, I think, a different respect after that. Michael signed autographs and took pictures with them.'

Acting was easy for Michael: he'd done a form of it onstage, singing, all his life. However, with ensemble-dancing, he found himself on uncharted terrain. Fans had never seen Michael in a Broadway-style setting, and some of them probably wondered why a hoofer like Michael needed someone to teach *him* steps, but choreographer Michael Peters succeeded in creating a dazzling, funked-up, *Chorus Line*-like dance effect. It all looked so easy, it seemed that anyone could do it. But, just try. 'Looks can be deceiving, especially when it comes to dance,' Michael would explain with a grin. Overall, the clip is rock theatre at its best. Its style and artistry actually succeeded in making the music more interesting, which has always been the ultimate goal of music videos.

What's really interesting about Michael's *Thriller* videos, however, is how they boosted the popularity of the then-fledgling MTV network. MTV, the twenty-four-hour-a-day cable station that plays only music videos, became a phenomenon when it began airing in 1981, yet by 1983 it rarely played the videos of black artists. The station's format was 'strictly rock and roll', said Bob Pittman, the executive vice-president and chief operating officer of Warner American Express Satellite Entertainment Company and the driving force behind MTV. Pittman's definition of rock and roll excluded most black artists from the station's play lists. In fact, of the over 750 videos shown on MTV during the channel's first eighteen months, fewer than two dozen featured black artists. It was acceptable to have Phil Collins sing The Supremes' 'You Can't Hurry Love' and Hall and Oates singing other black-sounding material, yet the real thing was completely unacceptable on MTV at that time. When videos of black artists were submitted, they were quickly rejected as not being 'rock and roll'.

MTV's research and marketing departments had somehow decided that white kids in the suburbs did not like black music and maybe were intimidated by black people. There was nothing wrong with that, Bob Pittman reasoned; after all, 'Bloomingdale's wouldn't work if it carried every kind of clothing ever made.'

Bob Giraldi, director of Michael's 'Beat It' video, best summed up many black critics' opinions of MTV when he said that the station was run by 'racist bastards'. Motown recording artist Rick James, whose videos had been rejected by the station, also charged that the network was racist and had set black people back four hundred years. Bob Pittman was probably not a racist, but he and MTV certainly catered to white suburban racism.

When CBS submitted Michael Jackson's 'Billie Jean' to MTV, the cable station quickly rejected it. CBS then threatened to pull all of its other videos from MTV unless they ran 'Beat It'. Michael Jackson had become so popular, Bob Pittman – and suburban white America – simply could not ignore him. Finally, in early March 1983, the 'Billie Jean' video was played on MTV, and in so-called 'heavy rotation', meaning often during the day. 'Beat It' followed. After that, MTV began to play a few more videos by black artists, and though the network still leans heavily towards white rock and roll, at least some black artists – though not many – receive airtime, mostly as a result of the Michael Jackson breakthrough so many years ago.

Managerial Trouble

By June 1983, Michael and his brothers had still not renegotiated their contract with their father, nor had they decided to re-sign with co-managers, Ron Weisner and Freddy DeMann. Though the brothers were ambivalent about re-signing, they were willing. They really didn't have any options, anyway. Of course, Michael was the hold-out. He was disenchanted with his father and, now, also with Ron Weisner and Freddy DeMann. Because Michael was taking his time in making a decision about the matter, everyone involved was concerned. His decision meant a great deal to a lot of people, in terms of money and power. If he signed, everyone else in the family would follow suit. If he didn't, it was possible that there could be other defections.

Joseph hadn't been doing much for Michael lately, especially since John Branca came into his life. Michael trusted John implicitly and tried to make certain he – not Joseph – was involved in every decision. No surprise, then, that Joseph wasn't one of John's biggest fans (and vice versa) and only spoke, begrudgingly, to him if he couldn't speak to Michael, directly. Ron and Freddy handled whatever John chose not to, so in a sense, though not technically or officially (or, even legally, for that matter), John Branca was as much a manager to Michael as he was an attorney.

Michael had complained to John during the last two years that Ron Weisner and Freddy DeMann were not creative individuals. 'I don't even know why they're here,' he said. 'They don't know what they're doing, do they?' But whenever John would discuss Michael's feelings with Ron and Freddy, they wouldn't know what he was talking about. They both felt that Michael was pleased with their work, since he had never told them otherwise. Michael picked up a lot of Joseph's business traits, but the art of confrontation was not one of them. He'd do it, if he had to . . . but he'd rather not have to do it.

'You remember their idea for the "Beat It" video,' Michael reminded John. 'They wanted me to have bows and arrows,' Michael complained. 'Now, come on, Branca. That's stupid.' It was true that Ron and Freddy had a concept for the 'Beat It' video that would have seen Michael dressed as a Robin Hood character in England. However, why not? It's all in the implementation, isn't it? If one was to describe the 'Beat It' video as it actually exists – Michael inspires two rival gangs to understand that *dancing* will bring about a peaceful solution of their disagreements – that might sound silly, too.

Because Joseph was nervous about his tenuous position with Michael, he reacted impulsively and hoped to force Michael's hand where Weisner and DeMann were concerned – thereby leaving *him* the only sure thing in his son's career, just as it had been in the past. 'It's over,' Joseph told *Billboard* magazine of Ron and Freddy. 'My boys are not re-signing with them. There are a lot of leeches trying to break up the group,' he observed, possibly referring to Ron and Freddy's continued emphasis on Michael's solo career. 'A lot of people are whispering in Michael's ear, but we know who they are. They're only in it for the money.' Then, as if to put pressure on Michael, he added, 'I was there before it started, and I'll be there when it ends.'

The brothers were not happy with Weisner and DeMann, anyway, because of all the attention the two had lavished upon

Michael in recent months. For that matter, they wanted to leave Joseph, too. However, they were waiting for Michael – not Joseph – to make an announcement. They knew that there would be trouble now.

They were right. Michael was angry with Joseph for taking matters into his own hands, and even more outraged that his father would talk to a reporter about their private business affairs. It was as if Joseph wanted the world to know what was happening so that Michael would then be reluctant to move against his own father. However, the more Joseph talked, the worse things got for him. 'There was a time when I felt I needed white help in dealing with the corporate structure at CBS,' Joseph explained. 'And I thought Weisner-DeMann would be able to help. But they never gave me the respect you expect from a business partner.'

For their part, Weisner and DeMann said to the press that, yes, they did have problems with Joseph, 'but we have no problems with Michael or The Jacksons,' and that Joseph had not been involved in any major business decisions in recent years. 'We don't have a good relationship with him,' Freddy admitted, 'but I don't think he enjoys a good relationship with anyone whose skin is not black.'

'People have called me a racist. I am not a racist,' Joseph countered. 'If I were a racist, I would not have hired a lot of white people to work for me. I'm not a racist. I'm an American. I gave my children one hundred per cent of my know-how, knowledge and time trying to develop them to be what they are today, and it has paid off and is still paying off.'

Finally, Michael realized that too much was being said to the press, especially about race. He decided to cut to the chase and fire Weisner and DeMann; he was going to do it, anyway, so his father didn't really need to do anything but seal the deal. 'They said *Thriller* would only go two million and it's *way* over that,' Michael reasoned to John Branca. 'So who needs them? They told me not to do *Motown 25*. And look what kind of bad advice *that* was.'

John reminded Michael that he had not wanted to do the Motown special, anyway. Michael argued, 'That's not the point. Ron and Freddy *agreed* with me when they *should* have tried to convince him otherwise. Do it,' he told Branca. 'They're finished.'

Ron Weisner and Freddy DeMann got their walking papers from

Michael on 22 June. Oddly, Ron had talked to Michael earlier that morning and, during their conversation, Michael acted as though no problem existed between them. When he then received the letter of dismissal from John Branca, Ron was astonished. Obviously, it wasn't the bravest way to handle the problem, having someone else do his dirty work, but for Michael it proved the easiest and, besides, John Branca made a lot of money doing the things Michael would rather not have to do himself. Though Michael may not have been influenced by Joseph's contentious nature, he was definitely his father's son when it came to dealing with those he felt crossed him, and he remains the same today: once someone falls from Michael's grace, that person disappears from his thoughts – as though he or she never existed.

As for Joseph, Michael made a public statement to distance himself from his sentiments. 'I don't know what would make him say something like that,' Michael told a reporter, referring to Joseph's comments about 'white help'.

'To hear him talk like that turns my stomach. I don't know where he gets that from. I happen to be colour-blind. I don't hire colour. I hire competence. The individual can be of any race or creed as long as I get the best [representation]. Racism is not my motto.'

With Ron and Freddy gone, and Joseph not re-signed, it looked like the number-one artist in the world, Michael Jackson, now had no manager. His team now consisted of his attorney and chief adviser, John Branca; his security man, Bill Bray; his accountant, Marshall Gelfand; and a secretary. When 'Beat It' and 'Billie Jean' were both in the Top Ten, Quincy Jones asked for a three-way-conference telephone call among himself, Michael and John Branca.

'It's unbelievable what's happening here, Michael,' Quincy said. 'You need a manager, man. How could you fire Weisner and DeMann? What are you going to do now?'

'Branca can handle it, Quincy,' Michael said, according to Quincy's memory. 'He's brilliant. I'm not nervous, why are you?' Before Quincy could fully respond, Michael cut the conversation short and hung up.

Later, Quincy telephoned John Branca.

'John, I'm worried, man. This thing, Michael's career, it's like a plane with no pilot,' he said. 'This kid's career is in trouble.'

John couldn't believe his ears. 'What? He's got two records in the

Top Ten and his career is in trouble?' he asked with a laugh. 'Hey man, don't worry about it. It's going to be fine.'

Quincy was perplexed; he didn't understand how Michael was going to have a flourishing career without managerial guidance. If the sales of *Thriller* slowed down because there was no manager calling the shots, it would affect everybody's bank account, including Quincy's. However, at this time Michael was the Golden Child; the public was pulling for him, and the music spoke for itself.

'Mike knows what he's doing,' John told Quincy. 'This kid is a genius. And we got CBS and Walter [Yetnikoff] covering the bases. All we have to do is follow Michael's instructions.'

'But—' Quincy began again.

John cut him off. 'This is our chance, man, and I'm just gonna go on out there and kick ass for this kid because he's got it, Quincy. I love this kid and I just want to do his bidding.'

Son vs. Father

As angry as Michael was with Joseph, taking that next step – severing his professional relationship with him – was still difficult for him to do.

Just as he had felt it important to give Berry Gordy a chance to redeem himself before the group took their first steps away from Motown, Michael now hoped his father would do something to ingratiate himself. However, Joseph simply couldn't rise to the challenge . . . mostly because he didn't even know he was being tested. Joseph never tried to impress his children. In his view, getting them to Los Angeles and making them stars had been impressive enough. He had proved himself, he felt, and that was the end of that.

'He's finished,' Michael decided of Joseph. Katherine may not have been able to get rid of him as a husband, but Michael was sure able to unload him as a manager. Once Michael Jackson made up his mind to fire someone, he stuck to the decision, no matter who the person was – even his own father.

'Joseph knew it was coming,' said Joseph's friend of fifteen years, Larry Anderson. 'He knew his time was up.'

Michael had John Branca draw up the official documents informing Joseph that his managerial services would no longer be required. Michael then left the house the day he knew they would be delivered by messenger. He stayed away from home until Joseph had time to get used to the idea. 'It's not easy firing your father,' he would later explain, in what was quite an understatement.

In a rare show of unity, the brothers acted as one on this decision. They wanted Joseph out too and if Michael was prepared to take the first step they would follow suite. *None* of them renewed his contract with Joseph.

Joseph was angry at first, but soon he was crushed. 'I can't believe they're leaving me,' he told Katherine. And his despair caused great conflict in Katherine. Of course she was livid with him about his treatment of her; the divorce was still pending. However, her heart went out to him over the matter of their sons. 'I knew how much he had done for them,' she would later say, 'and this . . . well, this was just plain suffering. I didn't want to see him suffer.'

According to one of Michael's advisers, Michael had a meeting with Joseph in the living room of the Encino house to discuss the matter. Michel asked his adviser to be present because he didn't want to meet with Joseph alone.

'The fact that you can't even talk to me unless you have *this* guy here,' Joseph said, motioning to the adviser, 'it hurts me, Michael. Do you know how it makes me feel?' He had tears in his eyes; he looked broken. 'You know how I feel about you. Why do I always have to *say* it?'

Michael averted his eyes; he didn't even want to look at his father. 'You never said it, Joseph,' he said, venomously. 'Don't act like you ever said it, even once, because you never said it.'

'After all I've done for you and your brothers?' Joseph asked. 'Think about it. It's always been about you and your brothers. That's how I say it.'

Michael shot him a look of disdain. 'Oh yeah?' he responded, bitterly. 'And what about all you've done to Kate? What's *that* been about, Joseph?'

Michael's comment set Joseph off, according to the witness's memory. 'That ain't got nothin' to do with nothin',' he said, raising his voice to a level that made Michael recoil. Joseph rose so that he was standing above his son, who was still seated. 'My marriage has nothing to do with you, Michael,' he shouted at him. 'You know I love your mother. It's between her and me.'

Michael stood up to face his father, his dark eyes were blazing. 'It's between *all of us*, Joseph,' he exclaimed. 'If you can't see that, then I don't know what to tell you.' He stormed out of the room.

Joseph then turned on the adviser. 'It's because of you,' he said in a hurting but still furious voice. 'You put this bullshit in my son's head and you're ruining our family. It's because of *you*.' He then crumpled into a chair. Joseph appeared to be reeling as if, for him, all logic, fairness and common sense had suddenly been suspended and now . . . *this*. He put his face in his hands and sat in his chair, shaking his head in disbelief.

In the summer of 1983, those Jacksons living at the Hayvenhurst estate – Michael, Janet, LaToya, and Joseph and Katherine – existed in a state of emotional siege. Imagine it: Michael had fired Joseph as his manager, yet they were still living in the same house together. Katherine had filed to divorce Joseph, yet he was sleeping down the hall. Of course, the sensible thing would have been for him to move out. However, Joseph wasn't going anywhere. The fact that he didn't even own the house any longer was irrelevant.

'My father's very stern, very strict,' LaToya complained to freelance writer Todd Gold at this time. 'Deep down inside, he's a wonderful guy, but you have to know him. If you don't, you can get the wrong impression. You'd think that he's mean and whatever he says goes, which it does. Sometimes, though, if you really fight it out, you can have your way.' She let out an exasperated sigh. 'But it's just not worth it.'

As soon as Joseph would leave the estate for a day of work elsewhere, a sense of relief washed over the premises. On Saturdays, for instance, when he went to visit Joh'Vonnie, the Hayvenhurst household came alive. LaToya told Todd Gold, 'We invite lots of kids over and play some movies in the theatre, and the popcorn machine's going, the animals are all out, and everyone's dancing to music.'

Throughout the week, Michael tried to make certain that he never crossed paths with Joseph. Should the two accidentally meet, a loud argument would be the inevitable result. Michael would end up in his room, sobbing, Katherine trailing him there. Joseph would follow. There would be shouting, then more crying. Doors would slam all around. The tension affected everyone; Janet and LaToya spent a lot of time in their bedrooms with their music turned up.

Of course, the Jacksons may have been having tough personal times, but they were still the Jacksons and therefore lived with a sense of entitlement that was, sometimes, astounding. They all expected devotion from their staff; employees had no lives of their own. Steve Howell, Michael's videographer at the time, remembered what happened when he took a vacation to Lake Tahoe. 'I was there with my girl and made the mistake of calling the house to see if everything was okay. "You have to get back here right away," Bill Bray, Michael's security man, told me hysterically. "There's no television reception and Michael needs to watch TV! Get back here right away. So I cancelled the rest of my trip, flew back to Los Angeles, bee-lined it to the house, only to discover that the cable wire was unplugged. I plugged it into the wall and the TV went on, and Michael sat down to watch TV. "Thanks," he said.'

Good help was hard to find, even in Encino. At one point, money was stolen from one of the bedrooms. The Jacksons suspected a maid. They then began leaving money out in view, and would then sneak about and peer around corners to see who would take it. Ah-ha! It *was* the maid. Michael was the one who busted her; twenty bucks! After that, the family employees were often tested. Katherine would leave the alarm on the closet unarmed, the one in which she kept her minks, chinchillas, and other expensive furs. She would leave the door slightly ajar so anyone walking by could see what was inside. She would then stand very still at a nearby vantage point to see who expressed the most interest in the furs. That person would be scrutinized very carefully from then onward. 'Keep your eye on that one,' she would tell Michael. 'I don't trust her as far as I can throw her.' Perhaps this kind of surveillance kept their minds off their troubles with Joseph.

During this time, outsiders were not welcome at Hayvenhurst, especially the press who might sniff out any trouble on the home front. Of course, persistent fans were always a problem. 'I love my fans, but I'm afraid of them,' Michael told photojournalist Dave Nussbaum. 'Some of them will do anything to get to you. They don't realize that what they are doing might hurt you.' Michael talked of a fan who had managed to get beyond the gate. 'We woke up and found her sitting by the pool. She had jumped the gate. Luckily our dogs were caged at the time. They're usually out, and they would have *destroyed* her. We brought her inside. She demanded not to leave, in a very rude way, so we held her there until we had somebody come and take her out.'

On his way out, the reporter asked Michael if he would like to join him for a bite to eat.

'Oh, no,' Michael said, shaking his head. 'I can't go out there.' He motioned beyond the electronic gate. 'They'll get me for sure. They're around the corner, and they want to get their hands on me.' The terror in his eyes seemed genuine. 'I just don't want to go out there.'

As Michael talked to the reporter, his security man, Bill Bray – a former police officer – stood nearby watching.

Bray, who worked with Michael until his recent retirement, was formidable in his day. Once, when a Jackson employee left the estate, a fan slipped in as the gate opened.

Steve Howell recalled, 'I was talking to Mike in the front yard. It was about three in the afternoon. I remember the time of day because at three – when the kids got out of school – two guards went on duty, instead of one. Mike and I were talking, and the next thing I knew this girl walked up to us and said hello. Then, she gave him a big bear hug. With her back to me, Mike motioned to me with his arms helplessly as if to say, Who is this person? I was about to say something when, suddenly, I felt the air break. Something moved like – *whoosh!* – the speed of light. It was Bill Bray.

'He grabbed that chick, smacked her to the ground, handcuffed her and dragged her out of there. The cops came, took her away. She was crying hysterically, probably scared to death. Michael took it all in, turned to me and without missing a beat, said, "So, anyway . . ." And we went back to talking like nothing had happened.

'We had a lot of fifty-one fiftys around there, so that was nothing new.' A 51-50, Steve Howell explained, was police terminology for a mentally unbalanced person.

*

How long could the siege continue? Joseph had a good deal of resolve and, as he may have put it at the time, 'It will continue for as damn well long as I *want* it to continue.'

Finally, Katherine had enough of the divorce drama – which was dragging on throughout this parallel family crisis. Years later, she explained her predicament. 'I was stuck between a rock and a hard place,' she recalled. 'Even though I wanted Joe out, I didn't want to go public by having him forcibly removed. I knew that the press would jump on the story, and I couldn't bear the publicity. It was the strangest of times for me. Some days, just the sight of him would fill me with anger. Other times, I found myself talking to him as if nothing had ever happened between us.'

After ten months, Katherine decided to withdraw the divorce papers. Without Joseph, she decided she would only lead an empty and shallow existence, anyway. She loved him still, she told herself, though she said she didn't know why she felt that way.

'A part of me believes that a person hurts herself more than the person she's feuding with by holding a grudge. Also,' she explained, 'I subscribe to Christ's teaching on forgiveness. How many times, He said, do you forgive a person? Seventy times seven . . . as many as it takes.

'But I'm not going to pretend that suddenly everything was the way it used to be between Joe and me,' she concluded, perhaps somewhat romanticizing her tumultuous history with him. 'Because it wasn't.'

Putting Pressure on Michael

Michael Jackson suspected that, with his parents now reconciled, Joseph might expect to be welcomed back into the fold not only as Katherine's husband, but also as the boys' manager. 'And that's not gonna happen,' he told Janet, according to her memory. 'Mother may want him back, but I don't, and I don't think my brothers do, either. There's no way they'll let him back in.'

Joseph was a bit craftier, however, than Michael may have thought because he did have a plan to get 'back in' and it was one he knew that Michael's brothers would find irresistible: a reunion tour.

Many of the artists who participated in the Motown anniversary television special felt a new sense of brotherhood and camaraderie with the label. After the programme, Berry Gordy re-signed The Four Tops to the company and teamed them with The Temptations on vinyl, just as they had been united on stage that evening in Pasadena. Other artists began to negotiate with Berry, as well. Holland-Dozier-Holland were back, and even Diana Ross was socializing with Berry again. It was as if they were all trying to recapture the feeling they had had during the glory days of Motown – everyone, that is, except Jermaine Jackson.

After the show was taped, Jermaine began meeting with his brothers and Joseph about the possibility of his leaving Motown, reuniting with the group, and going out on the road again, together. Michael knew nothing about these meetings. 'Michael's success can only help us,' Tito said. 'He's way up there above us, and maybe he can throw down a rope and let us climb it.' A tour would also relieve Marlon of certain financial pressures. He and his wife, Carol, had separated but were now reconciled. They were determined to make their marriage work, despite their financial challenges. They needed some assistance, however.

At this time, the brothers also prepared a new Jacksons album for CBS called *Victory*. Michael did not want to be involved in the project. He would write and sing only two tracks and participate in the writing of a third, and even that much participation was too much for him. However, as they recorded the album, the brothers became excited at the prospect of touring to promote it once it was released.

No one wanted to consider Michael's reaction to the possibility of a tour, probably because they knew in their hearts that he might present a problem. 'The thing is, we've *always* worked really hard,' Marlon observed at this time. 'As far back as I can remember, since the time Michael and I were six and seven, we were going to school, doing homework, attending rehearsals, and then on weekends we'd play nightclubs, stayin' up till four in the morning, then get up and go to school come Monday. It was real, real hard for us. And I don't think you can outgrow your brothers and sisters, and Michael feels the same way. We're blood. You just don't sever those ties.'

By the summer of 1983, Jermaine had become excited enough about the prospects of a tour with his brothers that he asked Berry for a release from Motown. He wanted to look at his options, he said. Arista had offered him a deal (which he would take) and he also wanted to be free to tour with The Jacksons.

Sadly, Jermaine's solo career had never taken hold at Motown. All of that family *angst* – and for what? One Top Ten record: 'Let's Get Serious', which sold 722,737 copies, and not until 1981, some six years after the night at the Westbury Music Fair when he had to choose between his family and the Gordy family. However, in the company's defence, some felt that Jermaine wasn't motivated; he didn't hunger for stardom, like Michael. Many of his fans felt he should have stayed with the group, stayed married to Berry's daughter . . . and hoped for the best.

'Sometimes I have this dream that I'm onstage with my brothers,' he told me in an interview in 1983. 'And I'm countin' off the songs like I always used to do when we performed together. We're all onstage and the crowd is goin' crazy. All of a sudden I wake up. What a let-down. We all started here at Motown,' he said, 'and if anybody left anybody, I feel *they* left *me* at Motown. If we were to perform together again, there'd be no end to the things we could do, the excitement we'd create.'

Berry gave Jermaine his release, sealing an anticlimactic ending to his days at Motown.

Finally, Joseph called a meeting of all of the brothers in the family's living room. He announced that it was time for them to go back out and tour, the original Jackson 5, plus Randy. Michael's response was swift and to the point: 'Count me out.'

Joseph tried to reason with Michael. A major tour could solve many of his brothers' financial problems, and they all had them. No one had been making money lately, but Michael. Of course, Michael realized that none of his brothers had become as wealthy as he had become since *Thriller*. However, he also knew that if they curbed their extravagant tastes, they would be in good shape. 'Michael's money didn't matter to nobody but Michael,' Joseph maintained. 'And he was always very secretive about that. More important, the brothers needed to enhance their own situation. Like any other group, they needed to tour.'

Next, Joseph tried guilt, accusing Michael of turning his back on his brothers now that he was a superstar. If Michael, never selfish in regard to his family, had sensed need, not greed, he might have responded. However, he knew when he was being used. He also realized that even if he agreed to the tour, his superstar status would be ignored. He would be just one vote in six – the odd man out, as usual. 'No,' he said, 'I'm not going.' The brothers stormed out of the meeting. 'See that,' Joseph said, pointing a finger at him. 'Now, they're mad atcha'.'

'So?' Michael said. 'Big deal.'

About a week later, the brothers and Joseph had another meeting with Michael and, this time, tried humour on him. They brought along a life-sized stand-up poster of Michael. 'If you don't come with us, we're gonna put *this* onstage in your place,' Jermaine told Michael, a grin playing on his face. It was always hard to resist Jermaine's smile; he and Michael had always been close. The brothers laughed, and Michael said he would think it over.

A few days later, when Michael still had not made up his mind, Joseph tore into him. 'Look, we don't need you anyway,' he shouted at him. 'In fact, I think it would be *better* if you weren't on this tour. Jermaine can sing some songs, and Jackie and Marlon and Randy can all have songs. Tito, too. So, the hell with you, Michael. The hell with you.'

Joseph's reverse psychology worked like a charm; Michael was upset by his father's comments. He told John Branca: 'Branca, what's he talking about? The brothers can't sing. Only *I* can be the lead singer.'

Just as Michael was on the brink of making up his mind in favour of the tour, lest they go without him and maybe – though not likely – show that he was dispensable, Joseph pulled out the big gun: Katherine, who was made co-promoter of the tour. Her chief responsibility would be to turn the new family dream into reality by, once and for all, convincing Michael to be involved in the tour. 'When Mother speaks, we listen,' Jermaine once said.

It could have been successfully argued that Michael had done more for Katherine over the years, financially as well as emotionally, than any of his brothers. It seemed unfair, then, that she would now be coaxing him to do something that he clearly didn't want to do, just so that she could appease his brothers and make more money for the family. However, Katherine loved all of her children, not just Michael. She knew that they were in financial straits, and that only a tour *with* Michael would help them straighten out their lives. In her view, it was the least Michael could do. After all, they were family.

Katherine met with Michael privately and asked him to consider the possibility of a tour – for her sake. How could he resist such a request? For Katherine he would agreed to continue being held down as part of a family act rather than do what was natural at this time in his life and career: soar on his own. It didn't particularly matter to Joseph or the brothers that Michael's heart would not be in the upcoming tour, as long as his body was on that stage.

In any case, Michael had his mind on other things at this time. In October 1983, he and Jackie Kennedy Onassis met at the Encino home to discuss the possibility of his writing an autobiography to be published by Doubleday, the company for which she worked as an editor.

Five years earlier, in 1978, Michael had befriended John Kennedy, Jr., and Caroline after meeting the two while he was in New York to film *The Wiz*. So determined was he to meet their mother he decided to try to date Caroline (then twenty) thinking, perhaps, that she might introduce him to the former First Lady. 'I remember that Michael began to call Caroline constantly, even hoping that maybe Jackie would answer,' recalled, LaToya, who was staying with Michael in New York at the time. 'Finally, she agreed to go out on a date with him. They went to an ice-skating rink and then to dinner. Caroline ordered veal osso buco, which Michael said he had never heard of before. After dinner, Michael said he tried to kiss her, and she said, "If my mother finds out I kissed a black boy, she will absolutely kill me." Michael came home crying, but it didn't stop him from wanting to meet Jackie.' (Many years later, when Michael asked Jackie about Caroline's comment, Jackie was angry. She insisted that Caroline made up the excuse just to avoid kissing him.)

LaToya says that she discovered a naked photograph of Jackie in

Michael's room in New York, hidden in his sock drawer. Apparently, an embarrassed Michael explained that he had recently visited a *New York Daily News* reporter at his home for dinner. While the two rummaged through the writer's showbiz memorabilia, they came across the picture of Jackie. Michael was perplexed as to why she would pose for such a photographer, while unclothed. The reporter explained that the picture was taken by a paparazzo, obviously without her permission. Then, the scribe gave him the photo as a souvenir. 'I just can't stop looking at it,' he told LaToya. 'I must meet her.'

'What will you do when you meet her,' LaToya asked.

'I don't know,' Michael answered. 'Faint, I guess.'

By the fall of 1983, Michael was a world-famous superstar and Jackie a Doubleday editor who wanted to edit his memoirs. Finally, Michael would have his chance to meet her when Jackie asked to have lunch with him in Los Angeles. However, on the day of the scheduled luncheon, Michael suffered a panic attack. 'She's the most famous woman in the world,' he explained to one family member. 'And I'm, well, I'm just me.'

Michael spent the afternoon at Hayvenhurst vomiting and hyperventilating while Jackie and a couple of assistants waited for him in a Beverly Hills restaurant. The next day, Michael invited Jackie to his home in Encino.

'On the day she was set to come by the house, everyone was excited,' Steve Howell remembered. 'Naturally, we all wanted to meet her but would have settled for just a glimpse of her going from the limo to the house. The buzz around the house was 'Jackie O's coming, Jackie O's coming.' Her driver called from the car to alert Michael that they were about thirty minutes away. 'Okay, everybody out,' Mike said. 'You can all go home. Out, out, *out*!' Though nobody wanted to leave, everyone had to go. Michael wanted the entire staff to vacate the premises so that he would be able to be alone with Jackie. "But I want to meet, Jackie O, too," Katherine said. "Nope," Michael told her. "Not this time, Kate. Maybe next time."'

Another friend of Michael's remembered, 'Jackie wanted to talk book business, but Michael had other things on his mind. He wanted to know how she felt about always being photographed everywhere she went. He wanted to know how she handled her celebrity. He asked her for tips on how to avoid paparazzi. He admired her and was hoping to figure out what makes her tick.'

Michael was twenty-five years old and felt uneasy about writing his memoirs. 'I'm still trying to sort it all out myself,' he told Steve Howell. Indeed, some of his life did deserve close examination, but most people who knew Michael at this time agreed that he was not the most impartial person for the job. Michael was much too concerned about his public image, and that of his family, to write the real story. He certainly had many personal problems, most of which Jackie was not aware of, but he would do anything to protect the family's dignity. 'I don't want to let my fans down by having them know the whole truth,' he said. 'They'll be crushed.'

Michael knew that baring his soul in a book at this time was not something he could do, so he asked Jackie to consider a scrapbook concept, a book illustrated by such novelty items as his first report card, early pictures and poetry. Jackie tried to act interested, but she really wasn't enthralled by the notion. She wanted his whole life on paper, but she agreed to the scrapbook idea, at least for a while.

The next day Michael took Jackie to Disneyland. Jackie wore a sleek leather jacket with belt fastened around her impossibly thin waist, along with playfully striped pants. Michael was in the requisite military-styled, sequined jacket adorned with silver zippers and buckles. They both wore sunglasses.

'Afterward, he told me he thought she was strong and intelligent, and the fact that she survived JFK's death made him feel that she was someone he should have in his life as a mother figure,' said LaToya. 'I told him, "But, Michael, we already have a mother," and he said, "Yes, but we have to take care of Kate because of all she's going through with Joseph. Who is there to take care of us?" I didn't know the answer to that,' concluded LaToya, 'but I felt sure it would not be Jackie O.'

Meanwhile, Michael struck up the first of many friendships with young boys, this one being the twelve-year-old actor Emmanuel Lewis. Emmanuel was three feet, four inches tall at that time; Michael enjoyed carrying him in his arms as if he were a toddler. Emmanuel had come to Hollywood to star in the sitcom *Webster*; Michael had seen him on television commercials and had always wanted to meet him. He telephoned the boy's mother and invited him to visit Hayvenhurst. When he did, the two became fast friends. In truth, Michael nearly became obsessed with Emmanuel Lewis. They would play with Michael's pets, run around the estate like little kids playing 'Cowboys and Indians', roll around on the lawn together, laughing. It appeared to observers that Michael was trying to live the childhood he feels he missed. Today, of course, this is 'normal' behaviour for Michael. Everyone is used to seeing him rolling around with kids. However, in 1983, this was considered unusual, even for him.

One visitor at the Encino estate recalled watching as Michael read the story of Peter Pan to Emmanuel. Afterwards the two of them imagined themselves as characters in the story. According to the eyewitness, twenty-five-year-old Michael and twelve-year-old Emmanuel sat on the floor with their eyes closed and fantasized that they were flying over Never-Never Land. 'Believe it and it'll be true,' Michael whispered. 'Now, are you ready? Do you believe? Do you?'

'Yes, I believe,' Emmanuel said, his eyes closed tightly. 'I do believe.'

They then began to recite dialogue from the story. After a while, the two broke up laughing and began to wrestle on the floor like puppies.

Emmanuel Lewis's family reportedly became concerned about the friendship after Michael and Emmanuel checked into the Four Seasons hotel in Los Angeles – as father and son. It's not known what fantasy they were acting out at that time. However, shortly afterwards they stopped seeing as much of each other.

Once Michael had agreed to a reunion tour with his brothers, Joseph and Katherine asked Don King to assist in promoting the venture. Don is a flamboyant, outrageous and controversial black man considered by many at the time to be the leading boxing promoter in the world. Raised in a Cleveland ghetto, he went to prison in 1966 for second-degree murder after killing a man in a street fight. He served four years and then began promoting prizefights.

King was best known for his huge boxing promotions of Muhammad Ali's 'Thrilla in Manila' and Sugar Ray Leonard/

Roberto Duran fights. When the Jackson sons met with him, though, they were not impressed. During the meeting, King wore a white fur coat, diamond rings and a gold necklace on which hung a charm: a crown with the name DON on top of it. His grey hair stuck straight up, as if he'd just been electrocuted. The brothers decided that he was too ostentatious, not the type of man they wanted representing them in the public arena. However, their negative judgement about Don King shifted when he came up with three million dollars to give them as a show of good faith, against concert earnings – $500,000 to each member of the group. The brothers were ecstatic, Joseph was happy, and Katherine content. Michael was not impressed.

'I think he's creepy,' Michael told one friend. 'I don't trust the guy. He just wants a piece of the action, that's all.' It wouldn't be a small 'piece', that much was certain. Forty shows were planned, with a projected gross revenue of thirty million dollars. Deducting six million dollars for expenses would leave twenty-four million dollars net profit – 85 per cent of which would go to the group, 7.5 per cent to Don King, and 7.5 per cent to Joseph and Katherine. That amounted to $3.4 million for each Jackson member – enough to get the brothers back on their feet, for a while anyway – as well as $900,000 each for Joseph and Katherine, and a $1.8-million pay-day for Don King.

Once aboard, Don King contacted Jay Coleman, an enterprising promoter who specialized in obtaining tour sponsorships from major corporations. Don told Jay about the Jacksons' tour and their need for a big-money sponsor. 'And you, my man, are just the white boy who can walk into a corporation and tap them for the change,' he said. He was right about that: Jay recruited the Pepsi-Cola Company to pony up another five million dollars to sponsor the tour.

Jackie, Tito, Randy, Marlon and Jermaine all voted to work with Don King as promoter. After all, an extra five million dollars *was* impressive. However, for Michael, five million dollars was, as they used to say back in Gary, 'chump change', especially after it was split six ways and 15 per cent was taken off the top for Don, Joseph, and Katherine – leaving Michael with $700,000 and not much incentive. Michael reluctantly agreed to allow Don King to promote the tour, but he wanted Pepsi out of the picture. 'Forget it,' Michael said. 'I don't drink Pepsi. I don't *believe* in Pepsi.'

The family then worked on Michael to accept the Pepsi endorsement; there was too much money involved to let it go, and it *was* a viable and impressive sponsorship whether Michael drank the soft drink or not. The Rolling Stones had only received a half million for their endorsement. In fact, up until that time, the biggest deal in Madison Avenue history had been actor Alan Alda's for Atari, and that was only a million. The brothers thought Michael was crazy. 'I just don't want to do it,' Michael insisted. 'I have a bad feeling about it.'

Finally, after a weekend of intense pressure, Michael signed the contract at four o'clock one Monday morning. A rider made it clear that he would not have to hold a can of Pepsi, or drink from one, in any commercial or publicity photo.

'You know something? I don't know what that boy has against making money,' Joseph said later, in regard to Michael's reluctance about the Pepsi endorsement. 'You can always have more money. You never get to a point, I don't care how much money you have, where you don't need more money. And at that time everybody in the family, except Michael, I guess, needed it.'

On 30 November 1983, a press conference was organized at the Tavern on the Green restaurant in New York City to announce the Jacksons' reunion tour, and the fact that Don King would be promoting it. By this time, Michael had had two more major hit singles, 'Human Nature' and 'PYT', so it was expected that the site would be mobbed with fans, which it was; there were over a hundred police officers guarding the Tavern.

The press conference began on an odd note . . . and went downhill from there. In his introductory remarks, Don King spoke of God, then love and 'enrapturement', and the fact that 'Michael has soared the heights to the unknown'. Then, said the master promoter, 'It is so fortunate for all of us and so symbolic that we have such a beautiful family to use for all the world to see. They are humble. They are warm. They exude charming magnetism. The love that emits from these guys is so contagious,' he enthused. 'It's so captivating and infectious and it got me into this whirlwind of a musical spell that I can't seem to get out of . . .' On and on he went, for almost a half-hour. Then, he showed a fifteen-minute documentary – about himself. Katherine, Joseph, LaToya and Janet watched with confused looks on their faces as Don King then paraphrased Malvolio's speech from Shakespeare's *Twelfth Night*. 'Be not afraid of greatness,' he said, his chest puffed with pride. 'Some men are born great. Some achieve greatness. And others have greatness thrust upon them.'

Joseph leaned over to Katherine and was overheard asking, 'Is he talking about us or himself?' She shrugged.

'Does anything he's saying make any sense at all?' she asked, bewildered.

Don King then spoke of the upcoming forty-city tour, a concert film and a live satellite broadcast. He also announced that Pepsi-Cola had ponied up five million dollars for the privilege of sponsoring the event. The Jacksons would star in two commercials for Pepsi as part of the deal. 'It is going to be fabulous. The highest-grossing tour, the most amazing tour ever in history by these extraordinary men . . .'

Finally, Michael, Marlon, Tito, Jermaine, Randy and Jackie walked out to great applause from the press corps; they sat on the dais with glum faces, their eyes hidden behind sunglasses. None of them looked amused by the manner Don King continued to grandstand for the media. Finally, Don urged Michael to speak. 'I really don't have anything to say,' Michael began. 'I guess I would like to introduce the rest of my family. First my mother, Katherine—'

'Yes, that's the mother, Katherine,' Don King butted in. 'The backbone, the strength, the heart and soul—'

'And this is my father, Joseph.'

'Hmm-hmm, that's him. Joseph Jackson. I love that man. That man has truly mesmerized me.'

'And that's LaToya and Janet,' Michael said, now frowning at Don.

'Yes, aren't they truly lovely? The Jackson sisters, LaToya and . . .' Don's voice trailed off when he noticed Michael's expression.

'And my brothers' beautiful wives are here,' Michael continued. 'Hazel, Carol, Enid and Dee Dee. My sister Maureen is not here because she is doing an album for CBS. Thank you very much.'

Michael then refused to answer questions.

'Thank you, Michael, the golden voice of song,' Don said, quickly.

'So, what's this tour going to be called?' a reporter asked.

'They haven't named it yet,' King answered.

'Excuse me, but yes, we have,' Marlon cut in. 'We're calling it the Victory tour.'

'So there you have it, ladies and gentleman,' Don proclaimed. 'That is the name of the tour. The Victory tour. And what a heck of a name that is, too.'

'And what's the point of this tour?' someone else asked.

'The tour will mean that the brothers are getting together once again,' Jermaine said, 'to unite and work close with each other, to show the world that we can make everybody happy. And everybody in the whole world will unite as one, because we want to bring this together in peace for everyone,' he concluded, making about as much sense as Don King.

'Why can't Michael say more?' asked another reporter.

'Uh, well . . .' Don shot a look at Michael. Michael shook his head emphatically, no. 'He, uh, his voice is a problem because he has been working so hard singing those songs and makin' all those hit records,' said Don. 'He will not be able to continue talking now. Isn't that right, Michael?'

Michael seemed to glare at the promoter behind his shades.

Later, Washington reporters Maxwell Glen and Cody Shearer would dub the event 'one of media history's most abominable press conferences, ever.' Another observer called The Jacksons' tour 'The Nitro Tour', explaining that 'at any minute the whole thing is gonna blow sky-high.'

Michael had arranged to have the press conference video-taped. A few hours after it was mercifully over, he, John Branca and a few other trusted associates watched the tape in Michael's suite at the Helmsley Palace. 'It's a mess, isn't it?' was Michael's verdict.

John observed that Don King was actually the star of the show, and that The Jacksons had been 'some kind of sideshow'.

'Well, that really stinks, doesn't it?' Michael said, angrily. 'We gotta show this tape to the brothers.'

Michael then called a meeting in his room. Jackie, Tito, Jermaine, Marlon and Randy showed up within minutes. After the press conference, even they had their doubts about Don King. 'Look at this terrible thing,' Michael said, putting in the video tape.

'What's wrong with you guys?' Michael wanted to know after the tape finished. 'Can't you see that this man is using us? This is the Don King show, and The Jacksons are an opening act. Can't you see how bad this looks?'

'You're right, Michael,' Jackie said, shaking his head in despair. 'The guy is a complete jerk.'

'Unbelievable,' Jermaine agreed. 'Mike is right. I've never been so embarrassed. That was bad, real bad.'

The rest of the brothers agreed. Participating in the press conference had been a bleak enough proposition, but seeing how it looked from the other side of the dais was more than the brothers' pride could bear. 'Well, look, you guys chose this creep,' Michael said. 'Now, Branca and I are going to choose someone else, a tour coordinator who's going to really handle the business, someone like Bill Graham or Irvin Azoff, someone big in the business,' Michael said, referring to two giants in the concert promotion world. 'Do we agree?' he asked, taking charge. 'Is it time to take back some power?'

The brothers nodded their heads in agreement.

Another Bombastic, Attention-getting Melodrama?

By 1984, despite his tremendous fame and great fortune, Michael Jackson still continued door-to-door proselytizing for the Jehovah's Witness faith, 'twice a week, maybe for an hour or two,' according to Katherine. He also attended meetings at Kingdom Hall with his mother four times a week, when he was in town.

An example of a typical day of spreading The Word: wearing a disguise – a moustache, hat and glasses – and a tie and sweater, and holding a copy of *Watchtower*, Michael stood at the door of an apartment in suburban Thousand Oaks, California, one morning in early 1984. 'I'm here to talk to you about God's word,' he told the young girl who answered the bell.

She slammed the door in his face.

He went to the next apartment.

'Today, I'm here to talk to you about God's word,' he said when the door opened. He was invited into the apartment, and the door closed behind him. Louise Gilmore recalled the day Michael came to visit: 'It was very odd. At first I thought it was some kind of a trick-or-treat gag. A young black man came to my door wearing what was obviously a phony moustache and beard, and a big hat. His face was too smooth for all that facial hair. He looked like a little boy playing grown-up. He had this soft little voice and looked harmless enough. 'Can I talk to you for just a moment?' he said politely. I decided to let him in.

'He sat down and pulled out all of these books and pamphlets from a bag. "You should read these," he said. He gave me a little speech about the Jehovah's Witnesses, which I paid no attention to, so I can't tell you what he said. He then had a glass of water, thanked me, and went on his way. I didn't think anything of it, except, My, what a polite little boy.

'The next day my neighbour said to me, "Did Michael Jackson come to your house too?" I said, "What are you talking about?" When I put two and two together, I almost fainted. I've kept the material he gave me as souvenirs. No, I didn't join the religion.'

More than ever before, Michael considered himself a strict Jehovah's Witness. He didn't believe in blood transfusions, Easter and Christmas (which he viewed as 'pagan holidays'), or the celebration of his own birthday. He also did not believe in pledging allegiance to the flag. (In April 1984 he would attend the T. J. Martell Foundation's dinner honouring Walter Yetnikoff, president of CBS Records. Michael refused to be seated at the dais until after Monsignor Vincent Puma delivered the invocation and the crowd pledged allegiance to the flag and then sang the national anthem.)

Despite the fact that Michael was devout – and no doubt had donated quite a bit of money to the religion – the church's elders were upset with him in 1984, mostly because of the 'Thriller' video.

Michael had been so impressed with the horror-fantasy film *An American Werewolf in London* that he employed the services of John Landis to repeat his directorial duties and then he hired Rick Baker to create special effects on the 'Thriller' video. The fourteen-minute video was budgeted at $600,000. At this time, an artist could make a decent video for about $25,000. John Branca felt that Michael was overextending himself and advised him that they should find another way to pay for the 'Thriller' video.

John and Michael came up with the idea of a video entitled *The Making of Thriller*. At the same time that the video was being taped, extra footage of how it was done, including interviews with some of the key figures and even Michael himself, would be shot. John then approached Vestron Video, a video distribution company, and had them pay approximately $500,000 for the right to distribute the product.

Afterwards, John went to MTV and told executives there that Michael was doing a sixty-minute documentary and that if they wanted to show it, they'd have to pay for it. At that time, MTV didn't even pay record companies for the right to air videos because it was considered terrific promotion to have an artist's video aired on the cable-music station. While today there is much negotiating of money between MTV and an artist's managers, attorneys and record label executives, that was certainly not the case in 1984. However, because Michael was so popular, MTV quickly agreed to finance part of *The Making of Thriller* – if Michael would license it to the station for an official debut. The video would end up costing a little over a million dollars. The Showtime cable network also paid for second rights to the video. In all, MTV and Showtime put up nearly the whole second half of the million dollars.

The 'Thriller' video combined illusion and reality, skilfully weaving one into the other. The story opens with Michael pulling his white Chevy convertible over to the side of a wooded road. In a line that has been around since ten minutes after the first Model T rolled off the assembly line, Michael turns to date Ola Ray (a former *Playboy* centrefold) and says, 'I'm afraid we're out of gas.' However, instead of staying put and romancing, they start to walk.

He asks her to be his girl. She accepts. 'I'm not like other guys,' he then tells her in a soft and whispery voice.

'Of course not,' she says, brushing off one of the great understatements of all time. 'That's why I love you.'

'No,' Michael insists. 'I mean I'm different.'

As the moon comes out from behind a cloud, Ola discovers how different Michael really is: how many other guys sprout fangs, claws and whiskers and bray at the moon as they turn into werewolves?

He chases her through the woods. She trips. She is flat on her back. He hovers over her, clearly up to no good.

Just as the monster is about to attack, the camera focuses on Michael and Ola as part of a movie theatre audience, dressed in a more modern fashion than their 1950-style counterparts on the screen. She is cringing in horror while he is clearly enjoying the scene. 'I can't watch,' she says, getting up to leave.

Reluctantly putting aside his popcorn, Michael follows her out of the theatre, playfully taunting her about her fears. He begins singing 'Thriller' as they walk along the deserted streets. When they pass a graveyard, an assemblage of ghouls emerge from their graves and crypts to surround the couple. With skin the colour of mushrooms, blood dripping from the corners of their mouths, and eyeballs bulging halfway out of their heads, they look as though they have been moldering for a long time.

Ola escapes to find shelter in a deserted house. Meanwhile, Michael leads the grotesque company in dance, his features contorted and menacing, his blood-red clothing contributing to his sinister appearance. He leads the other ghouls to Ola and, as she trembles in fear, Michael and his gruesome company break through the walls, the windows, the floor. Ola huddles on the sofa, screaming as Michael reaches out for her.

Suddenly, they are in Michael's home. 'Hey, what's the problem?' a smiling Michael asks. Ola looks up at him with confused eyes. Was it all a dream? Michael puts his arm protectively around her shoulder. But, then, as he turns to face the camera his eyes are bestial, his smile ominous.

There's little doubt that Michael never intended the video to advocate Satanism or the occult. He was so engrossed with fantasy, 'Thriller' was no scarier to him than Halloween. After all, when he finished a hard day's work on the set, he went home to a bunch of dead-eyed mannequins in his bedroom. Before he had even finished work on it, though, the video brought to a head an ongoing conflict between Michael and the church elders of the Encino Kingdom Hall. After the elders heard about the concept, they summoned Michael for a meeting, during which the state of his soul was discussed. He was not receptive. He didn't want to be told what to do, not by his father and not by his church, either. He refused to make any kind of statement repudiating his work, as the church insisted he should. 'I know I'm an imperfect person,' Michael said. 'I'm not making myself out to be an angel.'

Finally, when the elders threatened to banish him from the religion, Michael became worried. He telephoned John Branca's office. When John's secretary picked up the phone, there seemed to be no one on the line. All she heard was the sound of desperate breathing, as if someone was trying to catch his breath in between sobs. 'I don't know who it is,' she told John. 'It might be Michael.'

When John got on the line and heard nothing but panting, he became concerned. However, before he could figure out what was going on, the line went dead. John telephoned Michael, but there was no answer.

The next day, Michael called back and whispered that he had 'a big problem'. Then he abruptly hung up again. Could he be any more dramatic? These kinds of maddeningly cryptic telephone calls went on for several days until John was extremely worried about Michael.

Finally, Michael got a hold of himself, apparently, and called John to ask if he had the tapes to the 'Thriller' video. When the attorney said that he didn't have them, that they were in the processing lab, Michael instructed him to retrieve them. 'Then, I want you to destroy them,' Michael said. He sounded desperate. 'No one must ever see the video.'

Before John had a chance to respond, Michael hung up.

Michael called back the next day, wanting to know if his attorney had gotten the tapes. By this time, John was tired of playing games. He wanted to know what was going on, especially since Michael had already spent a million dollars of MTV's, Showtime's and Vestron's money on 'Thriller'. How could they now destroy the tapes?

When Michael explained that his church had threatened to expel him if the 'Thriller' tape was released to the public, John was astounded. He tried to convince Michael that he should not allow the church elders to dictate his artistry, but Michael wasn't interested in his opinion at that point.

Michael called back the next day. 'Do you have the tapes?' he asked John. John did. When Michael asked, 'Did you destroy them?' John said that he had done just that; actually, though, they were sitting on his desk. 'Okay, then fine,' Michael said. He hung up.

Coincidentally, at this same time John had been reading a book about Bela Lugosi. After thinking about Lugosi and his Dracula character, John called Michael back and engaged him in a conversation about the horror star, explaining to Michael that Lugosi had been a religious man but that, as an actor, he played the demonic Dracula and actually built a career for himself by doing so. Michael listened intently as John then told him that Lugosi's religious beliefs had no bearing on his art, and that the fact that he portrayed a vampire in movies didn't make him any less religious in real life. He suggested that Michael might want to reconsider issuing the 'Thriller' video with a disclaimer at the beginning stating that the work was not reflective of Michael's personal or religious convictions. Michael thought John's suggestion was brilliant. He wasn't even angry when John confessed that he'd not destroyed the tapes, after all.

The next day, John telephoned the video's director, John Landis, to tell him that there would have to be a disclaimer. 'Bullshit,' Landis said. 'No way.'

'Look, man, if there's no disclaimer then there'll be no video,' John told him. He then explained the entire story to Landis. 'Jesus Christ,' Landis said, 'this kid's in bad shape, isn't he?'

John Branca couldn't really disagree, though out of respect for his client he didn't comment. Michael had handled the entire matter in a manner that was so odd, it was actually eerie. What kind of madness was this behaviour, calling and hanging up, panting and sobbing? In a sense, the scenario was reminiscent of his dramatic declaration that the *Thriller* album be cancelled. It's difficult to know if Michael was really upset (and if he was, one would think that there might have been a better way to handle it) or, again, orchestrating a bombastic, attention-getting melodrama around a new and upcoming project.

In the end, the 'Thriller' video was released with the following disclaimer at its beginning: *Due to my strong personal convictions, I wish to stress that this film in no way endorses a belief in the occult – Michael Jackson.*

As part of the Michael Jackson merchandising bonanza, *The Making of Thriller* video cassette was eventually released – one video showing how the *other* video was made. According to the Record Industry Association of America, Jackson's first release for the home-video market was the first music video cassette to apply for immediate gold and platinum certification. It was, by far, the best-selling music video to date. Michael would make millions from it.

The week before the 'Thriller' video was released in late December 1983, *Thriller*'s sales had slowed down to 200,000 copies a week, more than respectable for an album that had been out for a year. According to *Time*, the week after the video was issued and televised on MTV for only five days, the album sold another 600,000 copies and shot back up to number one on the *Billboard* charts.

PART SIX

Michael Gets Burned by Pepsi-Cola

The first order of business for 1984 was the filming of the two Pepsi-Cola commercials. Michael was still unhappy about the endorsement, especially when the Quaker Oats Company offered to support the Jackson's tour with a sum that was 40 per cent more than offered by Pepsi-Cola. Though the contract was already signed with Pepsi, John Branca did try to get Michael out of the agreement. However, Katherine was asked by Don to 'talk some sense into Michael'. The Pepsi deal was back on.

From the beginning, it was understood by everyone involved that Michael would have complete quality control over the commercials. His brothers could have no say about the footage, which was fine with them. They were being paid a hefty sum to do the commercials, and were satisfied.

After a few meetings with Michael, the Pepsi-Cola executives were worried. As it happened, Michael's friends Paul McCartney and Jane Fonda had told him he had made a mistake in agreeing to the commercials because the result would be overexposure for him. Michael decided that one way to rectify the problem was to make sure his face should only be on camera for one close-up, and only for a maximum of four seconds. In other words, he wanted to make a cameo appearance in his own commercial – and for that, Pepsi would have to pay five million dollars.

'There are other ways to shoot me rather than push a camera in my face,' Michael insisted to three exasperated Pepsi-Cola executives in a meeting at his home. 'Use my symbols. Shoot my shoes, my spats, my glove, my look – and then, at the end, reveal me.' He offered to allow the Pepsi executives use of 'Billie Jean', for which he would write new Pepsi jingle lyrics. Michael wasn't trying to get out of the deal, he just wanted the commercials to be special. If he was going to do them, he'd decided, they may as well be worthwhile. When Michael met with Roger Enrico, president and chief executive officer of the Pepsi-Cola Company, he told him, 'Roger, I'm going to make Coke wish *they* were Pepsi.'

Though trying to be a team-player, Michael still had reservations. 'I still don't have a good feeling about it,' he said about the Pepsi endorsement. 'In my heart, I feel it's wrong to endorse something you don't believe in. I think it's a bad omen.' He shrugged his shoulders and added, 'But I guess I just gotta make the best of it.'

On Friday 27 January 1984, the time had come to film the commercial. Three thousand people were seated in the Shrine Auditorium in Los Angeles, in order to simulate a live concert audience. The Jacksons were to perform 'You're a Whole New Generation', which were special lyrics to the music of 'Billie Jean'.

Prior to one of the takes, the brothers were preparing themselves for the shooting – adjusting their outfits, putting on their makeup – when Michael had to go to the bathroom. 'Go ahead, use mine,' director Bob Giraldi suggested. 'Don't worry, I'll just be a minute,' Michael said. He went in and closed the door.

Thirty seconds later, a bloodcurdling shriek came out of the bathroom.

'Jesus! What happened?' Bob Giraldi started banging on the door in alarm. 'Michael, Michael. Are you okay?'

When Michael slowly opened the door, Bob and a bunch of others rushed into the bathroom. 'I dropped my glove,' Michael said, embarrassed.

'Where?' asked Bob.

'In there,' Michael said, meekly. He pointed down to the toilet bowl. Floating in the water was a lone, white, rhinestoned glove.

'Oh, okay,' Bob said, trying not to burst out laughing. 'Somebody get a hanger or something. We'll just have to fish it out of there.'

Everyone scattered about in search of a hanger. Finally Michael said, 'Oh, forget it.' He reached into the toilet and pulled out the soaking-wet glove. 'Anyone have a hair dryer?'

*

It had been a long day. All of the brothers except Michael had arrived at nine in the morning. Tito acted as his brother's stand-in, taking Michael's place for the purpose of camera angles and other technical positioning. Michael, the star of the show, would not arrive for hours.

By about six p.m., the group performed their number for the sixth time that day – this time so that Bob Giraldi could make technical adjustments. Finally, tape began rolling at 6:30. As he had done during each rehearsal, Michael began to descend from a podium by going down a staircase amid brilliant illumination. His brothers were lined up on the stage, playing. A smoke bomb and pyrotechnics exploded, as planned, momentarily blocking Michael from view.

First a pose; that unmistakable silhouette.

Then, a magnesium flash bomb, which went off with a loud bang two feet from Michael's head.

As Michael headed down the stairs, the smoke became thick. Something wasn't right. He began to dance. He did a turn. And another, and another. After spinning three times, he popped up on his toes. He was hot – literally. When he turned, their was an audible gasp from the audience. The explosion had set his hair ablaze. He would later remember feeling the heat, but said he thought it was generated by hot stage lights. He continued to perform, but not for long.

When he felt the burning pain, Michael pulled his jacket over his head and fell to the stage floor. 'Tito! Tito!' he yelled.

Bob Giraldi would recall, 'The film would later show that while his hair was burning, he was trying to get his jacket off. Maybe he thought it too was on fire. He did two quick spins, though, and put out the fire by his own force.'

The first to respond was Miko Brando, Marlon's twenty-two-year-old son and one of Michael's security staff. 'I ran out, hugged him, tackled him, and ran my hands through his hair,' reported Brando, who burned his fingers in the process.

For a few disturbing moments, no one seemed to know what had occurred, or how to respond to it. There was chaos and pandemonium. Jermaine would later say he thought Michael had been shot. The crew rushed on to the stage, threw him down, and covered his head with a blanket to put out the fire. After a handful of ice was applied and a T-shirt borrowed to make a cold compress, Michael was taken off the stage.

When Michael was taken away, and did not return to the stage, it was difficult for the authorities to keep the crowd calm and orderly. Screams filled the auditorium. Since no óne in charge could give an accurate report, audience members began to develop their own theories. Most believed that it had been an assassination attempt on Michael.

In order to avoid fans and news media, the authorities hoped to transport Michael through an exit from the back of the theatre. However, Michael insisted on exiting where the crowds and photographers could see him. He said that he wanted to be able to to show the assembled crowd that he was all right. In truth, though, he also knew a *moment* when he saw one coming; no one could ask for better public relations. 'No, leave the glove on,' he told the ambulance attendants as he was being prepared for the stretcher. 'The media is here.' No matter the pain, shock, or hysteria, the showman prevailed.

The videotape of Michael being loaded into the ambulance became the lead story on all news broadcasts that evening. There he was, strapped in a stretcher, covered up to his nose, his bandaged and taped head resting on a pillow, one sequined-gloved hand protruding weakly from blankets. Michael lifted his hand with what appeared to be his very last bit of strength . . . and waved to the cameras. 'If E.T. hadn't come to Elliot, he would have come to Michael's house,' Steven Spielberg had earlier said of Michael. Now, Michael *was* E.T., an odd little creature, hurt by grown-ups who had been playing with fire, being carted away to who-knows-where, by who-knows-whom, and for who-knows-what purpose.

As he was being wheeled out, as he would later tell it, he noticed several Pepsi executives huddled together with anxious expressions. They must have realized that the accident could become the catalyst for one of the biggest lawsuits in show-business history: Michael Jackson could *own* Pepsi by the time the smoke cleared.

The next day, photos of Michael as E.T. were on the front pages of newspapers all over the world. Michael would call it 'that famous shot of me'.

Michael was taken to the emergency room at Cedars-Sinai Medical Center, where he was treated with an antiseptic cream and bandages. He was offered a painkiller, but because of his disdain for narcotics, he turned it down. Soon, though, he realized he needed it and accepted one. Then, accompanied by Joseph and Katherine, Bill Bray, his brother, Randy, and his doctor, Steve Hoefflin, Michael was transported to Brotman Memorial Hospital in Culver City.

I attempted to get an interview with Katherine and Joseph as they rushed into the hospital, arm in arm. 'How do you feel about this?' he asked.

Katherine kept walking, but Joseph stopped. He glared at me. 'That's my son in there,' he said, clearly upset. 'How do you think I feel? How does any father feel when his son is hurt?'

'You and Michael have had your differences, though,' I observed.

Joseph studied me for a moment. 'Hey, man, do you have any kids?'

I shook my head no.

'Then you can't understand how I feel. Whatever happens, a father will always be a father. His son will always be his son. All right?'

Michael spent Friday evening in room 3307, resting. In a short time, though, he was bored and asked for a videotape player. Because no one on the staff had the key to the cabinet where the hospital's video equipment was kept, someone broke the padlock to get Michael a machine and an assortment of tapes. He chose the science-fiction film *Close Encounters of the Third Kind* – directed by his friend, Steven Spielberg – and watched it until he fell asleep at one a.m. after taking a sleeping pill.

Outside his room, Katherine, Joseph and Bill Bray prepared to go home. They looked relieved. It had been a tense, exhausting experience. Joseph noticed a group of Pepsi executives standing together, still looking upset. As he walked by them he asked, 'Why the long faces? Jeez. The burn's only the size of a half-dollar.'

Michael had been fortunate; his face and body escaped injury in the accident. He suffered a palm-sized patch of second- and third-degree burns on the back of his head. Only a small spot – smaller than a half-dollar, actually, more like a quarter – received a third-degree burn. Doctors said most of his hair would grow back. Ironically, Michael had visited burns patients at the same hospital on New Year's Day. He had been particularly affected by one patient, twenty-three-year-old mechanic Keith Perry, who had suffered third-degree burns on 95 per cent of his body. Michael had had photos taken of himself holding the patient's hand, with his sequined glove on. When asked why he was wearing the glove, Michael responded, 'This way, I am never offstage.' The photos were quickly distributed to the media.

By Saturday, according to nursing supervisor Patricia Lavales, 'Michael was singing in the shower.' He spent the morning watching *American Bandstand* and *Soul Train* on television when he wasn't talking on the telephone. Diana Ross called, as did Liza Minnelli. Michael was released later that day. According to Lavales, before he left the hospital, Michael, wearing turquoise hospital scrubs over his street clothes and a black fedora covering his wound, went from room to room saying goodbye, taking photographs and signing autographs for the other burns patients.

After being released from the hospital, Michael checked into the Sheraton Universal for a night in order to be away from his family. John Branca met him there.

'Mike, I think God is trying to tell you something about this commercial,' John told him. 'We should never have done it.'

'I know, Branca.'

'You know what? You've got Don King to thank for this,' John added.

'Look, don't remind me,' Michael said. He was clearly disgusted.

That evening, Michael, Steve Hoefflin – who had performed Michael's rhinoplasty surgery and is chief of plastic surgery at Brotman – and others in the Jackson entourage, including John Branca, watched a videotape of the accident to determine just what had happened. (As soon as the accident occurred, John's partner, Gary Stiffelman, seized the tapes from the cameramen. Pepsi didn't have any footage, at all. Michael had it.)

After Michael saw the tape, he became enraged. 'I could have been killed,' he said. 'Did you see what they did to me? Did you see that? Man, I can't believe it.'

Though the others tried to calm him down, it was useless.

'Show it again,' Michael ordered.

Someone popped the tape back into the VCR, and everyone watched again.

'That's it,' Michael said. 'I want the tape released to the public. I want the public to see it. I'm gonna ruin Pepsi. After my fans see this tape, Pepsi will be history.'

'But, Mike—' one of his associates began.

'No. I'm serious,' Michael said, cutting him off. 'Release the tape. I want it on the news right away. I want everyone to see what happened to me, and I want it released on Monday. Pepsi's gonna be sorry.'

'You can't do it, Mike.'

'You wanna bet? I sure can,' Michael insisted. 'And I'm going to.'

By Sunday, word of Michael's decision got back to Roger Enrico, president of Pepsi-Cola. John Branca showed him the tape. 'Did the press reports say his hair was on fire?' Roger later recalled. 'To me, it looked like his whole head. Like a human torch. No way can *anyone* see this footage. It's grotesque.'

Roger knew he had to change Michael's mind or no Michael Jackson fan on the planet would ever again drink Pepsi after they saw 'what Pepsi did to him'.

'With more anxiety than I've ever felt in my life,' Enrico telephoned Joseph Jackson to ask what should be done about this problem.

'What problem?' Jackson asked.

'Michael wants to release the film with his hair on fire.'

'Why would he want to do a thing like that?' Joseph asked, perplexed.

Roger didn't know the answer to that question. He could only assume that Michael wanted revenge. He told Joseph that if Michael allowed the film to be released, people would always associate him with the burn accident, the way, he said, the public equates the Zapruder assassination tape with President John F. Kennedy.

Joseph didn't know what to say. 'Try telling Michael what to do these days,' he said. 'There's no way. He does what he wants to do. All I can say to you,' he concluded, 'is lotsa' luck.'

The tape would be released early the next week, Michael finally decided. He was bent on revenge. It would have been distributed sooner, except that his associates were unable to locate a lab that could process the film on a Sunday at such short notice.

First, to whet everyone's appetite, a blurred photograph of Michael descending the stairs with his hair on fire – it looked in the photo as if he had a halo – was distributed by the Associated Press. It made the front pages of practically every daily newspaper.

After that photo was released, John Branca felt that Michael had had ample time to cool off, and he tried to talk Michael out of releasing the tape.

'It's morbid, Mike,' John told him in a meeting with associates. 'Don't do this to your fans. And besides that, I think we should just settle with Pepsi and get on with our lives. Why infuriate everybody, Mike?'

'Why not?' Michael wanted to know.

'C'mon, Mike. You're bigger than this,' John said.

Michael cracked a smile. 'I'm being dumb, huh?' he asked, sheepishly. He'd recognized his own petulant behaviour. 'You're right,' he told his lawyer. 'Let's just end this thing, but I want them to pay, Branca. I mean it. They should pay big time for this.'

Though Michael was only paid $700,000 to do the Pepsi commercial, the publicity he would receive because of the accident would prove invaluable. It triggered an outpouring of public sympathy from around the world. The hospital where he was first taken for treatment was even forced to add six volunteers to answer telephone calls from fans and well-wishers. At Brotman, thousands of calls, letters, and cards were received.

Even Ronald Reagan got in on the act with a fan letter to Michael dated 1 February 1984: 'I was pleased to learn that you were not seriously hurt in your recent accident. I know from experience that these things can happen on the set – no matter how much caution is exercised . . .'

'What really pissed Mike off,' recalled Steve Howell, 'was when attorneys for Bob Giraldi [producer of the video] tried to put the blame for the burn on the hair grease Mike used. They said that this product was responsible for his hair catching fire. He thought Giraldi was his friend and wondered why he would do such a thing. The stuff he uses on his hair is, he told me, like everything else he uses on his body, one hundred per cent natural, no chemicals.'

When Michael got home to the Encino compound, one of the first things he did was call Steve Howell: 'Can you come up here and set up the video equipment in my room so I can watch the Three Stooges?'

That afternoon, Michael took a spin around the property in his electric car, a close copy of the vehicle from Mr Toad's Wild Ride at

Disneyland. From the street, outside the gate, his fans – who were always there – could see him whizzing up and down the driveway like a little boy so happy that his mother had finally let him out to play. After he put away his expensive toy, Michael playfully tossed the gown he wore in the hospital over the gate to the fans.

To this day, Michael experiences some pain in his scalp where he was burned. 'They knew I could have sued them,' Michael wrote of Pepsi in his book *Moonwalk*, though most people felt that it was probably the production company, not Pepsi, that was responsible. 'But I was real nice about it.'

Well, he wasn't *that* nice. At Michael's request, John Branca pressured Pepsi-Cola into a monetary settlement. He wanted $1.5 million. The company argued that the sum was way too high. They would pay, but the accident wasn't even their fault; they blamed the production company. 'How about a half mil?' one of the soft drink's lawyers suggested. Finally, under threat of a lawsuit, Pepsi-Cola paid Michael $1.5 million.

Michael Jackson accepted the money, then donated it to the Michael Jackson Burn Center, which had been established in his honour at Brotman after the accident.

'I never smile when I dance'

By February 1984, Michael Jackson's accident had been the subject of news reports for weeks. The publicity had only served to heighten the suspense about the forthcoming Pepsi commercials, which were to be aired for the first time during the upcoming Grammy Awards programme. Some people began talking about their 'debut', as if they were among the most newsworthy events of the century. Before the Grammys, the commercials would be 'unveiled' at a black-tie event for one thousand bottlers at New York's Lincoln Center; the commercials would also be screened for the press in New York, have their world premiere on MTV at no cost to the sponsor, and then, finally, appear as consecrated commercials during the Grammy telecast.

Down to the very last minute, though, Michael gave the Pepsi-Cola Company a difficult time. When he saw the finished product (actually two commercials: the concert scene and a 'street' scene featuring Michael with dancer, Alfonso Riberio), Michael adamantly insisted that they were not good enough; Michael hated them. There was too much of his face in the concert spot, he said. The bigger problem was that Michael wouldn't talk directly to the Pepsi executives about his concerns. Either he was acting spoiled or he was shy. No one was sure.

Roger Enrico then telephoned Joseph to complain that they couldn't make the commercials 'better' if Michael refused to talk about them. No matter what people may have thought about Joseph personally, they respected the fact that he was usually willing at least to listen to them. If he thought an idea had merit, he would do his best to convince Michael to consider the proposal favourably.

'Look, it's not easy for Michael,' Joseph Jackson told one Pepsi executive. 'He's got great ideas, but he can't always express them. Let me help. I can act as a go-between and make it easier on everybody. I know the kid. I know how he thinks.'

A few hours later, Joseph called Roger. 'I have Michael here,' he said, 'and I'm sure you guys can work things out.'

There was a pause.

'Go ahead. Talk to the man?' Joseph urgently whispered. 'Get on the phone, Michael.'

Michael got on the line. He then complained to Roger that he was made to take off his sunglasses during the taping, and that he really hadn't wanted to do that. He had been promised, he said, that there would be only *one* close-up without the shades, 'and now I see lots of close-ups of me with my glasses off.' Moreover, he fretted that there was too much of him in the commercials, '*way* over four seconds of my face.' The film was too dark. He spins *twice* during the routine. 'And I only agreed to one spin,' Michael reminded Roger. Also, in the commercial with Alfonso Riberio, which he liked and said was 'magic, just magic', he wanted bells to sound when Alfonso bumped into him as they danced, 'like the sound of a wind chime.'

'Bells?' Enrico asked, dazed.

'Yes, bells.'

Both commercials were quickly re-edited with Michael's changes in place. Michael then took a look at the new product and telephoned Roger Enrico with the verdict. 'Hello, Mr Enrico. This is Michael Jackson,' he said. 'You know, the person you spoke to the other day about the commercials.'

Roger remembered.

The commercial with Alfonso Riberio was fine, he said. However, there was still too much of him in the concert endorsement. He was seen for a total of five seconds. There should only be four seconds of his image, he said. Also, he was seen smiling in one dance moment.

'So?'

'So, I never smile when I dance,' Michael explained.

'Oh.'

On 7 February Michael was inducted into the *Guinness Book of Records* during a ceremony at the American Museum of Natural History in New York City, in recognition of *Thriller* having broken all records for album sales at twenty-five million copies. CBS Records held a black-tie party for fifteen hundred guests at the Museum of Natural History. Michael was accompanied to the event by actress Brooke Shields. *Her* 'people' had gotten in touch with *his* 'people' and suggested that she would be the perfect date. 'Why not?' Michael decided.

When Michael got back to Los Angeles, he met with Joseph, Katherine, his brothers and Don King to tell them what he had decided about the tour. 'I want to rename it,' he said. 'I don't like "Victory Tour" I want to call it "The Final Curtain".'

Michael wanted to make it clear that the upcoming tour would be the end of the road for him and his brothers. Once they finished, he would not work with the Jacksons again, thus 'The Final Curtain'.

'None of the brothers liked that name at all,' Marlon recalled. 'Our parents didn't like it either. Michael was making it sound like a funeral, like someone had died. But we weren't dying.'

Michael wasn't happy with the name 'Victory tour' because of the obvious implication that the tour was, somehow, a victorious occasion. Actually, he felt that he'd been defeated by being coaxed by his mother into participating in the event. As far as the new name was concerned, however, he was, not surprisingly, outvoted.

'How many Grammys do you think I'll win?' Michael asked Quincy Jones.

Quincy shrugged. Smart man. He knew better, after the *Thriller* outburst, than to make any predictions.

'Well, all I can say is I hope I win a lot of 'em,' Michael said with a smile.

A review of the history of the Grammys – the awards programme that the National Academy of Recording Arts and Sciences established in the late 1950s as a pop music equivalent of the Oscars – reveals that Grammy winners are not always the true pre-eminent artists and recordings of their time. For example, Elvis Presley never won a Grammy for any of his major pop vocal performances, even though he was the most influential pop artist of the last forty years. Chuck Berry was also routinely omitted. The Beatles only received four Grammys, which is amazing considering their impact on popular music and our culture. Bob Dylan's ground-breaking *Highway 61 Revisited* album won no Grammys in 1965. David Bowie's important *Ziggy Stardust* collection didn't even win a nomination in 1972. James Brown, The Rolling Stones, Sly Stone and Diana Ross have never received Grammy Awards. Quite simply, the six thousand notoriously conservative people who vote for those awards are not apt to quickly recognize the importance and significance of new artists.

There are also other, political considerations. It has long been rumoured that both the nominating process and the final electoral process of the Grammy Awards are dominated by major record companies that have turned the award into a self-congratulatory sham. By 1983, this contest had come down to a struggle between two large superpowers – the Warner Brothers/Elektra-Asylum/Atlantic-Atco faction (WEA) and the Columbia/Epic faction (CBS). As a result, it was very difficult for non-WEA and non-CBS recording artists to win Grammys. Motown artists, with the exception of Stevie Wonder, were usually not even in the running. In fact, in 1982, CBS won twenty-one of a possible sixty-two awards, including all the major citations.

Michael wasn't interested in the politics of the Grammy Awards. 'Who cares?' he once told a friend. 'All I want is as many of 'em as I can get.'

He needn't have worried. Michael Jackson was, quite simply, too popular for the Academy to ignore. He was so popular, in fact, that everyone agreed on his importance; he had become rock music's most commonly celebrated hero, and he was a CBS artist, to boot. When the Grammy nominations were announced, he received an unprecedented twelve nominations – the highest number of mentions for any single performer in Grammy history – including Record of the Year ('Beat It'), Album of the Year (*Thriller*), and Song of the Year ('Beat It' and 'Billie Jean'); a nomination for Best Children's Recording for his narration of E.T.; nominations for the engineers who remixed the instrumental track of 'Billie Jean' for the B-side of a single, and for the songwriters who wrote 'PYT' for his album; nominations for his producer, Quincy Jones; and an additional Best Producer nomination jointly shared by Michael and Quincy. In fact, Jackson's closest competitor was his producer and occasional arranger, Quincy Jones, who received six nominations.

Along with *Thriller*, the Police's *Synchronicity* and the Flashdance soundtrack also received nominations for Album of the Year, as did Billy Joel's *An Innocent Man* and David Bowie's *Let's Dance*.

The Grammys

On Tuesday, 28 February 1984, Grammy night, the scene at the Shrine Auditorium in Los Angeles was one of pure pandemonium. Giant klieg lights cut dramatic white patterns in the dark sky above. Fans in their roped-off areas were ready to scream and call out the names of anyone they might recognize. When twenty-five-year-old Michael Jackson arrived for his coronation as king of the pop music world, he wore a spangled uniform with epaulets and the rhinestoned glove on his right hand. With him was Brooke Shields.

Actually, Michael didn't want to go to the awards show with Brooke. Shortly before the ceremony, she came by the Encino house unexpectedly to ask him if he would consider taking her to the show. Although they had been friends for two years, it's unclear whether Brooke, eighteen years old at this time, actually felt attracted to Michael, or whether she knew that going with him to the Grammys would generate enormous publicity for her. She had already accompanied him to the American Music Awards in January when Michael swept the night (winning eight trophies) and to the Guinness Awards in February. Her picture, with Michael's, had been in every newspaper across the country.

Brooke Shields was instantly recognizable back in 1984, but not really a major star. Her career had not been critically acclaimed; her later films usually flopped. Her famous jeans commercials were no longer airing, and a movie called *Sahara* had temporarily been shelved. Smart and well-spoken, she was attending Princeton University in New Jersey at the time. Brooke and Michael enjoyed each other's company and related to one another in that both understood the pressure of being a child star with demanding parents. Brooke's mother-manager, Teri, was delighted by her daughter's association with Michael.

LaToya and Janet were in the kitchen when Michael rushed in to tell them of Brooke's request. 'I don't want to take her,' he said, according to LaToya's memory. 'I really, *really* don't.'

'Well then *tell her*, Michael,' LaToya said. 'Tell her no if you don't want to take her.'

'But I can't.'

'Why not?' Janet asked.

'Because I don't want to hurt her feelings,' Michael explained. Visibly cringing, he then went back into the living room.

A few moments later he rejoined his sisters, wearing a sheepish grin.

'Well?' LaToya asked.

'I'm taking her,' Michael said, sounding defeated. How ironic that the pop star who had not been intimidated by record business honchos Berry Gordy and Walter Yetnikoff had been hectored by Brooke Shields into doing what he did not want to do.

Months later, Michael and his employee Steve Howell were

reviewing photographs from the awards show. One was of him with Brooke Shields. 'What's she like?' Howell asked.

'Oh, she's okay,' Michael said, nonchalantly. 'But I only took her to help her out,' he added. 'There was no romance. All of this was strictly for her, for the sake of publicity.'

Indeed, when Michael and Brooke arrived in a white Rolls-Royce just moments before the ceremony began, there was such hysteria from the fans one might have thought they were visiting royals. Poor Tatum O'Neal was at the entrance door with four friends, watching the madness. Michael, Brooke and a coterie of security guards rushed right by her. 'Michael. Hey, Michael!' Tatum shouted. Too late. He was gone. She turned to her friends. 'I'll introduce you to him later. I promise.'

Michael, wearing heavy pancake makeup and loads of eyeliner, sat in the theatre's front row with Brooke and Emmanuel Lewis, who had met them there. Brooke seemed uncomfortable about having to share her date with a twelve-year-old. Earlier, when photographers descended upon them, Michael held Emmanuel with one arm and hugged Brooke with his free hand. It was as if he was trying to remind Brooke – and maybe the public – that the presence of a child on their date meant that he really wasn't serious about her. 'Let's get out of here,' Brooke was heard saying to Michael. 'People are making fun of us.'

During the ceremony, cheers rose from fans in the balcony and from industry colleagues who filled the orchestra seats every time Michael's face flashed on the studio monitors or his name was even mentioned. When the two Pepsi commercials 'premiered', the audience reacted with a tidal wave of applause and whistles. It was obvious that he was the man of the moment, and before he had even won a single award. Comedienne Joan Rivers noted in an explanation of how the votes were tabulated, 'The reason we're reading the rules is so that all the losers will know why they lost to Michael Jackson.'

That night, Michael made Grammy history when he won eight awards out of a possible ten wins on twelve nominations (three of his nominations were in one category).

Not since the brilliant maturation of Motown's Stevie Wonder in the mid-seventies (he won five Grammys in 1973 and 1974) had the public, press, and industry – three factions that seldom see eye-to-eye on anything – agreed so wholeheartedly on an entertainer's importance to our pop culture. In a sense, the unanimous recognition of Michael Jackson at the Shrine Auditorium meant that fans, critics and voters had agreed on a new pop music king.

Accepting the Best Album award for *Thriller* (which, by this time, had sold twenty-seven million records, was the biggest-selling album in history and still number one on the *Billboard* charts), a nervous and shy Michael said, 'This is a great honour. I'm very happy.'

When he later picked up the seventh and record-breaking Grammy, he took off his dark glasses in a victory salute – 'for the girls in the balcony'. Katharine Hepburn ('my dear friend') had scolded Michael for wearing the shades at the American Music Awards and told him he was 'cheating' his fans by not allowing them to see his eyes.

Michael accepted one award with the comment, 'I have something very important to say . . . really,' and proceeded to pay touching tribute to legendary rhythm-and-blues star Jackie Wilson, who had recently died.

Jackie was one of Michael's show-business idols. After suffering a heart attack onstage in New Jersey in 1975, Jackie lay in a helpless, practically vegetative condition in a nursing home. All of the Jackson children went to visit him one day in 1977. His primary caretaker was Joyce McCrae, who would go on to work for Joseph Jackson Productions. She was Gina Sprague's nemesis in the work place. Jackie couldn't speak; he could only blink once for no and twice for yes. All of the Jackson siblings were gathered around his bedside, trying not to cry, as Joyce introduced them, one by one. When she got to Michael, Jackie smiled and blinked twice. McCrae recalled, 'There was a happiness on his face that was just so precious, so deep, and so moving. He was so glad they were there. It was a special moment.'

Michael also won Best Record ('Beat It') and Best Vocalist in three areas: pop ('Beat It'), rock ('Thriller') and rhythm and blues ('Billie Jean'). He also won Best Children's Album (*E.T.*), Best Rhythm-and-Blues Song ('Billie Jean') and Best Record Producer, an award he shared with Quincy Jones. Jackson's two losses were to The Police, who copped three Grammys in all for the *Synchronicity* album and the single 'Every Breath You Take'. All told, his eight wins topped Paul Simon's previous record of seven in a year, earned in a 1970 sweep for *Bridge over Troubled Water*.

In one acceptance, he called CBS head Walter Yetnikoff to the stage with him. Later, he invited LaToya, Janet and Rebbie to join him.

Backstage, after the awards, Michael didn't have much to say to the press. It had already been made clear to the media that he would not be available for interviews – he would allow photos only. The assembled media, having been deprived of the opportunity to ask Michael questions about his winnings, had no choice but to ask all of the other winners how *they* felt about Michael's achievement. 'I've seen four phenomena in my lifetime: Frank Sinatra, Elvis Presley, The Beatles and Michael Jackson,' Quincy Jones noted.

'What's your favourite song?' someone shouted out to Michael as he walked away.

' "My Favourite Things" by Julie Andrews,' Michael responded.

'You're kidding, right?' the reporter asked.

'Nope.' Michael started singing the song, 'Raindrops on roses and whiskers on kittens . . .' while he skipped down the hall, accompanied by four security men. As he left the auditorium with Brooke and Emmanuel, fifty people were elbowed out of his way by his guards – including Tatum O'Neal and her four friends. 'I'll introduce you to him later,' she promised them, again. As Michael's Rolls-Royce sped away from the auditorium, he rolled down the window and leaned out, both arms raised in triumph, clutching and waving a Grammy in one hand. 'All right!' he yelled out. 'All *right*!'

Michael Jackson had become one of the most sought-after celebrities in Hollywood, always invited to a multitude of A-list parties. Often he needed an escort and, uncomfortable in his new role as a social butterfly, he sought someone safe – and older. Liza Minnelli was one of his favourites, partly because Michael had always been fascinated by the mystique of her mother, Judy Garland, but also because Liza had grown up in Hollywood, knew her way around, and was able to keep Michael comfortable and relaxed.

Besides, in 1984 it was Liza, not Michael, who received the coveted invitation to the 10 April party hosted by famed literary agent, Irving 'Swifty' Lazar. Held every year right after the Academy Awards, the event had once been so prestigious that even big-name stars considered it an honour to be invited. Celebrities often instructed their publicists to hound 'Swifty' for months in advance for an invitation. In 1984, the party was held at the Bistro in Beverly Hills. Guests included Orson Welles, Cary Grant, Jacqueline Bisset and Linda Evans.

It was obvious that no matter how famous Michael had become, in his heart he was just another star-struck fan. Judging from the expression on his face, his success didn't diminish his awe, but it did allow him to observe his idols up close. In return, the celebs fell all over themselves for a chance to meet Michael, a guy who had made only one movie (and that one a flop!).

Michael never strayed from Liza's side. Wearing one of his blue glitter military outfits, dark aviator shades, and the requisite rhine-stoned glove, Michael looked around the room and probably couldn't help noticing that everyone was gawking at him. For her part, Liza strolled about proudly with Michael on her arm, as if to say, Yes, *I'm* with Michael Jackson. What do you think of *that*?

'Let me have a scotch and Coca-Cola,' Liza instructed the waiter. 'And Mr Jackson will have the same.'

'Oh, no,' Michael protested. 'I'll have a . . .' He hesitated. 'I'll have an orange juice, please.'

'Oh, of course he will,' Liza said. 'And so will I. With *scotch*.' She laughed merrily.

The waiter walked away. 'Yoo-hoo,' Michael meekly called out after him. 'No scotch in mine.'

Joan Collins sauntered over to the couple. 'Michael, my dear boy, how truly wonderful to see you.' She embraced him warmly and winked at Liza, as if sharing a joke with her. Michael looked confused.

'Quick, stand right next to him; let's get a picture.' A woman shoved her husband next to Michael. 'This is for our daughter, Natasha,' the man sheepishly explained. Michael, who has no doubt heard a similar line a thousand times before, nodded patiently.

'Oh, by the way, my name is Michael Caine,' said the actor after the photo was taken. The two shook hands as Caine's wife, Shakira, snapped another picture of them.

Joan Collins turned to a friend. 'You know, I must get the name of his plastic surgeon,' she said. 'I simply *adore* his nose, don't you?'

Johnny Carson, seated with his girlfriend Alexis Mass, took in the scene and walked over to Michael just as his orange juice was being served to him.

'Nice to see you, Michael,' Carson said with a firm handshake.

Michael seemed dazed. 'I . . . uh, gee, nice to see you again too, Mr Carson.'

'Call me John.'

'Oh, okay. Call me Mike.'

Liza Minnelli grabbed Michael's hand. 'Now look, Johnny, he's *my* date,' she told Carson with a big smile.

'Wow! What a nice guy that Johnny Carson is,' Michael was overheard saying as Liza dragged him away.

'Oh, yes, he's a dear,' she agreed. 'Now we're going to call my father.'

'We are?'

Liza then led Michael off to a payphone.

After Liza dialled the number, she began doing a soft-shoe dance routine and started singing, 'Forget your troubles, c'mon get happy,' she sang. She was feeling . . . good.

Michael laughed. 'I love being around you, you know that?' he told her.

'*Shhh*,' Liza said. Her father answered the phone. 'Daddy, listen, I want you to meet Michael Jackson.'

'Who?' was apparently the question back to her.

'Why, he's a *wonderful* singer and one of my *best* friends,' she explained. 'Now just say hello.' A pause. 'Oh, Daddy, just say hello. Now, *c'mon*.'

She handed the phone to Michael. 'No, I can't,' Michael protested, his hand over the mouthpiece.

'Oh, but you *must*,' Liza insisted.

'But he's my idol.' Michael had always enjoyed director Vincente Minnelli's films.

'Well, then say *hello*.' Liza punched him on the arm playfully. 'He doesn't bite.'

Michael took his hand off the mouthpiece. 'Hello, Mr Minnelli,' he whispered. He listened for five seconds, his eyes darting left and right. With a giggle, he handed the phone back to Liza. 'God, he's so *nice*,' Michael gushed.

Liza got back on the phone. 'Now listen, Daddy. Put on your velvet jacket. We'll be over in twenty minutes.'

Pause.

'Yes, I'm bringing *him* over *there*.'

A pause.

'Never mind what he's wearing.'

Another pause.

'Okay, he's wearing one sequined glove, all right? Now, are you satisfied?'

Michael doubled over, laughing.

'Okay, then fine. Goodbye.'

As Liza and Michael pushed through the crowd and out the door to the waiting limousine, Jimmy Stewart was overheard saying, 'Well, there they go, Dorothy's little girl . . . and the Wiz.'

Almost twenty years later, 'the Wiz' would be part of the star-studded wedding party when 'Dorothy's little girl' married for a fourth time, in New York. Michael was best man and Elizabeth Taylor the matron of honour when, in March 2002, Liza wed David Gest in a well-publicized, star-studded extravaganza. Unfortunately, the union would end after sixteen tumultuous months.

'Believe me, trouble's ahead'

The upcoming Victory tour promised forty concert dates and, at least as far as Michael was concerned, forty million opportunities for something to go wrong as long as Don King was in the picture. Michael felt that he needed someone to protect his interests. John Branca was an excellent attorney, but now he needed a hands-on manager since Weisner and DeMann were gone and Joseph was no longer managing him.

As it happened, Motown had just released a collection of songs by

Michael that he had recorded in the early seventies. The album was called *Farewell My Summer Love 1984*, a misleading title since the songs were recorded more than ten years earlier. The record only sold about a hundred thousand copies, a minuscule number considering the thirty-three million copies of *Thriller* that had by then been moved in record stores. Michael believed that Motown was trying to cash in on his fame, and he didn't like it. 'It's not fair,' he said. 'I had no control over that music. I don't even like some of those songs. I need someone to stop things like that from happening in the future.'

Michael took meetings with a number of managers, including Colonel Tom Parker, Elvis Presley's Svengali, hoping to find the most qualified person. When it came to choosing a manager, Michael was extremely cautious. He questioned everyone he knew about certain people, trying to determine their worth in the entertainment industry. He would talk to his brothers to see what gossip they had heard; he would check with record company executives. In the end, his choice would surprise many observers.

Seven months earlier, in August 1983, Michael had asked Epic Records head of promotion, Frank Dileo, if he would be interested in managing him. The two were having a meeting about *Thriller* in a bungalow at the Beverly Hills Hotel. Michael firmly believed that Frank was largely responsible for *Thriller*'s success, and also for the huge sales of all of its single releases. After his search, he again went back to Frank Dileo, even though the man had virtually no experience as a manager. Many industry observers wondered, why Frank? ('I asked Michael the same question: why me?' Dileo said.) Michael felt that the aggressive way Frank worked in the record industry could prove an asset to him. In Frank Dileo, Michael knew he was hiring a terrific record promoter, who may or may not turn out to be a good manager – but he was willing to take a chance.

At the time, Frank Dileo, whose nickname is 'Tookie' (Michael used to call him Uncle Tookie), was thirty-six, born and raised in Pittsburgh. He had got his start in the record industry as an assistant to a record promoter in the Midwest, and in the early seventies when he was twenty-one, landed a job with RCA Records in New York as national director of promotions. While at RCA, he turned that label's promotion department into the record industry's finest. In 1979, Frank was named Epic's vice-president of promotion. There, he developed a reputation at the label as being a confident man in complete charge of everything around him – even matters that didn't concern him. A flashy character, he would wear a sweat suit to the office, along with an eight-thousand-dollar Rolex watch given to him by the Epic recording group REO Speedwagon. He was largely responsible for successes by Meat Loaf, Culture Club and Cyndi Lauper.

A few years after joining Epic, Frank was invited to the recording studio to watch as Michael recorded *Thriller*. It was then that he and Michael developed a rapport, though opposites in almost every way: Michael was shy and retiring, Frank was loud and boisterous; Michael was a health-food junkie, Frank liked a good hoagie and a Budweiser with which to wash it down; Michael never smoked, Frank loved cigars, the smellier the better; Michael weighed about 120 pounds; Frank weighed twice that. Still, Michael admired the way Frank set goals for himself and then achieved them. 'I'd like to be like Frank Dileo,' he said. 'He gets the job done.'

Also, Frank was a close friend and confidant of Walter Yetnikoff, president of CBS Records, and socialized with attorney Nat Weiss, one of Yetnikoff's trusted friends. Michael understood how politically valuable those relationships could be to him. However, Michael told Frank that if he took the job as his manager, he would not be allowed to manage anyone else. He had to be exclusive to Michael. Frank agreed.

By March, the Victory tour battle lines were drawn. Though the point of the tour was that the family presented a united front to the public, the business behind the scenes was so fragmented, it was almost impossible to find any commonality among the participants.

If Michael had to do the tour, he wanted more control of it. Not only was he exerting his independence at this time, he knew that if the show flopped it could hurt his career. Whereas his brothers only wanted to make a decent living, that was the least of Michael's concerns; he already had plenty of money. Still, since Michael now had his own manager, the brothers felt they had to have one, too. Therefore, they hired Jack Nance, who had been the group's road manager during the early days at Motown. So, now he had *his* manager, and they had *theirs*.

Making matters worse, Michael wanted nothing to do with Don King, especially when Frank filled Michael in on Don's reputation. Frank told Michael that Don had been criticized for his handling of the defunct US Boxing Championships on ABC Television. He also heard of charges, which King has denied, that he skimmed money from closed-circuit fights and sold five-hundred-dollar tickets to boxing matches but did not report the sales. If Michael had to do this tour, he decided, he would do everything in his power to distance himself from Don King. 'I can tell you one thing,' he told John Branca. 'I don't want that guy telling *me* what to do, and I don't want him to touch *one single penny* of my money.' Or, as Don King would later say, 'With Michael, you're always on trial.'

Through John, Michael dispatched a series of instructions to Don stating:

1. King may not communicate with anyone on Michael's behalf without prior permission.
2. All monies will be collected by Michael's representatives and not by King.
3. King may not approach any promoters, sponsors or other people on Michael's behalf.
4. King may not hire any personnel or local promoters, book halls, or, for that matter, do anything at all without Michael's prior approval.

Don appeared perplexed by Michael's demands but he had no choice but to abide by them. Still, Don felt that Michael was too easily swayed by the opinions of his white manager, Frank Dileo, and white lawyer, John Branca. 'I see that Michael has nobody black around him,' Don said to a reporter. 'Nobody.' That might have been true, but it was a mistake for Don to say it to the press. 'Fire him,' Michael said, angrily. 'Who does that guy think he is?'

But Don had a contract, and he wasn't going anywhere.

John and Don then had dinner at the Beverly Hills Hotel to try to work matters out. 'Look, Johnny, there's no reason why you and me gotta be on bad terms,' King told Branca. 'I like Michael. I like you. Let's work with one another.'

They agreed that they should try to work things out. However, by this time, the brothers were also ambivalent about Don King, especially after that press conference.

At this time Chuck Sullivan, head of Stadium Management Corporation, of Foxboro, Massachusetts, and former owner of the New England Patriots football team, was brought in to watch over Don King. He would be organizing the concerts. Michael was also able to convince the brothers to allow Irving Azoff, head of MCA, to come aboard as a tour consultant. Meanwhile, in the background, there was still Joseph Jackson, who did everything he could to stay involved and not allow Don to overshadow him. Then, there was Katherine, watching and waiting until the next time she would have to speak to Michael in order to get him to do something he didn't want to do.

'I said the Pepsi accident was a bad omen,' Michael told Frank Dileo one day as they sorted out all of the characters. 'But I didn't know what it meant. Now I know. Believe me when I say that trouble's ahead.'

Another Nose Job, and Katherine's Party

In the spring of 1984, Michael arranged for Dr Steven Hoefflin, his plastic surgeon, to give him another rhinoplasty – a third nose job. 'He was determined that the last two weren't good enough,' said a source who once worked in Hoefflin's office. ' "It has to be thinner," he insisted. "Did you see the way it looked on the American Music Awards when I was standing next to Diana?" he asked. "Hers was so thin and mine looked so fat. I hated it." He didn't come out and say he wanted Diana Ross's nose, but it was pretty obvious it was the shape he was after.'

'I saw him after that third operation,' Steve Howell recalled. 'I was at the house dropping off some film and Mike was home. He didn't know I was there and our paths crossed. He shrieked, "Oh no!" and ran off. It was like seeing a woman you don't know in her underwear and without her makeup on, that was his reaction. His face was black and blue. There was a gauzy bandage over his nose. He looked like a guy who'd been in a boxing match and forgot to put his hands up.

'A couple of weeks later, we were talking and I was standing very close to him. I noticed what I thought were blemishes around his nose. I thought, All those natural creams and other cosmetics he uses, and he still has blemishes? However, studying the area on the other side of his nostril I realized those weren't blackheads, they were six small stitches around his nose. There was more work in weeks to come: his skin looked like it was being stretched, or peeled, or something. The reason I'm vague is that it was not something people around the house discussed.'

In May 1984, Michael hosted a birthday gathering with his brothers and sisters in honour of their mother, Katherine, at the Bistro Garden restaurant in Beverly Hills. No matter what was going on in their lives, the Jacksons loved their mother. Among her gifts, Katherine received a diamond ring and a rose-coloured, beige-topped Rolls-Royce. 'The press later reported that the Rolls was from Michael,' said his sister-in-law, the late Enid Jackson. 'Actually, we all chipped in on it. How do you think that made the brothers feel, the fact that the world thought the gift was from Michael? But that's the kind of thing they had to get used to over the years. Little things like this can be very hurtful. If, God forbid, they all got into an airplane crash, it would all be about Michael dying in a crash . . . and the brothers were also there.'

Much of the extended Jackson family attended Katherine's party. Her children flew Katherine's father in from Indiana as a special surprise. As a Jehovah's Witness, some of her friends thought it strange that she would agree to a birthday celebration.

Michael hired Steve Howell to videotape the proceedings. Not to be outdone, Jermaine had *his* videographer do the same thing.

Steve's video of the gathering is revealing. On it, the family did not appear to be close, though everyone seemed cordial enough as they exchanged pleasantries in the formal setting. When Janet walked in with her date, a singer named James DeBarge, everyone scattered. It was obvious that no one liked him.

The most emotional moment of the evening was between Michael and Katherine. Michael, wearing an expensive-looking, sparkly silver suit and tie, walked up on to the stage and said to his mother, 'This is one of your favourite songs. I'd like to do it for you.' He seemed nervous, even embarrassed. He can sing before thousands of people with no problem, but intimate gatherings truly rattle him.

Michael was accompanied by country star Floyd Cramer, playing a Fender Rhodes piano. (Cramer had been flown in for the party because Katherine is such a big fan of his.) As Cramer played, along with a three-piece band, Michael sang the Kris Kristofferson country song 'For the Good Times' to Katherine, reading the lyrics from cue cards.

When Michael sang the first line – 'Don't look so sad, I know it's over' – Katherine's eyes immediately began to well up with tears. Any observer might have thought that she was thinking of her marriage to Joseph, who was not even sitting with her but, rather, elsewhere in the room. As Michael sang the song – his voice pure, his delivery eloquent – Katherine rocked back and forth in her chair, looking as if her son's performance had completely swept her away. No mother had ever gazed upon her son in a more loving manner, and Michael's expression was equally moving.

Michael Meets the President

Around this time, John Branca received a telephone call from Transportation Secretary Elizabeth Dole asking if Michael would donate 'Beat It' as background music for a thirty-second television commercial and sixty-second radio spot on drunk driving. When John presented the idea to Michael, his reaction was swift. 'That's tacky,' he said. 'I can't do that.'

John told Michael he would call Elizabeth Dole and tell her that they were not interested. However, Michael then got an idea. 'You know what?' he mused. 'If I can get some kind of an award from the White House, then I'll give them the song. How about that?' he said, now excited. 'See what you can negotiate with them, Branca.'

'What do you want?' asked John, bemused.

'Well,' Michael said, like a kid coming up with a Wish List. 'I want to go to the White House. I want to be on a stage with the President [Ronald Reagan], and get an award from him. And I sure want to meet Nancy [First Lady, Nancy Reagan]. The whole works.

Why not? You think you can do that, Branca. Can you get me an award from the President?'

John laughed. 'Well, I can sure try.' The next day, John Branca went to work on the idea. He telephoned Elizabeth Dole and told her that she could have the song for her drunk-driving campaign if she dreamed up some kind of humanitarian award that the President could present to Michael. She agreed. The President agreed, as did the First Lady.

The presentation was set for 14 May 1984. It had started out as an exciting day. In fact, it was said that there hadn't been that much excitement at the White House since the day the hostages came home from Iran. For the occasion, the President wore a navy blue suit, navy blue and grey striped tie and white shirt. Nancy was chic in a white Adolfo suit trimmed with gold buttons and gold braid. It hardly mattered what she wore, though, for anyone standing next to Michael Jackson that day would pale in comparison. Michael appeared resplendent in an electric-blue sequined jacket adorned with sequined braid, a sequined gold sash, and sequined gold epaulets. He also wore his trademark single white, rhinestoned glove.

Hundreds of White House officials and secretaries, many of them clutching cameras, gathered on the sun-speckled lawn to catch a glimpse of Michael. More than a hundred yards back from the stage, the White House fence was lined solidly with fans, many wearing a single white glove like the one Michael sported.

Two thousand people cheered as Ronald Reagan stepped on to a stage on the White House South Lawn with Nancy and Michael. 'Well, isn't this a thriller,' he said. 'We haven't seen this many people since we left China. And just think you all came to see me.'

As Michael, the President and the First Lady walked to the Oval Office, one middle-aged White House office worker standing across from the Rose Garden shrieked, 'I saw his foot. I saw his foot!'

A special metal detector was constructed in the Jacqueline Kennedy Garden to screen Michael and his entourage of eight security men; Frank Dileo, John Branca and publicist Norman Winter. There was also a young man with Michael, a person no one seemed to know, except for Michael. He was dark, in his early twenties, and good looking. Dileo, Branca and Winter were perplexed as to who this person was, and when Michael was asked how the man should be identified to the press, he said, 'He's a close friend of mine. I don't care what you tell people. It's no one's business.' Norman Winter must have known that the presence of this mystery friend would raise some eyebrows. In order to protect Michael from controversy, he identified the man as a Secret Service agent.

Once at the podium, the President noted that Michael was 'proof of what a person can accomplish through a lifestyle free of alcohol or drug abuse. People young and old respect that. And if Americans follow his example, then we can face up to the problem of drinking and driving, and we can, in Michael's words, beat it.' After the President handed him a plaque, the only words Michael nervously spoke – or whispered, rather – were, 'I'm very, very honoured. Thank you very much, Mr President.' A pause. 'Oh, and Mrs Reagan, too,' he added as an afterthought. Then, he giggled as if it suddenly occurred to him that yes, he really *was* standing there with the President of the United States.

Six news photographers covering the event wore white gloves on one hand as they shot pictures of the Reagans and Jackson. The whole event took about nine minutes. Afterwards, nine police motor-cycles and several vans and mounted police escorted Michael from the White House.

But before they left, the entourage was given a special tour of the White House; Michael was particularly fascinated by a portrait of Andrew Jackson in a military jacket very much like the blue-sequinned one he wore that day. After the tour, the group was scheduled to spend time with the President and the First Lady.

Things took a turn for the worse, though, when Michael arrived at the Diplomatic Reception Room where he was to meet privately with the Reagans. He had been told that only a few children of staff members would be present. Instead, there were about seventy-five adults. Michael put one foot into the Reception Room, took a quick look around, and then ran out, down the hall and into the bathroom off the Presidential Library. Frank Dileo and the rest of the entourage followed him. However, before they could reach him, Michael closed the door and locked it.

'Hey, Mike, come on out,' Frank said.

'No. They said there would be kids. But those aren't kids,' Michael shouted back.

'But there *will* be children. We'll go get the children,' a White House aide promised. Then he turned to an assistant. 'Listen, if the First Lady gets a load of this, she's going to be mad as hell. Now you go get some kids in here, damn it. Get James Baker's kid. She's cute. [Chief of Staff James Baker had brought his six-year-old daughter, Mary Bonner.] I don't care *who* you get, just get some kids in here.'

Frank then addressed the closed bathroom door, again. 'It's okay, Michael. We're going to get the kids.' His voice had a patient tone, as though he were soothing a disturbed child. John Branca stood near by, watching with a bemused expression on his face.

'Well, you'll have to also clear all of those adults out of there before I come out,' Michael warned.

'Done.'

Someone ran into the Reception Room. 'Okay, out!' he said. 'Everybody out. Out, out, *out*!'

Senior staff and cabinet members cleared that room so quickly, an observer might have thought there had been a bomb threat.

'What's happening?'

'Where's Michael Jackson?'

'Has he left?'

Everyone spoke at once as they were ushered from the room.

The aide then ran back to the bathroom door, where a cluster of men with worried looks had congregated. He conferred with one of Michael's people. 'Okay. You can come out now, Michael,' Norman Winter said, finally. 'Everything is okay.'

'Are you sure?' came back the soft voice.

Frank Dileo knocked on the door with his fist, one loud thud. 'Okay, Mike, outta there. I mean it.'

The bathroom door opened slowly. Michael appeared. He looked around, slightly embarrassed. Frank put his arm around him. 'I'm sorry,' Michael told him, 'but I was told there wouldn't be so many people.'

Michael was then ushered back into the Reception Room, where awaiting him were just a few officials and their children. Elizabeth Dole was the first to approach Michael. She handed him a copy of *Thriller* and asked him to sign the record jacket.

Then Ronald and Nancy Reagan arrived and led Michael into the Roosevelt Room to meet some other aides and their families.

Nancy Reagan whispered to one of Michael's staff. 'I've heard that he wants to look like that singer Diana Ross, but really, looking at him up close, he's so much prettier than she is. Don't you agree? I mean, I just don't think *she's* that attractive, but *he* certainly is.'

The First Lady waited for a response. There was none.

'I just wish he would take off his sunglasses,' she said. 'Tell me, has he had any surgery on his eyes?'

The aide shrugged. He knew better than to discuss Michael's private life, even with the President's wife.

She studied Michael closely as he spoke to her husband on the other side of the room. 'Certainly his nose has been done,' she observed, her tone hushed. 'More than once, I'd say. I wonder about his cheekbones, though. Is that makeup, or has he had them done too?'

By this time, the First Lady didn't act as if she actually expected an answer, but the aide shrugged again anyway.

'It's all so peculiar, really,' Nancy observed as Ronald Reagan shook Michael's hand. 'A boy who looks just like a girl, who whispers when he speaks, wears a glove on one hand and sunglasses all the time. I just don't know what to make of it.' She shook her head in dismay, as if at a loss for words.

Finally, the Jackson employee broke his silence. 'Listen, you don't know the half of it,' he said, rolling his eyes. He looked at her with a conspiratorial smile, expecting her to laugh. She didn't. Instead, she stared at him for a cold moment. 'Well, he *is* talented,' she said as she walked away, 'and I would think that's all that *you* should be concerned about.'

'Their last shot'

Michael may have been treated like an American hero in May 1984, but the tide would turn in June when the plan for distribution of tickets for the Victory tour – now scheduled to begin in Kansas City on 6 July – was announced. Joseph Jackson, Don King and Chuck

Sullivan came up with a unique concept: tickets would be thirty dollars each and sold in lots of four *only*. Ordering tickets did not guarantee getting them. The names of those who ordered would be selected at random by a computer drawing coupons that had to be cut out of advertisements published in local newspapers. Therefore, the Jacksons fan had to send a $120 postal money order* – *plus* a two-dollar service charge for each ticket – *and* the coupon, all in 'a standard Number Ten envelope', to the ticket address printed in the advertisement.

Promoters predicted that as many as twelve million fans would mail in $1.5 billion in money orders for the twelve-city, forty-two-concert Victory tour, but only about one in ten applicants would actually receive tickets. In order even to be considered, the money orders were to be postmarked at least two weeks before the concert. With the delay in returning money to the unlucky ones – four to six weeks – the promoters and the Jacksons would have use of it for six to eight weeks. Assuming the tour sold $144 million in tickets, as the promoters estimated, $1.4 billion in excess payments would have to be returned. In a common money-market deposit account in a bank, which paid about 7 per cent interest, that money would earn eight million dollars a month for the promoters and Jackson family. The Jacksons' spokesman, Howard Bloom, said that whatever interest that would accrue on each $120 order would go toward costs of handling and postage for unfilled orders.

If you were a lucky winner and allowed to see the Victory show, you wouldn't know if you were going to go – or which show you would attend – until two days before the concert. If the mail was delayed, the tickets could easily arrive *after* the concert.

The tickets were obviously priced too high for even white middle-class kids if they had to buy them in lots of four. It's almost impossible to imagine that many of Michael's most loyal followers, kids from the ghetto, would be able to afford the luxury of seeing the concert.

*The United States Post Office must have been particularly happy about the plan, as each money order cost $1.55. If twelve million fans purchased money orders, post offices would collect $18 million. In all of 1983, the Postal Services collected $124 million in money orders.

Making matters more distasteful, The Jacksons and their promoters said that they would like to not have to pay for the advertisements from which the coupons were to be clipped, saying that those ads should be run free of cost as 'public service advertisements'. Of course, most newspapers didn't see it that way. 'It's just a way to make more millions for the Jacksons,' said Bob Haring, executive editor of the *Tulsa World*.

Before the outrageous plan was announced, Michael and John Branca met with the brothers to try to talk them out of it.

'We got to get as much as possible for the tickets,' one of the brothers said. 'The sky's the limit.'

'No,' Michael argued. 'That's not the way to do it. There's going to be a backlash. The tickets shouldn't be more than twenty bucks each. And the mail order idea is terrible.' In fact, the tickets for concerts by the Rolling Stones and Bruce Springsteen at this time were sixteen dollars each. Michael had wanted a simple twenty dollar ticket price, no lots of four, no money orders, no coupons.

The brothers voted against Michael, five to one.

'Okay, that's it,' Michael decided later in a meeting with John Branca and Frank Dileo. 'This is going to be my last tour with the guys. I'm very serious. So I don't want you to try to run anything. Let them do it all their way. I'm just one vote out of six. Let them do their thing. This is their last shot. I'm out of it.'

'But why, Mike?' Frank wanted to know. 'They're gonna fuck it up.'

'Because if anything goes wrong I don't want to hear about it,' Michael explained. 'I don't want to hear about it from my mother, my father or my brothers. Let them do it their way and I'm out of it. Maybe the money they make from this will set them up comfortably. Then, I'm out of it.'

When the plan was made public, fans from coast to coast were outraged. The *Los Angeles Herald Examiner* ran a telephone poll with the question: Are Michael Jackson's fans being taken advantage of? Of the 2,795 people who responded, 90 per cent said yes.

The newspaper published an editorial chastising the Jacksons: 'It's hard not to conclude that the Jacksons' promoters, if not the young stars themselves, are taking advantage of their fans. It's been said that all the Jackson brothers, including Michael, helped plan the tour. If so, they should have shown a little more consideration for the fans who have made them so rich and famous.'

Other newspapers across the country followed suit, lambasting the Jacksons and, because he was the most famous one, Michael, in particular. 'The Jackson tour has not been about music. It's been about greed and arrogance,' wrote the Washington columnists Maxwell Glen and Cody Shearer. 'What good does a drug-free, liquor-free, I-brake-for-animals image do when the overriding message is "Give Me Your Piggy Bank."'

As a youthful role model, the press was terrible publicity for Michael. 'I didn't even want to do this tour,' he complained, exasperated. 'Now look what's happened.'

Despite the furor, when the first coupons were printed in the *Kansas City Times*, scores of fans waited in the dark for the early morning papers to hit the streets. The *Times* published an extra 20,000 copies to meet the demand. Postal employees were ready with 140,000 money order forms for the expected avalanche. The tickets sold out rapidly.

Still, it looked bad for Michael. Frank Dileo advised him that if he didn't take a position against the brothers' and the promoters' apparent greediness, his reputation could be damaged. 'They don't care about your future,' Frank told him. 'Their only concern is their present, to make as much as they can, while they can. You have a career that's gonna be longer than this tour. They probably don't.'

Michael wasn't sure how to handle the matter. 'What I really want is for all of it to just go away,' he said, which wasn't much of a problem-solving strategy. Finally, an open letter appeared in the *Dallas Morning News* that impacted Michael. Eleven-year-old Ladonna Jones wrote that she'd been saving her pennies to see The Jacksons but that she couldn't possibly save enough to buy four tickets. She very pointedly asked Michael, 'How could you, of all people, be so selfish?'

When an aide showed Michael the letter, he was upset by it. Greed and selfishness really had been at the heart of the tour plans; he knew it. But hadn't his family already made more money than most people would ever make in their lifetimes? Of course they had. It took a child's sadness, however, to force him into action.

Though he hadn't wanted to make any major decisions about the tour in order to be distanced from the drama of it, he now realized he had to take action. He called a meeting with Joseph, Don King and Chuck Sullivan. 'Change the ticket policy,' he told them. 'It's a rip-off. You know it. I know it. Now, change it. Or I won't tour.'

'But, Mike,'

Michael wouldn't discuss the matter. If the situation wasn't changed, he said, the brothers would have to tour without him.

The next day, plans were made to change the system.

The Misery of the Victory Tour

Michael, who had dropped to 105 pounds from his normal weight of 125 pounds – the skinniest he had ever been – looked as if he was under a great deal of stress when he and his brothers arrived at the Hyatt Hotel in Birmingham, Alabama, on 26 June for a week of meetings about the tour. As Michael checked in, he had become so dizzy he had to lean on one of his bodyguards for support. When a hotel cook approached to say hello to him, the guard released his grip and the star nearly crumpled to the floor. It seemed to some observers that Michael barely had the strength to walk. How was he going to perform?

Perhaps the problem with fatigue had to do with Michael's eating habits. At Michael's orders, his Sikh cook, Mani Singh Khalsa, fed him a diet of cashews, pecans, seeds, herbs and spices. 'He's a health nut,' said his cousin Tim Whitehead, a roadie on the tour. 'People don't know that the reason he's a vegetarian is not so much because of what meat does to a person, but because he can't stand the idea of having an animal killed so he can have dinner. I've often wondered how he gets by on the little food he does eat.'

'If I didn't have to eat to live, I'd never eat at all,' Michael once told his mother.

Later that day, a difficult meeting with the brothers, attorneys and managers on telephone conference calls took place. By the time it was over, Michael was fed up. When he got into the freight elevator (he always travels in freight elevators rather than public ones), he leaned back against the wall and just slowly slipped down until he was sitting on the floor. Someone tried to help him to his feet, but he was too exhausted to stand. 'Just leave me alone. Let me rest here for a second,' he said as he went up to the sixteenth floor. Witnesses to these kinds of scenes began whispering that Michael was suffering from anorexia nervosa, which wasn't true but certainly seemed plausible from the way he looked and acted.

It was time to announce the new ticket-buying arrangement. Michael held a midday press conference on 5 July, the day before the first concert was to take place. He wore a white sequined jacket and a red-and-white striped sash. Marlon, Randy and Tito accompanied him. To counteract the charge that he was greedy and doing the show only for profit, Michael announced that he intended to donate all of the money he made from this controversial tour to a favourite charity. Moreover, close to two thousand tickets in each city would be donated to disadvantaged youths who would not otherwise be able to attend the concerts.

Michael added, 'We've worked a long time to make this show the best it can be. But we know a lot of kids are having trouble getting tickets. The other day I got a letter from a girl in Texas named Ladonna Jones. She'd been saving her money from odd jobs to buy a ticket, but with the current tour system she'd have to buy four tickets and she couldn't afford that. So I've asked our promoter to work out a new way of distributing tickets – a way that no longer requests a one-hundred-twenty-dollar money order. There has been a lot of talk about the promoter holding money for tickets that didn't sell. I've asked our promoter to end the mail-order ticket system as soon as possible so that no one will pay money unless they get a ticket.' Michael said that details of the new over-the-counter system for buying tickets would be announced shortly. (It was implemented by the tour's third stop in Jacksonville.)

Michael took no questions. Suddenly he and his brothers were surrounded by security men. And then they were gone.

'Why did he decide to donate all his money to charity?' one reporter asked Frank Dileo, who stayed behind.

'Because he's a nice guy,' Frank said.

Michael's estimated worth at the time came to seventy-five

million dollars, so donating to charity the approximately three to five million dollars he would make on the tour would be a generous gesture but not one that would cause him to change his lifestyle. His brothers, however, couldn't possibly have afforded such a gift. Also, Michael did not – perhaps could not – address any of the other problem issues. According to Cliff Wallace, who managed the Louisiana Superdome, Joseph and Katherine Jackson, Don King, Chuck Sullivan and The Jacksons had asked for free stadium rent; a waiver of city, state, and federal taxes; a share in the profits of the food, beverage and parking concessions; and free advertising to boot. Meeting their demands would have cost city taxpayers $300,000. And gross five million dollars for the Jacksons.

Michael arranged for Ladonna Jones to receive a set of four complimentary tickets to the show, to which she would be chauffeured by limousine. Michael met with her after the show. 'He asked me if I had good seats,' she recalled. 'They didn't turn out to be very good, but it was fun anyway.'

At this time, CBS released the *Victory* album. Not counting 1981's live album, it was the first Jacksons album in four years, so it was widely anticipated. The album featured Michael's duet with Mick Jagger on 'State of Shock', which wasn't so much a song as it was a glorified Rolling Stones riff. The best cut on the album was written by Jackie and entitled 'Torture', a high-tech rocker of a song on which Michael wails up a storm. The album featured songs written by all of the brothers – and leads were split among them as well – so it was the kind of group effort that was the perfect vinyl kick-off for the tour.

The long-anticipated and controversial Victory tour finally began on Friday 6 July 1984, in Kansas City, Missouri. 'Anybody who sees this show will be a better person for years to come,' Don King told the press that day. 'Michael Jackson has transcended all earthly bounds. Every race, colour, and creed is waiting for this tour. The way he shall lift the despairing and the despondent enthralls me. Only in America could this happen, only in America. Oh, I am so *thankful* to be an American . . .'

'Can't someone shut that man up?' Michael asked one of his associates. 'Isn't there enough pressure?' To complicate matters, Jackie injured his leg and would not be able to join his brothers until a later date; Jermaine, Marlon, Randy, Tito and Michael would have to appear without him.

❦

Jackson vs. Jackson on the Road

On the day of the first show, fans began to assemble outside Arrowhead Stadium hours before sunrise. Inside the auditorium, a five-hundred person security force and one thousand other stage workers geared up for the mass event. Two giant tapestries of a forest scene bordered each side of the stage, and a wooden barrier was erected fifteen feet in front of it to keep fans from rushing the Jackson brothers.

'Arise, all the world, and behold the kingdom,' a voice boomed as the show began for the 43,000 fans. Elaborate George Lucas-style computerized stage and lighting systems were the hallmark of the concert, including a hidden hydraulic stage that presented the group – Michael in zebra-print, vertical-striped pants; spangled shirt; white socks; 1950s-type penny loafers; and the white glove – as if they were appearing from under the earth on a waffle grid of two hundred blinding lights. Seen in silhouette, the brothers marched slowly down a staircase, approached the microphones, removed their sunglasses, and broke into the first song, Michael's 'Wanna Be Startin' Somethin''. There were red and green lasers, crimson strobe lights and purple smoke bombs – magic, illusion and fireworks. Eighteen songs boomed from a hundred outdoor speakers. Everything from 'I Want You Back' to 'Shake Your Body (Down to the Ground)'. (Oddly, the brothers performed no numbers from their new *Victory* album. It was later explained by Marlon that Michael refused to rehearse them or perform them before a live audience.)

Jermaine performed three of his own songs. Michael's solo hits 'Billie Jean' and 'Beat It' were saved for the end of the concert. He was in excellent voice, more of a real *singer* now than ever before. By the time the group finished their performance, the audience had been whipped into a frenzy even though most of the audience members had to settle for the distorted images of the brothers that appeared on huge overhanging television screens throughout the gargantuan football stadium. It was clear, though, they had paid the high ticket prices to see only one person, Michael Jackson.

Thanks to his music – not to mention the advent of the video age – Michael's stardom had reached such mythic proportions by this time, no one could share a stage with him. As Jim Miller wrote for *Newsweek*, 'He dances with the breathtaking verve of his predecessor James Brown, the beguiling wispiness of Diana Ross, the ungainly pathos of Charlie Chaplin, the edgy joy of a man startled to be alive. The crowd gasps and screams . . .'

After the first of three shows in Kansas City, the truth was painfully clear: Michael should never have agreed to do the tour, but for more reasons than the problems with ticket prices and promotion. He was a front man for an act he no longer felt a part of, and the brothers weren't comfortable in their roles as his supporting players, either. Or as one critic put it, 'Marlon, Jermaine, Randy and Tito seemed mostly ill-at-ease extras at their own celebration.'

Jermaine's odd comments to reporter Simon Kinnersley at this time brought to light the dissension and fraternal jealousy running rampant within the group. He said, 'Even though Michael is very talented, a lot of his success has been due to timing and a little bit of luck. It could have been him, or it could just as easily have been me. But now I'm doing a lot of things. I'm the hottest brother. It'll be the same when my brothers do their thing.'

To Michael's audience, though, none of the controversy they kept hearing and reading about mattered when *he*, the undisputed star, appeared on stage. All that mattered was his talent, his passion for his work, his charisma, his voice – and the way he could execute one of those impossible, backward glides across the stage. The audience roared its appreciation for him with every song. Not only had he outgrown any family pageantry, one sensed that he was constrained by a fear of upstaging his brothers.

Also, there was a feeling – imaginary or not – that Michael couldn't wait for the show to end. At the same time, the brothers, who entertained with great hunger and eagerness, looked as if they knew that their performance represented the chance of a lifetime for them . . . and maybe their last chance. However, never for a moment did they appear to share any common values or goals of showmanship with their star performer. And never did it appear that Michael wanted anything more to do with them than necessary. By trying to prove his loyalty to his family, he had distanced himself even further from them. Moreover, maybe he had lost a little of his soul in the process. Certainly he must have felt as if he'd lost *something* when James Brown – one of his idols – refused his invitation to perform onstage with him at Madison Square Garden in New York.

James, always a big fan of Michael's, felt that the steep ticket prices would preclude the attendance of many of the group's black fans. That decision had to hurt Michael, and make him think about whether the tour was worth it to him.

The agony of *Victory* would continue through 9 December 1984 – same show and dialogue each and every performance. Michael is not a spontaneous performer. In concert, he has a set routine, and he rarely veers from it. Bruce Springsteen went to see the show in Philadelphia and afterwards he and Michael had a conversation backstage.

'Do you talk to people during your concerts?' Michael asked him. 'I heard that you do.'

'Yeah. I tell stories,' Bruce said. 'People like that, I've learned. They like to hear your voice do something besides singing. They go wild when you just talk.'

Michael shuddered. 'Oh, I could never do that. To me, it feels like people are learning something about you they shouldn't know.'

The closer the time came for the tour to be over, the more anxious Michael was to see it end. 'The way we planned it, this was going to be the greatest tour of all time,' Joseph Jackson would say in retrospect. 'But outsiders interfered. Soon the brothers were at each other's throats.'

Without a doubt, the most annoying thing about the Jacksons' behaviour over the years has been their frustrating inability to take responsibility for their own actions. Over the years, all of them have pointed fingers to external sources for their internal problems. Either it's managers, promoters, the public or, their favourite foe, 'the media', that is held responsible for their problems – never themselves. Of course, the truth is that they almost always create their own internal dysfunction.

Touring can be a stressful, lonely business for an entertainer, even under the best of circumstances. However, to feel isolated from the people with whom you are performing, let alone if they happen to be your family members, is devastating – especially to someone as sensitive as Michael. The family had already begun to fall apart; the Victory tour seemed to be hastening its complete destruction. At one point in the tour, Michael was so upset with his brothers, he suffered from exhaustion and dehydration and had to be put under a doctor's care.

As a result of such pressure, Michael became increasingly difficult. Some of his demands were unreasonable. At one point, he threatened not to perform unless a certain publicist working on the tour was fired. The publicist had apparently allowed something to be printed that Michael did not appreciate. The brothers ignored the threat. Then, at the last possible minute, right before the show was to start, Frank Dileo announced that Michael would not appear unless the publicist was dismissed on the spot. Of course, *then* the publicist was fired.

In the beginning of the tour, it was agreed that only the performing members of the family would travel in the Jacksons' van. However, when Michael started showing up with Emmanuel Lewis, nothing could have been more annoying to the brothers. Before the tour was even half over, the brothers began travelling in separate vans and limousines – Jackie (who joined the tour midway on crutches, but did not perform), Marlon, Randy and Tito in one vehicle, Jermaine in another by himself, and Michael in still another, alone. When they had to travel by air, the brothers used a commercial airline; Michael travelled by private jet. (A couple of times, Pia Zadora's multi-millionaire husband, Meshulam Riklis, who was friendly with the Jacksons, took mercy on the brothers and allowed them to use his private aircraft.) In New York, when the group had to fly by helicopter to Giants Stadium, they agreed that no outsiders would be in the helicopter. Michael then showed up with Julian Lennon, John's son. The brothers glared at both of them during the brief flight.

At one point, the Jacksons received an offer from a producer who wanted to pay them millions of dollars to film the show and release it to the home-video market when the tour was over. They took a vote. Everyone was for the idea, except for Michael. He threatened that he would not perform if they struck such a deal. Furthermore, no one was to videotape the show. Without any recourse, the brothers bitterly turned down the deal, and all of that money.

Then, three nights later, the group was onstage with cameras all about them. Michael, himself, had arranged for the show to be video-taped. 'I'll give you copies, don't worry,' he promised his brothers when they confronted him after the performance, but they never saw a copy. (When Michael tried to get them to agree to let him release the video to the marketplace, they blocked him from doing it.)

The brothers stayed on separate floors of hotels in each city; they refused to talk to each other on their way to the stadiums. Every time there was a meeting about anything, there would also be side meetings among the different factions in the group, including the pair of lawyers who represented Michael, the one who worked for Jermaine, and the two who spoke for the rest of the brothers. 'It was devastating,' said long-time family friend Joyce McCrae. 'It amounted to the worst experiences Michael had ever had with his brothers. His success had affected every member of the family. Some were jealous, there was denial, the whole gamut of human emotions.'

During the final week of the tour, Joseph and Don King began making plans to take the Victory tour to Europe. When Michael heard about the possibility of European dates, he couldn't believe his ears. He sent a succinct message to Joseph and Don through Frank Dileo: 'I will absolutely not be going to Europe with the Victory tour. Good luck to you. Michael.'

On 9 December 1984, after the last song of the evening, Michael hollered out from the Los Angeles stage, 'This is our last and final show. It's been a long twenty years, and we love you all.' The brothers looked at Michael with surprised expressions, as if his declaration was news to them. 'What a little prick,' one of the brothers said of Michael afterward. 'How dare he? The little creep.'

'There's no way Michael Jackson should be as big as he is and treat his family the way he does,' Don King fumed after the final show, when it was clear to him that he would not be taking the show abroad. 'He feels that his father did him wrong? His father may have done some wrong, but he also had to do a whole lot right.'

He went on, 'What Michael's got to realize is that Michael's a nigger. It doesn't matter how great he can sing and dance. I don't care that he can prance. He's one of the megastars of the world, but he's still going to be a nigger megastar. He must accept that. Not only must he understand that, he's got to accept it and demonstrate that he wants to be a nigger. Why? To show that a nigger can do it.'

If it was possible for Michael to blow sky high when he read those comments, he would have done it. 'Sue his ass,' he told John Branca. 'That guy has been pushing my last nerve since Day One.' John knew better than to drag the Don King experience into a new year with fresh litigation. He calmed Michael down, as he always managed to do, and convinced him to let it go.

As if to rid himself of the bad taste in his mouth left by the Victory tour, Michael donated all of his proceeds from it – nearly five million dollars – to the T. J. Martell Foundation for Cancer Research, the United Negro College Fund and the Ronald McDonald Camp for Good Times.

When Michael wrote of the Victory tour in his autobiography, *Moonwalk*, he didn't mention Don King, Joseph and Katherine Jackson, Chuck Sullivan, or any of the other principal players behind the scenes. Of his brothers, he took the high ground, as he always does, 'It was a nice feeling, playing with my brothers again,' he wrote, graciously. 'We were all together again . . . I enjoyed the tour.' Whether or not he wanted to admit it publicly, the real victory for Michael Jackson was that he and his brothers were finally finished as a performing group.

Their future as a family didn't look very promising either.

Janet Elopes

While Michael Jackson and his brothers were preoccupied with the Victory tour, trouble was brewing at home too. Much to everyone's dismay, Janet (who turned eighteen on 16 May 1984), had become involved with a young singer named James DeBarge. James is from a large singing family from Grand Rapids, Michigan (the same DeBarge that had been the Jackson's stable-mates at Motown), and he and Janet seemed to have common ground, at least superficially, since both were from show-business families. Joseph and Katherine disapproved of the relationship, saying that James was combative and unpredictable. Plus, in their view, Janet was young and inexperienced. James would later insist, though, that he and Janet were first intimate when she was just fifteen, and, he added somewhat indelicately, 'that was some real lovemaking.'

When the Jackson parents finally figured out that James was abusing drugs, it was the end of their daughter's little romance, as far as they were concerned. However, Janet told them that she was in love with him and determined to marry him, despite – or perhaps even because of – their disapproval. She was aware that he had a drug problem, she said, but she thought she could handle it, and maybe even be of assistance. 'You always think you can change people,' she said in retrospect. 'And I knew that he so badly wanted to change. He was trying, but he wasn't trying hard enough.'

They eloped on 7 September 1984, in Grand Rapids, DeBarge's hometown. Their wedding night was a disaster, as James recalled it: 'I spoiled it completely. Janet had been shaking in her shoes at the wedding ceremony, and I thought the least I could do was to give her a night to remember. I booked the top suite of the Amway Plaza Hotel, which cost me a small fortune. But then I went out and got rotten drunk with some friends. I finally got back to the hotel at three a.m. and Janet was waiting for me, crying.'

The next day, Janet telephoned LaToya to tell her the news of her marriage. LaToya was then charged with breaking the startling news to Joseph and Katherine who, predictably, did not take it well. She also telephoned each brother, except Michael. They were all upset and angry, Jermaine in particular. 'I know that he would have killed her if he could've gotten his hands on Janet,' LaToya would remember.

The question, then, was how to tell Michael. Actually, no member of the family wanted to be the one to do it. It was as if they felt they would somehow be forever tainted in his eyes by being the person most remembered for having passed on such awful news. Michael had always felt protective of Janet; he used to say that she was his best friend in the family, 'like a twin'. The news was sure to be upsetting, and the Victory tour was difficult enough for him without having to deal with such domestic turmoil. So, no one wanted to be 'the one'. Finally, Quincy Jones's daughter, a friend of the family's, called Michael to tell him; she didn't have anything to lose. As expected, he was filled with anxiety by the news. 'It killed me to see her go off and get married,' Michael would say later. 'I didn't know how to handle it.'

For a month, Janet and James lived at Hayvenhurst with Janet's family, much to James's dismay. 'He wanted them to have their own place,' explained his mother, Etterlene. 'He felt that they needed to be alone to give themselves a chance to grow in their marriage. However, Janet didn't want to leave that house. She was still like a little girl, who never wanted to leave her bedroom.'

'James DeBarge would come to the house completely out of his mind on drugs,' Steve Howell remembered. 'He would be so high on coke and alcohol that, on two occasions, the guards tried to stop him from going inside Hayvenhurst. "If you do, Mr Jackson will kill you," they'd warn him, speaking of Joseph. However, he was belligerent and didn't care. The funny thing was that when he wasn't high, James was the nicest guy in the world. He was like Dr Jekyll and Mr DeBarge.'

'You leave my husband alone!' Janet was heard screaming at Joseph on several occasions.

'He's not good for *you*, Janet,' Joseph shot back. 'And if you think you're going to ruin this family by staying married to this guy, you can forget it.'

Katherine tried to find a reasonable solution to the problem: she offered to enroll James in a rehabilitation programme. He refused to go.

In an interview, James DeBarge remembered the Encino estate as 'The House of Fears' and painted an eerie picture of Michael, who was at home for a short time in the middle of the tour schedule. 'It was while I lived there that I came to realize what a sad, lonely figure he is,' James said. 'He was like a ghost, wandering around the place looking for friendship. He would come to our room late at night, tap softly on the door, and say, "Is it all right if I come in?" One time, Janet and I were making love, and he came right on in! He got into bed with us and poured his heart out. He said, "I envy you two, because you have each other and love each other. But, I haven't got anyone." There was never a sign of a woman in his life, ever.'

'He really was a very lonely man-child,' James DeBarge recalled of his brother-in-law, Michael. 'The only time he had any fun was when he had friends over to play in his two-million-dollar amusement arcade, but they had to let Michael win most of the time. If they didn't, they wouldn't be asked to come back.'

James has a litany of amazing memories about his life in the 'House of Fears'. He recalls the day it rained and Michael danced naked around the pool. 'His mother screamed from the house, "Put your clothes on, Michael. Your father will be home soon." Fear of Joseph was what controlled them all,' James said. (Of course, James was on drugs, so who knows how reliable his memory is of that time.)

After a few months, James and Janet moved into their own condominium at 12546 The Vista, in Brentwood. 'They moved out of the house because Joseph was gonna kill James,' recalled Steve Howell. 'I'm serious.'

'James had it out with Joseph a number of times,' confirmed his mother, Etterlene. 'They were enemies. They detested each other.'

Janet wanted nothing to do with her family as long as they could not accept her husband. Actually, Janet had begun distancing herself a couple of years earlier when she began working as an actress on the TV show *Fame*. 'My parents were very strict while I was growing up,' she once told me. 'It was really our music and our work. We missed out on our childhood, getting to know what really goes on out there. It was bad, because once you step out there for the first time, it stuns you. I saw a lot of things I'd never seen before.'

In a short time, Janet was miserable in her new marriage. She had wanted her independence, and she got it, but at what cost? Now, she found herself staying up nights worrying about James, who was rarely at home.

According to Jerome Howard, Joseph and Katherine's former business manager, 'Janet would get phone calls in the middle of the night from James's friends telling her where he was, which was usually out in the ghetto, about twenty-five miles from Encino, buying or doing drugs. Janet, who'd never been there in her lifetime, would get up and drive out to the ghetto to find him. In time, she got to know the ghetto better than any other Jackson. She loved him and would do anything for him.'

With the entire Jackson family opposed to the marriage, each member took turns trying to persuade Janet to end it with James. The problems the newlyweds were having in their marriage, especially the drugs, went against everything Michael stood for personally and spiritually. Besides, he could see what the marriage had done to his sister emotionally. At one point she collapsed and had to be rushed to a hospital. She was exhausted, physically and emotionally. Michael was the only person to whom she would now listen. He begged her to leave James, crying on the phone with her from different stops along the Victory tour. Janet was finally convinced.

'God, I felt like my whole life was falling down, and I could see him [James] going down, but there was nothing I could do,' Janet said. 'And he said to me, "Well, you haven't tried to help me," but I thought, What about helping yourself? I thought, Well, I can either go down with him and that's the end of my life, or I can let go and continue on, alone.'

Janet left James on 7 January 1985, and immediately filed for a petition to nullify her marriage and restore her former name, Janet Dameta Jackson. On the petition, she listed her total gross monthly income as just $3000 – a minuscule amount considering the millions she would earn later. She said the amount of her husband's income was 'unknown' to her. When she got home from the courthouse, she called her friend René Elizondo and said, 'God, I can't believe what I've just done.'

(The annulment was finally granted on 18 November 1985. By then, Janet was back at Hayvenhurst.)

James claims that Janet terminated a pregnancy while he was married to her. 'I don't think she told many family members,' he said, 'but, her mother knew. I wouldn't have minded a child, but it had to be Janet's decision. I think her career, her plans, her family had a lot to do with it. We went to a clinic in Los Angeles but we had to go in and out the back door because we were so well known. It was real scary. Afterward, I took her home and held her in my arms and told her everything would be okay.'

For years, Janet has dealt with the rumour that she actually did have the baby she was carrying at the time, and that this child is secretly being raised in Europe. Janet denies it. Of course, she spent almost ten years denying that she was married to René Elizondo when, the entire time, she actually *was*. It was only when he filed for divorce that the truth came out . . . would it surprise anyone, then, if Janet Jackson one day reveals that she and James de Barge had a child so many years ago, and that rather than having an abortion she thought it better if he or she was raised away from the limelight?

'Michael is *not gay*'

It was difficult to imagine Michael Jackson viewing romantic relationships in a positive light when he was surrounded by such poor examples. His parents' marriage had rarely been happy. Marlon's marriage to Carol had been troubled, though they had reconciled. It was difficult to know what was going on with Jermaine's relationship, but Hazel seemed domineering to most observers. Jackie's marriage was also in trouble at this time, because he had cheated on Enid. The two would end up divorcing, and the final decree would not occur until August 1987, after they had put each other through as much misery – and litigation – as possible. Luckily, Tito seemed to be faring well with Dee Dee. Still, Michael had learned early on to be cautious before committing himself to any relationship that could become serious. Therefore, he stayed alone – except for the occasional youth, such as Emmanuel Lewis and, in 1984, a ten-year-old kid named Jonathan Spence who had become a constant companion. The two were seen nuzzling and hugging throughout the fall of 1984.

Along with Michael's huge success came a resurgence of rumours about his sexuality. Michael had always been extremely sensitive about the issues of sexuality, and nothing annoyed him more than the fact that it kept coming up every few years. Yet, by September 1984, the question remained: was Michael gay?

However, being a twenty-six-year-old virgin teen idol devoted to a sexually repressive religion is not easy, especially when show business dictates that a male celebrity be 'romantically involved' – to use Michael Jackson's words – with a woman, thus the existence of Tatum O'Neal and Brooke Shields in his life. But the public could see through those charades, and tongues continued to wag.

One rumour had it that, when Michael was younger, Joseph had ordered him to be injected with female hormones to ensure that his voice would not change with maturity. He wanted it to remain high-pitched and, thus, commercial. 'Not true,' said Michael's vocal coach, Seth Riggs. 'He started out with a high voice, and I've taken it even higher. It's ridiculous. I don't even know if it's possible to do that.'

During one break in a vocal lesson, according to Seth, he said to Michael, 'You know, everybody thinks you're gay.'

Michael nodded his head and told Riggs this story: a tall good-looking blond approached him one day and said, 'Michael, I think you're wonderful. I sure would like to go to bed with you.'

Michael glared at him. 'When's the last time you read the Bible?' he asked.

The blond said nothing.

'You know, you really should read it, because there is some real information in there about homosexuality.'

'Sure, I guess if I was a girl, it would be different story,' said the fellow. '*Then* you'd have sex with me.'

'No, I wouldn't,' Michael told him. 'There are some very direct words on *that* in the Bible too.'

Still, there were some odd reports about Michael. For instance, reporter Denise Worrell was writing a story about him for *Time* and had tried to arrange an interview with him, but to no avail. Instead, she interviewed his parents. Unbeknownst to Michael, Joseph decided to give the reporter a tour of the house. He knocked on Michael's bedroom door. There was no answer. 'Michael I have someone I want you to meet,' Joseph said. He opened the door. 'Can I bring her into your room?'

Denise reported that Michael was inside with a male friend, about twenty years old, watching television. The glow from the set was the only light in the room. She noticed the outline of Michael's man-nequins against a wall.

Michael was startled by the presence of his father and his guest.

He nervously introduced Joseph to his friend, using just a first name. Michael then shook hands with the journalist who reported that his handshake 'felt like a cloud'. He 'barely said hello'. Michael's friend then nervously extended his hand; she reported that it was 'damp'. Michael stared at the writer for a moment and then began watching television, again.

As Joseph and Denise backed out of the room, Joseph had the look of a man who'd just opened Pandora's box. 'Michael has a friend over,' Joseph explained. 'He isn't about to give any interviews. You got pretty close, though,' he added, with a nervous chuckle.

After Denise left the house, a security guard came running after her. Joseph and Katherine wanted to speak to her again. Joseph must have told his wife what had occurred in the bedroom.

'We were hoping you'd set the record straight and put a stop to the rumours,' Katherine said as soon as she saw Denise. 'They say Michael is gay. Michael is not gay. It's against his religion. It's against God. The Bible speaks against it.'

'Michael is *not gay*,' repeated Joseph, emphatically.

Perhaps Michael is *not gay*, but he was curious about the lifestyle just the same. One friend remembered the day he and Michael went into a gay bar on Santa Monica Boulevard in West Hollywood. 'Michael was recording at Larrabe studios, which is across the street from a bar in a predominantly gay section of Hollywood,' the friend recalled. 'I said to him, "Hey, man, let's go get a drink at that bar." He told me he didn't drink, but perhaps he could get an orange juice. "You know, it's a gay bar," I warned him. "Really? I've never been to a gay bar," he said. "What goes on there?" he asked. I told him he should go and see for himself. He hesitated. "Well, I've always wanted to. Okay, let's do it." So, in we went.

' "Why is it so dark in here?" Michael wanted to know. I had the impression he had never been in *any* bar, let alone a gay one. There were a few guys in there, but it was early, so there weren't many. Michael took a deep breath and went up to the bartender and ordered an orange juice. The bartender said, "Hey, aren't you Michael Jackson?" He said, "Nope. But I'm told I look like him." He turned to me and winked.

'He and I sat in a corner and watched all the guys. He was recognized by a few, but they left him alone. Not one person came up to him.

' "Is this all they do here?" Michael asked me. "They just drink and talk and watch videos?" I wondered what he *thought* people did in bars. As we were sitting there, two men walked in and immediately began kissing each other. When Michael saw them making out, I could feel him tense up. Finally he said, "Okay, I've seen enough. Let's leave." So we got up and walked out. On the way out, Michael said, "I can't believe those two guys kissed one another. How can they do that?"

' "Maybe they liked each other," I told him.

' "Well, if that's what they do in gay bars, then I don't think I'll be going to any more," Michael decided.'

This same friend remembered the day he and Michael went into Drakes, a novelty store on Melrose Avenue in Hollywood that specializes in sex toys and pornography. In the back of the shop, behind a gated area, a browser could find gay reading material and photo magazines.

'Hey, what's back there?' Michael wanted to know as soon as he walked in.

'You don't want to know,' said his friend.

'Yeah, I *do* want to know,' Michael insisted. He then proceeded to go boldly where probably no Jackson had ever gone before.

Thirty seconds later, he came running back. He looked shaken, as if he had just seen a ghost. 'We gotta go, now,' he said nervously.

'Why?'

'You don't want to know,' Michael answered.

The more enigmatic Michael remained, the more people would talk, and even joke, about him. His videographer, Steve Howell, once asked him about a comedy sketch Eddie Murphy had performed on *Saturday Night Live* in which he played an effeminate and affected Michael as a guest on a fictional talk show, *Guy Talk*, along with an equally fey Liberace played by another actor. The two bragged about their sexual exploits with women; it was ludicrous and extremely funny.

Michael had smiled. 'I don't mind it,' he said softly. 'The more they make fun of me, the more people are going to wonder what I really am. I don't care when people call me a fag. No one knows the truth. No one knows who, or what I am.'

'You don't care what people say about you?'

'They can say what they want to say, because the bottom line is they don't *know* and everyone is going to continue searching to find out whether I'm gay, straight or whatever,' Michael explained. 'It doesn't bother me, and the longer it takes them to discover this, the more famous I will be.'

Perhaps that's how Michael *sometimes* felt, but he was also a man who told *Rolling Stone* writer Gerri Hirshey that he lives his life with obsessive caution, 'just like a haemophiliac who can't afford to be scratched in any way.'

In August 1984, a tabloid alleged that Michael was having an affair with British pop star Boy George, an allegation which was not true. Michael was livid. His publicist, Norman Winter, recalled, 'Michael was angry that there were these stories about him being gay, that little kids who could barely read were hearing about these rumours, maybe from their mothers who buy the tabloids and talk to others about them. Who knows? The point is that he felt that he was getting a reputation he didn't want. He told me that he wanted to organize a press conference to refute the stories. I told him I thought it might not be a good idea. 'Why give them any credibility? Maybe they'll just blow over,' he said. 'No, they just keep getting worse. I have to do something now.'

'Frank [Dileo] was against the idea, but Michael is a very strong-minded person. He told me what he wanted to say, I wrote the text of the statement, he approved it, and we went from there.'

The problem was that Michael decided that he did not want to appear at the press conference; he was too shy to face the press and discuss such a personal matter.

On 5 September 1984, a major news conference was arranged in a West Hollywood sound studio. Frank Dileo – in dark sunglasses and with a cigar in his mouth – stepped in front of a podium to announce that he was about to read a two-page statement from Michael, 'who, as you all know, has risen to the pinnacle of success in his field.'

In a gruff, tough-guy voice, the burly manager read: 'For some time now, I have been searching my conscience as to whether or not

I should publicly react to the many falsehoods that have been spread about me. I have decided to make this statement based on the injustice of these allegations and the far-reaching trauma those who feel close to me are suffering.

'I feel very fortunate to have been blessed with recognition for my efforts. This recognition also brings with it a responsibility to one's admirers throughout the world. Performers should always serve as role models who set an example for young people. It saddens me that many may actually believe the present flurry of false accusations. To this end, and I do mean END: NO! I've never taken hormones to maintain my high voice; NO! I've never had my cheek-bones altered in any way; NO! I've never had cosmetic surgery on my eyes. YES! One day in the future I plan to get married and have a family. Any statements to the contrary are simply untrue.

'Henceforth, as new fantasies are printed, I have advised my attorneys of my willingness to institute legal action and subsequently prosecute all guilty to the fullest extent of the law.

'As noted earlier, I love children. We all know that kids are very impressionable and therefore susceptible to such stories. I'm certain that some have already been hurt by this terrible slander. In addition to their admiration, I would like to keep their respect.'

After reading the statement, Frank refused to answer questions from the assemblage of reporters, and left the podium.

No celebrity had ever gone to such lengths to proclaim his or her heterosexuality. The fact that Michael didn't appear in person dampened his declaration. Also, his statement was full of half-truths. Perhaps he hadn't had surgery on his eyes, as he claimed, but he certainly had surgery on his nose, and three times. How could he repudiate one story relating to plastic surgery without admitting the whole truth about work done on his nose? Because of this obvious omission, one was forced to wonder what else Michael was not revealing. In the end, the press conference backfired; if anything, it raised more questions than it answered.

PART SEVEN

Michael Buys the Beatles' Songs

While Michael Jackson was on the road with the Victory tour, he made further headlines – this time on the business pages – by purchasing the ATV Music Publishing Company for an astounding $47.5 million. The purchase, believed to be the biggest publishing acquisition of its kind ever by an individual, was actually the culmination of ten intense months of negotiation. The seed of this venture had been planted a few years earlier when Michael was in London to record the number one hit 'Say, Say, Say' with Paul McCartney at Abbey Road Studios. Michael had become friendly with Paul and Linda McCartney during his stay; he ate most of his meals at their home outside of London. One evening after dinner, Paul displayed a thick booklet of song titles to which he owned the rights, including most of Buddy Holly's material, and standards such as 'Autumn Leaves', 'Sentimental Journey' and 'Stormy Weather'.

'This is the way to make big money,' Paul said. 'Every time someone records one of these songs, I get paid. Every time someone plays these songs on the radio, or in live performances, I get paid.'

'You're kidding me, right?' Michael said.

'Do I look like I'm kidding you?' Paul answered, seriously. In truth, Paul reportedly earns more than forty million dollars a year from record and song royalties not of his own personal composition.

Michael was intrigued. He owned the publishing rights to his own songs – obtaining that right was one of the reasons he and his family had left Motown and Berry Gordy's Jobete publishing house – but he always thought of publishing as a tedious business primarily concerned with collecting royalties and licensing material for other media. Paul explained that the world of publishing can prove lucrative, especially thanks to the CD explosion and the increased use of popular songs in advertisements, movies and televisions. Songwriters often lose their copyrights for one reason or another: sometimes they sell them for profit – a shortsighted thing to do, especially nowadays when so much money is generated in the music industry – and often they lose them out of ignorance, as in the case of The Beatles, who simply signed away their rights when they were naive and didn't know any better.

As it happened, Paul McCartney and John Lennon had sold their copyrights to a publisher named Dick James when they were young. James ended up making a fortune on The Beatles' songs. Then, in the late sixties, while McCarney and Lennon were each on their respective honeymoons James sold Northern Songs – the company that continued to hold the rights to the Beatles' compositions – to Sir Lew Grade's ATV Music Limited. ATV's assets were later purchased by Australian businessman Robert Holmes à Court's Bell Group. McCartney and Lennon's estate split with ATV the songwriting revenue generated by 251 of their songs written between 1964 and 1971 – including 'Yesterday', 'Michelle', 'Help', 'A Hard Day's Night', 'The Long and Winding Road', 'Hey Jude', 'Let It Be', and many others. ATV also held the publishing rights to thousands of other compositions, including songs by The Pointer Sisters, Pat Benatar and Little Richard (including 'Tutti Frutti', 'Long Tall Sally', 'Rip It Up' and 'Lucille').

When Michael told Paul, 'Maybe someday I'll buy your songs,' Paul laughed.

'Great,' he said. 'Good joke.'

Michael wasn't joking. Paul would one day regret their conversation.

'I gave him a lot of free advice,' he would later say. 'And you know what? A fish gets caught by opening his mouth.

'Michael's the kind of guy who picks brains. When we worked together, I don't even think he'd had the cosmetic surgery. [He actually did have surgery by that time.] I've got photos of me and him at our house, and he looks quite different. He's had a lot of facial surgery since then. He actually told me he was going to a religious retreat, and I believed him. But he came out of that religious retreat with a new nose. The power of prayer, I guess.'

Michael and Paul remained somewhat friendly, but Michael also kept his distance. He didn't want Paul to perceive him as being anything more than an acquaintance, perhaps because he had a plan.

When Michael returned to the United States, he mentioned Paul's book of titles to John Branca and said that he wanted to buy some copyrights himself, 'like Paul'. John did his research and presented Michael with a list of songs that were for sale. Michael's first purchase was the Sly Stone catalogue, including all of Sly's pop classics of the 1970s, such as 'Everyday People', 'Hot Fun in the Summertime', and 'Stand!' ('Stand!' was the song The Jackson 5 performed the first time they appeared on *The Ed Sullivan Show*. Now, Michael owned it.) For less than a million dollars, Michael also secured a few other titles, including two of Dion's hits, 'The Wanderer' and 'Runaround Sue', Len Barry's '1-2-3' and the Soul Survivors' 'Expressway to Your Heart'.

For the next couple of months, Michael was too preoccupied with the Victory tour to concentrate on any publishing deals. But then in September 1984, when John Branca flew to Philadelphia to meet with Frank Dileo and Michael about the Victory tour's problems, John casually mentioned the availability of the ATV catalogue. Michael wasn't sure what kind of music ATV represented.

'Well, it happens to include a few things you might be interested in,' John teased.

'Like?' Michael asked.

'Northern Songs.'

Michael became excited. 'You don't mean *the* Northern Songs, do you?'

'Yeah, Mike,' John said. He couldn't contain his enthusiasm. 'We're talking The Beatles, man. *The Beatles*.'

In fact, Paul McCartney had tried to buy ATV in 1981. He asked Yoko Ono to purchase the publishing house with him for twenty million dollars, ten million each, but she thought that was too much money and declined. Because Paul didn't want to spend the twenty million dollars himself, the deal fell through.

As Michael skipped about the room, whooping and hollering, John warned him that there would be stiff competition in a bidding war for such popular songs. 'I don't care,' Michael declared. 'I want those songs. Get me those songs, Branca.'

John said he would see what he could do. He then telephoned John Eastman, Paul McCartney's attorney and brother-in-law, and asked if Paul was planning to bid on the catalogue. 'No,' Eastman said. 'It's too pricey.'

A few days later, Yoko Ono telephoned John and said that she had heard a rumour that Michael was interested in purchasing ATV. Then, she spent forty-five minutes trying to make John believe that buying the catalogue was a terrible idea. John discussed the conversation with Michael. 'Man, she obviously just wants it for herself,' Michael said, 'but doesn't want to spend the bucks. She's hoping the price will go down if I don't buy it. So, buy it, Branca.'

The next few months were filled with intensive and frustrating negotiations. Bidding against Michael were Charles Koppelman and Marty Bandier's Entertainment Company; Virgin Records; real estate tycoon Samual J. Lefrak; and financier Charles Knapp. At one point, John Branca called off the negotiations, completely.

During those eight tense months, Paul McCartney again tried to convince Yoko Ono to join him in a bid. When Yoko repeated that she was not interested, Paul decided not to bid.

Meanwhile, Michael telephoned John Branca once a week for news.

When Koppelman and Bandier had beaten Michael's offer of $47.5 million with one of $50 million, Michael was crushed. 'Branca, we can't lose this, now,' he said. 'You gotta do something. I know we agreed that we wouldn't spend more than $41 million, but I'm willing to do it.'

The Koppelman and Bandier offer was being financed by the MCA company, so John made a telephone call to the head of the company, Irving Azoff. 'Man, you can't give these guys money to buy this catalogue,' John told Irving. 'Did you know that they're competing against Michael for it? Remember, you were a consultant for the Victory tour?'

'Johnny, don't worry about it,' Irving Azoff said. 'I'll take care of it.'

Azoff then pulled the rug out from under Koppelman and Bandier by refusing to finance their offer. John Branca had put Michael back in the driver's seat.

Soon, Robert Holmes à Court was telephoning John Branca and

practically begging him to go to London and close the deal. John played hardball and acted as if Michael wasn't interested. Holmes à Court offered to pay for John's plane fare, but John could afford his own ticket, and didn't want any favours at this stage of the game. John agreed to go to Europe, and Holmes à Court even said that if the deal wasn't closed on that trip, he would reimburse all of John's travel and accommodation expenses.

After Michael gave John power of attorney, he went to England and closed the deal in twenty-four hours. Michael Jackson never signed the important, history-making contracts; John Branca did. John then telephoned Michael long-distance to give him the news, bad and good. The bad news: he was out $47.5 million. The good news: he owned ATV.

Michael couldn't believe his good fortune. The same could be said for Paul McCartney, who said, 'Someone rang me up one day and said, "Michael's bought your songs." I said, "*What??!!*" I think it's dodgy to do things like that,' Paul complained. 'To be someone's friend and then to buy the rug they're standing on.'

After the deal was struck, Michael did attempt to telephone Paul to discuss the matter. Knowing his personality, that probably wasn't an easy thing for Michael to do, still he at least tried. However, when he called, Paul hung up on him. Finally, Michael concluded, 'Paul's got a real problem, and I'm finished trying to be a nice guy. Too bad for him. I got the songs and that's the end of it.'

Robert Hilburn, in an analysis of the ATV acquisition for the *Los Angeles Times*, explained Michael's purchase in dollars and cents: 'If, for instance, "Yesterday" earns $100,000 a year in royalties from record sales, airplay and live performances, the Lennon estate and McCartney – as co-writers – divide about 50 per cent of that income, about $25,000 each. The publisher – now Michael Jackson – collects the other 50 per cent. The publisher also controls the use of the song in terms of films, commercials and stage productions.' *Yesterday* in particular probably earns considerably more.

As soon as Michael made the purchase, he and his representatives investigated tactics to make it pay off for him. He hired a staff to develop an anthology series and four films using The Beatles' music, including *Strawberry Fields*, an animated feature; *Back in the USSR*, a movie based on Russian rockers; and films based on 'Eleanor Rigby' and 'The Fool on the Hill'. Michael also planned musical greeting cards and music boxes. When he licensed 'Revolution' to Nike for a sneaker advertisement, he obtained Yoko Ono's consent, but not Paul McCartney's. In fact, Paul, like many Beatles fans, felt Michael was cheapening the music.

In the end, though, Paul had to accept Michael's decision. Every time Paul performed one of the songs he wrote between 1964 and 1971, he had to pay Michael.

When Michael sold 'All You Need is Love' to Panasonic for $240,000, Paul finally called him and told him he was going too far. Michael didn't even hang up on him. He explained that he felt using The Beatles' songs in commercials enabled the music to reach an entirely new generation of fans who would then buy Beatles' records. 'I just don't like the idea that Michael Jackson is the only guy in the world who gets to sit in judgement as to which Beatles songs can be used in commercials,' Paul later said. 'He's drawn up a list! I don't see how he should have that power.'

Paul said he had hoped that 'All You Need is Love' would remain an anthem of the sixties, not become a jingle for 'a friggin' loudspeaker system. And I also don't want "Good Day Sunshine" to become an Oreo cookie,' he complained, 'which I understand he's done. I think that's real cheesy. I don't think Michael needs the money.'

On the other hand, Paul owns the Buddy Holly catalogue and had exploited Holly's songs commercially many times over, because, as he's reasoned, 'Buddy himself did commercials, and his widow actively wants us to earn money via commercials. It's her call.'

Yoko seemed satisfied with what Michael did with The Beatles' catalogue and called his ownership 'a blessing'. She said in November 1990, 'Businessmen who aren't artists themselves wouldn't have the consideration Michael has. He loves the songs. He's very caring. There could be a lot of arguments and stalemates if Paul and I owned it together. Neither Paul nor I needed that. If Paul got the songs, people would have said, "Paul finally got John." And if I got them, they'd say, "Oh, the dragon lady strikes again." '

In 1990, Paul and Michael met to discuss what Paul called 'this problem of publishing'. Paul recalled, 'I put it to him this way: "When we signed our deal, John and I didn't even know what publishing was. We thought songs were in the sky and everyone owned them. These days, even kids know better than that. Last year, "Yesterday" passed the five-million-plays mark in America, which no other song has ever done. Not even "White Christmas". But no one has ever come up to me and said, "Hey man, I really think you need a bonus. You've done great for this company." So what the fuck is going on? You mean I've got to be content for the rest of my life to be on this deal I signed when I was a fresh-faced twenty-year-old? I've done a lot for this company.'

Michael acted as though he didn't understand what in the world Paul was telling him. Therefore, Paul spelled it out for him. 'I wanted him to recognize in the deal that I'm a big writer for this company that he now owns,' McCartney recalled.

Michael told Paul that he didn't 'want to hurt anyone', and Paul said he was happy to hear that. 'He's a genuine bloke, Mike is,' a placated Paul would then say of him. Michael promised that he'd try to work something out.

The next day, John Eastman, Paul's attorney, telephoned John Branca and told him that Paul and Michael had agreed to renegotiate a higher writer's royalty for his songs. John checked it with Michael. 'Heck, no, I didn't tell Paul that,' Michael said, annoyed. 'In fact, he's not getting a higher royalty unless *I* get something back from *him*, in return.'

John passed Michael's comment on to Paul's attorney.

'Okay, then fine. We'll sue,' Eastman threatened.

'Hey, be my guest,' Branca told him.

When John told Michael that Paul might sue him, Michael laughed out loud. 'Cool. Let him sue,' he said. 'Meanwhile, go license some more songs, Branca. Let's make some money. Let's run this thing like a business.'

An associate of Michael's said, 'Privately, Michael's feeling was: Paul had two chances to buy the company. Both times, he was too cheap to spend the money. Mind you, Paul is said to be the richest entertainer in the world, worth about $560 million. His royalties in one year come to $41 million. As Mike told me, "If he didn't want to invest £47.5 million in his own songs, then he shouldn't come crying to me now." He's a hard-hearted son-of-a-gun, Michael Jackson is, just like his father. And when it comes to Paul, Michael doesn't want to know anything. "I got those songs fair and square," he's said.

"They're mine, and no one can tell me what to do with them. Not even Paul McCartney. So, he'd better learn to deal with it.'"

By acquiring ATV, Michael Jackson proved himself a perceptive, hardheaded businessman, exactly the kind of entrepreneur his father, Joseph, would like to have been, but wasn't. Where Joseph bullied, Michael ingratiated. Where Joseph shouted, Michael usually listened – but he, too, could be unreasonable. Where Joseph rushed in unprepared, Michael usually studied every angle before reaching a decision – or, at least, he had someone else do it for him, namely John Branca. Indeed, Michael had the wisdom to surround himself with brilliant people, and then allow them to do their jobs without interference; Joseph never did. He always felt that he had to have final-say over everything. It's almost as though Michael had studied Joseph's technique and then tried to do exactly the opposite. However, what father and son did share back then – and still do today – is that they trust no one and can be ruthless to those they have vanquished. Rarely do they allow anyone a second chance.

'We Are the World'

By January 1985, the Victory tour was history. Though it hadn't been an easy experience, Michael did find a pot of gold at the end of the rainbow: Chuck Sullivan gave him eighteen million dollars, *cash*, to develop a clothing line. Michael barely got a few fashions into the stores – which didn't sell – when Chuck went bankrupt. Michael got to keep the eighteen million.

The Jacksons made a lot of money on the Victory tour, even if the promoters didn't; each brother made about $7 million, one-sixth of the share after all expenses, net. Michael donated his take to charity; his brothers spent theirs on a lavish lifestyle and, before very many years, would need to work again.

Michael has never again gone on the road with his brothers – though they have repeatedly tried to convince him to do 'just one more tour'.

Once he got home to Encino, one of the first things Michael did was get into LaToya's black Mercedes-Benz 450 SEL and speed off without any security. He simply wanted some freedom – as if he could ever have it! As always, there were about two dozen fans waiting at the front gate for someone – anyone – who looked like a Jackson. They never dreamed they might actually catch a glimpse of *the* Jackson. When they saw him pull out of the gate, they jumped into their cars and followed in hot pursuit. Michael tried to lose them, but to no avail. He was almost to Quincy Jones's house, miles away, when the vehicle car ran out of gas. Michael jumped out of the car, leaving it in the middle of the street, and then ran for blocks, with his stalkers following him, until he reached Quincy's home, where he found refuge.

After the Victory tour, Michael became involved in 'We Are the World', the historic effort to feed the hungry of Ethiopia. For some time, Harry Belafonte had been making plans to draw together some of the biggest artists in the entertainment business to record a song, the proceeds of which would go to a new nonprofit foundation, USA for Africa, to feed the starving masses. In addition to providing emergency food, medical relief, and self-help programmes to stricken areas of Africa, the undertaking was also to set aside funds for hunger relief in the United States. Harry contacted Ken Kragen, an entertainment manager with a history of fund-raising, to ask if he could enlist his clients, Kenny Rogers and Lionel Richie, in the endeavour. Kenny and Lionel, in turn, obtained the cooperation of Stevie Wonder to add more name value to the project. Lionel then telephoned Michael to ask if he would perform on the recording. He not only wanted to sing on the song, Michael said, he also wanted to help Lionel write it.

Michael has always been empathetic to the plight of the hungry, homeless and sick, especially children. In the past, Frank Dileo has told many heartbreaking stories of Michael's influence on dying children. It is as though an unexplainable part within Michael is able to reach children close to death; his touch seems to act as some kind of soothing balm for kids facing a frightening time. It's an important, positive side of Michael, and one he thinks is the best thing about himself.

For instance, a small child suffering from a brain tumour and spinal cancer was brought to Michael on a stretcher one night after a show. When the boy reached up to Michael, Michael grabbed his hand and held tight. The child smiled. Frank Dileo turned away and broke into tears. 'He's not afraid to look into the worst suffering and find the smallest part that's positive and beautiful,' Frank concluded.

Seth Riggs, his voice teacher who has travelled with Michael on tours, recalled, 'Every night the kids would come in on stretchers, so sick they could hardly hold their heads up. Michael would kneel down at the stretchers and put his face right down beside theirs so that he could have his picture taken with them, and then give them a copy to remember the moment. I couldn't handle it. I'd be in the bathroom crying. The kids would perk right up in his presence. If it gave them a couple days' more energy, to Michael it was worth it.'

While working on 'We Are the World', Lionel Richie went to Hayvenhurst every night for a week where he and Michael sequestered themselves in Michael's room to labour on lyrics and melodies. They knew that what they wanted was some sort of anthem, a song both easy to sing and memorable. Though Michael and Lionel have never said as much publicly, LaToya – who watched the pair work – claims that Lionel only wrote a couple of lines of the song. She contends that 99 per cent of the lyrics were written by Michael, 'but he's never felt it necessary to say that.' The lyrics and the melody were finished on 21 January 1985, just one night before the recording session.

While Michael and Lionel were composing, Ken Kragen went about the business of lining up the all-star cast: Bruce Springsteen, Tina Turner, Bette Midler, Billy Joel, Ray Charles, Diana Ross, Dionne Warwick, The Pointer Sisters, Stevie Wonder, Cyndi Lauper, Willie Nelson, Smokey Robinson, Bob Dylan and many others, forty-five in all. Another fifty artists had to be turned down to keep the project from becoming too unwieldy. Michael asked LaToya to show up, and she did. (She got to stand next to Bette Midler in the line-up.) Marlon, Jackie, Tito and Randy were also there.

Quincy Jones took time away from producing the film *The Colour Purple* to produce and arrange (with Tom Bahler) the Jackson–Richie collaboration at A&M Studios in Hollywood. Because the American Music Awards had been held that same night, many of the artists came directly from those festivities. When the performers showed up, the first thing they saw was a sign outside Studio A: 'Please check your egos at the door.' It was astonishing that so many artists of diverse backgrounds and individual renown were able to do just that: there were no ego problems, at all. Diana Ross could not conceal her excitement and asked the other stars for autographs. The Pointer Sisters took pictures of Michael. 'I've never before felt that strong sense of community,' Kenny Loggins observed.

At around ten p.m., the proceedings turned solemn. Ken Kragen addressed the group to assure them that money generated from the recording would, indeed, 'go to the right places'. Bob Geldof, the leader of the Boomtown Rats and organizer of the British Band Aid musical charity effort, which produced the single, 'Do They Know It's Christmas?' told of his visits to Ethiopia. Two Ethiopian women, whose presence had been arranged by Stevie Wonder, reported on the horrible suffering there.

Finally, Michael addressed the assemblage of stars. Very quietly and somewhat awkwardly, he explained his and Lionel's composition as 'A love song to inspire concern about a faraway place close to home.'

The musical tracks had been recorded earlier in the day, so it was just a matter of fine-tuning the lyrics – 'Should it be "*brighter* day" or "*better* day"?' – and adding the voices. Michael taught the artists the melody and lyrics – most had already been sent taped demos of the song with Michael performing – and worked with them on vocal arrangements.

As integral as Michael Jackson had become to the process, he was also very much separated from it. Whereas everyone else present was filmed (by six cameras) as they performed for the 'We Are the World' video, Michael's solo was taped later, privately, and spliced into the final version. He never took off his shades. Some people speculate that he chose not to record with the rest because he was so awestruck by his fellow celebrities. The ultimate perfectionist, he would feel that he could not perform to the best of his abilities in front of them. Others offer a more cynical explanation: Michael likes to feel he is different from everybody and emphasizes this difference by erecting barriers between him and his fans, his peers and his family. Indeed, in the video of 'We Are the World', the shot of Michael begins at his Bass Weejun shoes and trademark sequined socks, and then pans upward to his carefully made-up face, all at Michael's direction. 'People will know it's me as soon as they see the socks,' he said, proudly, and he was right about that. 'Try taking footage of Bruce Springsteen's socks and see if anyone knows who they belong to,' he added with a grin.

The recording and taping session took all night. Who would sing what and with whom had been decided a couple of days earlier by Lionel Richie, producer Quincy Jones, and arranger Tom Bahler. Some of the interesting vocal pairings included Tina Turner with Billy Joel, Dionne Warwick with Willie Nelson, and, of course, Diana Ross with Michael Jackson. The only hint of things not going as planned involved the pairing of Michael and Prince. Michael didn't like Prince, but for charity he would sing with him. However, Prince didn't even show up. At six the next morning, he called the studio to ask if he might come in and lay down a guitar part. Quincy told him it was too late.

By seven-thirty in the morning, the job was done and the artists began to leave. 'Michael was as exhausted as anyone,' Jeffrey Osborne reported. 'He didn't say much, maybe something about being very happy, but I could tell that he was delighted.'

'I did expect to see more ego,' Paul Simon reported. 'You know, "The Gloved One" meets "The Boss" and things like that, but it just didn't happen.'

'I just don't want this night to end,' Diana Ross said as she hugged Tina Turner.

It would seem that everyone who participated in the 'We Are the World' recording session shared Diana's sentiments. The gentle, uplifting spirit of the song also touched the public's emotions when it was finally released on 7 March 1985. The initial shipment of 800,000 records sold out within three days of its release. The song was number one in America for a month, and also spent a couple of weeks at the top spot in Britain, as well as in other countries. The 'We Are the World' video lent itself well to the benevolent spirit of the celebration and helped to sell four million records in all, earning about eight million dollars for the USA for Africa fund.

A Prank That Didn't Work

The 1986 Grammys set the stage for one of Michael's more bizarre pranks – but one that didn't pan out as he had expected.

Frank Dileo, John Branca, Norman Winter and Michael Jackson had often discussed the careers of show-business icons like Frank Sinatra and The Beatles, and how their representatives were known to sometimes hire teenagers to scream and weep at the sight of them at public appearances. Hysteria does photograph well. Michael always believed that hiring youngsters to holler, faint and sob was a masterful public relations stroke.

One evening Michael and Frank telephoned Norman to tell him of an idea. Michael wanted to cause a commotion during the televised Grammy Awards presentation in February. It had been decided that Quincy and Michael would accept the award if 'We Are the World' won for Record of the Year, accompanied by some of the other participants on the record. It's not known whether it was his intention to do so, but it would seem that Michael wanted to steal a little of Quincy's thunder during the acceptance. He and Quincy always had a strange relationship, symbiotic but also competitive.

Michael's plan was to have a female teenager run out on to the stage from the wings and jump him as he stood next to Quincy. Bill Bray's security staff would be ready and waiting to pull the girl off Michael, who would then act surprised and frazzled. Since the Grammys are televised internationally, the whole world would witness this mad scene. The next day, Michael's popularity, and the hysteria it had caused at the Grammys, would be the subject of worldwide news. The scene caused by Jackson's 'overwrought fan' would probably even overshadow the fact that 'We Are the World' had won the coveted Grammy for Record of the Year. Certainly, Quincy's acceptance speech would be overlooked in favour of Michael's manic adoration.

Frank and Norman were against Michael's idea. If word ever got out to the press that the girl who had attacked Michael had actually been hired by him to do so, it would be embarrassing to everyone involved. 'But it'll never get out,' Michael said, enthused. 'So, who do we get? Who can we hire to do this thing?'

Frank and Norman didn't have a clue. Finally, a female publicist who worked in Norman's office found a teenager who she felt was savvy enough to pull off the hoax. She was hired for the job.

The night of the awards, those involved in the trickery held their breath as 'We Are the World' was announced by presenters Sting and Phil Collins as Record of the Year. Michael, who was wearing a black military jacket, red shirt and red brooch, rose from his seat. Frank, seated behind Michael, smiled broadly, a cigar hanging from his mouth. Michael then walked up on to the stage with Lionel Richie.

Before long, Quincy Jones, Dionne Warwick, Kenny Rogers and Stevie Wonder were also on stage. As Quincy gave his speech, Michael nervously rocked from side to side. He kept looking off into the wings, as if he was wondering when the girl was going to make her move.

Unbeknownst to Michael, the teenager, who had full backstage credentials, was having a difficult time trying to break through the crowd of people – technicians, production people, members of the press – who had gathered in the wings to gawk at the celebrities on stage. Before the hapless 'attacker' knew what was happening, the speeches were over and she had missed her moment. The scheme didn't work.

'What happened? What happened?' Michael wanted to know later. 'I'm standing there waiting and waiting, and nothing?'

When Frank Dileo explained, Michael cracked up into laughter. 'The joke's on me, I guess,' he said. 'I couldn't even concentrate on what was going on because I'm waiting for this girl to come out and jump me . . . and she never did it. Quincy said I was squirming so much, he thought I had to go to the bathroom! Next time, we'll have to plan it better,' Michael concluded, with a wink.

More Plastic Surgery

In June 1986, Michael Jackson underwent another operation to have his nose made slimmer, his fourth rhinoplasty. He also wanted Steven Hoefflin to create a cleft in his chin. Years later, he would tell one associate that the 'greatest joy I ever had was in knowing I had a choice about my face.' This same associate asked Michael for advice about rhinoplasty surgery, and Michael recommended that Steven Hoefflin operate on him. 'There's nothing to it, man,' Michael said. 'After the first one, it doesn't even hurt that much. Once you have it done, you'll never stop looking in the mirror. That's how great you'll feel about yourself. Do it. You'll love it.'

When Michael told Katherine he was going to have a cleft put into his chin, she thought he was going, as she put it, 'overboard'.

'Why?' she wanted to know. 'I just don't understand.'

As Katherine told a friend of hers, Michael explained, 'I can afford it, I want it, so I'm going to have it.' It was as if he were buying a new car instead of undergoing painful, appearance-changing plastic surgery. Whereas most people can only fantasize – 'Wouldn't a new nose be nice, and maybe a new chin too?' – Michael could afford to make those whims a reality. 'And I think if more people could afford it, they would do it too,' his sister Janet has reasoned. 'I see nothing wrong with it.'

One psychologist has speculated that it was Michael's narcissistic side that dictated he have a cleft carved into his chin. 'Michael Jackson was obviously becoming more and more enchanted by his own image,' Dr Raymond Johnson said. 'He is apparently continuing his quest for the perfect face.'

'I *do* want to be perfect,' Michael confirmed. 'I look in the mirror, and I just want to change, and be better. I always want to be better, so maybe that's why I wanted the cleft. I don't know how else to explain it.'

Of course, one of the public's favourite theories about him is that Michael was trying to transform himself into the image of Diana Ross – as if Diana has a cleft in her chin! Mostly this theory is the result of the popular connection between the two stars over the years, and some family members' recollections of Michael making statements to Janet and LaToya such as, 'You're not pretty until you start looking like Diana.' After surgery and with the help of carefully applied makeup, Michael sometimes *did* resemble Diana, with tweezed, arched eyebrows, high cheekbones, and a tapered nose (actually much more tapered than Diana's). Still, the resemblance was in the eye of the beholder. When an associate told Diana that Michael was trying to look like her, Diana was dismayed by the notion. She sized Michael up and snapped, 'I look like *that*?'

In fact, Michael does not want to look like Diana, even if he was enraptured by her image, allure, glamour and, also, her power. He did try to recreate her from time to time, though, by playing out certain 'Miss Ross' fantasies in front of witnesses. Beverly Hills limousine chauffeur, Ralph Caricosa, recalls having driven Michael to a destination. He looked into the rear view mirror and asked, 'Where to now, Mr Jackson.' Michael said, 'Call me Miss Ross, won't you?' Then, there was the night Diana caught him putting on her makeup backstage at Caesars Palace in Las Vegas. Former Supremes star Cindy Birdsong reported that when Diana scolded him ('How many times have I told you to stay out of my makeup!'), Michael responded by saying, 'But, Diana, it's *magic*.'

Once, when Michael checked into the swank Helmsley Palace in Manhattan, he telephoned the front desk from a house phone in the lobby and, in front of amused witnesses, used his best imitation of Diana's speaking voice to hoodwink the operator. 'My suite is not good enough,' he said, acting like a disgruntled diva. 'How *dare* you put me in that suite? There are no flowers, and I think I saw a mouse, and I'm, well, I'm just really *upset*. I can't even go back up there.'

'Who is this?' the surprised operator apparently asked.

'Why, it's Miss Ross,' Michael answered, trying to suppress a giggle. 'Miss *Diana* Ross. Who do you think it is? How dare you even ask?'

By the time the operator put him on hold, Michael was grinning from ear to ear. 'She believes me,' he whispered, excitedly. 'She thinks I'm Diana Ross!'

The operator came back on the line. 'Diana Ross isn't staying here.'

'Oh, she's not?' Michael responded. 'Sorry.'

Then he quickly hung up, laughing so hysterically he could barely catch his breath.

Most people who know Michael agree that there are two reasons why he has had so much plastic surgery. First of all, he strove for some ideal of physical perfection, or his version of it, anyway. He spent most of his life studying pictures of himself, not to mention the hours dancing in front of mirrors, looking at videos, deciding which are his best features and which are not. 'I just want to look the best I can look,' he told Frank Dileo.

'But when do you stop?' Frank asked.

Michael shrugged. 'I'm a work in progress,' he said with a gentle smile.

Publicly, Frank never had much patience for questions about Michael's plastic surgery, mostly because he could not explain it. 'Okay, so he had his nose fixed, and the cleft – big deal. I got news for you,' he said, 'my nose has been broken five times. It's been fixed twice. Who gives a shit? Who cares? Elvis had his nose done. Marilyn Monroe had her nose done, had her breasts done. Everybody's had it done.'

As well as improving his appearance, Michael also had another reason for the operations. All of the Jackson boys grew up to resemble their father, Joseph. Michael could not have imagined a worse fate for himself, and he did everything he could do to destroy the resemblance. Certainly, he has many of his father's character- istics, whether or not he recognizes them: Joseph's determination to the point of ruthlessness, his coldhearted business sense, and on the plus side, his love of family. Emotionally, Michael may be a lot like Joseph – though he would never emulate Joseph's coldhearted unfaithfulness in love – and, he has said, it frightens him. Outside, though, he isn't like Joseph at all.

'He told me so himself,' said a former girlfriend of Berry Gordy's who has known Michael for years. 'He would do *anything* not to look like Joseph. Believe me, the last thing he wants to see when he looks at the man in the mirror is his father. With each operation, he distances himself not only from his father but from the whole family. I'm afraid that's the sad point of all the surgery.'

'The tragedy is,' concluded Joyce McCrae, a longtime intimate who worked in Joseph's office, 'no matter how much Michael tries to scrub Joseph off his face, he's still there.'

Or as Joseph Jackson so aptly put it, 'It takes a father to make a son.'

It was after Michael's operation to have a cleft in his chin that he first began being seen wearing a surgical mask with a black fedora and sunglasses. The press speculated that he was obsessed with catching germs, reminiscent of Howard Hughes' fixation with health issues. Michael said nothing publicly. 'If you knew Michael well enough, you knew what was going on,' Joyce McCrae said. 'As soon as I saw him wearing the surgical mask, I said, "Oh, he's had the cleft done." People told me, "What? That's ridiculous." Well, sure enough, that's what was going on.'

At this time, Michael appeared at a movie memorabilia showcase at the Continental Hyatt Hotel in Hollywood wearing a blue surgical mask and a black fedora. To say he looked conspicuous would be an understatement. When the vendors saw him coming their way, they would triple the prices of all of their goods just because they knew Michael represented a windfall for them. He was shopping for Disney memorabilia with a young boy and Bill Bray, his security man. Whenever he saw something he liked, he mumbled through his surgical mask for Bray to purchase the item. Bray would then pull out a wad of hundred-dollar bills, pay the vendor, and move on to the next display. The fact that the prices were raised especially for him did not escape Michael. 'They see me coming, and they feel like I have a lot of money, so they take advantage of me,' he told me. 'That's not really fair, is it?'

'No, it's not, Michael. But what's with the surgical mask?' I asked.

'I had my wisdom teeth taken out,' he told me. 'Oh, man, the misery. You can't believe what I have been going through.'

'Sounds awful,' I said.

Michael shook his head, sadly. 'It is awful.'

When Michael did not cover his face with a surgical mask, he would venture forth in public wearing a hairy gorilla head mask with fur and beady eyes. 'I love it when people stop and are scared,' he said. 'And I love it when they don't know that it's me inside the mask. I just love that.' It's a great paradox about Michael that he is as much a public show-off as he is a recluse. Sometimes, though, his exploits can prove embarrassing. Once, while walking through an airport wearing the gorilla mask, he tripped over a sand-filled ashtray and fell to the floor in a heap in front of a host of paparazzi, all because his vision was obscured.

When the bandages came off after the cleft operation, Michael concentrated more than ever on his appearance. The new cleft seemed oddly out of place on the bottom of his soft, ingénue-like face. After all of the procedures, Michael's nose was slimmer than ever. It also pointed upward, an odd touch. Tweezing his eyebrows gave him a softer, even more feminine look. His skin seemed to be getting lighter with each passing day. He had begun using an over-the-counter skin-bleaching cream called Porcelana to achieve that look. LaToya used it as well. They had crates of this cream stored at Hayvenhurst, hording it as the most valuable beauty product ever produced.

Also, Michael existed on a strict macrobiotic diet that had left him quite thin and made his face look even more sculpted. 'If I ate like him, I'd be dead,' Frank DiLeo said succinctly.

In truth, Michael Jackson had begun looking more than a little unusual. It was difficult to be in the same room with him and not stare in disbelief, especially if you had known him since he was a child. Comedian Eddie Murphy probably put it best when he said, 'I love Michael, but the brother is *strange*.'

Duets Gone 'Bad'

At twenty-seven years of age, Michael Jackson faced the challenge of recording an album that would top the tremendous success of *Thriller*. Could he do it? Could *anyone*? In the summer of 1986, when he began working on the follow-up album, which would be called *Bad*, Michael put himself under enormous pressure. Extremely competitive, even against himself and his own achievements, he felt that if he did not top *Thriller*'s record sales of nearly 38.5 million, he would be perceived as a failure. Moreover, he needed to have success with the single releases. Once, he discussed the phenomenon of the four hit singles from the *Off the Wall* album, which had preceded *Thriller* in 1979. He told writer Gerri Hirshey, 'Nobody broke my record yet, thank God. Hall and Oates tried, but they didn't.' Eventually he matched his own record with the *Thriller* album, the final US tally being: 'This Girl is

Mine', number two; 'Billie Jean', number one; 'Beat It', number one; 'Wanna Be Startin' Somethin'', number five; 'Human Nature', number seven; 'PYT (Pretty Young Thing)', number ten, and 'Thriller', number four. He needed to do better than that with *Bad*.

When he began working on the album, he taped a piece of paper that said '100 million' to his bathroom mirror. He wanted *Bad* to be, as he put it, 'as perfect as is humanly possible'. Before they started to record the album in August 1986, Michael and Quincy Jones chose from sixty-two songs Michael had written. 'Fifty per cent of the battle is trying to figure out which songs to record,' Quincy said. 'It's total instinct. You have to go with the songs that touch you, that get the goose bumps going.' In the end, eight of the ten songs on *Bad* would be written by Michael. Interestingly, Michael cannot read music. He writes his songs in his head, sings them on to a tape, and then hires musicians to put them down on paper. He is an incredibly musical person, however. The notes he imagines, and the way he hears them composed in song, often astound the most trained of musicians.

One song planned for the album was a rhythm-and-blues-tinged number intended as a duet, 'I Just Can't Stop Loving You'. Michael had wanted Barbra Streisand to record the song with him, but she turned him down. 'I can't believe she would turn me down,' he said. 'Doesn't she know that this is going to be the biggest album in history?' Michael suggested that 'my people' get back in touch with 'her people' and 'tell her she's about to make a big mistake'. Barbra explained she wasn't interested because she was worried that the age difference between them would make the lyrics seem unbelievable, plus she didn't like the song. Frank Dileo was unfazed. 'I knew the song was a hit – with or without Barbra Streisand,' he said.

'Forget her,' Michael reasoned. 'Let's get Whitney Houston.' However, Whitney wasn't interested either. 'Believe me, I didn't lose any sleep over it,' Frank Dileo said of Houston's decision. Someone suggested Diana Ross. 'No way. Bad idea,' Michael responded, straightaway.

Michael didn't explain that Diana was angry with him for a recent misunderstanding. He had made plans to go to dinner with her at a Hollywood restaurant called Le Dome. However, Elizabeth Taylor telephoned and invited him to a meal that same evening. Wanting the best of both worlds, Michael asked her if she would like to join him and Diana. Elizabeth, who must be the centre of attention, accepted his offer, as long as Diana met them at the restaurant. In other words, Elizabeth did not want to join Diana's party. She wanted a party of her own. Michael didn't understand the ego game involved in her decision; he just thought she was being friendly. Anyway, the only thing on his mind was how 'magical' it would be to have Diana Ross and Elizabeth Taylor sitting at the same table with him.

Once he and Elizabeth arrived at Le Dome, Michael telephoned Diana to ask her to join them there. Diana was not pleased. She had been under the impression that *she* was supposed to be his date that evening. 'This is not the way to do things, Michael,' she scolded. She told him that the two of them would have to dine some other time, and *not* with Elizabeth Taylor. She was angry, and Michael knew it; she wouldn't return his calls. It wasn't the right time to ask Diana to record a duet with him. Instead, Quincy recruited singer Siedah Garrett to do the song with Michael, and it would end up the first single release from *Bad*.

(A few years later, in 1990, Michael did the same thing to Elizabeth Taylor that he had done to Diana Ross. He was scheduled to have dinner with Elizabeth at the Hotel Bel Air restaurant in Bel Air, California. However, he left her waiting for more than an hour. She ate *Sevruga* caviar, drank Cristal champagne, waited and became increasingly infuriated. When Michael finally showed up, he explained that he had been in the parking lot in his Rolls, talking on his cellular telephone to Jackie Kennedy Onassis. According to the maître d' who had escorted Michael to her table and was still standing beside him, Elizabeth said, 'I will not play second fiddle to any woman, not even *that* woman. How dare you do this to me, Michael?' Michael protested. 'But, Elizabeth, I have a gift,' he offered in his own defence. From his vest pocket, he pulled out a pair of earrings that appeared to be two ovals of turquoise embellished with diamonds. They weren't even in a box. Without a word, Elizabeth grabbed the earrings. She then donned her fur wrap and sunglasses (at night!) and flounced out of the restaurant, leaving Michael standing there with the maître d'. He couldn't help but break out into laughter; it had been one of the best exits he'd ever seen. 'Oh my God! I can't believe she just did that,' Michael exclaimed, his face lit with delight. 'Did you see that? Wow.')

*

For some reason, Michael had his heart set on recording duets for the *Bad* album, but the plans never seemed to work out for him. While writing the album's title track, he decided he wanted Prince to join him on the recording of it.

A couple of years earlier, Warner Bros. had sponsored an afternoon screening of the Prince movie *Purple Rain* for company personnel and film critics. The word in Hollywood was that the film, a drama with music, was so riveting, it would make Prince a major movie star. Michael was deeply disappointed that he had not been able to make a strong impression in films. Being so competitive, he had to see *Purple Rain* before it was distributed to the public; he arranged to attend the Warner Bros. screening.

When the house lights dimmed, Michael slipped into the small theatre on the Warner Bros. Burbank lot, wearing a sequined jacket and sunglasses. He looked as if he were about to go on stage to accept an award. He sat in the last row and watched the film, never once taking off his shades. About ten minutes before the movie was to end, he rose and walked out. Later, a member of his entourage asked Michael what he thought of the film. 'The music's okay, I guess,' Michael asked. 'But I don't like Prince. He looks mean, and I don't like the way he treats women. He reminds me of my relatives. And not only that,' Michael concluded, 'that guy can't act. He's not good.' Then, Michael let out a sigh of relief.

Though he didn't seem to appreciate Prince's talent, Michael realized that singing a duet with him could generate interest not only in the title track, 'Bad', but in the entire album. His concept for himself and Prince was actually ingenious.

The plan was that a month before the single release of 'Bad' was to be issued, Frank Dileo would plant stories in the tabloid press suggesting that Michael and Prince were bitter rivals. Michael's representatives would criticize Prince, and then Prince's friends, a few of whom would be let in on the hoax, would condemn Michael. To then confound the public, Frank would then tell a *Rolling Stone* reporter that the rivalry did not exist and that his client was disgusted with the rumours since he and Prince were great friends, 'and who believes the tabloids, anyway?'

In a month, rumours about him and Prince would be flying – are they friends or aren't they? – with the general consensus, hopefully, being that they were not. At the height of such controversy, the 'Bad' single and video would be released. In the video, as Michael planned it, he and Prince would square off against one another, taking turns vocalizing and dancing, in order to determine, once and for all, who was *'bad'*.

Quincy arranged for Michael to meet him, feeling that the two were creative geniuses and should know one another, whether they ever sang together or not. According to writer Quincy Troupe, 'It was a strange summit. They're so competitive with each other that neither would give anything up. They kind of sat there, checking each other out, but saying very little. It was a fascinating stalemate between two very powerful dudes.'

However, when Michael telephoned Prince and told him about his idea, Prince was not enthusiastic. He said he wanted to hear a tape of the song. Michael sent him one. After hearing it, Prince decided that he didn't like the tune and wanted nothing to do with the hoax. That was the end of it. When word got back from Prince's representatives that he was not going to cooperate, Michael was disappointed, but not really angry. 'What do you think about this guy turning you down?' Frank Dileo asked him.

'Figures,' was all Michael would say, shaking his head in disgust.

The Hyperbaric Chamber

In September 1986, Michael Jackson's *Captain EO* was set to premiere both at Epcot Center in Orlando, Florida, and at Disneyland in Anaheim, California. It was probably the most expensive and most ballyhooed short subject (seventeen minutes) in film history, and it took over a year to complete it. *Captain EO* was directed by Francis Coppola. The executive producer was George Lucas. Estimates of the 3-D film's budget ran as high as twenty million dollars. Both parks had to build special theatres for the film with floors that tilted to coincide with the space-age action on the screen. It was also a light-and-sound show, with smoke emanating from the screen. Michael played a space commander with a crew of robots and fuzzy creatures battling a hideous queen (Anjelica Houston). Through song and dance, a planet's inhabitants are transformed into peace-loving creatures. Michael performed two songs, 'We Are Here to Change the World' and 'Another Part of Me'.

Michael felt that he needed some kind of dazzling gimmick to promote the film. The publicity designed to create a buzz about Michael and his *Captain EO* is an excellent example of how he could manipulate the press to do his bidding.

Earlier, in 1984, when Michael was burned while filming the Pepsi commercial, he saw an oxygen chamber at Brotman Memorial Hospital called a hyperbaric chamber, used to help heal burn victims. The machine is about the size and shape of a casket with a clear, plastic top. It encloses the patient in an atmosphere of one hundred per cent oxygen under increased barometric pressure up to several times the pressure at sea level, thereby flooding body tissue with oxygen. When administered by trained medical personnel, hyperbaric therapy is safe. However, in the hands of the untrained user, risks include oxygen toxicity, seizures and danger of an oxygen-fed fire. When Steven Hoefflin told him that he had a theory that sleeping in this machine could prolong life, Michael became fascinated by it and, immediately, wanted one for himself. The cost was about $200,000.

Though Michael could well afford it, Frank Dileo talked him out of wasting his money on such a contraption. 'Well, I'd at least like to have my picture taken in it,' Michael decided. When Frank arranged for Michael to be photographed in the chamber, at the hospital, word began to spread that he was interested in the chamber and, eventually, the story found its way to the tabloid, *National Enquirer*. 'I had a phone-in from a source in Los Angeles who said that Michael was seen going to a hospital and taking pictures in this chamber,' said reporter Charles Montgomery who worked for the *Enquirer* at the time. 'It sounded like a sensational story. I wanted to be the one to break it.'

Charles met with Frank Dileo and asked for details. 'He didn't want to discuss it, told me to get lost,' Charles said. 'I got some information on the phone from Steven Hoefflin, but not much. Without cooperation, the story had to be put on hold.'

Not for long, though . . .

When Michael heard that the *Enquirer* was asking questions about him, his wheels started turning. Earlier in the year he had given Frank Dileo and John Branca a copy of a book about P. T. Barnum, his theories and philosophies. 'This is going to be my Bible and I want it to be yours,' he told them. 'I want my whole career to be the greatest show on earth.'

Michael's idea was to promote the story that he was sleeping in the hyperbaric chamber in order to prolong his life to the age of 150. He would add that he planned to take the machine on the road with him on his next tour. He wasn't certain that the public would believe such a fantastic story – at this time, such wacky stories were not as associated to Michael as they are today – but he was eager to see how much of a buzz he could start. John Branca thought the idea was odd, but it seemed harmless enough as far as publicity stunts go.

It fell upon Frank Dileo to find a way to disseminate the fabricated story. He called Charles Montgomery and gave him the information he had sought earlier and, to make the story even more irresistible, he promised a photograph of Michael actually in the chamber – as long as Charles could guarantee the weekly's cover. He also made Charles promise not to reveal his source for the information.

'I honestly didn't know if the story was true or not,' Charles Montgomery said. 'But Michael Jackson said it was true, his manager said it was true, and his doctor verified it. How many more sources do you need? Then, there was a picture. It turned out to be a great shot, the guy laying there in the chamber. We knew what they were after in giving it to us, though. They said they wanted us to use words like 'wacky' and 'bizarre'. We knew the *Captain EO* thing was coming up, and figured he was probably trying to promote some kind of sci-fi image. Still, it was a good story.'

With the *Enquirer* in place, Frank wanted to strategize a way to distribute the story to the mainstream press, but without anyone knowing he was involved with it. Planting it in the *Enquirer* did not risk his credibility since he could easily deny having had anything to do with it. Certainly, no one would take a *National Enquirer* reporter's word over Frank Dileo's. However, other more legitimate press might be tougher to crack. Since the media knew that veteran publicist Norman Winter worked for Michael Jackson, Norman could not be the one to promote the bizarre story to the press. Frank would have to hire an outside publicist for the job.

As it happened, Frank's Sunset Strip office was next door to that of leading show-business publicist Michael Levine. Frank invited Michael to his home in Encino and told him about his idea, but with a few embellishments. Frank took Michael's idea a step further. He wanted the press to believe not only that Michael was sleeping in the chamber, but also that he and Michael were locked in a strong disagreement about its safety, and that Frank did not want him to take the machine on the road with him during his next tour. Michael Levine was told that if he wanted to represent the story to the media, he would have to do so without having any contact with Michael Jackson – and without informing the media that he (Levine) was involved in any way. In other words, Michael Levine's task was to publicize one of the most ridiculous stories ever concocted without anyone knowing he was doing it.

The next day an envelope was delivered to Michael Levine's office. The messenger had strict instructions that only Levine be privy to its contents. He opened the envelope to find a single colour transparency of Michael Jackson lying in the hyperbaric chamber in his street clothes, but without shoes. There was no covering letter or return address.

It was time for Michael Levine to go to work. He brought a well-known Hollywood photographer to Brotman to take pictures of the empty hyperbaric chamber for any publication that might need additional photos.

One reporter recalled, 'Levine telephoned me and said, "Look, I don't represent Michael Jackson. I don't even know Michael Jackson. But I was up at Frank Dileo's house, and I overheard that there's this wild feud going on.' Then he told me this story about Michael sleeping in an oxygen chamber and the fact that he and Dileo were feuding about it. In about three days, I was hearing this damn story all over town.'

About a week later, the pieces of the puzzle came together. The picture of Michael lying in the chamber made the front page of the *National Enquirer* on 16 September 1986, as planned. Most people had never heard of a hyperbaric chamber, so it was difficult to know if the picture was a set-up. In truth, patients and medical personnel who enter such a chamber must wear fire-retardant clothes due to the high concentration of oxygen, not street clothes as Michael had on in the photograph. And why take off his shoes?

With Michael Levine's assistance, word of Michael Jackson's exploit quickly spread around the globe, a perfectly orchestrated public relations coup. If his goal was to appear 'wacky' . . . he certainly achieved it. The hyperbaric chamber story was carried by the Associated Press and the United Press International. It appeared in *Time*, *Newsweek* and practically every major newspaper in the country. Television and radio news covered it. Suddenly, the words 'hyperbaric chamber' were on the lips of many people as they gossiped about crazy Michael's plan to live to 150 and how he and his manager were fighting about it.

When contacted by the Associated Press, Frank Dileo confirmed the report. 'I told Michael, "That damn machine is too dangerous. What if something goes wrong with the oxygen?" But Michael won't listen. He and I are in disagreement about this. He really believes this chamber purifies his body – and that it will help him accomplish his goal of living to be a hundred and fifty.'

And to *Rolling Stone*: 'Michael knows if I tell him something, it's the truth. I don't have to agree with things if I don't want to. In other words, because I know this is eventually going to come up in this interview anyway, the hyperbaric chamber. I'm one hundred per cent against that. I don't want it around. I've spoken about it publicly. Some managers couldn't have that conversation with their artist. They'd be too afraid. He respects my opinion. He doesn't always listen.'

He added to *Time*, 'I can't figure him out sometimes.'

Even Michael's plastic surgeon, Steven Hoefflin, got in on the act and said he tried to talk Michael out of 'this wacky idea'. However, Michael ignored everyone's fears and made room for the chamber in his bedroom.

When Joseph Jackson heard the story on the TV news, he ran up to Michael's bedroom to see if Michael had a hyperbaric chamber in there. 'But I didn't find anything,' he recalled. 'So I figured, well, either the story is untrue . . . or the chamber is on its way.'

'I don't think I allowed Michael to have that thing in the house,' Katherine added.

Michael's family was obviously not let in on the joke. 'Joseph always stood behind Michael when it came to these kinds of rumours,' said his friend of twenty-five years, Jack Richardson. 'He'd say, "Michael's not sleeping in no chamber. Don't believe what you hear about my son."'

'I never asked him about that chamber thing,' Janet said. 'I have no idea what that was about. It's not in the house, or I would know it. But knowing Michael, if he is doing something like that, it probably has to do with his voice.'

'I realized then that Michael Jackson liked to see himself portrayed in an absurd, bizarre way,' Charles Montgomery said. 'In the years to come, I would do the biggest number of stories on Michael in the *Enquirer*. Before I ran anything, I would always check its accuracy with people close to Michael. I almost always had full cooperation from his camp. Michael is one of the smartest entertainers in the business. He knows how to get his name out there. He knows about PR. He knows how to control his career. I think he's brilliant.'

Michael was astonished by the way his fiction made headlines. Many untrue stories had been written about him in the past, and he had been angry about them. Now, he was exacting his revenge against the media. 'I can't believe that people bought it,' he said of the hyperbaric chamber idea. 'It's like I can tell the press anything about me and they'll buy it,' he added, as if recognizing the full potential of his communications power. 'We can actually *control* the press,' he concluded. 'I think this is an important breakthrough for us.'

Once, Frank Dileo was asked about the wisdom of doing whatever he could do to make Michael seem as incredible as possible or, as he put it, 'to keep him as popular and in demand as anyone can be.' 'Might all this hoopla damage the singer's already fragile psyche?' asked reporters Michael Goldberg and David Handleman for *Rolling Stone*.

'It's too late anyway,' Dileo responded. 'He won't have a normal life even if I stop.'

The Elephant Man's Bones

Another publicity gimmick sprang forth from Michael Jackson's imagination in May 1987, one that was just as fantastic and – as it would happen – as damaging to his image as the hyperbaric chamber scam.

For years, Michael had been fascinated by the 1980 film about John Merrick, *The Elephant Man*, starring John Hurt. When he screened it in his private theatre, he sobbed his way through the entire film, he was that moved by it. John Merrick, the hideously deformed, Victorian sideshow-freak, was an outsider in a seemingly endless search for love and acceptance – just like, in his own view, Michael. In researching Merrick's life, Michael heard that his remains were kept in a glass case at the London Hospital Medical College. He wanted to see the ninety-seven-year-old skeleton, of course, and during a trip to England he obtained special permission to inspect the exhibit. (Because it attracted droves of tourists to the hospital, it had been removed from public view after the movie was released.) Michael was awe-struck by the exhibit and, as he examined the skeleton, said to Frank Dileo, 'I sure would like to have these bones at Hayvenhurst house. Wouldn't it be cool to own them?'

'Yeah, well forget it,' Frank said.

'But . . . hmmmm.' Michael looked as if he had an idea.

'Uh-oh,' Frank said.

Remembering the hyperbaric chamber hoax, Michael came up with the idea that he should make an offer to the hospital to buy the John Merrick exhibit just to see what kind of press it would generate. 'Man, that is crazy,' Frank told him.

'I know,' Michael said, excited. 'That's why we have to do it.'

In truth, Frank was all for it; he liked a good show as much as anyone else, and certainly as much as Michael. Therefore, claiming that Michael's absorbing interest in the remains of John Merrick was based on his awareness of 'the ethical, medical and historical significance of the Elephant Man', Frank told members of the press that he had offered a half-million dollars to the hospital for the bones. The offer was not publicized in the complex, cloak-and-dagger manner by which the hyperbaric chamber hoax made news. Rather, Frank called a couple of writers himself and gave them the scoop; the rules for such madness had, it seemed, become somewhat more flexible.

'What's he gonna do with the skeleton, Frank?' a reporter wanted to know.

'I don't know,' Dileo said, 'except that he'll probably put it in the room while I'm trying to have a meeting with him.'

As expected, the media was interested in the story. The pop star who sleeps in a hyperbaric chamber wanted to buy the Elephant Man's bones. How could that *not* cause a stir? The wire services – Associated Press and United Press International – both picked up the story. By June, much of the public interested in such things was talking about Michael's latest eccentricity. The British media began referring to him as Wacko-Jacko.

Michael and Frank failed to realize, however, that the media might check with the London Hospital Medical College to verify that an offer had been received by them. In fact, when contacted by the press, officials at the College said they had received no such offer, that they had only heard about Michael's interest in Merrick's remains by reading about it in one of the British tabloids. Even if they did get an offer, the spokesman said, 'We would not sell the Elephant Man. It's as simple as that.'

'Oh, man, why didn't we think to cover our bases,' Michael said to Frank. 'Now we gotta make a real offer. And, anyway,' he added, 'of course they'll sell it if the money is right. Every man has his price.'

'You serious now,' Dileo asked. 'You really want them, now?'

'Yeah, I do,' Michael said. 'Let's get 'em.'

Now, Michael actually wanted the skeleton, but not because of any devotion to John Merrick but rather because he was told he couldn't have them.

Frank telephoned the hospital and made an offer of a *million* dollars for the Elephant Man's bones. The hospital officials said they were insulted. A spokeswoman told the press, 'Indeed, he offered to buy it, but it would be for publicity and I find it very unlikely that the medical college would be willing to sell it for cheap publicity reasons.'

Back in America, Katherine Jackson figured out that the story was bogus. However, she thought it had been Frank's idea; she never dreamed that it was Michael's. She called Frank and said that she was upset; 'you're making Michael look like an idiot.' Frank told her that all he was doing was trying to make Michael appear to be more interesting. Katherine didn't like his explanation, though, and made her feelings clear. However, when Frank asked Michael what he thought about his mother's concern, Michael said, 'Kate doesn't understand show business. So, don't worry about it.'

At this same time, the Jehovah's Witnesses' elders in Woodland Hills, California, began pressuring Michael again. They felt strongly that the recent publicity was doing him great damage, and that it reflected poorly on the Witnesses, because Michael was so representative of the faith. Michael was becoming disenchanted with the church's elders by this time, mostly because he didn't want to be told what to do. What's more he couldn't reconcile his lifestyle and career to the religion's strict tenets. In truth, it's almost impossible to be a Jehovah's Witness and be an entertainer. Therefore, in the spring of 1987, Michael withdrew from the Jehovah's Witnesses. A letter from the Jehovah's Witnesses headquarters in Brooklyn, New York, sent out as a press release, stated that the organization 'no longer considers Michael Jackson to be one of Jehovah's Witnesses.' Gary Botting, coauthor of *The Orwellian World of Jehovah's Witnesses* and a Witness himself, said that leaving the religion 'is worse than being disfellowshipped, or kicked out.' He observed, 'If you wilfully reject God's only organization on earth, that's the unforgivable sin . . . the sin against the Holy Spirit.'

Michael's decision to leave the church puzzled his mother, Katherine, and caused her great despair. Katherine wasn't sure she knew her own son any longer. However, there was no discussing the spiritual matter with him – literally. As it is strictly prohibited for a Witness to discuss matters of faith with ex-members, even if they are family, Katherine says that she has never asked Michael what happened, and she says that she never intends to ask such questions. 'I was not required to "shun" my son,' she claimed, referring to rumours of that nature. 'But we can't talk about matters of faith any longer, which is a shame.'

Katherine maintained that her relationship with Michael continued to be warm. 'Michael still asks my advice,' she said. 'And he helps me choose my clothes. He tells me to put on lipstick when company's coming. He has encouraged me to lose weight. He said, "Elizabeth [Taylor] lost all that weight. If she has, you can. And if you don't like it, you can always have plastic surgery." But I wouldn't do that,' Katherine hastened to add.

Michael soon lost interest in the Elephant Man's bones. As expected. It had certainly generated a great deal of press for Michael, though none of it favourable. *Playboy* magazine facetiously reported, 'Rumour has it that the descendants of the Elephant Man have offered $10,000 for the remains of Michael Jackson's nose.' In time, the controversy blew over. Gone, but not forgotten. Ever.

Michael's phony quest for John Merrick's bones created a domino effect in the tabloids, one from which his image would never truly recover. After the Elephant Man's Bones story, unscrupulous journalists began creating their own fictions about Michael, and they did so with a vengeance. After all, if Michael wanted the kind of publicity he had been diligently courting, why not accommodate him? Crazy-Michael stories sold millions of magazines.

In a short time, according to the tabloid press, Michael had asked Elizabeth Taylor to marry him and said, 'I could be more special than Mike Todd. I could be more attentive and generous than Richard Burton, but she turned me down.' He also apparently tried to convince Elizabeth to sleep in his hyperbaric chamber; was convinced that the world would end in 1998; refused to bathe in anything but Evian water; and had seen John Lennon's ghost (who convinced him to use The Beatles song 'Revolution' in a Nike ad). And the stories about Bubbles the Chimp seemed to never end. None of the stories was true, though, and Michael went on to complain bitterly about them, never admitting (and maybe not even understanding) that he was the one who had thrown the first punch. Since Michael refused to do any interviews in an effort to maintain his inscrutability, the stories just spread without contradiction or explanation.

CBS Records executive Bobby Colomby recalled, 'Michael kept asking why so many bad things were being said about him. He didn't understand it. He said it really hurt to read all that stuff. I tried to tell him that the problem was his. I explained to him that he'd never seen Bruce Springsteen on the cover of the *National Enquirer* in a hyperbaric chamber. Even if that picture came in, they wouldn't believe. I said, "But you, Michael, spend so much time working on your mystique, on being reclusive and unusual, that people will buy anything with your name on it." He said he understood . . . kind of.'

To this day, the stories continue. Some true, some false, all mad.

Since the time of the hyperbaric chamber and Elephant Man's bones, Michael has never stopped complaining about the press, and has even written songs about his victimization at the hands of the media; for instance, 'Leave Me Alone'. In 1993, Oprah Winfrey asked him about the hyperbaric chamber during her televised interview with him. 'I cannot find an oxygen chamber anywhere in this house,' she said in mock exasperation. 'That story is so crazy,' Michael remarked, annoyed. 'I mean, it's one of those tabloid things. It's completely made up.' He explained that what happened was that he saw the chamber at the The Brotman Burn Center and decided to 'just go inside it and hammer around, and somebody takes the picture. When they process the picture, the person who processes the picture says, "Oh, Michael Jackson!" He made a copy and these pictures just went all over the world with this lie attached to it. It's a complete lie. Why do people buy these papers?'

In May 2003, when he was about to release the tamed *Michael Jackson's Private Home Movies* documentary to combat the sensational one by Martin Bashir, he told *People*, 'I want people to see the real me. I don't have sex with little kids. I don't sleep in hyperbaric chambers, and don't have elephant bones in my body. So many things are said about me, and I have no idea where they came from.'

In the end, the hard truth probably hurts more than any wacky fiction: Michael Jackson is responsible for his own image. He's given the media plenty to work with over the years and, in turn, the media has assisted him in achieving what he once stated was his ultimate goal, that of making his life 'the greatest show on earth'.

Jackie, Jermaine and Janet

By August 1987, after many years of acrimonious litigation, Jackie Jackson's marriage had officially ended, mostly due to his unfaithfulness to Enid. Two months later, Jermaine's marriage ended after almost fourteen years. Again, his relationships with other women was key to the marriage breakdown. He even had a child with another woman, a baby Hazel had considered adopting rather than end her marriage over it. Then, she became pregnant at the same time. It was an emotional rollercoaster for everyone involved. To some family members, the scenario eerily resembled that of Joseph, Katherine and Joh'Vonnie.

One had to wonder who could be blamed for such emotional bankruptcy. Had Joseph's influence been so damaging to his sons that they just didn't know how to conduct themselves in a relationship? Had Katherine's acceptance of Joseph's philandering warped their view of fidelity? Or was show-business excess responsible for their behaviour? Were they so accustomed to entitlement brought about by fame, they knew no boundaries? Today, the brothers look back on the 1980s and regret many of their personal decisions. 'It's not easy growing up,' Jermaine has said. 'We made mistakes. We all make mistakes.'

While Hazel and Jermaine litigated their divorce, Hazel continued living at the couple's Benedict Canyon home in Beverly Hills with their children. Meanwhile, Jermaine, his girlfriend Margaret and their new baby moved in with . . . Joseph and Katherine!

Katherine was opposed to having her son, his new romantic interest and their baby living at Hayvenhurst since he was not yet divorced from his wife. To her, the living arrangements did not seem, as she put it, 'moral'. However, when Joseph insisted that Jermaine and his new family moved into the estate (which Michael owned), the debate was over.

For Michael's part, he didn't approve of anything that had occurred in the marriages of Jackie and Jermaine. Even Tito was having trouble with Dee Dee. However, he seemed to sense that the brothers were doing the best they could, under the circumstances of the way they were raised. 'We have had to learn a lot of stuff on our own about how to treat people,' he told LaToya. 'That's what's so hard, isn't it? I mean, no one taught us anything.'

'Except for Mother,' LaToya added.

'Except for Mother,' Michael agreed. Then, after a beat. 'Still, look at how hard she has had it. What are we supposed to learn from that?'

By June 1987, Michael Jackson still did not want the *Bad* album to be released. He didn't think it was ready for commercial consumption and was nervous about the public's reaction to it. He was also understandably concerned about comparisons to *Thriller*. 'He's afraid to finish the record,' said Frank Dileo. 'The closer he gets to completing it, the more terrified he becomes of that confrontation with the public.'

While Michael was sweating out *Bad*, his sister Janet was finally having her first major recording success with the A&M album *Control*. At this time, Janet was in the thick of a power struggle with her father over just that – control: of her music career and of her life.

Janet had recently aligned herself with thirty-one-year-old A&M Records executive John McClain. It had actually been Joseph's idea that John – a brilliant songwriter and session guitarist turned manager – take Janet under his wing. John had been a friend of the family's for years; Tito taught him to play his first licks.

After Janet had two commercially unsuccessful A&M albums, Joseph insisted that if she stayed with him and worked hard, she'd be 'as big as Michael'. However, Janet had her doubts. 'She's no dummy,' Joyce McCrae said. 'She knew there was a reason why Michael and her brothers left Joseph, and she didn't trust her father's management. She started listening to outsiders.'

Joseph hoped that John McClain would work with Janet to polish her image and enhance her career. To that end, John encouraged Janet to diet and exercise, and sent her to Canyon Ranch in Arizona for ten days to get her in physical shape. More importantly, he teamed her up with the writing-producing team of Jimmy Jam and Terry Lewis for what would go on to become the *Control* album. He sent her to a vocal coach, teamed her with choreographer Paula Abdul for her videos, and, in short, made her a major star, almost overnight. In doing so, of course, he also made an enemy out of Joseph; Janet now trusted John, not her father. He had lost the boys, and now he was losing his daughter, too. All he would have left was LaToya . . . and, bless her soul, no matter what she did she wasn't going to be 'as big as Michael'.

'We're the dog with the bone that all the other dogs are trying to get,' Joseph said at the time. 'And the pressure is always on you to hold on to what you've got. As for Janet, I was putting her on stage in Vegas back when she was still a little girl. The wheels had already been set in motion for Janet Jackson 'and anyone who jumps on now will be getting a free ride. I don't intend to let that happen.'

Joseph didn't want Janet to work with Jam and Lewis; when he first heard the *Control* album, he didn't like it − especially the title track and 'What Have You Done for Me Lately?' (which went on to become a huge hit). It was little wonder that Joseph didn't appreciate the concept. The album represented a personal declaration of Janet's freedom from her father and her family; in the title track, she claims that she will now have control over all her own affairs. She sings as if still stung by her family's meddling in her marriage to James DeBarge.

Control was one of the ten best-selling albums of 1986, so Janet had reason to question Joseph's judgement. John McClain said that he would have been 'scared' if Joseph had championed the record because, as he put it, 'I wasn't trying to get a fifty-year-old audience. I was trying to get these kids out here. And because I'm a lot younger than Joseph, I have a clear vibe on how to do it.'

When Janet's album sold six million copies worldwide, Michael was ambivalent about its success. One of the reasons he had such difficulty conceptualizing the follow-up to *Thriller* was that he was so rattled by Janet's *Control* and the public's overwhelming reaction to it. 'Michael is used to being the star of that family,' a family friend said. 'He was not used to seeing anyone get as much attention as Janet got. It got to the point where he didn't want to dance around her because he was afraid she'd steal his steps. That's how bad it got. Janet is also competitive but has always been afraid to admit it. She didn't want to admit to herself that what she really wanted out of her life was to be as big, as famous, as Michael Jackson.'

'God, you make me sick,' Janet Jackson told her brother Michael one day. 'I wish *Thriller* was *my* album.' They laughed, but Janet wasn't kidding.

'Well, Michael may not want her to be as big,' John McClain observed at the time, 'but it's no sin for *her* to want it.'

How 'Bad' Can It Get?

Finally, in July 1987, Michael Jackson's *Bad* was released to the public. If every artist on the planet envied the record-breaking success of *Thriller*, surely none of them wanted to be in Michael Jackson's Bass Weejuns when he tried to follow it up with a new record. *Bad* was a pleasing offering and probably would have been considered first-rate if it didn't have the dubious distinction of having to follow up not only *Thriller*, but also the masterful *Off the Wall*. Ironically, in trying to lead themselves out of the woods, Michael and Quincy Jones followed the *Thriller* formula too closely. Songs like 'The Way You Make Me Feel' and 'Another Part of Me' were dance-floor marvels, but the pseudo-romance of 'Liberian Girl', the album's answer to *Thriller*'s 'Lady in My Life', didn't work as well. Nor could 'Dirty Diana', the production's appointed rock song – featuring Steve Stevens, former Billy Idol guitarist – hold a candle to the more convincing 'Beat It'.

The problem with *Bad*, critics argued, was that unlike *Off the Wall* and *Thriller*, it offered few truly memorable songs. Michael wrote most of *Bad* himself, perhaps propelled by his newfound interest in music publishing and the millions in songwriting royalties he garnered from songs he wrote for the last two albums. Rod Temperton, whose talents helped make *Off the Wall* and *Thriller* such outstanding albums, was not represented. The album's most intriguing moment is the reflective 'Man in the Mirror', written not by Michael but by Siedah Garrett and Glen Ballard. Having gospel stars Andrae Crouch and the Winans sing on the track seemed a weak attempt to musically endear Michael to a black audience.

However, it was the album's title track that came under the most fire from the black music community because it seemed that it should have been the easiest thing for Michael to pull off. Michael was black, his critics reasoned. He began with Motown. He's a funky dancer. Vocally, his roots are steeped, at least to some extent, in gospel. Is 'Bad' the funkiest – the *blackest* – he could get? At best, noted most critics, 'Bad' was a lightweight attempt at a serious, black music.

The 'Bad' video was directed by Martin Scorsese, at Quincy Jones's suggestion. Michael was unfamiliar with Scorsese's work, having seen only one film he directed, *New York, New York*. He had wanted George Lucas or Steven Spielberg to direct the video. However, at this time, Frank Dileo was trying to toughen Michael's Peter Pan image and felt that another Spielberg-style fantasy would be counter-productive. Street music – particularly the rap and hip-hop genres – had begun to dictate pop music and fashion. As a result, Frank thought it would be beneficial for Michael to get back to 'basics'. He believed the image of a street-tough cat would serve his client well.

From the start, there were problems on the set, especially when Michael tried to tell Scorsese how to direct the video. According to a friend of Scorsese's, the filming of 'Bad' was 'a nightmare'. Scorsese has said that the cost of the production went 'two or three times over budget', reaching about two million dollars. However, Scorsese has made no negative comments about Michael and says he found him to be 'sympathetic, sweet, and open'.

The 'Bad' script, written by novelist Richard Price, was inspired by the story of Edmund Perry, a Harlem youth who was educated at a prep school and was shot to death by a New York plain-clothes policeman who claimed he had tried to mug him. What began as a good idea – an attempt to recapture the rebellious spirit of 'Beat It', probably Jackson's most important video – ended up an ill-conceived, albeit entertaining, parody.

'Michael loves *West Side Story*,' said dancer Casper, who danced in the 'Bad' video. 'He had us watch the film one night. He sat on the bed and we dancers – me, Jeffrey, Daniel, Greg Burge and some others – were sprawled all about in a hotel room. He'd have us watch some scenes, and when he saw something he liked, he'd let out a yelp. "*Oooh*, did you see that? Did you feel that?" he'd say.

That was the attitude he said he wanted in the video, *West Side Story*.'

The video's storyline is about a lonely, sheltered school kid, constantly badgered by peer pressure and neighbourhood street toughs. The youngster transforms himself into a bold, avenging hell-raiser. It all goes awry for the viewer, however, because of Michael's ridiculous-looking outfit. Clad in black — boots with silver heels and buckles; a leather jacket with zippers, zippers and more zippers; a metal-studded wristband and a wide belt with silver studs and chains — Michael was slightly overdressed for the ghetto.

The video's debut produced a cynical reaction. Radio stations and newspapers held contests to see who could correctly guess how many buckles were on the costume. *The Los Angeles Times*, for instance, was deluged with responses from readers:

'There's one buckle no one will ever detect, and it's located at the back of his head, to pull the flesh snugly over his ever-increasing new features.'

'The buckles are part of the continuing treatment he is under-going to alter his appearance to that of Liz Taylor as she looked in *National Velvet*.'

'Sixty-six buckles — left over from his oxygen gizmo . . .'

More than the buckles, Michael's concept of what really *is* bad — as in 'tough' and 'streetwise' — seemed distorted and caricatured. He shouted; he stamped his feet; he flicked his fingers and shook his groin. He tugged at his crotch repeatedly. Is *this* what Michael sees from the tinted window of his limousine?

Michael may have been a little overdressed for an urban subway rider, but the surrounding players and dancers certainly looked the part. However, it was difficult to imagine their being so quick to follow anyone — black or white — who looked as effeminate as Michael did in this video. There was something disconcerting about Michael — wearing more pancake makeup than Joan Crawford ever did and flaunting Kirk Douglas's chin cleft — shrieking at a group of tough, black gang members, 'You ain't *nothin*'.' The viewer couldn't help but think, *This boy is going to get hurt*. As one observer noted, 'In Michael Jackson's loathsome conception of the black experience, you're either a criminal stereotype or one of the Beautiful People.'

The original photograph intended for the cover of the *Bad* album was a close-up of Michael's heavily made-up face superimposed with black floral lace. Walter Yetnikoff, president of CBS Records, purportedly phoned Frank Dileo and said of the feminine-looking picture, 'Look, this cover sucks.' The photo eventually used – Michael in a tough-guy-with-fists-clenched-at-his-side pose, wearing his leather outfit from the 'Bad' video – was taken as an afterthought during a fifteen-minute break while shooting the video.

Michael's first single from *Bad*, 'I Just Can't Stop Loving You', was released worldwide on 27 July 1987, and went straight to number one in America, and to the same position in the UK after just two weeks.

Then, Michael's *Bad* album debuted at number one on the *Billboard* charts, an amazing feat proving that even when Michael does wrong, he can do no wrong. The album received generally lukewarm reviews, but that didn't matter either. 'We win,' Frank Dileo said. 'We're into winning.'

The second single, 'Bad', also went to number one in America, Britain and countries around the world. (In the UK the album was even number one for five weeks, and remained on the charts for an amazing 109 weeks. It sold 350,000 copies in five days, the first time that had ever happened in Britain for any artist.)

Michael had a hit on his hands with the *Bad* album, but certainly nothing as big as *Thriller*. However, could it ever have attained *Thriller* status? Isn't it enough that Michael managed such a feat once in his amazing lifetime?

In September 1987, the month his Bad tour kicked off in Tokyo, *People* published a cover story on Michael with the headline, 'Michael Jackson: He's Black. He's *Bad*. Is This Guy Weird, Or What?'

Apparently, such coverage was what the Elephant Man had wrought . . .

Cutler Durkee, the writer of the feature, explained that the public's perception of Michael Jackson had shifted from 'Here's a really interesting guy' to 'Here's a guy I don't understand any more'. Durkee hastened to add, however, that that's precisely why people continued writing about him.

Of course, Michael had good reason to be unhappy with the story. 'They made me sound like a freak,' he said. 'None of that stuff is true.'

Because of such adverse publicity, Michael's tour had a shaky start. Michael thought the act still needed work, but he had no choice but to begin the schedule. The dates were set. Therefore, in September 1987, he reluctantly began what would end up being an exhausting, eighteen-month-long world tour. 'Whatever we play,' Michael and his crew members would yell while clapping their hands and stomping their feet just before hitting the stage, 'it's got to be funky!'

After a successful kick-off in Japan, where he was dubbed 'Typhoon Michael' (and grossed twenty million dollars), Michael had problems in Australia. Ticket sales proved low. Foreign newspapers had latched on to that 'Wacko-Jacko' moniker and the Aussies thought he was a head case. 'He's giving the world a gift, his talent,' complained his former sister-in-law Enid Jackson, 'and, in return, the world tries to crucify him.'

While Michael was on tour, he wrote a letter to *People* and asked that it be published. He wanted to make known his feelings about the adverse publicity he'd received of late. In an odd writing style – no margins, no indentation, and childlike penmanship – Michael wrote:

'Like the old Indian proverb says, do not judge a man until you've walked 2 moons in his moccosins [*sic*]. Most people don't know me, that is why they write such things in wich [*sic*] most is not true. I cry very often because it hurts and I worry about the children. All my children all over the world, I live for them. If a man could say nothing against a character but what he can prove, his story could not be written. Animals strike not from malice, but because they want to live, it is the same with those who criticize, they desire our blood, not our pain. But still I must achieve. I must seek truth in all things. I must endure for the power I was sent forth, for the world, for the children. But have mercy for I've been bleeding a long time now. MJ.'

'I'm not sure I even understand this letter,' Frank Dileo said to an associate after it was published in the magazine as a cover story. 'If you read it carefully, it doesn't make sense. "They desire our blood, not our pain." What the fuck does that mean?'

The associate studied the letter again. 'You know, it's not really about the letter,' he told Frank. 'It's what it says about Michael. He's losing it . . . the man is losing it. Can't you see that?'

Frank began to shake his head in despair. 'Jesus Christ,' he exclaimed. 'What have we done? What's going on with this kid? *What the fuck is going on with this kid?*'

The White Man Won't Let Him . . .

In January 1988, Michael was well on his way to his thirtieth birthday. Despite his best-selling records, his celebrity and his great fortune, he had recently begun to lament that he felt undervalued not only by the music industry, but by the public, as well. 'They call Elvis the king,' he complained to Frank Dileo. 'Why don't they call *me* that?'

One would think that, given all he had achieved, Michael would have been satisfied. He wasn't. Indeed, ever since he was a child, he had been taught that being number one was the most important thing he could do with his life. Because it was a goal he had worked toward for years, reaching it before his thirtieth birthday seemed anti-climactic. After all, what was left for a recording artist to do after selling more records than any person ever in the history of popular music?

Michael never strategized his career in terms of artistic development. He couldn't imagine recording an album for any purpose other than for it to be the biggest and best, ever. He needed to have his work acknowledged in a huge way, or he simply was not going to be satisfied. Perhaps such determination can be traced back to his days as a youngster when The Jackson 5 competed on talent shows, when the only goal was to be the winner. That forum was Michael's original training ground.

Maybe one of the reasons Michael was not respected by the public and music industry is because the masses sensed in him the lack of two essential qualities possessed by artists such as Bruce Springsteen, Bob Dylan, John Lennon, Elvis Presley: humour and humanity. It had become increasingly difficult in recent years to relate to Michael as he stood onstage in his military outfit, accepting his many awards, whispering his thanks in an odd, highly pitched tone, and then taking off his sunglasses for a quick moment because his friend Katharine

Hepburn told him to do so. It was as if he was from some other planet, not earth.

While there was still something about Michael's humility that was engaging, especially considering his many gifts, there was still a nagging problem with his image. Certainly, his fans admired his prowess as a vocalist and his stylized genius as a dancer: he was – arguably, still is – the quintessential entertainer. While the public could identify with many other rock stars whose humanity and accessibility supersede their stardom, it was unable to identify with Michael. After all, who knows *anyone* like Michael Jackson?

After, *Thriller*, Michael saw himself as bigger than The Beatles and more important than Elvis. 'They call Bruce [Springsteen] the boss and he's really overrated,' Michael complained. 'He can't sing and he can't dance. And if Elvis is supposed to be the king, what about me?'

The fact that Michael is black complicated matters. Promoter Don King had preyed on his insecurities in 1984 during the Victory tour by telling him, 'You're the biggest star ever, but the white man will never let you be bigger than Elvis. Never. So, you can forget that.' Michael was stung by Don's observation, so much so that he telephoned his attorney, John Branca, in the middle of the night and, without explanation, blurted out, 'They'll never let me be bigger than Elvis.'

When John asked what he was talking about, Michael answered, 'The white man – because I'm black.'

John reminded Michael that he had already outsold Elvis in record sales. He said that he believed Don had filled Michael's head with racist notions.

However, for the next couple of days, Michael continued to complain about being victimized by his race until, finally, John became so upset he refused to speak to him. When Michael began leaving desperate messages on John's answering machine, begging him to return his call, John finally wrote him a letter. In it, he expressed how much he loved and admired him, and why he felt Michael should rise above the kind of racist thinking Don King propagated with his hare-brained theory about Elvis and the white man. If Michael didn't get over Don's remarks, John wrote, he wasn't certain he would be able to continue representing him, that's how much such thinking hurt him. When Michael read the letter, he was moved. Though he promised to try to forget Don King's words, he never really did that. (Wisely, he also never mentioned the subject to John Branca, again.)

By 1988, Michael seemed to have found a variation on the theme: he began complaining about feeling undervalued by white America, griping that he had an 'image problem'. By this time, though, no one in Michael's camp had a clue how to solve such a problem; it was a little late now to start worrying about his nutty image. Even if Norman Winter or Michael Levine, the two publicists who'd worked with Michael to help create the 'problem', could fathom a way to promote him as an accessible *human* artist with goals that were artistic instead of just commercial, it would never work. No one would believe it; Michael simply wasn't that way and didn't even know how to act that way.

Michael has always been myopic in his thinking about the music business: how many records are being bought by his fans? How long does it take to get to number one? How many tickets are sold? For Michael, commercialism is key, and he doesn't understand any artist who doesn't understand *that*. After all, Joseph dedicated himself to getting his kids out of Gary so that they could have a better life, not so they could make important contributions to the music industry. In his mind, Michael was still there with Joseph, trying to out-do the other acts at the Apollo. Any artist he perceived as being a threat to his dominance on the pop charts, was viewed with scepticism.

For instance, Michael has never been a fan of Madonna, a woman who has managed to combine commerciality with artistic vision because, from the start, she has had something she wants to communicate with her music and, usually, a clear-eyed vision as to how to go about it. She gives interviews; she has a point of view. Other than lamenting about his lost childhood and his victimization at the hands of the media, Michael has never had much of a public viewpoint about anything. He's not what one would call articulate, not by any stretch of the imagination. He's a genius on stage, but in the public eye he's stilted. He is constrained by his insecurity, his bashfulness and his deep fear that he will be revealed as being less than what he would like to be for his public. It's understandable, considering his life, considering the way he was raised by Joseph to think so little of himself.

'She just isn't that good,' Michael told one associate of Madonna. 'Let's face it. She can't sing. She's just an okay dancer. What does she do best? She knows how to market herself. That's about it.'

In 1989, Madonna was named 'Artist of the Decade' by many newspaper and magazine polls. Warner Bros., her record label, even paid for an advertisement in one of the industry trade publications pronouncing Madonna 'Artist of the Decade'. It was the kind of empty compliment record labels often give their artists in paid promotions, but Michael was incensed by it just the same. He telephoned John Branca and Frank Dileo and complained that Madonna didn't deserve such an award. 'It makes me look bad. *I'm* the artist of the decade. Aren't I? Did she outsell *Thriller*?' Michael asked, his vast insecurity coming forth. 'No, she did not,' he said.

John who, lately, was in the business of problem-solving for Michael, suggested that he could approach MTV with the idea of a fictional award. Off the top of his head, John came up with something he called 'The Video Vanguard Artist of the Decade' award. That title sure sounded impressive to Michael; he was happy, again. 'That'll teach the heifer,' he said, speaking of Madonna.

And so it came to pass that at the MTV Awards in 1989, Michael was presented with the 'Video Vanguard Artist of the Decade' trophy. Peter Gabriel handed over the honour, certainly not the most meaningless award ever offered at such a festivity, but sad in that it was given to a fellow who really wanted people to know he deserved it. (To this day, the Michael Jackson Video Vanguard award is presented to artists who excel in that medium, a testament not so much to Michael's amazing videos, but to John Branca's amazing ability to placate his client.)

It's ironic, considering Michael's obsession with Elvis Presley, that John Branca represented the Presley estate. John once mentioned to Frank Dileo that Elvis used to give his trusted employees Cadillacs. He suggested to Frank that it was time for Michael to start taking care of his trusted associates in that same fashion, especially considering all of the bullets John had dodged on Michael's behalf over the years. John was only half-joking. Who wouldn't want a new car?

'Hey, Johnny, that's a damn good idea,' Frank said, seriously.

Later, Frank had a talk with Michael. 'Hey, Mike, listen up. You think you're as good as Elvis?'

'Yeah, I do. Of course I do,' Michael answered.

'Well, you know what? Elvis used to give his people Cadillacs,' Frank said. 'You're a little cheap sometimes, Mike,' Frank added with a grin. He nudged him, good-naturedly.

'What do you mean cheap?' Michael asked, defensively.

'Well, hey, Mike, you got sort of a reputation. No big deal. Let's change the subject.'

Frank had planted the seed.

A few months later, when Michael and John Branca were in London negotiating the ATV acquisition, Michael said to him, 'Branca, if you get me The Beatles catalogue, I'll buy you any car you want, just like Elvis would have done.'

'Including a Rolls-Royce?'

'You got it,' Michael said.

Of course, John Branca later brilliantly closed the deal . . . and Michael bought him that Rolls. The only problem was that he didn't buy one for Frank Dileo. Frank was on the phone to John as soon as Michael told him he had bought him a car.

'He got you a fucking Rolls-Royce?' Dileo asked, bewildered. 'I can't believe this. It was *my* fucking idea, and you ended up with the Rolls!' The two had a good laugh. Finally, Frank got a Rolls from Michael as well. Both guys had played Michael, no doubt about that. John deserved a vehicle, that much was clear, if only for clearing the way for *Thriller* to be released, both the album and the video. One has to wonder about Frank Dileo though, considering the undeniable damage he had done to Michael's image. However, in truth, he was doing exactly what Michael had asked him to do . . . so, yes . . . he probably deserved a Rolls-Royce, too.

On 23 February 1988, Michael Jackson brought the Bad tour to the United States for the first time at the Kemper Arena in Kansas City, Missouri. By this time, the three single releases from *Bad* – 'I Just Can't Stop Loving You', 'Bad' and 'The Way You Make Me Feel' – had all gone to number one. Michael was in good spirits, especially since Frank Dileo predicted that there would probably be two more number-one hits.

Before the show, the Jackson crew unloaded eight truckloads of equipment, including seven hundred lights, one hundred speakers, a massive stage, two huge video screens, and eighty-five costumes. On the night of the concert, banks of floodlights rose from the stage bathing the audience in blinding white light before *he* appeared, frozen still onstage in a line of dancers. Dressed in a black toreador's outfit with buckles down the trouser seams, Michael exploded as a supernova of energy in motion to the strains of the opening number. 'Wanna Be Startin' Somethin''.

There were startling and grandiose effects: bullet-like, multi-coloured laser beams, smoke bombs and explosions, all of which were effective and *loud*. There was also plenty of shtick: Michael dis-appearing from one side of the stage and reappearing on the other in a puff of smoke; Michael swinging out over the audience on a boom crane during 'Beat It'. In terms of pure stagecraft and showmanship, it was impossible to fault Michael and his huge supporting cast, including four male dancers who took the place of Michael's brothers.

In this show, Michael also became much more sexually sugges-tive. He grabbed his crotch at least five times during the opening number. His ungloved hand hovered around his groin during most of 'Heartbreak Hotel', 'Bad' and 'Beat It'. It was an odd gesture coming from someone like Michael, but the seventeen thousand mostly middle-class white fans seemed to love it; the audience was on its feet for the entire slick, demanding, two-hour performance. Every time Michael moonwalked across the stage the audience would cheer and Michael's face would light up. It was clear that he still enjoyed performing.

'The word "superstar" became meaningless compared with the power and grace pouring from the stage,' wrote Gregory Sandow, who reviewed the concert for the *Los Angeles Herald Examiner*.

Vocally, Michael was in terrific shape; his voice teacher, Seth Riggs, travelled with him for much of the tour. 'He's a high tenor with a three-and-a-half octave range,' Riggs said. 'He goes from basso low E up to G and A-flat above high C. A lot of people think it's a falsetto, but it's not. It's all connected, which is remarkable. During his vocal exercises he would put his arms up in the air and start spinning while holding a note. I asked him why he was doing that, and he said, "I may have to do it onstage, so I want to make sure it's possible." I'd never seen anything like that before. I thought maybe I should stop him so he can concentrate on his voice now, and dance later. But I figured if he can do it, let him do it.'

A good third of the show consisted of material Michael and his brothers had used in Kansas City four years earlier when the Victory tour opened, right down to some of the dialogue. This time, though, Michael performed 'Thriller' in his act – complete with werewolf mask and the kind of high school jacket he wore in the video – now that he no longer considered himself a Jehovah's Witness.

When Katherine and Joseph saw the show, they were disturbed by it. 'He should have his brothers with him,' Joseph said, not letting go of that idea. 'What the hell's the point in not having them? I don't get it. He's got a good show, but with his brothers it's a better show.'

Katherine told Frank she thought Michael was better when he performed with his brothers. Frank laughed in her face. 'You are crazy,' he told her. Imagine, telling Michael's mother that she was crazy! Of course, she was offended. 'I am not crazy,' she shot back. 'The show would have been better with the brothers, and that's that.'

'Yeah, well . . .' Frank said before walking off.

Just prior to going onstage in Kansas City, Michael was handed a copy of the *Star*, a tabloid, with the cover headline, 'Michael Jackson Goes Ape. Now He's Talking with His Pet Chimp – In Monkey Language'. The story claimed that Michael was now obsessed with learning how to communicate with his pet monkey by making chimp sounds. 'Did Frank plant this?' Michael wanted to know. 'Where'd they get these pictures of me and Bubbles?'

Michael's aide shrugged his shoulders.

'Well, I don't like it,' Michael said. 'I don't want to see this. Don't show me this kind of stuff before I go onstage. What the hell's the matter with you?'

Like many stories published about Michael, the tale of his fixation with Bubbles – a three-and-a-half-year-old chimp who had been released to Michael from a cancer lab in 1985 – was false. Michael enjoyed his ape, the way he enjoys all of his animals, but even though master and ape sometimes ate together at the dinner table – good enough material for a story in and of itself, one would think – he wasn't speaking chimp language to his pet, not that anyone knew, anyway. (Incidentally, contrary to some reports, there has only been one Bubbles – not a series of monkeys named Bubbles. Just the one.)

Katherine had been after Frank for months to stop promoting her son as 'Wacko-Jacko'. She later said, 'I spoke to him about it on numerous occasions. I knew it was not a good idea, it was backfiring. But, there was nothing I could do about it.'

Partly as a result of the bizarre image Michael had cultivated, it seemed that some of his public had begun turning against him. *Rolling Stone*'s readers voted him the worst artist in nearly every category in its yearly poll. Still, he hoped for some redemption at the Grammy Awards on 2 March.

He decided to perform on the telecast, the first time in five years he had entertained on television. 'Michael wanted to erase all the negative publicity that had been trailing him and replace it with a positive image of him doing what he does best,' said Bob Jones, vice president of communications for MJJ Productions. He wanted to prove to the world that he is serious about entertaining, that the very essence of him is a performer, not an eccentric. He did it, too. Anyone who saw his riveting performance that night would have to agree. He is an intensely competitive person; he wanted to leave an unforgettable impression of himself with the academy and with his audience.

However, after truly inspiring, absorbing performances of 'The Way You Make Me Feel' and 'Man in the Mirror', Michael then had to sit in the first row of Radio City Music Hall, in full televised view of millions, and suffer one humiliating defeat after another. Out of four nominations – Album of the Year, Best Male Pop Vocal, Best Male R&B Vocal Performance and Producer of the Year – he had no wins. The last time Michael appeared at the Grammys, with *Thriller*, he had received more awards (eight of them) than anyone else in the history of the event. This time, he got nothing. Most of all, he had craved the Grammy for Best Album for *Bad*. However, much to his dismay, U2 won it for *The Joshua Tree*.

'He couldn't have looked any more heartbroken if someone had walked away with his pet chimp,' wrote Robert Hilburn, the *Los Angeles Times* pop music critic.

'He went back to the Helmsley Palace, where he was staying, and cried,' one friend said. 'He and Frank had made a vow that they would at least win Album of the Year and, of course, they didn't. He thought the whole thing was unfair. It wasn't about the music. It was about the image. Would the Academy give Record of the Year to a guy who sleeps in an oxygen chamber? Not likely.'

There was little time for Michael to feel sorry for himself, though. The next day he was due to give a concert at Madison Square Garden. After the show, he and a representative from the Pepsi-Cola Company (which had sponsored the Bad tour) presented a $600,000 cheque, the proceeds from the concert, to the United Negro College Fund. Four years earlier, Michael had endowed a scholarship programme at the UNCF with a portion of his earnings from the ill-fated Victory tour. By 1988, seventy students at UNCF member schools had received Michael Jackson scholarships. (At some of the country's smaller black colleges, that could be an entire graduating class.) Michael maintained a low profile when it came to such donations. Perhaps if his generosity were better known, he would not have been so roundly criticized by many African-Americans for not having a so-called 'black consciousness'. In truth, he has given many millions of dollars to black charities over the years.

Most people who accompanied Michael on his Bad tour also recall how generous he was to children who wanted to see him perform. At every concert stop on his Bad tour, he set aside a portion of tickets for underprivileged youngsters who otherwise would have been unable to attend his shows. All of the royalties from his number-one single 'Man in the Mirror' were donated to Camp Good Times, a charity for terminally ill patients in Los Angeles.

Though his good deeds were going unnoticed, his eccentricities were still getting the once-over by the media. While on stage at Madison Square Garden, Michael shared a kiss with model Tatiana Thumbtzen, who appeared in his video 'The Way You Make Me Feel'. A week later, the photo showed up in the *National Enquirer* with the headline, 'Michael Jackson and Model Fall Head-Over-Heels in Love'. The story said that Michael and Tatiana were having an affair (which was not true) now that Michael's romance with makeup artist Karen Faye was over (the two were never romantically involved).

Later, the *National Enquirer* would run with the story that Michael saw Jesus Christ materialize from a cloud of smoke while he performed onstage. That same week, *Star* would print that Michael had fallen in love with Princess Diana and wanted her to star in his next video. When Michael demanded to know where these stories came from, all fingers pointed at Frank Dileo. By this time, though, Frank wasn't doing anything to promote such stories. The media was acting on its own, providing Michael with the image it felt he wanted.

A favourite story among those in Michael's inner circle also appeared in the *Enquirer*. It claimed that Prince had used ESP to drive Bubbles the chimp crazy. 'Prince has gone too far this time,' a furious Michael was quoted as saying in the article. 'What kind of sicko would mess with a monkey? This is the final straw. Poor, poor Bubbles.'

Actually, Michael liked that one. John Branca and Frank Dileo had never seen him laugh so much.

Buying Neverland

In March 1988, while he was still on the road, Michael Jackson finalized the purchase of his new home, a twenty-seven-hundred-acre estate in the Santa Ynez Valley then called Sycamore Ranch. He had become enchanted by the ranch when he stayed there during the time he and Paul McCartney filmed the 'Say, Say, Say' video in Santa Ynez; Paul had leased the home for the duration of his and his wife Linda's stay.

At Sycamore Ranch, there would be plenty of room for Michael's menagerie, an important consideration, and the location was far enough from Encino to guarantee space between Michael and his pesky family members. The property was owned by developer William Bone, who had spent many years and a fortune building it to his specifications; the main house is thirteen thousand square feet. The asking price was $35 million furnished, or $32.5 million unfurnished. Michael toured the estate by horse-drawn carriage provided by Bone.

John Branca had advised Michael that, from a business standpoint, the ranch was not a good investment. Michael intended offering 50% of the asking price, but even so the re-sale opportunities would be limited: there are not many buyers for a twenty-seven-hundred-acre ranch that costs seventeen million dollars. John wrote Michael a letter and told him that if he really wanted to buy the ranch, he shouldn't do so with any 'future profit motive'. He felt it would be a more sensible idea to purchase the property that was once used as the estate on *The Beverly Hillbillies* television show. He also suggested that Michael buy the surrounding property, demolish the houses that were there, and then he could have five acres of property to do with what he pleased.

Michael couldn't understand why he should settle for only five acres when he could have almost three thousand. When he used to visit Paul McCartney, he was always impressed with Paul's sumptuous acres and acres of verdant property. 'My guests expect something grand,' Michael told John. 'It's gotta look like I've made it big, because I have.'

A difficult and lengthy negotiation with William Bone ensued because John was determined to secure the best possible deal possible for Michael. However, Michael was impatient; he called John three times a day, prodding him on. Finally, Michael decided that John really did not want him to have the property, that his stalling could lose the deal altogether. He became angry. He wanted that estate, and that's all he wanted. He went right off the deep end over it, and reportedly asked another of the attorneys at John's law firm to break into John's office and steal the file on Sycamore Ranch . . . and then get to work on closing the deal. Of course, the lawyer didn't do it and, in fact, informed John, who was astonished. He telephoned Michael and asked how he could think to do something so terrible.

'Because I think you don't want me to spend too much money,' Michael said in his own defence. 'You don't want me to have the ranch.'

John told him he was right, he didn't think Michael should make the purchase. However, he intended to follow Michael's wishes, anyway. He hoped that Michael would never again pull a stunt like that one. John was genuinely hurt by it, but it also showed him how irrational Michael can be at times – not that he needed further proof of this fact.

At the last minute, William Bone began having second thoughts about selling the ranch to Michael. He said that he didn't want to lose his emotional connection to the property; he treasured it that much.

More than likely, he realized that he was losing a lot of money and was getting 'cold feet' about it. John submitted an offer of fifteen million dollars, which was not accepted. After a series of counter-offers, Michael's final offer of seventeen million dollars was accepted, certainly a let-down for Bone, considering his thirty-five-million-dollar asking price. Why William Bone took such a loss is still an open question, except that he may have just wanted out of Sycamore Ranch. Michael also got all of the furnishings and eighteenth- and nineteenth-century antiques as part of the purchase. A fully stocked wine cellar went along with the deal. Because Bone started causing a fuss – and John knew that if he lost this deal, Michael would become a real liability in his life – he came up with a clause in the sales agreement that allowed Bone to spend one week out of every year at the ranch for the next three years, subject to Michael's schedule. Therefore, Bone wouldn't feel that he was losing the property entirely. The sale was concluded, successfully. The press reported that Michael paid twenty-eight million dollars for the estate, which was fine with Michael, for obvious reasons.

The first thing Michael did was change the name of the ranch to 'Neverland Valley', though it is usually called, simply, Neverland. When Michael had to conduct business in Los Angeles, he would stay in a condominium he leased in Westwood, which he called his 'hide-out'. Otherwise, he would stay at Neverland, and never again at Hayvenhurst.

Leaving his parents' home was obviously a big deal for Michael. He was sad to leave his mother, but eager to view Joseph as someone to whom he no longer had any responsibility. Still, he couldn't actually face them with the news. In fact, he didn't tell them anything about his negotiation for Neverland Valley, nor did he tell them when it was purchased. Katherine and Joseph found out that Michael was leaving Hayvenhurst while watching the American television programme *Entertainment Tonight*. Panicked, Katherine telephoned Marlon to ask him if he knew anything about it. Marlon then called Michael. Michael said it wasn't true.

Apparently, Michael didn't want anyone to know what he was up to, lest they all gang up on him to talk him out of it – which they definitely would have done. The next day, Michael instructed certain employees of his to go to the Encino home and take from it the possessions he now wanted at Neverland. 'I was waiting for Michael to come to us and say something,' Joseph said, sadly. 'But he never did.'

A few weeks later, Michael hosted a housewarming party for his relatives, but he did not invite Joseph or Katherine. 'That hurt us both,' Joseph recalled. 'We'd seen a lot from that boy, but this was really something we couldn't figure out. I don't know why he would be so hurtful to us, and especially to Kate. I couldn't understand it,' he said.

As it happened, Michael's name was not on the original purchase agreement for the estate. Rather, the agreement was signed by his lawyer, John Branca, and his accountant, Marshall Gelfand, all at Michael's instruction. He had told them that he didn't want anyone to be able to check public records of property ownership and figure out where he lived. Marshall suggested that a trust be set up with himself and John as trustees. Michael owned the trust and could fire both men at any time. The two could do nothing with the property without his permission. To Michael, it was a good idea . . . but only for a couple of days. He's too insecure, and maybe too paranoid, to allow such a situation to exist very long. It was Bill Bray who had a talk with Michael about the property, stoking the fires. 'Man, you don't own this place, they do,' said Bill, being completely unreasonable and naive. 'You need to check this out, Michael. What's gonna happen if they decide to kick your ass out. What'chu gonna do then, Michael? Huh?'

The next day, Michael called Marshall and demanded to know why he didn't own his own property.

'But you *do* own it,' Marshall explained. 'It's set up as a trust, Michael. It's what you asked for.'

'Well, I don't like it,' Michael said, curtly. 'I think it sounds fishy. Change it. I didn't spend all of this time working on this negotiation to now not own the place. It's *my* house.'

'Fine, we'll terminate the trust,' Gelfand responded. 'It's done. Terminated.'

On 11 April 1988, John Branca and Marshall Gelfand signed individual grant deeds turning over the property to Michael Jackson, thereby dissolving the trust.

Michael hoped for a serene lifestyle in his new, palatial estate. He said he needed space, a place to think, time off after the Bad tour.

However, his family now felt that he'd distanced himself from them geographically, as well as emotionally. As much as they missed him, they were also worried about their futures without him. What could the Jacksons do without Michael? Not much. Joseph, Katherine and the brothers were thinking about another reunion tour, and it would only be a matter of time before they approached Michael with the idea. As it would happen, the Victory tour fiasco of 1984 would pale in comparison to what they now had in mind. However, this time Michael would not be quite as accommodating.

PART EIGHT

Enter the Moonies

In the spring of 1988, Jerome Howard, the thirty-five-year-old president of business affairs for Joseph and Katherine Jackson's many entertainment corporations, received a telephone call from someone named Kenneth Choi, a Korean businessman who desperately wanted to arrange a meeting with Joseph. Kenneth, who had already been booted out of Michael Jackson's office – as well as the offices of his accountant, Marshall Gelfand, and attorney, John Branca – told Jerome that he was from a wealthy family interested in spending millions to organize and promote a Jackson family concert tour in Korea. Realizing, of course, that just such a reunion was always on Joseph's and Katherine's minds, Jerome arranged a meeting between Kenneth and Joseph.

'Millions of dollars were offered at that meeting,' Jerome remembered. 'The guy was talking ten to fifteen million. Whatever it would take to get the Jackson brothers to come together for these concerts, that's what he and his family wanted to spend. Joseph was excited. Choi invited us to go to Korea to check things out. We didn't know what was happening; all we knew was that the guy had a lot of money – and he wanted to give it to us.'

Joseph, Katherine, Jerome and Kenneth took a four-day trip to Korea, paid for by Kenneth. They were wined and dined and introduced to several wealthy and influential business people, celebrities and politicians. They also met a gentleman who could not speak English, named 'Mr Lee', who was introduced as Choi's brother. They were told that Lee, who owned a shipping company, would be the primary backer of the proposed Jacksons concerts, along with the *Segye Times*, a Korean newspaper. Through his interpreter-secretary, Mr Lee said that if the concerts were successfully organized, he would also invest two million dollars in a record company for Joseph. Of course, Joseph was intrigued and eager to move forward with the deal.

'These people knew the strengths and weaknesses of the Jackson family,' Jerome Howard recalled. 'They knew that Joseph was interested in getting money for his company, and for himself. They understood that Katherine's interest was for her family. She wanted to make money for her children. They seemed to know everything about the Jacksons, and they knew how to play all the angles.'

In the course of meetings, Jerome soon discovered that the *Segye Times* is owned by the Reverend Sun Myung Moon and the Unification Church. The so-called Moonies, as it turned out, were actually to be the ones primarily backing the tour.

Although many people have joked over the years about being hassled for small change by young Moonies in airports, Moon's followers have actually raised a lot of money, which Moon has invested in a number of diversified enterprises, including banks, restaurants, fisheries and the media. However, the Unification Church has been a lightning rod for controversy: Christian fundamentalist groups have charged that the Church is not Christian; liberal groups have accused them of being too right-wing; parents have hired deprogrammers to kidnap their children who are living in Moonie compounds. Although membership has rapidly declined, the Unification Church is still wealthy.

What Moon craved most for his church was respectability. If he could align himself with Michael Jackson (the biggest-selling and most clean-cut pop artist of all time) and the Jackson family (still perceived by many as being one of the most wholesome families in the United States), Moon would benefit, greatly. The price would be high, but the prestige would be well worth the cost.

When Jerome told Joseph and Katherine that the Reverend Sun Myung Moon was involved in the proposed Jackson deal, Joseph was fascinated; he had heard that Moon was wealthy. However, Katherine was upset. 'I don't want to have anything to do with anything religious,' she said. 'Business is business, but I don't even want to know anything about the religious ties.' Katherine did not tell Jerome to stop the negotiations. She just didn't want to know the details.

From the beginning, Jerome was suspicious of the people working on Moon's behalf. 'They always spoke Korean behind your back,' he said. 'They'd say something in English and then turn to someone and say something in Korean, and who knows what they were saying? I worried that we were missing out on important information. It would be my job to protect the Jacksons as best I could in these sorts of circumstances.'

It was a job Jerome often performed admirably. At about this time, Katherine and Joseph purchased a six-bedroom house in Las Vegas, Nevada, where they eventually plan to retire. The house was being offered for $570,000. The Jacksons brought Jerome Howard to Las Vegas with them to negotiate a deal. Before they went to meet the sellers, Jerome told Katherine and Joseph to strip off all their jewellery – probably a quarter of a million dollars' worth – and put it in the glove compartment of the car. Then, Jerome brought them into the home to meet the owners. Katherine and Joseph acted like 'everyday folks', never mentioned their famous history, and must have done a fairly convincing job of acting because, in the end, they bought the house for only $292,000.

Of the cost of the home, $200,000 came from money that Michael had given Katherine. She then mortgaged the balance.

A month after their first visit to Korea, Joseph, Katherine, Rebbie and Jerome returned for more meetings. They attended a meeting with a Reverend Dr Chung Hwan Kwak, president of the *Segye Times*. A large, framed picture of the Reverend Sun Myung Moon hung in his office; Katherine tried to ignore it. Kwak told Jerome to put together a proposal, ' "and whatever my son wants to do, we'll do it." ' He kept saying "my son" throughout the whole meeting, and we were under the impression that Choi was his son [he wasn't],' Howard recalled. Kwak may of course have meant the reference in a spiritual, rather than strictly familial, way.

Katherine and Joseph then met privately with Reverend Kwak in their suite. They had a sumptuous breakfast and exchanged gifts; Katherine gave him autographed pictures of her family members. After that meeting, Katherine and Joseph went shopping in Etaewon with a tour guide, all to keep them busy while Jerome started talking 'real business'.

Working with Kwak's special assistant David Hose, Jerome

Howard began structuring a deal at the Ambassador Hotel. Joseph, Katherine and Jerome agreed that the way to structure it was to make the Moonies the sponsors of the show and Katherine and Joseph the promoters. Katherine and Joseph would establish a company for this purpose, which they would call Jackson Family Concerts International. Reverend Kwak's representatives then took what Jerome had outlined, left the hotel, and brought the papers to their lawyers. They returned three and a half hours later.

'They came back with a contract that was so wild I couldn't believe it,' Jerome said. 'They wanted Michael to begin the show by singing the Korean national anthem and then perform three Korean numbers in Korean costumes. I looked at that contract and thought, Oh, man, this is ridiculous. Michael is not going to learn any Korean songs, and he is certainly not about to wear any Korean wardrobe onstage! When I showed the deal to Joseph and Katherine, they busted up laughing and were almost rolling on the floor. "I want to see Michael sing in Korean," Joseph said. "Now, that is too much! It's gonna be hard enough to convince him to go along with this, but wait'll we tell him he has to learn Korean."'

Jerome negotiated an outstanding deal. The Jacksons would perform for four nights, one two-hour show each night, at the Olympic Stadium in Seoul, for which they would be paid $7.5 million. There would also be a $1.5 million production budget; whatever was not spent of that budget would go to the Jacksons. One hundred per cent of the profits from broadcasting rights outside of Korea and 50 per cent of the merchandising profits would also belong to the family. However, the Moonies would hold broadcasting and video rights in Korea, as well as 100 per cent of the ticket sales. The clauses about the Korean songs and costumes were deleted from the contract. There was further talk that the Moonies hoped to send Michael and his brothers to Russia and China, and would offer them up to thirty million dollars in advance for those tours. Joseph, Jerome and Kwak signed the contract. Katherine didn't sign; she doesn't sign anything, which is why she is the one with good credit, and not Joseph.

'The Jackson–Moonie Project,' which is what it became known as among the family members, had become a major, multimillion-dollar proposition for the family. As it happened, most of them needed the money.

Janet and LaToya were not approached because the Koreans only wanted the brothers, plus Janet was immersed in the recording of a new album for A&M and would never have toured with the family at this stage of her life. Jackie, Tito, Jermaine, Marlon and Randy would not be a problem, or at least that's what Joseph and Katherine speculated. Rebbie had consented to appear but, again, this tour was only for the brothers. Of course, the entire deal was contingent upon getting Michael, who was in Europe on the Bad tour at the time, to agree to it.

'How will we get Michael to do this?' Jerome asked Joseph.

Joseph turned to Katherine with a smile. 'The question,' he said, 'is how will *she* get Michael to do this?'

'But what about Michael?'

In September 1988, Michael telephoned Katherine and Joseph from Liverpool. He was lonely, and missed his family. His tone was weary. 'I need a break. I've been thinking about all of us. The family is falling apart, do you know that?'

Katherine told Michael she agreed with him. 'What can I do, Michael?' she asked.

Michael let out a long sigh. 'I'll talk to you and Joseph when I get back,' he offered.

He asked to speak to Joseph. Michael then apologized to his father for some of the material written in his autobiography, *Moonwalk*, which had eventually been published by Doubleday. He explained that he hadn't written the book himself, and that the critical portions were written by 'someone else'. Whenever Michael is publicly critical of Joseph, he feels badly.

Joseph wanted to know if Michael was planning to rejoin his brothers after the Bad tour. Why, one might wonder, would he try to push that sensitive issue when Michael was clearly reaching out to him? Michael was firm about it; he told him he didn't want to rejoin the brothers, 'and please don't push me about it.' Joseph then told Michael that anything he had ever heard about him wanting to exploit him or profit from his success was simply not true. 'I don't want to be involved in your business, Michael,' Joseph said, according to Katherine's memory. 'I have money problems, yeah. But all I want is for us to be a family again. Don't you want that?'

'I do want that,' Michael said. 'I really do, Joseph.'

The conversation ended on a hopeful note. Katherine and Joseph felt optimistic that they would soon have their son back. For Joseph, the timing couldn't have been better. He was in serious financial trouble after having lost $700,000 in bad oil well investments, and over $250,000 in his JoCola beverage company. Plus, a judgement had been entered against him. Three years earlier he had entered into an agreement with real estate developer and entrepreneur Gary Berwin to purchase the Berwin Entertainment Center complex in Hollywood for $7.1 million. 'Joseph indicated that money was not a problem,' said Gary. 'I had no reason to doubt him. Michael had just bought The Beatles' catalogue for forty-seven million dollars, so I believed that the family had access to money. In fact, Joseph laughed when I brought up the question of finances. "With the kind of family I've got, money's no object," he said.'

Gary and Joseph entered into a deal by which Gary would own 15 per cent of the real estate, Joseph the other 85 per cent. The two would be equal partners in a recording studio, nightclub and private club in the building. Joseph shamelessly bandied about the notion that Michael would somehow be involved. 'He told me that Michael would come and visit the club often, and that his presence alone would make the place a success,' Gary said. 'He said that Michael could come in through the guard gates, take the private elevator, and no one would know when he was coming or going, which Michael would like. He said that access to the recording studio would be secretive, which was also good for Michael.'

'What makes you so sure that Michael is going to want to be involved in this?' Gary asked.

'Look, if I'm involved, then it's a known fact Michael Jackson will be involved,' Joe answered, confidentially. 'You can bank on it. If I'm here and Katherine's here, Michael's here.'

Joseph decided to pay for the building in cash, rather than attempt to secure a mortgage with his poor credit. He wrote a cheque for the full $7.1 million and gave it to Gary, telling him not to deposit it 'until Friday'. On Friday, he called and told him to 'wait until Monday'. On Monday, he called and said 'wait until Friday'. This went on for a few weeks until, finally, Gary deposited the cheque – which was promptly returned for lack of funds.

A year later, the matter was resolved in court; it was ruled that Joseph had to either buy the property or be responsible for damages incurred by his having stalled the sale to another buyer. He could not afford to buy it. Gary said, 'We finally got Michael served to find out if and how he had led his father into thinking he would help out. He was in a limousine at the time, and somebody walked up to him and handed him a paper. He went to sign it, thinking the person wanted an autograph. It was a summons.' One can only imagine Michael's annoyance, to be served a summons in a bad business deal involving his father. It certainly wasn't the first time, nor was it the last. He ignored the demand to appear for a deposition.

In October 1988, damages to Gary Berwin had been assessed at three million dollars. Since Joseph did not have the money, Gary obtained a judgement against him. To this day, he has not collected on it. 'It was a debacle,' he said, 'and all because I got myself into this Jackson family mess. It was the sorriest thing I'd ever done in my life.

'I couldn't imagine that Michael Jackson, who earns all of these millions, could not give his father the money. I couldn't believe that he would let his father go down like that. This building would have put Joseph on his feet once and for all, and independently of the family. He would never have had to deal with the kids any more, professionally. I tried to appeal not only to Michael but also to the other kids, all of whom are isolated by hard-nosed lawyers. Not one of them cared about Joseph's security. As much as I grew to dislike Joseph, I also felt sorry for him.'

In fact, Michael never misled his father into thinking he would assist him in the investment. Joseph had telephoned Michael before he attempted to buy the complex to ask for assistance. Michael made it clear to him that he wanted nothing to do with it and warned Joseph not to get involved in it. Still, Joseph wrote the cheque out . . . and then hoped to find a way to cover it. When he couldn't, he called Michael, again. 'It's only a few million bucks,' Joseph said. 'Help me out, Michael.'

Michael said no, absolutely not. He was not going to bail his father out, and he could not be convinced to do so, even by Katherine. 'He has to learn,' Michael told one of his associates. 'If I give him the money, he'll be back for more, and more, and more. Damn it, I'm just not going to do it. *I'm not doing it.*'

Joseph also asked some of his other children for help, including Janet, all of whom told him they could not, or would not, assist him. Perhaps they didn't think the investment was a good one, considering Joseph's track record. Larry Anderson, a friend of Joseph's for fifteen years, explained, 'Joseph loves his kids. He hoped they would help out. It seems like a lot of money, but really it isn't when you think of all that was made in that family.'

By December 1988, the proposed Jackson reunion shows in Korea had to come to pass, or Joseph Jackson would forever have the large Berwin judgement hanging over his head. 'I met with Jerome Howard,' Gary Berwin said. 'We started comparing notes on how this wacky family was being run. In the final analysis, it didn't look good for either one of us.'

At this time, Michael was in Japan on his Bad tour. Joseph thought if he could obtain his brothers' cooperation, he may have some leverage with which to obtain Michael's. Therefore, a Jackson family meeting was set up at Hayvenhurst, in the family's movie theatre.

First, Joseph and Katherine spoke to Jackie, Tito, Marlon, Randy, Jermaine and Jermaine's fiancée, Margaret Maldonado. (Jermaine and Hazel divorced in July 1988. He and Margaret would eventually have a second child.) The brothers had to be approached carefully, on the chance they might not agree to go to Korea. For Joseph, it was as if he was going into the lion's den, that's how suspicious the brothers were of him and of anyone who would have anything to do with him – like Jerome Howard. After about two hours, a relieved Joseph came out of the theatre. He was sweating, as if he'd just run a triathlon.

'So, now, look,' he told Jerome, who had been waiting for him in the living room. 'You go in there and do what you can. But don't talk to them about nothing but contracts. Don't mention the Moonies and all that stuff, 'cause then they're not gonna want to do it. Just talk to them about all the money they're gonna make. That's it.'

When Jerome went into the thirty-two-seat theatre, he found Jackson family members scattered all about it. 'I thought, Damn! These people don't even want to sit near each other,' Jerome recalled.

Jerome stood in front of the screen and delivered a speech about the proposed concerts. He talked about the millions that could be made, and how much publicity could be generated. He didn't mention the Moonies, or much about the financial backing other than Kenneth Choi's involvement. Immediately afterwards, Marlon rose from his chair. 'No way,' he said. 'Forget it. No more family tours for me. I don't care how many millions are involved, I learned my lesson the last time. Count me out.'

Marlon was finished with The Jacksons, and he had ambivalent feelings about Michael. The brothers had hoped to go with Michael on the Bad tour, if not in a full-reunion capacity, maybe just as part of the act, singing a medley of old hits. Michael was elusive about the possibility, and never actually said that he wouldn't be using them on the show. He's the one who had mentioned it to them but, given the family dynamic, who knows – or remembers – why. In the end, though, he decided against the idea. 'I'd hear from friends what was going on,' Marlon complained later, in an interview. 'If he didn't want to tell me the truth, he shouldn't have said anything. But instead, he lies. The last time I got a straight answer from Michael was back in 1984.' No doubt, Marlon was still stung from the most recent fib Michael had told him, which was that he was not moving out of Hayvenhurst and into Neverland.

Still, Marlon had a warm spot in his heart for his brother. When he had trouble extricating himself from his mediocre CBS recording contract, Michael called the company's president Walter Yetnikoff and secured his brother's release. 'I just don't want anything to further ruin the way I feel about Mike,' he said. 'I don't think we should work together. It's better when we don't.'

'Well, too bad for you,' Jackie said to Marlon. 'Because I'm in.'

'Me too,' said Randy.

Jermaine conferred with Margaret; the two whispered back and forth to each other, urgently. 'Okay,' he said, finally. 'I'm in, too.'

'Count me in too,' Tito piped up.

'But what about Michael?' Randy wanted to know. 'What are we gonna do about Michael?'

'We don't need him,' Jackie said. 'We can do it ourselves, without him.'

Katherine agreed. 'Oh, let's not bring Michael into this,' she said. 'Please. Isn't there some way to do this without him?'

Jerome shook his head. He had to be careful how he put it, but the fact was that the Olympic Stadium in Seoul seats sixty thousand people, and the brothers would not be able to fill it on their own. They'd never performed without Michael, and this was no time to start. Besides, the Koreans wanted Michael Jackson a lot more than they wanted the rest of them. 'I think it would be best if we approached Michael,' Jerome said cautiously. 'We should at least give him the opportunity we have to make this much money.'

'Look, just leave him to Mother and me,' Jermaine offered, impatiently. 'We'll talk him into it.'

'How?' Randy wanted to know.

Jermaine turned to Katherine. She took a deep breath and sighed wearily. 'I'll see what I can do,' she said. 'I'm just afraid that if we push too hard, we'll lose Michael forever. And then, what will we do?'

●

'Attack him – with love'

The final date of Michael Jackson's Bad tour was at the end of January in 1989 at the Sports Arena in Los Angeles. Diana Ross, Elizabeth Taylor, Dionne Warwick, and many other celebrities attended the concerts, as well as Katherine and Janet Jackson. Michael dedicated his Motown hits medley to Berry Gordy, who was sitting with Diahann Carroll and Suzanne dePasse. 4.5 million people had paid to see Michael perform since the tour began in September 1987. Over the last year and a half, he had performed 123 concerts in fifteen countries on four continents. The show's weekly expenses were between $500,000 and $650,000. The tour grossed over $125 million at the box office.

It hadn't been all work, however. 'He would always take time to see the sights,' recalled Seth Riggs. 'When we were rehearsing in Liverpool, he stopped the practice session so that we could look at some beautiful clouds that had wafted in. That's Michael. They closed down the Louvre in Paris for a whole day while Michael and the rest of us went through. In Rome, Franco Zeffirelli gave him a big party. All of the crème de la crème were there, and suddenly Zeffirelli couldn't find Michael. He looked all over and found Michael in a room with a bunch of little kids in their pyjamas, playing. He's the most natural, loving person I've ever known, a very good person, as corny as that sounds,' continued Riggs, who still works with Michael on a regular basis.

'He'll see a picture of a baby, and if it's a cute kid, he will go gaga over the picture. During the tour, on his nights off, he would go into a toy store and buy ten of this and ten of that and then stay up all night long putting batteries into toys, making certain each one worked so that he could have them ready to give to kids backstage the next day. As if he didn't have enough to worry about.'

On one leg of the tour, Michael brought along his ten-year-old friend, Jimmy Safechuck. Michael had a copy of one of his stage uniforms made for Jimmy so that they could dress alike. Most people found the relationship strange, especially when Michael would take him on shopping sprees. He spent thousands of dollars on toys for Jimmy in London. At one point, Michael had to cancel two shows because he caught a cold from the kid.

Another young friend of Michael's, Jonathan Spence, said, 'When we hang out. He's just like any other guy. He never talks about himself, only about what is going on with others. We never talk about show business. Sometimes he'll put on a disguise when we're in public. When we go to Disneyland, we'll go through the back and take all the alleys and back ways and get in front of the lines. He can't wait in the line, no way. He would cause a riot. We move fast through Disneyland; if people get a good look at him, that'll be it for that outing.

'He's one of the nicest people I've ever known. He's smart. He knows a lot about everything. He's a kid. He never really had a childhood, and he's having it now. The stuff I read in the papers about him, I know it's all a bunch of B.S. I just ignore it. A couple of times I've asked him about girlfriends and stuff, but we never really get into that. We don't talk about the plastic surgery either, because it's none of my business. He never brings it up. It's not like he says, "Well, how do you like my new chin?" It's hard to get in touch with him, though. I usually have to call his secretary, and then a couple of days later, he'll call me.'

After Michael gave Jimmy Safechuck's parents a hundred-thousand-dollar Rolls-Royce, Frank Dileo became concerned about the way it looked. It seemed inappropriate. He suggested that Michael break off his friendship with Jimmy. Michael was hurt, then angry. 'No way,' he told Frank. 'Forget it.'

'But I don't like it, Michael,' Frank insisted. 'It looks bad, you and all these kids.'

'Mind your own business then,' Michael snapped back, 'and maybe it won't look so bad. How's that sound?'

With the tour finished, Michael and Jimmy holed up at Neverland, recharging their batteries, so to speak. Meanwhile, unbeknownst to Michael, someone named Kenneth Choi wanted his signature on the contract for the Jackson–Moonies Project. 'I was getting faxes left and right,' Jerome Howard recalled. 'The heat was on. We had to get Michael. But the timing was wrong. It was a bad time to approach him.'

'We're giving Michael his space now,' Jermaine said at the time. 'But after he finishes his tour, we're all going to attack him – with love.'

Michael might have responded by saying, 'Please, don't do me any favours.'

None of the Jacksons was even able to contact Michael. It was sad that he didn't feel comfortable contacting his family members, but he sensed that whenever he opened himself up to them they ended up wanting something from him, and he had nothing else to give. 'Dirty Diana' realized Frank Dileo's prophecy of five number-one hits from the *Bad* album, the first album in pop history to generate five number-one singles. Yet, despite all of the touring, his last two singles, 'Another Part of Me' and 'Smooth Criminal' did not make number one. Michael wants *every* record to go to number one. The sales of the *Bad* album stalled at seventeen million, amazing but still a far cry from *Thriller*'s sales of almost forty million. It was obvious that Michael would not break his own sales record, which depressed him.

'They think he's shy and he's evasive and all of this,' observed his guitarist David Williams. 'No. He's just fucking scared and tired of people bugging him.'

Whenever Michael went out, it was in disguise. For instance, he visited a pharmacy in Westwood disguised with a large Afro wig and dark glasses. Still, he was picked out by the store's manager. 'I recognized him the minute I saw his nose and chin,' he said. When asked what Michael had purchased, he answered, 'A hand-held power vibrator.'

One does have to wonder about the true reasons for Michael's outrageous disguises. It seems that when he truly *wants* attention, he wears a costume so ridiculous he gets the desired result. Occasionally, though, matters get out of hand. For instance, Michael once went into a jewellery store in Simi Valley, California, wearing a wig under a baseball cap, a phony-looking moustache, and fake buck teeth. He was accompanied by a young boy. Nervously, he continually adjusted his moustache while looking into a mirror. When employees feared the suspicious character was 'casing the joint', a security guard asked him to step outside and demanded an explanation. 'I have to wear a costume,' Michael said. 'I'm Michael Jackson.' Michael then removed the disguise. By that time, however, three squad cars had arrived, as had a huge crowd. Michael's presence, along with the police, had caused such hysteria, everyone present had to have his autograph. He happily signed for all. Perhaps the get-up did serve a purpose, but not the one most people thought it was supposed to serve; he clearly wanted the attention. He loves his fans, and he also loves knowing they still love him.

Another time, though, things didn't work out as well. When Michael was driving his Rolls while wearing a disguise, he was stopped by a police officer who thought the automobile 'looks like a stolen car'. (Of course, there is a prevailing racism among some police officers in America who routinely stop blacks who are driving expensive cars.) Michael didn't have his licence with him. Worse, he had an outstanding ticket. The officer didn't believe he was *the*

Michael Jackson, even when he removed the disguise. The next thing he knew, he was in the Van Nuys jail. Bill Bray bailed him out. Afterward, Michael said, 'It was the coolest thing, ever. I never thought I'd get to go to jail. I loved every second of it.'

◆

LaToya Gets Naked

Michael was only able to avoid his relatives for about a month before, at the end of January, his sister LaToya created enough familial chaos to make it necessary that he re-surface. Michael was now thirty. He had spent the last twenty years concerned with the public's perception of him and his family. Ever since the day in 1969 when Berry Gordy and Diana Ross taught him to lie about his age, Michael had understood the importance of public relations. He had always helped to present an image of solidarity where the Jackson family was concerned, even embarking on the Victory tour with his brothers when he really did not want to do so. Now, LaToya threatened to shatter the family's carefully constructed image of wholesomeness by stripping naked for *Playboy*.

The *Playboy* lay-out was the culmination of a chain of events that had all but destroyed LaToya's relationship with her family. She had been unhappy because the albums she had thus far recorded were all poor sellers. 'I want platinum albums,' she complained. However, Joseph realized that LaToya had limited vocal ability and stage presence; there wasn't much he could do with her. He had tried to convince her to model, but she was ambivalent about it even though she was a beautiful young woman. She, like Michael, has had her nose operated on more than once, though she denies ever having rhinoplasty, and other work, as well. 'I don't know who she's trying to fool,' Marlon laughed.

When LaToya decided that she no longer wanted Joseph to manage her, she followed the example set by Michael, her brothers and Janet: she fired him by having her attorney send letters of dismissal to him at home, even though she still lived there with him.

Of course, Joseph ignored the letters. Finally, she decided to confront him. 'I will sit on you for five years before I ever let you go,' he then told her, angrily. After all, she was the only Jackson he had left. There had to be *something* he could do with her, he decided. Later, he thought that he might be able to get her involved in the Jackson–Moonies Project.

'But they don't want her, Joseph,' Katherine told him. 'They just want the boys.'

'They'll take her if I tell them they have to take her, or they don't get Michael,' Joseph said.

Katherine wasn't so sure about Joseph's logic, especially since she didn't know how they were even going to convince Michael to do the tour.

If Joseph couldn't represent LaToya, then he wanted to be sure no one else could, either. 'In other words, he was saying I'd never get anywhere on my own,' LaToya recalled, 'and he'd make certain of that.' When LaToya asked Katherine for assistance, Katherine said, 'I don't want to get in the middle of it. It's between you and your father.'

Hoping to placate their daughter into remaining with Joseph, he and Katherine hired an outsider, Jack Gordon, to manage LaToya, under Joseph's direction. Her parents hoped that she would no longer feel as trapped. Jack, who was in his mid-forties – had served time in prison for trying to bribe the Nevada State Gaming Commission. He has also been linked to underworld dealings and allegedly ran a brothel in Nevada for four years. In a short time, Jack became more than LaToya's business associate. Before anyone in the family knew what was happening, he and LaToya were plotting a way to extricate her from Joseph and Katherine's hold.

'When I questioned him about some major expenses he and LaToya were running up on Joseph's account, Jack threatened my life,' Jerome Howard recalled. 'The man was dangerous, but LaToya felt that Joseph was dangerous, too. "Do you know my father?" she asked me once. "No, you don't," she answered for me. "You don't know what he's like, Jerome. You don't know what I've *been* through."'

In March 1988 – just three days after Michael moved out of the Encino home – LaToya took off with Jack Gordon. She took just two suitcases, left her Mercedes in the driveway, and didn't look back.

The family blamed Jack. They all hated him, and he returned the animus. 'I love Joseph like poison,' Jack said.

In order to boost LaToya's career, Jack made the deal with Hugh Hefner that she would strip for a photo lay-out. He reported that she would receive a million dollars for disrobing. She probably was paid half as much. LaToya explained her decision, to Hollywood columnist Frank Swertlow: 'It was a matter of my letting my family know I am an individual and I want my independence. That's very difficult when you come from a large family and you've been controlled all of your life.'

When Katherine heard about the photo essay, she couldn't believe her ears. Neither could anyone else who had known LaToya. 'LaToya was always the puritanical one,' said longtime friend Joyce McCrae.

'I used to always cover my body from head to toe,' LaToya told Playboy. 'I guess my shyness came from growing up the way I did, being so sheltered and having a strict father.'

Katherine telephoned LaToya and asked if it was true. 'Are you posing for a Playboy centrefold? Please, 'Toya, tell me it's not true.' One wonders why Katherine even bothered. Did her famous children ever tell her the truth about their activities?

'Oh, Mother,' LaToya said, 'where do you hear these things? Of course it's not true.' She then did what Michael always did – she blamed the media for lying about her. 'Don't believe what you hear, Mother,' she said. 'You should know better.'

Later LaToya would explain why she lied to Katherine. 'Mother did ask me if I had posed for Playboy. She asked very specifically, "Did you pose for the Playboy centrefold?" I told her no, and that was the truth. I did pose for Playboy – but not for the centrefold. It was for elsewhere in the magazine.'

After speaking to LaToya, Katherine telephoned Michael and, with a sigh of relief, told him that everything the family had heard about her and Playboy was a lie manufactured by the media. However, Michael had already begun his own investigation into the matter and realized that there was more to the story. He decided to take matters into his own hands.

After making a few more telephone calls, Michael learned that a meeting at Hugh Hefner's mansion had been scheduled for the next day, regarding LaToya's pictorial. That day, he drove to the mansion and, under the guise of wanting to visit Hugh's menagerie of animals, snooped around the estate with one of his young friends. When he walked into one of the parlours, he found a group of men sitting around a table, nervously stuffing colour photographs into their briefcases. 'What's goin' on in here?' Michael asked with a 'caught ya' grin. Hugh walked over to Michael and shook his head. The two then had a discussion about LaToya, during which Hugh promised to send Michael the pictures by messenger later in the week, 'after they've been touched up.'

A week later, Michael received the photographs. 'I can't believe this is my sister,' he told a person who still works for Michael today. 'This ruins the family image. That's it. There's nothing left.'

Michael's employee said, 'All he cared about after seeing the pictures was his mother and her blood pressure. "I'm afraid that when Kate sees these pictures, she'll have a heart attack," he told me. "I'm not even going to tell her I have them. Hopefully, they'll touch up 'Toya's, uh, her, uh, nipples, at least. I mean, do we have to see her *nipples*?"' Michael hoped that the photographs he received did not represent the actual lay-out. Perhaps all of them had not been utilized in it. Perhaps LaToya's nipples *had* been camouflaged in some way. He telephoned LaToya.

She says he told her he thought the photos were lovely, which doesn't seem likely. When he asked if she had an advance of the final lay-out, she confessed that she did have it. Would she send it to him? No, she said.

A month later, the lay-out was published. Michael's worst fears about the spread of eleven photos were realized. Could that really be LaToya, posing nude with a sixty-pound boa constrictor slithering between her legs? 'Boas aren't dangerous unless they're hungry,' she observed in the accompanying text.

After the initial shock, there was shame and embarrassment. Katherine and Rebbie were both humiliated; not only had Latoya disrobed, but she had clearly had some work done on her breasts. Whereas they had once been small, they were now . . . *bountiful*.

For Joseph, seeing his daughter sprawled out in *Playboy* with a snake was an agonizing experience. One of his friends claimed that he and Katherine sequestered themselves at Hayvenhurst for a month, not because they were afraid to be confronted but rather because they were heartsick over what LaToya had done to them. They also blamed Jack Gordon for convincing her that posing for *Playboy* would be a good career move.

Michael, too, was irate with his sister, but not only for her career choice and the fact that she had further damaged the family's image. He certainly did not find artistic merit in the photographs and told one friend that, as far as he was concerned, they represented pornography. However, Michael was more angry with LaToya because she publicly claimed that he had *approved* of the pictures, and was glad she had taken them. 'When he started hearing LaToya say on television that he was the only one in the family who approved, he went nuts,' said Steven Harris, a former associate. 'He called his mother, and they had a long, painful conversation about it. "How can I talk to her about anything if she twists what I say for her own purposes?" he asked. Katherine and Michael decided it was best if Michael never spoke to LaToya. He changed his number and didn't give it to her. Of course, she couldn't get it from anyone else in the family. No one would dare give it to her once Michael made it known that he didn't want her to have it. It was a shame. They had been so close.'

'You know what?' he told his attorney, John Branca. 'I can't control her, just as they [presumably his family] can't control me. So, good for her, I guess. She did what she had to do and she didn't care about any of us, did she? When I do that kind of thing, they all come down on me, hard. So, good for her if she can take it. Good for her.' Michael then instructed the rest of his staff never to bring up the subject of LaToya's *Playboy* lay-out in his presence. 'I don't want to hear one more word about my sister's big breasts,' he concluded. 'I just want to forget the whole thing ever happened.'

A Million-dollar Bounty on Michael's Head

'We need Michael Jackson.'
    'We must have Michael Jackson.'
    'How do we get Michael Jackson?''

In February 1989, faxed communications from Kenneth Choi flooded into Jerome Howard's office regarding the 'Jackson – Moonie Project'. Still, no one wanted to approach Michael just yet; they were afraid he would give them an instant 'no,' and that would be the end of it. 'Finally, in desperation, the Koreans came up with an idea,' Jerome recalled, 'a reward. A bounty was placed on Michael's head. The price: one million dollars. Anyone – family member or business associate – who could get Michael's signature on the contract would get a million dollars, money which would come straight from the Moonies. Now, *everyone* wanted to approach Michael,' Jerome concluded with a chuckle, 'and right away.'

Katherine decided to take the proverbial bull by the horns and telephone Michael at Neverland to give it her best shot. As she gently tried to explain the proposed tour, feeding him information about it as gingerly as possible, Joseph stood nearby, pacing. Finally, he was about to burst. He snatched the phone from her hand. 'Michael, now you listen here,' he declared. 'You said you wanted us to be a family again,' he said, referring to their last telephone conversation from Japan. 'Now, look. I got these rich Koreans and they got this big deal and I want you to do this thing, Michael, 'cause we're gonna make a lot of money and we *need* this money and you *know* we do and—'

'Joseph, put Mother back on the phone.'

Michael then told Katherine to forget about it. He wouldn't even consider another family venture, especially if Joseph was involved in it. He reminded Katherine of the time (in 1985) when Joseph aligned with a Hollywood producer to develop a film based on 'Beat It' which was to star Michael – and Michael didn't know anything about it. He later had to disavow the project which, he said, was embarrassing. 'He's always doing things to get me involved in projects with him, and I'm not going along with it,' Michael said. He didn't want to tour with the brothers again, either. 'That's over,' he told his mother. 'I mean it,' he concluded. 'Forget it, Kat. [Michael often calls his mother 'Kat'.] I won't do it and I want you to please just drop it. Do you understand?'

The good ol' days when Katherine was able to convince Michael to do anything she asked of him were clearly in the past.

By February 1989, financial matters had gotten so desperate for

Joseph and Katherine that they could no longer afford to pay Jerome Howard his salary; he had settled for $3,000 a month, even though they had originally agreed to pay him $10,000, and now he wasn't getting anything. Therefore, he became even more interested in concluding the Jackson–Moonie Project not only to generate revenue for the family, but for himself, as well. He decided to go directly to Frank Dileo for assistance. Unfortunately, no one in the family knew how to get to Frank. The brothers barely knew him, and Katherine and Joseph never liked meeting with him about anything because, they claimed, he would then go back to Michael and misrepresent what they had said. Katherine, in particular, didn't like Frank – especially after he said she was 'crazy' for thinking Michael could do a better show with his brothers.

Jerome finally had to pay an associate of Frank's $2,000 for an introduction to Frank, who, as it turned out, was at a weight-reduction centre run by Duke University in North Carolina. Jerome called Frank and arranged a meeting for them with Kenneth Choi. It took place in a North Carolina hotel room at the end of February 1989. Frank told Kenneth that if Katherine was involved in the deal, he would talk to Michael about it. 'He loves his mother,' said Frank. 'I don't know. I ain't promisin' nothin'. But, maybe . . .' At that point, Kenneth opened his briefcase and took out two cashier's cheques made out for $500,000.

'These are for you,' he declared. 'A million dollars.'

Frank laughed in his face. 'I can't take a million bucks from you. What, are you crazy?' he said. 'I can't guarantee Michael Jackson will do anything for you. Michael is a smart man. He makes up his own mind. No one *tells* him to do anything. Do you understand that?'

As promised, Frank then discussed the situation with Michael. Michael said he didn't want to be involved. Frank told him to think it over, 'and maybe you'll change your mind, maybe you won't. It's your decision.'

'It was business as usual,' Frank recalled. 'Everything was hunky-dory.'

Michael and Frank were inseparable. He was prominently featured on the *Bad* record jacket, a picture of him and Michael which was captioned 'another great team'. Michael also devoted a full page to photos of him and Frank in his lavish concert tour booklet. In fact, Frank had often said that he thought of Michael as a son, 'and he referred to me as a second dad.'

'I was with the kid every day,' he recalled. 'Some days you could have a decent conversation with him. Some days he was on another planet. But I got closer to him than anybody else in his life.' Frank had even advised Michael about the taboo subject of plastic surgery, telling him that when he was a youngster he, too, had wanted a cleft in his chin like Kirk Douglas. 'But that's enough,' he told Michael. 'No more surgery.'

After five years of working for him, Frank Dileo may have thought he was in good standing with Michael Jackson, that their relationship was, as he put it, 'hunky-dory'. He would have been wrong.

Michael Fires Frank Dileo

Three days after the brief telephone conversation about the Jackson–Moonie Project, Frank Dileo was fired. Michael's publicist, Lee Solters, issued a terse statement: 'Michael Jackson and Frank Dileo have announced an amicable parting. Jackson said, "I thank Frank for his contribution on my behalf during the past several years."'

Perhaps Michael felt he had valid reasons for firing Frank, but he did it in a cowardly way: he had John Branca do it.

'Look, man, I hate to have to be the one to tell you this,' John said, 'but Michael doesn't want to work with you any more.'

'What? No shit? You're kiddin' me, right?'

'Sorry, Frank,' John told him. 'It's no joke.'

After some more discussion about the matter, Frank said, 'Okay, fine with me, then. I just want to get paid whatever is owed me, and then I'll be on my way.'

'Are you pissed off, Frank?' John asked. He felt badly about it. He liked Frank and knew that Frank truly cared about Michael.

'Hell no,' Frank said, trying to be the tough guy. 'Look, Johnny, if the kid doesn't want me, I don't want to be around. See you later.'

With that, Frank hung up. He then left the weight-reduction centre, 'because I had to get to work,' he recalled. 'I was out of a job.'

The next day, Frank telephoned Kenneth Choi, who was in San Francisco. 'I just wanted to tell you that Michael and I broke up,' he said.

'What? What's that mean, "broke up"?' Kenneth asked. 'I don't understand.'

'The kid fired me, I'm tellin' ya. I'm finished. *Ka-put*.'

'Oh,' Kenneth said. '*That* I understand.'

Immediately, word circulated within Michael Jackson's camp that Frank had taken the million-dollar reward money, that Michael found out about it, that this was why he fired him. Of course, this was not true. Kenneth Choi later recalled, 'That impressed me a great deal. Frank said that if Michael did end up going to Korea, *then* he might take some money as a bonus, but not before.'

'Frank could have had one million bucks that day, but he didn't take it,' Jerome Howard confirmed. 'He could have accepted the money, never gotten Michael's signature, and it would have taken a lifetime in court before he'd ever have to return it, if ever. But he's an honourable man. Later, Frank told me that he very gently talked to Michael about the Korea plan. He said, "You can't just ask Michael straight out to do something, like Joseph did on the phone. Michael has to be stroked. His ego has to be massaged thoroughly before he will agree to do anything." I wondered if he had massaged it maybe one time too many . . .'

Actually, Michael was upset with Frank for a number of reasons.

First of all, Michael felt that Frank had taken too much credit for his success. He was tired of other people taking credit for what he felt was his own destiny. Because Michael refused to be interviewed, Frank had developed a high media profile as his spokesman. Many celebrities – and Michael is one of them – do not like it when their representatives also become celebrities. Michael's ego is fragile. Frank was becoming too well known for Michael's taste, giving interviews to the press touting his accomplishments for Michael. Every time he did so, Michael cringed.

'Frank isn't even creative,' Michael told an associate. 'Let's face it. I come up with all of the ideas.'

Michael felt that Frank had also become too dictatorial. For instance, when the Bad tour played Pittsburgh, Frank's hometown, he arranged a gathering so that he could introduce Michael to his close friends and relatives. 'Michael, I expect you to be there at eight sharp,' he said. 'Do you understand?' He knew Michael well enough to know that he might show up, or he might not. He hoped not to be embarrassed in front of people who mattered to him. 'So I will expect you there, right?'

Michael didn't say anything. Later, he complained, 'Who is *he* to tell me what to do? Screw that. *I* tell *him* what to do.'

Michael showed up, but an hour late, no doubt on purpose. Afterwards, Frank let him have it. 'You embarrassed me,' he screamed at him. 'What's wrong with you? How could you do that to me?'

Michael seethed as Frank laid into him. Finally, Bill Bray began shouting at Frank to leave Michael alone. 'Fuck you, man,' Bill said. 'He don't work for you. You work for him. You better check yourself.' It was an unpleasant scene.

Another matter had to do with a deal that some thought Frank had bungled on Michael's behalf: a multimillion-dollar contract for domestic theatrical release of Michael's ninety-minute video *Moonwalker* (which is part clip compilation and part musical autobiography).

The film features Michael's innovative video of 'Leave Me Alone', in which he spoofed his image by showing a shrine to Elizabeth Taylor, a newspaper headline that read 'Michael Confides in Chimp' and a discomforting segment in which he dances with the Elephant Man's skeleton. In the video, Michael moves through a surreal world of floating chairs, huge chomping teeth and amusement park rides. It took twenty-five people six months to make the four-minute-and-forty-five-second video.

The project cost Michael Jackson about twenty-seven million dollars. *Moonwalker* was released theatrically in Japan, but not in the United States because of numerous disagreements. It had been reported that Frank was behind the decision not to release *Moonwalker* domestically, angering international distributors who had bought the film for theatrical releases. When the announcement was made that there would be no domestic deal, many overseas theatres pulled the film, or scaled down its promotion and publicity. This decision cost Michael many millions of dollars in lost box office revenue.

Frank eventually did come up with a multimillion-dollar offer to distribute the film domestically, but someone else in Michael's organization talked him out of it. Therefore, while Michael may have been angry at the way distribution of *Moonwalker* was handled, he didn't blame Frank for it – not entirely, anyway.

Most of Michael's associates felt that Michael *should* have been angry at Frank, however, for allowing him to spend twenty-seven million on *Moonwalker*, a video project whose budget should not have exceeded five million dollars. In the end, the video made approximately thirty million dollars in over-the-counter sales and other deals, another tribute to John Branca's negotiating savvy and Walter Yetnikoff's persistence (CBS Music Video Enterprises distributed the tape). No home music video had ever come close to generating that much money for its artist. Still, after *Moonwalker*, Michael would say that he felt 'poor' and didn't want to spend any more money on major projects 'for a long, long time'.

Another problem with Frank was that Michael had become disgusted with the tabloid image of himself that he believed Frank was continuing to propagate. But the hyperbaric chamber and Elephant Man's bones stories were Michael's ideas – not Frank's.

One story that appeared in the *Star* (on 2 August 1988), was particularly disturbing to Michael: MICHAEL JACKSON BANS 4 PALS FROM TOUR AFTER THEY FLUNK AIDS TEST. The article said that Michael fired four employees because they had tested positive for HIV. 'I'm really afraid of AIDS,' Michael was quoted as having said. 'I think about having lunch with these guys and shaking hands and spending so much time together.' The article also said that Michael was spending a fortune having his own frozen blood moved around with him wherever he goes. 'You never know when you may need blood, and the only blood I can be sure of is my own,' Michael supposedly said.

Apparently, Michael was paying the price for the idea he had had years ago to have a Plexiglas shield constructed between him and his audiences to protect him from germs during the 1984 Victory tour. He realized at the time that the plan was absurd, and dropped it. Someone on his team remembered it, though, and after embellishing it with an HIV twist, then sold it to the tabloid.

The peculiar idea came to Michael during the time, after his burn accident, when he had become fascinated with medicine. He'd become a ravenous reader of medical books and enjoyed reading and hearing about dreadful diseases. For a while, he also became obsessed with learning about different surgeries, going so far as to witness operations at UCLA Medical Center.

'Michael's curious about surgery,' said one former associate. 'He gets off on it. He can watch for hours. He especially likes to watch plastic surgeries – tummy tucks, liposuctions, he's into all of that. He has even witnessed brain surgeries.'

While he was interested in medicine, he was not obsessed with catching AIDS and had only empathetic feelings about the disease. 'When Michael read that report, he became upset,' said Michael Tucker, a friend of the Jackson family (not the actor). 'Of all diseases, AIDS is one that Michael is most sensitive about. "Why would they write this about me?" he said. "That isn't me at all. What if people believe this of me? What are they going to think of me?"

'He became furious and wanted to know where the report originated. "If I find out that anyone in my organization planted these hurtful stories, that person will be fired. I mean it," he said.'

It's not known if Michael fired Frank Dileo because he wanted to end his wacky image in the tabloids. After Frank was gone, though, the stories continued. It wasn't necessary for anyone on Michael's staff to plant them; writers just made them up as they went along . . .

The primary reason Michael dismissed Frank was because he was disappointed that *Bad* was not as successful as *Thriller*. It had 'only' sold about twenty million copies worldwide, roughly one-fifth of what Michael had hoped for it. *Thriller* sold twenty-four million in the United States; *Bad* sold six million.

'Michael was pissed off,' said one friend of Frank Dileo's. 'He had his heart set on another huge album. When he didn't get what he wanted, he acted like a spoiled, little kid. He threw temper tantrums. He cried. He can be very dramatic. Frank had his hands full. He had a lot to deal with.'

'But we did the best we could,' Frank said of *Bad*. 'We made the best album and the best videos we could. We don't have anything to be ashamed of.' While that may be true, some were whispering in Michael's ear that Frank should have done a better job. Doubt began to creep into Michael's mind. He had to blame someone for what he thought was a weak showing for *Bad*. Therefore, he blamed Frank Dileo.

About a year later, Frank would say there was 'No warning. Did it anger me? Yes. The way it was done was an insult. He took away my faith in people. For a long time, I've not been as trusting.'

Frank felt that the least Michael could have done was fire him personally. However, Michael is not a sentimental person, and never has been one. To Michael, Frank was not 'a second father'. Rather, he was a capable businessman who had, in Michael's view, exhausted his usefulness.

Michael's Mother Gets the Reward Money

After Frank Dileo's firing, Katherine Jackson's campaign to get Michael Jackson to go to Korea with his brothers continued, but Michael could not be swayed.

Now that Frank was out of the picture, Jerome Howard telephoned Michael's accountant, Marshall Gelfand, to ask for help in getting Michael to commit to the Korean venture. 'By all means,' Marshall told Jerome. 'We're always looking for ways to make extra money for Michael. Call John Branca, tell him I told you to call, and *he'll* convince Michael. Michael *loves* to work, so sure, he'll go.'

'At this time, the Koreans said, "But what if he won't go?" They were panicking,' Jerome recalled. '"Fine, then offer him *ten* million to come," they said. That's ten million *above* the seven point five million the brothers would get and split among themselves. And they said they were going to give him an airplane from Korean Airlines to travel in, and another plane for the brothers. This way, Michael wouldn't have to even see his brothers, except onstage. I faxed all of this to John Branca, who got back to me right away and said, "No, Michael doesn't want to go." So, then the Koreans sent a gold bust statue of Michael over to him to try to convince him. Still, Michael wouldn't budge. He didn't want to go, but no one was listening to the guy.

'Then the Koreans offered *me* a gift, a car, because they thought I might have some influence on Michael, which I did not have,' Jerome continued. 'I already had three cars; I didn't need another. But they wanted to buy me a seventy-thousand-dollar Mercedes. I told Katherine and Joseph, and Joseph said, "They're not gonna buy you no car." Well, the Jacksons weren't paying me any more, so I accepted the Mercedes. When I drove that Mercedes on to the Jacksons' property, Katherine was happy for me. I told her I was going to sell the car and use the money to cover my expenses until she and Joseph could pay me again. She said, "No, you need that car for business. They gave you that car. You keep it and don't you ever sell it." But Joseph was pissed off, because they gave me a car but didn't give him one. "Those are *our* kids, Katherine. Why should Jerome get a car, but we get no car?" he wanted to know. From that time on, Joseph's attitude about me began to change. I began to feel I was about to get cut out of the deal.'

The Koreans still felt that if anyone could talk Michael into going on this tour, Katherine could. Therefore, they upped the ante and actually gave her the million-dollar bounty – on condition that she get her son's signature on the contract within fourteen days. Jerome Howard handed Katherine the two $500,000 cashier's cheques.

'I don't want that money, Jerome,' Katherine insisted. 'Don't give it to me.'

'If I don't give it to you, then I have to give it to Joseph,' Jerome warned her. Katherine took the money.

'Do you think you can convince Michael?' he asked.

'Well, I can only try,' Katherine said. 'Michael has a mind of his own, you know.' She shook her head in disbelief. 'A million dollars, I guess we *have* come a long way.'

Joseph never imagined that Katherine had a million dollars stashed away somewhere in Hayvenhurst. Jerome Howard feared that if Joseph knew about it, he would have cashed the cheques immediately, signature or no signature from his son. Katherine apparently agreed, because she did not tell him she was in possession of the reward money. If she got Michael's signature on the contract, she said, she fully intended to give Joseph half of the reward.

In the last year, Michael had made over sixty-five million dollars. According to *Forbes* magazine, he had been one the highest-paid entertainers in the world in 1988. He could be generous when he wanted to be, but when it came to his family, he had reservations. However, his family needed his help and believed that Michael should come to their rescue.

It's true that the brothers did feel that Michael owed them. 'Michael is very popular right now,' Jermaine said at the time, 'and I feel I've contributed a major part to it. Not just me, but my brothers too. What's happened to Michael has *a lot* to do with what we *all* did as The Jackson 5.'

In March 1989, Jerome Howard and Kenneth Choi were at the Jacksons' estate in Encino with Katherine, Joseph and Jermaine, discussing the problem at hand. 'I think the best thing would be for him to get closer to his family,' Jermaine said. 'Once you make so much money, it's just another dollar. At some point, you have to start looking at the important things, like love, family and health.'

As they were talking, the phone rang. Katherine took the call upstairs. Joseph followed.

A few minutes later, Katherine came running down the stairs, huffing and puffing and saying, 'Michael's on the phone. Michael's on the phone! Joseph's talking to him right now.' Jerome Howard recalled, 'She was very worked up about it.'

Jermaine ran to the staircase where Katherine was standing and, in a very excited tone, said to her, 'Mother, let Kenneth talk to Michael. Let Kenneth try to convince him. After all, he convinced you and Joseph in the first place. *He* should talk to Michael.'

Katherine was sceptical. 'I don't know if that's a good idea,' she said as she ran back up the stairs. It was all so . . . frantic. 'But pick up the phone and try,' she hollered back at them. 'It can't hurt.'

According to Jerome, Jermaine ran back over to Kenneth. 'Look, man, you gotta persuade Michael.'

'But . . . how?' Kenneth asked, helplessly. 'How do I do this?' He looked bewildered.

'Man, I don't know,' Jermaine answered. His brow was furrowed; it looked like he was trying to think of something, quickly. 'But you gotta do it. Cry on the phone to him if you have to,' he said, facetiously. 'Whatever. Just do it, man. Do it.'

Kenneth Choi picked up the telephone.

'Michael, please, my country wants you to come and perform,' he said in broken English.

There was a pause. Apparently, Michael was explaining why he didn't want to do the tour.

'But, please, Michael, I beg of you . . .'

Another pause.

Suddenly, Kenneth began to weep. 'But, Michael, if you don't come to my country to perform, I have no choice but to *kill* myself,' he said, his tone theatrical. 'I mean it. I'll do it.' In moments, Kenneth was sobbing, uncontrollably.

Jermaine took one look at him and fell to his knees, laughing. He had to hold his hand over his mouth to stifle the sound. Then, Jerome fell to the floor, as well, laughing hysterically.

Kenneth ignored them both. 'You see, this is my mission,' he continued on the phone, tears cascading down his cheeks. 'My mission is to bring you, the great Michael Jackson, to Korea to perform for all of the people there. I must see you. Please, I beg of you. Michael, please. *Please.*'

Finally, Michael agreed to meet with Kenneth Choi. He never could resist a crying man.

According to Jerome, when Kenneth got off the phone, his demeanour immediately changed and he began dancing around the room, merrily. 'My God, I can't believe it,' he whooped. '*I talked to Michael Jackson on the phone.* Oh my God!'

Meanwhile, since the two weeks Katherine had to convince Michael to sign the contract had passed, she had no choice but to return the million-dollar reward money. Joseph was upset with her when he found out she had the money, and even angrier when he heard she had given it back. 'We coulda' used that money, Katie,' he said, angrily. 'Oh my God. The world is going crazy when my own wife has a million dollars and doesn't tell me about it.'

Soon after that, Jerome Howard quit working for Katherine and Joseph Jackson. 'I discovered that Kenneth Choi was meeting with Joseph and Katherine behind my back, cutting a side deal. When I saw this happening, I quit.'

It had been twenty years since the Jacksons moved from Gary to Los Angeles in search of fame and wealth. All of them had come to enjoy a privileged lifestyle. However, somewhere in the process, they seemed to lose all perspective on reality. It seemed that none of them knew when to stop; they wanted more, always more. When the Koreans figured out how to appeal to this acquisitive streak, a new, Moonie-induced decadence spread like a cancer throughout the family.

The Moonies gave Joseph a Rolls-Royce Corniche; later he would get more than fifty thousand dollars because, after all, he was Michael Jackson's father and, it was thought, he must have *some* influence on him.

Then, Katherine got thirty-five thousand dollars, because she was Michael's mother.

Then, Jermaine got a Range Rover, because he was the brother who, it was felt, had the most power over Michael. (He gave the automobile to Hazel, as part of their divorce settlement.)

Then, Michael got sixty thousand dollars and expensive artwork, because he was, after all, the man of the hour. That wasn't enough, however, so the Koreans sent over a white Rolls-Royce Corniche, which Michael happily accepted. Why not? If they were dumb enough to give it to him, he figured, he was smart enough to take it. He wasn't even sure where it came from, he said. 'Who are these people, and why are they giving me a car?' he asked John Branca.

Other people were getting many thousands of dollars just because they knew Michael and, it was hoped, had some sway over him. Jerome Howard said. 'To the Moonies, this was just so-called seed money, funds they had to spend in order to get close to Michael.' Even Michael's bodyguard, Bill Bray, got half a million and, today, no one even remembers why or how he got it.

Everyone was greedy enough to accept what they could before the Koreans finally realized that the chance of Michael Jackson ever doing those concerts was nil. The nadir of the debacle was reached when one of Bill Bray's girlfriends went to Kenneth Choi and said, 'Listen up, you. My boyfriend controls Michael Jackson, and *I* control my boyfriend. So, if you want this concert to take place in Korea, then you'd better give *me* something.'

'Well, what do you want?' Kenneth asked, hopefully. Maybe *she* could do the job no one else was able to do. She mulled it over. 'How about that 560 SEL Mercedes-Benz you have parked in your driveway?'

'It's yours,' Choi said. He handed her the keys.

Finally, Kenneth Choi got the meeting with Michael Jackson he had so desired. Katherine brought him along with her to the *Soul Train* Awards where Michael was an honouree. When Katherine introduced him to her son, he dropped to his knees and kissed Michael's hand. 'My people need you,' he told Michael. 'You must perform in Korea. After all, Japan attacked our country two times, and you performed in Japan two times. You even held a Japanese baby in your arms.'

'Huh?' Michael asked. He looked perplexed. 'Who the heck are you? Mother, who is this person?'

'Why, Michael, this is the nice man I told you about,' Katherine said, eagerly. 'Kenneth. You know, the man who is putting together the concerts in Korea?'

From the look on his face, Michael didn't have the vaguest idea who his mother was talking about, or why the man in front of him was on his knees.

'My people need to see you,' Kenneth continued. 'You are a hero, a saint of men.' He then pulled out a video camera and began taping Michael. 'No, wait!' Michael said, putting his hands in front of his face. 'Stop! Is this that reunion thing? Is that what this is?'

'Yes, Michael,' Katherine said. 'Yes! This is him. Kenneth Choi.' She was brimming with excitement.

'But I don't do business with my family,' Michael said, turning to Kenneth. 'And stop taping me. Stop it, I said.'

By June 1989, after almost six months of feeling pressured by everyone around him, Michael finally signed a contract to appear in Korea for four shows that would take place in August. 'I can't take another second of it,' he said in explanation of his decision. 'These people are going to drive me crazy until they get what they want. So, let's just do the shows and get it over with.'

He would perform only four songs, however, as well as a medley with his brothers. The rest of the show would be done by the brothers, without Michael.

'I'm doing it for Katherine,' he said of the Korean deal.

The family was elated. Finally, Michael had committed to the Jackson–Moonie Project. No one received the reward money, however, because Michael had made up his own mind. '*He* should have gotten the million dollars,' said John Branca, 'for turning himself over to the Koreans.' (Until the first edition of this book was published in 1991, Michael didn't even know that there had been a reward offered to any family members who could secure his services.)

Amazingly, considering all that had occurred in the recent six months, when the deal was signed and it was time to pass the promised millions on to Michael, the Reverend Moon, who was to fund the venture, decided that the agreed-upon amount was too high a price. According to Jerome Howard, Moon wanted Michael's payment lowered: first to $8 million, then to 7, then 5, then 4.5, and finally to $2.5 million. Finally, the deal fell apart, completely.

As a result, Michael Jackson ended up being sued by Segye Times, Inc. – which is financed by Reverend Moon. Moon wanted his money and all of the gifts to be returned. Also named in the suit were Joseph, Katherine, Jerome Howard, Jermaine Jackson and Bill Bray.

Michael, in turn, sued Segye Times, Inc. for eight million dollars saying that he was not giving back any of his gifts, and not demanding that anyone else give back theirs, either.

There is disagreement among the participants of the Jackson–Moonie Project about who is responsible for what had occurred, but most associates of Michael's agree that none of it would ever have happened if Frank Dileo had still been Michael's manager. After all, in the past, Frank had intercepted many deals having to do with the family before they even reached Michael.

Even John Branca could not have protected Michael from the debacle because by the time Michael went to him for advice, he had made up his mind to sign the deal. Also, it seemed to some observers that Michael, now seeming more paranoid than ever, was beginning to lose confidence in John as well.

'I don't even know how this whole thing happened, or how I got involved in it,' Michael said at the time. 'All I know is that I kept saying no, no, no, *no*. But my family would not take no for an answer. Look what happened as a result. The whole thing made me sick. Just sick.'

LaToya's Drama

In the summer of 1989, after the Jackson–Moonie Project was no longer an issue for them, the Jackson family braced themselves for more distress from LaToya, who was thirty-three years old. They had heard that she was now writing a book of her own, one that would be nothing like the one penned by Michael. Hers, LaToya threatened, would tell the 'whole truth about my dysfunctional family'. (One would think the family wouldn't be so worried, though, since in April of 1988, LaToya told a reporter, 'To my knowledge, Michael has only had one nose job.')

According to Marjorie Walker, a friend of the family's at the time, 'Katherine telephoned LaToya to ask if it was true that a book was being planned. LaToya said it wasn't true. Meanwhile, she had been negotiating with G. P. Putnam's Sons publishing house. When Katherine found out she had a deal, she was hurt. Once upon a time, LaToya never lied. If you knew LaToya, you'd understand how out of character her behaviour had been since she'd met Jack [Gordon]. She is a girl who was scared to death to go out of the house, who felt her family could do no wrong. Now, she was planning to write a book about just how wrong they all were.'

LaToya signed a deal with Putnam, which advanced her more money for her autobiography than Michael had received for his from Doubleday. Michael's was reportedly a $300,000 deal; LaToya's $500,000.

'It won't be so bad,' Katherine reasoned. 'What can she write about anyway?'

For starters, LaToya was going to claim that Michael had been sexually molested as a child. When word of this allegation got back to Michael, he was incensed by it. 'She can do what she wants, if she wants to get back at Joseph and Katherine for whatever,' he stormed, 'but don't drag my ass into it. I never did one damn thing to hurt that girl. So, stop her, Branca,' he told his attorney, John.

John Branca arranged a meeting with Jack Gordon to discuss the matter. During it, he told Jack that Michael did not want his sister writing that he'd been molested.

'Why not?' Jack demanded to know. 'It's the truth.'

'Look, man, I don't know if it's true or not,' John told him. 'But I do know that if she writes it, Michael will sue her. That, I fucking *know* is true.'

Rumours that Michael was sexually molested as a child had been circulating for years within the entertainment industry. Michael denies it. With that denial in place, there's not much more anyone else can say about it. It certainly seems that if such a thing were true, it would be known by now considering how exposed Michael's life has been in recent years.

In subsequent letters to LaToya and Jack, John Branca reiterated his position at the meeting: Michael would litigate against his sister if she made any claim about him being sexually abused. He also indicated that Michael would make himself available to read whatever it was she eventually wrote in order that he be able to review it for 'accuracy'.

After he received that particular letter, Jack Gordon telephoned Katherine's ex-business manager, Jerome Howard, to inquire as to whether he still had the power to arrange a meeting with Katherine. According to Jerome, Jack wanted to offer Katherine a deal: if she and Joseph paid LaToya five million dollars, LaToya would cancel her memoirs. 'It's the least they can do for her,' Jack reasoned, 'considering all they have done *to* her.' Moreover, if Jerome was the one who could convince the Jackson parents to pay LaToya the money, he would be paid ten per cent of the total: $500,000.

'Man, that's blackmail,' Jerome said, according to his memory.

'No, it's not,' Jack responded. 'It's business. Plain, simple business.'

'Well, I don't want anything to do with it,' Jerome told him. 'I'll present the deal to Katherine and have her get in touch with you about it.'

'*What?* You don't want $500,000?' Jack asked, incredulously.

Jerome said no. 'I telephoned Katherine and then met with her,' Jerome recalled. 'I told her what was going on. If she wanted to stop her daughter's book, it was going to cost her five million bucks. She wasn't pleased. I also told her I didn't want to get involved, that Jack had offered me a percentage but that I didn't think it was fair money. I suggested she should have her lawyer deal with it. I suppose she did.'

After that, someone in LaToya's camp apparently fed a story to the media that Michael had offered her twelve million dollars to kill the project. It was not true. However, in an apparent attempt to maintain heightened interest in her project, LaToya charged that 'Michael's offer is awful, a sign of bribery. Nothing is going to stop me,' she said, as if a war cry, 'no matter how much I'm offered.'

Jack Gordon then made the ludicrous allegation that Michael had offered to *purchase* G. P. Putnam's Sons, for eighty-four million dollars just so that he could prevent the book from appearing.

According to an associate of Michael's, 'What really happened is that someone representing LaToya – and I'm not saying it was Jack and I'm not saying it wasn't, because, frankly, I don't know – got in touch with Michael's people and said that Mike had better come up with millions if he didn't want that book to be published. Mike was hurt. He had never done anything to LaToya to cause her to be so unkind to him, and he felt that Jack was orchestrating all of it. Still, it was LaToya who was responsible for the final outcome of it. "She doesn't get a free ride just by saying Jack is the one doing the dirty work," he said. "She has to take responsibility, just like I do." I was in the room when Michael made his final decision. "I'm not going to let my own sister, a person I loved, a person who has known me all my life, blackmail me. This is as low as you can go," he observed. "Tell LaToya I said she can go jump in a lake. She's not getting one fucking dime from me." '

For LaToya, family loyalty was clearly a notion now relegated to her recent past. In fact, to keep the pot stirred, Jack claimed that LaToya's years at Hayvenhurst had made her so angry and bitter that she would include yet another allegation in her book: that Joseph had sexually molested her.

Katherine was stunned when she first heard the charge from Jack. 'Why, it's just not true,' she insisted.

'Oh, yes, it is,' Jack said.

'But who told you this?' Katherine demanded. 'Did LaToya tell you?' Jack said that it had been Rebbie who told him.

By the time Katherine confronted Rebbie, she was seething. However, Rebbie denied ever having told Jack that LaToya was sexually abused by Joseph.

Michael then telephoned LaToya and, as she later recalled it to me, 'We fought about many things, but the main thing was the book.' When Michael wanted to know if there was anything critical of him in it, she refused to get into details. The true issue was not her book, she told me, but the fact that Michael 'is jealous of all the great exposure I'm getting. He wants to hog the limelight.'

'Look, I've been doing this since I was five years old,' Michael told her, according to her memory. 'And here you come out of nowhere. What justifies your fame? You're not entitled to it yet, LaToya. You haven't *done* anything, yet.'

'Why, how dare you?' LaToya exclaimed. 'After all I've been through with this family, how can you say that to me?' She had apparently confused familial dysfunction with artistic achievement. At any rate, she said that she never wanted to speak to Michael again, and then slammed down the phone.

On 5 September 1989, LaToya, now thirty-three, and Jack Gordon, fifty, were married in Reno, Nevada. Two days earlier, LaToya telephoned Katherine and said, 'I don't have a family any more. I don't have a mother, father, or brothers or sisters. I've disowned you all.' The Jacksons firmly believed that LaToya didn't love Jack, that she only married him in order to disassociate herself from the family. Jack said that they had six security guards with them at all times to prevent her from being kidnapped by the Jacksons. 'Jack used to tell me all the time how Joseph was trying to kidnap LaToya, and that LaToya was scared to death. From what I understand, Joseph used to beat her when she was a child,' recalled Gary Berwin, whose business dealings with Joseph went sour in 1985.

'LaToya was not a very happy person. She'd had a hard life, and she found someone to love and rely on – Jack Gordon,' Gary continued. 'Finally she had escaped from that family. I asked Jack specifically why he married LaToya. I asked him, "Did you marry LaToya because you really love her, or did you marry her as a convenience for you and herself?" He said, "No, man, I really love her." I said, "C'mon, man, be honest with me." He replied, "I'm telling you, I love her very much." '

In August 1989, Michael Jackson turned thirty-one years old. Recent years had not been easy for him. Family pressures and demands, as well as career concerns, seemed to keep him in a continuous state of anxiety. Though he had left home, he never really left the womb. As much as he tried to shun his family, except for Katherine, he just could not seem to do it – mostly because they wouldn't cooperate in that regard. They just get coming back for more. Somehow, their problems always ended up his.

Despite the fact that he was now in his thirties, many people in his circle felt that Michael had never grown up, that he was still an adolescent at heart, playing with his teenage male friends and entertaining handicapped youngsters at his palatial estate. He liked wearing his many disguises and was agitated when people pointed him out, not so much because he didn't want to be identified as because he had left home thinking he had such a swell costume, no one should ever have been able to recognize him. Visiting Disneyland, Disney World and Universal Studios was still his favourite leisure-time activity; fantasy was a major part of his life.

On the career front, there had been much discussion as to how to follow *Bad*. Just as when he was attempting to conceptualize a successor to *Thriller*, Michael was concerned about competing with himself. *Bad* had not sold as many copies as *Thriller* and Michael was disappointed. Still, rather than try to compete with the previous two albums by issuing another one of new material, John Branca convinced Michael that he should release a Greatest Hits collection, entitled *Decade*, which would also include a few new songs. It was a good idea. It would take some pressure off Michael at a time when he did need a break in his life.

Michael intended to deliver *Decade* to the Sony Corporation, CBS Records' parent company, in August of 1989. It was scheduled to be released in November in time for the Christmas sales rush.

'I want more money than anyone else has ever gotten,' Michael told John when the attorney began negotiating with CBS Records for the new album. John did not let him down. He arranged an eighteen million dollar advance, which was, indeed, 'more money than anyone else has ever gotten'. The deal included a fifteen million dollar straight advance – which CBS would recoup from Jackson's royalties before he would make a profit on the album – and a non-recoupable three million dollars which was a gift for Michael from his label. (On each of the three album deals John Branca negotiated for Michael Jackson at CBS he succeeded in getting for Michael three million as a bonus.)

Prior to the latest Michael Jackson deal, the Rolling Stones, who were also represented by John Branca, held the record for the most lucrative contract, with five-million-dollars-plus per album. According to the *Hollywood Reporter*, Billy Joel had $1.7 million as an advance at the time, Bruce Springsteen $2.5 million, and Madonna $1 million before bonuses, which could make it several times that.

Michael Jackson's album royalty was forty-one points. What that means in terms of percentage of retail sale varies with each formula, from CD to tape to disc; however, the album came to approximately 25 per cent of the retail price of each record. Michael's 25 per cent translated to $2.50 per album sold. However, when the three-million-dollar non-recoupable gift was added to Michael's royalty rate, it actually jumped to about 29 per cent of retail.

To put Jackson's royalty into perspective, Madonna made 18 per cent at the time. Most other acts of superstar status made 12 per cent.

In its entirety, Michael's new deal with CBS would be worth as much as fifty million dollars because, in addition to the advance and non-recoupable gift, John Branca had negotiated a joint business venture with the company. According to that arrangement, CBS would finance a custom label for Michael Jackson – a subsidiary of CBS Records which would be Jackson Records (shades of Joseph!) – which Michael would oversee. CBS would provide 100 per cent of the funding for the new label, and then split the profit equally with Michael. He would also own half the stock and thereby be entitled to half the assets if the label was ever sold. This was a coup for Michael and still yet another tribute to John Branca's masterly negotiating skills.

Since Janet Jackson had constantly called upon her brother for advice and guidance, John felt that she would be the most logical choice as first artist to sign to the label. Michael was elated at the possibility. (It didn't happen, though. Instead, Janet signed a contract with Virgin Records for an estimated thirty-two million dollars. When finalized, in March 1991, it was said to be the largest recording contract in history, but these deals are always said to be just that. There's always a way to calculate ambiguous figures and money not yet earned but projected in such a way to make any decent, big-money record deal 'the largest in history'.)

In the final *coup de grâce* for Michael, as far as *Decade* was concerned, John Branca negotiated a five-million-dollar advance from Warner-Tamerlane Publishing Corporation, the Warner Bros. publishing arm that administers the copyrights on Jackson's songs. (Michael owns all of his copyrights. Warner-Tamerlane has no ownership, but, for a small fee, the company does collect money generated by publishing deals around the world involving his compositions.) For an artist, five million dollars is a huge advance from a music publishing company; most superstars get about one million.

All of the pieces of the puzzle were in place for a tremendous *Decade* kick-off. However, by January 1990, it was obvious that Michael would fail to deliver *Decade*. He was ambivalent about the format, there was some confusion as to which songs to include on it. The original plan was for the package to consist of four cuts from *Off the Wall*, seven from *Thriller*, six from *Bad*, three to five new songs, 'State of Shock' (the hit duet with Mick Jagger); 'Heartbreak Hotel', 'Someone in the Dark' (from Michael's *E.T.* narration album), 'Come Together' and two vintage Motown songs that Michael was re-mastering. However, Michael kept vacillating about the plan, and, in the end, his close friend, entertainment mogul David Geffen, finally talked him out of putting out the album, altogether. Rather, Michael would produce an album of new material. (The deal John Branca negotiated for him at CBS and with Warner-Tamerlane applied to any product Michael chooses to issue.) Here we go, again, John Branca must have thought.

David Geffen Influences Michael

Though Michael is the sole director of all of his companies, he has an investment committee that meets informally about once a year to discuss his many investments. In 1990, that committee consisted of John Branca and his partner, Kenneth Ziffren; Jackson's accountant, Marshall Gelfand; John Johnson of Johnson Publishing Company (which publishes *Ebony* and *Jet*); and David Geffen. The committee had no real power; Michael could veto any decision five minutes after it has been made.

None of the members pocketed any money from investments made on Michael's behalf. Mostly, the committee was formed by Michael so that these powerful men would be well acquainted with one another and be able to follow one another's activities throughout the year. Michael believes in having his associates watching over one another to see who may be taking advantage of him. Because his investments are so fascinating – and because it seems an honour for these gentlemen to be involved, even if it does not mean a personal profit for them – Michael has no difficulty in organizing such an investment committee.

In recent months, David Geffen, who had been a member of the investment committee for about ten years, had begun to exert great influence over Michael. At one point, Michael had signed a development deal with David's production company to do a film. David's task was to procure a script that would meet with Michael's approval. However, the two couldn't agree on one. (Michael still wants to do a movie that would be a fantastic, big-budget combination of *Star Wars* and Busby Berkeley.)

It's easy to see why Michael – a man who is most impressed by wealth and power – would be enamoured of David Geffen. In its 24 December 1990, issue, *Forbes* dubbed David, 'the richest man in Hollywood' and, indeed, he probably was then, and still is, today with an estimated worth of over $100 million.

David has a reputation as being shrewd and savvy, an intuitive show-business genius who knows when to buy and, just as important, when to sell. He is intelligent and witty. He can also be temperamental, and is considered by some associates to be conceited and arrogant. Over the years, David earned a respectable reputation in the music world (with his Geffen Records) and film world, producing movies that were distributed by Warner Bros., including *Risky Business* and *Beetlejuice*. In addition, he made money in the theatre, co-producing the Broadway hit *Dreamgirls* with Michael Bennett and helping to finance Andrew Lloyd Webber's *Cats*.

Michael admired David's business savvy and vision. 'Michael told me he thinks David is the most amazing man he has ever met,' said a Jackson associate. 'He felt that if he listened to David's advice, he, too, could become a mogul, like David. He hung on to his every word the way he used to hang on to John Branca's. Unlike Branca, though, Geffen really kissed up to Mike, flattered him constantly. He and David became extremely close in many ways. Not only did they have a professional relationship, they also had a close personal relationship. David was the one who told him that *Decade* was a mediocre idea and that Michael shouldn't waste his time on it. He convinced Mike to do an album of new material, and Michael agreed. So, obviously, John Branca is not a fan of David Geffen's.'

There was some talk that Michael would hire Quincy Jones for the new project. However, Michael no longer wanted to work with Quincy because he felt that the producer had become too possessive of him and his work, and had taken too much credit for it. Michael was still miffed that Quincy gave him a tough time about 'Smooth Criminal' – Quincy didn't want it on the *Bad* album. For Quincy's part, he felt that Michael had become too demanding and inflexible. With emotions running so high, the partnership that had once sold millions and millions of albums had soured. Still, Quincy figured he would work with Michael, again. He was never informed otherwise. Michael just began work without him; he hasn't worked with Quincy since *Bad*.

David Geffen had obtained all of Michael's financial information – it is quite possible that Michael gave him the documents – and started discussing with him his relationship with CBS Records. He pointed out to Michael that he had spent about forty million dollars making music videos for *Bad* (including the cost of *Moonwalker*), an exorbitant amount to spend on video production. David was right about that. However, John Branca had made back an enormous amount of money for Michael on these videos as a result of distribution and other sales deals, and Michael's net loss was 'only' ten million dollars. Practically no one in the record industry makes thirty million dollars from music videos. But, still, Michael began to believe that CBS Records was making more money on him and his videos than he was making for himself. Soon, he was riled up enough to want to leave CBS altogether.

Prior to this time, Walter Yetnikoff and Michael Jackson had had an outstanding relationship. Michael brought him up on to the stage during the 1984 Grammys. Walter was appreciative and felt that Michael's public show of gratitude helped him earn millions of dollars for himself and his label. 'You don't bring record executives up at the Grammys, 'cause no one's interested,' Yetnikoff told *Rolling Stone* in 1988. 'I went back to CBS and I said, "Give me another two million dollars for that."'

Walter Yetnikoff had been one of the most powerful men in the record business for many years. By 1990 his line-up of superstar recording artists included Michael, Bruce Springsteen, The Rolling Stones and Bob Dylan. But his power had slipped during the year due to a deteriorating relationship with CBS Records' new parent company, Sony, and, in part, to his estrangement from Bruce Springsteen and Springsteen's attorney, John Landau. Now, without Michael Jackson in his corner, Yetnikoff's future looked cloudy.

The Still-Struggling Jacksons

By 1990, Janet Jackson had come into her own with the biggest success of her career, the A&M album *Janet Jackson's Rhythm Nation 1814*, a string of hit records – 'Miss You Much', 'Escapade', 'Rhythm Nation', among others – and her first national tour. Charming and timid, talented and driven, Janet has turned out to be one of the better-adjusted Jackson siblings. With the exception of a relationship she maintains with her mother, she keeps her distance from the rest of the family. Though she is no longer managed by Joseph –

the break was predictably volatile – he does profit from *Rhythm Nation*.

'I've studied the best – Michael Jackson,' Janet said in April 1990. 'I'm not saying that just because he's my brother. I really feel he's the best. I saw how hard he works, his ambition. It's so strange to read things about him, because people just don't understand Michael much.'

Janet also noted, 'Michael has said that, out of everyone in the family, we're the two that think the most alike.' Janet is the only family member who makes it a point to show up at the taping of Michael's videos, just so that she can sit and watch him work. Still, she has to admit that a rivalry does exist between them. 'He's very competitive,' she said in November 1990. 'And so am I.'

Surprisingly, Michael is not as competitive with Janet as people might think. Mostly, he supports her efforts and offers advice whenever she asks for it. He thought *Rhythm Nation* was the work of a genius, and his biggest concern was not that it had sold so many copies, but that it hadn't sold enough. 'Why did it only sell five or six million copies?' he asked a former associate. 'And what does this mean for *me* and my next album?'

Like Michael, Janet has not been resistant to the plastic surgeon's knife. She has had at least two nose jobs, and some have speculated that she has had surgery on her breasts. But she knows how to make plastic surgery work to her advantage. She looks stunning, especially after shedding, on a nine-hundred-calorie-a-day diet, the weight she'd been trying to lose for years.

The rest of the Jacksons have not fared as well in their recordings without Michael. Solo albums by Jackie, Jermaine, Marlon and Randy all had disappointing sales. So too did an excellent group album (recorded by Jackie, Jermaine, Tito and Randy) called *2300 Jackson Street*, after the street on which the family lived in Gary.

Michael was bothered that *2300 Jackson Street* had not been a commercial success, especially since he had telephoned Walter Yetnikoff and specifically asked him to take a special interest in the album. But CBS Records could not successfully promote the Jacksons without Michael. It's not that the brothers have no talent; they do. After decades of experience, most of the Jacksons are first-rate vocalists, and they are all champion entertainers. However, trying to pursue their own careers while Michael Jackson's shadow looms is not easy. The public doesn't seem to want Michael's brothers; it just wants Michael.

CBS did not renew its relationship with the Jacksons after *2300 Jackson Street*. There was no fanfare, as when the Jacksons left Motown for CBS. Rather, the label just did not pick up the brothers' contracts. The Jacksons simply fizzled out.

Without Michael in the lead, his brothers have not been able to secure a new record deal.

Rebbie, by far the most resourceful singer of the three daughters, no longer records.

LaToya's memoirs, '*LaToya – Growing Up in the Jackson Family*,' was published in September 1991. In it, she was extremely critical of her family, but generous to Michael (and did not suggest that he had been molested). While she did not claim to have been molested by Joseph in the book – the publisher did not want to risk legal liability on such a volatile issue – she did so in her promotional tour. On talk show after talk show, she spoke of Joseph having forced her into sexual relations with him, and Katherine having told him, 'Not tonight, Joseph. She's had enough.'

Again, who can truly know, considering the personalities involved in such madness, if the awful charges LaToya made against her father were true, or not?

Losing Count of the Plastic Surgeries

There has always been a great deal of speculation about Michael's nose; it's the first of his features referenced when discussing, or even joking about, the extent of his plastic surgery. By the end of 1990, most people had lost count of how many surgeries Michael had undergone on his nose, but some in his camp have figured that it had to be at least ten. For years, plastic surgeons not related to his case have speculated as to whether the nose – which has an elfin quality to it – is made of bone, cartilage or latex. It's part of the public discourse when speaking of Michael: what is the truth about his nose?

The truth is that the structure of Michael's nose collapsed years ago, a consequence of extensive trauma from previous surgeries on it. One subsequent operation was to add cartilage into the tip, to support and reshape it. However, that procedure was not completely successful. Therefore, when appearing in public, and often in private, Michael wears a latex appliance, a prosthetic nose-tip, which he camouflages with stage makeup.

Interestingly, when Michael is seen wearing the surgical mask that is so much a part of his image, it's not always because he is attempting to hide his identity or even avoid germs. Sometimes, it's simply because he was not inclined to wear the prosthesis. Putting on the appliance is an annoying and frustrating process. It's his cross to bear on a daily basis, and there are days when he simply can't bear it . . . thus, the mask.

In March 2003, *Vanity Fair* reported that, without the prosthesis, Michaels 'resembles a mummy with two nostril holes.' This is not true. Without the device, his nose appears flatter, more blunt – not pointed – and he doesn't really look like . . . Michael Jackson. Self-conscious about his face, he refuses to be seen without it. If nothing else, the prosthesis must be a painful and daily reminder to Michael of his past choices where plastic surgery is concerned, and the impact they have had on his life.

It has been suggested that Michael is somehow addicted to plastic surgery. 'People can easily get addicted to plastic surgery, as they can to alcohol, drugs, or food,' according to Dr Alfred Coodley, associate clinical professor of psychiatry at UCLA.

'Actually, it's more of an obsession than an addiction,' Dr Robert Kotler, a Beverly Hills plastic surgeon who has not treated Michael, observed. 'I think you have to know when to quit. That's the greatest message a cosmetic surgeon can bring to his patient. A conscientious surgeon will say to a patient, "Enough is enough."'

There are several reasons for Michael's extremely pale skin, especially on his face. First, he used to bleach his skin with different chemicals. Is it possible for a black person to make his skin lighter? 'Yes,' said Robert Kotler. 'You can't make it white, but you can make it lighter. There are classic bleaching compounds that are commonly found in over-the-counter bleaching creams like Porcelana. Also, there are known bleaching agents, a class of compounds called Hydroquinones, that will make a black person's skin lighter.'

One employee of Michael's recalled, 'He used to rub a cream on his face and neck in the morning and, again, at night. He had all of these little tubes in his makeup kit. I asked him what it was, thinking it was some kind of skin nutrient. He told me it was 'medicine'. I left it at that. I then noticed that whenever Michael would go out into the sun, he would cover his face with his hand or wear a big hat. He seemed petrified of sunlight, as if he was afraid he would burn.'

According to *The Handbook of Nonprescription Drugs*, 'As the sun's ability to darken skin is much greater than that of Hydroquinone to lighten it, strict avoidance of sunlight is imperative. Although sunscreens may help, even visible light will cause some darkening. The preferable packaging of Hydroquinone is in small squeeze tubes. The dosage is a thin application of 2 per cent concentration rubbed into affected areas twice daily. Once the desired benefit is achieved, Hydroquinone can be applied as often as needed to maintain de-pigmentation.' Some have noted that Michael's fingernails seemed brown and discolored on Martin Bashir's 2003 documentary about him. One possible reason for this is that Hydroquinone stimulates pigment-producing cells in the nail plate, making them darker rather than lighter.

In the 1980s, he was diagnosed with the skin disease Vitiligo. (Some doctors have speculated that the Vitiligo is not as much hereditary as it is the consequence of damage done by bleaching chemicals over the years. Vitiligo makes the sufferer sensitive to sunlight.)

In the late 1980s, Michael's dermatologist, Dr Arnold Klein, diagnosed him as having discoid lupus – an auto-immune disease that causes darkening or lightening of the skin – on his scalp.

There are two variations of lupus: discoid, which is skin deep, and systemic, which can be deadly. As a part of the treatment for discoid, Michael's doctor prescribed the skin lightening creams, Solaquin, Retin A and Benoquin. As a result, Michael was told that, more than ever, he had to avoid all sun exposure – which is one of the reasons he is often seen shielding himself with an umbrellas on sunny days. Also, Michael had to endure the direct injections into his scalp of hydroxy chloroquin – a steroid – in painful, recurring treatments.

Presently, his lupus condition is in remission.

Michael also uses plenty of pancake makeup to even out his skin, which makes him appear even lighter.

In terms of specific plastic surgeries, he will admit to only two nose jobs and the cleft in his chin, but it does not take a cosmetic surgery expert to see that cheek and chin implants and all sorts of other work, including on his eyes and lips, are not beyond the bounds of possibility. Trying to actually detail the work Michael had had done is simply not possible; only he and his surgeons can fully document the extent of it – and it also seems, at least to people who know him well, that he truly doesn't remember it all.

Some professionals have gone on the record saying they believe Michael suffers from body dysmorphic disorder, a psychological condition of people who are obsessed with their appearance, work on it constantly and have no concept of how they are perceived by others.

Certainly, Michael has not had it easy. In 1995, when he released his composition 'Childhood', on *HIStory – Past, Present and Future, Book I*, many people were bored to tears by the notion of him still going on and on about his missing boyhood. However, the song is about more than just his lost youth; it's a plea for compassion and understanding. If one truly contemplates and reviews the challenges he has faced with his appearance, the fact that Michael Jackson is ever able to muster the self-confidence to make well-scrutinized, public appearances seems almost a miracle.

A Maddening Decade, An Uncertain Future

By 1990, both family and career pressures continued to take their toll on thirty-two-year-old Michael Jackson.

In June of that year, Michael was in negotiations with Disney Studios to lend his name to a new robotic attraction at their theme parks. At the same time, David Geffen, who was affiliated with MCA (a division of Universal), wanted Michael to appear at the opening of the Universal Theme Park in Florida, as did Steven Spielberg. However, Michael Eisner, head of Disney, told Michael that if he had anything to do with MCA-Universal, he would never be able to be associated with Disney again. This was pressure.

Michael desperately wanted Disney, and Michael Eisner, in his corner, but he also wished to maintain his friendship with David Geffen and Steven Spielberg. He anguished over this matter for weeks until, in his mind, the dilemma became overwhelming.

On 3 June 1990, Michael was admitted to St John's Hospital and Health Center in Santa Monica. Accompanied by Steven Hoefflin, he was gripping his chest and looked dizzy, pale and weak. It was later reported that he had suffered chest pains while doing his Sunday dance exercises.

The hospital immediately ran a battery of diagnostic tests, including an HIV test. Michael's blood work came back from the lab negative, as expected. However, it was determined that he suffered from an enzyme deficiency and was anaemic, probably due to his strict vegetarian diet.

Michael's hospitalization made headlines for days. President Bush, Liza Minnelli and Elton John all telephoned to wish him well. Katherine and other family members visited. LaToya sent a dozen black roses, an odd gesture, but, said LaToya, 'I think they're beautiful.' Fans held all-night vigils outside of the hospital.

It was reported that Michael was diagnosed as having a condition called costochondritis, a cartilage inflammation in the front part of the ribs, an ailment most commonly found in young athletes who exercise sporadically. The condition is caused by overexertion and stress.

'What bullshit,' one of Michael's former close associates noted. 'The kid had an anxiety attack.'

Indeed, Michael had exhibited the symptoms of sweating, shaking and panting often associated with a classic 'panic attack', a psychological problem sometimes suffered by people under great stress and anxiety.

Michael had suffered such attacks when he was a teenager; he still has them from time to time, today. After his hospital stay generated such worldwide publicity, he was apparently embarrassed to say that he'd had a panic attack, had his representatives come up with a disease no one on the planet had ever heard of, and the public had to accept it.

Michael's spokesman, Bob Jones, did admit that Michael had been 'under some stress, lately.' He said that Michael was particularly saddened by the AIDS-related death of his friend, eighteen-year-old Ryan White, who won a long court battle to attend public school and overcame prejudice against himself and other AIDS victims. Bob also said Michael was still upset over the deaths of his maternal grand-mother, Martha Bridges, who died in May, and Sammy Davis, Jr., who also died that month. Moreover, Michael was agitated because work on his album was not progressing quickly. He didn't mention the real problem: whether Michael should be loyal to Universal or to Disney – not to mention what he'd been through recently with his family members and business associates.

After Michael was released from the hospital, he went about the business of reorganizing his affairs. He had said privately that when he returned from the Bad tour, he would fire everyone on his staff. 'I don't trust anybody,' he said to one associate. 'Except Katherine.'

Frank Dileo had been dismissed after the tour was over, and Michael apparently felt no regret over the decision. He still com-municated with Frank, but only through middlemen, and only when he was agitated about something. For instance, when Michael heard that someone was again spreading rumours that he was a homosexual, he had an associate telephone Frank demanding to know if it had been he who was the source of the story. Frank was hurt. He later said he wondered how a person he once considered to be a son could be so mistrusting of him. However, he'd always known Michael was a suspicious person. Two months before Michael fired Frank, he purchased from a New York-based security firm a briefcase featuring a hidden tape recorder for himself and six Voice Safe telephone scramblers for his home. The briefcase could be used to tape meetings secretly, and the scramblers made it impossible to tape the user's conversation off a telephone line.

After the Bad tour, Marshall Gelfand, Michael's accountant of seven years, was given his walking papers by John Branca. Michael felt he was too conservative in his investment strategies and had John hire a new accountant, Richard Sherman, who also worked for David Geffen.

By the summer of 1990, Michael had also begun to have doubts about John Branca. In recent months, despite John's many professional strengths, Michael allowed his insecurities – and it was said by his associates, David Geffen's personal feelings about John – colour his perception of the high-powered attorney. For instance, Michael suddenly became overly concerned about the identities of John's other clients. Frank Dileo was not permitted by Michael to even have other clients, but John was an attorney who had been practising law before that day in early 1980 when Michael came into his office. By 1990, he had twenty-five clients in addition to Michael.

Earlier, in 1988, John Branca had represented The Rolling Stones' Steel Wheels international tour. When Michael telephoned him one day about a business matter, John mentioned that he would be in Barbados for a week. Michael wanted to know the reason for the trip. When John told him it was for business purposes, Michael became suspicious. He wanted to know what kind of business John had in Barbados. Rather than lie, he told him that he was meeting with Mick. 'Mick? You mean *Mick Jagger*?' Michael wanted to know. He was upset.

John finally admitted that he was representing The Rolling Stones tour. 'Well, is it a big tour?' Michael asked. 'It's not going to be as big as mine, is it? It's not going to be *bigger* than mine, is it?'

There was probably no way to calm Michael down at that point. Next, he wanted to know where the Stones would be playing. When John reluctantly told him they were thinking about the Los Angeles Coliseum, Michael became even more anxious. 'The Coliseum!' he exclaimed. 'The Coliseum! Why, that's bigger than the [Los Angeles] Sports Arena, where I played. How many dates? They're not playing as many dates as me and my brothers played at Dodger Stadium, are they?' He was frantic. The only way to end it with him was for John to beg off the line, saying he had another call.

When John Branca took on Terrence Trent D'Arby as a client, Michael was again upset. He considered D'Arby competition, just as he did Prince. Michael asked John to drop D'Arby. John said he would do it if Michael absolutely insisted upon it. However, Michael then telephoned D'Arby, with whom he had never spoken, to let him know that he (Michael) had no control over John Branca, and that if the attorney should ever drop him as a client, it would be entirely his decision because, as Michael told D'Arby, 'I have no problem with Branca representing you.' Actually, Michael was trying to maintain friendly relations with D'Arby in case the two should ever decide to record a duet sometime in the future.

When John Branca found out what Michael had done (Terrence Trent D'Arby's manager telephoned John immediately after D'Arby had hung up with Michael), he was as disappointed in Michael as he was angry. In the end, John decided *not* to drop D'Arby as a client; Michael just had to live with it.

Most observers felt that representing Michael had become more taxing and demanding than ever for John Branca. In the spring of 1990, John and Michael had a meeting during which John said he felt the time had come for him to share in the equity in Jackson's publishing company. He explained that he wanted to devote as much time to developing Michael's publishing holdings as possible, and in return he wanted five per cent of those profits. John must have known that it would be risky to make such a proposition because Michael is known to be thrifty when it comes to compensating his repre-sentation. He feels that the occasional Rolls-Royce or expensive watch is a fair demonstration of his appreciation to his advisers; he doesn't favour giving them extra percentages. Up until this time, John had worked for Michael on a monthly retainer. On certain extraordinary deals, a percentage would be worked into the deal for him. For instance, he did receive five per cent of the profit on the Victory and Bad tours. (In contrast, though, Mickey Rudin, Frank Sinatra's attorney for years, received ten per cent of Sinatra's tours.) At this time, Michael was feeling psychologically poor as a result of the *Moonwalker* debacle. He told John he would consider his proposal. Then, he decided to talk the matter over with David Geffen.

At this same time, David Geffen was trying to convince Michael that he should break his CBS Records deal by utilizing a contract loophole. Michael's contract with CBS had been signed in 1983, and then amended after *Thriller* in 1985. David felt that the seven years that had lapsed since the original agreement gave Michael an edge in renegotiating the entire deal because California state law forbids personal service contracts of a longer duration. Industry observers felt that David was trying to lure Michael away from CBS so that he could sign him to his own label.

Though Michael's contract with CBS had expired, he still owed four more albums to the label. Yes, after the seven-year duration, Michael could probably have left CBS Records. The company could not enjoin him from recording for another label. However, it *could* sue him for damages, the amount of which would be based on the estimated loss of profits from the albums he did not deliver. This dollar amount would be derived from the combined sales figures of *Off the Wall*, *Thriller* and *Bad*. CBS Records could have mounted a huge lawsuit against Michael. David was willing to overlook the possible litigation ('It'll all work itself out,' he said), however John Branca was not willing to do so, and *he* was the one representing Michael, not David.

When John and David engaged in a heated argument over the logic of trying to extricate Michael from his recording contract with CBS Records, John told him to mind his own business. David hung up on him.

David then telephoned Michael and, apparently, tried to sour him on John Branca by saying that John had been uncooperative, and that the reason Michael didn't have 'a good deal at CBS' was because of John's close relationship with the company president, Walter Yetnikoff. Michael allowed himself to be swayed by David, never stopping to consider that he truly did have the best deal in the record industry and that John Branca was the man who had secured it for him.

John Branca's work with Michael Jackson can only be compared to Colonel Tom Parker's representation of Elvis Presley. Even though John was not Michael's manager, he certainly had the kind of impact on his career that Colonel Tom had on Elvis's. In 1980, when John began representing him, Michael's net worth was barely a million dollars. Ten years later, in great part due to John's negotiating skills, the net worth was close to $300 million, including the publishing holdings, which were valued at close to $200 million. That leap in holdings was a tribute to Michael's artistry, no doubt; but it also spoke well of John's negotiating skills. Despite all they had been through together, Michael now doubted John.

A couple of days after John's difficult conversation with David Geffen, John met with Michael. Something had changed in Michael, and it became clear as the two of them spoke; Michael barely listened to what John said and he seemed hostile towards him. The two engaged in a heated discussion about CBS and whether or not Michael was obligated to record for them. The meeting did not go well.

When it ended, John went back to his office in Century City. The next day, he received a letter by special messenger from Michael's new accountant, Richard Sherman, whom John had recently hired: John's 'services were no longer required by Michael Jackson.'

Michael was sorry to lose John Branca, but he didn't get sentimental about the loss. The way he looked at it, John made a fortune doing what he loved to do, representing Michael in major show-business deals. When it was over, it was over. Michael swiftly replaced him with three seasoned law veterans: Bertram Fields (for litigation), Alan Grubman (for negotiations with CBS), and Lee Phillips (for music publishing) – all closely associated with David Geffen.

In March 1991, Michael Jackson finally came to terms with CBS Records, now known as Sony Corp. The deal was structured on groundwork laid by John Branca – including a 25 per cent royalty rate and Jackson's own label (then called Nation Records). Michael's spokespeople claimed that the contract guaranteed a return of hundreds of millions. Press reports implied that Sony actually handed over a *billion* dollars to Michael. In fact, Michael could receive $120 million per album for the next six *if* sales matched the forty-million-plus level of *Thriller*. If they didn't, he wouldn't. With advances and financial perks, the deal was worth about fifty million dollars to Michael, nicely eclipsing Janet Jackson's thirty-two-million-dollar contract at Virgin Records.

Where Michael Jackson's career was concerned, the future seemed to rest on the commercial success or failure of his next album. That was the case in 1991, and remains so, to this day.

PART NINE

Michael Meets Jordie Chandler

May 1992. Imagine Michael Jackson standing on the side of Wilshire Boulevard in Beverly Hills, his jeep steaming at the side of the road while other cars whisk by in two busy lanes in both directions. With so little knowledge about automobiles, Michael had always wondered what he would do if he was ever alone when his car broke down. He reached for his mobile phone and called 911. He was told that a disabled automobile did not qualify as an emergency situation, and that he should call Directory Assistance to locate a tow-shop. 'But I'm Michael Jackson,' he protested. 'Can't you help me?' The answer was, 'No.'

As he stood next to the car fretting about his next step, Michael was spotted by the wife of Mel Green, an employee of a nearby car-rental business, called Rent-A-Wreck. She telephoned her husband and said, 'You will not believe who I just spotted on Wilshire Boulevard kicking the tyre of his broken-down car. Michael Jackson! You should go there and see what's up.'

Mel Green raced to the scene and, sure enough, there he was: Michael Jackson wringing his hands, pacing back and forth and kicking the tyres of his vehicle. 'I got him,' Mel said, calling Dave Schwartz, owner of Rent-A-Wreck.

'What? You gotta be kidding me?' said Dave. 'Is it really Michael Jackson? Are you sure? Maybe he's one of those wacky impersonators. It can't be *the* Michael Jackson.'

'It sure is,' Mel said. 'I'm bringing him in, now.'

'Then I gotta call June,' Dave said, now excited. Dave and his wife, June, had been having marital difficulties and, more often than not, he was not staying at their home, although they were still on friendly terms. He called June and told her to bring her son Jordie to 'the shop' for 'a big surprise'.

June and Jordie arrived on the scene before Michael. When Michael finally showed, he presented quite a sight wearing a black turban with a veil over his face and dark, over-sized sunglasses. He also wore a long-sleeve black silk shirt, jeans and tennis shoes. The only parts of his body visible were his hands, which seemed pale.

Whenever June Chandler-Schwartz walked into a room, heads turned. A striking woman of Asian extraction, she wore her dark hair to her shoulders with bangs cut straight above her eye line. Her smile incandescent, her manner outgoing, she moved with elegance and grace. Michael was quickly taken by her as she excitedly introduced herself and then Jordie.

Actually, Jordie had seen Michael on several occasions over the years, the first time being at a restaurant in Los Angeles when he was about four. The young boy didn't approach Michael, of course, but instead gawked at him while the entertainer ate his food.

That same year, 1984, was the year Michael was burned filming the Pepsi commercial. Like thousands of fans, Jordie – still just four – sent a letter and picture of himself to the Brotman Memorial Hospital where Michael was recovering. He included his telephone number in the note. Two days later, much to his parents' excitement, Michael called Jordie to thank him for the note, and to also tell him that he thought he was 'a beautiful young boy'.

In 1989, when Jordie was nine, Michael's manager Frank Dileo contacted Jordie's mother to ask if she and her family would like four tickets to see Michael in concert in Los Angeles. Of course, she accepted. They enjoyed the show but, though they attempted to do so, did not meet with Michael backstage after the concert. As the years went on, Jordie continued with his adolescent fan-worship of Michael Jackson.

In the spring of 1992, Jordie got the idea for a spoof of Kevin Costner's film, *Robin Hood: Prince of Thieves*, which he called *Robin Hood: Men in Tights*. For a twelve-year-old, he was amazingly creative. Jordie and his father, Evan, wrote the script (along with Evan's friend, J. D. Shapiro) and with the help of some of Evan's show-business friends, father and son actually got their script produced into a major movie. Though the movie, produced by Mel

Brooks, was not a commercial success, the youngster had two more ideas in mind and was working with his father on them. To young Jordie Chandler, it seemed as if almost anything was possible. Now, he was face to face with his idol, the so-called 'King of Pop'.

Jordie was dark-haired with big, luminescent eyes. He was on the verge of manhood, but certainly not there yet. His face was lean and angular, its raw-boned sharpness softened by its olive complexion. Anyone looking at him would say, 'That kid is going to be stunning in about ten years.' However, standing before Michael, he was just a boy with a big smile on his face.

June wrote down a telephone number and handed it to Michael. 'You should call Jordie sometime,' she suggested, as if the notion of a twelve-year-old being 'friends' with a thirty-three-year-old pop star was the most natural thing in the world.

'Mom!' Jordie protested, embarrassed.

'No, Jordie,' she said, according to a later recollection from, Jordie. 'You guys can be friends.'

'For sure,' Dave Schwartz said as he walked into the room. 'Give him a call, Michael. He's your biggest fan.'

'Yeah, okay,' Michael said as he signed the final paperwork for the rental car. He took the paper from June and stuffed it in his pocket. Michael then looked over his glasses and took in the twelve-year-old. 'So, look, I'll call you, Jordie,' he said. 'Okay?'

'Sure,' the youngster answered. He flashed a dazzling smile at the singer. 'Oh, boy!'

'Yeah,' Michael exclaimed, seemed tickled by the youngster's enthusiasm. 'Oh, boy!' he repeated.

Have You Seen His Childhood?

Of course, Michael Jackson had long associated himself with children, regularly visiting with ill children on his concert tours and inviting underprivileged youths to tour his ranch. His philanthropic activities, including those executed by his Heal the World Foundation, were well known. In the past, Michael had often been seen in the company of young celebrities, such as Emmanuel Lewis and McCauley Culkin, as well as with many youngsters who are not famous, which was why Jordie's mother and stepfather saw nothing unusual about encouraging a friendship between the pop star and their son.

'One of my favourite pastimes is being with children,' Michael had explained in an interview, 'talking to them and playing with them. Children know a lot of secrets and it is difficult to get them to tell. Children are incredible. They go through a brilliant phase, but then when they reach a certain age, they lose it. My most creative moments have almost always come when I am with children. When I am with them, the music comes to me as easily as breathing. When I'm tired or bored, children revive me. Two brown eyes look at me so profoundly, so innocently, and I murmur, This child is a song.'

In the early nineties Michael Jackson's interest in children was viewed by most quarters where it was known about as odd, but not necessarily inappropriate.

Michael was thought of as not only a virgin, but asexual. He was viewed as 'damaged goods', a brilliant entertainer who gave his all to his work because he had no personal life in which to find satisfaction. No one believed he actually had romances with girls like Tatum O'Neal or Brooke Shields, no matter how much he insisted that such affairs of the heart had taken place in his life. Mostly, where Michael's personal life was concerned, one felt a sense of sadness about it. He was an oddity, a brilliant performer and legendary recording artist whose image was perplexing and eccentric, but not sexual. Even when he grabbed his crotch during his performances, the action didn't have a sexual connotation to it as much as it did the imprint of another clever bit of choreography. Then, of course, there was all of that business about his 'lost childhood' . . .

'He's a man who has never had a childhood,' Bert Fields, one of Michael's attorneys, explained to me – as if I wasn't aware of Michael's background. 'So he's having his childhood now, you see? His friends are little kids. They have pillow fights. It's all innocent.'

I had a discussion with Michael along those same lines in 1991, after the original publication of my biography of him. I saw him and LaToya at a Record Collectors' Convention in the parking lot of Capitol Records in Hollywood. He was wearing a bright red shirt, black satin pants . . . and a black surgical mask. When LaToya went off in search of records by The Partridge Family, Michael and I began talking about the music of our youth and, somehow, we began talking about his childhood. 'I missed my childhood,' he said, sadly.

Having personally witnessed just a bit of Michael's childhood in Encino, I offered the opinion that perhaps his childhood wasn't as bad as he remembered it. The biggest misconception about him is that he has lived his life sheltered from 'the real world', and that this is why he has practically withdrawn from society. In fact, Michael has had more life encounters than most people. An immensely gifted performer, he has travelled the world many times over, entertaining people of all colours, races and religions. He is intimate with the exhilaration of a thunderous ovation, of a standing-room-only crowd. He knows what it is to be 'special', to be able to make demands and expect them to be met because of who he is. He knows what it's like to have great wealth, to be able to give his mother a million dollars so she won't have to work. He has experienced the pleasure of giving, of being charitable, of seeing the faces of deathly ill children light up just because he is who he is.

'A lot of kids starve, Michael,' I reminded him. 'A lot of kids are poor, they become addicted to drugs. A lot of kids don't live in mansions with servants. A lot of kids have it a lot worse that you did. In fact,' I said, maybe feeling a little too self-confident, 'I think you had a pretty good childhood. You travelled. You had friends. You did what you wanted to do, didn't you? You performed. You entertained. It was fun. I think you miss your childhood, yes. But I don't think you missed out on it.'

Michael stared at me, angrily. 'No, it was horrible,' he countered. 'I had a terrible childhood. All of that performing. All that recording. The fans took over my life,' he said, pointing at me. 'I never got to play,' he complained. 'It was awful.'

'See you 'round,' he said, turning his back on me. 'I'm going to find 'Toya.'

The memory of that brief exchange has stayed with me over the years, especially when the common explanation to Michael's increasingly unusual behaviour became that he had 'missed out' on his youth.

A week after meeting him, Michael Jackson telephoned Jordie Chandler. As the two discussed their lives and hobbies, Jordie expressed an interest in playing video games. Michael then invited the boy to his 'hide-out', an apartment he maintained in Century City, California, which most of Michael's family and staff members had only heard about, but had never actually seen. Michael explained that he had an arcade at the apartment and felt sure that Jordie would have fun there. Of course, Jordie wanted to go. However when he asked his mother for permission, she denied it citing upcoming school tests for which the youngster needed to study. But in the weeks to come, Michael continued telephoning Jordie; the two became fast friends.

On 27 June 1992, Michael embarked on his Dangerous concert extravaganza, the first of thirty-nine performances on the first leg of the tour taking place in Munich, Germany, at the Olympic Stadium. It was a complex production with the expected bombastic special effects and lighting, dancers, musicians and others involved in the fantastic multimillion-dollar presentation. In all, Michael would perform eighteen numbers – including hits such as 'Wanna Be Startin' Something', 'Thriller', 'Billie Jean' and 'Beat it' – and four from the current *Dangerous* album. At the end of the show, in front of nearly 75,000 people, Michael appeared to strap on a jet and rocket right out of the stadium. (Actually, a stunt double did the trick, which was orchestrated by illusionist, David Copperfield.) Even without John Branca at the helm, Michael was making winning decisions; he sold the rights of his Dangerous tour to HBO for twenty million dollars, the highest sum ever paid for a live concert. When the network broadcast the final show of the first leg of Michael's tour, HBO gained its highest rating up until that time.

Because Michael was involved in every aspect of the show, from sound to lighting to costumes all the way down to ticket sales, it demanded all of his focus. How he managed to even give Jordie Chandler a second thought during this time is remarkable, yet he did just that. For the next nine months while on the road, Michael telephoned his new friend on a weekly basis. For Michael, it was as if

Jordie had become his lifeline to the real world, to his home, as he performed in front of hundreds of thousands of adoring strangers. In fact, Michael also had eleven-year-old Brett Barnes with him from Australia, as well as nine-year-old Prince Albert von Thurn und Taxis, son of Gloria von Thurn und Taxis of Bavaria and already one of the richest kids in the world. His staff was used to having to accommodate children while on the road with Michael, no one ever questioned it. However, even though he had other youngsters with him, Michael's thoughts were of Jordie. According to what Jordie later recalled of his late-night, long-distance conversations with him, Michael told him about Neverland. 'It's a place where boys have rights,' Michael said, promising to take Jordie there as soon as the Dangerous tour was completed.

Michael also told Jordie about his charity work, how he had raised funds for needy children's organizations round the world with his Heal the World Foundation, and his plans for a World Congress of Children to bring together youngsters from one hundred nations. 'Children,' Michael explained, 'are the hope of the world.' Sometimes, Michael said, he sent his staff members to a toy store in one of his pick-up trucks. The employees fill the truck with toys until 'there's not a single inch left' in the pick-up bed, and bring them to Neverland. Then, 'as they gather all around me, smiling and laughing,' Michael distributed the toys to all the needy children. He promised to introduce Jordie to Elizabeth Taylor one day, telling him, 'she's really old, but she's still cool. She's won, like, fifteen Oscars!' (Taylor has actually won two.)

When Michael returned home from the final stop on the tour's first leg, Japan, on 31 December, he found that Elizabeth Taylor had decked out Neverland for the Christmas holidays, with hundreds of thousands of dollars' worth of elaborate decorations. Though Michael, raised a Jehovah's Witness, never celebrated Christmas, he was still overwhelmed by Elizabeth's kind gesture. He called Jordie to tell him about it. 'You should see it,' he said, the youngster later recalled. 'It's like a Winter Wonderland. The only thing that would make it better would be having you here. Then, it would be absolutely perfect.'

Michael was too busy in January, however, to entertain any guests at Neverland. On his agenda was the NAACP [National

Association for the Advancement of Colored People] Image Awards on 16 January, President Clinton's Inaugural Ball on the 19th and then the American Music Awards on the 25th – each performance requiring days of rehearsal time. Then, he had the Superbowl on the 31st, where he performed with a 750-member choir and a 98,000-person flashcard stunt to promote the Heal the World Foundation. At the end of the show, 3,500 children joined Michael on stage for 'Heal the World'. 120 million people watched Michael's performance.

On 10 February 1993, Michael gave an internationally televised interview to Oprah Winfrey. During it, Michael and Oprah gave the world a nighttime tour of Neverland and Michael then revealed, for the first time, he suffers from Vitiligo. He also spoke of his 'girlfriend' Brooke Shields. When Oprah pushed to learn if Michael was still a virgin, he clarified that he was 'a gentleman. You can call me old-fashioned, if you want.' When asked about plastic surgery, he said he had 'very little. You can count it on two fingers.' Elizabeth Taylor made a surprise appearance, as if just passing through, to declare that Michael 'is the least weird man I have ever known.' (Michael later presented her with a $250,000 diamond necklace to thank her for the compliment.) It was a terrific, ratings-winning broadcast, drawing an audience of more than ninety million; the fourth most-watched entertainment show in US TV history.

The next day, Michael called June Chandler to invite her, Jordie and his half-sister Lily, to his estate for the weekend. With Michael so much in the headlines as a result of the interview with Oprah, it must have seemed surreal to June that he had invited her and her family to the same place she had just seen displayed on television, even offering to put them up for the night. June accepted Michael's invitation.

June and the children arrived at Neverland Ranch early on Friday afternoon. The servant who greeted them suggested that they be seated in the parlour and wait for 'Mr Jackson' as he scurried off to fetch soft drinks. June, Jordie and Lily sat side by side on one of the couches and looked at their surroundings, their mouths agape. Simply put, they could not believe their eyes. Was it possible that they knew a person who lived *here*?

Though the twenty-five-room, mock-Tudor mansion's living room was large-scale and packed with opulent furnishings, there was also a sense of warmth and elegance about it, with pine-panelled walls, fine Italian antiques (a little over-done but, of course, for Michael excess is never enough), and big, over-stuffed furniture, the kind into which one would sink six inches upon being seated. Here and there, were eccentric treasures: life-size mannequins of senior citizens and youngsters having tea; giant oil paintings of Elizabeth Taylor hanging in elaborate, carved and gilded frames; the white, bugle-beaded gown Diana Ross wore in the final scene of *Lady Sings the Blues* encased in a large glass box – with pink lights glowing around it. There were pictures of children, everywhere, both boys and girls. The house was perfectly still; nothing stirred. It was quiet as a tomb, no music, not a sound.

Outside, as far as the eye could see, were more than 2,000 verdant acres of bucolic landscape, reminiscent of the English countryside. It was impossible to imagine that anyone *owned* this place, it was so expansive, with its deep blue four-acre lake way off in the distance. Statues paid homage to Scottish author J. M. Barrie and his creation Peter Pan. From more than a hundred speakers, disguised as rocks in the flowerbeds, emanated Disney music (never Michael's own music, to which he rarely listens). There was a zoo with a menagerie of alligators, giraffes, lions, a twelve-foot albino python and a seventy-thousand-pound elephant named Gypsy (a present from Elizabeth Taylor). There was also 'Cricket', the thirty-four-inch-tall stallion and Petunia, the potbellied pig, and Linus, the two-foot-tall sheep. Of course, Bubbles the chimpanzee also lived on the property, often sitting in the cinema with Michael, eating free candy from the sweets counter. 'Sometimes he takes off his diaper and goes on the floor, but mostly he's very clean,' Michael had told Jordie. Then, of course, there were the many rides: the Ferris wheel, bumper cars, steam trains . . . and, for the little ones, a carousel, fire trucks and frog hoppers. Some might have found it disturbing that hundreds of security cameras were positioned all over the estate, hidden inside little birdhouses. However, Michael viewed it as a necessary precaution. If any one of the thirty full-time gardeners or ten ranch hands didn't smile enough, or seemed otherwise unhappy, he would be dismissed – another necessity. After all, this was supposed to be a happy place.

'So, how do you like my home?' It was Michael, walking into the room, flashing a smile of genuine pride and satisfaction, and holding a tray with four soft-drink bottles. 'I was going to put them in glasses,' he said of the refreshments. 'But I couldn't find any in the kitchen,' he joked. 'I've been gone so long, I was lucky to even find the kitchen.' He was funny, June later recalled, funnier than she imagined he would be.

For the rest of the day, June, Jordie and Lily played games, swam, zipped about in the master's $7,000 black-and-lavender golf cart, and then watched first-run films (loaned to Michael by major Hollywood studios) late into the evening in his private screening room. The next day, Michael took them all to a toy store an hour away, which had been closed by the managers for a few hours to allow the Jackson party private shopping time. 'You can have anything you want,' Michael told Jordie and Lily. As June watched, the two children ran through the store, pulling more than ten thousand dollars' worth of toys from the shelves and piling them into three shopping carts.

Saturday night was spent enjoying Michael's amusement park under a full and magical moon, first on the rollercoaster and then the Ferris wheel. When the cart carrying Michael, Jordie, June and Lily got to the top of the Ferris wheel, the operator stopped the rotation, just as Michael had earlier instructed. The four of them then sat high above the ground – June, Michael and Jordie shoulder-to-shoulder, and Lily on her mother's lap – surveying all that was Michael's pride-and-joy. A slight breeze rustled the leaves of old trees. There seemed to be twinkling lights as far as the eye could see. 'I don't know where there are more lights,' June said, breathlessly, 'in the sky or on the ground.' All four were lost in their own thoughts as they sat in silence, the moon bathing them with silvery radiance. However, Michael looked glum in the dim light.

'Do you know how much time I spend up here alone,' Michael said, softly, 'just sitting up here by myself? I have all of this,' he declared, motioning to the acres below, 'yet I have . . . nothing. The things I really want in my life are the things I don't have.'

'You have us, now,' Jordie said, putting his arm around Michael's shoulder.

Michael smiled. 'My new little family,' he concluded. 'The only thing that matters in life is having someone who understands you, who trusts you and who will be with you when you grow old, no matter what.'

On Sunday morning, June, Jordie and Lily departed for Los

Angeles after their unforgettable weekend. Another visit was planned.

The following Saturday night, Michael showed up at June's home in a limousine ready to whisk them back to Neverland. However, when June, Jordie and Lily got into the stretch automobile and greeted Michael, they discovered another boy sitting on the singer's lap, eleven-year-old Brett Barnes, who Michael introduced as his 'cousin'. (They're not related even though the youngster did introduce himself as 'Brett Jackson'.) Apparently, Jordie would not be the sole focus of Michael's attention during the weekend ahead.

As June tried to keep the conversation going, Brett and Michael appeared to be in their own world with an easy rapport between them, one that made what Michael had with Jordie seem, perhaps, not so unique. It was a tense drive to Santa Barbara.

When Michael and his guests finally arrived at Neverland, they were immediately surrounded by uniformed guards, maids, butlers and other functionaries, all gathering and grinning to one another excitedly. Michael nodded and smiled and shook hands. He then instructed two of the guards to take June's suitcases to one of the guest cottages. 'Oh, and Brett's belongings go in my room,' he added nonchalantly as Brett ran off with one of the maids. Michael then embraced and kissed his remaining guests. 'You have Neverland at your disposal,' he told June, 'so have a ball. I love you all,' he said with genuine warmth. 'And just wait,' he added, 'tomorrow will be another great day.'

'Never do that again, Jordie'

Like many celebrated people, at his core, Michael Jackson was conscious of a certain emptiness. He admitted it, and often; it didn't take much prodding for him to describe himself as 'the loneliest person on the planet'. Over the years, especially as he got older, bleakness crept into his soul. When he was on stage, he came to life and was without peer; offstage, he felt . . . joyless. However, when he met Jordie Chandler, all of that seemed to change.

'Michael is a sad person,' confirmed someone who has been associated with him for twenty years. 'He has had a difficult life, always been a loner, a misfit. If he hadn't become a star, he would be the guy living in Gary, Indiana, alone in a one-bedroom apartment with no friends and a job developing film at a photolab. What really attracted Michael to Jordie, was the youngster's humour. Whenever a person can make him laugh, that's someone he will want in his life. Jordie made him laugh. He would make fun of Michael, of the way he dressed, of his clumsiness, his driving. Michael was amused by Jordie's irreverent manner. He felt he could be himself around him.

'They used to dance together, Michael showing Jordie choreography steps and Jordie catching on remarkably fast. Jordie was intelligent; Michael loves smart kids and Jordie was tremendously creative. Michael said that Jordie could one day be an amazing film director. "He has a vision," he told me. "I think he could do wonderful things." '

They probably would have been a perfect couple of buddies – if not for the fact that Jordie was thirteen and Michael was thirty-four.

'I truly don't think there's a devious bone in his body,' June said of Michael. If she thought anything was unusual about Michael and Brett at Neverland, she didn't indicate as much after she and her family returned to Los Angeles.

It wasn't long before Michael invited them all to his 'hide-out' on Wilshire Boulevard in Westwood, about ten minutes from June and Dave Schwartz's home. 'Do you have an amusement park there, too?' Jordie asked him. Michael laughed, 'No, silly. It's just my place to go where no one can find me.' Then, lowering his voice as if to share an important confidence, he added, 'As soon as someone finds out about it – whoosh! – I move to another hide-out. Once,' he continued, 'a person knocked on my door that I didn't know and – whoosh! – I moved to another hide-out, the next day.'

Why?'

'Because if one stranger knows where I live,' Michael answered, 'then millions more will follow.'

'So how many hide-outs have you had?' Jordie asked.

'Hundreds,' Michael said, grinning. 'Hundreds and hundreds and hundreds.'

Jordie, Lily and June had fun at Michael's hide-out, as expected, and, as the days passed, became privy to more of his secrets. For instance, on 9 March, Michael was honoured with a *Soul Train* award for Best Album (*Dangerous*) and Best Song ('Remember the Time'). At the show, he sat in a wheelchair on the stage and performed 'Remember the Time' while surrounded by a host of dancers. He explained that he had hurt himself during rehearsals.

However, the next day at Neverland, he threw the crutches aside. 'It's a miracle! I can walk! I can walk!' Michael exclaimed, the jokester in him coming forth. Michael had never been injured; it appeared he had used the wheelchair and crutches as a publicity gimmick.

A couple of days later, Michael took Jordie, Lily and their mother to Las Vegas where they all stayed at Jackson's private, $3,000-a-night suite in the Mirage Hotel. Michael and Jordie stayed in separate rooms, while June and Lily shared another suite.

The night after their arrival, June and Lily turned in early, exhausted by their fun time in Las Vegas. Meanwhile, Michael and Jordie watched *The Exorcist*. Jordie was so frightened by the film, he asked – or Michael suggested, depending on which of them tells the story – that he be allowed to stay with Michael in his room. In whatever manner the circumstances evolved, the two ended up sleeping together, Michael in silk pyjamas, Jordie in a T-shirt and sweat pants.

The next morning, when June went to Jordie's bedroom she found that he had not slept in his bed. As she stood in the doorway trying to figure out what had happened, she caught Jordie slipping out of Michael's room. 'What is going on?' she asked. 'Where were you?'

'Oh, I slept with Michael,' answered the boy, casually, according to a later recollection.

'What?' June exclaimed. 'What are you talking about? You don't do that,' she said, now scolding him. 'Never do that again, Jordie.'

'Why?'

'Because it's not right,' June said, upset. 'Promise me you will never do that again, ever, Jordie.'

'But, Mom—'

'But, *nothing*,' she cut him off. 'Promise me!'

'I promise,' said Jordie, sounding defeated.

The next day, Jordie told Michael about June's concern. Now, Michael was the one who was upset. He didn't understand why June would so object to his sleeping with her son. Did she not trust him? With Dave Schwartz not around the house, it seemed right that Jordie have a male influence, Michael reasoned. He decided to take up the matter with June. According to what June later recalled, Michael pulled her aside and, fixing her with an earnest look, said, 'Jordie and I share a special and innocent friendship. Why did you tell him he can't sleep with me?'

'Because it's completely inappropriate, Michael,' June said, holding her ground. 'And I don't want Jordie to be hurt.'

'But I'm not like that,' Michael said. 'How could you think I would hurt Jordie?' he asked. 'We have a friendly, honest, true and loving relationship.' Michael then told June his theory about 'conditioning'. That children are innocent until conditioned by the world to be otherwise, at which point they become cynical, judgemental adults who lie, cheat, gossip and treat each other poorly. It would be his desire, he said, that Jordie remain pure and untouched by the adult world, unconditioned. Michael began to cry.

June didn't know how to respond to Michael's heart-felt monologue. His theory, while idealistic and naive, was probably harmless. However, there was still something disconcerting about the proposition that Jordie never be permitted to grow into a well-adjusted adult. After all, it couldn't always be moonbeams and lollipops for her son. Did she really want him to end up like the thirty-four-year-old man standing before her, sobbing? Or, was she now just being 'cynical and judgemental', thereby proving Michael's point? At a loss, she apologized to Michael for hurting his feelings. The two embraced. 'You must trust me,' Michael said.

'I do,' June assured him. 'I do trust you.'

The next day, Michael gave June a $12,000 ruby-and-diamond bracelet from Cartier's. June stared at him as he presented the gift, dumbfounded. 'A token,' Michael told her. 'It's nothing. I just love you.'

Afterwards, Michael continued telephoning and visiting Jordie, with June's approval and much to the astonishment of many in the

Chandler and Schwartz families. Why would a wealthy, world-famous and busy superstar work so diligently to forge a deep and meaningful bond with one of his teenage fans? No one seemed to have the answer to that question. However, the scenario wasn't quite as odd to those witnessing it from Michael's camp. Many of them had seen young friends of Michael's come and go over the years and had long ago learned not to question their employer about it. Though clearly obsessed with certain boys along the way, no one ever saw him do anything inappropriate with them, no one ever accused him of anything improper . . . and, so, that was the end of it. The explanation always had something to do with Michael's 'lost childhood' and his having young friends because they were innocent and trusting . . . a bit of a tiresome excuse. Therapy might have been a better way to go but, as one of his long-time associates put it, 'Don't even go there with Michael.'

On Friday, 2 April Jordie Chandler and his mother and sister again went to Neverland to visit Michael. While there, they noticed that a pair of mannequins, both dressed as fierce-looking Sikh Indian guards, had been positioned in front of the heavy, mahogany double-doors leading to Michael's bedroom. Michael said he had them placed there in order to keep ghosts away from the room.

Inside his bedroom, Michael had a giant, gold throne placed directly in front of the fireplace. It was very strange.

That night, June and Lily stayed in the guest quarters. Jordie stayed with Michael in a room fit for a king.

Either Jordie's Mom Trusts Michael . . .
or She Doesn't

June Chandler spent much of the next five days at Neverland walking alone and mulling over the odd goings-on. On one hand, she trusted Michael and didn't believe that anything inappropriate was going on between him and Jordie. But the fact that Michael and Jordie were now sleeping in the same bed was troubling. However, it was Michael

Jackson with whom Jodie was sharing a bed. *Michael Jackson.* June and her children were staying at Neverland, receiving expensive presents and being treated like royalty. She was swept away by it. Today, a parent might conclude that precisely because it *is* Michael Jackson with whom he or she is dealing, she might have had good reason to err on the side of caution if only because of his controversial reputation with children – deserved or undeserved. However, ten years ago, June simply did not know what to make of the situation. Therefore, she allowed it to continue, especially since her husband was not living with her and the children and, she reasoned, a strong male influence on Jordie might not be a bad thing.

Michael accompanied June, Jordie and Lily in the limousine back to Los Angeles. However, he did not then return to Santa Barbara, deciding instead to retreat to his Westwood hideaway. He had a medical problem, and needed to be close to his dermatologist.

In fact, a week or so earlier, Michael had decided to bleach his scrotum with Benoquin, a bleaching cream prescribed to him many times over the years by his dermatologist, Dr Arnie Klein. Michael had been using the cream for years to bleach his skin. However apparently, he had never tried it on his scrotum. As it happened, the cream burned and stung, causing a great deal of discomfort. Debbie Rowe, the assistant to Michael's dermatologist attended to him. To show his gratitude, Michael gave Debbie a white GMC truck.

No sooner was Michael settled in at his home that he began to long for Jordie. He had to speak to him; he called him.

June didn't like the way the conversation unfolded as she listened to her son's end of it. He responded to questions with what sounded like a code of simple answers, 'yes,' 'no' and 'maybe'. When he hung up, June asked him what he and Michael had discussed. He was evasive.

Five minutes later, Michael's telephone rang. It was June calling to tell him that, again, she was concerned about his relationship with Jordie. Michael was bewildered. Hadn't they already covered this territory? Either she trusted him, or she didn't . . . however, she had to make a choice, as Michael told her.

Michael suggested that she come to his hide-out so that they could discuss the matter personally. When June arrived, she found Michael in his pyjamas. Once again he pleaded with June to give him a chance.

He had often been misunderstood in the past, he told her, and he truly did care about her and her children. Hadn't he proved as much? It seemed unfair, Michael pointed out, that after all he had done for her and her family she would now doubt his motives. He had only been kind and generous to them, he reminded her. June had to agree.

Michael then told June that he was lonely at his hide-out and asked if she would take him back to her home. She complied. Without changing from his pyjamas, Michael got into the car with her. It's no wonder, as she later told it, that she felt as if she was dealing not with an adult, but with a child.

Once at the Schwartz home, June suggested that Michael retire to one of the guest rooms. However, perhaps testing her to see if she really did trust him, Michael asked that he be allowed to sleep in Jordie's bed . . . with Jordie.

The next weekend, June, Jordie and Lily were again guests of Michael's at Neverland. The weekend after that one, Michael had to leave Los Angeles on a business trip. He didn't want to go, telling his associates that he had become so attached to Jordie and his family that he couldn't bear to leave them. At the Burbank airport Michael sobbed as he hugged Jordie, telling him that he would 'do anything' to not have to go to Philadelphia. 'I'm going to miss you so much,' he told the youngster, as June and Lily looked on.

'But you'll be back soon,' the little girl offered.

'I know,' Michael said, still hugging Jordie tightly and crying. 'But it's just that I love you guys so much. You're my true, true family.' He sighed as he buried his face in Jordie's hair. Then, he embraced Lily. Then, June. 'I'll be back,' he told them, 'and we'll have more fun. I promise.' He then turned to Jordie and said, 'Don't forget the wishes. Always say the wishes.' He winked at him, conspiratorially.

'I won't forget,' Jordie promised. He winked back.

By the time Michael left Burbank, Jordie, June and Lily were so emotional they couldn't stop crying. It was as if they had all been swept away by some surreal melodrama. After all, Michael would only be gone for a little more than a week. They really didn't know Michael that well, and he didn't know them, either – not really. Yet, the relationship had become so intense, June couldn't help but feel a little uncomfortable about it. 'What wishes?' she wanted to know when she and Jordie were alone.

'Nothin',' he said. 'It's between me and Michael.'

'I don't like that, Jordie,' June said. 'You know I don't like you keeping secrets.'

Jordie didn't respond.

In truth, the 'wishes' were six rules that Michael and Jordie had come up with, mostly as a joke between them. However, the wishes seemed to have real significance to Michael, and he often reminded Jordie of them. He said that if they repeated these wishes three times a day, perhaps they would actually come true for them:

1. No wenches, bitches, heifers or ho's (whores).
2. Never give up your bliss.
3. Live with me in Neverland forever.
4. No conditioning.
5. Never grow up.
6. Be better than best friends.

Michael Meets Jordie's Father

One person was not as taken by Michael Jackson's relationship with Jordie as everyone else: Jordie's father, Evan Chandler.

The odd situation between Jordie and Michael Jackson evolved so quickly, Evan couldn't seem to keep track of it. When June would telephone him to tell him about their Neverland visits, he found it difficult to believe that a world-famous entertainer would have that much time to spend with his ex-wife and their child. Also, June and Evan had been arguing about Evan's involvement in Jordie's life; June didn't feel that Evan was spending enough time with his son. Evan disagreed. However, he couldn't help but feel that he might be losing his place in Jordie's life to Michael. He didn't believe that Michael was doing anything wrong with Jordie. Rather, he simply felt the presence of another man, an influential male figure, in his son's life – and he didn't like it. It didn't help matters that June would often make reference to the fact that Jordie saw Michael more than he did his own father. 'Michael is completely influential on your son,' she told Evan during once conversation, 'and he's taking over where you have left off.'

When he learned that Michael was sleeping with Jordie, Evan became upset. 'It's preposterous,' he told his ex-wife, according to what he later recalled. 'It isn't right.'

'Well, that's what I thought, at first,' June explained to him. 'But you have to be there. You have to see how kind and gentle Michael is with Jordie.'

'Bullshit,' Evan said, angrily, according to his memory. 'It's not right and I want it to stop.'

'Well, it's not going to,' June told him. 'I've already been through this with Michael, and I know it's fine. I'm Jordie's mother,' she said, 'and I know what's best for him.' How dare Evan try to tell June how to raise their son? She was doing the best job she could do, she felt, and had given the matter regarding Jordie and Michael serious consideration. She did not want Evan to second-guess her.

When Evan polled his friends, they agreed that there was something inappropriate about Jordie sleeping in the same bed with Michael Jackson. One of his patients – Evan was a dentist – suggested that, 'just to be on the safe side', he should insist that such behaviour stop. She was familiar with Michael's dermatologist, Arnold Klein, and, at Evan's request, called the doctor to inquire about Michael. Klein told her that Michael was 'absolutely heterosexual' and, according to him, there was no reason to be concerned about him and Jordie. 'He's the sweetest guy in the world,' Arnold said, 'and, I swear to God, you would be making a mistake separating him and Jordie. He's completely innocent, like a kid himself.' Still, despite Klein's reassurance, Evan Chandler's patient said that, at least in her opinion, an adult should not be sleeping in the same bed with a youngster, unless he is the child's parent – and even then such sleeping arrangements should be closely monitored. Another of Evan's friends, Dr Mark Torbiner, had to agree: something *was* wrong with the arrangement as it existed between Jordie and Michael, and it should be stopped, he insisted. 'It's not normal,' said Torbiner. 'C'mon! Be realistic. In the real world, this is crazy.'

On Sunday 18 April, Michael returned from his business trip to the East Coast. As soon as he got to Neverland, he picked up the telephone to call Jordie and invite him and his mother and sister to the ranch for a five-day 'vacation'. Now Evan was closely monitoring the frequency of Jordie's visits with Michael, and becoming unreservedly uncomfortable about them.

On 22 April, much to Evan's chagrin, Michael took June, Jordie and Lily to Disneyworld in Florida for three days, utilizing Sony's company jet. When they returned to Los Angeles Michael asked if he could stay at the house with June and her children. Again, Michael slept in the same bed with Jordie. About a week later, Michael bought Jordie a computer. The youngster was thrilled with the present; Evan was not happy about it. He had planned to buy his son the exact same computer and Michael had beaten him to it.

It was decided by Michael and Jordie that the computer would be set up at Michael's hide-out so that when Jordie spent time there he would have access to the Internet. Jordie now felt that the more time he spent at the hide-out, the better off he was – and June agreed, since she trusted Michael with her son – and maybe to spite Evan, or maybe not – she allowed the visits, most of them overnight, to continue.

In early May, Michael offered to take June, Jordie and Lily to Monaco for the World Music Awards where Michael was being honoured with three trophies including 'World's Best-selling Record Artist of the Era'. The Jackson entourage would be travelling first class, and would stay in the $2,000-a-night Winston Churchill suite at the Hotel de Paris, the finest such establishment in the principality. It promised to be an exciting vacation for June and her family. For his part, having his friends with him on this overseas trip meant that Michael did not have to leave them behind; he couldn't bear the idea of that.

On the day they were to leave, Evan Chandler came by the Schwartz house to say goodbye to his son. Though he still had not met Michael Jackson, he had no choice but to trust that June knew what she was doing when she agreed to the trip. Disturbingly, though, Evan noticed that Jordie now seemed oddly cold towards him. Evan would later remember feeling that his son had changed, that he no longer seemed to care about his father. As Jordie climbed into the limousine with June and Lily, Evan stood at the curb and watched them chatter among themselves and, as he recalled it, felt left out of the proceedings. Later, he would say, 'I felt then that maybe

June should just divorce Dave, since they were having problems, and maybe hook with up Michael. After all, they were having a good time, even if I had some reservations about it. Maybe I was wrong, I reasoned. Maybe I was wrong.'

In Monaco, Michael was often photographed with June, Jordie and Lily. In several pictures, he is seen holding Lily in his arms while walking next to June. Jordie, in a red shirt and large, oversized hat that clearly belonged to Michael, walked ahead of them. During the show, Michael sat next to Prince Albert, with Jordie in his lap.

On Sunday 16 May Michael and his guests returned from Europe. While browsing in the airport's gift shop, they found a feature story in the *National Enquirer* tabloid about 'Michael's new, adopted family'. Along with the article were photographs of Michael with Jordie at Disneyworld. 'Oh, no, don't believe that stuff,' Michael told his friends, even though the article was obviously true. 'The stuff they wrote about me is all lies.'

Unbeknownst to Michael, Evan Chandler had also seen the article. He worried that such publicity might set Jordie up as a target for kidnappers and, in his opinion, the situation between his son and a man he had never met — Michael Jackson — was out of control. Evan had a tense telephone conversation with June about the situation; he also telephoned Dave Schwartz to tell him how he felt about the article, which resulted in a loud argument between the two men.

Though Dave had been on his estranged wife's side, his position changed after the article came out, and his friends began calling to express sympathy that he had lost his family to Michael Jackson. He demanded that June break off her friendship with Michael. She refused, saying that Michael had been kind to her and the children and that for him to try to interfere at this point was 'just plain selfish'.

Afterwards June told Michael Jackson about the many emotional and argumentative conversations relating to him and Jordie which had taken place in just a few hours. Concerned, Michael felt that what had transpired was typical of the behaviour of adults. 'See, grown-ups don't trust each other, and that's the real problem here,' he told June. 'It's such a shame that this kind of thing happens, isn't it?'

*

During the first weekend of June 1993, Jordie Chandler was entertaining Michael Jackson at his home when his father, Evan, stopped by for a surprise visit. Michael and Jordie were playing in Jordie's bedroom when Evan entered the room. Shy about meeting Evan, as he is about meeting most people for the first time, Michael ducked into a corner.

Evan walked around the room with his mouth agape, unaware that Michael was in the shadows. 'My God, look at all this stuff, Jordie,' Evan said, astonished by the sight of so many thousands of dollars' worth of compact discs, videos, Nintendo cartridges and toys, many of them still in boxes. 'Where'd you get all of this stuff from?' he asked.

Just as Evan asked the question he caught a glimpse of movement in the corner. It was Michael. Evan's first impression of Michael was that he was an odd person. Michael had on full makeup, including red lipstick and black eye-liner. He had on his black hat; a band-aid on his nose. He was chewing gum. 'Hello, Mr Chandler,' he said, his voice a delicate whisper. Michael extended his hand. When Evan shook it, as he later remembered, it was a weak, limp handshake.

At that moment, Evan's five-year-old son, Nikki, from his second marriage, ran into the room. 'Wow. Michael Jackson,' exclaimed the youngster. Within moments, Nikki was on the floor with Michael playing with action figures and wrestling with him, as Evan and Jordie looked on. Later, all four went into the backyard to play with slingshots. Maddeningly, Michael kept touching his nose, every few minutes. No one knew why; no one asked. By the time he left the house, Evan was completely taken with Michael. He had been kind and considerate to the children, funny and 'completely normal acting', as Evan later recalled it.

A few days later, Michael felt comfortable enough with Evan to invite him to the hide-out. He suggested that Evan bring Nikki. When father and son arrived, they found Jordie and Michael waiting for them. Michael then presented Nikki with an assortment of toys, and Evan with a Cartier time-piece. Later, as the boys played, Michael told Evan that he hoped to be able to take Jordie with him on the second leg of his Dangerous tour, which would begin on 24 August 1993 at the National Stadium in Thailand, Bangkok. He felt that Jordie might obtain a unique education on the road with him in countries such as Taiwan, Japan, Russia, Israel and Turkey and Mexico. Michael hoped that Evan would think of his offer as a rare opportunity for Jordie, and perhaps discuss the matter with June.

Evan would later recall again feeling uneasy about Michael. He had to ask the question: 'Michael, what exactly is the nature of your relationship with Jordie?'

'Well, I don't know what to say,' Michael responded, 'except that it's . . . it's . . .' He seemed to search for the right word. 'It's cosmic,' he finally said.

Evan got to the point. 'Look, are you having sex with my son?' he asked. One would think such a question would be asked by Evan while his hands were wrapped around Michael's throat, but Evan recalled his demeanour as having been calm and collected.

Michael was shocked. He couldn't believe Evan would ask him such a question, and in such a straightforward a way. 'My God, I can't believe you would ask me that,' he said.

The two men stared at each other for a few moments, apparently not knowing what to say. Evan decided not to push the issue. Instead, he asked, 'What if you don't want to be friends with my son in the future? He'll be so hurt.'

'Not want to be friends with Jordie?' Michael asked 'But that'll never happen. No one is more loyal than me. I will always be Jordie's friend.'

An awkward silence hung between the two men. Finally, Evan suggested that he and Michael join the youngsters in Michael's arcade.

At this point, as Evan Chandler later recalled it, he truly did not know whether to approve of Michael or not. He vacillated between feeling exhilaration and uneasiness. After all, Michael didn't really deny that anything inappropriate was going on, nor did he admit it.

In a few days' time, Evan was again awe-struck by Michael's presence in Jordie's life, enough to suggest that Michael even spend more time with him. The suggestion came when Michael showed up at Nikki's birthday party on 22 May 1993, astonishing all of the guests who couldn't fathom that *the* Michael Jackson was playing with their children at a friend's birthday party. 'Who wouldn't want his kid to be Michael Jackson's pal,' Evan said at the time. He even suggested that Michael build a new wing on to the home so that he wouldn't have to make the trek from Santa Barbara to Los Angeles just to visit Jordie. 'You can just stay here,' he offered, 'but you'd be more comfortable building an addition to the house, I think.'

Michael took the offer seriously enough to have his representatives check with the zoning division of the county in which Evan lived to determine if it would be possible to build such an addition to the house.

That night, Michael stayed at Evan's home, sleeping in the same room with Jordie and Nikki. After the two boys watched a video of *Peter Pan* with Michael, Evan bid them good night and closed the bedroom door. The last thing he saw was Michael Jackson tucked into a roll-out bed, and his two sons in bunk beds – Jordie in the bottom bed and Nikki in the top. Those would remain the sleeping arrangements at Evan's home for the next two nights.

What a strange scene: Michael Jackson, arguably the wealthiest and most accomplished entertainer in show business curled up in an uncomfortable, roll-out bed while sleeping in a room with two youngsters.

Didn't he have any responsibilities? It was as if the person in Jordie's room had no plans for the future, certainly no recording dates or concert commitments.

Wasn't he known to rub shoulders with movies stars, magnates and members of royal families such as Diana, Princess of Wales? Why did he never mention them? Where was his family? Why did he never speak about them? He never once mentioned his brothers, or the names of any of his siblings.

And wasn't he supposed to be wealthy? According to *Forbes*, he had earned fifty-five million dollars the year before. Why then did he dress only in old jeans and T-shirts? Why did he wear the same black loafers every day? When, on occasion, he did refer to his wealth, it seemed incongruous. For instance, Evan once watched Michael and Jordie shoot water pistols at tomatoes lined up on a ledge. Michael told the youngster, 'I'm thinking about buying my own private jet.' Jordie shrugged. Then, Michael said, 'You know what? I'll bet if I stand back three more feet I can still hit that tomato right over there.'

If anyone had told Evan that the person sleeping in his son's bedroom was actually a Michael Jackson impersonator, he would have believed it – that's how little the life of the man on the roll-out bed seemed to have with the genuine-article King of Pop.

Over the next couple of days, Evan and Michael forged ahead with their own friendship. They discussed family matters as well as Jordie and Nikki's education. Michael mentioned that Jordie had often described Evan as a terrific father, and Michael noted his own admiration of Evan's dedication to his children. They also discussed Dave Schwartz, and his displeasure over the *National Enquirer*'s assertion that Michael had 'stolen' his family. Evan said he had to agree with Dave that the story was 'in bad form'. Michael explained that he had learned to live with sensational articles about himself and his friends, and he hoped Evan would not hold this one against him. Evan said he liked Michael very much and would happily allow him to continue to be friendly with Jordie and Nikki.

The two men shook hands and agreed to keep open the lines of communication between them.

In days to come, however, Evan had more time to think about Michael's analysis of his relationship with Jordie as being 'cosmic' and the fact that he had been so curiously reticent to characterize their relationship in specific terms. Michael hadn't been responsive to the direct, albeit disconcerting, question of whether or not he was having sex with Jordie. Rather, Michael just seemed embarrassed by it. Evan, as he would later tell it, began to experience a sinking feeling in the pit of his stomach. Small incidents over the next few days made a bigger impact on him.

For instance, there was the evening the family was together watching television with Michael when Michael seemed unable to take his eyes off Jordie. When Evan asked Michael if something was wrong, Michael said, 'No, I'm just looking at things.' However, when Jordie rose to go into the kitchen to fetch a snack, Michael followed. When Jordie went outside to speak to a visiting friend, Michael followed. Finally, when Jordie got up to go to the bathroom and Michael also rose, Jordie said, 'Michael, I'm just going to the bathroom. You can stay here.' Embarrassed, Michael laughed and said, 'Oh, okay. That's fine.'

Evan understood that teenagers have all manner of relationships with non-family members and that those with peers can sometimes have a greater influence on their values and behaviour. However, was

Michael a peer? Not really. Also, his influence on Jordie was troubling because there were so many unanswered questions about it. Why did Michael and Jordie have so many inside jokes between them, as if sharing their own language? Why were they always whispering to one another? Why would they speak softly to one another and then, as soon as they would hear one of Jordie's parents enter the room, clam up? Why was Jordie beginning to dress like Michael, with black hats and mirrored sunglasses? Most importantly, why were they sleeping in the same room?

Over the next few weeks, Evan continued to press Michael about the nature of his relationship with Jordie, so much so that Michael began to distance himself from Evan rather than have to undergo any further interrogation. Michael seemed to not understand why Evan was confused about what was going on between him and Jordie. Hadn't he already explained that he was Jordie's true, loyal friend? Didn't they have an agreement to forge ahead with Michael as an accepted part of the family? Again, as Michael had earlier told June, Evan either trusted him or he didn't. The problem was that Michael was unprepared for what might occur if Evan did not trust him. Would he abandon his friendship with Jordie because the boy's father did not trust him? No.

When Michael was unhappy with a person, that person was usually ousted from his world. Many important people had shown up in his life and then been banished from it over the years. Some of them, like John Branca, had considered themselves long-time friends of Michael's, but such status did not save them from being terminated. If Michael could let go of John after more than ten years, where then did Evan Chandler stand after just a few weeks? Michael stopped returning Evan's telephone calls when Evan became a problem in his life. If he could have fired him, or had someone else do the job, he would have done it.

However, Michael had seriously underestimated Evan. He wasn't an employee who could be easily dismissed. Rather, he was the father of the boy upon whom Michael had fixated, for whatever reason. He wasn't about to allow Michael to cut him out of his life, and out of his friendship with Jordie, especially since he wasn't sure he even trusted him. There was something not right about Michael's friendship with Jordie, he decided, and he was going to set it straight if, for no other reason, than to prove to Michael Jackson that he couldn't get away with it.

❦

Dirty Minds

In June 1993, Jordie Chandler was scheduled to graduate from junior high school's seventh grade. For months, he had anticipated the students' party that would commemorate the milestone for them. Though Jordie had always been a popular student and had many friends, lately he seemed not to be in communication with many of them. He had become so antisocial since meeting Michael Jackson, his parents were concerned. However, the fact that he was still enthusiastic about going to the end-of-the-year dance did suggest to Evan and June that their son was still a normal teenager.

However, when Jordie walked into his mother's bedroom to announce that he had decided not to attend the school function and wanted, instead, to spend the evening with Michael Jackson, she was worried. He had more fun with Michael than he did with his school chums, he told June, and if he could have it his way he would just as soon be with Michael. June, according to her later recollection, tried to convince Jordie that he should not abandon friends his own age for Michael. It was possible, she told him, to cultivate relationships with his school friends as well as with Michael. 'You don't have to choose one over the other,' she said. However, Jordie didn't see it that way; as far as he was concerned, his fellow students didn't understand him the way Michael did and, worse, he said, they were unkind to others because they had been 'conditioned' to hate, just like adults. June was at a loss. Hearing her son parrot Michael's philosophy was disconcerting. 'You'd better talk to your dad about it,' she suggested.

Evan Chandler's position about Jordie's decision was absolute. 'Over my dead body,' he told him, angrily. 'You can not spend all of your time with Michael Jackson. I won't allow it. Enough is enough.'

'Well, you can't stop me,' Jordie said, defiantly. 'I'll do what I want to do.'

Evan, as he would later recall it, had begun to think that Michael was gay and that perhaps Jordie might be, as well. There was no other explanation, he thought, to such obsession. Whatever was going on, though, he felt that he needed to reconnect with his son. If the two could better communicate, he might then be able to figure out the problem. 'I'm sick about all of this,' he told Jordie. 'We love you so much. Why have you turned your back on us? You can have Michael in your life,' he concluded, 'but you can also have us, and everyone else.'

When Evan went to embrace his son, Jordie was stiff and unaffectionate. Jordie didn't want to hear what Evan had to say and didn't want to engage with him on any level. Evan would later say that he felt then that he was losing his son to another man, and that he became more determined than ever to stop that from happening. He had no recourse but to lay down the law: 'You're going to that damn dance, Jordie. You are not spending the night with Michael Jackson.'

'No, I'm not,' said the youngster. 'You never liked Michael,' he said, as he stormed off. 'You *acted* like you did. Michael told me that's what was going on, and he was right.'

In the end, Jordie did not attend the school dance. He spent the night with Michael.

Though Michael Jackson may not have intended to do so, his presence in Jordie's life had caused a terrible turmoil for the youngster, as well as for his parents, Evan and June, and even his stepfather, Dave Schwartz. The emergence of Michael into their lives had thrown everything into wild disarray, pitting the three adults against one another, and then Jordie against all of them, resulting in distrust and frustration for all. Without effective communication, it was inevitable that there would continue to be serious problems at home for Jordie.

Was Michael aware of his part in what was happening to Jordie's family? One of his advisers recalls a conversation with him about Jordie, which took place while the two were sitting in a golf cart on the Neverland acreage, star-gazing. 'You know, maybe you should just leave Jordie alone,' suggested Michael's adviser.

'Nope,' Michael said succinctly, recalled his adviser.

'Why?'

'What can I say?' Michael asked. His expression was serene as he stared into the infinite space.

'But look at all of the chaos your friendship with him is causing Jordie,' observed the adviser. 'Don't you think you should back off?' the adviser asked, still pushing.

Michael became angry; he could go from calm to fury in seconds. 'Look, I'm not the one causing problems,' he said. 'It's Jordie's parents. They can't accept that my relationship with him is innocent. They have dirty minds. There is nothing sexual going on. Why can't people just get that?'

'But, Mike . . .'

Michael rose and walked away before the conversation could be finished.

If what those who know him best say is true, that Michael is a child at heart, there's definitely a flip side to such immaturity: he acts like a spoiled little kid when he can't have his way. He is often unable to see any point of view other than his own.

On 7 July 1993 Evan Chandler struck a damaging blow to Michael's friendship with Jordie and also, as it would happen, to his own relationship with his ex-wife, June, when he filed for a modification of her custody agreement. The documents petitioned the courts to forbid Jordie from going anywhere near Michael, and from visiting him at any of his homes, or anywhere else. Evan requested that Jordie receive psychiatric help to determine the full extent of Michael's influence on him. He also accused June of 'nurturing' the relationship between Jordie and Michael, which he viewed as unhealthy, 'because, according to what I know, she [June] receives expensive gifts, cash and vacations from Jackson'.

In the affidavit, Evan declared that he had discovered that Michael 'routinely spent the night with my son and they slept in the same bed. I then asked him directly if he was having sex with my son. Jackson refused to give me a straight answer. He rather told me that he would continue sleeping with my son and that he thought it was "cosmic" and that he and Jordie were made to be together.'

Michael was hurt and, of course, angry. He was also still unwilling to consider the option of sacrificing his own wants and needs in order to allow Jordie some space to reconnect with his parents. Rather, he viewed the adults in Jordie's life as validation of his personal philosophy that grown-ups cannot be trusted, are certain to act in irrational ways and can be counted on to sink to the lowest, most base behaviour. If Evan had Jordie's best interest at heart, Michael reasoned, surely he would allow such a loving friendship to continue without questioning it and assuming the worst about it. Plus, the heart wants what it wants – and Michael Jackson wanted to be with Jordie Chandler.

The Secret Tape Recording

Now that Evan Chandler had filed such damaging court papers against June, there was no way she could trust him. June's estranged husband, Dave, agreed with her that Evan was a threat. Would he take his claims against June further by claiming that she had been an unfit parent by allowing Jordie's relationship with Michael to continue? Would he try to obtain complete custody of Jordie?

On 2 July 1993, Evan and Dave met at Rent-A-Wreck to discuss what was going on in the family. During the meeting, Evan made it clear that he wanted Michael's reign over Jordie's life to come to an end, and that he was about to start taking action to see to it that it happened. He asked for Dave's assistance. However, Dave made it clear that he did not agree with Evan and did not wish to interfere with Jordie's relationship with Michael. June had been monitoring the situation, he said, and he wasn't going to second-guess her. If he did so, he argued, he would risk a deeper wedge in his marriage to her, and he would probably alienate Jordie, as well.

Over the next week, Evan continued to be a problem. Michael, June and Jordie did not trust him and wanted as little to do with him as possible. They had not returned his telephone calls; it had been almost a month since Evan spoke to Jordie. Now, Evan was pushing for a meeting with the three of them. He knew that June and Jordie intended to accompany Michael on his upcoming tour, and that they would be gone for five months. He didn't want them to go, felt it was unsafe for Jordie. He called June and left a message on her answering machine during which he insisted that she, Jordie and Michael meet with him on 9 July.

Dave called Evan to ask him what it was he hoped to accomplish by demanding such a meeting. 'You're not going to get anywhere that way,' he told him.

'Listen, you dumb ass,' Evan told him. 'I'm worried about my kid. I want him with me, now. I don't know what's going on with you people and Michael Jackson, but I don't like it.'

The two men then argued for about an hour, hurling insults at one another.

Perhaps in order to learn what Evan had in mind, Dave decided to secretly tape-record a telephone conversation with him. An hour after their argument, he called Evan, again.

During that 8 July conversation, transcripts of which were later filed with the Los Angeles County Court House, Evan said that he was angry because Michael had stopped telephoning him and no longer wanted a friendly relationship with him. 'There was no reason why he had to stop calling me,' Evan told Dave. He added that he'd recently had a long conversation with Michael and told him 'exactly what I want out of the relationship with him.' (He didn't say during the conversation with Dave, however, what it was he wanted from Michael.) He also maintained that, in his view, Michael was spending too much time with Jordie, and that something was 'not right about it'. He was furious with June, he said, who had told him to 'fuck' himself, when he tried to discuss Michael with her. When pressed, Evan said that he believed Michael Jackson had 'broken up the family' and that Jordie had been 'seduced by this guy's money and power'. He didn't say, during the conversation, that he suspected Michael might also be having sex with Jordie. However, he did allow that he had hired an attorney to start looking into the matter, his friend, Barry Rothman.

As it happened, Barry had been in Evan's dental chair one day for work when Evan began to confide in him about certain changes in Jordie's personality. He became so emotional when recounting recent events, he began to cry. There was a wall between him and his son, he told the attorney, and he simply didn't know how to scale it, or tear it down. He was losing Jordie, he said. As the two discussed the matter, Barry recalls Evan saying that he had begun to believe that Michael and Jordie's relationship may have become sexual. If that was the case, Barry Rothman suggested, perhaps Evan might need an attorney. They agreed to trade services, dental for legal.

'I picked the nastiest son of a bitch I could find,' Evan told Dave, speaking of Barry Rothman who had, in the past represented Little Richard, the Who, the Rolling Stones and Ozzy Osbourne. 'All he wants to do is get this out in the public as fast as he can, as big as he can, and humiliate as many people as he can,' Evan continued. 'He's nasty, he's mean, he's smart, and he's hungry for publicity. Everything's going according to a certain plan that isn't just mine. Once I make that phone call, this guy [Barry Rothman] is going to destroy everybody in sight in any devious, nasty, cruel way that he can do it. I've given him full authority to do that.

'Jackson is an evil guy,' Evan continued, sounding fired up. 'He is worse than that, and I have the evidence to prove it. If I go through with this, I win big-time. There's no way I lose. I will get everything I want, and they will be destroyed forever. June will lose [custody of the son] and Michael's career will be over.'

Evan and Dave then discussed June's plans to take Jordie on Michael's Dangerous tour in the fall. 'Well, they may think so,' Evan said, 'but they're not going anywhere.'

Clearly baiting him for more information, Dave asked Evan how his plan might help Jordie. Evan's response was disconcerting. 'That's irrelevant to me,' he said. 'The bottom line is, yes, his mother is harming him, and Michael is harming him. I can prove that, and I will prove that. It cost me tens of thousands of dollars to get the information I got, and you know I don't have that kind of money. I'm willing to go down financially. It will be a massacre if I don't get what I want. It's going to be bigger than all of us put together.

'I believe Jordie is already irreparably harmed,' Evan continued. 'The whole thing is going to crash down on everybody and destroy everybody in sight. This man is going to be humiliated beyond belief,' Evan concluded. 'You will not believe what's going to happen to him. Beyond his worst nightmares. He will not sell one more record. The facts are so overwhelming, everyone will be destroyed in the process.'

Did Evan Chandler know he was being tape-recorded? Did he also suspect the recording might one day be played for Michael Jackson? Was he being melodramatic and intimidating just for the sake of scaring Michael off? Or, did he really plan to ruin him? Only he knows what was in his head at this time . . . and he hasn't said.

The day after Evan Chandler's inflammatory comments about Michael Jackson were tape-recorded by Dave Schwartz, Evan hoped to have the family conference he had long sought to discuss Jordie. However, no one showed up at the meeting. Now, he was more infuriated than ever. Finally, he got June on the telephone. According to June's former attorney, Michael Freeman, Evan reiterated his concerns that something improper might be going on between Jordie and Michael. June said that Evan was 'full of baloney'. Moreover, she told him that she and Jordie still intended to go on tour with Michael, and that Evan would 'just have to get used to the idea'.

Michael Freeman recalled, 'Evan then said that he was going to go to the media. Right away, we thought, Why would he do that? If he really believed Jordie was being abused, why would he not go to the police instead of the press?'

That same day, June and Dave decided to meet with Michael to tell him there might be trouble ahead where Evan was concerned. However, Michael didn't take them seriously. 'Oh, this kind of stuff happens to me all the time,' he told them. 'People are always trying to get money out of me. I'll have my people work it out. Don't worry about it.' However, when they played Michael the tape Dave had made of his conversation with Evan, Michael became anxious. 'He sounded so angry,' Michael told me of Evan Chandler in an interview months later. 'I knew then and there that it was extortion. He said it right on the tape. So what I did then,' Michael told me, 'was turn it over to Bert [Fields] and [private investigator] Anthony [Pellicano] and I decided to try to forget about it.'

'Were you angry?' I asked Michael.

'No,' Michael told me. 'I knew I didn't do anything wrong, so why would I be angry?'

'Because you believed you hadn't done anything wrong, yet you were being accused of a horrible crime?' I offered.

'I don't think like that,' Michael said, bluntly. 'I don't live in fear.'

In retrospect, it seems that Michael may have been feigning nonchalance with me, perhaps because I was in my reporter's role and he was saying what he felt was appropriate for an interview. Later, one of his closest advisers told me that he truly was angry when he heard the tape of Evan. 'He said, "After I've been good to him and his family, he says these terrible things about me? After I took his family around the world, after I bought them presents, after I let them into my life, allowed them into my home? Tell him Michael Jackson said he can go to hell."' That was his reaction.

'I asked him if it was true, or not. Was something going on with him and Jordie? "Of course not," he said. "It's absolutely ludicrous, and it's not even the point. Tell Evan that Michael Jackson said go to hell. *That's* the point."'

On 9 July 1993, June and Dave Schwartz met with Michael Jackson's investigator, Anthony Pellicano, in his Sunset Boulevard office to play for them the tape Dave had made of his conversation with Evan Chandler.

A tough, no-nonsense kind of personality, Anthony could be intimidating, always getting his way and representing his clients fiercely. Interestingly, he got his start in 1977 by finding the bones of Elizabeth Taylor's third husband, Mike Todd, under a pile of leaves. Todd's corpse had been stolen from an Illinois cemetery by mobsters looking for a ten-carat diamond ring, a gift from Elizabeth which they thought had been buried with the deceased.

Today, Anthony's career is in tatters. In November 2002, he was arrested following a probe into allegations that he had hired a man to threaten a *Los Angeles Times* reporter researching a story about a Mafia extortion plot targeting actor Steven Seagal.

Michael's attorney, Bertram (Bert) Fields, was also present. Fields is, today, still one of the most daunting and influential attorneys in show business with a client list that has included some of the biggest names in show business from The Beatles to Tom Cruise to John Travolta. He's never lost a trial in which he was lead attorney. He was determined to represent Michael in as aggressive a manner as possible, especially after he heard the audio tape June and

Dave brought with them. 'I was concerned,' Bert recalled. 'It sounded bad. It sounded like extortion.'

The next day, Anthony Pellicano arranged a meeting with Jordie Chandler at Michael's hide-out in Los Angeles. He asked Michael, June and Dave to leave the room so that he and Jordie could be alone. His intention was to interrogate the youngster about his relationship with the pop star. 'I decided to be straight with the kid,' Anthony would later recall. 'This was serious business. There was no time to be delicate. I asked him, have you ever seen Michael Jackson naked? Has he ever seen you naked? Have you ever done anything sexual with him? The kid looked me straight in the eye and said, "No. No. No." I believed him.' Anthony spoke to Jordie for more than an hour and, he says, was convinced that nothing inappropriate had ever occurred between him and Michael.

After that meeting, Bert Fields (working on behalf of June Chandler as well as Michael) and Barry Rothman (Evan's attorney) negotiated an agreement whereby Evan would have custody of Jordie for a week. Reluctantly, June agreed to the terms, not wanting to keep the boy from his father. Anthony Pellicano and Bert Fields gave personal guarantees that Jordie would be delivered as promised. Barry Rothman then gave his word that Evan would return the boy on schedule.

At the appointed time and place, Evan waited for his son to show up, but he never did. Instead, June decided to take Jordie and his sister, Lily, to Neverland to celebrate Lily's birthday with Michael Jackson.

While in the limousine on the way from Los Angeles to Santa Barbara, Michael and company stopped at the beach house of financier Michael Milken, the so-called junk bond king who had just been released from prison after serving a couple of years for securities fraud. He was a friend of Michael's and the two had been in discussions to set up an educational cable TV network for children.

While at Michael Milken's, Michael Jackson telephoned Anthony Pellicano to tell him of the change in plans: they had decided not to allow Evan to have Jordie for the week. This decision put both Anthony and Bert Fields in difficult positions; they had given their word, and now they appeared to be liars. Anthony was furious; he let Michael have it. 'You're being ridiculous,' he recalled telling him,

'Now you get that kid back here, and you do it right now, Michael. You and Jordie apparently share a brain. So, *use it*. Do you hear what I'm saying?'

'Listen, you don't tell me what to do,' Michael shot back. 'I tell *you* what to do, Anthony. Not the other way around. Do *you* hear what *I'm* saying?'

As Michael's side of the telephone conversation became more heated, June became uncomfortable.

Michael continued. 'Evan gets to see Jordie when I . . .' He corrected himself. 'Evan gets to see Jordie when *we* say so, not when he says so. And we don't say so. So that's the end of that. Got it?' Michael slammed down the telephone. He clenched his fists and made an angry face, so furious he seemed as if he was about to explode. 'Why does he treat me like I'm an idiot?' he asked no one in particular. 'I'm not an idiot. I'm Michael Jackson. *I'm Michael Jackson*.' He kicked a wall. 'It's offensive and insulting, damn it!'

June, Jordie and Lily looked at one another with surprised expressions. 'Gosh, Mommy, Michael's so mad,' Lily said, surprised.

After witnessing Michael's unexpected tantrum, June no longer wanted to go to Neverland with him, saying she wasn't in the mood. 'Whatever,' Michael told her, annoyed. 'Do what you want to do.'

June, Jordie and Lily called a cab and went back to Los Angeles.

Meanwhile, Michael proceeded to Santa Barbara alone. When he finally got to the ranch, he was greeted by his housekeeper, Adrian McManus. 'Where are the guests of honour?' she asked. 'Is there still going to be a party?'

'There's not going to be a party,' Michael said. 'So, forget it. Throw the food away. Just throw it all away,' he said. 'And tear down those decorations, too,' he added, motioning to colourful streamers hanging from the doorway.

Michael then stormed off to his bedroom and slammed the door.

Michael in October 1978 as the scarecrow in *The Wiz*, a huge box-office disaster.
(J. Randy Taraborrelli Collection)

Jermaine Jackson with author J. Randy Taraborrelli, 1980. Jackson was ambivalent about his decision to stay with Motown when his brothers signed with CBS Records. He told Taraborrelli, 'I don't feel I left them. I feel they left me . . . here at Motown.'
(Mike Jones)

In July 1980, Joe Jackson celebrated his fifty-first birthday. Left to right: Joe's mother, Chrystal; Joe; Gina Sprague, nineteen; Marlon, twenty-three; Janet, fourteen; and Randy, seventeen. Michael did not show up. Katherine, who suspected that Gina and Joe were having an affair, was seated with LaToya at a nearby table when this picture was taken. (J. Randy Taraborrelli Collection)

By the time this photo was taken, 7 February 1984, Michael Jackson was sitting on top of the world, thanks to his *Thriller* album. 'You get one frame,' Michael told photographer David McGough, who had waited five hours to take this picture. 'That's it. If I close my eyes, too bad.' McGough took his 'one frame', and this was the result. Michael is wearing a hat because his scalp was burned less than two weeks earlier while taping an ad for Pepsi. (David McGough/DMI)

On 7 February 1984, Michael was inducted into the *Guinness Book of World Records* for recording the most successful album in music industry history, *Thriller*. Right, Michael with his manager, Frank Dileo. (David McGough/DMI)

Michael Jackson set a new music industry record on 28 February 1984, when he walked off with an unprecedented eight Grammy Awards, the most won by an artist in one year. Michael gives the thumbs up to photographers as he drops off his date, Brooke Shields, at her Los Angeles hotel following the awards after-party. (John Paschal/DMI)

On 30 November 1983, a press conference was held at Tavern on the Green in New York to announce that the Jackson brothers would be reuniting for a tour. Left to right: Marlon, twenty-six; Michael's friend, Emmanuel Lewis, twelve; Michael, twenty-five; Randy; twenty-one; Tito, thirty; Jackie, thirty-two; and Jermaine, twenty-nine. Promoter, Don King, with the 'interesting' hair-do, is posed flashing the peace sign. (David McGough/DMI)

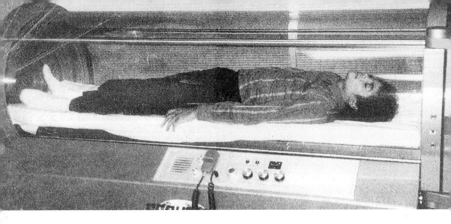

Michael's bizarre hyperbaric chamber hoax made worldwide headline news. To this day, many people believe that Michael sleeps in such a contraption, when actually the whole thing was a publicity stunt concocted by Michael. (Transworld Feature, Synd.)

Twenty-nine year-old Michael on stage in March 1988 during the *Bad* tour. (David McGough/DMI)

Michael receives the BMI Michael Jackson Award on 8 May 1990, in Beverly Hills. (Kevin Winter/DMI)

Top left Michael and his friend Jordie Chandler (far right) and Jordie's mother, Lily, in 1993 at the World Music Awards in Monaco. It was during this trip, Jordie alleged, that the sexual misconduct began between him and Michael. (Rex)

Top right On 22 December 1993, Michael gave a speech from his Neverland ranch about the allegations. 'I ask all of you to wait and hear the truth before you condemn me,' he said, holding back tears. 'Don't treat me like a criminal.' (Corbis)

Left Was he telling the truth? Though Michael denied that anything sexual happened between him and Jordie, pictured here in 1993, he ended the ordeal with a huge cash settlement to the youngster and his family. 'I had to go on with my life,' Michael explained to the author of this book. 'Too many people had already been hurt.' (Rex)

On 26 May 1994, after the Jordie Chandler scandal, Michael went on to marry Lisa Marie Presley. At the time, most observers viewed the union as a public relations manoeuvre. However, as it happens, the truth is stranger than fiction: he and Lisa Marie had a strong sexual chemistry; it was the first time Michael had ever felt so intensely about another person. (Corbis)

On 13 November 1996, Michael married Debbie Rowe. And it was Debbie who gave Michael his longed-for child. (Corbis)

Michael with his daughter, Paris (left), and son, Prince Michael I, on a public outing, in 2002. He covers their faces, he says, in order to avoid kidnapping attempts. (Corbis)

Above left This is the photo that caused a huge sensation in November 2002, when Michael dangled his nine-month-old son, Prince Michael II from a balcony in Germany. He apologized for it, but will he ever be able to live it down? (Corbis)

Above right When Michael testified in a lawsuit against him in 2003, most people were a little startled by his odd appearance, as well as his eccentric behaviour in court. Michael was unhappy with this photograph when it was published around the world, feeling it did not do him justice. (Corbis)

'How can I get past the pain?' Michael recently asked. 'I'm so tired of being controlled by fear.' For him, the first step has been coming to terms with his father, Joseph. It's not been easy, but he's working on forgiveness. His relationship with Joseph is much improved. (Corbis)

Say what you will about him, Michael Jackson remains one of the greatest entertainers of our time. He truly comes to life once on stage, performing before an audience. (Corbis)

Michael Feels Betrayed

On the way back to Los Angeles, June Schwartz had time to think about the way matters had evolved with her son and Michael Jackson. When she got home, she called Evan. She'd had a change of heart, she said. Perhaps when she saw Michael lose it the way he had, she realized that *someone* needed to put things into perspective. Though Jordie didn't want to go, she now felt it important that he visit with his father for the week.

In young Jordie's world these days, no one ever seemed to do anything he didn't want to do. Therefore, he was sullen and disagreeable when he finally got to Evan's house. He said he missed Michael.

Evan had heard enough about Michael Jackson in recent months. As soon as he had his son in his custody, he instructed his attorney to draw up papers that stipulated that June would not be permitted to take Jordie out of Los Angeles county, meaning she would not be able to see Michael at Neverland (in Santa Barbara county), and most certainly not on tour.

Surprisingly, when she got the news the next day, June wasn't angry. She didn't even fight the stipulation, mostly because she no longer knew what to think about Michael. She needed time to figure it all out, especially after she and her attorney had a meeting with two LAPD officers who claimed that they'd recently discovered a youngster who'd been molested by Michael (even though they refused to identify him). Recalled June's lawyer, Michael Freeman, 'With serious expressions on their faces, they said, "We're convinced Michael Jackson molested this boy because he fits the classic profile of a paedophile, perfectly." June started getting scared. She was scared for her son.'

June decided to telephone Michael. Perhaps they could meet and discuss the matter; after all, they had been friends. When she saw him face to face, she would be able to look into his eyes, she believed, and then know the truth. She finally got Michael on the phone.

'I'm sorry, June,' he said, 'but things are so out of hand now that my lawyer has told me that I can't speak to you, or even see you.'

'But, Michael . . .'

'Evan is the one who started this mess, not me,' Michael said, his tone surprisingly cold and deliberate. 'Evan ruined our beautiful friendship, not me. I'll have Bert call you and answer any further questions. Goodbye, June. I'm sorry.'

June couldn't believe the way Michael had talked to her. Now, she didn't know what to think of him. Because she still leaned towards his innocence, perhaps he would have been better advised to have been less dismissive, if only to keep her as an ally. However, he was so cold to her, he left her with no choice. She decided she had to agree with her ex-husband that Jordie not be permitted to visit Michael, at least for the time being, and not accompany him on his tour, either. She even agreed to allow Evan to keep custody of Jordie 'for a while'.

Michael learned of June's about-face from one of his staff members during a meeting in his bedroom at Neverland. Having just finished with a costume-fitting, he hadn't changed out of what he called his 'uniform': a glittery, red military outfit trimmed across the shoulders with jet-bead embroidery. He was seated on his bed.

'There had been a sadness about Michael in recent days, but after he learned of June's decision, it was more acute than usual,' recalled the employee. 'After all, she was handing Jordie over to Evan, which would not bode well for Michael's friendship with him.'

After discussing the matter with his adviser for a few minutes, Michael fell back onto the bed heavily and began to cry. 'Why do people hurt the ones they say they love?' he asked.

'It's going to be okay,' said the staff member, now seated on the bed next to him. 'Don't cry, Mike.'

Then, typical of his mood swings, especially lately, Michael went from zero to ten in anger within seconds. 'She betrayed me,' he said, bolting upright, his eyes ablaze. 'I can't believe June buckled like that, after all I did for her and her kids. Now I'll never get to see Jordie. I didn't even do anything wrong,' he insisted. Then, ashen-faced and his dark eyes raging, Michael repeated: 'I didn't do anything wrong. *I didn't.*'

The next day, Anthony Pellicano received a telephone call from

Evan Chandler. He wanted to meet with Michael, 'man to man', he said.

Anthony passed the message on to Michael. 'No way,' Michael said, according to Anthony's memory. 'I'm not meeting with the guy and giving him more ammunition to use against me. His heart is filled with hatred, Anthony, and you know it's the truth. Tell him I said no way.'

'But it might be a good idea,' Anthony suggested. 'Maybe we can work this thing out.'

Michael was adamant that he would not meet with Evan. He said that he had been thinking it over, and the truth had hit him as if an epiphany. 'Evan's pissed off at me because I have the kind of relationship he *wishes* he had with Jordie,' Michael said. 'That's what's really going on here. He's completely jealous of me.'

Anthony couldn't disagree; to him, Michael's analysis of the situation sounded plausible.

Jordie's Confession

On 2 August, Evan Chandler extracted a troublesome tooth from his son, Jordie, in his Beverly Hills clinic. During the procedure, he decided to intravenously administer the drug sodium Amytal. Mark Torbiner, a dental anaesthesiologist (who had been the one to introduce Evan to his attorney, Barry Rothman in 1991 when Rothman needed dental work), was present during the surgery. Evan has since confirmed that his son was given the drug, but only as a part of the dental procedure. While under the influence of sodium Amytal, says Evan, Jordie finally began to speak openly about sexual activity he claimed had occurred between him and Michael Jackson.

Sodium Amytal has erroneously been called a 'truth serum'. Actually, most doctors agree that patients are extremely susceptible to suggestion while under the influence of the drug. 'You can't trust it,' said Dr Lewis Strong, a Los Angeles psychiatrist (who does not know Evan or Jordie Chandler). 'I never use it in my practice. I have found it to be unreliable. It's certainly not a truth serum. Sometimes it is used for the treatment of amnesia, but it often provides false memories.'

Why did Evan Chandler use sodium Amytal on his son in order to perform dental work on him?

'It's absolutely a psychiatric drug,' observed Dr Kenneth Gottlieb, a San Francisco psychiatrist who has administered sodium Amytal to amnesia patients. 'I would never want to use a drug that tampers with a person's unconscious unless there was no other drug available,' he added, 'and I would not use it without resuscitating equipment, in case of allergic reaction, and only with an MD anaesthesiologist present.' (Mark Torbiner is a dental anaesthesiologist.)

Dr John Yagiela, the coordinator of the Anaesthesia and Pain Control department of UCLA's school of dentistry, confirmed, 'It's unusual for it to be used for pulling a tooth. It makes no sense when better, safer alternatives are available. It would not be my choice.'

Perhaps Evan felt that he had no choice but to administer the drug to his son in order to get him to finally open up about the true nature of his relationship with Michael Jackson. 'Did Michael ever touch your penis?' Evan asked Jordie. Groggily, Jordie said in a soft voice that, yes, Michael had done it. Evan then grabbed his son and hugged him tightly, as if never wanting to let him go. 'I'm sorry, Jordie,' he said, according to a later recollection. 'I'm so sorry.'

In his heart, Evan would later say, he always knew what was going on between his child and the pop star. He said that he only needed confirmation from Jordie before he could, in good conscience, go up against Michael in such an explosive and life-ruining campaign. It wasn't much to go on, though if, in fact, it was even true that Michael had touched Jordie's penis. However Evan believed there was more to it. He didn't need all of the details, anyway, he said. In the end, he had what he wanted: Michael Jackson's neck in a noose. But the question remained: how much of what Jordie had confessed while under the influence of a psychiatric drug was the truth?

PART TEN

Michael Meets with his Accusers

After obtaining what he believed to be the truth from Jordie, Evan Chandler demanded another meeting with Michael Jackson. Anthony Pellicano managed to arrange it. The show-down between the teenager's protective father and the man he believed had molested his son would take place on 4 August 1993 at the Westwood Marquis Hotel. 'No good can come of it,' Michael predicted, 'but I have to see Jordie, somehow, so let's do it.'

At the appointed hour, Evan walked into the room, trailed by his anxious-looking son. As soon as Jordie saw Michael, he ran to him and embraced him. They kissed each other on the cheeks. 'Oh my God, how I've missed you,' Michael said, visibly choked up. He stroked Jordie's hair. 'How are you? Are you okay? Tell me you're okay.'

'I've missed you, too,' Jordie said. 'I can't believe what's going on, Michael. Yes, I'm okay,' he said, 'but you should know that . . .' The teenager's voice trailed off.

'What?' Michael asked. 'I should know what? Never mind,' he decided, his tone now reassuring. 'We'll work it out, I promise.'

Evan then walked over to Michael and embraced him. 'Nice to see you, Michael,' Evan said. Michael stared at Evan with cold, dark eyes. Under the circumstances, it was an odd greeting by Evan. Later, Anthony Pellicano would say, 'If I believed somebody molested my kid and I got that close to him, I'd be on death row right now.'

They were seated, Anthony next to Michael on one settee, Jordie next to his father on another.

Evan got to the point quickly. 'I believe that Michael has acted inappropriately toward Jordie,' he said. 'In fact, I'm sure of it.'

'What's he talking about, Jordie?' Michael asked, turning to the youngster.

Jordie made eye contact with Michael and nodded his head slightly, as if trying to pass a secret message. Michael looked at him, quizzically.

Evan then reached into his vest pocket, pulled out an envelope and took a document from it. He explained that it was a psychiatric evaluation of Jordie's relationship with Michael. He read from it; the last paragraph encapsulated the analysis: 'The minor is in danger whether the relationship continues or ends. The impact that would be caused in other family members of the minor should also be considered. These circumstances create the possibility that there exists negligence toward the child, even as far as prostitution.'

'What does that mean, exactly?' Michael wanted to know.

'It means that this doctor thinks you had sex with my kid,' Evan said, his temper rising. Michael remained calm, which seemed to infuriate Evan all the more. 'You and Jordie are having sex, aren't you?' he shouted at him. 'Just fucking admit it, Michael. Be a man. Admit it.' By this time, Evan had tears in his eyes. 'How could you do it, Michael?' he asked. 'My God. How could you do it? How could you do this to Jordie?'

'I already told you that I didn't do it,' Michael said, remaining composed. 'That's preposterous. It never happened. I don't even know that doctor.' He turned to Anthony. 'Do we even know that doctor?'

Anthony, now an irate contrast to Michael's demeanour, said, 'Hell no, we don't know that doctor. This meeting is over,' he told Evan. 'Get out of here. Now.'

'Wait,' Evan said. He then read from another document written by the same psychiatrist: ' "A thirty-four-year-old man constantly sleeping with a thirteen-year-old boy when other beds are available constitutes," Evan raised his voice, *"perverse and lewd conduct."* Perverse and lewd conduct, Michael. Do you hear what I'm saying?'

Michael seemed stunned. He looked at Jordie for help, but now the youngster wouldn't make eye contact with him.

'I said, that's it,' Anthony again insisted. 'This is war, now,' he added, using a favourite phrase. 'Who do you think you are, coming in here and accusing Michael Jackson of a crime? Are you crazy? Get the fuck out of here!'

'Wait,' Evan said, again. 'Look, if he's willing to take a lie detector test, then fine,' he added, pointing at Michael. 'If it comes back that he didn't do it, fine. I'll be out of your lives for ever. He can take Jordie on tour with him and I won't have a thing to say about it.'

'That's fucking preposterous,' Anthony shot back. 'Michael will never take a lie detector test. And besides,' he added, 'I was in army intelligence. Do you think I couldn't teach him to pass a lie detector?'

It seemed an odd statement for one of Michael's advisers to make during such an important discussion. For a second, Evan didn't know how to react to it. 'Great,' he finally said. 'And maybe you can also teach Jordie to lie, too.'

Anthony stood up. 'Hear me, and hear me good,' he said, pointing aggressively at Evan. 'Michael Jackson did not have sex with your son, and he will not take a lie detector test.'

'I hear you,' Evan said. 'But I don't understand you. Why not?'

'Because it's an *insult*, that's why,' Anthony said loudly.

All eyes fell on Michael who was now looking straight ahead as if in a trance.

'Then, there's nothing more to say,' Evan concluded. 'This meeting is over.' Evan didn't mention that Jordie had said that he and Michael had been intimate. Perhaps he didn't want to play that hand, yet. 'I'll see you in court, Michael,' he said. Maddeningly, there was still no reaction from Michael.

Jordie stood up and followed his father out of the room. As he walked through the door, according to Anthony Pellicano, the youngster turned to face Michael with a sad expression. Michael stared at Jordie, probably never dreaming that it would be the last time he would ever lay eyes on him.

'Oh, and one more thing,' Evan said, pointing to the singer. 'I'm going to ruin you,' he said. 'You're going down, Michael. You are going *down*.'

Finally, Michael and Anthony were alone. 'Oh, my God,' Michael said after a few moments. He now looked drained and pale, as if in shock. He rose from his chair and gazed out the window. 'Oh, my God,' he said, again, tears now streaming down his face. 'Oh, my God.'

Unsuccessful Negotiations

The 'smoking gun' letter by Beverly Hills psychiatrist Dr Mathis Abrams, which Evan Chandler had produced at the meeting with Michael Jackson, was solicited by Evan's attorney, Barry Rothman. As it happened, Rothman had sought an expert's opinion in order to establish what may have transpired between Michael and his client's son Jordie. During a telephone conversation with Dr Abrams, Rothman explained the evidence he thought he had against Michael, presenting the scenario as a purely hypothetical situation. Though Abrams didn't even meet with Evan, Jordie or Michael, his opinion of what had transpired would be devastating. After the telephone conversation with Barry Rothman Dr Abrams wrote the letter (dated 15 July 1993) in which he observed that, at least based on what the lawyer had described, it sounded as if something sexual had transpired between the parties. He also noted that if the incidents had occurred as explained by the lawyer, he would have no choice but to report the matter to the Los Angeles County Department of Children's Services.

After his father's show-down with Michael, Jordie was more depressed than ever before in his young life. The thought that he might now have to testify against Michael was more than he could bear. Before he went to bed, he drew what looked like suicide art: a stick figure jumping off the roof of a five-storey building, and then landing in a bloody heap on the ground.

The next morning, when Evan went into Jordie's room to say goodbye to him before going to work, he found the chilling drawing on the floor. Jordie was still asleep. Evan wrote on the top of the paper: Don't Let This Happen, underlining each word. He then put the drawing back where he found it. Turning to leave he changed his mind and decided to take the drawing. It would become evidence of Jordie's state of mind.

The next evening Evan and Barry Rothman met with Anthony Pellicano. 'They put their cards on the table,' recalled Anthony. 'Twenty million. That's what they wanted.'

In fact, Evan wanted the total sum of twenty million dollars to be deposited in an interest-bearing account. Five million would then be paid out to Jordie in four instalments over a four-year period. 'Maybe that amount of money will teach Michael Jackson not to abuse any more children,' Evan explained to Anthony. 'It'll pay for Jordie's education, for psychiatric evaluation. Some will be donated for child abuse foundations. I'll be able to retire and spend more time with my son and help him through this time. If not, then fine. We'll have a trial and see how that goes.'

Though Anthony felt sure Michael wouldn't consider paying a single dime to the Chandlers, he was duty bound to pass the offer on to his client.

Evan had already hand-written a letter to his attorney, Barry Rothman (dated 5 August), outlining his intention if Michael decided not to pay the twenty million. In the missive, he explained that one of the reasons he had hoped to avoid a trial was because he realized the devastating impact it would have on Michael's career. 'I believed that Michael was a kind, sensitive, compassionate person who made a mistake in judgement born out of an honest love for Jordie,' he wrote. 'I now know I was wrong.'

Evan then recounted his version of the events that took place at the meeting with Jordie, Michael and Anthony Pellicano. He wrote that Jordie had acknowledged that he [Evan] had evidence that Michael had sexually assaulted him. (Anthony Pellicano, however, says that Jordie never said anything at that meeting about Michael having molested him.) 'Michael responded with a cold, mocking smile that you often see on the face of criminals who proclaim their innocence even in the face of irrefutable proof of their guilt,' Evan wrote. 'It was a chilling sight. He showed no sign of remorse for his actions and he was completely indifferent to Jordie's suffering.'

Evan then opined that if Michael were to see a psychiatrist, it would surely be determined that he is a paedophile. Therefore, Evan wrote, he had no sympathy for Michael whatsoever, and no interest in protecting him from prosecution. In fact, he wrote, he now believed that Michael should be jailed to prevent him from sexually assaulting other minors. He added that he believed that Michael's incarceration would be the inevitable result of any investigation by the District Attorney, and that if Jordie would need to be called as a witness, he would eagerly testify against Michael. Jordie would only have to tell the truth, Evan wrote, perhaps not taking into consideration the emotional ordeal such gut-wrenching testimony might exact on his son.

'I would like you to continue to negotiate with Mr Pellicano,' Evan concluded, 'but if those negotiations are not successful then as your client I am instructing you to file a complaint against Michael Jackson for the sexual assault against my son.' In a postscript, he wrote of the drawing he had found in Jordie's bedroom. 'I thought you should see it,' he wrote. 'I'm very frightened. One way or the other, please get this over with as quickly as possible.' He enclosed a copy of Jordie's drawing.

When Anthony presented Evan's offer to Michael, the reply was swift: 'No way,' he said. 'We have a love that's pure and eternally innocent. I'm not gonna ruin it by paying that man money. No way in hell.'

On 13 August, Anthony offered Evan a counter-offer, with Michael's approval: three film scripts over a three-year-period, each valued at $350,000, in a million-dollar-plus deal that would have attached to it the promise that a major studio would review any script Evan and Jordie may write as a follow up to their Mel Brooks movie. Not only did it sound speculative to Evan and Barry Rothman, it was also a small amount of money considering their original multimillion-dollar demand. 'You guys aren't even in the ball park,' Evan told Anthony. 'Pass.' Then, oddly, Evan asked Anthony if Jordie could take possession of the computer Michael had purchased for him, and which he had set up at his Los Angeles hide-out. Anthony couldn't believe Evan's gall. Michael had never bought that computer for Jordie, he answered quickly (though it seems doubtful Anthony even knew what Evan was talking about) and Jordie would never see it again, 'so forget about it.' Evan stormed out of the office.

The next day, Barry Rothman proposed a counter-offer to Anthony Pellicano: a deal for three screenplays that would amount to about fifteen million dollars. Through Anthony, Michael declined the counter-offer. Then, inexplicably, Anthony came back with another offer so low he didn't even expect Evan to take it: $350,000 for *one* film deal, to be paid directly out of Michael's pocket. He had gone from an offer of three movies down to one . . . not the best of negotiating tactics, one might argue. Of course, Evan turned it down.

He now felt that the discussions were being conducted in bad faith, and that there was little point in continuing them.

With all battles now seemingly lost, the war was about to begin.

Jordie Sees a Psychiatrist

On 16 August 1993, after negotiations broke down between Evan Chandler and Anthony Pellicano, Michael Freeman (June's attorney) alerted everyone that he was going to petition the court to demand that Evan return Jordie to his mother. June didn't know what to make of the discussions between Evan and Anthony Pellicano. If Evan was certain Michael Jackson had molested Jordie, why was he trying to extract twenty million dollars from him instead of reporting him to the proper authorities? She began to question Evan's motives; she wanted her son back. A court date was then set to determine who would have custody of Jordie.

However, Evan did not want to return Jordie to June, no matter how a judge might rule. He felt sure that she would simply hand him right over to Michael Jackson. They would live happily ever after at Neverland, he feared, and he would never see his son again.

Not knowing what course of action to take, and feeling pressured to do something, Evan made an appointment for Jordie with Dr Mathis Abrams, the psychiatrist who provided the letter in which he speculated that, based on the hypothetical case proposed by the attorney, sexual abuse had occurred. He told the doctor that the case wasn't imaginary, after all, and that it actually involved his own son and Michael Jackson. Evan realized that once Abrams met with Jordie, the real drama would most certainly begin. After all, the doctor would be required to file a report with the authorities, which would be the end of any confidentiality where the matter of Jordie and Michael was concerned. However, as he later would tell it, Evan felt pressured to protect his son, and if it meant sacrificing Michael Jackson then that was a small price to pay, especially since negotiations with him had ended so badly.

At the hearing, on 17 August 1993, Evan's attorney agreed that Jordie would be returned to June by seven o'clock that night. In fact he was stalling for time – he had no intention of returning Jordie to his ex-wife. At the very hour of the hearing, Jordie was meeting with the psychiatrist.

During a gruelling, three-hour session with the doctor, Jordie told of many incidents of masturbation and oral sex with Michael Jackson. In fact, he claimed, he and Michael had been having sex for months.

Just as expected, the psychiatrist reported everything Jordie said directly to the Department of Children's Services. Within hours, the youngster was interviewed by a caseworker with the Los Angeles County Department of Children's Services and an officer with the Los Angeles Police Department.

The caseworker's eleven-page, hand-written report began with a description of how Evan and Michael met, when Michael's car broke down. Jordie said that he and Michael became friends and that Michael would telephone him almost every day for 'long conversations about video games'. The conversations continued, he said, even when Michael was on tour. In February (1993) and in succeeding weeks, Michael began seeing more of him and his mother, June. He bought toys for Jordie and took him, June and his half-sister, Lily, to Las Vegas. There, Jordie recalled, they watched *The Exorcist*. The film frightened Jordie, he said, and that night he slept in the same bed as Michael – a pattern, he said, that was repeated several times, including during visits to Neverland. During those initial encounters, however, sexual abuse was not alleged. According to the report, at first Michael would merely 'cuddle and kiss him [Jordie] on the cheek'. However, on one occasion at the ranch while June slept in guest quarters and Michael and Jordie shared the same bed, the pop singer began to 'rub up against me'.

'Over time,' claimed Jordie in the report, 'Michael graduated to kissing me on the mouth. One time, he was kissing me and he put his tongue in my mouth. I said, "Don't do that". He started crying. I guess he tried to make me feel guilty.' The report then alleged that Michael told the boy their relationship was 'meant to be' and was 'in the cosmos'.

According to the report, Michael's relationship with Jordie

became sexual when he took the family to Monaco, and then continued to be sexual from that time, onward. The details Jordie provided were graphic.

Jordie also claimed that Michael had threatened that if he ever told anyone what had transpired between them, they would both be in trouble and he [Jordan] would be sent to Juvenile Hall, a young offenders' institution. 'Minor also said Mr Jackson told him about other boys he had done this with,' wrote the investigator, 'but did not go as far with them. Minor said Mr Jackson tried to make him hate his mother and father, so that he could only go with Mr Jackson.' The report ended with Jordie's wish to remain in his father's custody, and his belief that his mother liked the 'glitzy life' that surrounded Michael.

Later, when Jordie was interviewed by the police department, he relayed the same anecdotes of sexual encounters and also gave officers what he said was a detailed description of Michael's genitalia.

With such stunning disclosures of a sexual nature involving a star as world-famous, as controversial and as seemingly androgynous as Michael Jackson, there was no way the story would not emerge with some of the most sensational headlines in show-business history . . . It was just a matter of time.

'Jordie will never forgive me . . .'

The next day, 18 August 1993, Bert Fields and Anthony Pellicano gave Michael Jackson the stomach-churning news that the Los Angeles Police Department's Sexually Exploited Child Unit had begun a criminal investigation of him. 'Oh, my God,' Michael asked, 'is my life over?'

'No,' Bert answered. 'We'll defend it, Michael. And the odds are that we'll win.'

'And you know how it goes with you and the odds,' Anthony added, optimistically.

'That's what I'm afraid of,' said Michael, miserably.

Anthony embraced Michael. 'Man, you never lose,' he said, according to his later recollection. 'Look at your life, Michael. Look at who you are. You're not gonna start losing now.'

Michael began to sob. 'I have worked so hard,' he said. 'All of my life, I've been working so hard. I can't lose it all now, Anthony. I just can't lose it all.'

'You won't,' Bert injected. 'I swear to you, you won't.'

That same day, June and Dave Schwartz were interviewed by the police. They weren't so sure, they maintained, that Michael was guilty of abusing Jordie. They both felt that the youngster was so controlled by Evan, they didn't know what to believe, they said. 'I think I believe, maybe, half of it,' she said, reluctantly. Now, June would lose custody of Jordie, at least for the time being. She was heartbroken by this decision made by Child Protection Services, even if it was said to be temporary, however there was nothing she could do about it. Anyway, Jordie had told the authorities he wanted to be with his father, which was persuasive.

Later that day, Michael met with another one of his associates, a publicist who had to determine a course of action to take if the allegations were made it into the press. 'I met him at the Los Angeles hide-out,' recalled the representative. 'He looked absolutely terrible, as if he hadn't slept in days. He wasn't wearing his makeup, so his face seemed broken out, splotchy. He looked thin and sickly. He had on his pyjamas. "What am I going to do now?" he asked. "I can't believe this is happening to *me*, Michael Jackson. Do you think the police will ask me questions about me and Jordie?"'

The publicist told Michael that there was little doubt he would be questioned by the authorities, and soon. Michael began to cry. 'But I can't answer questions,' he said through his tears. 'I can't talk about Jordie. Don't you get it? He's my soul mate. I won't know what to say.'

'Just tell the truth, Mike,' suggested the publicist as he patted Michael on the shoulder.

'But no one will believe me,' Michael said, sounding defeated. 'It's my word against Evan's. Poor Jordie,' Michael added, wiping his eyes with the backs of his hands. 'I can't believe his father would do this. We were so close. Evan is so jealous of me, so, so jealous of me.'

The publicist then asked how Michael wanted to handle the media when the allegations became news. 'Oh, screw the media,' Michael said, going from sadness to fury in a nanosecond. 'I don't care what they say about me. They're gonna make stuff up, anyway. Screw them. Screw them all. It's because of *them* that I'm in this trouble, anyway.'

The publicist recalled being confused by Michael statement. 'How is the media responsible?' he asked.

Michael began jabbing his finger at his associate as he spoke. 'It's because of *you* allowing the media to write these things about me that people think I would do this thing,' he said, furiously. 'It's *your* fault. No. It's *their* fault.' Michael collapsed in a chair, looking bereft. 'I have been trying to stop the rumours and for years and years and they've just been going on and on and on,' he said. 'The oxygen chamber. The Elephant Man. The plastic surgery. Now, this.'

On 20 August 1993, Michael left for Bangkok on the second leg of his Dangerous tour. How ironic for him to start again in a city known as the sex capital of the world.

Michael was swamped with feelings about leaving Los Angeles. He could not fathom that Jordie would not be with him on the road. He had planned an exciting time for the two of them on continents all over the world, and the only reason to even go, in his view, would have been to be with his 'soul mate'. Now, he would be going alone. Of course, he would be with about 250 people, all integral to the massive, multimillion-dollar production, from musicians and stage hands and dancers to bodyguards, secretaries and assistants. However, as far as Michael was concerned, he was alone if he was to be without Jordie.

Also, he didn't want to leave home because he simply wasn't sure what would occur in America during his absence. Yet, he also couldn't wait to go, just to get out of town and not have to deal with whatever terrible thing was about to happen. He felt he needed to escape from his life, if at all possible. As it would happen, Michael Jackson left town just in time because, the next day, all hell would break lose.

On Saturday 21 August 1993 a search warrant was issued for the police to gain access to Michael Jackson's Neverland Ranch at 5225 Figueroa Mountain Road in Los Olivos, Santa Barbara. The authorities hired a locksmith in order to gain access to all of the many rooms on the estate, including Michael's private quarters. Moreover, the search warrant permitted the authorities to search Michael's 'hideout' at 1101 Galaxy Way, #2247 in Century City, California, for evidence. Of course, anyone who thought the authorities would find anything incriminating during such searches would have been naive. Obviously, because of the chain of events that had led up to the day, Michael's camp expected that a search warrant would be issued.

Adrian McManus, Michael's personal maid and the only employee with access to his Neverland bedroom, recalled, 'People were running all about the place, employees taking things off the property in boxes and crates, as if they couldn't get the stuff out fast enough. They took sheets, pillows, bedspreads, towels and wash clothes. They took boxes of makeup and eyeliner and lipstick and creams and gels. They took stacks of magazines. They took pictures. I remember that one person who worked for Michael held up a photograph and everyone else gathered around to ask, "Who is that? Who is that?" "Is that Macaulay Culkin in his underwear? It is!" Then, they would take the picture and put it in a box with a lot of other pictures of children in their underwear. I heard them mumbling things like, "This guy is nuts, isn't he?" as they went through his things. "How many pictures of Elizabeth Taylor does one person need?" I felt badly about the whole thing.

'My job was to hide all of Michael's women's perfumes, of which he had many bottles. He only used female fragrances, no male, and I guess they thought that might look bad.

'The next day, when the police came they looked around and one of them said, "Hmmm. Slim pickings, I see." They knew. Of course, they knew.'

When the authorities found a large, walk-in, black safe the size of a closet, they could not contain themselves. Imagine what might be found in such a thing owned by the enigmatic, secretive Michael Jackson. The officers ordered the locksmith to figure out the combination. For hours, he worked on the safe. Finally, *voilà*. It was opened. It was also empty, except for one small black briefcase. 'Open it. Open it,' the officers exclaimed. Inside was a single slip of paper. On it was written the combination to the safe. Someone in the Jackson camp had quite a sense of humour.

Despite the earlier clean-sweep, the police did manage to seize books, videos, pictures, scrapbooks and anything else they could find that they thought might be evidentiary. A year later when I conducted a telephone interview with Michael, he told me of the search: 'Imagine having someone going through all of your stuff while you're a million miles away. They took all kinds of things, stupid things like videotapes of me at Disneyland, pictures of my friends, boxes and boxes of personal things. And diaries! Imagine having some stranger reading your most private thoughts, his filthy hands turning all of those private pages, thoughts about [my] Mother and the way I feel about God. It was vicious. And we still haven't gotten back a lot of that stuff. It makes me cry when I think about it. But in all of my private stuff, there wasn't one piece of evidence to prove I had done anything wrong.'

The authorities took photographs of the rooms at Neverland in order to be able to compare them to Jordie's descriptions, as evidence that he had complete access. They seized Michael's telephone and address journals and would use them to later question more than thirty children and their families. (Those interviewed included Emmanuel Lewis, Jimmy Safechuck and Jonathan Spence; all three insisted that Michael had never acted in any improper way toward them.)

On 23 August, a Los Angeles television station reported the startling news that a police raid had occurred at Neverland. Michael Jackson was suspected of committing a crime, the police confirmed. However, the officers would not be more specific. Even with the lack of details, the story became the focus of more than seventy news broadcasts and Special Bulletins in the Los Angeles area alone over the course of the next day. Within hours, the investigation was the subject of international headlines. The *New York Post* ran with a dreadful photo of Michael looking his worst, and the blazing headline: 'Peter Pan or Pervert?' One thing was clear: nothing would ever be the same for Michael Jackson.

Though the television reports about Michael did not mention the subject of child molestation, rumours about it were strong enough for the Jackson camp to decide to just come out and deny them. It fell upon Anthony Pellicano to make the statement that, indeed, Michael was being accused of sexually abusing a minor, that he was innocent of any wrong-doing. Anthony's comments were the first the public had to confirm that it was, indeed, a matter of molestation about which Michael was being investigated. The police department then held a press conference to reveal more details. They had reason to believe, they said, that Michael had molested a thirteen-year-old boy. This was a shock. The pop star who was regularly seen in the company of youngsters, and who was known for his interest in children and in charities devoted to them, might actually be a paedophile? In a matter of hours, Los Angeles was descended upon by reporters from foreign countries doing their own independent investigations into what Michael had done, and to whom. He had always been so secretive, so strange. Now, it was assumed, the questions about him had been answered. Anyone who knew Michael feared that his career, and maybe even his life, was now ruined. 'I thought he would kill himself,' said one of his staff members at the time.

The next day, Anthony Pellicano explained to the media that Michael had been the 'victim of an extortion attempt gone awry', and one which his camp had been investigating for the last four months. 'A demand for twenty million dollars was made,' he told the Associated Press. 'It was flatly and consistently refused. The refusals have, in our opinion, caused what has transpired in the last few days.' He didn't mention the fact that the Jackson camp had entered into negotiations that involved proposals and counter-proposals.

Michael's camp hired high-powered criminal defence attorney Howard Weitzman to represent him; he read a statement prepared by his client: 'I am confident the department will conduct a fair and thorough investigation and that its results will demonstrate that there was no wrong-doing on my part. I intend to continue with my world tour.'

On 25 August, in an effort to do more so-called 'damage control', the day after Michael performed his first show in Bangkok, Anthony Pellicano arranged that the media have access to two young friends of Michael's, Brett Barnes and Wade Robson. In front of lights, cameras and microphones from news outlets around the world, Brett admitted that he and Michael had slept together on many occasions, but with no sexual overtones. 'He kisses you like you kiss your mother,' said the eleven-year-old. 'It's not unusual for him to hug, kiss and nuzzle up to you, and stuff.'

Wade, who was ten, also said he had slept in the same bed as Michael, but 'just as a friend'. He said, 'Michael is a very, very kind person, really nice and sweet. Sure, I slept with him on dozens of occasions but the bed was huge.'

Anthony Pellicano's offering of Wade and Brett to the press did little to help Michael's case: in fact, it was thought by many observers to have made things worse. Michael was actually unhappy about Anthony's decision to put the boys forth when he heard about it in Thailand. 'That's not good,' he said according to an adviser of his at the time. 'That makes me look even worse, I think. It's not good.'

Rarely had a show-business story taken flight like the Michael Jackson molestation scandal, with the world's press running blazing headlines that strongly implied that Michael was guilty, even if not yet charged. When the confidential and sexually charged statements Jordie Chandler gave to the authorities about his sleepovers with Michael were released, all objectivity about how the story should be reported seemed to go right out the window. The press had a story allegedly rife with sexual content and illegal activity between the biggest pop star in the world and a thirteen-year-old. It seemed impossible for much of the media to remain objective about it. Michael certainly appeared to be guilty, at least if Jordie's statements were to be believed.

On 26 August 1993, I appeared on CNN stating my view that we in the press might use some restraint in reporting the story. To my surprise, after the worldwide broadcast of my appearance, Michael telephoned me from Bangkok.

A day earlier, Michael had performed for an audience of 70,000. He ended his show accompanied by a stageful of young children while singing his personal anthem, 'Heal the World', to the appreciative crowd. He had seen the CNN report while backstage, he said, and called to thank me for my remarks. 'How are you feeling?' I asked him.

'Bad,' he said. He sounded weak, his voice a whisper.

'Is there anything I can do?' I asked.

'No,' he answered. 'I'm just very, very . . . sad. It's such a terrible world, isn't it? No love in the world at all.'

He promised to send a gift from Neverland to show his appreciation for my report. 'Maybe a llama,' he said, his spirits seeming lifted by the thought. 'Do you have room for a llama? I'll send you a nice, big llama!' He chuckled, softly.

'Tell me, how you are able to perform with all of this business going on?' I asked.

'Last night's first show was good,' he said. 'But after every song I had to run backstage and get oxygen. It was so hot and humid, I thought I would die. Now, I'm sick. I think I'm dehydrated. I can hardly take a deep breath. I don't know how I will ever be able to sing tonight.'

'Have you talked to any of your family?' I asked. 'Did you know they are planning a press conference in support of you.'

'Oh, great,' Michael said, sounding unenthused about the notion. 'That's just . . . great.'

That same evening, Michael was scheduled to give his second concert in Bangkok. However, the show was cancelled, the first to be cancelled over the next few months with excuses that would range from dehydration to migraine headaches to dental work.

Shortly thereafter, the Jackson family held their press conference to 'take this opportunity, when our family has come together in unity and harmony, to convey our love and unfailing support for Michael.' In front of camera crews from around the world, the family members said that it was their 'unequivocal belief that Michael has been made a victim of a cruel and obvious attempt to take advantage of his fame and success. We know, as does the whole world, that he has dedicated his life to providing happiness for young people everywhere. We are confident that his dignity and humanity will prevail.'

Also at the press conference, the family confirmed that they would soon leave the country to be at Michael's side.

In truth, Joseph could not have been more bereft about what was going on with his son. They had their differences, obviously. However, it was almost more than he could bear to see the televised news broadcasts relating to the scandal. In his view, Michael's success reflected upon him in a good and positive way. He felt that all Michael had achieved as a superstar was inextricably tied to what he had been in his son's life. He was proud of Michael. The last thing he wanted to do was see Michael's world laid to waste, yet there was nothing he could do about it, other than to be supportive. The problem, of course, was that Michael didn't want Joseph's support. Their history had been so volatile for so long, Michael had a strong, negative reaction to Joseph.

As for Katherine, Michael didn't want her involved in his life at this difficult time, either. He felt that she could be manipulated by the family to convince him to do the one thing he didn't want to do: another reunion show with the brothers.

Michael had always been the son Katherine was the proudest of, her favourite from the time he was a little tyke. However, lately she had been disapproving of him because she couldn't condone his private life. She simply didn't understand it, and with good reason: he wouldn't explain it. All she knew was that he was . . . *different*. Unlike his siblings, he had never been in a serious, romantic relationship. She was worried about him. She would also support him, regardless of his quirks and eccentricities, and be the first to speak in his defence. In truth, though, she didn't really know Michael. She only knew the parts of himself he felt free to reveal to her, certainly not unusual in many complex, mother-son relationships.

Before the scandal broke, the family told him of plans they had for an upcoming Jackson Family television special revolving around an achievement award that would be given to certain celebrities. Again, it was Jermaine's concept. Michael was clear; he wanted no misunderstanding about it: he wanted just limited participation in the special; the best they could expect of him was that he might give out an award and sit in the audience. In a manner so typical of Jackson family business, there was a great deal of back-and-forth about Michael's participation and, at one point, he wanted to back out, altogether. Now, with the family coming forth with their support at this difficult time in his life, he felt as if he was being backed into a corner where the programme was concerned. How could he disappoint them after they'd been so publicly loyal?

Enter: Lisa Marie Presley

Lisa Marie Presley, daughter of rock and roll trailblazer Elvis Presley, had known Michael Jackson since 1974; the two met in Las Vegas during one of the Jackson family's engagements at the MGM Grand. Lisa was six, Michael, sixteen. Elvis brought her to see the show because she was a big fan of the group's. 'I always liked him,' Lisa Marie, who prefers to be called Lisa, recalled. 'Michael fascinated me with his talent. I loved watching him dance. He wanted to know me better, but I always thought he was sort of freakish. I didn't really want to know him any better than I already did.'

Born on 1 February 1968 to Elvis and Priscilla Presley, Lisa Marie was destined for controversy just by virtue of her illustrious lineage. She had a privileged childhood. Her father lavished her with gifts, including jewels and a fur coat – for a five-year-old! Or, as her mother once put it, 'She had everything a child shouldn't have and couldn't appreciate.' She was spoiled or, as she bluntly recalled it, 'When I was a kid, forget it! I was a fucking little tyrant.'

She would also say of her childhood, 'There is not one bad memory about any of it, I have to admit. There was always a lot of energy around him [Elvis] and all over the house [at Graceland] when he was around. He was very mischievous.'

She would sit outside his bedroom at Graceland for hours, just waiting for him to awaken. Then, she would cuddle in his lap and, for no apparent reason, say things like: 'Daddy, please don't die.' She sensed that his time on earth would be brief. 'I was aware of the drug use,' she would later admit. 'I sensed it, knew it. His temper was bad at times. He didn't seem happy. I saw him taking pills, like cocktails of pills. But I think he tried to hide it from me as best he could. Still, I knew. I felt sort of helpless. It hurt. It still hurts. He was such a good man, so decent.'

Lisa was nine when her father died in 1977. Horribly, she was present when his body was found on a bathroom floor, and watched as people attempted to revive him. 'What's wrong with my daddy?' she tearfully demanded to know. At the funeral, she seemed in complete shock as she walked about Graceland in a daze, saying to relatives, 'You know, I just can't believe that Elvis Presley is dead.'

In October 1988, Lisa married musician Danny Keough, already pregnant with their first child. Danielle Riley was born the following year, and Benjamin Storm in 1993. The relationship would last six years.

In February of 1993, Lisa and Michael were brought together again at a private dinner in the Los Angeles home of artist Brett Livingston-Stone, a mutual friend. At this time, Lisa had recorded four songs produced by her husband. She felt she had a lot to say about her unusual life as daughter of an icon, and was looking for a way to say it through her lyrics and music. 'I had a voice,' she once told me, in retrospect, 'but I didn't have the experience. Things always got too wild when people found out that Elvis's daughter wanted to sing. It became a matter of deals and money, money, money: I lost my fire for it. I lost the urge to create. I was scared, I guess, so I pulled back.'

'She had no confidence in herself as a vocalist,' said Brett Livingston-Stone. 'She was afraid of being compared to Elvis, afraid of rejection. When I suggested that Michael could help her, she said, 'He's a superstar. Do you really think he'd help me?' After dinner at my house, Lisa played tapes of some of her music, and Michael was blown away. He told her, "You have real talent . . . a fine voice. You could be a star. Let me see what I can do for you." '

As she sat with him and listened to stories about his life in the business, she found herself falling under his spell. According to Brett Livingston-Stone, when Michael was about to leave, he offered Lisa a penetrating look and, in a conspiratorial voice, said, 'You and me, we could get into a lot of trouble. Think about that, girl.'

In days to come, Michael and Lisa forged a surprising friendship, speaking on the telephone nearly every day. They realized that they shared the same kinds of backgrounds, both had been sheltered and protected from the real world, both felt they had missed out on their childhoods, both were mistrustful of outsiders after having spent most of their lives feeling exploited by outsiders. They had problems with the media. She was raised in Graceland. He lived in Neverland. On some strange level that only they understood, as Lisa recalled it, they seemed to be soul mates. 'The difference between them was that Lisa was working on herself, trying to come to terms with her celebrity,' said Brett Livingston-Stone. 'She didn't see herself as a victim. Michael did. I think she wanted to help him view himself in a different way.'

He truly was misunderstood, he told her. 'I know you think I'm gay,' he said. 'But I'm not. I get tired of people thinking I am gay. But, oh well, fuck them. I know you have heard a lot of things about me, in fact,' he continued, 'but most of it isn't true. And the stuff that is true, you shouldn't hold against me.' He winked at her.

'Hey, I'm a married woman,' Lisa said. 'And you're coming on to me.'

'Yes, but are you happy?' Michael asked.

'No.'

'See?' Michael remarked. 'I knew that. You look like a woman who needs to let go and have some fun. You look like a woman who needs to hook up with *me*.'

Lisa was unable to disguise her surprise at his candour and his . . . normality. She recalled staring at him thinking, Who *is* this man? She was right to be perplexed; he sure wasn't acting like the Michael Jackson others had known over the years. It was as if he had taken macho lessons from Joseph! Unbeknownst to Lisa, many people along the way had tried to put together the puzzle pieces of Michael's mercurial psychology, often flattering themselves into thinking they and they alone understood him better than others. It usually ended badly for them; they would learn that Michael is truly the only one who understands Michael.

Lisa recalled, 'I thought to myself, Wow, this is a real guy. He swears. He's funny. I told him, "Dude, if people knew who the hell you really are, they would be so surprised. People wouldn't think I was so crazy for being into you if they saw who you really are; that you sit around and you drink and you curse and you're fucking funny, and you have a bad mouth and you don't have that high voice all the time."'

'He said, "Well just don't tell them." I thought he was normal and that everything you saw of him publicly was just a mask.'

Lisa recalled, 'As time went on, Michael and I talked more, I thought, I'm getting to know the real man here. He puts on an act for outsiders, this sort of victim thing, I thought, but I'm the one seeing the real deal, the real person. I started thinking I was special, that he was opening up to me as he never had to anyone else. He made me feel that way. He can be very seductive when he's pulling you in.'

In truth, as a potential mate, Michael did seem to have it all: intellect, drive, brains, energy, vision, success . . . money. As for his appearance, well that, admittedly, was a bit off-putting, with the plastic surgery and pale skin colouring. And his sexuality still seemed ambiguous. However, he was kissing her fairly passionately and, from many accounts, in public places. He seemed to enjoy doing it, too. Either he was playing some kind of manly role, perhaps an emotional consequence of the damaging allegations, or he was really interested in her. Lisa was definitely into him. 'I'm not a woman who goes for the norm, anyway,' Lisa said in explaining her attraction to him. 'I like strange guys, the ones on the edge, the ones *with* an edge, the ones with fire in their bellies. That was Michael, to me.'

Lisa was Elvis's kid; she'd been around 'strange'. When she was seven, she and her daddy were eating breakfast in front of the TV when singer Robert Goulet happened to appear on the screen. For some reason, Elvis hated Robert Goulet. When he saw his image before him, he pulled out a .22 shot gun and blew the TV away, blasting it to smithereens. Then, he calmly went back to his ham and eggs. Lisa just sat in her chair, stunned. At least Michael was afraid of guns . . .

As far as Lisa was concerned, she and Michael were dating, and her motive was to see where it could take her, romantically. Most people in his circle, though, were not as certain as to his motives for being with Lisa, though he did seem to like her. There was talk that he was after her money, which was ludicrous – as if he didn't have enough of his own.

As Elvis's sole beneficiary, Lisa would come into a fortune of about $300 million, but not until she turned thirty. Most of Lisa's money would be the result of the savvy Priscilla Beaulieu Presley's business acumen. While Elvis had earned roughly $250 million in his life, by the time he died his estate was valued at $5.4 million. It was his ex-wife, Priscilla, who turned Elvis's failing Presley Enterprises around to make a profit. Turning Elvis's fourteen-acre estate, Graceland (purchased by him in 1957) into a tourist attraction, in 1982 was one stroke of genius on her part. It brought in $20 million a year.

Throughout 1993, during the time Michael seemed obsessed with Jordie Chandler, he was dating Lisa, intermittently. When the molestation allegations surfaced in his life, however, Michael's relationship with Lisa became a more urgent matter to him. Ironically, if not for Jordie's accusations and the ensuing scandal, he and Lisa may never have become anything more than just friends, a coupling similar to the innocuous, non-sexual 'romances' he had with Brooke Shields and Tatum O'Neal. However, after Michael began the second leg of his Dangerous tour and the investigation intensified, he began to depend on Lisa for emotional support, telephoning her from overseas, seeming desperate and alone. During such anguished calls, Lisa would attempt to counter his sadness with humour, cheerfulness and good advice. As he grew to depend upon her, their relationship strengthened.

'I was in on the beginning of the molestation stuff, and I was getting the phone calls, and he was telling me that it was extortion,' she recalled. 'I believed him at the time. I mean, I was convinced. He was freaking out. I believed that he didn't do anything wrong, and that he was being wrongly accused and, yes, I started falling for him. I wanted to save him. I felt that I could do it.'

Elizabeth Taylor to the Rescue

In the midst of all of the turmoil, there was some good news for Michael Jackson when he heard that Elizabeth Taylor and her husband, Larry Fortensky, would be joining him in Singapore, his next tour stop, to lend their emotional support and celebrate his thirty-fifth birthday with him.

Many people have wondered about Michael's relationship with Elizabeth, thinking it an unlikely friendship. However, they actually have a great deal in common – and much more than just having been child stars. Like Elizabeth, Michael has known loneliness, he has lived in fear of not being able to fully love . . . and of not having love returned.

Michael once explained to me that he and Elizabeth first met in the early 1980s. Out of the blue, he had sent her a dozen tickets to one of his Los Angeles concerts at Dodger's Stadium. 'I didn't know it, but it was her birthday – February 27,' Michael recalled. 'I thought I was giving her great seats because they were in the VIP box. But when Elizabeth got there, she became very angry because the seats were so far away from the stage. And she left, upset! The whole time I was performing, I was thinking, Oh my God, Elizabeth Taylor is watching me. Elizabeth Taylor is watching me! But, she wasn't even there. When I got offstage, they told me she had gone home, mad. The next day, I called her, and I cried because I felt so awful.'

According to Michael's memory, Elizabeth was cordial, but direct. 'Michael,' she said, 'a major star such as myself *never* sits in the cheap seats.'

'After that, we talked on the phone every day, on every stop of my tour,' Michael said. 'And I thought, Wow. Doesn't she have other things to do? After all, she's Elizabeth Taylor! At the end of the tour, I asked her if I could come by for tea. She said, "Yes." I brought Bubbles along. She didn't mind . . .'

When asked, Michael will always say that no one is a better, more understanding friend than Elizabeth Taylor. She can deal with any problem; nothing shocks her and she is always available with a warm hug and an understanding ear. Because she is also extraordinarily charismatic, it's easy to become swept away by Elizabeth – just as it is easy to be swept away by Michael. The two became so fascinated with one another so quickly that, in 1989, Elizabeth toyed with the idea of moving Michael into her home so that they could spend all of their waking hours together. At the time, Michael was about to move out of his family home in Encino, and was considering buying Neverland.

'But why do you need all of that space when you and I can live together in my home,' Elizabeth suggested, according to what Michael told me. 'Imagine the fun we'll have. Maybe we'll even get married.' She was probably being facetious; she, no doubt, realized that the ever-so-secretive Michael was troubled and in need of love and acceptance. Maybe she also sensed that he was ashamed of his inability at that time to truly connect with and be intimate with anyone, male or female. 'But will we have to have sex?' an alarmed Michael wanted to know. 'Oh, of course not, you silly boy,' Elizabeth told him, cackling in her inimitable way. 'Why, I don't know *any* married couples who have sex!' Michael considered her proposition. 'In the end,' he said, 'I thought that might be taking things too far.' Instead Michael bought Neverland, but he and Elizabeth remained close friends. In fact, Elizabeth married her seventh husband, Larry Fortensky, under a gazebo at Neverland in 1991 – amidst swans, doves and at least one giraffe – in a million-dollar ceremony.

It speaks well of Elizabeth that she was so vociferous in her defence of Michael, especially since it wasn't a popular stance; such public support was certainly not forthcoming in the same degree from his other high-profile friends, such as Diana Ross, Jackie Onassis or Liza Minnelli.*

'Michael is one of my best friends in the world,' Elizabeth Taylor told a reporter on the plane to Singapore; she and Larry Fortensky took the trip surrounded by a coterie of press people. 'I can't think of anything worse a human being could go through than what he's

*In 1993, Michael sent Jackie an extravagant gift, perhaps trying to win her over. Recalled Stephen Styles, who was a close friend of John F. Kennedy Jnr's, 'Michael was pushing for a deeper relationship, I think. But you just didn't do that with Jackie; she was the one to set the boundaries. One day, my phone rang and it was John. "You will never guess what's going on around here," he said. "My mother is fit to be tied." Then, he explained to me that a big screen TV had been delivered to Jackie's apartment building from Michael, and that was so large they couldn't even get it in the front door of the lobby. It was just out in the middle of the sidewalk on Fifth Avenue, with a giant pink bow on it that said, "For Jackie. The Most Wonderful Woman in the World." A big crowd had gathered, hoping that the most wonderful woman in the world would come down and claim her prize. "My mother is having a fit, about it," John said, laughing. They finally got it up to her apartment, but they had to disassemble much of it just to get it in the lobby.'

going through now,' she observed. 'He's a very sensitive, vulnerable, shy person. I believe that he will be vindicated.' When asked about the reason for such allegations, Elizabeth became irate. '*Ext-oooooor-tion*,' she exclaimed in a shrill voice. 'I think that's clear. *Well, isn't it?*' she demanded, wanting the writer to agree with her.

On arrival, Elizabeth and Larry checked into the same hotel in which Michael was staying, the exquisite Raffles. As soon as she checked in, she rushed to her friend's room. When Michael answered the door, he collapsed into her arms in a heap. 'Oh, there, there, you poor thing,' she said, patting him on the back. 'I'm here, now. Elizabeth is here.'

Michael did manage a show that night, 29 August, his birthday. At the end, forty thousand people sang 'Happy Birthday' to him. Later, Elizabeth hosted a small party for him in his suite.

The next stop was Taiwan, which is where Joe, Katherine and some of the Jackson boys had decided to join Michael. 'Just what I need,' he told Elizabeth, according to a witness. 'Why do they have to come?'

'They are your family, Michael,' she said. 'You must put up with them.'

'My father,' Michael said, burying his face in his hands. 'I can't even stand to be in the same room with that man.'

'Neither can I, dear,' Elizabeth said, massaging his back, sympathetically.

When he finally got to Taiwan, Michael simply refused to see his visiting family members. Bob Jones, his long-time publicist, was even assigned the task of keeping them from him. Katherine was hurt. 'Why does Elizabeth Taylor get to see him any time she wants,' she complained, 'but I have to make an appointment to see him for five minutes?'

Dealing with the allegations against Michael was hard on Katherine. It affected her blood pressure, and the family was worried about her. It was even tougher on her when she realized that she couldn't see him, couldn't comfort him. She and the family members felt isolated in the hotel, wondering when they would ever have a private audience with the King of Pop. Later, Jermaine would complain bitterly about it on *The Larry King Show*. 'Michael's handlers don't want us to get to him,' he said.

As his family waited to see him, Michael had lunch with Elizabeth Taylor. Holding a messy slice of carrot cake with frosting in her hand, she urged him to eat it. He had lost six pounds since the second-leg of the tour began, just a short while ago in Bangkok. 'Take this,' she insisted. Michael sneered at the cake, seeming repulsed by the sight of it. 'No, take it away,' he said, begging her.

'Michael, if you don't eat this cake, I swear to God, I will call your family in here and let them have a go at you,' she warned. 'And you know I'll do it, too.'

Michael laughed. 'Give me that goddamn cake,' he said, scooping it out of her hands. He wolfed it down.

'Good boy,' she exclaimed with delight. 'Good boy!'

The next day, Michael gave in and hosted a luncheon for Katherine, Joseph and the rest of his visiting family. Mostly, he sat in a corner quietly. Before the luncheon was over, though, Jermaine approached him about participating in the upcoming Jackson Family television programme. No longer in a position to avoid the question, he agreed.

By the fall of 1993, as the legal manoeuvrings continued, Michael was in worse shape than ever, physically and emotionally. He was devastated by an interview with Evan and Jordie – although neither was identified by name. 'I imagine Michael Jackson is pretty scared right now, really scared,' the kid was quoted as having said. 'And he should be, because what he did to me is a really bad thing. Michael hasn't called me or anything . . .'

June and Dave Schwartz decided to align with Evan against Michael. It was said by her friends that June feared reprisals from Evan if she continued to oppose him. She thought it possible that if Michael was found guilty, Evan might then accuse her of neglect. Meanwhile, her lawyer, Michael Freeman, quit saying that he was 'uncomfortable' with her decision and had a bad feeling about Evan, whom he later described as 'not a genuine person'.

Then surprisingly, Evan's lawyer Barry Rothman resigned from the case too and was replaced by civil attorney, Larry Feldman. So it was on 14 September 1993, Evan Chandler filed a civil suit against Michael for the sexual molestation of his son. It was effectively an insurance policy should the criminal system not work for him. Plus, it was a sure way to see that Michael paid in financial terms for what Evan said he had done to Jordie. Jordie would be represented in the legal action by attorney Feldman, who said at the time, 'Michael was in love with the boy. It was a gentle, soft, caring, warm, sweet relationship.' Larry also believed his client when told that the relationship was sexual, thus the lawsuit.

Though the lawsuit seemed to double the trouble for Michael, some of his advisers hoped it might actually provide a catalyst to end the matter. If the lawsuit could be settled with money, they reasoned, the police investigation might go away, as well. Though a trial for the civil case was set for 21 March 1994, there was still hope that a deal could be brokered before that time. There was a sense that Evan Chandler would accept money from Michael, and with good reason. They had already tried to negotiate a deal with him, albeit unsuccessfully, when he originally asked for twenty million dollars, before he went to the authorities. The problem, though, was that it was well-known within Michael's camp that he would never pay Evan a dime. Michael still maintained his innocence in the matter and was certain that any cash settlement would suggest otherwise; he wasn't going to do it, not without a fight. However, it was decided, as one adviser put it, 'to cross that bridge when we come to it.'

Though some secretly felt the matter might actually be settled given a little time and a lot of cash, others in the Jackson camp weren't as optimistic. According to a person familiar with the case, Elizabeth telephoned Michael to tell him that 'things do not look good back here.' She said, 'You've got to take action.' Michael asked for details, telling her not to 'hold anything back'. She said, 'All hell is breaking loose.'

Recalled one of Michael's representatives, 'Miss Taylor and I were on speaker phone with Michael. Michael was crying, asking, "What should I do? What can I do?" She became impatient. "Michael, you mustn't substitute my judgement for your own," she said. "You need to stop freaking out. You need to take charge of your life."'

In August 1994, Michael would tell me, 'I swear to you, I didn't know how bad things were. If I had known, maybe things would have been handled differently.' It does seem, in retrospect, that he knew more than he said he did, and was actually just in a state of denial about it.

Elizabeth told him that, in her view, no one was handling matters for him in the States in a way that would benefit him. 'I think they need to be kicking ass, and they're not,' she said. 'Then *you* be the one kicking ass, Elizabeth,' Michael said. At that, I cringed,' recounted the adviser. 'All we needed to make things worse was Elizabeth Taylor handling the defence. Much to my chagrin, and that of others on Michael's team, Miss Taylor offered to hold strategy meetings at her home two or three times a week, and then report back to Michael what had been said, and by whom.'

In the next few weeks, Elizabeth Taylor hosted many conferences at her house with about ten of Michael's team and was often critical of those handling Michael's public relations, though not so much his legal defence. Some on Michael's team did not want to attend the Elizabeth Taylor summits, protesting that for a movie star to have such control over his career was ridiculous. They dubbed her 'Queen of the Defence'. In truth, she wasn't spearheading any legal tactics, as much as providing a forum for attorneys, publicists and other strategists to brainstorm so she could then keep Michael apprised of their view points. Of course, some of Michael's staff did not wish to attend Elizabeth's meetings for fear of a negative report being sent back to the boss.

During one meeting, Elizabeth said, 'I'm afraid he will never sell another record again if we can't get this goddamned ridiculousness straightened out. I think we have to make sure there's something left for Michael after this is resolved.'

'He just might be in jail after this goddamned ridiculousness is resolved,' muttered one of Michael's advisers.

Elizabeth looked down and scribbled on her legal pad. She then looked back at the adviser. 'I just made a note to remember to tell Michael you said that,' she told him.

He lowered his head, duly chastised.

Anthony Pellicano simply refused to attend the Taylor meetings. 'What are you, kidding me?' he asked when asked why he wasn't present. 'I'm fucking busy. I'm out here working for Michael. I don't have time for tea with movie stars.'

Elizabeth was unhappy with Anthony, anyway. 'He's not a team player,' she said. 'We can't keep track of him. He does his own thing in his own way, and we don't know what he's thinking. I don't like it. He makes me nervous.'

During another of her home meetings, Elizabeth, Sandy Gallin (Michael's manager at the time) and Howard Weitzman telephoned Michael overseas to discuss the matter of Anthony. According to a witness, all three were on 'speaker phone', talking to Michael.

'Look, Mike, maybe he has to go,' Howard said of Pellicano. 'I like the guy, but I'm not sure about him, any more . . .'

'I think so, too,' Elizabeth concurred. 'Absolutely.'

'Well, I've had my run-ins with him, too,' Michael admitted. He sounded lethargic, drugged. He said that while he admired Anthony, he still felt that his idea to present Wade Robson and Brett Barnes to the public wasn't a good one. He felt that the investigator should have checked with him first before exploiting the youngsters. 'And it really pisses me off that guy tries to tell *me* what to do,' Michael said, 'like I work for him instead of the other way around. And, also,' he concluded, 'I think he scares the public, he's that intimidating. John Branca, now *he's* a good spokesman.' Indeed, after having let him go so unceremoniously, Michael had recently asked John to return to the fold. He knew he could always count on him and, of course, he was right: Branca was back and loyal as ever.

After that conversation, Michael wrote a detailed memo to Howard Weitzman explaining why he believed he and John should take over as his spokesmen. He told him that he trusted them, they were believable, and had the respect of the legal profession – unlike Anthony Pellicano who he now felt was perceived as being a man on the edge, a rebel. 'If Anthony worked for Motown,' Michael observed, 'he'd be someone Berry would keep behind the scenes. Having him out there speaking for me now is almost like having Joseph out there. He's intimidating. Right now, we don't need that.'

Michael Proposes to Lisa Marie

It was difficult to imagine how things could get much worse for Michael Jackson in the fall of 1993. In just a matter of months he had, without a doubt, experienced the 'swift and sudden fall from grace', he would later write about in his self-revealing song, 'Stranger in Moscow'.

Certainly, no one had counted on Michael becoming addicted to drugs, thereby raising the stakes in terms of the precarious nature of his future and well-being. Yet, anxious, unable to sleep and, he said, in pain because of dental work and a recent surgery to his scalp (a consequence of the burn he suffered during that Pepsi commercial), Michael began taking more of the painkillers, Percodan, Demerol and codeine, as well as tranquillizers Valium, Xanax and Ativan. Such dependence was uncharted terrain for him. In the past, he had made an effort to not over-medicate during recovery from plastic surgeries, explaining to doctors that he wanted to remain 'sharp' for the purpose of making sound business and career decisions. However, with all that was going on in his life at this time, Michael no longer cared to be quite so focused. In fact, he wanted to forget, escape. It didn't take long before he was completely dependent on the drugs. It happened so quickly that his team in the United States didn't even realize what was going on with Michael, until it was too late to do anything about it.

Everyone was stunned to learn that Michael had a problem with drugs. Of course, Elizabeth Taylor understood and had empathy for his plight. She'd been there, with her own, well-publicized battles. Lisa Marie Presley was also sympathetic; she, too, was a recovering addict.

'When I was a teenager, I was completely out of control,' she told me. 'I started doing drugs when I was fourteen. I had been spinning for quite some time, years, when I finally hit bottom. That was when I found myself on a seventy-two-hour bender of cocaine, sedatives, pot and drinking, all at the same time. I woke up and there were all of these people, friends of mine, passed out on the floor. My coke dealer was in the room trying to sell me more stuff. I just said, 'That's it. Everybody get the fuck out.' I don't know why I got addicted, I just know that I was going to die if I didn't get help. Finally, my mother and I decided I would go to the Scientology Center in Hollywood for detoxification. It saved my life.'

When Michael telephoned Lisa from overseas in September 1993, he was high, incoherent and delusional. Alarmed, Lisa attempted to convince Michael to do as she had once done, enter a rehabilitation centre. For Lisa, the quest to pull a drug-addled superstar back from the edge had great significance. She had shared with friends earlier the guilt she had suffered as a child, seeing her father falling into his own bottomless pit of addiction. She was still married to Danny Keough, but unhappily. She was restless and felt that she had no real purpose; she wanted more than motherhood, she said. Michael's dilemma seemed to provide an outlet for her. 'Absolutely, I felt that I had a *responsibility* to save him,' she said. 'I don't know the psychology of it and what it had to do with my father. I only know what I felt.'

There was one major obstacle that lay before Lisa if she was going to help quiet the demons haunting Michael: access. It was well known that Jackson had done a very thorough job of insulating himself from the outside world. Often, he would start casual relationships with people, many of whom were certain that their relationship would grow, only to find that Michael had left them behind. Calls would go unanswered, sometimes letters would be returned, unread. Lisa had heard of Michael's reputation for tossing aside new-found 'soul mates', and saw this pattern as a liability if she was going to complete her task of rebuilding his crumbling life. She would have to proceed with caution.

In her frequent telephone calls to him, Lisa maintained that Michael could not go on much longer with his personal life and career in such disarray. He was immobilized by uncertainty and a sense of hopelessness, which had contributed to his addiction. She suggested to him the idea others in his camp had begun to secretly discuss: that Michael end his misery with a cash settlement to Evan Chandler. Michael was, predictably, against the idea. A man who'd been building an image for himself since the time most children were building tree houses, Michael cared deeply about what people thought of him. Even if the image he had fostered over the years was, arguably, not the best one for him, it *was* the result of a great deal of strategizing on his part, and on that of his handlers. 'He felt that this thing of him being wacky and weird and crazy worked for him,' Lisa recalled, 'and maybe for a time, it did. I don't know. I was always against it. I always thought he was bigger, better, than the image. I always thought the image did him an injustice.'

One thing was certain: by 1993 Michael was lonelier than he'd ever before been, and that was really saying something. He had to face the fact that his career, his most enduring passion, was in jeopardy, a possible fatality either of an unlawful, immoral love affair with a minor or of poor judgement in having aligned himself so stubbornly with the wrong people and at the wrong time. If he wouldn't settle with money, Lisa suggested rehab at the very least. She cared deeply about him, she told him, and she wanted to be sure he knew it.

One night, while abroad, Michael found himself, as he often would, feeling trapped in a plush hotel suite, alone with the constant drone of a chanting crowd below his room. After a string of phone calls from lawyers and publicists, Michael decided to calm himself by calling the one person who could somehow help him forget that his career hung in the balance: Lisa.

She had certainly been persistent in her pursuit of him. She left telephone numbers for a house she was renting in Canoga Park, California.

She also left the number of the new three-acre estate which she had just purchased and was getting ready to occupy on Long Valley Road in Hidden Hills (an exclusive gate-guarded equestrian community in Calabasas, California, where she still lives, today).

Then, just to be sure, she left the number where she could be reached in Clearwater, Florida, where she was planning to spend time at the Scientology retreat. She even sent him party balloons with messages attached. Somehow, she could always put a smile on his face, even if it was just her raspy voice proclaiming, 'Oh, fuck them!' He found her in Canoga Park.

Michael valued Lisa's settling effect on him, so much so that during his phone conversation, he posed a question that surprised both of them. 'If I asked you to marry me, would you do it?' Was this a joke? A hypothetical? Or was it a dare for Lisa to take him seriously? If it was a dare, Lisa was just the woman to take it – even though she was still married to Danny Keough. Without missing a beat, she replied, 'I would do it.' Michael didn't say a word, at first. He then said, 'Hold on, I have to use the bathroom.'

When he finally did speak into the phone again, he was speaking to his new fiancée. 'My love for you is real,' Michael told Lisa. 'Please believe me.' Michael didn't realize, however, that whether or not

Michael loved her wasn't the *real* issue for Lisa. His proposal served a greater purpose. It would give her access, she hoped, to enter his secret world. Then, from the inside, she would begin to put the pieces of this broken man together, and this time she would not fail.

'You'll all be fired'

By the time Michael Jackson's tour took him to Mexico City, on 24 October 1993, there was talk of a pending warrant for a police strip search of his body. This seemed odd, almost unthinkable. Making matters worse, the Los Angeles Police Department had seized medical records from the offices of two of Jackson's physicians, Beverly Hills dermatologist, Arnie Kleins and Santa Monica plastic surgeon, Stephen Hoefflin. 'What do they want my medical records for?' a bewildered Michael asked one of his team members in a long-distance telephone call. 'They can't do that, can they?'

'Hell, yeah, man, they can do that,' confirmed the associate. 'They think they can do anything they want to do. When the rest of the troops get down there, you'd better whip them into shape. Things are bad here, Mike.'

The records were needed to verify aspects of Jordie's testimony. Did the authorities really think such documents would still be in place? All of Michael's medical records from both doctors were long gone by the time the police arrived to take them.* Still, one can only imagine the stress for a person as pathologically private as Michael

---

*Later, Arnold Klein was forced to testify at a Grand Jury. He brought along his assistant, Debbie Rowe. The two testified that Michael had been a patient since 1983, was diagnosed with Vitiligo and acne in 1986, and was given his first of many prescriptions of Benoquin, a bleaching cream, in 1990. Klein said he had never seen Jackson's penis, but – on one occasion – saw his buttocks when Michael had tried using his Benoquin bleaching cream there. Klein also confirmed the incident with Michael's scrotum, when he tried to bleach it in the spring of 1993. However, Rowe treated him for that particular problem, not Klein.

Jackson, to know that the police were trying to locate his confidential medical records.

The heat was on. The investigation would not let up, that much was clear.

At this same time, the police raided Michael's Hayvenhurst estate in Encino. When the Jacksons went to Phoenix for the funeral of Joseph's father, the police used the opportunity to inspect the estate and look for evidence there. A locksmith helped them gain entrance.

The officers seized books, magazines, photos, tapes and anything else they thought might be interesting – including Katherine's high blood pressure pills. They also found a videotape called *Chicks*, which promised to be valuable evidence since the slang word 'chicks' is sometimes used by paedophiles when referring to young boys. When the cops got back to the police station, the first thing they did was review the tape. Much to their frustration, what they saw was a video about . . . chicks, as in birds.

The 'troops' to which Michael's adviser had referred were those Jackson team members on their way to Mexico City: attorneys John Branca, Howard Weitzman, Bert Fields, as well as Dr Arnold Klein (to deal with a skin condition brought on by Jackson's anxiety) and Elizabeth Taylor. They hoped to convince Michael to return to the States. The longer he stayed away the guiltier he looked to his fans. Lisa Marie Presley also hoped to go on the trip.

For the last few years, Elizabeth had been trying to convince Michael to open himself up to a romantic relationship. However, when it began to happen with Lisa, she suddenly felt left out. 'She has a deep insecurity about other women, especially younger women,' says a friend of Michael's. 'I spent a great deal of time in her company and saw for myself the competitive way she dealt with Lisa.'

One of Jackson's associates was with Elizabeth and Lisa during a meeting. Both were sitting in the adviser's office, discussing their concern about Michael. Elizabeth looked grand in a black, turtleneck sweater and matching skirt, her hair in a bouffant style. Her eyes, the world's most famous violet pair, were concealed by large sunglasses, which she even wore indoors. By contrast, Lisa looked like a punk rocker in torn denim slacks, a white T-shirt and a black leather jacket.

('I can understand if she doesn't want to be a star like her father,' Elizabeth said of Lisa, later. 'However, one would think she would at least want to *dress* like one.')

'I think we should get him into rehab,' Lisa said, speaking of the beleaguered Michael. 'Fly to be at his side. Do whatever it takes.'

Liz gave Lisa an icy stare. 'It's taken care of, dear,' she said. 'I've been rescuing Michael for years.'

'Well, maybe that's the problem,' Lisa countered. 'Maybe he needs to grow up, do things on his own—'

Elizabeth cut her off. 'Or maybe *not,* dear,' she said. With her tone sickeningly sweet, she made her point: Lisa was an interloper. Perhaps she realized she'd acted rudely, because Elizabeth then apologized and blamed her attitude on the stress of the times.

Still, Lisa was chagrined and felt that Elizabeth had treated her as if she was one of Michael's groupies, rather than a trusted friend. She decided not to go to Mexico City because, as she later explained, she didn't want to make things worse for Michael. However, from that point onward, Lisa considered Elizabeth to be, as she put it, 'opposing counsel'.

Shortly after the arrival of the Jackson contingent, a shouting match erupted between Bert Fields and Michael's loyal head of security, Bill Bray (who had known and worked for Michael since the star was about twelve years old). The protective Bray accused Fields of mishandling the case. In front of witnesses, he screamed at the attorney, 'You're blowing the whole damn thing! Mike is gonna end up in jail. What is going on?'

One witness said, 'Elizabeth agreed with Bill that the attorneys weren't being aggressive enough. It was as if they were waiting for time to pass to see what would happen next. 'You need to get out there and start deposing these people,' she said. 'There are liars all over the place, and they need to be revealed for who they are . . . all these housekeepers and maids and butlers. I know good help is hard to find, Michael,' she said turning to him, 'but where did you find *these* people? Look at how they turned on you.' Michael sat staring at her with his mouth open. 'My maid turned on me?' he said. 'Not my sweet Blanca?' he asked, sounding pretty dumb. [He was referring to his maid, Blanca Francia.]

'Where she once felt that Michael was capable of taking charge, she could see that he was now in bad shape. He was so drugged out, he couldn't handle anything. "I think now that he can't make important decisions," she said. "Look at him! What do you expect of him? I've been there," she said, referring to her own drug use, "and I know he can't make any decisions right now. We have to help this boy. Enough is enough."

'She was angry at just about everyone in Michael's camp. Michael was so affected by Elizabeth's outburst, he collapsed into racking sobs. "What am I going do?" he asked. "If you people can't figure this goddamn thing out, how can I?" Elizabeth went over and embraced him. "We're fighting, Michael, but it's because we love you," she said, almost as if she was talking to a child whose parents were divorcing. It was touching. "And I'll be goddamned if you have to suffer another second over this bullshit. We will work it out. I promise you."'

Michael pulled away from Elizabeth. 'I want you people to fix this thing, now,' he said, addressing everyone in the room. 'I'm serious,' he added. 'My life will not end this way. You'll all be out – *fired* before that happens.'

'Hear, hear,' said Elizabeth, clapping her hands. 'That's telling 'em, Michael. Right out on their asses!' Then, after a beat, she added, 'Just to be clear, you don't mean me too, now do you, dear?'

He couldn't help himself; Michael burst into laughter, as did everyone on his team.

After that day's discussions, it was decided that attorney Johnnie Cochran, well respected in Los Angeles' black and legal communities, would be added to the legal team. Elizabeth had said that she wanted her own attorney, Neal Papiano, to join the team. However, she eventually agreed with Branca and Weitzman that Cochran (who would later successfully defend O. J. Simpson of charges that he had murdered his wife and a friend of hers) was the man for the job. Johnnie would have one job and only one job: to settle 'this goddamn thing' with money. There would be no trial, it was agreed. Michael would not, *could* not survive it. He was now too emotionally devastated to present a strong image for himself on the witness stand. Whatever it would cost, it was decided, he would have to pay it. If the public construed any financial settlement as an indication of guilt, it was decided, there was nothing anyone could do about it. 'He will just have to say he didn't do it, as he has been saying, and that's going to have to be the denial that lasts through the ages,' said one of the attorneys. 'The thing for us to do now is to save the man's life, not worry about the superstar's image.'

Chaos and Rehab

On 12 November 1993, looking thin, tired and haggard, Michael Jackson performed what would turn out to be the final show of his Dangerous tour at El Estadio del Azteca in Mexico City. The rest of the engagements were cancelled.

Apparently, Michael's mental state had truly disintegrated while in Mexico City; the damage to his $12,000-a-week, five-room suite on the forty-second floor of the Hotel Presidente was evidence of his serious abuse of drugs. After he checked out, the hotel staff was stunned to discover that the carpets in the living room and in Michael's bedrooms were stained with vomit. There were deep dents and cracks in the plaster of the living-room wall, as if someone had either banged his head, or his fists, against it. There was enough rubbish in the room to fill two large, trash bags. There were scribblings on the walls ('I love you. I love you.'), and even on the fabric of some of the furniture. Chewing gum was squashed into the carpet, everywhere.

After the final show, Michael, Elizabeth and Larry boarded an MGM Grand 727 jet, chartered for the occasion by Elizabeth, to London. When they arrived at Heathrow Airport, bodyguard Steve Tarling met them at the tarmac. All three had on dark glasses and long coats with hoods covering their heads, as if on some kind of espionage mission. Michael seemed drugged as he walked to the waiting van, held up on one side by a cloaked Elizabeth and on the other by her husband. 'He looked like a transvestite who'd had the same makeup on for a couple of weeks,' recalled Tarling. 'What shocked me most was the tip of his nose, which was like an open cut when it congeals into a scab. It looked awfully painful.'

The strategy had been to drive Michael directly to Charter Nightingale Clinic. However, that plan had to be changed when it was learned that reporters had begun to stake out the hospital because word had leaked that Michael might be showing up there. Instead, Michael was whisked off to the home of Elton John's manager, John Reid.

He didn't even make it inside the house. As he stepped from the van, he crumpled on to the ground. 'That's it,' Elizabeth decided. 'The press be damned. He has to go straight to the clinic. Now.'

In a matter of hours, Michael was at the Charter, taken in through the laundry entrance in what turned out to be a successful effort to avoid the paparazzi awaiting his arrival in front. He was immediately searched for drugs and, sure enough, eighteen vials of medicine were found in one of his suitcases. Of course, they were confiscated. After a quick induction meeting, Michael was officially enrolled in the centre – albeit in a way befitting the King of Pop: he took over the entire fourth floor of the hospital, at fifty thousand dollars a week, and was expected to remain there for about a month and a half. Michael was immediately put on Valium IV, part of the process of weaning him from painkillers.

The next day, 13 November, Michael announced in a press statement that he was cancelling the remainder of the tour because he was now an addict. He explained that he had begun using painkillers seven months earlier after having undergone reconstructive surgery for a scalp burn suffered during the filming of the Pepsi commercial in 1984. 'The medications were used sparingly at first,' Michael said, but increased as the molestation allegations consumed him.

'As I left on this tour, I had been the target of an extortion attempt and shortly thereafter was accused of horrifying and outrageous conduct. I was humiliated, embarrassed, hurt and suffering great pain in my heart,' he said in the statement. 'The pressure resulting from these false allegations coupled with the incredible energy necessary for me to perform caused me so much distress that it left me physically and emotionally exhausted. I became dependent on the painkillers to get through the days of the tour.' Of Elizabeth Taylor, he said that she'd been 'a source of strength and counsel as this crisis came about. I shall never forget her unconditional love and encouragement in helping me through this period.'

Many observers felt that the drug addiction was a perfectly timed hoax designed solely to keep Michael away from the United States and, thus, allow him to evade prosecution. Bert Fields addressed the cynicism directly, saying, 'The last thing in the world he would want would be the humiliation of admitting that he has become an addict. He's a man who has hated drugs all his life. If we wanted a smoke screen,' allowed Bert, 'we would have stayed on tour. That was the perfect one.' Bert also told reporters that Michael was 'barely able to function adequately on an intellectual level.'

Others in Jackson's camp thought it a mistake to portray Michael as being out of control. John Branca would later send a news clipping to Michael quoting Bert as having made such a statement. Michael was angry about it, even if it was true. 'That pisses me off,' he told John. 'Bert's not thinking about my fans. How does that look to them? And my mother? How must she feel?' In his own defence, Bert explained, 'I felt that honesty was important. Larry [Feldman] was trying to make a case that Michael wanted to evade prosecution. I wanted to dispel that notion.'

It was true that Larry Feldman had encouraged the critical press to be sceptical of Michael's motives in cancelling the tour, particularly because it happened just prior to its Puerto Rico date. It *was* suspicious. Puerto Rico is a United States territory. Michael could have been arrested there under United States law. All of this was occurring against a backdrop of persistent news reports that Jordie Chandler had described Michael's genitals in detail, and the authorities were serious about having Michael stripped and photographed so that they could inspect hidden evidence. 'You've got to be kidding,' exclaimed Howard Weitzman when asked about it at a press conference.

Meanwhile, Michael got his first taste of much-needed counselling.

Rehabilitation is never easy, but it's even more challenging for people who have lived privileged lives. During his first night there, he roamed the halls asking other patients if they knew 'a secret way to get out of here'. He didn't want to listen to the authorities. No one told him what to do in his private world, and he expected that it would be the same at Charter. It wasn't. Soon, he found himself mopping floors, which he hadn't done since he lived in Gary.

In the days to come, group therapy also proved to be difficult. Michael had never been in any type of therapy programme. How could he now be expected to sit in a room full of strangers and be candid about his personal life?

Led by well-known therapist Beechy Colclough, Michael's private sessions were more intense and productive than the group ones, during which he hardly spoke for fear that someone there might go to the tabloids. It was during private sessions, according to someone still close to Michael, that he began to finally deal with the root of so many of his problems: his anger at Joseph. It was a fine line, though, between blaming his father for everything that had ever happened in his life and taking responsibility for some of it, himself. In the past, Michael had never been one to own up to his actions, always intent on blaming family members, the press and even his fans for actions that have caused him unhappiness.

'In therapy, he began to see that he was his own worst enemy,' said his associate. 'It was slow-going, though. He was not eager to accept that he could change his life if he would just change his mind about it. Old habits die hard. He was determined to dwell on his lost childhood, on how mean Joseph had been to him, how cruel Evan had been to him. He practically equated them as one and the same.'

After many hours of therapy at Charter, it seemed as if Michael had a sudden rush of clarity. 'It's me,' he told his associate. 'It's not Joseph. It's me. Not Evan. I'm the one who blew it, and I need to start over again. I want another chance.'

'You can have it, Michael,' said his associate.

'I deserve it,' Michael said, crying. 'Do you still believe I am innocent?'

'I do.'

Michael didn't say anything for a few moments. Then, finally: 'When I get out of here, I'm starting over. Let's end this thing with Evan. I want my life back.' He always referred to the molestation business as a matter having to do with Evan Chandler because, in his mind, Jordie could never have truly been behind what he viewed as a nefarious plot against him.

*

Back in the States on 23 November, Bert Fields made what some thought was another serious blunder when, while standing in front of a judge and arguing the motion to have Michael's civil case delayed to the year 2000 – the year the criminal statute of limitations would expire – he indicated that a Grand Jury was about to convene in Santa Barbara, and that a criminal indictment against Michael was imminent. Though Bert claimed that he got his information from Howard Weitzman, it was news to everyone in Jackson's camp that an indictment was 'imminent'. Bert's reason for making the statement, as he later explained, was that he felt the civil suit should be delayed so that any impending criminal case could be tried first. He wanted to prevent information obtained for the criminal case from being used against Jackson in the civil suit. He was being a good lawyer. However, the strategy did serve to make Michael look as if he was trying to evade responsibility, at least in the eyes of the suspicious public and cynical media.

Immediately afterwards, Howard Weitzman attempted to deflect Bert Fields' comments. With a chagrined-looking Bert standing next to him, Howard said that Bert had 'misspoke himself'. No Grand Jury was convening at that moment; no indictment was 'imminent'. Who knows what kind of behind-the-scenes battles the two attorneys were having, but there was obviously a communication problem between them, one that served to make Michael look like he was trying to weasel out of the civil trial.

'I don't want to start more trouble,' John Branca told Michael, according to his memory. 'But you know that people here think you're trying to delay the trial for six years?'

'Six years? What are you talking about, Branca?' Michael wanted to know. 'I don't want to delay the trial, not even a day.'

John explained to Michael what happened in Los Angeles between the other two attorneys. 'No way, Branca,' Michael said of Bert's strategy. 'That's not what I want. I'm not guilty. I want this over with.' He was angry. 'What's Bert doing? No wonder everyone thinks I'm running scared.'

Later that same day, Michael came up with a pretty good line when talking to another associate on the telephone: 'I got a ship of fools representing me, and we're all going down.'

The issue of postponing Jackson's trial, as it happened, would be a moot one. The judge denied Bert Fields' petition, setting a trial date for 21 March.

Then, in a few weeks, a Santa Barbara Grand Jury *did* begin hearing witnesses, so Bert Fields hadn't been completely wrong. Furious with Howard Weitzman for making him look foolish, Bert resigned from the case, later calling the change of events 'an outrage. It was a nightmare and I wanted to get the hell out of it as soon as possible.'

At the same time, Anthony Pellicano, who had tired of the flak he had received for his aggressive tactics, resigned.

When Michael heard about all of the upheaval on his team, he telephoned Elizabeth Taylor to tell her that he was 'surrounded by people who don't know what the hell they're doing.' He had lost all hope, he said, according to what Elizabeth later recalled to one of Jackson's attorneys. 'He's threatening to kill himself,' she said, dramatically. 'And if he does, his blood will be on all of our hands.'

'Well, we're doing all we can do,' said one of Michael's advisers. 'What else can we do?'

'We can pray,' answered Elizabeth Taylor. 'At this point, I think that's about it.'

It was soon suggested that Michael Jackson wasn't being treated like the other patients at Charter when, after just a few days, he was granted permission to move his rehabilitation to the bucolic home of Elton John's manager, John Reid. Shortly thereafter, he was seen at Manor Farm, the estate of seventy-year-old British banking mogul Jack Dellal, a friend of Beechy Colclough. Hopefully, he was still getting his fifty thousand dollars a week's worth of mental health assistance. To a lot of people, including Elizabeth Taylor – who has had hardcore rehabilitation in her lifetime – it appeared that Michael was having some kind of 'quick fix'. Surely, it would take more than a few days, even a few months, for Michael to deal with so many years of dysfunction. All his friends could do was hope that he was on his way to being able to at least partially understand himself and his choices.

However, the fact that Michael was still doing business during this time was disconcerting. In fact, a big deal was struck while he was supposed to be in rehabilitation. He consulted with John Branca on the biggest music publishing agreement in history: one hundred and fifty million dollars with EMI to administer his ATV catalogue. John faxed the agreement to him at John Reid's. Upon signing it, seventy million dollars was deposited into Michael's bank account. 'The deal was already negotiated,' John later explained. 'A couple of phone calls to Michael for some fine-tuning. It wasn't much of a distraction, believe me, or I wouldn't have even called him. He was okay with it. It was good for him to know that things were going forward, that his life was far from over.'

Indeed, despite the turmoil in his life, Michael was still making money, and a great deal of it. *Dangerous* had thus far sold twenty million copies worldwide. In the UK, the record had debuted at the number one position. Propelled by a hit single, 'Black and White', and an accompanying controversial video (where Michael takes out his anger on an automobile, seems to pleasure himself with his own gyrating dancing, and then transforms into a panther), it was the fastest-selling number one album of all time in the UK, and remained on the charts for ninety-six weeks, a performance only exceeded in America. 'His past royalties were huge, especially for *Thriller*, and his residuals from The Beatles' catalogue, his stocks and other investments,' noted one advisor. 'The kid had plenty of money, millions.' One point was clear, however: he was determined not to give any of his money to Evan Chandler, despite whatever strategy his legal team had been considering with Johnnie Cochran, and despite his own determination that the matter be settled. An associate who was with him at Dellal's home recalled having asked him about a possible settlement the morning after the ATV deal was final. 'I said, "Mike, you can give up twenty million dollars of the new ATV money,"' he remembered. '"It's found money, anyway. For twenty million dollars, the whole Chandler thing can go away."

'"No way," he told me. "I want it settled, yeah, but with apologies all around, some kind of press release, whatever. I don't care. All I know is I'm not giving anyone a single dollar. I'm not pissing away my money on this lie. Forget it."

'His eyes were blazing. He insisted that he didn't do anything wrong, and he wasn't going to pay money to settle it. "I never touched that kid," he told me, "and that's the end of it. Believe what you want. See if I care."

'I said, "Mike, I believe you, of course." He looked at me angrily and said, "Yeah, right. Sure you do."'

Michael Stands Naked

On 10 December 1993, Michael Jackson returned to the United States after having been discharged from Charter clinic. Of course, he didn't simply hop on a commercial airline to cross the ocean. Rather, he flew back to the States in a private 727 owned by the Sultan of Brunei, said to be the wealthiest man in the world and an admirer of Michael's.

When Michael disembarked in Santa Barbara, he looked healthier than he had in recent months while wearing a red hat and matching silk shirt, black slacks and . . . surgical mask. He also had two youngsters with him, Eddie and Frank Cascio, from New Jersey, who had been travelling with him on his tour. Eddie was about ten; Frank fourteen.

Michael had befriended the Cascios about ten years earlier; their father, Dominic was the manager of New York's Helmsley Palace Hotel. Michael asked to meet the boys after seeing a picture of them on the wall of Dominic's office; they were just babies at the time.

Dominic accompanied his children on their 1993 travels with Michael; Michael was not alone with them. However, such chaperoning was not the impression given the media since Dominic was nowhere in sight when Michael made well-publicized appearances with the boys. They had even gone to Elizabeth Taylor's Swiss chalet in Gstaad (in September) and been photographed all over the small village, looking for toy stores, all three wearing large sunglasses, Michael in a big hat with surgical mask.

Eddie and Frank are in their twenties today, and are still good friends of Michael's. In court papers connected to one of the many suits filed against Michael in recent years, one by a business manager, Myung Ho Lee, states that Michael once loaned Dominic Cascio $600,000 to start a restaurant in New Jersey. However, the restaurant was never opened. Today, Frank Cascio goes by the name Frank Tyson, and is one of Michael's most trusted assistants.

Some in his camp had serious reservations about Michael continuing to be seen in the company of children at such a critical time in his life. Was he still so out of touch he didn't realize how inappropriate, not to mention dangerous, such behaviour was? Or, as one adviser put it, 'I guess the therapy thing didn't take, did it?'

Michael could not be swayed from continuing his friendships with children publicly. In fact, after being in therapy at Charter, Michael was more emboldened to live his life on his own terms, rather than consider any restrictions.

'Look, I almost died,' he told one associate. 'Do you know how close I was? Now that I am past it, no way am I not going to do what I want to do, when I want to do it and how. It's plain and simple,' Michael concluded, 'and anyone who doesn't like it can just go to hell.'

Michael Jackson has been hailed as a genius of a businessman. No matter how eccentric he seemed, it was said, he was actually a shrewd marketing genius – and the joke was on us. Maybe on some level that was true. However, one can't help but wonder if such a 'genius' would not know when to just . . . stop. Many of Michael's actions, especially in the last ten years, have caused observers to question if the perception of ingenuity in the 1980s was actually just good timing, and his willingness to take full advantage of it. Is it possible that Michael just made a couple of amazing albums, and then inherited the world because of his showmanship and ability to surround himself with *others* who were true marketing geniuses, like John Branca?

Others have argued that Michael's insistence that he be seen in the company of young boys demonstrates a consciousness of innocence on his part. If he had been guilty of the crime for which he had been accused, would he continue to flaunt his relationships with youngsters?

The bottom line is that Michael has done whatever he has wanted to do for most of his life, living in a world of privilege and entitlement simply because he is who he is. He has never understood the notion of 'appropriate behaviour' because, in truth, he's never had any reason to live appropriately. It's a strange commentary on celebrity and fame that the public's perception of Michael as being bizarre has had its advantages. After all, how can he be judged by normal, common-sense standards when he's 'Wacko-Jacko'?

However, in December of 1993 Michael was about to experience, if just for one day, what it might be like in the real world, where people often have to do things they may not necessarily want to do.

Upon Michael's return to the United States, he was immediately served with a warrant for the long-threatened strip search by the police. According to the order, officers expected to examine, photograph and videotape Michael's entire body, 'including his penis, anus, hips, buttocks and any other part of his body. Michael Jackson should be notified,' according to the order, 'that he has no right to refuse the examination and photographs. Any refusal to cooperate with this order will be admissible in a court and an indication of his guilt.' Also, it was explained to his attorneys that if he didn't cooperate, the police would probably just arrest him on 'probable cause' and take him away in handcuffs, in front of photographers. This scenario was more than anyone in his camp could even fathom.

Apparently, Jordie had claimed that Michael had distinguishing marks on his genitals. He even drew a diagram of Michael's penis on a napkin for police, and wrote on it: 'Michael is circumcised. He has short pubic hair. His testicles are marked with pink and brown marks. Like a cow, not white but pink colour. He has brown patches on ass, on his left glut.'

The police were now determined to learn if Jordie's description was accurate. If so, then he obviously had seen Michael Jackson unclothed.

The photo session, set for 20 December, promised to be as torturous an experience as Michael ever had in his life. Present from Santa Barbara would be its District Attorney, Thomas Sneddon, as well as a detective, photographer and a doctor. From Los Angeles, were Michael's attorneys, Johnnie Cochran and Howard Weitzman, and Dr David Forecast, one of Michael's physicians from the United Kingdom, as well as another detective and another photographer (employed by Michael), all of whom had arrived by helicopter.

After everyone arrived at Neverland, it took Johnnie Cochran and Howard Weitzman an hour to get Michael to leave his bedroom and go into the parlour, where the photos were to be taken. Finally, Michael came into the room, wearing a brown robe. It was agreed that his attorneys and Sneddon would leave the room and not be present for the photos. Bodyguard Bill Bray was allowed to remain, as would the two detectives and two photographers and two doctors.

As everyone was getting settled, Michael took a look at one of the detectives and, for no reason anyone could think of (except that he may have mistaken him for someone he knew), began shouting at him. 'You! Get out! I don't want you here for this. Get out!' Michael then tried to storm from the room. However, one of the doctors grabbed him. 'Hold on, Michael,' he said, 'hold on.' Johnnie and Howard, upon hearing the ruckus, came back into the room. 'Get these sons of bitches out of here,' Michael screamed at them, now referring to everyone in the room. He was agitated beyond all measure and actually seemed high, though everyone present hoped that was not the case.

The District Attorney's photographer, Gary Spiegel, began taking photographs of Michael while he was still seated on the couch. Michael blocked his face with his hands, as if thwarting a paparazzo.

Finally, an anguished Michael was told to stand on a platform in the middle of the room as if about to have his pants hemmed by a tailor. He was still wearing a bathrobe. 'Please don't make me do this,' he said, his doe-like eyes watery. 'This is terrible. Don't make me.'

'Sir, we have no choice,' said one of the detectives.

Then, while standing on that platform and staring at a picture of Elizabeth Taylor on the wall, Michael took off the bathrobe. Under it, he wore a bathing suit.

'You'll have to take it off, sir,' said the detective.

Still staring at the photograph of Elizabeth, Michael slipped the bathing suit off . . . under which he had on boxers.

'Sir, please.'

Crying softly now, Michael slipped off the boxers and stood, naked, stripped not only of his clothing but of the one illusion he'd always had: that of his invincibility. All eyes went right to his penis, which did not appear to be circumcised.

'Is the subject uncircumcised?' asked the doctor. Everyone stepped in for a closer look.

'Yes, he is . . .'

'No, he's not . . .'

'Yes.'

'No'

'Oh my God,' Michael whimpered. He looked dizzy, as if about to faint.

'You don't know?' asked one of the detectives of Michael's physician.

Michael's medic became indignant. 'Sir, I have never seen his penis before now.'

'Well, the subject is clearly *not* circumcised,' decided the other doctor, finally. He made a note of his finding.

As everyone circled him slowly, they began making other feverish notations about Michael's body.

Yes, he did have patchy-coloured skin on his buttocks, as Jordie described.

Yes, he had short pubic hair.

Yes, his testicles were marked, pink and brown.

However, no matter how many different ways they looked at it, all seemed to agree that his penis was uncircumcised. But, did that matter? In fact, an uncircumcised penis can look circumcised when aroused. If Michael had been sexually excited when seen by Jordie, would anyone, let alone a thirteen-year-old know if he was circumcised or not? But there was now doubt about the identity of the person in question.

'I then took several photographs of Jackson's penis,' said Gary Spiegel. 'First the right side, then the left. When I was photographing the left side, the D.A.'s doctor told Michael Jackson to lift up his penis. He didn't want to, so there was a lot of discussion about that. Finally he did it. Then, he angrily jumped off the platform. 'That's it,' Jackson said. 'That's enough.' He put on his robe and ran out of the room.'

The detectives looked at each other, one of them moved towards the room in which Michael's attorneys had been waiting. Then, as the detective headed back into the living room, Michael's lawyers stomped down the hall to get their client back before the waiting cameras. The cops were uncomfortable as they listened to what most would have guessed to be a rebellious teenager arguing loudly with strict, disappointed parents. Then, after fifteen minutes of cries, shrieks and pleas – silence. A moment later, the sound of one loud plaintive wail resonated through the house. Michael Jackson had been broken. He pounded his bare feet hard against the wood floor, moving towards the room he had worked so hard to make perfect for waiting guests.

'When this whole thing is done, I want pictures of *you*,' Michael said, pointing angrily at one of the photographers, 'and you, too,' he said, jabbing his finger at the other one.

Again, Michael stood naked. More pictures. Then, videotape.

'Please,' Michael said, his tone now pleading. 'Can we stop now?' One of the doctors pulled out a ruler.

'That's it,' said Michael's physician. 'Mike, get dressed. This is a joke. I can't believe it myself.'

Michael quickly put on his robe. 'Don't you ever, ever, *ever* let that happen again,' he said, unleashing his anger on poor Bill Bray, who just sat in the corner the whole time looking mortified.

'But I didn't do nothin', Mike,' Bill said. 'Why you hollerin' at me?'

Ignoring Bill's question, Michael stepped off the platform and ran from the living room. 'How could this happen to me?' he screamed on his way out. He was shaking. Observers said it looked as if he was about to have a melt-down. '*How could this happen to me?*' he kept repeating.

LaToya in Madrid

It was in the winter of 1993 that perhaps the most damaging blow of all to Michael Jackson's image was struck, and it came from a family member: his own sister, LaToya. Though she had not seen or talked to him in a number of years, LaToya claimed to have exclusive information about Michael. As it happened, like many of Michael's household employees who had sold stories to the tabloid press, LaToya and her husband, Jack, had their own sliding scale of scandal: for a fee of $50,000 she would come forth with certain secrets about familial abuse that she had not yet revealed in her many interviews about the subject. However, for twice that, she would open up twice as much – and for a half-million she would throw caution to the wind and just come out and admit that Michael was a paedophile, and that she had proof to support her allegation.

The bidding war began with the British *News of the World* tabloid, who ponied up a substantial amount of money, only to be topped by the American *National Enquirer* and *Star*. However, during the course of the week, as editors pushed for details of LaToya's revelations, negotiations collapsed. It became clear that she didn't have much to offer, after all. Left without his planned windfall, Jack then arranged for LaToya to hold a press conference in Tel Aviv, Israel, where she was on tour.

'Michael is my brother and I love him very much,' she said, reading from a prepared statement, 'but I cannot and will not be a silent collaborator in his crimes against young children. If I remain silent, then that means I feel the guilt and humiliation that these children are feeling, and I think it is very wrong. Forget about the superstar, forget about the icon. If he was any other thirty-five-year-old man who was sleeping with little boys, you wouldn't like this guy.'

She also said that she had seen cancelled cheques made out to several boys for large sums of money, shown to her she said by her mother, Katherine, suggesting that Michael had bought their silence. She said that she sympathized with the children, 'because I am a victim myself. When parents abuse their children, the children go on to be abusers themselves,' she said. 'Do you know how many children are going to psychiatrists because of Michael? So many, many children.'

The Jackson family, understandably upset by LaToya's position, then hosted a press conference at their Encino estate. Distraught, Katherine said, 'LaToya's lying. I'll tell her to her face she's lying. I can't believe I have a daughter out there saying these things to sell her brother down the river. She's been brainwashed by her money-grabbing mongrel of a husband.'

For weeks to come, LaToya's charges made big news, while she finally started making big money. That she is Michael's sister gave her point of view special credibility; her stories did more damage to Michael than anything that had ever been charged by any house-keeper in his employ. From country to country, LaToya and Jack ventured forth, pitting television producers and newspaper editors against one another in bidding wars for her anecdotes about Michael. Meanwhile, family members continued to vilify LaToya. 'But Michael supports the entire Jackson family, financially,' LaToya said. 'They have to support him.'

In December 1993 I was asked by the producers of a Spanish television show in Madrid called *La Máquina De Mentira* (*The Lying Machine*), to appear with LaToya and discuss with her the allegations she had made against Michael. As it was explained to me, LaToya would be hooked up to a lie detector machine. Then, I was to ask her questions about why she believed Michael was a paedophile. The television audience would be able to judge, by virtue of how LaToya fared on the test, the veracity of her observations.

Coincidentally, 22 December, the day we were in the studio and waiting to go on the air, was the same day Michael gave a four-minute speech from Neverland, first carried live by CNN and then re-broadcast all over the world.

'I ask all of you to wait and hear the truth before you condemn me,' he said, holding back tears. 'Don't treat me like a criminal, because I am innocent.'

Dressed in a red shirt with red lipstick, false eyelashes and long strands of hair framing his heavily made-up face, Michael had harsh words for the media which, he charged, 'has dissected and manipulated these allegations to reach their own conclusions.' He grew more emotional when describing the examination and subsequent photo session of his body: 'I have been forced to submit to a dehumanizing and humiliating examination by the Santa Barbara County Sheriff's Department and the Los Angeles Police Department earlier this week. They served a search warrant on me which allowed them to view and photograph my body, including my penis, my buttocks, my lower torso, thighs and any other areas they wanted. They were supposedly looking for any discoloration, spotting blotches or other evidence of a skin colour disorder called Vitiligo, which I have previously spoken about.

'It was the most humiliating ordeal of my life, one that no person should ever have to suffer. And even after experiencing the indignity of this search, the parties involved were still not satisfied and wanted to take even more pictures. It was a nightmare, a horrifying nightmare. But if this is what I have to endure to prove my innocence, my complete innocence, so be it.'

'Don't treat me like a criminal,' Michael insisted, 'because I am innocent.'

As LaToya stared at the TV screen, tears sprung from her large, expressive eyes. She seemed lost in thought until Jack Gordon burst into the room and laid waste to her reverie. 'The show is off,' he said. 'I'm not allowing LaToya to be hooked up to any damn lie detector.'

'Why?' LaToya wanted to know.

'We agreed on fifty thousand dollars,' Jack explained. 'But with Michael crying his eyes out on TV, I'm doubling her fee to a hundred thousand. I just told the producers, and they said to go to hell. So, we're out of here. The hell with *them*.'

Jack grabbed LaToya by the arm.

'I'm sorry you came all the way to Spain for nothing,' she told me, looking victimized. 'What a waste of time for you. You must think I'm a terrible person, now. But, really, I'm not.' She was then hustled from the room by her husband. 'Tell Michael I'm sorry,' she said, while being whisked away.

Years later, LaToya would insist that the allegations she'd made against Michael were all Jack's fabrications, which she was made to repeat against her will. Though it would take a few years, by 2003 she and Michael had cleared the air between them and were, again, close. LaToya also apologized to the rest of her family members; they then all accepted her back into the fold.

Michael Pays Up

By 1 January 1994, nearly two million dollars had been spent by prosecutors and police departments in California jurisdictions on the investigation of Michael Jackson. Two Grand Juries had questioned more than two hundred witnesses, including thirty children who had been friends of Michael's over the years. Not one witness could be found who could corroborate Jordie Chandler's story, and without other witnesses the authorities' case against Michael was weak. Perhaps Michael had the undying loyalty of the youngsters with whom he'd had sex? Or, maybe all of those who had investigated the singer were inept? Or was it possible that he was innocent?

11 January marked Jordie's fourteenth birthday, but he had no party. He wasn't in the mood to celebrate, he said. When he blew out the candles on his cake, Evan asked him to make a wish. 'I wish this nightmare would end,' he said. As a gift, Evan gave him a bottle of mace, for his protection.

On that same day, more damage was done to Michael's image when transcripts of depositions in the Jackson–Chandler civil suit were filed in Los Angeles Superior Court as part of a motion brought by attorney Larry Feldman. Arguing that he should be allowed access to Michael's financial records since, as he put it, 'there is substantial probability' that his client would prevail in the suit, Feldman filed the transcripts as a demonstration of the evidence against Jackson. Also included was a new declaration from Jordie, who had repeated the original allegations he had made about Michael to police and social workers.

Transcripts filed by Larry Feldman included sworn depositions from Michael Jackson's former chauffeur, former maids and secretaries. Truth or fiction, it didn't matter; all of it was now a part of the public record. Composed mostly of hearsay, speculation and innuendo, and much of it from people who'd already been paid handsomely by tabloid television programmes and newspapers to 'reveal all' about their boss, it was difficult to imagine that such statements would have been given much credence by a jury.

No doubt, Jordie Chandler's detailed testimony would have been the most damaging to Michael. One wondered, though, how a jury would have reacted to the fact that the original allegation, that Michael had touched his penis, was given while under a mind-altering drug? And what of the question of Michael's being circumcised or not? In the end, it would be Michael's word against Jordie's, because there were no witnesses to any episodes of molestation (but, then again, there are rarely witnesses to such events).

Due to his celebrity status, it was possible that Michael could prevail at the civil trial. A mountain of circumstantial evidence (not to mention the impact that might be made on a jury by his wrong-minded determination to continually flaunt young boys in public) was probably not enough to secure a verdict against him. However, the question then was: was it worth it for him to find out? His attorneys didn't think so, feeling that more harm than good would occur by having so many disclosures made public. Plus, what if he really *was* guilty? What would such a trial do to the already-victimized Jordie Chandler? Though Jordie certainly wasn't the primary concern of Michael's attorneys, they empathized with him and felt a sense of responsibility to him simply because of his youth. They probably didn't care much about his father, though, not after all that had occurred.

When Larry Feldman began nosing into Michael's finances, he had crossed a line. 'A lot of terrible business had gone down for Michael, but once Feldman started demanding information about his bank accounts, we knew the game was over,' said one of Michael's advisers. 'You can take pictures of Michael's dick, and he's not gonna like it. But once you start trying to figure out how much money he has, that's where he stops playing around.'

Unbeknownst to even Michael's attorneys, Lisa Marie Presley had also tried to influence his decision to settle. A seasoned survivor of many publicity wars, she had long thought that Michael should end the matter with a cash pay-out. She was finally able to convince him that, as she later put it, 'some things, like a good night's sleep, are more important than public opinion.'

He wanted to get on with his life, Michael said, so that he could finally marry Lisa. Not much movement had occurred in their relationship since his odd proposal to her on the telephone, and he was afraid that she was becoming impatient with him. 'The only thing I got out of therapy is that it's my responsibility to have a good life,' he said, 'and maybe I can have that with Lisa. I don't want to lose her, now.'

Indeed, Michael Jackson was finally leaning toward paying Evan Chandler the money Jordie's father had originally sought. 'They've worn me down, I admit it,' he told one of his attorneys. He wondered what more 'they can do to humiliate me, to ruin me? I don't know what else to do but pay the guy.'

The attorney suggested that, perhaps, they should have done as much at the beginning of the debacle.

'It's not like we didn't try, now is it?' Michael observed, wryly. 'What a nightmare this has been, to now only end up back at square one.' He concluded that he was so unhappy about all of it, he wished he could 'just crawl into a hole.'

Another thing had also changed for Michael: he no longer wanted to think about Jordie Chandler. No one could mention the youngster's name to him. If, as they say, a thin line exists between love a hate, Michael seemed to cross it after he was forced to pose naked for the police. The subject of Jordie was off limits from that day onward.

On 16 January, Michael hosted a party for two hundred underprivileged children at Neverland. There he was, on news broadcasts all over the world, cavorting with children and gaily leading them in their fun day, like a Pied Piper. Some observers wondered if he had any sense, at all. His advisers were more frustrated than they were angry. ('I give up,' said one. 'I *fucking give up*.')

Michael's behaviour would never change, that much was clear. True to form, he was going to continue doing what he wanted to do, and that would have to be the end of it.

On 25 January 1994, Michael Jackson agreed to pay twenty-two million dollars to Jordie Chandler, Evan Chandler, June Chandler-Schwartz and attorney Larry Feldman. Twenty million of it was earmarked for Jordie. One million each went to Evan and June. Larry Feldman then got about five million from all three of them in contingency fees. Jordie's money would be held in a trust for him, to be paid out over the intervening years under the supervision of a court-appointed trustee.

'He had sex with Jordie, and he paid a price,' said a member of Jordie's family of Michael. 'He ruined the kid's life. I hope he learned a lesson, the pervert. But I doubt it. He should be in jail. But he's not, so good for him.'

In the end, no criminal charges would be brought against Michael by the police or the Grand Juries, citing a lack of evidence. They had many witnesses, said the police, but no victims who actually wanted to testify against Michael Jackson.

'All's well that ends well,' said Anthony Pellicano, bitterly. 'From the beginning, this case was always about how much money the father could get out of Michael Jackson. So he got what he wanted, I guess.'

Attorney Michael Freeman, who had represented June Chandler-Schwartz, says that, in his opinion, Michael was innocent of any wrong-doing. 'I think he was wrongly accused,' said the attorney. 'I think that Evan Chandler and Barry Rothman saw an opportunity and went for it. That's my personally held opinion. I believe it was all about money, and their strategy, obviously, worked.'

Elizabeth Taylor's comment about the end of the investigation and litigation was classic spin-doctor Liz. 'Thank God this case is being dismissed,' she said. 'Michael's love of children is one of the purest things I have ever seen, it shines like an extra sun, despite the media's distorted lens. I always knew this would be thrown out of court, and I am so grateful.'

The Last Word on the Matter

When I conducted a telephone interview with Michael in August 1994, after the allegations were settled, he told me, 'Too much damage had already been done to everyone involved. I don't care what people think. I know the truth. If anyone has ever gone through something like this, they'd know you'll do anything to end it.'

Of the case, Michael suggested extortion, but without actually saying as much since he was not supposed to speak about the case by legal agreement (which didn't stop him, though, in other instances). 'Lots of people are always trying stuff like this, trying to hurt me, embarrass me. I thought this was just another one of those things. I never dreamed it would blow up to be the mess it became. I'd never hurt a child, and any child who has ever been my friend knows that. I'd never, ever, ever hurt any child on this planet.'

'I want to go on with my life,' he said, passionately. 'I want to make records. I want to sing. I want to perform again. Tell my fans I have supreme confidence that they'll judge me on stage and in the recording studio, just as they always have. I don't believe this nightmare will interfere with my career,' he added, 'because I've spent too many years developing my relationship with the fans. They should just know that, yes, I paid some money. So what? But no, I'm not guilty. I did nothing wrong.'

I asked him if he was concerned that, his fans aside, he would be thought of by much of the general public as having been guilty because of the way he settled the case. His answer was direct: 'It's my talent. My hard work. My life. My decision.'

Today, Jordie Chandler is twenty-three years old and living on eastern Long Island near the beach in a $2.35 million home, under an assumed name. He and his family also own a high-rise apartment in Manhattan and a condominium in Santa Barbara.

Evan Chandler also lives in Long Island – under an assumed name.

June Chandler and David Schwartz are divorced.

Jordie hasn't seen Michael Jackson since that day in Anthony Pellicano's office a decade ago when Evan and Michael had their final show-down. The last instalment of Michael's payments to Jordie was paid in June 1999.

PART ELEVEN

Michael and Lisa Marie Become Lovers

On 1 February 1994, Michael telephoned Lisa Marie Presley at her estate in Hidden Hills, California. He was at his hide-out in Westwood. 'Hey, listen up, girl,' he said, according to her memory, 'I'm heading up to Las Vegas to see The Temptations and the Fifth Dimension. Come with me. I'll get us a suite at the Mirage and we can party like there's no tomorrow.'

'Am I staying in the suite with you?' she asked

'Hell, yeah,' Michael said. 'What do you think, girl?'

'I think I'm still married,' Lisa said.

'Then separate rooms, if that's what you want,' Michael responded.

Lisa agreed to go; the next day, the two flew up to Vegas in Michael's private plane.

Otis Williams of The Temptations once told me, 'Man, we were backstage after the show, and here comes Mike with this chick, and he's all up in her face, kissing on her, and we were saying, "Who the heck is this girl?" Finally, he introduced her: Lisa Marie Presley. You could have knocked me over with a feather. I said to the guys, "Check this out. The King of Pop and the King's daughter, together. It had to happen. They looked pretty cosy."'

Two weeks later, Lisa accompanied Michael again to the MGM Grand in Las Vegas for his appearance on *The Jackson Family Honors Special* (the programme Jermaine had been working on for months). Designed to pay homage to Elizabeth Taylor and Berry Gordy, the television special was also an attempt by the Jacksons to project a wholesome image to a now-suspicious public.

Janet made a quick appearance performing her hit 'All Right', before vanishing from sight as if embarrassed for herself and every-one else on stage. She had little to do with any of her family members, and steadfastly refused to appear in the planned finale. She even checked into the Luxor Hotel, rather than take a chance on running into anyone named Jackson at the MGM Grand, where most of them were staying. Michael also wanted little to do with his father or siblings, which was not a surprise. Though Jermaine had generously offered him a suite at the MGM Grand, he chose to stay at the Mirage.

'When does the boy grow up and not have to go to the family reunions?' Lisa has said he asked her. He said that it was taking 'everything I have' to show his face in public again after all that had happened with the Chandlers, 'and to now have to do it at one of these things is really hard for me.' If it wasn't for his mother, he said, he would never even attempt it.

'But if you weren't here, there wouldn't even be a show,' Lisa observed.

'Exactly,' Michael said, dryly. He adjusted the red arm band on his black military jacket. 'If I could, I think I would pay twenty million dollars for them to be more famous than me.' He seemed exhausted. 'What a relief it would be to accept their love and not have to wonder what they have planned for me, next.'

It was then that Lisa had an uncomfortable encounter with Elizabeth Taylor, who had tried to coax Michael into performing. He didn't want to sing. Rather, he just wanted to make an appearance, present an award, and then sit in the audience. As Elizabeth tried to change his mind, an already-protective Lisa intervened. 'Look, he's not going to perform,' she told Elizabeth, 'so you might as well just leave it alone.' Elizabeth, taken aback, gave Lisa a once-over and remarked, 'Well, you're the boss, I guess,' and walked away.

(In the end, after the show was broadcast, Michael ended up getting dragged into a messy lawsuit between the producers of the show against the Jackson family.)

When they got back from Las Vegas, on 21 February, Michael invited Lisa to Neverland. The two spent hours walking hand in hand on the well-manicured property, as Lisa's children, Danielle, five, and Benjamin Storm, eighteen months, played with their nanny. Workers at the estate recall seeing Michael and Lisa kissing while high atop the Ferris wheel, then nodding graciously to the Neverland staff members as they sauntered from one ride to the next.

There were times when Michael seemed unable to contain his laughter; he seemed to appreciate Lisa's sharp and clever mind as much as he relished her new role as protector and sounding board. 'I can run anything by her,' he said, 'and she has a good point of view about it. She's on top of everything, she knows so much. I've never known a person like her.'

He made sure all of her needs were met in an instant. If she got thirsty, he would clap his hands once and, as if by magic, a waiter would appear with an aperitif. If she was too tired to walk, someone driving a golf cart would appear to take her back to her room for a nap.

For the first two days, Lisa and her children stayed in one of the visitors' units on the property. On the third night, Michael ordered a dinner of poached salmon and cucumber salad to be served to him and Lisa on one of the candle-lit terraces. Afterward, he presented Lisa with a gift: a three-strand, pearl choker with a diamond clasp at the front, worth about $50,000. That evening, while her children and their nanny slept in the guest quarters, Lisa stayed with Michael in his bedroom.

Did they make love? Lisa, say her friends, is a woman who enjoys physical intimacy and would not become involved in a relationship that was not sexual. She was aware that her mother and father had stopped being intimate shortly after she was conceived. Elvis met Priscilla when she was just fourteen; he was twenty-four. The two lived together for six years before marrying in Las Vegas, but were never intimate. Then, on their honeymoon, Priscilla got pregnant. Eight months later, Lisa was born. After that, Elvis would never touch Priscilla again saying he felt weird having sex with his child's mother. 'I was young and accepted his way of life as normal,' Priscilla recalled. Though she was one of the most publicized women in America, Priscilla then lived in a sexless marriage for a couple of years before she got involved with her karate instructor – and that was pretty much the end of her marriage to Elvis. Lisa was not about to find herself in the same situation.

In truth, Lisa and Michael had an intense and active sex life, which came as a surprise to many people. According to all available evidence, it was the first time he had ever experienced such chemistry with a woman, or with *anyone*, for that matter. His associates say the early stages of the romance impacted his personality in positive ways, in terms of his self-confidence and self-image. 'Apparently, Michael Jackson is a freak in bed,' said Lisa's friend Monica Pastelle. 'Lisa said he was amazing, and she's been around. Everyone was saying, "No way, Lisa. It can't be true. Michael Jackson? Are we talking about *the* Michael Jackson, the one with the glove?" However, she wasn't joking, and it wasn't long before she didn't think it was funny, either.'

Who knows why it became so intense for Michael with Lisa. However, it was this surprising – some may think of it as astonishing – sexual component that most cemented the relationship between Michael and Lisa.

The 'first time' for them was in Florida, during a weekend stay at Donald Trump's Mar-A-Lago estate in Palm Beach. Donald recalls seeing Michael and Lisa walking hand in hand on his estate, seeming lost in a mutual dream. In a photograph taken that day, Lisa was elegantly dressed in a severely tailored, black silk dress that fell in fluid lines around her shapely figure. Michael was wearing a sharp, black suit, scarlet-coloured shirt and matching tie. At one point, he dropped to one knee and kissed her hand. She urged him to his feet; the two embraced. Michael gazed at her intensely, mesmerized by her face. They kissed. He pulled from his vest pocket a small, wrapped box. When she opened it, Lisa's face lit up. Pearls.

'It was romantic,' Donald Trump recalled. 'Later, I asked Michael how things were going and he said, "Great. I just got to kiss the most beautiful girl in the world. I hope I'm worthy of her. I think I might marry her."'

'They made love at the Trump estate,' said another one of Lisa's confidantes. 'She said it was intense, it took her breath away. I have no idea what they were doing, or what *he* was doing to her, but since she gravitates toward the unconventional, she was out of her mind over this guy. Maybe it's hard for some to believe,' she concluded, 'but true, just the same.

'After that first time, she went to turn on the lights, and he leapt out of bed and ran into the bathroom so she wouldn't see his body. He emerged twenty minutes later, in full makeup and wearing a silk robe.

Then, they went at it, again. He liked her to wear jewellery in bed. They were into role-playing games, though Lisa would never say who was playing what kind of role.'

To say that Michael wanted children is to understate the way he felt about procreation. He craved offspring. When Lisa didn't become immediately pregnant, even before they were married, he began to express his disappointment. 'I want children,' he said, 'and I thought we would be expecting one within a couple of weeks of making love. But Lisa says it takes time. I don't have time,' he said. 'I want it to happen, now. I want children so badly.'

Michael and Lisa Marie: Happily Ever After?

On 26 May 1994, Michael and Lisa were finally married in the Dominican Republic after a brief and, according to her, 'uneventful', courtship. Lisa's divorce from Danny Keough had been finalized twenty days earlier.

Lisa's mother Priscilla had married the most famous singer of her time back in 1967, and now Lisa followed suit with a man who was, arguably, pop music's biggest star. Though Michael and Lisa claimed to be crazy about one another, much of the public just thought they were crazy. 'I actually did fall in love with him,' she told *Newsweek* in the spring of 2003, 'but I don't know what was on his menu.'

The close relationship they had forged during the time of the allegations was known only to those in Michael's and Lisa's inner-circle. The two had managed to keep the fact that they even knew each other out of the press. Therefore, when they married, it was like a bolt from the blue.

Lisa was in love with Michael; did he feel the same about her? Always painfully conscious of the emptiness of his life, he said that he'd been missing out on 'too much' and wanted to now jump-start his life. After the Jordie Chandler business, the gnawing, empty space in his heart somehow seemed more terrifying than ever. He was determined to now 'start living', he insisted and, at the time, that meant being in love with a woman, marrying and having children with her. Lisa Marie Presley was that woman.

'When he nearly lost everything because of the allegations and then the drug abuse, he was determined to set things straight,' recalled one of his associates. 'He may have been in love with her, I don't know. I think he was actually in love with what she represented: conformity and kids. Everyone who knew him felt it was too soon after rehab for him to be jumping into a marriage, especially since he'd never been married and had no idea what he was doing. I knew he wasn't emotionally equipped for it. I also think the physical relationship was a powerful tool in convincing him that, yes, she was the one. However, as far as I know, she had been the *only* one.'

Michael was deeply disappointed in the wedding ceremony, he later admitted. He's a romantic. He'd always hoped for a grand, opulent and loving affair, like Jermaine's wedding had been so many years earlier. It was significant to him that he one day have a ceremony to join him with someone he loved and to express his affection for that person before family and friends. Sure, he had romanticized the notion over the years, but so what? People have done so throughout the ages, and have seen those dreams become reality in their lives. Michael never imagined that he would run off and marry a person in secret, as if ashamed of his relationship.

What Michael and Lisa ended up with was a fifteen-minute ceremony in front of a judge at his home in La Vega, eighty-five miles east of Casa de Campo, a resort owned by fashion designer, Oscar de la Renta (where Michael and Lisa had sequestered themselves in a four-thousand-dollar-a-night oceanfront villa). The ceremony was conducted in Spanish, and translated to Michael and Lisa by one of the attorneys present. Instead of the tuxedo he had dreamed of wearing on his wedding day, Michael wore black pants and matching shirt with a cowboy belt, bolero and black flamenco hat. Lisa also wore black. They exchanged heavy gold wedding bands. Michael later said he missed having Katherine present and to some extent, even Joseph. 'It just didn't feel right,' he said. 'It felt empty, like everything else in my world.'

Rather than blame his frustration on his and Lisa's lack of preparation for the event, Michael blamed it on the media saying that there was no way he could have had the ritual of his dreams, 'because the press would have made it a fiasco.' It was a shame, felt those who knew him and cared for him, that he kept missing out on a good and fulfilling life because of his celebrity, and that he continued to blame such intangibles as 'the media' for his grief over it. After all, even his friend Elizabeth Taylor managed to have big and wonderful wedding ceremonies along the way.

Perhaps it's a clue to their insecurity about what they were doing that Michael and Lisa didn't warn their families and friends about the wedding, lest someone try to induce them to reverse their decision. It wasn't a surprise, perhaps, that Michael didn't confide in Katherine, Joseph or his siblings, considering his complex relationship with them. However, that he didn't tell Elizabeth Taylor in advance was really startling – especially to her. When Michael finally telephoned Elizabeth from the Dominican Republic to give her the news, she was so distraught she spent the next day on the telephone with friends saying that she was, as she put it, 'so worried about Michael, I don't know what to do. I'm pulling my hair out over it! What has he done? *What has he done?*'

That night, Elizabeth was with friends at the Polo Lounge in the Beverly Hills Hotel. When a reporter asked her if she would confirm rumours of Michael's marriage, she snapped at him, 'I am *not* in the business of clarifying rumours. Now, be gone!'

The fact that Lisa kept the news from her mother, Priscilla, to whom she is close, also spoke volumes. It would be almost a week before Lisa confirmed to her frantic mother that she had married Michael Jackson.

Feeling strongly that Michael was exploiting her daughter and using her to rehabilitate his damaged image, Priscilla was not happy about the news. 'Can't you see what he's up to?' she asked her, according to what Lisa later recalled. 'It's so obvious.'

Lisa disagreed. She felt that Michael truly loved her. He had said as much and she had no choice, she felt, but to take him for his word. 'I can't say what his intentions were with me, but I can say it was the most real thing I think he's had,' Lisa noted in the spring of 2003. 'My mother was like, "Timing! *Hello?*" But I rebelled against my mom, of course, and tried really hard not to think like that, not to believe that.'

'My God! Use your instincts,' Priscilla admonished her. She

could not believe her daughter would marry, of all people on the planet, Michael Jackson. 'What does your gut tell you?'

'It tells me that you should mind your own goddamn business,' Lisa shot back. 'It's time for me to lead my own life and for you to stay out of it.' Clearly she and Priscilla had issues that pre-dated her marriage to Michael. Also, her sexual chemistry with Michael was so intense, Lisa wasn't about to give it up.

'All I wanted at the time was to believe what he was telling me, and that was it. It was this whole psychodrama that was going on, and I really put my mother through it. She thought he was lying to me, using me.'

Lisa's ex-husband, Danny – still a trusted friend – was also unhappy about the union. He knew better than to drag her into a fight with her about it, though. However, he told her that he was concerned, about her and about their children. It seemed to him, as it did to everyone else in her life, that she had made a big mistake.

Michael decided that he didn't want to announce the marriage. He said he wanted them to have their privacy. However, Lisa disagreed. 'The more we hide it, the more interest there will be in it,' she argued. 'Shouldn't we just announce it so that the interest will die down?' She didn't know Michael very well, did she? Of course, what he really wanted to do was to create a big, worldwide controversy about his relationship with her; he just couldn't help himself.

His strategy worked. For the next two months, the press ran with headlines speculating as to whether or not Michael and Lisa had been married. Meanwhile, the two took a duplex apartment suite in Trump Tower in New York (directly below Donald Trump's), while Michael began work on a new album.

If Lisa thought she was famous before, she would discover an entirely new – and unwelcome – sort of celebrity, as Michael's wife. One of his bodyguards remembered, 'It was chaos with the media and fans suspecting the newlyweds were in the suite, but not able to confirm it. One morning, we were getting ready to leave, and Mike had to explain the strategy involved in getting them out of there. He didn't want them seen together. For him, everything was a big drama. Nothing could just occur easily; it had to unfold with loads of bedlam and confusion. That's just what he's used to, and I think he thrives on it.'

As Michael was putting on his hat and his surgical mask and his sunglasses and his makeup, he explained to Lisa, 'See, first you leave, and they'll take you downstairs in the back, and then – *whoosh!* – off you'll go in the car with the smoky windows. Then, I will do the same. And we'll meet up later, and nobody will be the wiser.' He seemed delighted by the intrigue.

'He was all ready to go, looking like Michael Jackson looks with the mask on his face and hat on top of his head,' said the bodyguard. 'She sized him up from head to toe and said, "Fuck, no. Screw this shit." And she just got into the front elevator and went down to the lobby, alone. He started screaming, "Lisa! No! It's dangerous out there! They'll eat you alive!" Then, he turned to me and said, "Don't just stand there you big idiot, follow her." So, I raced down after her in another elevator. When I got there, she was gone. When I went back up and told Michael, he freaked out. "My poor wife! She's been kidnapped," he said, acting like the biggest drama queen, ever. "How will I live with myself? Call the police," he shrieked. "No, call the FBI. No, call the CIA." I said, "Look, man, she's probably in a coffee shop somewhere eating a doughnut. Let me find her." I did find her, an hour later, in a bar down the street, having a martini with some guy she'd just met, and it was ten in the morning. I thought to myself, What a match-up *this* is.'

Finally, in July, Michael and Lisa announced that they'd been married the previous May.

When I appeared on the United States news programme, *Good Morning America* to report on the news of Michael's marriage, I joked that 'the newlyweds are registered at Toys 'R' Us.' There was, I felt at the time, little choice but to remain light about the subject, the reaction to the news had been so cynical in America. After the show was broadcast, I received a telephone call from an irate Michael. 'How could you say that?' he demanded. 'How can you make light of my marriage? I love Lisa. Why won't people believe that? Why won't people let me be happy?'

'You have to understand that it does seem odd,' I explained. 'The marriage came out of nowhere. There are people who don't believe it's legitimate.'

'You know what? I don't care what people think,' Michael said angrily. 'She's my wife, I love her.'

I took the opportunity to ask Michael a few questions about the relationship. Did he and Lisa have a pre-nuptial agreement? 'No way,' he said. 'What kind of marriage would that be?'

Was Lisa pregnant, as had been reported? 'No,' he said, 'but we want children and we *will* have children. But don't rush me,' he said, now giggling.

There had been recent reports that Lisa had plastic surgery in a Los Angeles hospital, her breasts enlarged and liposuction on her hips, at Michael's behest. It was preposterous, but I decided to ask him about it, anyway. 'Ridiculous,' he told me. 'Just try telling Lisa Marie what to do. It would never happen. I would not be able to convince her to do anything. The truth,' he said, 'is that she had scar tissue removed from an appendectomy, and dermabrasion on her face to get rid of old acne scars.'

He also volunteered an anecdote about giving her an engagement ring (after his telephone proposal, once they were in Los Angeles, together). 'Lisa and I were in the living room [at Neverland] having a glass of wine,' he said. 'We had just finished watching *All About Eve*, starring the great Bette Davis. We both love that movie. I walked over to her, reached into my pocket and pulled out this huge, diamond ring. "So what do you think?" I asked her. "You wanna?" She screamed out, "Yes, yes, yes." So, anyway, I gotta go,' he concluded. 'Just tell people to leave us alone, will you? We're happy. That should be the end of it.'

As it turned out, even though Lisa was in love with Michael, *she* – not he – was the one with certain goals she hoped to achieve as a result of the marriage; chief among them was the realization of her musical career. 'Michael told Lisa that he would attempt to get her a record deal at Sony,' says her friend, Monica Pastelle. 'Yes, she loved him. She didn't marry him because of the offer to help her career, but it was on the table as something he was going to work on for her.'

For the next year, the newlyweds divided their time between Michael's 27,000-acre ranch in Santa Ynez, California, and Lisa's one-acre estate in Hidden Hills, a hundred miles away. Some thought Lisa and her two children would move into Neverland. No chance. She wanted to maintain her independence. Plus, her kids thought Michael was a little strange, especially five-year-old Danielle. No matter how hard he tried with her, Michael could never win over the girl. He was usually so good with children, but not with Danielle. She would take one look at him, squeal and run in the other direction. 'What'd I do? What'd I do?' Michael would ask. Therefore, whenever Lisa and her offspring went to stay at Neverland, she would tell her housekeeper, 'Just pack our toothbrushes and a few comfortable pairs of walking shoes, 'cause I don't think we'll be staying very long.'

Once she started living with him in their residences, Lisa was even more amazed at the degree to which Michael was emotionally repressed. Determined to 'fix him', she busily went about the work of peeling away layer after layer, as if he were an onion. However, it was difficult; the protective layers around him were thick and impenetrable. It had taken years for him to become who he was, and he wasn't going to easily change. He didn't *want* to become more communicative, as Lisa had insisted. He didn't *want* to become more extroverted, either, as she had suggested.

Most maddening to Lisa, her new husband continually blamed other people for problems that were clearly of his own making. Lisa, a Scientologist, maintained that she was the architect of her own life and had no one to blame but herself for the aspects of it that had not worked out for her. When her first marriage to Danny Keough ended, she didn't blame the press or her fame, she blamed herself and later felt that she had made a critical mistake in ending it. She wished she could go back, but she couldn't – so she moved forward and found a way to incorporate Danny into her life, as a best friend.

'Lisa felt Michael was too much into playing the victim,' said Monica Pastelle. 'Maybe it was understandable, given all he'd been through in the last year. Their relationship became strained as she tried to prod him along, make him feel less sorry for himself, lift his spirits. She said he was like a young boy, angry at the world. She had no patience at all with the lost childhood routine. "Who hasn't had a miserable childhood?" she would say. "Show me someone who loved every single second of their childhood, and I'll show you a person who has deluded himself into believing such a thing." '

Michael and Lisa certainly didn't make many television appearances, but the two that they did agree to do together are memorable. In September 1994, they made their first television appearance as husband and wife on the MTV Awards in New York, in front of two hundred and fifty million television viewers.

Backstage, according to Lisa, Michael announced to her, 'Now, check it out, girl. I'm going to kiss you when we get out there.'

'Oh no, you're not,' she said.

'Oh, yes I am,' he said, smiling. He thought they were bantering, but Lisa wasn't kidding.

'No, Michael,' she said. 'That's bullshit. Absolutely not. I don't want to do it.'

'Oh, sure you do,' he remarked. 'It'll be great.'

'I'm telling you, don't you fucking do that, Michael,' she warned him. 'I'm serious.'

About an hour later, they walked on to the stage to thunderous applause, holding hands. Lisa didn't know when the kiss was going to happen, she would recall, but she knew he was going to do it because 'by this time I realized that he does whatever he wants to do.' She said that, as they walked out from the wings, she was squeezing his hand so hard, 'I think I cut off the circulation.'

'Just think, nobody thought this would last,' Michael told the audience with a grin. He motioned to Lisa. Then, he embraced her and kissed her fully on the lips.

'It looked awkward because I wanted out of my skin,' Lisa said, years later. 'I hated it. I felt used, like a prop,' she said. 'It was awful.'

'Afterward, they had a huge fight about it,' said Monica Pastelle. 'Her whole thing was, "I told you no, and you just disregarded it." But Michael thought it was great, a showstopper. He was all about the show, you know? What could they do that would cause headlines? That's where his head was at. "But people will be talking about that kiss for decades," he said. "Don't you see? They're gonna run that clip over and over." Lisa was pissed off for days. "Don't you fucking even come *near* me," she told him.'

That same week, Michael became annoyed by newspaper reports that suggested that if Elvis Presley were alive, he would not approve of the marriage. 'I think we need to find out,' he said. He suggested that he and Lisa have a seance to contact the King. He was serious. He told Lisa he had friends who could communicate with the deceased, and that they could make it possible for him and Lisa to talk to Elvis and ask his opinion of the union. Lisa thought the idea was tasteless. When Michael continued to push it, she lashed out at him. 'I said no,' she told him, angrily, 'and if you stay on this particular road, they're gonna need a medium to contact *you* in the great beyond, because I'm about to put you there, right now.' Michael never mentioned the idea, again. 'Jeez, it was just a suggestion,' he said, later. 'Can't a guy even have a suggestion?'

Nine months later, in June 1995, Michael and Lisa were interviewed on the American television programme *Dateline* by reporter Diane Sawyer.

While it is true that Michael rarely grants television interviews (the last one had been in 1993 with Oprah Winfrey), one would have been hard-pressed to remember any time Lisa had ever been seen answering questions on television. Prior to this highly anticipated broadcast, only frozen images of her came to mind – photographs of a fragile blonde child with a droopy glare and sad, pouting expression reminiscent of her father's. It was easy to imagine her as a poor little rich girl, victimized by her privileged, heavily scrutinized circumstances. That wasn't really true of her as an adult, though. After years of therapy through Scientology, she had long ago come to terms with her celebrity. 'My best trait is that I don't put on a front for anybody,' she observed. 'I'm honest. Scientology has helped me a lot. It teaches you to stay what we call "clean", to understand your feelings and not hold things in. Yeah, I've had a difficult life, in some ways,' she allowed. 'But I've gotten through it, and have done all right for myself.'

On the night of the television interview, Lisa appeared to the world as a sophisticated, twenty-seven-year-old brunette, gorgeous and, it would seem, anyway, nobody's victim.

As the Jackson couple sat side by side, they fielded questions from

Diane Sawyer about their private life. In talking about the allegations, Michael said, 'I could never harm a child or anyone. It's not in my heart. It's not who I am and it's not what I'm even interested in.' Diane then asked, 'What do you think should be done to someone who does that?' Michael responded, 'To someone who does that? What do I think should be done? Gee, I think they need help in some kind of way, you know?'

He then explained why he decided to settle the Jordie Chandler case. 'I talked to my lawyers and I said, "Can you guarantee me that justice will prevail?"' Michael recalled, 'And they said, "Michael, we cannot guarantee you what a judge or a jury will do." With that, I was like catatonic. I was outraged, totally outraged. So I said, "I have got to do something to get out from under this nightmare, all these lies and all these people coming forward to get paid and these tabloid shows, just lies, lies, lies, lies." So we got together and my advisers advised me. It was hands down, a unanimous decision to resolve the case.'

Throughout his explanation, Diane had continually attempted to interrupt him to ask how much money he had spent on the settlement. Finally, a protective Lisa abruptly cut her off and said, 'He's been barred to discuss it.'

Diane asked, 'The specific terms of the agreement?'

Lisa confirmed, 'The specific terms, *and* the specific amounts.'

It was going fairly well, until Diane Sawyer asked the loaded question to which no one ever has a good answer: 'What is a thirty-six-year-old man doing sleeping with a twelve-year-old boy, or a series of them?' Michael fumbled for a bit, giving his usual monologue about the innocence and purity of such behaviour, until Lisa, looking frustrated, decided to put the matter into perspective.

'Let me just say,' she began, 'that I've seen these children. They don't let him go to the *bathroom* without running in there with him. They won't let him out of their sight. So when he jumps in the bed, I'm even out [of the bed], you know? *They* jump in the bed with *him*.' Lisa – mother of two – was on the spot; her credibility was in question just by virtue of the fact that she was sitting there with her husband, on TV, trying to explain why it was okay for him to sleep with children who were not his own. She had to at least give it her best shot.

Unrelenting, Diane followed up, 'But isn't part of being an adult and loving children keeping them from ambiguous situations? And again, we're talking about over an intense period of time here. Would you let your son, when he grows up and is twelve years old, do that?'

Lisa gamely jumped in for more of the impossible. 'You know what? If I didn't know Michael, no way,' she said. 'But I happen to know who he is and what he is and that makes it, you know . . .' Her voice trailed off. 'I know that he's not . . . you know? I know that he's not like that and I know he has a thing for children . . .' Her voice trailed off, again. 'Sorry . . .' she finally said, at a loss.

'I just wonder, is it over?' Diane asked, turning to Michael. 'Are you going to make sure it doesn't happen again? I think this is really the key thing people want to know.'

'Is what over?' Michael asked.

'Are there not going to be more of these sleepovers in which people have to wonder?'

'Nobody wonders when kids sleep over at my house,' he said. 'Nobody wonders.'

'*But are they over?*' Diane pushed. 'Are you going to watch out for it?'

'No,' he answered. Then, acting as if he didn't know what she was talking about – or, maybe he really didn't – he did a double-take and asked, 'Watch out for what?'

'Just for the sake of the children and because of everything you've been through?'

'No, because it's all moral and it's all pure,' Michael said, stubbornly. 'I don't even think that way. It's not what's in my heart.'

'So you'll do it again?' she asked.

'Do what again?'

'Have a child sleeping over?' Diane clarified, now looking annoyed.

'Of course,' he answered. 'If they want. It's on the level of purity and love and just innocence, complete innocence,' he concluded. 'If you're talking about sex, then that's a nut. It's not me. Go to the guy down the street, 'cause it's not Michael Jackson. It's not what I'm interested in.' (A consequence of this interview was that Evan Chandler sued him – again! – claiming that he had breached the terms of the settlement with Jordie. Michael's lawyers eventually got the suit dismissed.)

It was a shame that Michael couldn't have conceded to Diane

Sawyer that he may have used poor judgement in the past. She was on his side, trying to work with him, and pushing for him to do the mature thing – or at least the responsible thing – and say that he would exercise more caution in the future where youngsters were concerned. There were many ways he could have approached the matter, but being obstinate and haughty was not the best way. 'I had off-the-record information that there were some ambiguities about the case in Jackson's favour,' Diane Sawyer later explained. 'Still, I have heard people say, after seeing him during that interview, that a parent would be crazy to let their child be alone with him.'

Later, in the interview, when asked whether her marriage to Michael was a sham, Lisa said of such rumours, 'You know it's crap. I'm sorry. It's the most ridiculous thing I've ever heard. I'm not going to marry somebody for any reason other than the fact that I fall in love with them, period. And they [the public] can *eat* it if they want to think anything different.'

Lisa hoped the couple would be perceived as serious, not silly, during the televised interview. However, Michael's mugging and clowning – as if he was testing to see how many faces he could get away with before his strict mother would send him to his room – undermined her efforts. She was exasperated, especially when he put his two fingers behind her head as if making devil-horns. However, the interview was emblematic of their relationship: she was the adult, he was the child.

'What a fucking disaster,' Lisa said the day after the interview. She was mortified, and angry. 'I am so pissed off at that Diane Sawyer, the way she pushed and pushed and pushed about our sex life. Jesus, that was terrible. Oh my God. I can't believe it,' she said, shaking her head miserably. 'I can't even fucking believe that was on TV.'

'I don't know, I thought it was pretty cool,' Michael said, thoughtfully. 'I mean, we made some good points about the allegations. We made a good-looking couple, too. People loved it, Lisa.' He reached over and put his arm around her, lovingly. 'Don't worry,' he said, 'it was all right.' Lisa rolled her eyes.

What originally brought Lisa and Michael together was the drama of molestation allegations and subsequent drug abuse. Her desire to work out a crisis for him was a powerful, motivating force in their relationship. However, once the drama was over, they had little more to fall back on but their surprising physical relationship. 'It was right after the Diane Sawyer show that things started going bad,' says Monica Pastelle. 'Lisa started to wonder if she'd made a mistake in choosing him as a life partner. The great sex continued, though. It was the thing that made it difficult for her to see straight where he was concerned. Whatever was going on in the privacy of their bedroom was enough to keep her hooked into the relationship. However, things were getting strained. When they weren't in bed making love, they were fighting.'

One adviser recalled, 'I was in the studio with him as he cut some new music when Lisa walked in. She slumped down next to Michael, looking miserable. They didn't say one word to each other. He just played with his knobs and dials, ignoring her. Then, after about five minutes of silence, Lisa gave him a long look. She got up. On her way out the door she said, "Nice talkin' to you, as always." He ignored her. I said, "Yo! Mike! What's up? Is everything okay with you two?" He said, "Sure. We're doing just great. I don't know why she's so pissed off at me." Then, as if hit by a sudden thought, he said, "Wait! Do you think she's on her . . . you know . . . her . . . you know . . . her," and he lowered his voice dramatically, "her *period*?" '

Lisa Marie Wants to Know Why Michael is 'So Selfish'

In October 1994, about six months after Michael and Lisa were married, the two of them and some friends were invited to dine with Elizabeth Taylor at her Bel Air home. Sixty-two-year-old Elizabeth took twenty-six-year-old Lisa aside to offer some hints as to how she might keep her husband happy. 'Always look your best,' she told Lisa. 'He's into glamour, and you must be into it, too. And if you don't like the jewellery he gives you, fake it; act like you do. And keep separate bedrooms to keep him guessing. Also,' she said, 'find the right colours and wear the hell out of them.'

Later, when Elizabeth was out of ear shot, Lisa asked Michael, 'What era is *she* living in? No wonder she's been divorced seven times!'

'Now, Lisa,' Michael said, with a wag of his finger. 'Be nice.'

Lisa also found it amusing that Michael was, as she put it to one intimate, 'an absolute cosmetics freak'. He would spend hours in the bathroom, she said, putting on and taking off different kinds of makeups. In fact, she never saw him without his makeup. If they slept together, in the morning Michael would be gone before she awakened – in the bathroom, applying his morning makeup. She'd look at his pillow and find it smeared with makeup. 'It didn't bother her,' said one friend. 'She thought of it as being sort of rock and roll, freaky, you know? "Lots of rock stars wear makeup," she said. "Whatever. I don't care, as long as he's happy. What do I care?" Lisa would try to surprise him, though, by waking up before him and then tapping him on the shoulder. The sun would be up, and there he would be, with smudged makeup in the light of day. "No, Lisa," he would shriek, "don't look. Please, don't look!" Then, he would jump out of bed and scamper into the bathroom. Lisa would crack up.'

However, light moments like that one between Michael and Lisa had become rare. A major problem for them in their marriage was that Michael insisted that he still be free to go on vacations with young male friends, even though he was now a married man. Lisa did not believe her husband was a paedophile; she made that much clear. 'I wouldn't have let him near my kids if I ever thought that,' she later said. 'Never once did I see him do anything inappropriate, ever.' However, she was dismayed that he would still want to be seen in the company of youngsters, considering all that they had been through with the Jordie Chandler matter. She felt that any public display with youngsters, and especially with boys, would only serve to spark more rumour and innuendo about him and, by extension, her. While many in her husband's 'world of wonder', as she called his insulated environment, put up with Michael's poor judgement, she wasn't going to be one of them. However, Michael was not going to compromise; he had no experience with the notion. When the two fought about the ongoing presence of youngsters in his life, he laid down the law: he was going to do what he wanted to do and, if Lisa loved him, she would have to accept his choices.

'Lisa didn't understand how Michael could disregard her

feelings,' said James Cruse, who knew her well at the time. 'It was embarrassing for her to constantly defend his actions, always explaining that he was not a paedophile, he was misunderstood, he was a child at heart and, blah, blah, blah . . . the same stuff you always hear about the guy. He didn't seem to care that it was hard on her. He just wanted to live his life the way he had always lived it. 'What I do is none of your business,' he told her. That really set her off. 'How can you say that? Of course it's my business,' she told him. 'You're my husband. *You're* my business."

'Why are you so selfish?' Lisa hollered at Michael one evening in front of staff members at Neverland. They had just finished dinner and settled themselves in front of the fireplace, the blazing logs casting a warm glow over them. As they all talked, Michael slipped into the conversation that he was considering a vacation to France with the Cascio brothers from New Jersey, Eddie II and Frank. Lisa was stunned.

'How did you get to be this way?' she demanded, her eyes hard and condemning. 'Do you care how that makes me look, you going on vacation with two kids? Don't you care about me, at all?'

'Me? Selfish?' Michael asked, seeming dismayed. 'But look at the money I give to charities. Why, Lisa! I love all the little children of the world.'

According to witnesses, Lisa stared at him, her mouth agape. 'What does that have to do with anything?' she countered. She was furious and getting more so by the second. 'I'm talking about you and me, Michael. Not, *all the little children of the world*. In fact,' she concluded, 'you are the most selfish person I have ever known.'

Michael grimaced, as if struck in the stomach. Quick tears sprung to his eyes. No one had ever talked to him like that before, not since Joseph, anyway.

'Oh, what's the use?' Lisa asked, ignoring his hurt. 'You don't get it, do you? The little children of the world,' she repeated, angrily. 'I can't even believe you would say that to me.'

'I got into this whole "I'm going to save you" thing,' Lisa admitted in 2003. 'I got some romantic idea in my head I could save him and we could save the world. I thought all that stuff he was doing, philanthropy and the children thing and all of that, was awesome. OK. *Hello*. I was delusionary.'

Later, when Michael recounted the incident to another associate, he said of his wife, 'Man, she's so mean to me. I'm like, why are you being such a bitch to me? What'd I ever do to you?'

'It's too soon after your rehab, Mike,' said the adviser. 'This kind of conflict isn't good for you. You should be working on staying drug-free.'

'Eddie and Frank and I have been friends for years,' Michael said, not seeming to hear his friend's remarks. He shook his head in disbelief. 'We've been all over the world together. It's all innocent. Now, Lisa hates me because of it.' He stopped, as if hit by a bolt of lightning. 'Oh my God, she hates me. It's Katherine and Joseph all over again, isn't it?'

'Look, forget about those Cascio kids,' offered the adviser. 'Come on, Mike. You can see them, any time. Why mess things up any more with your wife?'

'Because I'm a grown man,' Michael said as he rose to leave the room. 'And I don't need anyone's permission to go on a vacation with my good friends. That's why.'

Michael did have his vacation in Paris with Eddie and Frank Cascio, in July 1995 . . . and without Lisa.

Michael Goes on the Record

In September 1995 rumours surfaced that Michael and Lisa Marie were ending their marriage, causing an international firestorm of headlines. I managed to get Michael on the telephone for an interview for the Australian magazine, *Woman's Day*, to check it out. 'Let me just say this,' he told me, impatiently: 'No. No. No. *No*. These stories are damn lies made up by people who hope they'll get lucky with one of them and hit it big.'

I asked if he wanted to further respond to reports that Lisa did not know about his vacation to Paris with the Cascio brothers. 'Like I wouldn't have told her?' Michael asked. He sounded tense, stressed out. 'Like she wouldn't read about it anyway, or see us photographed by every newspaper photographer in the world? Neither one of us could have a secret from the other, even if we wanted to,' he said. 'We're so happy,' he added of his marriage. 'We do it our way. I don't know if it's conventional. My parents have been married for forty years. Is their marriage conventional? Were Lisa's parents in a conventional marriage? I don't think so. I love being married, knowing that Lisa is there,' he continued. ' She's strong. She's smart. She's on my side, listens to me, understands me, understands my world.'

The child molestation allegations came up, once again. There had been a report that the twenty-five-million-dollar settlement would be paid to Jordie Chandler in instalments of $466,000 a year over forty years. It wasn't accurate. However, the report further indicated that Michael spends more than that amount on toys. 'That's not true, either,' he confirmed. 'I probably don't spend more than,' he paused, as if calculating the figure in his head, 'about a hundred and fifty thousand a year on toys.'

Also at this time, Santa Barbara District Attorney, Tom Sneddon, was quoted in a *Vanity Fair* article as saying that the criminal investigation against Michael was not over. 'It is in suspension,' he said, 'even if the civil case has been settled with cash.'

'What the heck does that mean?' Michael asked, heatedly. 'Either there is an investigation, or there isn't one. It's over. Let it rest.'

During the course of our conversation, the subject of the photo session with the police came up. 'Those photos did not match [Jordie's description],' he told me. 'How many times do I have to say this to you? *They did not match.* Now, I'm hanging up,' he told me, 'because you crossed the line with that question.'

'Wait,' I said. 'One more thing: do you know that a writer says he found a videotape of you with some kid. Do you want to respond to that, Michael?'

'It's not true,' he said, sounding dismayed. 'Even if I were the most deviant person in the world, why would I keep a tape like that?'

In fact, Michael Jackson sued Victor Guitterez (author of a book about Jordie and Michael for private publication, called *Michael Jackson Was My Lover)* for claiming that such a videotape existed, and challenged him to produce it. Apparently, no such tape existed. Victor lost the suit and ended up owing Michael almost three million dollars. He declared bankruptcy, moved to Chile, and hasn't been heard from since.

'People will believe anything about me. I don't care any more. Is that what you want to hear? Then, fine,' he concluded, lashing out at me. 'In fact, why not just tell people I'm an alien from Mars. Tell them I eat live chickens and that I do a voodoo dance at midnight. They'll believe anything you say, because you're a reporter,' he concluded, spitting our the word *reporter*. 'But if I, Michael Jackson, were to say, "I'm an alien from Mars and eat live chickens and do a voodoo dance every night at midnight," people would say, "Oh, man, that Michael Jackson is *nuts*. He's cracked up. You can't believe a damn word that comes out of his mouth." '

Finally Michael said in a weary voice, 'People don't know what it's like for me. No one knows, really. No one should judge what I've done with my life,' he concluded, 'not unless they've been in my shoes every horrible day and every sleepless night.'

Enter: Debbie Rowe

Michael first met Debbie Rowe in the early 1980s when he went to his dermatologist to complain of a skin condition. Panicked because of the emergence of mysterious blotches, he was certain he had a deadly skin cancer. Ace Johnson, who worked as an assistant for Joseph Jackson at the time, recalls, 'That was when Mike was told he had Vitiligo. "Oh no," he said, "I *am* a freak." I distinctly remember him telling me that there was a white girl named Debbie in the doctor's office, a nurse and receptionist, who was helping him through the ordeal, always there for him.'

Dr Arnold Klein suggested to Michael that if he needed someone to talk to about his medical condition, he should call Debbie any time, day or night. For a short while, Michael did telephone her daily to ask her medical questions, and cry on her shoulder. They were soon good friends. 'At the time, his brothers thought maybe this would be the beginning of a romance for Michael, since all he talked about was Debbie,' recalled Ace. 'Jermaine said, "I want to meet this Debbie chick. Mike's got it bad for her." Michael giggled and laughed, like a kid with a crush.'

Whenever Michael came to the office for treatment, Debbie would fuss over him. In reciprocation, whenever Michael released a new CD he would send her an autographed copy. Debbie would hang his CD picture jackets on the walls of her office until, one day, Arnold Klein asked her to remove them, saying that such a display of affection for a patient could be misconstrued.

Tanya Boyd, who was a good friend of Debbie's, remembered, 'She would obsess about Michael saying, "I'm going to talk to him about opening up more, he's too inhibited." She cared about him, would be up all night long on the phone with him. She said he was best on the telephone. "All of his defences break down when he doesn't have to look at you, face to face," she said. She felt that he was sweet and misunderstood and also a rebel.' Echoing Lisa Marie's sentiment about him, Debbie told Tanya. 'If people knew him like I know him, they would not think he was so strange. He's unique, kinky, actually. I like that in a guy.'

'Some thought they'd end up together. When I asked Debbie if she was romantically interested in Michael, she became evasive. She ended up marrying someone else for a few years – divorced him [in 1990] because she said she felt trapped – but I believed she was interested in Michael.'

Over the years, Debbie and Michael continued their friendship, often confiding in one another about their unhappy marriages.

By 1995, Deborah Jean Rowe was thirty-six, about ten years older that Lisa Marie Presley. Born in 1958 in Spokane, Washington, to Gordon Rowe and Barbara Chilcutt, she had been relocated to Los Angeles by the time she was fifteen. At that time, her parents divorced, and her father left the United States for the Middle East. She graduated from Hollywood High School in 1977, and began working as an assistant to Arnold Klein. In 1982, she married Richard Edelman, then a thirty-year-old teacher at Hollywood High. They moved to a small apartment Van Nuys, California, where Edelman started a computer consulting business. Their marriage began to crumble in 1988; a year later they filed for bankruptcy with assets of forty thousand dollars and debt worth twice that much.

Debbie was truly an unusual character. When she was just a bit younger, she was a biker chick who enjoyed dressing up in black leather and roaring around Los Angeles at breakneck speeds. Mario Pikus, a friend of hers at the time and a fellow biker, recalled, 'She had so many crashes that her powerful 2000cc machine was covered in dents. And she swore like a sailor. Everything she said was peppered with four-letter words. She was like one of the guys. She used to drink beer and tequila, and she had this habit of punching you in what was supposed to be a friendly gesture. After she had a few drinks, her friendly jabs could knock the wind out of you.

'She never had any money, she was always broke. But one day, after a road trip, she said she had to stop by her parents' place. I was stunned. It's near Bruce Willis's home in Malibu, and it makes his house look like a shack. It's got to be worth four million dollars.' Inside the home, Pikus (who is a professional artist) estimated that there might have been ten million dollars in paintings and sculptures. Debbie explained that her step-father was a real estate magnate. 'They seemed to have a warm relationship, but it was clear that Debbie didn't take any money from him. Her apartment, which cost her about seven hundred dollars a month, was a dark little place, kind of cheap and depressing. But it was a shrine to Michael Jackson. Every inch of wall space was taken up by posters and photographs of him. Lots of them were signed, 'To Debbie – Love , Michael.'

It's fascinating that Michael was able to have someone in his life like Debbie, a person about whom the public was completely unaware. It had been presumed by his fans – mostly because of the way Michael complained about his lack of privacy – that if ever a woman became a part of his life in any meaningful way, the world would know about it, instantly. It would make headlines. However, somehow, Debbie was kept a secret from Michael's fans and the press for more than a decade.

'When he went into the rehab for the drug problem, Debbie was relieved,' says Tanya Boyd. 'She'd been so worried about him, never out of touch with him during any of the Jordie Chandler business. He may have been talking to Lisa on the telephone a lot, but he was also speaking to Debbie – though I suspect Lisa did not know about that.

When he got out of the hospital [Charter], he started dating Lisa, but he never stopped seeing Debbie, either, even after he married Lisa.'

Lisa's friend, Monica Pastelle, recalled, 'Lisa once told me that she heard Michael was interested in a white nurse who worked for his dermatologist. She laughed it off. She thought he was probably trying to make her jealous, playing games. Still, she was interested enough to go to the doctor's office and sneak a look at this generously proportioned blonde, blue-eyed nurse named Debbie. After she saw her, she said, "I'm not sure Michael would ever be interested in her. She's not his type. He likes glamour. However, I think *she's* into *him*. I think they're, I don't know, *dating*, or something. It's crazy."'

It turned out to be true. While he was with Lisa, Michael *was* seeing Debbie secretly, if only as a friend. When Lisa found out about it, she thought it odd that he would keep it from her. However, she suspected that he had many secrets and this one was probably the least noteworthy of them. She did some research and realized that Debbie was, as she put it in 2003, 'a nurse who had a crush on him.'

Lisa called her 'Nursey', she didn't seem concerned about her. One friend recalled, 'One afternoon, in passing, she said, "So, Nursey called about ten times today looking for Michael. I finally had to tell her, *please*, he will call you back, *okay?* Jesus Christ!" I said, "Lisa, what is that about?" She said, "Oh, I don't know. She's got it bad for him, I guess. I have no idea what her thing is. I have enough trouble trying to figure out Michael. I'm not about to start trying to figure out his friends, too." That was her feeling about Debbie Rowe. She didn't think of her as a threat.'

Lisa Marie Confronts Michael in Hospital

When in September 1995 Michael and Lisa appeared together at the MTV Awards, she sat at his side looking pissed off and miserable. She was tired of arguing, tired of trying to save him from himself. She had recently called Katherine Jackson to ask what she thought she should do about Michael's insistence that he continue to have young boys in his life. 'I want to save this marriage, but I also want to save Michael,' she said, according to what Katherine later recalled to a friend. 'He's just looking for trouble. What can I do? This whole thing is freaking me out.'

'I don't know what you can do, but I know what you can't do: you can't try to tell him what to do,' Katherine advised her daughter-in-law. She told her what many people already knew: 'Michael does what he wants to do.' She also suggested that Lisa call Johnnie Cochran, saying that the attorney might be the one to address the issue with Michael. Lisa called Johnnie. 'My God! It's all so innocent, this business with kids,' Johnnie told her. He suggested that if she wanted to save her marriage she would 'have to let Michael be who Michael is.'

'You think she could have hid it for just one night in front of the cameras,' Michael later complained to his mother about Lisa's glum appearance on the MTV Awards. 'But, no, not her. She puts her feelings right out there, doesn't she? She's so open.'

'But that's what you liked about her,' Katherine reminded him.

'Yeah, but now it's working against me,' Michael observed.

Despite the fact that their marriage seemed in trouble, Michael was still pushing for Lisa to become pregnant. Whenever he brought up the subject of having children, though, Lisa acted as if it wasn't a serious issue for them. 'I mean it,' he told her, according to a later recollection. 'I'm very serious. I want us to have children. I don't think you're hearing me,' he said.

However, Lisa had heard him loud and clear. She had two children with Danny Keough. She knew how much she loved them, could never live a single day without them. Projecting ahead, she wondered what would happen to the child they would have if the marriage ended. 'When I imagined having a child with him,' she confirmed in 2003, 'all I could ever see was a custody battle night-mare.' Also, after getting to know him better and watching his day-to-day interactions with people, she became convinced that he was too emotionally immature to raise a child. 'I think *he* needs a parent,' she told one confidante, 'and maybe shouldn't be one himself, yet.' However, she wouldn't tell him all of that, at the time. Instead, she just hoped he would give up on the idea, at least for the time being.

Also, by this time, the heated physical intimacy Lisa had enjoyed with Michael had cooled. It could have only lasted so long, without real communication between them. She decided to use their waning physical intimacy as an excuse. 'I think we have to have sex in order for me to get pregnant,' she told him, according to what she later recalled. 'And you know what? I ain't doin' it."

Michael wasn't convinced that he and Lisa had to engage in sexual activity in order to have a family of their own. He wanted children; that was his chief goal and he had made it clear. The question, then, became how to achieve it. Finally, one day over breakfast he told her, 'Look, my friend Debbie said she will get pregnant and have my baby. If you won't do it, then *she* will. How about that?'

Lisa didn't know how to take Michael's statement. Was it a challenge? A threat? Or just a fact? It certainly wasn't the kind of news most wives would welcome hearing from their husbands: if you don't have my baby, my nurse will. She was amazed by the seriousness of his tone. Who would then raise this child? She and Michael? Debbie? Or, just Michael, alone? Life with Michael Jackson was getting a little weird for her, as if it hadn't been weird enough up until that time. She met his direct gaze calmly. 'No kidding?' she remarked. 'Well, cool, then. That's fine with me,' she said in a controlled tone. 'Tell her to go ahead and do it.'

The weeks slipped into months. By the winter of 1995, Lisa and Michael weren't even speaking, and not because Lisa didn't want to communicate with him, but because she simply could not find him. She didn't know his whereabouts, only that he was not at Neverland – and no one in his camp would give her any information. After spending about a week trying to find him, there was a floral delivery from him at her home in Hidden Hills: dozens of red roses with a card that read, 'Love, Michael.' Under the circumstances, the gesture made no sense. Exasperated, she threw the flowers into the trash.

At about this time, she was already furious with him because of a cover story in *TV Guide* during which he was quoted as saying that she told him Elvis once had a nose job. 'He was quoting me, "Presley told me Elvis had a nose job," which is absolute bullshit,' she now recalls. 'I read that and I threw it across the kitchen. "I told you *what?*"'

'It was getting nasty,' she recalled, ten years later. 'I was ready to kill him, I swear to God.'

In December 1995, Michael finally returned to Neverland. Priscilla Presley decided to pay him a surprise visit to find out what was going on with her son-in-law. 'When she arrived, she saw Michael in the living room playing with about a dozen babies, all crawling about, some laughing, some crying,' recalled Monica Pastelle. 'It was like a big nursery, with a grown man in the middle of it all, seeming in a state of bliss. Though nothing wrong was going on, she was flabbergasted. It was so unsettling, Priscilla left, immediately.'

Lisa was speechless when her mother confronted her about what she'd seen.

A week later, Michael went to New York to begin rehearsals for a concert at the Beacon Theater, 'Michael Jackson – One Night Only', which was scheduled to be broadcast on cable television to 250 million viewers on 9 December. On 6 December, he collapsed during a practice session and was hospitalized at New York's Beth Israel North Hospital. His doctors said he was suffering from heart arrhythmia, or irregular heartbeat prompted by severe dehydration, gastroenteritis and a chemical imbalance affecting his liver and kidneys. He also had a viral infection. Yet earlier in the day, he seemed fine. Marcel Marceau, who was going to make an appearance on the HBO programme during Michael's performance of 'Childhood', had been at the rehearsal when Michael collapsed. 'He was so full of energy, in absolutely wonderful condition,' said the mime, who turned away for a moment during Michael's practice session of 'Black and White' under the hot and blinding lights.

'I heard silence,' said the mime, 'and everything stopped. I looked and he was on the floor.'

By the time medics appeared on the site, Michael's heartbeat was irregular and his blood pressure low. He had on so much makeup, they had to check his pallor by the color of his chest when they lifted his shirt.

As soon as he was checked into the hospital, Michael's press people telephoned Lisa in Los Angeles and, with frantic explanations, begged her to fly to her husband's side. 'Hell, no,' was her response. 'Screw him. I'm not going. Why should I?'

She wasn't going to get out of it that easily, however. Michael's collapse had made big news: 'Jacko on his Backo' screamed the front page of the *New York Post*. The hospital even set up a telephone number with daily, automatic message updates on his condition. The media had assembled in front of the hospital, waiting for his wife to arrive to be with him. His 'people' then badgered her 'people' about Michael's image and how it would 'look' if his wife wasn't at his side. After all, even Diana Ross had shown up. Finally – and surprisingly, to her friends, anyway – Lisa gave in. Arriving at the hospital the next day, wearing a black pea coat and sunglasses, she was whisked through a side entrance.

It's possible that Michael really did want Lisa to be with him. However, when she got there he must have been sorry she'd agreed to the public relations manoeuvre. She showed up with fire in her eyes. When she walked into the room, the first thing that hit Lisa were all the framed posters of Shirley Temple as a child-star, Mickey Mouse and Topo Gigio, the strange, little puppet-mouse popular from the old *Ed Sullivan Show* in the 1950s and 1960s. When Lisa looked down at Michael, he appeared to be on his death bed; it seemed as if he had tubes coming out of every limb. He reminded her, she would later say, of the pathetic creature from *E.T.* at the end of the movie when the alien has taken a turn for the worst. As she stood there, 'E.T.' gazed up at her weakly and, mustering all his strength, managed to say, 'Hi, Lisa. How are you?'

Lisa wasn't moved. She didn't care much about Michael's health, not at that moment, anyway. She suspected that he wasn't suffering from 'exhaustion' or 'dehydration'. He had long ago confided in her about his panic attacks. According to those who know her well, she figured that he'd suffered another and, based on his destabilized condition, that it had been quite a jolt to his system. Surely, though, it wasn't because of the upcoming concert, she speculated. He'd made many such appearances, why would this particular one cause such a reaction? The broadcast had actually now been postponed indefinitely, costing both Michael and HBO a fortune. (It would never happen.) Whatever was going on with him was serious. Now that Michael was a captive audience, she wanted to confront him. So where had he been? Why was he so anxious? Most importantly, where did she stand with him?

Michael usually tries to avoid confrontation. So, for his irate wife to barge into his safe, hospital haven was upsetting. His heart must have been thundering in his chest.

Making matters more tense was the fact that the Cascio brothers had just left the room five minutes earlier. Had Lisa seen them? It was difficult to tell; her face was that impassive. But it's likely she wouldn't even have recognized them now. Still, it was a close call.

Lisa closed the door behind her. She and Michael then engaged in a private and, judging from the shouting going on in the room – hers, not his – heated conversation. 'I'm like a lion, I roar,' she would say in 2003. 'I won't be a victim. I don't sulk, I get angry. I go immediately into retaliation.

'I couldn't figure out what was wrong with him,' she recalled. 'I started asking questions, and it was always a different story. He said I was causing trouble and stirring up problems. He told me, "You're making my heart rate go up," and asked me to leave. I said, "Good. I want out. This is insane, all of it."'

When the door to Michael's room opened, Lisa burst out as if shot from a cannon, past everyone in the hall and straight to the elevator. 'Mrs Jackson,' exclaimed one of the doctors. 'My goodness! Your husband cannot be upset like this. He's much too fragile. If you're going to do this, you'll not be able to visit him.'

Lisa gave him a sharp look.

Michael's mother, who had been pacing in the hallway, regarded her daughter-in-law intensely. She could not fathom that Lisa would fly all the way from Los Angeles to New York just to fight with her son. Janet, who had also rushed to be at her brother's side, had just gone to the ladies' room. As Lisa stood waiting for the elevator, Katherine walked up to her and exploded in stunned disbelief. 'What is *wrong* with you, Lisa,' she hissed. 'You are so *spoiled*. I can't believe that you would do this to Michael.' At that moment, the elevator opened and Lisa got into it. She turned, faced Katherine and gave her a critical look. Luckily for Katherine, the elevator's doors then slammed closed between them.

Lisa wanted to see Michael the next day. 'Absolutely not,' Michael's handlers told her. There had been a meeting with Jackson family members and it was decided that Lisa was an antagonizing presence in Michael's life, and that he should now be protected from her, at all costs. Furious, Lisa went back to Los Angeles.

Perhaps a clue to Michael's behaviour – his distancing himself from Lisa and his subsequent, apparent panic attack – can be found in analysing a chain of events from late 1995. It would be many years later that Debbie Rowe would reveal that she became pregnant that December. Michael had certainly given Lisa fair warning that Debbie would have his baby if she wouldn't do it. 'Tell her to go ahead and do it,' Lisa had said. If she was being sarcastic, perhaps Michael didn't catch the mockery.

Did Lisa know about the pregnancy? 'I don't think Debbie even knew yet,' observed Monica Pastelle. 'I think by the time Michael was on his back in the hospital, she was only a couple of weeks' pregnant. As for Lisa, if she had known, do you think Michael would have been still drawing breath when she left that hospital room?'

It certainly appears either that Michael was a fast worker when he realized his marriage was in trouble or that he had a master plan to father a child, once and for all, which did not involve his wife. Some have said that Michael and Debbie were intimate. Others have said Debbie is 'not his type' and insist that they underwent the process of artificial insemination shortly before Michael ended up in the hospital. Since no one who knows them well enough to be privy to such information wants to discuss it, Debbie's pregnancy remains one of Michael's most sensitive secrets. 'I can only tell you that I did not discuss it with him,' said one of his advisers. 'I did not want any more information about any of it.'

When Michael was released from the hospital after a week, he went off to Euro-Disney in France to recuperate. He must have had at least a half-dozen children with him, judging from photographs taken on his vacation.

On 18 January 1996, I appeared on CNN to announce that Lisa Marie Presley had filed for divorce from Michael Jackson. In her petition, she noted the 'Date of Separation' as 10 December 1995, just after she saw Michael in the hospital. 'This person is one of the biggest entertainers out there,' Lisa told *Newsweek* in 2003. 'He is not stupid. He's very charming when he wants to be, and when you go into his world you step into this whole other realm. I could tell you all about the craziness – all these things that were odd, different, evil or not cool – but it still took me two and a half years to get my head out of it.'

In March 1996, Debbie Rowe suffered a miscarriage. 'I was just devastated,' she has said. 'I thought I would never be able to have a baby, and I really wanted to have his. Michael was there to console me the whole time.'

It's fascinating, in retrospect, that Debbie's pregnancy and subsequent miscarriage – as well as her very existence in Michael's life – had still escaped public scrutiny. It seems incredible that someone of Michael's celebrity status could be married to one woman and planning a baby with another . . . and no one in the media would catch on to any of it. How, one wonders, did he manage it? 'Carefully,' responded someone in Michael's camp, only half-kidding. 'Very carefully.' Or, perhaps not very well at all, it could be argued . . . if, in fact, he had a panic attack over it.

Michael's divorce from Lisa was finalized on 20 August 1996. As part of the settlement, Lisa received ten per cent of royalties from Jackson's *HIStory* album. According to the agreement, she was allowed to write a tell-all book about her marriage, if she ever chose to do so; she did not sign a so-called 'confidentiality agreement'. At the time, though, Lisa just wanted to get on with her life and career. She said that she had great regard for Michael and refused to speak critically of him. She knew that he wasn't entirely venal . . . she just didn't know, at this point, what to think of him. So, she chose to preserve her dignity by keeping sacred their private life together. Seven years later, though, in the spring of 2003, Lisa began to discuss her frustration as Michael's wife during promotion of her long-anticipated debut album, *To Whom It May Concern*, on Capitol Records.

Michael was deeply conflicted by the end of his marriage to Lisa, his heart flooded with despair. Never before had he connected with a woman, or maybe even another person, on the level that he had with her. She had been there when he most needed her, during the dark days of allegations and drug abuse. 'She's like a force of nature,' he said of her, 'always there for me. I don't know how I'll be without her.'

He also had a strong sexual connection to her, and that had been a first for him. Previously, he hadn't been able to open himself up, feel uninhibited and truly, physically intimate with anyone. However, for some reason, he was able to let himself go with Lisa. Who knows why? It's easy to be sceptical of Michael's relationship with her, but doing so risks ignoring his obvious humanity. Despite the plastic surgeries and maddening friendships with boys, and all of the rest of the eccentric behaviour that goes into making Michael Jackson such a strange individual, he is still a human being with emotions, feelings and a beating heart – and, somehow, Lisa Marie Presley was the one to truly touch it, to truly affect him. 'I'm afraid it will never happen for me, again,' he said at the time. 'I'm scared to death that it's over for me, now.' Indeed, it was difficult for him to let it go.

Michael spent a couple of weeks lamenting what had occurred with Lisa. 'Lisa said that the part of him that is critical of himself – the beaten child part of him – really kicked in after the divorce was finalized,' said Monica Pastelle. 'He wanted to call and talk to his best friend, her. He didn't want to let go. She needed space, though. She really needed time away from him. She felt that he had really screwed with her mind, and she got sick and her body started breaking down after the divorce. She poured her life into him. Now, she needed to reclaim it for herself. He had a hard time with that.'

In the end, Michael Jackson had no choice but to go on alone. He was a survivor, he told himself. He had music to work on, career commitments – a huge, world tour coming up with a show that, as always, demanded his complete focus. Besides, he and Lisa had different goals in life. He wanted to raise children; she already had two, and had made it clear that she didn't want any more with him. Michael wasn't used to waiting for other people to catch up with him and with his goals. When Debbie Rowe said she would have his baby, he jumped at the opportunity. With glacial determination replacing his despondency, he was ready to push onward. That had always been his way; at the age of thirty-eight, he wasn't going to change.

Debbie is Pregnant

In September 1996, Michael embarked on a new worldwide concert schedule, the *HIStory* tour, the first leg of which began in Prague, Czech Republic, and would not end until Honolulu, Hawaii, at Aloha

Stadium in January 1997. The second leg would begin in Bremen, Germany, in May 1997 and end in Durban, South Africa, in October 1997. During the tour, Michael would perform eighty-two concerts in fifty-eight cities to over 4.5 million fans. It was a gruelling schedule. All told, the *HIStory* tour visited five continents and thirty-five countries.

A month after the tour began, and just a few months after his divorce was finalized, Michael made headlines again with another bombshell revelation: a woman was carrying his baby. Debbie Rowe was five months' pregnant, which meant she and Michael had been working on a baby while he was still technically married to Lisa. Debbie later explained, 'I said, "You deserve to be a father. Let me do this for you. Let me have your baby." He was surprised, but he said, "Yes. Let's do it."'

Debbie's existence in Michael's life – and her pregnancy – was finally revealed when she was tricked into discussing it with a 'friend' who was surreptitiously tape-recording the conversation. 'She just didn't know any better,' explained Tanya Boyd, one of the neighbours in the Van Nuys apartment complex where she lived at the time. 'She was an open-hearted girl who never dreamed that there were people out there tape-recording conversations for the tabloids.'

However, there it was, for all to see, on the front page of *News of the World* (3 November 1996). 'I'm Having Jacko's Baby,' blazed the headline, with individual photographs of Michael and Debbie. She was appalled. 'Oh, my God, no,' Debbie said to a friend who was with her when she saw a copy of the publication. 'Please, tell me it does *not* say that. It's my own fault. Look at this thing. *Look at it.* They're treating us like freaks!' Debbie took the newspaper and flung it across the room, angrily. Then, she sank into a chair, buried her face in her hands, and burst into tears. 'Those bastards,' she kept said. 'How can they do this to Michael? He doesn't deserve it. And he's going to be so mad at me.'

In truth, the article was fairly accurate, especially reading it retrospectively. In it, Debbie was quoted as saying that Michael was, indeed, the father of the baby, and that he'd be raising the child without her. She also said, according to what the *News of the World* reported as being on the tape-recording, that the two had engaged in sexual activity, but that when she did not immediately become pregnant, they decided to try what she said Michael referred to as 'a foolproof way of doing it': artificial insemination. She said that the process occurred at the Los Angeles Fertility Institute (on Brighton Way in Beverly Hills). The first time ended in miscarriage, she said. This time, she felt she would carry to full term. The article also said that Debbie would receive about $500,000 from Michael when she delivered the baby.

The revelation was almost as startling – and maybe more so – than the excitement that had resulted from Michael's surprise nuptials to Lisa Marie Presley. The questions from the media came fast and furiously: who was the expectant mother? What is she to Michael? Why is it that no one had ever heard of her before? It all seemed strange, almost like a publicity stunt.

Debbie's father, Gordon Rowe – a retired cargo pilot who lived in Cyprus – went on the record to say that the baby was conceived by artificial means at the Los Angeles Fertility Institute.

'She broke the news to me in a telephone call,' he said. 'I only speak to her once in a while, and I knew something was up. She said straight off: "I'm going to have Michael's child." After I recovered from the shock, Debbie said, "Come on, it's not so bad. We had the child by artificial insemination." I said, "Debbie, why artificial insemination? Isn't he capable of fathering a child like anyone else?" She laughed and said, "Michael doesn't do *anything* like anyone else." I said to her, "Isn't this the same man who was charged with child abuse?" She said, "He wasn't charged with anything, not at all." Then, she told me, "Dad you have no idea who the real Michael Jackson is. He is the most compassionate person I have ever met in my life. If you could only spend one day with him, you would love him like I do." '

Gordon had rarely seen Debbie since he and her mom, Barbara, divorced more than twenty years before; he had not been directly involved in her upbringing since the early 1970s. 'She's always been a rebel,' he said of Debbie. 'Maybe if I'd been more of a father, things would have been different.' After his comments received worldwide publicity, he issued a general retraction of everything he had said, each and every word. It appeared that Gordon spoke too soon, and that Michael was unhappy about his comments. The pop star soon issued his own statement: 'The reports speculating that Ms Rowe was artificially inseminated, and that there is any economic relationship, are completely false and irresponsible.'

However, Steve Shmerier, a California computer executive who dated Debbie for six months before her first pregnancy with Michael, insists, 'Debbie told me she had agreed to try for a baby using artificial insemination as a favour to a friend. No names were mentioned. But with hindsight, you don't need to be a genius to figure out who she was talking about. She is simply not the maternal type, though. She's always said she had no interest in having children. The only reason she agreed to do this thing for Michael was the under-standing that she would not become a traditional wife.'

Michael could insist that the baby was not the result of artificial insemination, and the public and press could either believe him or not. However, he went a step too far in also claiming that there was no 'economic relationship' with Debbie. Such a statement only weakened his credibility about the baby's conception. After all, who in his right mind would believe that he wasn't giving Debbie *some* money? Even the surrogate mother who comes into the picture as a complete stranger is compensated for her services, let alone those who are close friends of fifteen years. Is it logical that Debbie Rowe would have a child for one of the wealthiest entertainers in show business and that he, in return, would not give her even a dime for her trouble?

In fact, according to reliable sources, Debbie has received millions of dollars from Michael over the years, not as payment for her services but as 'gifts' to her. When Michael's former business manager Myung Ho Lee sued him for fourteen million dollars in 2002, among the court papers filed was Michael's *monthly* budget, which included 'payment to Debbie Rowe' for $1.5 million. Whether she's getting money from him every month, annually, or per child, she will never have to worry about finances again. Michael arranged for other financial annuities for her, as well as eventually buying her a $1.3 million home in the exclusive Franklin Canyon enclave of Beverly Hills, in the fall of 1997. He and Debbie would never live together.

'At the time that the story broke, Debbie was supposed to meet him in Australia,' said Tanya Boyd. 'She presumed that the trip would be off, that Michael would be so upset about what had happened that he would refuse to see her. She cried a lot that day.'

Debbie frantically attempted to locate Michael in Sydney to explain to him how she had been deceived by her 'friend'. However, before she could reach him, he was on the telephone, calling her. Contrary to what Debbie expected, as she recalled it, Michael could not have been more loving and understanding. She now says that it was during that telephone call that she realized that Michael was the man for her. 'Look, I can understand how this terrible thing happened,' Michael told Debbie. 'I've been tricked by the media before. Relax. It'll be okay, I promise.'

'Debbie so appreciated him,' said Tanya Boyd. 'Even though she had obviously created a huge jam, he didn't blame her for it. That went a long way toward making him a saint in her eyes. She was so relieved, she decided that she would be loyal to him, and once you have Debbie Rowe's loyalty, you have it for life – unless you screw up, royally.'

'Focus, Debbie,' Michael told her. 'Keep your eye on the goal, which is that you and I have this baby. Of course, the press would find out about it, eventually. I expected it. They have made my life miserable for years.'

Though he tried not to show it to the expectant mother, Michael actually was apprehensive about the news of Debbie's pregnancy being made public. First of all, would his fans put it all together and realize that he'd been working on having a baby with Debbie before he was even divorced from Lisa? How would that look? (Oddly, it would turn out that much of his public wouldn't figure it out, or, at least, care.) Not only was he unsure how his fans would take it, he was worried about the reaction of his mother, Katherine.

Indeed, Katherine, still a devout Jehovah's Witness, was not happy to learn from news broadcasts that her son was fathering a child with a woman to whom he was not married. 'This reminds me of what Michael's father did in the seventies,' Katherine said, privately, speaking of Joh'Vonnie. 'It broke my heart. I won't have history repeat itself with Michael. I just won't have it.'

After the news of Debbie's pregnancy broke, Katherine tried to reach Michael overseas. It was difficult because of his tight schedule but on the day the pregnancy story broke, Katherine managed to find Debbie, whom she had met on several occasions, at a neighbour's apartment, where she was hiding out from the stalking media. That neighbour recalled, 'I picked up the telephone, hoping it was Michael calling for Debbie from Australia, and this woman on the other end said, "Would you please put Miss Rowe on the phone?" I thought it was a reporter, so I said, "She's not here." And the woman said, "Well, this is Michael Jackson's mother. Can you help me locate her?" I have no idea how she got my number. I handed Debbie the phone.'

Katherine was, as Debbie's neighbour put it, 'sweet as she could have been to her.' For about thirty minutes, she talked to Debbie about the sanctity of marriage, and about the Jehovah's Witness faith. Debbie was impressed. In fact, by the time she ended her conversation with Katherine, she had not only agreed that it would be best if she married Michael, she was practically ready to convert.

When Michael found out that Katherine and Debbie had spoken, he probably sensed that his life might be about to change. Indeed, according to one of his associates, when Michael finally spoke to Katherine on the telephone, she asked him to marry 'that nice girl, Debbie' and 'give your child a name, not like your poor, half-sister, Joh'Vonnie.' Michael had never wanted to repeat the sins of his father, so Katherine perhaps knew how to appeal to him or, as the associate put it, 'She pushed all the right buttons.'

Michael agreed that he should marry Debbie. 'It's definitely the right thing to do,' he said.

When one reviews the chain of events described by their intimates, it's interesting that Katherine's telephone call to Debbie and Michael had such an impact on their future together. Prior to the Jackson matriarch's involvement, the plan was that Debbie was to have been a 'surrogate mother' for Michael – a close friend doing a favour for him by having a baby, which she would then give him to raise. After the birth of the child, Michael intended to issue a statement, and then keep the mother's identity a secret, in much the same way the identities of most surrogate mothers are protected. A good example of what he and Debbie intended is the way he has handled the identity of the woman who gave birth to his very blond third child, Prince Michael II. We don't know who she is, other than that she's not Debbie; Debbie has denied maternity. He has not divulged her name, and he hasn't married her, either. It wouldn't have been easy, of course, to keep Debbie's identity undisclosed, but since he has managed to keep the other woman's identity out of the press, it obviously can be done. Over the years, Michael had proven that, if he wishes to do so, he can keep secrets about his private life.

However, Debbie's having confided to a traitorous friend about the pregnancy, the resulting publicity, and then Katherine's concern, altered Michael's master plan – and also his life. As a result, he was not only going to be a father, but a husband – again.

While speaking to her on the telephone, Michael insisted that Debbie keep her plans to visit him in Australia and, in fact, take the next plane. She agreed to meet him at the Sheraton on the Park Hotel, where the Jackson contingency occupied forty rooms. However, she did not know then that she was going to be marrying him, there. 'She was surprised when she finally got there, and he told her of his plan,' said Tanya Boyd. 'She called me [on November 12, 1996] and said, "Guess what? I'm marrying Michael tomorrow." I asked her if she loved him. She thought it over for a moment, and answered, "Yes, I do, sort of." I pushed. "Romantically?" She paused, and said, "The kind of love I have with Michael is bigger, more important, than that. It's not the kind that most people can understand. Simple love affairs end. This relationship will never end."'

Michael's New Family

On 13 November 1996, Michael Jackson sat down at a grand piano in his two-bedroom suite at the Sheraton on the Park Hotel in Sydney. With a flourish, he played the Wagner march known as 'Here Comes the Bride'. Michael had on a creamy foundation and transparent powder that made his face almost stark white. He had extra eyeliner on his lids, emphasizing their almond shape; his eyes stood out like dark coals. He highlighted his nose and cheekbones with bronze tones. His eyebrows were tweezed and darkened. He had on a black hat and one long curl framing each side of his face. Also, he appeared to have fake sideburns. The total effect was nothing short of jaw-dropping, in that Disneyland sort of way.

From one of the other rooms came Debbie Rowe, six months' pregnant, wearing black and holding a small arrangement of flowers. It had just been ten days since the world knew that he was about to become a father and now, thanks to his mother, he was about to become a husband, again. As fifteen of their friends watched, thirty-eight-year-old Michael and thirty-seven-year-old Debbie – both wearing black – were wed in a simple ceremony. Michael's best man was a new friend of his named Anthony – who was eight years old. Michael identified him as a nephew. (However, unless there are relatives unknown to other family members, he doesn't seem to have a nephew by that name.) Michael further explained that the boy had been depressed by the death of one of his parents. 'I brought him with me to cheer him up,' he explained.

As they stood in the suite, decorated, wall to wall, with exotic orchids, roses and deep pink lilies, Michael presented Debbie with a $100,000 diamond and platinum ring. After being pronounced man and wife, they exchanged an affectionate look and a brief, tentative kiss. Debbie seemed tense, holding herself stiffly. When they drew apart, Michael held her away from him, gazing deeply into her face. He then leaned in and kissed her on the neck. 'You are so beautiful,' he said, holding her with his eyes. 'More beautiful than I ever imagined the mother of my child would be. Thank you so much, Debbie. Thank you so much for being . . . you.' It was a touching moment.

The next evening, Michael and Anthony attended the Australian premiere of Michael's short film *Ghosts* and walked side by side in front of the clicking and whirring cameras. Michael looked content in one of his military outfits and a black silk surgical mask. Anthony, who wore a simple, short-sleeved black shirt, was dark-haired, good-looking . . . and, in the opinion of most observers, a dead-ringer for Jordie Chandler.

Meanwhile, Debbie was in her hotel suite making long-distance telephone calls to friends in the United States. Marsha Devlin, another one of her Van Nuys neighbours at the time, recalled that Debbie told her she needed her to pay her telephone bill for her. 'She had left the States in such a hurry, she forgot to pay it,' said Marsha. 'It was disconnected already; she owed back money for the bill. If she had money from Michael by this time, you sure would never know it. She told me she had about three thousand dollars in the bank.'

When Marsha asked, Debbie told her that Michael did not stay with her in her suite at the Sheraton on the Park Hotel the night before they wed, nor on their wedding night. Instead, she said, he stayed with 'an assistant' in another room, 'so that I could get some rest. I was exhausted.' Less than a week later, Debbie returned to Los Angeles, never having slept with Michael in Sydney.

The day before he married Debbie Rowe, Michael telephoned Lisa Marie Presley in Los Angeles to tell her of his plans. He still cared deeply about her, he said, and didn't want her to 'read about the wedding in the papers'. He felt dreadful, he told her, about the way their relationship ended, 'with us saying mean things to each other. And now I'm moving on,' he told her, according to a later recollection, 'but I don't really feel that it's right, not without your blessing.' In fact, those close to Michael say that he was so anxious about his marriage to Debbie, he was jittery and would begin to sob at the slightest provocation, his tears flowing, unchecked. No wonder he was worn out; his life had been filled with such confusion and anxiety for as many years as he could remember, the stress of it keenly felt, especially while on the road with yet another strenuous tour. He was bone tired; getting up on that stage and executing his trademark dance steps had become more of an ordeal with each passing year. 'I'm getting too old for this shit,' he said.

Lisa didn't know how to react to Michael's telephone call. She still loved him, she said, but she was adamant that they would never be together, again. Therefore, he should go forth and do whatever he wanted to do with his life, with Debbie Rowe, or anyone else. She gave him her 'blessing'. Anyway, it was time for her to move past the madness of his world, to stop trying to fathom the unfathomable. After she and Michael ended their marriage, she fell into a serious health decline, 'the worst two years of my life,' as she put it. Privately, she said that she hoped he was content in his new life, but she knew him too well. His sadness sprang from so many years of distrust and unhappiness, how could a marriage to someone with whom he wasn't in love possibly end his misery, even if she was having a baby for him?

Lisa may have been concerned, but much of the public and media's reaction to Michael's second marriage was just cynical. It appeared that he married a person he didn't love, who was having a baby that may or may not have been his, or maybe conceived artificially. 'Please respect our privacy,' Michael said in a statement, 'and let us enjoy this wonderful and exciting time.' As for Debbie, many people didn't know what to make of her, either. On its front page, the *Daily Mirror* published a photograph of her on a hotel balcony in Sydney cradling her head in her hands in dismay, probably expressing exasperation at the presence of an army of paparazzi, below. However, the bold headline suggested otherwise. It read: OH GOD! I'VE JUST MARRIED MICHAEL JACKSON.

Prince Michael Jackson, Michael's son, was born in February 1997 at Cedars-Sinai Medical Center. (He is now known as Prince Michael I. Michael's grandfather and great-grandfather were both named Prince.) He and Debbie cut the umbilical cord together. The baby was weighed. He spent five hours in intensive care with a minor problem, and then Michael rushed him out of the hospital and off to Neverland.

When Debbie was released from Cedars, she recuperated at a friend's house.

'I have been blessed beyond comprehension,' Michael said in a statement, 'and I will work tirelessly at being the best father I can be. I appreciate that my fans are elated, but I hope that everyone respects the privacy that Debbie and I want and need for our son. I grew up in a fish bowl and I will not allow that to happen to my child. Please give my son his privacy.'

Michael and Debbie posed for photographs with Prince in March, at the Four Seasons Hotel. Though the poses seemed warm and Michael and Debbie appeared to be proud parents, it had actually been the first time Debbie had seen the baby since the day she gave birth to him six weeks earlier. She was smuggled into the hotel room, given the infant to hold, told to smile for the camera with Michael . . . and then, her work done, thanked profusely by Michael and sent on her way. She did seem very loving to her child – who was light-skinned with black hair and dark brown eyes – during the time she cradled him in her arms. No doubt, however, she would not want to have become too attached to Prince. It would just make matters more difficult for her. Under ordinary circumstances, a surrogate mother would never be called upon to have to pose for pictures with the baby she had given to someone else to raise. However Debbie Rowe, always amenable to whatever was asked of her, was in a different world . . . Michael's world.

A woman who worked as a chef at Neverland recalls the way Prince was nursed during his first six months. 'Debbie was not a significant presence,' she said. 'We never saw her. The baby was cared for by a team of six nannies and six nurses. They all worked eight hours each, in shifts, so the baby would always have two nurses and two nannies by his side. They were kept under constant video surveillance, which was monitored by members of Jackson's security team. The nannies all have special training. The day-team do exercise drills with the baby to build up his strength. The night-team began reading and singing to Prince when he was only three weeks old. When Prince cries, he seemed to be calling for his mama. It was eerie, almost as if the baby didn't have a mother at all. There are no pictures of Debbie. Mr Jackson has just one photo by his bed, and that's of Lisa Marie as a child in the year when the two of them met.'

She said Prince sometimes slept in Michael's room in a crib filled with stuffed animals. 'The room was more like a nursery than a room for a grown man,' she recalled. 'There were two life-sized figures outside, like a toy shop. One is a boy scout, the other is a girl in a British policeman's hat. Inside there was Peter Pan stuff on the walls and a bunch of Nintendo games we were told not to touch.'

One nanny who worked at Neverland said, 'There was a feeling of being a bit under siege. Nevertheless, the baby did get exceptional care. We had to measure the air quality in his room once every hour. When we fed him, all the utensils had to be boiled first and could only be used for one type of food. They were all thrown away after a single use.' Prince was given new toys every day and, apparently for sanitary reasons, Michael instructed his staff to discard his 'old' toys after Prince has gone to bed. 'Debbie Rowe really had no input,' the nanny said. 'I saw her maybe three times and she seemed very sullen.'

For Debbie, one perk of being Michael's wife was the opportunity to rub shoulders with the rich and famous. However, sometimes she didn't rub as closely as she might have hoped. For instance, she had been anxious to meet Elizabeth Taylor. However, Elizabeth was annoyed at Michael at this time because Michael had never introduced Debbie to her, and she couldn't fathom that he would go off and marry someone she didn't know. Michael told Debbie to go ahead and try to meet Liz if she wanted to, but that it wouldn't be a good time for him to be an intermediary. Debbie attempted to contact Elizabeth, telephoning her a few times. At one point, she gave Elizabeth's secretary her mailing address, so that Elizabeth would have it in her appointment book. One day, she received a note from the screen star: 'Thank you for your interest in my career. Enclosed, please find a signed photo. With affection. [signed] Elizabeth Taylor.'

'Debbie laughed when she got it,' said Tanya Boyd. 'She thought it was the funniest thing in the world. She even framed it! "So close," she said of Elizabeth Taylor, "yet so, so far."'

Lisa Marie has a Change of Heart

Michael Jackson is a powerful person who has a strong effect on people, even the most wealthy and famous who want nothing more than to be in his life. Apparently, Lisa Marie Presley was not immune to that influence. Despite all that had happened with him in their twenty-month marriage, she was compelled to keep abreast of the goings on in Michael's life. Maybe in an effort to achieve that goal, she suddenly began socializing with Michael's sister Janet. A few months earlier, the two were spotted together at a club in Manhattan called Life, seemingly enjoying each other's company and causing people to wonder what in the world they were doing together.

Lisa explained to friends that she was advising Janet on how to get back in shape for her upcoming *Velvet Rope* tour; Janet had apparently gained about forty pounds and was determined to lose them, and more. However, it's unlikely that Lisa and Janet were going to the gym together. It simply looked like they were having fun because, that same week, they were seen shopping, having lunch, going to the movies and even catching an off-Broadway play, both in disguises. In September 1997, Lisa attended the launch party for Janet's *Velvet Rope* CD. Shortly after, they attended the MTV Awards together.

When Michael heard from Janet that she was socializing with Lisa, he became intensely interested. 'Does she ever talk about me?' he wanted to know. 'I'll bet she hates me, now. Does she hate me, now?'

Janet told her brother that Lisa seemed to hold no grudge against him for what had happened in their relationship and, in fact, would actually like to see him. What she didn't tell him was that Lisa had been suspicious of Michael's marriage to 'Nursey'. She knew Michael well enough to know that his goal had always been to have children, and he didn't seem to care how he got them. He had wanted Lisa to bear him a child, but she drew the line there since she didn't want to bring a child into an unhappy union. She suspected that he and Debbie had an agreement to have a baby, and that their marriage was just a device to make it legitimate. Janet confirmed all of those suspicions, telling her that Michael 'did it [married Debbie] for Katherine, really.' Lisa didn't hold against Michael any of his choices where Debbie was concerned. 'You can't blame someone for being exactly who they are, can you?' she asked her friend, Monica Pastelle. 'A lot of people use surrogate mothers and, if you look at this and really kinda squint at it, I think that's what it is. But,' she hastened to add, 'it gives me a terrible headache if I think too hard about it, so I try not to.'

Michael then telephoned Lisa to ask if they could be friends. 'I've always loved you,' he said to her, according to a later recollection, 'and I hate that way it ended between us. I really do.'

Lisa told him that an important aspect of her Scientology training is that she not hold on to bitterness and anger, and that she had dedicated herself to get past any negative feelings about him. He was happy to hear it. He then invited her and her children to join him in South Africa where his HIStory tour was finally wrapping up. His mother and father would also be there, he said, so Lisa wouldn't have to feel awkward about the propriety of such a visit. They were helping him watch Prince Michael, he explained. (That may have been true, but Michael also had a team of nurses and nannies on hand.) Lisa couldn't resist; she said, yes.

Whatever Lisa's intentions had ever been involving Michael, she still had a deep connection with him – and seeing him building a family with another woman wasn't easy for her. It had been some time since she had immersed herself in his world, which as she once said, was 'the only way to figure out how he's doing. You can't ask someone how a rollercoaster ride is while they're still on it – you just have to hop on too.' Lisa had to see for herself how he had adjusted to life since they parted company. A lot had changed for him. He had sidestepped the molestation allegations, released new music, toured successfully, married, had a child. Finally, it appeared he was settling down, finding himself. Would she now find a new Michael Jackson, one that had risen from the ashes of the broken man she knew before. It was this curiosity that took her across the Atlantic, twice. She would first join him in London, where he would be playing Wembley Stadium (12–17 July). She had Scientology business there, she said. Then, she would return to the States, and rejoin Michael at the end of the tour in South Africa.

Perfect, Michael must have thought. As it happened, Debbie was joining him in France, Austria and Germany (25 June–6 July), just a week before Lisa's arrival, to see him and Prince Michael, who was about four months old. By that point, she'd only seen the baby once, maybe twice, since he was born. She was planning to leave before the London dates, which was fine with Michael because she and Lisa would then not cross paths.

In Germany, Michael was upfront with Debbie and told her that Lisa would be joining him on his next dates in England and then, later, in South Africa. Debbie wasn't thrilled with the news – she may have thought Lisa was encroaching on her territory – but she got over it, quickly. Their relationship wasn't such that she could tell him what to do, anyway, even if they were married. Plus, she didn't really care. 'Look, the thing is this,' she told a friend. 'I don't tell Michael Jackson how to live his life, and he doesn't tell me how to live mine. [Debbie always referred to her husband as "Michael Jackson".] And that's a fact,' she concluded. 'So if he wants to run around with his ex-wife, I'm not going stop him. Because I don't want him stopping me if I want to do the same thing with my ex-boyfriend.'

'But that's not a normal marriage, is it?' protested Debbie's friend.

'We're talking *Michael Jackson's* marriage, here,' quipped Debbie.

'Come on! Get real. I have it under control. I'm a grown-up, and I know what I'm doing, and so does he. Besides,' she said, 'I think we'll have a big announcement, soon.'

Debbie didn't explain at the time, but she and Michael either had sex (as they would later insist), or did something more artificial to make it happen, but while she was in Paris, staying at the Disneyland Hotel outside the city, she became pregnant with his second child. She knew her relationship with Michael – such as it was, whatever it was – was not in jeopardy. They had an arrangement; it seemed to work.

Meanwhile, in London, Lisa and her two children joined Michael and his parents in London. They all stayed in Michael's $10,000-a-night suite at the luxury Carlton Towers hotel.

Michael's three dates at Wembley Stadium were all sold out; he was in a terrific mood. However, as devoted as Lisa was to it during their visit, she didn't have enough quality time with him to get a handle on Michael's state of being.

Three months went by, and Lisa joined him again in South Africa in October. This time Lisa stepped off the plane with a shock of blonde hair, moderately resembling the shade of Debbie's hair. During this trip, she made a concerted effort to 'weasel' her way (as she later put it) into his busy days.

Lisa and Michael, and his parents, son and her children, all stayed at the Palace Hotel in the centre of Johannesburg. The former couple was seen holding hands and beaming at one another. Yet, beneath the veneer of her pleasant smiles, Lisa had begun to grow uncomfortable with the new Michael Jackson. While he was not nearly as troubled as he had been during her reign in his life, some of the changes she saw in him bothered her.

For one thing, the vulnerability that he had before, born maybe of paranoia or an impending sense of doom, had now been replaced with a kind of bravado. It appeared that Michael felt invincible. A particularly troubling fact for Lisa was the appearance of a thirteen-year-old Norwegian boy. He was a cute kid who wore a red baseball cap all the time, given to him by Michael. His presence, even if it was innocent, was disconcerting. Did Michael still not realize how dangerous it was for him, in terms of his public image, to have young boys with him on tour?

On Friday 10 October, Michael performed before 47,000 people at Johannesburg Stadium. Afterward, Lisa spent hours backstage with Michael. During that time together, she attempted to raise the topic of Michael's new friend. The appearance of impropriety was something that she felt had to be addressed. Yet, Michael made it clear to her that the issue would not be discussed. It seemed he no longer required, or at least welcomed, her counsel.

It had been the self-doubting, vulnerable part of Michael Jackson that had always been the bridge between him and Lisa Marie Presley. Now, without that part intact, and with the bridge of their sexual compatibility also broken down, Lisa felt not just powerless, she also felt like an outsider.

The next day, Lisa and her children were on hand for the formal ceremony when Michael was made an honorary member of an African tribe, Bafokeng Ka Bakwena (People of the Crocodile). The 300,000-strong Bafokeng is regarded as one of the richest in the country due to its ownership of the world's second-largest platinum reserve. Katherine and Joseph, who met the tribe a few days before, were also given 'citizenship' certificates.

Dressed in a military-style jacket adorned with gold badges on the chest and arms, Michael walked slowly through a crowd of native women and children in the town of Phokeng, ninety miles northwest of Johannesburg, after the ceremony. With Lisa clutching his arm proudly, Michael smiling benevolently and touched the hands of his admirers as if he was visiting royalty. At all times an aide carried a blue-and-yellow umbrella to provide shade for him and Lisa.

That afternoon, Michael and Lisa went water-skiing at South Africa's Sun City resort. Then, that night they had dinner with Katherine at the resort. During the meal, they applauded as youngsters dressed in leopard skin tribal garb performed for them.

The next day, Michael rehearsed for his concert at Johannesburg Stadium. Lisa, with her plans to depart already made, watched from backstage, waiting for Michael to finish so she could say her 'goodbyes'.

A small coterie of people watched Michael as he and the dancers rehearsed 'Thriller'. In the middle of the song, he halted the performance. 'Hold it, guys,' he said. 'That's all wrong. It goes like this. Watch.' He then glided across the stage effortlessly, as if on air, thereby demonstrating the correct moves for his troupe. Katherine, who was standing with Lisa, beamed.

'When I think of how bad it got with those damn lies, and how far he has come since then, I have to cry,' Katherine said, not taking her eyes off her son. 'He was almost destroyed. Now, just watch him, he's so darn good.' She then put her arm around Lisa and gave her a warm look. 'And it's because of you that he got through it. Do you know that? Do you know how much we appreciate what you did for him?'

Lisa smiled dimly and shrugged her shoulders. 'I don't know if I helped, or not,' she told Katherine, modestly. 'I did love him. That I know. But, face it, Katherine, your son is one big mystery.'

Katherine tilted her head back and laughed. 'Girl, tell me about it,' she exclaimed.

Michael came off the stage just as the two women were sharing their conspiratorial moment. 'Now, what are you two gossiping about?' he asked, good-naturedly.

'You!' they both said, in unison.

He executed a quick, soft shoe routine, made a funny face at them, and went back to work.

Lost Love

In November 1997, Debbie Rowe announced that she was pregnant with a girl, her second 'gift' to Michael. This was the child they said had been conceived in Paris. Michael was elated. At this time, he bought her a new house in Los Angeles. She moved in with her two pet dogs, and seemed happy with her life.

Michael anxiously prepared himself for the birth of another baby, excited to see his family grow. Though he and Debbie still did not live together – and never would – they got along well. She was his friend – the one who had his children. The other woman in his life, Lisa Marie Presley, was still the one who had his heart, and Debbie knew it. 'She told me that Michael had Lisa's picture in his bedroom, on his nightstand,' said Tanya Boyd. 'Debbie never had any misguided notion that Michael was in love with her, and she's never been in love with him either, I don't think. "What he has with Lisa, now that's true love," Debbie told me. "I have always known it," she said. "I've never fought it. I've only encouraged it." She never wanted to come between Lisa and Michael. "If Lisa would have had his children," she told me, "I never would have done it for him. There would have been no reason for it." '

On Saturday, 7 February 1998, Michael got together with Lisa for dinner at the Ivy in Los Angeles. He had telephoned her and said he wanted to take her out for her thirtieth birthday, which had been about a week earlier.

They arrived at the restaurant holding hands. Michael wore a black hat and matching surgical mask, Lisa a dark blue dress with a gold choker. Because they didn't have a reservation, the manager took them into his office and served them drinks while they waited for a table in a quiet, romantic corner. Once seated, Lisa enjoyed a plate of steamed vegetables. Michael ate crab cakes and fried chicken. However, he slipped the food underneath his mask, rather than take it off. One wonders what it might be like to sit across the table from a person who is eating while wearing a surgical mask. 'Once you get past the preposterousness of it,' Lisa explained, privately, 'and decide in your head, okay, now, look, the guy is *not* going to take the mask off . . .'

For dessert, they shared a piece of cake, decorated with a single candle – which Lisa happily blew out. 'How's it going with Debbie?' Lisa wanted to know, according to what she later recalled to a friend.

Half-heartedly, Michael said it was 'okay' with his wife. He had another glass of red wine, his fourth. He told her that as much as he cared for Debbie, when he was with her, 'I focus on what I don't have, instead of what I do have. I just want to be in love. Like what you and I had. I was so afraid,' he told her, according to her memory. 'I know now that I closed you out. What can I do now?'

Lisa says that she didn't respond. She no longer had the answers to his problems – not that she ever did – or the solution to his life. There wasn't much she could propose, except perhaps the most basic of offerings between two people with a history who still care about each other. 'I want you to know,' she told him, 'that if you ever need a friend, I'm here for you. You have such a good heart, Michael,' she added. 'But, dude, tell me this: why do you have to be so *fucking strange?*'

The two dissolved into laughter, probably realizing that there was no simple answer to that question.

After dinner, they strolled down Robertson Boulevard in Beverly Hills, window shopping under the watchful eye of paparazzi. At one point, Michael kissed the top of her head and put two fingers under her chin, lifting it so her eyes would meet his. His arms closed around her, enveloping her. They kissed through his silk mask, as if he was some kind of comic book super hero and it made all the sense in the world. She then snuggled against him. A paparazzo memorialized the tender moment, the photographs appearing five days later in a tabloid.

Later, they were driven to Santa Monica for a long walk on the beach, talking late into the night.

'I love her,' Michael told one of his associates the next day, 'more than anything, more than anyone, I still love Lisa. We have such a strong connection.' His eyes filled with tears. 'That was my one shot, man,' he said. 'I did a lot of foolish things. I may never get another shot, you know?'

'In another world, we would be together,' Lisa would say, 'just not in his world, I'm afraid.'

Two months later, Michael was the father of a new daughter.

Paris Katherine Michael Jackson was born on 3 April 1998 (named after the city in which her parents say the baby was conceived, and also after her grandmother and her father). Michael's associates contacted the Pope at the Vatican in Rome about the possibility of his christening the baby. However, a Vatican official sent a letter to Michael through his representation in Los Angeles explaining that The Pontiff would not want to be involved in 'what may be perceived by some as a publicity stunt'. (The Vatican had already been down this same road with Madonna a few years earlier when she attempted to have the Pope baptize her first child, Lourdes, but was also turned away.)

When their 'arrangement' no longer felt right to Debbie, she asked for a divorce, and he gave her one on 8 October 1999, no questions asked. He gave her about ten million dollars in a settlement, beginning with a first payment of $1.5 million in October.

Michael continued with his life and career in 2000 and 2001 – as noted later in this text. Then, another baby was born to him in 2002, a boy he named Prince Michael II. He has told confidants that he hopes to have more children in the future, and that all of the boys will be named Prince Michael (III, IV, etc . . .).

Prince Michael II has the nickname 'Blanket'. Michael has explained, 'It's an expression I use with my family and my employees. I say, "You should blanket me or you should blanket her," meaning like a blanket is a blessing. It's a way of showing love and caring.' It was this particular child, nine months at the time, whom Michael dangled off a balcony in Germany in November 2002, causing a flood of editorials speculating about his emotional stability and suitability for fatherhood. Michael was bewildered by his own actions and distraught by the media coverage. He was also embarrassed; what would his friends and family think? He publicly apologized for his behaviour, saying that he became caught up 'in the moment'.

Afterwards, Michael received a letter from Elizabeth Taylor, dated 19 December 2002, which lifted his spirits. 'Don't ever let them [the public] get you down, Michael. You're loved by too many, especially this kid. I love you just as much as I always have and understand you just as much as I always have. Don't hide. You haven't done anything to be ashamed of. Be proud of how you are bringing up your children. God knows I am. I love you with all my heart, and because I know you so well. I will always understand where others may not. But, you know something: screw the others. All my love, Elizabeth.'

Michael has not revealed the identity of the mother of his third child. He would explain that the two older children were 'a natural conception' – meaning, he said, that he and Debbie had sex – and that the new baby was the result of artificial insemination. 'I used a surrogate mother and my own sperm cells,' he explained. 'She doesn't know me and I don't know her. I didn't care what race she was as long as she was healthy and her vision was good. And her intellect – I wanted to know how intelligent she is.' He first noted that the mother was a black woman, then later changed the story and said he didn't know her identity. Prince Michael II is very blond. Debbie had confirmed that the child is not hers. If he knows who the mother is, he has decided not to reveal her name.

The Martin Bashir Documentary

In February 2003, another strange chapter in Michael's life opened with the highly controversial documentary, *Living with Michael Jackson*, which first attracted fifteen million viewers in the United Kingdom and more than double that in the United States. The programme made excitable headlines on both sides of the Atlantic for its subject, Michael, and interviewer/presenter, Martin Bashir.

Prior to the Michael Jackson interview, Martin Bashir was most famous for his 1995 television dissection of Diana, Princess of Wales. Almost twenty-three million people watched her confess royal unhappiness about her difficult marriage to Prince Charles, his relationship to Camilla Parker Bowles and the complex, personal embarrassment Diana called 'three in a marriage'. Soon after, the Queen urged Charles and Diana to divorce. Because Diana had won global sympathy with her interview, Michael believed Martin when he presented himself as 'the man who turned Diana's life around'. Actually, if he had examined the history of the Diana documentary, he would have found that it didn't help her. As she revealed details of her tragic recent life in a halting, hypnotic voice, it was as if she had decided to self-destruct, and do it on television. During her interviews, she seemed distant, aloof and damaged. To her advantage, though, she was the victim of certain challenges, such as eating disorders and marital discord, which could, at least, be understandable to the viewer. There was no way she would be viewed as a freak of nature. Instead, she appeared to be a sad woman whose life had spun out of control – and was still spinning, in fact – and who had decided to just come clean with it. However, Michael Jackson – with his plastic surgeries, babies with no maternal presence and intense fascination with youngsters – took a greater risk when he decided to allow Martin Bashir into the environment his first wife called his 'world of wonder'.

After his Diana extravaganza, Martin Bashir won an award from the British Academy of Film and Television Arts and was named the Royal Television Society's Journalist of the Year for 1996. He subsequently landed other high-profile interviews, including one with anguished gay British actor-comedian Michael Barrymore, in the news after the drowning of a young man during a party at his house.

Martin courted Michael Jackson for five years, trying to convince him to participate in the documentary. Finally, after being recommended by Michael's friend, the paranormalist Uri Geller, Martin was given an audience with Michael, during which he was able to convince him to cooperate. Michael then allowed him total access to his life for eight months, despite the fact that his advisers felt that such cooperation would not bode well for him. Martin Bashir spent time at Neverland in California, and travelled across the United States and Europe with Michael. (Uri would later regret having ever introduced Michael to Martin.)

The most interesting aspect of the documentary is not what it revealed, though much of it was astounding. What fascinates about *Living with Michael Jackson* is that its subject ever allowed it to be filmed, which suggests that Michael either still does not understand how he is perceived by much of the public or that he doesn't care. He truly believed, according to those who know him best, that it was a savvy public relations manoeuvre, to allow a stranger to document his world from an outside view point and in a way that would prevent Michael from having control over the final content. He wasn't thinking clearly about it. He thought it was a cool thing to do because Diana had done it, and he felt sure that the public would be interested in his life. He never imagined anyone would be shocked by it because he simply does not think he or his life is shocking.

Some in Michael's camp – like John Branca, it was said – never believed the project would be completed. Like many entertainers, Michael involves himself in many projects that never get past the developmental stage, and it was hoped that this one would be another on that list. Such a project would surely never have been released in days-long-gone when others had influence over him.

Some supporters of Michael's have tried to spin the Martin Bashir documentary as a positive in the star's life, saying that he presented a sympathetic image of himself in it. Of course, while watching him discuss the beatings he endured by his father, one's heart went out to him. Michael recalled that Joseph sat in a chair as the boys rehearsed, 'and he had this belt in his hand. If you didn't do it the right way, he would tear you up, really get you. It was bad. Real bad.' He is still traumatized by his childhood and it doesn't appear that he has come to terms with much of it. However, that said, most of the rest of the 110 minutes made Michael appear to be about as eccentric a character as pop culture has ever produced.

For instance, his description of Paris's birth: 'I was so anxious to get her home after cutting the cord – I hate to say this – I snatched her and just went home with all the placenta and everything all over her. I just got her in a towel and ran.'

Privately, Debbie Rowe takes the absurdity to a new level by confirming that Michael had the placenta frozen! (Of course he did, one might observe. How else could he keep it?)

Michael's constant complaining about sensational tabloid coverage of his life seems irrelevant when his actions are jaw-dropping enough to provide *true* material to such publications. 'Wacko-Jacko Kidnaps His Own baby Just Hours After Birth', screamed the front-page headline in *Star* in April 1998. ('He just snatched the kid away from her.') 'Jacko Snatches Baby Minutes After Birth' blared the headline in *National Enquirer* that same week. ('Michael gave Debbie a peck on the check, took Paris in his arms and whisked her off.') Who would have believed these stories? However, even the writers of those articles may have thought it a leap to report that Michael had the placenta *frozen*; that would have been too much of a stretch even for them!

Another scene showed him feeding Prince Michael II with a bottle. As he fed the infant, concealed by a green chiffon scarf, Michael vigorously bounced him on his knee. 'I love you, Blanket,' he cooed, 'I love you, Blanket.' Then, seeming somewhat wild-eyed and jittery, he recalled his actions on the balcony in Germany, explaining that he had the infant firmly in hand when he briefly dangled him off the side, and that it was the media that was responsible for the ensuing fracas, not him. 'Why would I put a scarf over the baby's face if I was trying to throw him off a balcony?' Michael asked, angrily. 'We were waving to thousands of fans below and they were chanting to see my child, and I was kind enough to let them see.'

Of his love for children, he noted, 'I'll say it a million times. I'm not afraid to say it. If there were no children on this earth, if somebody announced that all kids are dead, I would jump off the balcony immediately. I'm done. I'm done.'

Most maddening, perhaps, was Michael's insistence that 'I've had no plastic surgery on my face, just my nose. It helped me breathe better, so I can hit the higher notes.' He claimed that he's only had two surgeries, both on his nose. 'I'm telling you the honest truth. I don't do anything to my face,' he said. After all of these years, one would think he would have a better way to deal with the issue of plastic surgery. How about: 'Obviously, I have had plastic surgery. Next question, please.' Who could argue with that?

Throughout the ages, the one safe haven to which a celebrity can always retreat from an aggressive media is the 'No Comment' zone. It works. Jackie Kennedy, for instance, rarely had an interesting public comment to make about anything, and no one held it against her. It's often better, in fact, if celebrities have nothing to say, especially if they are unconventional people who behave in a way that, no matter how much they try, they simply will not be able to explain to anyone's satisfaction.

For anyone who knew Michael, watching the Martin Bashir documentary was painful. Lisa Marie Presley telephoned Neverland the next morning, telling his assistant that she wanted to speak to Michael as soon as possible. She was in another state, on a radio tour for her album. Still, she took the time to call to see how her ex-husband was handling the highly publicized controversy.

When Michael heard that Lisa was trying to reach him, his heart began to race. He still hasn't got over what he shared with her and, according to what he has said, believes that one day, somehow, they will be together again. When Lisa married actor Nicolas Cage in Hawaii in November 2002, Michael had been troubled. When they separated after less than four months, he called her to check in on her. 'Oh, don't worry about me,' she told him. 'It's just another shit storm in my life. I'm getting through it, just shovelling through the bullshit.' He laughed.

He called her at the number she left for him. 'Dude!' Lisa said as soon as she got on the line. 'That documentary fucking *sucked*, man. What were you *thinking*?'

They couldn't stop laughing. Leave it to her to lift his spirits. 'Oh, screw Martin Bashir,' she said. 'That guy's never gonna work again, Michael. Who would ever trust him? He's over. You fucking killed his career.'

'I think maybe he tried to kill mine, Lisa,' Michael said.

'Oh, please,' she told him, 'it's gonna take more than that shit head of a reporter to kill your career, believe me.'

It could be argued that Martin had exploited Michael with all of his leading questions, his presumptions, expressed fascination and bemusement. For instance, he encouraged Michael to climb the tree atop which he writes many of his songs while at one with the beauty of Neverland, his so-called 'Magic Tree'. One doubts he did so because he was trying to show Michael's playful side. What he got was the image of Michael sitting alone, on top of a tree. It worked; it was touching and even somewhat disturbing. When Martin later followed Michael on a Las Vegas shopping spree and observed him spending thousands of dollars on the worst, most gaudy furnishings, was he doing it for any other reason than to make Michael look like a spectacle? But why, by the same token, did Michael allow himself to be seen this way? There were also a number of sanctimonious voice-overs from Martin as he stood in judgement of Michael and his life.

Michael was at home, in Neverland, with a few friends and advisers when he viewed an advance copy of *Living with Michael Jackson*, just before it aired in the UK. He expected to be pleased with it. 'However, he knew within five minutes that he was going to be very unhappy,' said an associate. 'He watched quietly. You could hear a pin drop in the room, no one wanted to say a word. When it was over, he was quiet. He kept saying, "I can't believe he would do this to me." There was a lot of discussion about blocking the programme's broadcast, but not much hope held out for it. Mike drank a lot of wine, that night, trying to dull the misery. It wasn't until the next day that he became angry. Then, he was adamant that he didn't want it released. His attorneys said there was no way to block it. "Don't tell me that, now. Find a way," he said, angrily. However, they were never able to do that.'

In the final analysis, though, Michael did say what he said and was the way he was – tricky editing had nothing to do with him, at the age of forty-four, holding hands and giggling with a cancer-survivor, age twelve, and admitting that he sometimes sleeps in the same room with him. Recalled the youngster, his head nuzzling against Michael's shoulder, 'I was, like, "Michael, *you* can sleep in the bed," and he was, like, "No, no, *you* sleep in the bed," and I was, like, "No, no, no, *you* sleep in the bed," and then he said, "Look, if you love me, then *you'll* sleep in the bed." I was, like, "Oh, *man!*"' said the youngster. 'So, I finally slept in the bed.' (Michael slept on the floor.)

As the boy spoke, Michael gazed upon him steadily, clearly wanting to convey his affection and devotion. Once again, by his own doing, he had presented himself to the world in a way that would cause the raising of eyebrows and the wagging of tongues. Michael told Martin, 'I have slept in a bed with many children. Why can't you share your bed? The most loving thing to do is to share your bed with someone. When you say "bed", you're thinking sexual. They make that sexual; it's not sexual. We're going to sleep, I tuck them in and I put a little music on, and when it's story time, I read a book. We go to sleep with the fireplace on. I give them hot milk, you know, we have cookies. It's very charming, it's very sweet; it's what the whole world should do.'

Of course, talent and excess go hand in hand in the entertainment world, and in some ways Michael Jackson may be no more eccentric than certain other stars in pop history. Imagine what *Living With Elvis* might have looked like in his declining years, secluded at Graceland, paranoid and on drugs? The problem for Michael is that he has been publicly wigging out for more than fifteen years, since the hyperbaric chamber scam of 1986. 'No, I *am* Peter Pan,' he told Martin Bashir. 'I'm Peter Pan in my *heart*.' Such PR has never served him well in the court of public opinion; his wacky image only serves to diminish his important, hard-earned legacy in the entertainment field.

Perhaps Lisa Marie said it best to *Playboy* writer, Rob Tannenbaum: 'For a while, Michael was like the Wizard of Oz, the man behind the curtain. At one time, he was really good at manipulating a Howard Hughes type of image. He became this bigger-than-life figure. But at some point, it turned on him and he became this freak [in some of the public's view]. And now he can't get out from under it. When you're the king of your own palace, there are no morals or ethics or integrity. Everyone will kiss your ass and then give you the push that knocks you over.'

After *Living with Michael Jackson* aired in the United States, an unhappy Michael issued a statement saying that he felt 'devastated' and 'utterly betrayed' by the documentary, that he viewed it as 'a gross distortion of the truth' and a 'tawdry attempt to misrepresent' his life and his abilities as a father. Michael clearly felt that the journalist had let him down. Blaming the sensational tone of the documentary on its editing and on what he saw as Bashir's bad-faith intentions, Michael then launched a turn-about-is-fair-play offensive by releasing a sixteen-second extract of unreleased film that would, it was hoped, make Bashir look like a complete ass.

In *Living with Michael Jackson*, Martin accused Michael of having little time for his own youngsters: Prince Michael I, then five; Paris Katherine Michael, four; and baby Prince Michael II. Of the Jackson offspring, Martin noted, 'The children are restricted. They are over protected.' He branded Michael 'broken, childish and self-obsessed'. He said, 'I came away quite saddened and deeply disturbed by what I saw.'

However, on Michael's footage, Bashir gushes, 'Your relationship with your kids is fantastic. In fact, it almost makes me weep when I see you with them because your interaction is so natural, so loving and so caring. Everyone that comes into contact with you knows that.' Michael Jackson replies: 'Thank you.'

Did this film make Martin Bashir appear to be a liar, and Michael an exemplary parent? Perhaps, to some, it did. To others, it came as little surprise that an interviewer would attempt to ingratiate himself to the person that he's talking to in order to encourage him to be more candid.

It was then decided that Michael would release an entire two-hour documentary about his life, as seen by him and some of his inner-circle. Fox-TV, in America, paid him two million dollars for the rights to *The Michael Jackson Interview: The Footage You Were Never Meant to See*, and then the programme was sold around the world. Because his interpretation of Martin Bashir's un-released footage would not have been enough to sustain an entire documentary, Katherine and Joseph were brought in to defend him, as were others such as his brother, Jermaine, his makeup artist, Karen Faye, and Debbie Rowe.

Debbie's attempts to explain her relationship to Michael, and to their children, may have done him more harm than good. 'My kids don't call me Mom because I don't want them to,' she said. 'They're Michael's children. It's not that they are not my children, but I had them because I wanted him to be a father. People make remarks, "I can't believe she left her children." Left them? I left my children? I did *not* leave my children. My children are with their father, where they are supposed to be. I didn't do it to be a mother . . . If he called me tonight and said let's have five more [children], I'd do it in a heartbeat.'

She seems well-meaning; her heart in the right place. However, Debbie's unconventional relationship with Michael, and especially with her children, is perplexing, no matter how much logic she tries to ascribe to it. It's probably better left unpublicized, unexploited.

After the duelling documentaries were broadcast – Martin's and Michael's – Michael once again dismissed his longtime attorney, John Branca, this time, by fax. John was said to be sorry to go, but also a bit relieved. His had been an exhausting job, on and off for twenty-five years, made even more frustrating when Michael stopped taking his good advice. As a friend as well as his attorney for so many years, it was difficult for him to see Michael make some of his choices. Also, the woman managing Michael at this time, Trudy Green, quit her position – she, too, did not know Michael had finalized a deal with Bashir until it was too late to do anything about it. Then, Michael fired his accountant, Barry Siegel, as if completely cleaning out the shop.

At this same time, a website published previously unseen documents filed by authorities a decade before when Jordie Chandler detailed his alleged sexual abuse at Michael's hands. It had to happen; more reminders of the past misery with Jordie and Evan, and all as a result of the appearance of impropriety that resulted from footage of Michael holding hands with a twelve-year-old on the Martin Bashir documentary. After the release of the lurid five-page document, Michael issued a statement saying he 'has respected the obligation of confidentiality' and that Jordie's declaration was just being used to 'further sully' his [Michael's] character. 'It will never go away, will it?' he then asked one adviser, seeming miserable. Just when he was able to forget about Jordie Chandler for a time, he had to once again be reminded of him. 'It's not fair. Why won't the media leave me alone?' he asked. 'Why?'

If Michael truly wants to redeem himself, perhaps he should do the one thing he has never done: join us, the general public, in acknowledging the strange, disturbing aspects of some of his behaviour and attribute them to *something*, rather than continue to act as if they don't exist. Instead, he issues statements such as one after the Martin Bashir interview, in which he said, 'I am bewildered at the length to which people will go to portray me so negatively.' Then, he allows his enablers to come forth with their own proclamations: 'He's not crazy. It's the *public* that's crazy. He's not nuts. It's the *public* that's nuts. Why don't you understand? *Why don't you get it?*' Rather, one wishes Michael Jackson would be the one to finally 'get it', apologize for any perceived impropriety and say, 'To tell you the truth, I don't know *what* I was thinking.'

HIStory, Blood on the Dance Floor & Invincible

Michael Jackson survived the devastating child molestation allegations of a decade ago, but it could be argued not without considerable damage to his recording career. In fact, his record sales have dipped dramatically since 1993.

In 1995, a double CD was issued, *HIStory – Past, Present & Future, Book 1*. The package boasted fifteen of his greatest hits ('Beat It', 'Billie Jean', and the rest) and fifteen new songs, such as the thoughtful 'Stranger in Moscow', the elegant 'Earth Song' and 'Scream' (with Janet, the first single release from the package).

'You Are Not Alone', also included, remains among Michael's best songs; it made chart history in America by becoming the first song ever to go straight to number one on the *Billboard* charts in its first week. It also topped the chart in Britain, after debuting there at number three. On listening to 'You Are Not Alone', one wonders how many times Michael tried to tell himself, during his most desperate and anguished times, that he *did* have support in his life, from a higher power, or even friends and family, whether he actually believed it or not.

The only problem with 'You Are Not Alone' was the bizarre video for it, in which Michael and Lisa Marie frolic about semi-nude against an ethereal backdrop. 'I don't know why I did it,' Lisa says. 'I was sucked up in the moment. It was kind of cool being in a Michael Jackson video. Come on!' Actually, the semi-nudity made no sense and was a bit disconcerting; one wished they would put their clothes back on.

Another stand-out is Michael's version of Charlie Chaplain's 'Smile'. What a vocal performance and delivery he gives to this song! Never has he sounded more sincere, more gorgeous. The song was scheduled for release as a single, but cancelled at the last minute when it was decided it was probably not commercial. However, some promotional CDs – now collectors' items – did slip out, with pictures of Michael nattily dressed as Charlie Chaplain.

Huge statues of Michael were constructed and unveiled in a number of European cities to coincide with the record's release. (Leave it to Michael to have a huge statue of himself towed down the Thames as a publicity stunt!) Also, a controversy over the lyrics of 'They Don't Care About Us' broke out, with Michael accused of anti-Semitism because of his lyrics 'kike me' and 'jew me'. He replaced them with 'strike me' and 'do me' as a result.

However, any publicity for Michael is usually good publicity when he's promoting a record. *HIStory* went on to sell about fifteen million copies worldwide, a slip down from *Dangerous*, which had managed twenty-seven million (*Bad* sold twenty-five million; *Thriller* went on to fifty-two million, and *Off the Wall*, fifteen million). Still, *HIStory* was a major success – artistically as well as commercially – though one largely ignored by a media still distracted by his turbulent and vastly entertaining personal life.

Blood on the Dance Dloor – History in the Mix, Michael's 1997 album, contained five new songs and eight previously unreleased, kick-ass dance remixes of songs such as 'Scream', 'You Are Not Alone' and 'Stranger in Moscow' from *HIStory*. Several of the other songs on *Blood* are also memorable. 'Ghosts' stands out, perhaps because it's so evocative of Michael's spell-binding 'Ghosts' long-styled video in which he is transformed into an old, white man with no rhythm. (It's classic, must-see Michael Jackson.)

The bad news for Michael was that the collection was not a success in America; it was dismissed by critics and much of his audience, who seemed confused as to whether it was a new release or some kind of hybrid combination of songs. Michael's British fans, however, did not disappoint: *Blood* was a major hit in the United Kingdom, kicking off with the single release of 'Blood on the Dance Floor' debuting at number one, then the album. In truth, there may be nothing in his entire catalogue better than 'Blood on the Dance Floor', a song that many of Michael's American fans don't even know exists, it was so overlooked. He wrote and produced it himself.

Blood only sold about four million copies worldwide. While it's not fair to equate the sales of an album of mostly remixes with the sales of his other products, this was still a weak showing. It, and the 'Ghosts' video, like much of what Michael did at this time, was lost in the ongoing controversy of his world: the ongoing confusion about children, Lisa Marie, Debbie Rowe . . . Without that, this stellar work would no doubt have found an appreciative audience.

It should also be noted that it was because of its weak showing Sony executives no longer viewed Michael as being 'invincible'. Heads would *not* roll, it was learned, if he had a flop record, or if he was unhappy with the company. After *Blood on the Dance Floor* disappointed in the USA, he was never a company priority again.

Invincible (released in October 2001), was said to be the most expensive recording ever produced. Sony advanced Michael about forty million dollars to make it. They then spent another twenty-five million to promote it (though, it's difficult to specify how such funds were allocated because the promotion was so weak).

From the beginning, Michael didn't seem excited about the project, and perhaps his lack of enthusiasm and focus became apparent to some listeners. The fact that it took about three years to compose the album – more than fifty songs were produced, mixed and remixed with writers and producers being hired and fired and hired and fired – made some observers feel that Michael was, as one producer put it, 'sick to death of the whole thing.'

Also, Michael began battling with Sony early in the production of *Invincible*. He had thought that the licence to the masters to his biggest-selling albums (*Thriller, Bad, Dangerous*, etc . . .) were to revert back to him in 2000, and was counting the days until that would happen. He would then be able to market the songs himself in some way or with some other label, and not have to split the proceeds with Sony. However, when his advisers checked his contract, they found that the classics revert back to Michael only if he releases about one new CD for Sony every couple of years – which was never going to happen in Michael Jackson's world, one in which he spends *years* on just one project. There was even a Christmas CD specified in the deal (he's not done one of those since 1970, with The Jackson 5), which Michael said he didn't know about, as well as a couple of soundtracks. Michael was way behind in this proposed release schedule, would never be able to catch up, and wouldn't think to even attempt to do it. However, for each specified album he did not deliver (which was most of them), Sony was able to add a few more years to the countdown of rights reversion of the others. As it stood, Michael would be just a tad older than God before the rights to his top-selling albums would ever be reverted to him.

After some investigation into the matter, it was learned that the same attorney who represented Michael on this deal had also represented Sony. (How, one wonders, was *this* ever allowed to occur?) Thus Michael managed to extricate himself from the entire Sony deal, then, using the obvious conflict of interest in this negotiation as leverage . . . In the end, it was decided he would be able to leave Sony, but not until he had delivered *Invincible*, then a Greatest Hits package and *then* a Box Set.

Still, signed to the label or not, Michael would owe Sony hundreds of millions in advances, loans and other monies the company had invested into in his chaotic personal life and professional career. Michael was so chagrined by the situation with Sony that he really didn't want to produce another record for them.

If he received a telephone call while in the studio recording *Invincible*, it could mean the end of that day's work. 'Sorry, I've got business to take care of,' he'd announce while walking out the door. If he had to go to the bathroom, the production staff would fret because Michael would sometimes sneak out and not be seen or heard from for days. 'He's an artist,' explained one producer. 'They're usually pretty nuts.'

However, when the album was finally released, it demonstrated something many of Michael's supporters already know: he is best when recording his own material, such as the sublime 'Speechless', which is really the only track he solely wrote (in about forty-five minutes, he says, after a water-balloon fight with his children) and produced, from beginning to end. However, he doesn't seem to have the fire in his belly he once did to write and produce his own music, therefore *Invincible* was largely a compilation of material from outside songwriters and producers, such as Rodney Jerkins, the hit-making mastermind behind tunes by the Backstreet Boys, Britney Spears, Brandy and Destiny's Child. If Michael wants a huge-selling album in his future, perhaps he should write and produce it himself – *all* of it. He still has the magic touch, if not the drive, ambition and, perhaps, self-confidence.

The initial single release was the somewhat formulaic Rodney Jerkins song, 'You Rock My World'. It had been Sony's decision; Michael was against it and fought for the upbeat, probably more commercial 'Unbreakable' to be issued. He had already conceived of a video for the song. It's interesting that even at this stage of his career, his choices were vetoed by his label. In the end, 'You Rock My World' stalled at number ten in the United States. It debuted at number two in the United Kingdom, but dropped from there quickly. Sales in the rest of Europe were comparable; a Top Ten hit in most countries, but not a huge record.

The video for 'You Rock My World' was a miscalculation; it looked like a remake of the 'Smooth Criminal' short-film, but with Michael in a black suit instead of a white one. In most of the production, Michael seems to be camouflaging the top half of his face with his fedora, causing the viewer to wonder what he is trying to hide. Again, he didn't seem inspired by the concept, anyway – even if it did have a weird cameo appearance by Marlon Brando. There had been upsetting debates between Michael and Sony over the video's budget, and by the time he was to begin production he was, as one of his intimates put it, 'completely over it, done with it.' The dancers had rehearsed for days before Michael appeared on the set. When he finally arrived, he did pretty much the same variety of jerky, robotic steps he's been doing for years, as if trapped in his own myth and afraid to break out of it.

A stand-out on *Invincible* is Carole Bayer Sager's, Kenny 'Babyface' Edmonds and John McClain's sparkling, 'You Are My Life'. It was recorded just five weeks before the album was released – that's how late in the schedule they were considering material. The writers first played it for Michael on a Thursday, he loved it – changed the lyrics from 'You Are My World' to 'You Are My Life' (and got a songwriting credit in the process!) and then recorded it the next evening. John McClain, an executive at DreamWorks Records, has been one of Michael's most trusted and capable advisers for decades. He wrote the song based on a finger exercise he had created for his guitar practice!

The second release from the album was 'Cry'. However, Michael was so angry at Sony for the budget allocated for the video, he refused to even appear in it. Then, the delightful 'Butterflies' began receiving radio, and could have been a hit record. However, again, Jackson and Sony battled over the video, and production was cancelled – as was the commercial release of the song.

The battle lines were boldly drawn between Michael and Sony in a war that continued to be so bitter it would contribute to the commercial failure of *Invincible*. The executives at the label, all the way up to its chieftain at the time, Tommy Motolla, didn't care what Michael thought about anything, he was now that low on their priority lists. His very good song, 'What More Can I Give?' (recorded with a host of pop stars in the wake of 9-11 in an effort similar to 'We Are The World'), was shelved by the label. Of course, Michael didn't help matters when he hired a former gay porn director to direct the video; the man is a friend of his, and Jackson didn't feel that anything was wrong with the association. However, he inadvertently provided Sony with more ammunition to use against him. Frustrated and angry at the label for this and other sins, Michael then went on a terrible, ill-advised campaign against Tommy Motolla, holding a press conference and other public events in the summer of 2002 to call him a 'racist', insisting he is 'very, very, very . . . devilish.' This was not his best moment.

In the end, *Invincible* sold only about ten million copies world-wide – a crushing blow for Michael, as well as for loyal fans who campaigned for it with more devotion and organization than Michael's own label, Sony, possibly did. Even though it entered the *Billboard* charts at number one, it sank quickly, falling out of the Top Ten in a month. It also debuted at number one in the UK, Germany, Holland and a number of other countries, but didn't last long at the top of those charts either – except in France, where it was number one for three weeks. (In Britain, it fell out of the Top Ten completely in three weeks.) The reviews were, generally, dreadful, and often unfair, focusing on the artist's unusual nature, rather than his music. Maybe the expectations had been so high for a new Michael Jackson collection, there was no way for *any* recording to rise to the occasion, let alone one caught in the cross-fire of such acrimonious exchanges between artist and label.

Justin and Britney

Michael Jackson does try to stay current with musical trends, as evidenced by some of the hip-hop production work on *Invincible*. One way he attempts to do that is to keep the lines of communication open with popular young entertainers, such as pop heart-throb Justin Timberlake. Michael is a big admirer of Justin's and was determined to meet him. A couple of years ago, when Justin was about twenty, Michael asked Wade Robson (who, when he was a youngster, was brought forward by Anthony Pellicano to say that he slept innocently in bed with Michael), to arrange a meeting. Robson was a friend of Timberlake's and worked with him and 'N Sync as a choreographer.

'Are you kidding?' Justin said when asked by Wade if he'd be interested in meeting Michael. 'Hell, yeah. Who wouldn't want to meet Michael Jackson? He's my idol.' The meeting would take place at the Four Seasons Hotel in New York.

At the appointed hour, Wade, his girlfriend Mayte Garcia (ex wife of Prince), and Justin showed up in the hotel lobby . . . with Justin's then-girlfriend, Britney Spears. Britney, who is a big admirer of Michael's, simply couldn't resist tagging along.

'Oh no,' Michael said when told that Justin had brought Britney. 'I didn't invite her. Why'd he have to bring *her*?'

'Well, she's his girlfriend, Mike,' said one of his advisers.

'Oh man, you gotta be kidding me?' Michael remarked. 'He brought his *girlfriend*? Damn. I just wanted to see Justin. Maybe she should wait downstairs, or something?'

The notion that Britney Spears might wait in the lobby while Michael entertained Justin, Wade and Mayte was not an idea his associates felt they could suggest. 'Mike, look. You can't keep her waiting in the lobby,' said one of them. 'How's that gonna look? She's one of the biggest stars in show business, Mike. Come on!'

'Oh, man,' Michael protested again, chagrined by the turn of events. 'Damn. She's just gonna be in the way.'

On and on went the discussions. Finally, Michael agreed to allow them both up to his suite.

Once they got up there, however, Michael was enchanted by both Justin and Britney. They were so thrilled to meet him, the two lavished more praise upon him than he'd probably gotten in about a week.

'How about when you did the moonwalk on that Motown show?' Justin said, according to one recollection. 'Man, that was so fucking cool. You are the coolest, Michael. I can't believe I am standing here with *Michael Fucking Jackson*.'

'And how about that "Thriller" video?' Britney enthused. 'That was the best. You revolutionized videos, dude. You are the fucking *best*.'

His indelible influence on modern pop is so far-reaching and entrenched, it's probably not surprising that Justin and Britney were dazzled to be in his presence. Michael beamed; as far as the top teen stars of the day were concerned, he was still the man.*

'Everyone wants to be crazy'

Michael Jackson has earned an estimated $500 million dollars in his lifetime, about $100 million from 1982's *Thriller* alone. A report by the business magazine *Forbes* last year estimated his net worth at

---

*In 2001, Michael, Justin and 'N Sync made a couple of TV appearances together, on Michael's megalomaniacal thirtieth anniversary television special, and then on the MTV Video Music Awards that year. Britney also appeared on the anniversary programme, performing 'The Way You Make Me Feel' with Jackson. However the footage was cut from the broadcast due to contractual issues.

$300 million but warned that he had incurred big debts and that his spending seemed to be out of control.

Though Michael has made some canny investments, he has experienced financial difficulties in recent years because of his high overheads. He spends money like mad, as demonstrated when he appeared to shell out about six million dollars in minutes on baroque vases and urns, with Martin Bashir's cameras rolling in Las Vegas. 'I want that one,' he exclaimed, 'and that one and that one and . . . *yoo-hoo?* How much is *that* one!' (However, he did return much of that merchandise after the programme was broadcast – buyer's remorse, perhaps . . . or maybe just a reconsideration of his taste in furnishings.)

His staff of 120 people costs him about $300,000 a month. More than once, the company that leases much of the amusement park equipment has threatened to repossess it; Michael has had to come up with emergency payments, thereby not being able to compensate certain employees. Neverland's monthly expenditures amount to about $1.2 million.

A couple of years ago, Michael used his one-half share of the Sony/ATV music catalogue as collateral to borrow $200 million. (Michael bought ATV in 1985 for $47.5 million. Ten years later, in 1995, he sold 50 per cent of ATV to Sony for about $90 million. Sony/ATV, of course, owns the publishing rights to hundreds of Beatles songs, as well as more than 400,000 other songs, including some of Elvis's and even Madonna's.) Sony guaranteed the $200 loan for Michael. However, if he defaults, the company can then move to claim his share of ATV.

'He's a ticking financial time bomb waiting to explode,' claimed the attorney of Myung Ho Lee, his former financial manager from 1998 to 2001 who sued him for back payment. (The suit was settled in June 2003.)

More than likely, in order to meet the loan, Michael will borrow $200 million from someone else, pay back the original lender, and then owe the money to a new one. He's never going to be sensible when it comes to finances; yet he will always live like a king. According to different legal filings along the way, he owes hundreds of thousands of dollars to attorneys, publicists and even to limousine companies; people apparently work for him, and then wait to be paid, because it's worth it just to be able to be affiliated to him. He even still owes money to the contractor who built Neverland! Those who predict his financial downfall forget that he's a person with whom powerful people want to rub shoulders, no matter what, a famous man who traffics with the international elite. There will always be someone, somewhere, willing to bail him out, if it becomes necessary to do so, even if he's viewed as a poor risk. Why? Because he's *Michael Jackson*.

Besides, the $200 million isn't due until 2006. In Michael's world, that's a lifetime away. There are times when he's simply trying to get through the week; his eye certainly isn't on what will happen in three years. Also, he can take comfort in knowing that he can eradicate the entire matter by doing the one thing he most doesn't want to do: tour. A couple of unsuccessful CDs, videos and bad judgement calls can still not dim the glory that has been Michael Jackson's performing career for decades. His 1997 *HIStory* tour was a monumental success for him, setting attendance records at each stop along the way. The public might not be as supportive of his music as it was before the allegations, but Michael still sold out concert halls after the scandal.

For instance, he feared that he would have problems performing in the United States, and was particularly nervous about two January 1997 dates in Hawaii, his first American shows since the scandal (and his first US Tour stop since 1989). However, the two concerts (4 and 5 January 1997, in Honolulu) were hugely successful for him. While no other musical act had ever sold out the stadium, Michael's shows sold out in less than a day. Hawaii promoter, Tom Moffatt enthused, 'I've never seen anything like it . . . there's been nothing even close to this the Rolling Stones, Elton John, Julio Iglesias, the Eagles.' Evan Chandler may have thought he would 'ruin' Michael Jackson . . . and maybe he did do him significant damage where record sales are concerned, but not when it comes to his ability to draw concert goers.

In 2001, he was offered ten million dollars simply to perform two nights in Las Vegas. He also had $100 million guaranteed for a national tour. Imagine what he might command for a *world* tour? He could earn enough to handle his responsibility with the bank loan – plus whatever he may require to cover his annual Toys 'R' Us budget. 'But it takes too much out of me,' he told me of touring, back in 1995. 'It's like a two-hour marathon, every show. I swear, I must lose ten pounds a concert. The expectations are too high. It's hard.'

Michael also spends a fortune on presents for children around the world, some of whom he knows but many of whom he doesn't and who are connected to him through various charities. Also, of course, he splurges on himself: for instance, in June 1999 he paid $1.54 million at a Sotheby's auction to own David O. Selznick's Best Picture Oscar for *Gone With the Wind*. Moreover, he gives generously to friends such as Elizabeth Taylor, who is accustomed to receiving expensive baubles from Michael on a regular basis, and he doesn't disappoint. He recently spent $10,000 in Las Vegas, on perfume for her.

Unfortunately, making his life more complex is the fact Michael is always involved in lawsuits from people with whom he's done business in the past: former promoters, producers, managers, accountants, investment bankers, employees have all come after him for tens of millions of dollars. It seems that the lawsuits never stop coming. Brian Oxman, who has represented Michael and some of his siblings for more than ten years, says that Michael has given about 500 depositions in his lifetime and, amazingly, been involved in more than 1,500 lawsuits. If one figures that Michael didn't start becoming involved in litigation until he was a professional entertainer of about ten years of age, and it's unlikely that the suits started that early, it would amount to thirty-five years of lawsuits or an average of forty lawsuits a year.

Michael, of course, is not the only one giving depositions – all of the litigants are required to do so, as well. Such interrogations then become public record and, often, the foundation for interesting assertions. Earlier this year, as a result of depositions given during a lawsuit filed against Michael, it was reported by *Vanity Fair* that he hired a witch doctor named, Baba, to sacrifice forty-two cows in order to curse David Geffen, Steven Spielberg and dozens of others on a Hate List. Sure, it's preposterous, but in Michael's world – one in which he whisks his baby out of a hospital, 'with all the placenta and everything all over her' – it could be argued that anything goes.

In Michael's song 'Tabloid Junkie' he wrote, 'Just because you read it in a magazine or see it on a TV screen don't make it factual.' He might have added, ' . . . or read it in a deposition.'

Michael becomes anxious about each lawsuit filed against him, but often not until it involves his personal participation which is usually at the time of deposition. 'He has, on some occasions in the past, not eaten when he should,' says Oxman. 'He can become very concerned and nervous at depositions. He doesn't like lawsuits, and it makes him ill to have to cope with litigation that people heap on him. He is tired of being sued. But this is the kind of life that Michael leads. No one wants to be reasonable. Everyone wants to be crazy.'

Fathers and Sons

Perhaps it's not surprising that one person more moved by Martin Bashir's *Living With Michael Jackson* documentary than maybe anyone else in the Jackson family was Michael's father, Joseph. Every time he sees Michael on television describing how he was beaten as a child, Joseph can't help but cringe.

Today, Joseph regrets many of his actions, wishes he had made different choices as a parent – even if he does put up a tough front. Michael first spoke about his view of his father in a 1993 interview by Oprah Winfrey. 'There were times when he'd come to see me, I'd get sick,' Michael said. 'I'd start to regurgitate. He's never heard me say this,' Michael added. 'I'm sorry,' he said, looking into the camera. 'Please don't be mad at me.' He hastened to add, 'But I do love him.' Afterwards, a visibly hurt Joseph went on television and said, 'I didn't know he was 'gurgitatin', [sic] but if he did 'gurgitate, he 'gurgitated all the way to the bank.' True to the nature of their conflicted relationship, Michael then felt so badly about his words to Oprah that, to show his deep regret, he bought Joseph a new automobile.

'I was tough on him,' Joseph told me of Michael, a few years before Oprah's interview. At the time, he and Michael weren't even speaking; the subject of their disagreement was not known to me. 'See, the thing is that I wanted him to know that the world was not a nice place,' Joseph went on. 'He was so damn sensitive, more than the other kids, I was worried about him. Me and Katie both were. So, yeah, I admit it,' he said, a bit defensively. 'I was hard on him. Maybe too much, huh?' His eyes searched my face for an answer. 'Maybe I should have backed off, do you think? I don't know. I do know this. I would do it differently, today.' He shook his head, sadly and concluded, 'What father doesn't wish he had the chance to go back and do it . . . differently?'

By February 2003, Joseph's son, Michael, was four years older than Joseph had been on the day he took his talented boys to Motown to audition for the company. Then, Joseph was vigorous and full of fight, arguing with Berry Gordy and Ewart Abner, playing around behind his wife's back and ordering his boys about in his own inimitable way. Now, he's slowed down. He sometimes finds it difficult to rise from a chair.

Those who know him best say that seventy-three-year-old Joseph Jackson has become, in his senior years, sentimental and even sad about the past. He wishes his relationship with his wife and children had been better, more satisfying. Somehow, he has managed to set it straight with Katherine, especially in the last ten years. Despite all that has happened to their family – the in-fighting, family politics, hurt, anger, betrayal and disappointment – Joseph and Katherine, seventy-two, remain united as husband and wife. They have been married for more than fifty years. The names of the women who have come and gone from their lives have been relegated to the distant past. 'Now, what was that girl's name?' Katherine recently asked him in front of a family member. They were speaking of Gina Sprague, from almost twenty-five years ago. Joseph thought for a moment, and had to smile. 'I swear to God,' he said, 'I can't remember.' Katherine looked perplexed for a moment, then exclaimed, 'My goodness, Joseph. Neither can I. Oh, well . . .'

Given all the evidence, it could be said that what should have been the story of a family's transcendence and triumph over poverty turned out, instead, to be a tale of tragedy and disappointment. However, maybe that's a cynical view of the Jacksons' story. What if Joseph hadn't been so driven to transform the lives of his family? What if they'd never left Gary, Indiana? Would they have been better off there? It's doubtful. They've had a remarkable, thrilling life in Los Angeles, even with all of the intense, and often hurtful, melodrama.

'At the root of it, we love each other,' Joseph has explained, 'and

I guess that's what has kept us together all these years. Even when it got bad,' he said, before correcting himself with a smile, 'even when *I* got bad and I *did* get bad, that woman loved me, and my kids loved me, I like to think. You don't see that in this world so much. I'm a lucky man.'

Joseph and Katherine were both upset about the Martin Bashir documentary. They know how easy it is to paint a sensational picture of their most famous son. They felt that Bashir had exploited his obvious eccentricities, and were incensed by his machinations. They were also moved by Michael's recollection of his childhood. It was obvious from his demeanour that he was still in such pain.

When Joseph telephoned Michael early the next morning, he found him crying. Michael said he felt wretched about the way the documentary had turned out and, according to a family member, he told his father, 'I just hope that, in twenty years, my kids don't see it. What will they think of me, Joseph?'

Joseph said that he and Katherine wanted to visit him as soon as possible at Neverland. It had been some time since they'd been to the ranch. Michael was suspicious. In the past, whenever Joseph wanted to meet with him it had to do with a scheme to reunite him with his brothers. Michael didn't have the energy to turn him down again. 'I promise you, Michael, it's not about the brothers,' Joseph said. 'It's about us, you and me and Katherine. Plus,' he said, 'we want to see the kids. Please.' (He was referring to his grandchildren.) 'They're as important to us as they are to you, Michael.'

Michael must have been moved. Whereas show business was once paramount in his life, it's true that his children are, today, his primary concern, his great passion. Ironically, the allegations of sexual abuse levelled against him a decade ago, those charges that practically laid ruin to his life and career, had a surprising consequence: they were the catalyst for change. Evan Chandler, father of Jordie, had promised to ruin Michael. 'You're going down,' he told him. 'You are going *down*.' It was a terrible threat, one no person would ever want to hear. In an effort to reprioritize his world, Michael then reached within to learn what might truly matter to him. He wanted to be vitally involved in something meaningful, not just in show business, and he decided that it would be in the raising of his own children that he would find the most satisfaction. So, he had children – not in a conventional manner, but what else could one expect of Michael Jackson?

Katherine and Joseph arrived at Neverland a few days after the United States broadcast of the Martin Bashir programme. They would then spend the next five days with Michael and his children. Mornings would begin with the ritual of Katherine and Michael having breakfast together on one of the patios, the air thick with the mingled scent of the wildflowers Katherine has said she so enjoys. They would then feed the children in the expansive kitchen.

Meanwhile, Joseph would sleep late in one of the guest quarters. When he awakened, a personal butler, on staff at Neverland, would assist him with his morning needs. Joseph would then spend afternoons with Michael, taking in the well-manicured vistas of Neverland, talking privately. From all accounts, they looked happy to be together. One of the few associates of Michael's also present that week at Neverland recalled the afternoon father and son were seen having a picnic with Prince Michael I on one of Neverland's verdant lawns. Katherine and Paris were off with a staff member to a Toys 'R' Us store in nearby San Maria. (The baby spent the afternoon, sleeping.) Because it had rained earlier in the day, dampness lingered into the chilly February afternoon. Still, as they ate a fried chicken meal prepared by Michael's personal chef, the bright sun shone down upon them, three generations of Jackson men, laying on a blanket . . . talking, laughing and enjoying each other's company. 'I love him,' Michael later said of his father, 'and I totally, totally forgive him.'

Joseph and Katherine were delighted to check in on their grandchildren and see how Michael was progressing with them. They found that Prince Michael I and Paris are bright, confident, affectionate and considerate. They pray before meals. They are polite, thoughtful and funny. Michael becomes angry when they swear, as they sometimes do since most of their friends are adults. He never spanks them, however; he would never lay a hand on them, but as he puts it, 'No means *no*.' He doesn't raise his voice in anger, and doesn't seem to have to do so – they are generally well behaved. If one does act up, he or she has to endure a 'time out', which means standing in a corner, alone, to cool off.

Michael explained that he rations the youngsters' toys and sends presents they receive as Christmas gifts from his fans to orphanages around the world, allowing the children to keep just one. He has taught them not to refer to any of their toys as 'mine', when friends are over to visit; he wants them to learn to share. It's telling, maybe, that he doesn't like seeing his children stare into a mirror for too long when getting ready for the day. 'I look great,' young Prince once said, as he combed his hair. 'No, you look okay,' Michael said, correcting him. Though Michael has always been frightened of dogs (since being bitten as a child), he got over his fear in order to buy the children a much-wanted Golden Retriever. If they have a question (and children always have questions), Michael will not give them an answer unless he is sure it is accurate. He makes use of his expansive library to look up factual responses to even the most innocuous questions asked by his children.

Michael and his governesses dress Prince up as if he were little Lord Fauntleroy, whereas Paris wears dainty, lacy and velvet dresses. The baby, Prince Michael II, seems happy and well-adjusted. All three openly adore their father. Once a year, he dresses up in full clown regalia, and thrills them. 'If I could spend all my time with Daddy, I would do it,' Prince Michael I told Katherine. 'I think he's the best daddy in the whole world.' Michael scooped the boy up into his arms. 'And you're the best little Prince, ever,' Michael said, kissing his face. 'I love you,' said the child. 'I love you, more,' Michael responded.

While Michael was recording tracks for *Invincible* at The Hit Factory Criteria studio in North Miami, Prince Michael I spilled some popcorn on the floor. A producer was about to bend over to clean it up when Michael intervened. 'No, let me,' he said, apologetically. 'He's my kid. I'll clean up after him.' Then, according to the producer, 'I look down and there's Michael Jackson on his hands and knees picking up his son's popcorn. I'm not sure you would see Madonna doing that.'

Of course, there could be problems for his family in the future. The day may come when his three progeny will wonder why their mothers have decided to play such a small part in their lives. They could feel abandoned. Might they one day lament their childhoods, just as their father does his? Though there are never any guarantees in child rearing – only time will tell how these three will turn out – Michael Jackson's family is unique in almost every way. His children face challenges in life perhaps even greater than those faced by their famous father.

Their being made to wear brightly coloured gauze scarves that resemble burkas, and other kinds of disguises, in public is disturbing. The two older ones must watch television and movies and realize that they are the only kids on the planet earth wearing masks when it's not Halloween. Certainly, being forced to hide their faces in public puts the two Prince Michaels and Paris at risk of becoming antisocial, paranoid adults.

In the summer of 2003, Michael and his two oldest children went shopping in a Santa Monica store. He had on a red-and-white baseball cap, and a lavender surgical mask. Prince, then six, wore smart little slacks, a vest. Paris, then five, had on a red sweater and plaid skirt, with ruby-coloured shoes that resembled Dorothy's from *The Wizard of Oz*. Both children had on red-and-black Spider Man masks, which covered them from the neck up. Father and children were followed by LaToya, in a straw hat. What a scene.

Why does Michael think his children must be protected in such unprecedented ways from kidnappers? Again, using Jackie Kennedy Onassis as an example, no woman was ever more famous than she was, nor more protective of her and the President's children. Yet, she would never have thought to make them wear masks in public. In fact, no celebrity in recent memory – if ever – has seen fit to disguise his or her children in such an outlandish way. Even after Frank Sinatra's son, Frank, Jr., *was* kidnapped in 1963, Sinatra didn't make him wear a disguise to prevent future abductions! It begs the question of whether such costumes are for the children's sake, or a way for Michael to distinguish himself as the most prominent, sought-after man in the world, thus his offspring the most prominent, sought-after progeny? At the very least, he seems to be imposing his own fears on to them. However, they're his children, it could be argued, and he can therefore raise them anyway he sees fit, as long as he doesn't abuse them. (Also, Debbie Rowe has said it was *her* idea that the children wear masks and scarves. However, given Michael's ages-old habit of wearing disguises in public, that explanation doesn't seem likely.)

The weird ways he disguises his children aside, has Michael Jackson finally found happiness as a father?

On some days, yes, it would seem that way. From all accounts, he is a father who is good to, and for, his children. He has joyous times with them, watching them grow up, being completely involved in their lives. Hopefully, parenthood has been a self-educating experience for him and he's now setting straight for himself his history of abuse and yearning for a better childhood, by giving to his own children that for which he has so longed – love, with no strings attached, nothing expected in return, unconditional.

On other days, he remains one of the walking wounded, a lost boy holed up at Neverland, cowering from an ever-pressing world. 'How can I get past the pain?' he recently asked one associate. 'That's the question I ask myself. I'm so tired of being controlled by fear,' he admitted, 'and by my own bullshit.' He's working on himself, working on forgiveness. He has good days, he has bad – the latter spent sitting atop his so-called Magic Tree content to retreat into his imagination, reviewing his life, feeling unhappy about the way things are, coping as best he can with it and wanting to effect change in his life – just wanting some *relief* from it all. Who knows, but maybe when stripped of all of his fortune and celebrity – and his unconventional behaviour – it's in that very human place of restless discontent that some of us can find commonality with, of all people, Michael Jackson.

About two years before the Martin Bashir interview was broadcast, Michael gave a speech at Oxford University about raising children, launching his global initiative for his 'Heal the Kids' charity. Much of what he said was absorbing, especially in that it seemed to have as much to do with his feelings about Joseph as it did about his own experiences as a father. ' "What if they grow older and resent me, and how my choices impacted their youth?' Michael asked rhetorically of his children. "Why weren't we given a normal childhood like all the other kids?" they might ask. And at that moment I pray that my children will give me the benefit of the doubt. That they will say to themselves: Our daddy did the best he could, given the unique circumstances he faced. I hope,' he concluded, 'that they will always focus on the positive things, on the sacrifices I willingly made for them, and not criticize the things they had to give up, or the errors

I've made, and will certainly continue to make in raising them. We all have been someone's child, and we know that despite the very best of plans and efforts, mistakes will always occur. That's just being human.'

The week Michael's parents visited in February 2003, Michael enjoyed most of his time with them. Of course, as sometimes happens with families who've had a troubled history, there was a brief and sudden disturbance. On the third day, Michael and Joseph became embroiled in a disagreement. The specific subject of the quarrel is unknown, but witnesses recall Michael loudly insisting to his father, 'It's none of your business, Joseph. This is *my* house.' It sounded like the sort of argument that has been engaged in by grown children and their visiting parents throughout the ages. Joseph stormed off to his guest quarters, where he remained for about three hours. Katherine ran to be with Michael; the two had an intense conference in the kitchen, as Michael cradled Prince Michael II. By sunset, however, whatever it was that had caused the abrupt outburst had blown over; Joseph joined his wife and son, and grandchildren, for dinner in the ornate dining room.

On their final morning together, it again rained. As the black limousine approached that would take the senior Jacksons on their two-hour drive back to Encino, the day's first sun rays shimmered through dark clouds, suddenly filling the sky with incandescent light. Michael was dressed for a meeting scheduled that day with business associates; he was fashioned as if he were European royalty in a black jacket, a white-on-white tuxedo shirt and a tie with crests on it. An artificial mane of jet-black hair in a straight, pageboy cut fell just to his shoulders. He was also in full makeup, with thick eyeliner and densely pencilled eyebrows and lipstick. He even had powder on his hands. He and his mother embraced, holding on to each other for a long moment. Katherine whispered something into her son's ear. He smiled, broadly, and kissed her on the cheek. Affectionately, Joseph then took hold of Katherine's arm and helped her into the stretch vehicle. After Katherine was seated, Joseph turned to Michael and pulled him into a bear hug. Michael seemed to melt into his father's arms. The two held on for a long moment. When he finally released him, Joseph patted Michael on the shoulder, straightened his tie for him in a fatherly fashion, and then got into the car.

The tall, oak gates of Neverland opened before them as the Jackson parents were slowly driven away, leaving Michael at the foot of the long, long road leading out of the ranch. He waved goodbye. As they disappeared into the horizon, Michael lingered a while, perhaps with memories flooding him fully, carrying him back to Encino with his parents, farther back even, to Gary with the rest of his family.

While he stood there silently, a light rain began to fall. He tilted his head back, letting the gentle drops fall upon his face. As if on cue, a young male in his twenties, wearing a black silk shirt and slacks, hurried toward Michael, trailed by two uniformed, ageing house-keepers. The trio gained momentum as they realized the King was getting wet. The man opened a bright, red umbrella with a flourish, and held it above Michael's head. The women wrapped him in a scarf and cloak as he stood motionless, like a mannequin being staged for display. Michael attempted a small smile of appreciation to the three; their faces remained stoic.

As the rain began to fall harder, Michael turned away from those gates that opened to the outside world. The four then made the long trek back to the main house at a slow pace: Michael and his young man-servant, side-by-side under an umbrella; the two old maids dragging behind, becoming drenched in the downpour. An eerie parade of strangers in the rain. None of them speaking, all knowing their task. Onward, to Neverland.

Michael's World Caves In . . . Again

He thought being ten was hard, being famous before he knew what it was to be a human being. He thought being eighteen was hard, going through adolescence with the eyes of the world upon him. Twenty-one was hard, too, feeling like a phoney, not fitting in . . . choosing plastic surgery, hoping it would be the solution to all his problems. He came to thirty with a desire to do good, but it was hard. While his career was history-making, his life remained . . . hard. Forty. Then forty-five . . . harder than he ever dreamed possible.

The end of 2003 and beginning of 2004 has been the worst period of time in Michael Jackson's life. Making it even more unfortunate for him is that he had, at the time that the last edition of this book was published, been working, even if tentatively, on repairing his personal life as well as his career, trying to come to terms with the past, with his father and other family members, and making important choices about how to handle other problems in his life. Yet he still had not made the most important decision of all, the one having to do with the on-going habit of entertaining other people's children at Neverland. Such continual lapses in judgement and caution has caused another massive personal upheaval for him, a true crisis in his life.

What a shame. There are no other words to describe the sight of Michael Jackson being led away in handcuffs . . . then, the mug shot . . . then, the arraignment on child-molestation charges.

Michael was at the Mirage Hotel suite in Las Vegas on 18 November 2003 when a police raid of Neverland, the second one in ten years, occurred. He was shooting a video for a new song, 'One More Chance', written and produced by R. Kelly (who has also been arrested on child-molestation accusations, in a case that is still pending). However, there was no way for him to continue with the project. Seventy officers had descended upon the Jackson ranch and spent fourteen hours searching for evidence that might connect him to the latest charges. 'I don't think I'll be able to get through it,' he said, according to an aide who was present. Michael looked desperate and alone, said the aide, 'the very foundation of his soul, shaken. But, still, there was a strong sense among people present that he had somehow brought it onto himself.'

It's true that after the first allegations of molestation were made against him ten years ago, Michael Jackson had every opportunity to change his behaviour. He would have been smart to stop himself, not just from making obsequious comments about young people ('I would die if there were no children in the world') but from seeking out the company of other people's offspring. At the very least, it seemed unwise and even foolhardy for a man once accused of molestation to continue having sleepovers with the children of strangers.

After the Chandler case was resolved, many on Jackson's team hoped he would never again mention the subject of children – and certainly not be seen on television cuddling them, as he was on the controversial Martin Bashir documentary. As we have seen earlier, during his interview with Bashir, Michael admitted sleeping in a bed with many children. 'When you say bed you're thinking sexual,' Michael said. 'It's not sexual, we're going to sleep. I tuck them in. It's very charming, it's very sweet.' While watching Michael holding hands with the wide-eyed and star-struck youngster in the documentary, who was described as a cancer-survivor, anyone who had been following Jackson's chequered story over the years and knew his troubled history with the parents of young boys could sense trouble ahead. Indeed, a year later, that same boy is Michael's accuser.

What was Michael Jackson thinking? Had he been so emboldened by the solution to the Jordie Chandler problem that he was now arrogant about the way he lived his life? Did he not recognize the need to protect himself from the possibility of similar events? Was he so naive that he simply didn't understand the danger in which he continued to place himself by entertaining hundreds upon hundreds of children at his Neverland ranch? Or, one at least has to wonder, did he just have the misfortune to cross paths with a family that is now out to get him, and ruin him?

Of course, there is another possibility: Maybe Michael Jackson is a paedophile – a remote prospect as plain and simple as it is sick and twisted – and he got caught . . . again. The question remains unanswered at this stage, at least from a legal standpoint. There are many who believe in his innocence, and probably just as many who believe in his guilt.

Ten years earlier, even at the height of the Jordie Chandler scandal, matters hadn't escalated to the point where an arrest warrant was filed against Michael. During the latest raid in 2003, if Michael had been home, he would probably have been taken to jail and booked, immediately. The authorities had an arrest warrant with his name on it, and an ambulance present in case he fainted.

There was good reason for such concern about Michael's state of mind, though it seems unlikely that Santa Barbara District Attorney, Tom Sneddon, was genuinely worried about him. Michael is so fragile a person, the Chandler case almost sent him over the brink; he became addicted to drugs and, if not for the positive influence Elizabeth Taylor and Lisa Marie Presley, he might never have been able to recover. However, he did recover – and, then, paid Jordie millions of dollars to settle the matter in order that he be able to move forward with his life.

Though Michael was able to put the other case behind him without admitting guilt – in fact, with many declarations of innocence – his career never recovered; his record sales were never the same. There was hope that a 2003 CD, a greatest hits compilation called *Number Ones*, would help matters when issued in November. A single from it, 'One More Chance', a melodic tune with multi-layered and lush harmonies, in the vein of some of his best 1980s work, seemed poised for success. In the UK, the compilation found quick acceptance: *Number Ones* debuted at the top of the charts. 'One More Chance' was also a hit. It's clear that Michael's British fans remain supportive. He also has the support of legions of fans in most other countries, but not in America. In the USA, he may never be able to rebound, especially now that he has been arrested. Indeed, in America, *Number Ones* was a huge commercial disappointment, nowhere close to being considered a hit record.

'You have to stay strong,' Michael's aide told him on the day of the Neverland raid. 'For your children, you have to be strong.'

Michael crumpled into a chair. 'I'll do the best I can,' he said. 'But . . .' His voice trailed off as he buried his face into his hands. 'Oh, my God. What a shock. I can't believe this is happening to me . . . again.'

Explaining Away His Pain

Michael Jackson is always caught by surprise whenever something terrible occurs in his life. He never seems able to connect the dots of unfolding misery back to his own impulsive actions and questionable judgement.

For instance, he had never recognized that for every disadvantaged youngster who visited Neverland Ranch, there would always be a set of parents in the background. Some, such as those of his present accuser (and those of Jordie Chandler's), might be at war with each other in a battle that could involve child custody (as it has in both cases). Also, each child and each parent was likely to have his and her own dysfunctional history, as well as aggressive attorneys. Since there was no way to check the backgrounds of every child and every parent who entered his private domain, would it not have made more sense to keep strangers out of Neverland? If he was so determined to host an amusement park for kiddies, could he not have maintained Neverland for that purpose, but chosen to live elsewhere? The simple answer for Michael is: no. He must be around children. He must have them in his midst. Neverland is a shrine to adolescence. There are statues of youngsters and photographs of boys and girls all over the place. He's obsessed with kids.

How long, one wonders, can Michael and his enablers continue to explain his strange behaviour by saying that he is compensating for a childhood ripped from him by his career, his fame, his fans?

The duration of a person's conscious childhood probably spans the years between five and eighteen. Michael became famous at the age of ten. Not to be reductive of a person's dysfunction in such a complex world, but if one insists upon harping on the notion of a lost childhood, then it would seem that Michael 'lost' eight years. Michael bought Neverland in 1988. He has lived there, surrounded by a dreamy and fake adolescence, for roughly sixteen years. Therefore, it would seem that he has compensated for his 'lost childhood' two times over.

In truth, Neverland remains a monument to Michael's confusion and conflict about childhood, and not how much he missed out on it but, rather, how much he *misses* it. He clings to every vestige of youth with almost manic desperation, as if growing up would be the worst thing that could happen to him.

The ride on the private jet, a Gulf Stream G-4, from Las Vegas to Santa Barbara on 20 November 2003, the day Michael was arrested, was, of course, a difficult one. He was frightened and pessimistic about the future. 'Why does everyone else get to be happy, and I'm always thrashing through the mud?' he asked.

Michael arrived at the jail wearing a black suit with his hands cuffed behind his back. He was photographed and fingerprinted and handed over his passport; it took about a half-hour. He was charged with ten counts of lewd or lascivious acts with a child under age fourteen, each count punishable by three to eight years in prison. Michael was freed on $3 million bail, which means he had to come up with $300,000 – not a difficult thing for him to do.

Later, Michael would claim that he had been abused by police officers while at the station; they had even dislocated his shoulder! It was unlikely that Jackson suffered at the hands of law enforcement; there were video cameras everywhere. When did the abuse happen? He seemed fine when he arrived at the station, and was waving to people and flashing the victory sign when he left. The bruise Michael displayed to *60 Minutes* correspondent Ed Bradley (on 29 December 2003) as evidence of handcuffs that had been too tight was so high on his arm it had to be the result of some other occurrence. Some speculated that he had actually hurt himself during the caravan ride from Santa Barbara to Las Vegas, while shaking hands with fans out of the half-opened window of his automobile.

There was something about Michael's detailing of police abuse that felt impulsive in delivery, as if he hadn't thought about it in advance but, rather, made a snap decision in a desperate, anxious moment. It's doubtful that he discussed it with his attorneys in advance. Coming directly from Michael, the accusation of abuse truly was disconcerting. Everything Michael says these days has to hold up under scrutiny; his credibility is on the line now, more than ever. It's also doubtful that anyone in his camp would dare take him to task for such impulsive behaviour, though. It is more likely that, after they were caught by surprise, they scrambled to figure out how to handle it.

After the accusation of abuse made headlines, the police department retaliated by releasing a video in which it seemed Michael wasn't abused at all but, rather, actually treated well by the authorities. The suspicious allegation against the police made things worse for Michael; it looked like a diversionary tactic and caused some of his critics to speculate as to why he would need one.

The Way He Wants It

A compelling image and one his fans want to believe is the notion of Michael Jackson hunkering down with his staff in a boardroom, ordering people about, expressing his 'outrage' about whatever is going on that day, issuing edicts and pounding his fist on his desk as frightened minions scramble about him. Actually, there's little evidence to suggest that Michael is, at least in the last few years, the calculated strategist his handlers describe as they spin his present situation in the press. In truth, he spends most of his time with his three children, ignoring as much as he can the frightening details of his dilemma.

'When he is forced to become involved in meetings with lawyers and accountants, he is often in a tense, sullen and uncooperative mood,' says another person who knows him well.

Perhaps it is understandable that Michael would just as soon not face his troubles, and maybe he's lucky to be able to avoid most of the details. He has many people in his employ whose job it is to shield him from the reality of litigation, as well as the media coverage of the on-going molestation story. When he hears of a particularly controversial report – usually second-hand since he does not watch television or read the newspapers – he is 'appalled' by it. Someone then writes a statement expressing such empty emotion, and 'exposing' the untruth of the story. New people in his circle act as if we're living in a parallel universe, and that everything ever published or said about Michael or his family – including that which they have said and written about each other in the past – occurred in some *other* reality, not our own. The only history the public is supposed to have with Michael is one that begins on the morning someone in his inner circle appears on television to proclaim that all is well . . . and that we're wrong-minded for believing, or even suspecting, otherwise.

Unfortunately, coddling and indulging Michael serves to reinforce his own self-image of being a rich kid in a mean world of money-grubbing adults and, thus, unable – or unwilling – to deal with his responsibilities and obligations. When he does give a first-hand interview, he seems distracted, disconnected from reality. He expresses himself as if he's never been around adults, as if he has no social skills. He looks troubled, scared, sick to his stomach. He truly *is* childlike. However, it remains disconcerting to hear family members and reasonable-thinking, educated people describe him that way as if it's an admirable, even awe-inspiring, trait for a man in his mid-forties, instead of a troubling, worrisome one. What can be done to help Michael Jackson? Certainly more than just approve of him.

After his arrest, Michael came forth to say, once again, that he would never hurt a child and the public is 'crazy' to think that there is anything strange about his rapport with children. 'I love children. I would slit my wrist before hurting a child,' Michael told Ed Bradley in the televised *60 Minutes* interview. His eyes were wide and heavily lashed, the nose small and sharp. He seemed delicate, frail, almost like a geisha girl as he sat so primly in his turquoise-blue silk blouse. His hair fell to his shoulders, a jet-black swoop that contrasted with his whitish skin. Every now and again, someone would rush to his side, looking alarmed. He said he didn't feel well, he clearly wanted to wrap the interview up. He looked as if he was about to wilt under the pressure.

Later, his family members, in support of Michael, confirmed that he 'loves all children' and as Jermaine put it, 'he would never harm a child'.

Actually, the Jackson family's defence of Michael's obsessive love for children does little to help him. Rather, it tends to make them look out of touch with society and with what is considered appropriate behaviour in the real world. Simply put, loving children and not wanting to hurt them is no defence against child molestation. In fact, most child molesters express great affection for their victims and feel that they are not hurting them. Most would rather 'slit' their 'wrists' than hurt a child . . . and, horribly, they *all* end up hurting children.

'People in the real world will always out-number them in their world where, it seems, anything goes,' remarked one legal analyst. 'They are not going to be able to beat us, or change our minds about what makes sense and what looks inappropriate when it comes to kids and adults. They may as well join us in the real world, and maybe sit down and have a very strong talk with their son and brother.'

'After the *60 Minutes* interview, we looked at each other and said, "Holy Christ! That did not go well, did it?" says the former spokesman. "What happened there?"

'Michael has been around for so many years, one expects him to shine on camera. But people who know him well know that he does not do that. Instead, he acts as if he's never done an interview in his entire life.

'He tries, God knows he does, and it's hard for him. I saw it first-hand. He is sick before going on camera for an interview, throwing up, so nervous, so upset, so filled with anxiety. Your heart goes out to him. You wonder how he ever ended up in the public eye, and what an ordeal he has been through just to get this far in it.

'After he's on TV, his people have to do clean-up work to minimize all of the late-night talk-show criticism and joking, and explain that *he's* fine, it's the *public* that has a problem. "Focus on the message" was always my tactic. "Forget the messenger". He's innocent of any wrong-doing. I'm sure of it. Just stick to that truth and forget how much damage he's done by trying to express such innocence on television. Get him help? It's not an option. No one is close enough to him to even presume to suggest it.'

Some observers who are sceptical of Michael Jackson's innocence speculate that people in his life – his attorneys, publicists, accountants and even family members – believe in their heart of hearts that the man is guilty as sin. It is thought that such allies of his are merely exhibiting blind loyalty to him by publicly, and so vociferously, declaring his innocence. After all, they have jobs to do, or family allegiances to protect, it's thought. However, it's not true. If a person is around Michael Jackson long enough, he begins to believe in him. Michael is such an unconventional, curious person, the only way to truly fathom him and his world is to actually be in his presence, experience it and take it all in. While he welcomes the support of his inner circle, he does not appreciate it when they try to explain to him why outsiders are suspect of him and his behaviour.

'He doesn't want to hear it,' his former close friend Uri Geller has explained. 'I tried to tell him, "Michael, I know you are innocent but you have to understand why there are others who do not believe that.

You have to stop with the children in people's faces. You have to try to understand the public. It's not just you. You are in the world." He becomes sad, and his eyes glaze over. Then he becomes angry. No one can talk to him these days, not really. So I think that people in his life go about the business of defending him, and don't bring up anything with him that really matters or addresses the problem.'

Ten years ago, Elizabeth Taylor and Lisa Marie Presley stepped into Michael Jackson's world and attempted to bring some sense and wisdom to it. They were not paid to do so, they did it out of love. If not for them, who knows how the Jordie Chandler matter would have worked out for Michael.

Sadly, Michael no longer has allies such as Elizabeth and Lisa.

Elizabeth is too advanced in years and upset by the melodrama in her friend's world to be recruited for such hard duty.

For her part, Lisa simply can't become immersed in Michael's problems again. It was tough on her, last time. When she ended it with Michael, she suffered physical problems, a myriad of ailments, because she had been so anxious for so long about him. In order to protect herself, she now keeps her distance. Some have indicated that she is more concerned about her new recording career with Capitol Records than she is about Michael, and won't align herself with him because of her fear of bad public relations . . . as if Lisa Marie Presley has ever cared what the public thinks about her. Rather, she is taking care of herself, say her friends, the way she used to take care of Michael.

Today, Michael Jackson's best and most reliable support comes from people who are compensated by tremendous amounts of money to shield him from the ugly truth of his world – and then explain away his deep sadness and pain by acting as if it doesn't exist. It's not as if they have any choice. It's the way he wants it.

Michael's Latest Accuser

How credible are the present charges against Michael Jackson?

While Michael is most certainly guilty of creating the appearance of impropriety where his current accuser, Gavin Arvizo, is concerned, such wrong-minded choices about socializing with children – and making sure everyone knows about it – obviously don't make him a child-molester. As of this writing, the Santa Barbara District Attorney's evidence against Michael is sealed. Therefore, a firm opinion of his guilt or innocence is premature. Understandably, loyal friends and family members believe he is innocent based on little more than . . . their personally held beliefs about him. However, critical-minded people who have no emotional attachment to him have good reason for prudent scepticism. Still, the presumption of innocence is on Michael's side. That stated, the criminal case against him seems very weak, even at this early stage.

In the year 2002 and into 2003, Gavin Arvizo and members of his family had enjoyed being with Michael at Neverland Ranch on several occasions. The Hispanic boy with dark hair and dark brown eyes from East Los Angeles is a comedy aficionado who aspires to a career in that arena. At the age of ten he had been diagnosed with cancer so he was quite ill. He'd had an eight-pound cancerous tumour on his left kidney; doctors were forced to remove that kidney as well as his spleen.

While he was sick, the youngster was asked by a comedy club owner in Los Angeles what would make him happy. He said he wanted to meet certain celebrities – one of them being Michael Jackson. (Actually, Michael was third on the list, behind comedians Adam Sandler and Chris Tucker.) Unfortunately, Michael has always been a sucker for young kids who want to meet him. After the comedy club owner made quick arrangements with Michael's 'people', one thing led to another, and before anyone knew what was happening, Gavin and both his parents, younger brother and older sister were guests of Michael's at his Neverland ranch. It's a bit startling, actually, when one considers how easy it is to gain entrée into the King of Pop's castle.

Just as in the case of Jordie Chandler and his family, Michael became engrossed in the personal, complicated and troubled life of the youngster. He not only began paying the boy's medical expenses, and provided transportation for Gavin to get to and from chemotherapy, he took him, his mother Janet Ventura-Arvizo and two siblings, Daveline and Star Arvizo, into his confidence, into his secret world. He also extended his generosity to people *they* knew; for instance, he leased an apartment for the mother's boyfriend. He pushed and pushed until he was fully enveloped in their lives, exactly as he had with Jordie.

Caught up in the security of Michael Jackson's cushy lifestyle, the family settled in. Compared to their lower-middle-class existence in East LA, Neverland was ... well ... *Neverland*. They had safety and security – and the excitement of knowing a big star and trafficking in his exciting and privileged world. Janet encouraged the children to call Michael 'Daddy'. That was fine with Michael, but the immediate and inappropriate familiarity suggested by the new moniker was disconcerting to observers in his camp. Didn't he have three children calling him daddy, already – his own?

'It was too much,' recalled someone close to the situation. 'It was Michael not remembering what had happened with Jordie Chandler and his old man [Evan Chandler, his father], and then letting these new kids and their mom into his world, no holds barred. Whatever they wanted, man, they got. Money. Trips. Gifts. Toys. The whole Michael Jackson package. 360 degrees of everything ... and way too much alone time with the one boy [Gavin]. People in his [Jackson's] camp were worried about it, but there had been a lot of kids and a lot of families between Jordie and this new family, and Michael had let them all into his life too, with no consequences. You can't reason with him ... he takes his chances. The questions for me have always been, when does this guy have time for his career, how'd he even get to be the King of Pop when he's so preoccupied with other people's lives ... and how the hell does he keep track of all of these kids?'

When Gavin's health took a turn for the better, everyone was elated. Why, it was as if Michael was some kind of miracle worker! In just a few months, the youngster was born again. Of course, the fact that he was finally eating well and now able to afford the best medications in the world – thanks to Michael's largesse – didn't hurt.

The story might have had a truly happy ending if everyone had then gone their separate ways. Gavin and his family might have exited Neverland never to be seen again – with all being well that ended well.

However, at this same time, Michael was involved in the making of the Martin Bashir documentary. Bashir had heard about the youngster and the transformation he had undergone as a result of his connection to Jackson, and wanted to include his story in the documentary. Because it seemed like a good idea – he hoped people would *finally* understand his relationship with children if they were to see the footage – Michael agreed to it. When the documentary was first broadcast in the UK, and finally in the USA, Michael was seen holding hands with Gavin while giggling and discussing sleeping arrangements with him. He also made it clear that he saw nothing wrong with sharing his bed with children.

After the documentary aired on 3 February in the UK, and three days later in the USA, tongues began to wag about his odd interaction with Gavin Arvizo. It was then that Gavin's mother, Janet, complained publicly that Martin Bashir had allowed her son to appear on the show without her permission. Of course, Michael did not secure her permission, either. However, at that time, the family was still friendly with Michael and did not point out his lapse in judgement.

In truth, Michael Jackson isn't used to asking anyone permission for anything. He reasoned that, considering all that he had done for Gavin and his family, Janet wouldn't mind seeing her son featured on his show. After she complained about it, it was thought that she would simply have to get over it. However, Gavin was being ridiculed in public, other youngsters coming up to him and taunting him for being 'Michael Jackson's boyfriend'. It is understandable that Janet was upset. However, Michael had other problems, having to do with 'damage control'. There had been outrage about the Martin Bashir programme, and Michael charged Bashir with having taken statements and scenes out of context. 'That damn Martin Bashir show didn't work out as well as I hoped,' he told one of his staff members.

To set the record straight, Michael Jackson wanted to produce his own special and give his side of the story. He also wanted to press Gavin into service: would he be interviewed for the new documentary and confirm that Michael's behaviour toward him had always been innocent? Yes, of course he would, and this time with his mother's permission. Michael dispatched his so-called 'videographer', Christian Robinson, to tape an interview with the family. It seems unlikely that Michael Jackson would have charged Robinson with such a task if he thought the Arvizo family would ever allege he was a child-molester.

Denials All Around

Christian Robinson, who had been documenting Michael's experiences on the road and at home on video tape for about two years, sat down with mother and son at a private home to ask questions about the star's relationship with them. He asked if there had ever been any inappropriate behaviour on Michael's part. 'They [Gavin, his sister Daveline, brother Star and mother Janet] answered and were very upfront and said "absolutely not",' he later maintained. 'And during this interview, I told them to speak truthfully probably more than thirty times. I kept reminding them, I want you to tell the truth, tell your story.'

'They all felt that a miracle had taken place,' Robinson recalled when speaking of Gavin's recovery. 'He says that Gavin and Star insisted to him that whenever they slept in the same room with Michael, they slept on the bed and he slept on the floor. They were so resolute in their answers, almost as if they were getting mad at me. "Why are you asking me this? Michael is innocent." ' He says that 'the family was not coached', and 'the family was incredibly passionate, talking about Jesus and God and Michael as the ultimate father figure.'

As mentioned earlier in this text, Michael's rebuttal was finally broadcast – the awkwardly titled, *The Michael Jackson Interview – The Footage You Were Never Meant to See* – but it didn't change the way people thought about him. His supporters still believed in him, and his detractors remained critical of him.

The footage of Michael's accuser in the documentary is unsettling, especially in light of the new charges. Gavin is bald, a result of chemotherapy, and, according to the documentary, should have been dead by that time but was alive thanks to his association with Michael Jackson. There is footage of the youngster in his hospital bed, of him being pushed in a wheelchair with Michael at his side. There is more footage of him walking with Michael through Neverland, Gavin in a yellow baseball jersey and the superstar in head-to-toe black and holding an umbrella as a shield from the sun. The two are cocooned within the pleasant, familiar surroundings of Neverland, lost in conversation, in their own . . . world.

Camaraderie was evident between Michael and Gavin, the kind that springs from shared experiences and genuine affection. However, anyone who knows Michael and has a memory for the past could look at the footage – and also the scenes of the two in the Bashir documentary – and sense that, once again, Michael had gone way too far with this kid. As he did with Jordie, he gave himself over to the youngster. He has no boundaries with anyone under the age of fourteen. Michael Jackson puts himself right out there – no walls of defence, no safety zone, maybe, it might be argued, no sense, either. He simply hopes that the boy, and his family, will have the best intentions for him, just as he feels he has for them. In some ways, it's commendable. For a star of his magnitude to be so naive is somehow refreshing. However, there's still a dysfunction attached to such bonding with children who are not his own, and it's something that should be addressed in his life because, obviously, it can lead to big trouble for him – and also for the youngster. As a result of the footage, Gavin's entire world changed.

'Since Mr Bashir's documentary aired, [Gavin] and his mother have gone into seclusion, after being bombarded for requests for interviews from tabloids around the world,' intoned Maury Povich, the documentary's narrator. He also read a statement from Janet Ventura-Arvizo: 'I'm appalled at the way my son has been exploited by Martin Bashir. The relationship that Michael has with my children is a beautiful, loving, father-sons-and-daughter one. To my children and me, Michael is a part of my family.' In addition, concluded Povich, Janet was considering legal action against Martin Bashir for including her son in the special without her consent.

In truth, the boy should not have been on either show – Martin Bashir's *or* Michael Jackson's – and both are equally guilty of having exploited him for their own purposes. Some might argue that Janet doesn't acquit herself, either. However, parental guidance and direction in matters having to do with children at Neverland is always a big part of the mystery surrounding sleep-overs at the ranch.

Michael's documentary aired, and people quickly forgot about it. It was the Martin Bashir programme, however, that continued to pose a problem, especially when concerned mental-health professionals began to lodge complaints about it.

A number of psychologists, psychiatrists and other child advocates, including Dr Carole Lieberman of Beverly Hills, wrote letters of concern to the Santa Barbara Child Protective Services and the Los Angeles Child Welfare department. 'I felt that enough was enough,' said Dr Lieberman, who lodged her official complaint on 11 February 2003. 'I couldn't believe that the world was standing by and letting these children be potentially harmed.' Others, like school teachers in Los Angeles county, also voiced concern. One contacted the Los Angeles Department of Child and Family Services (DCFS) saying that she felt what was seen in the Bashir documentary between Michael and Gavin Arvizo looked strange and inappropriate. Not only did the teacher feel that the relationship between the two should be investigated, she also raised questions as to what kind of mother would allow her child to be seen in such circumstances.

After receiving a few letters himself, Santa Barbara District Attorney Tom Sneddon took the position that what appeared on screen 'was no substitute for credible cooperative victims'. He didn't seem interested in pursuing Michael Jackson again. However, he actually *was* interested; he just didn't want to tip his hand in the matter, at least not yet.

On 14 February 2003, the DSCS began its investigation.

Four days later, on 18 February, the Santa Barbara Sheriff's department began its own investigation, in secret.

Michael and his camp did *not* know about the Sheriff department's inquiry. However, they found out about the DCFS's immediately, because Janet Ventura-Arvizo telephoned as soon as she was contacted. Michael was perplexed. 'What the hell?' he asked one of his representatives. 'Someone can call out of the blue, and they start an investigation?' When told that such was the case, Michael decided he wanted to know as much as he could about the questions that would be asked by the officials . . . and the answers provided by Gavin and his mother.

Shortly thereafter, DCFS representatives arranged that two social workers meet with the family at the Los Angeles apartment of Janet's boyfriend. At the same time, Michael arranged to have his own representation present at the meeting – an investigator and, also, the fiancé of comedian Chris Tucker. (Tucker's future wife is a mutual friend of Janet's and Michael's.)

When the case workers arrived for the interview, the three children were sitting in front of a television, mesmerized by a video of Michael. According to the tape recordings made that day by Michael's camp, Janet said that she was unaware of the nature of the allegations that had been made against Michael. She said she wanted to be present for the interview with each of her children and wondered, 'What are my rights? What are their rights?' She seemed scared.

The social workers told her that their agenda would be made clear to her during the course of questioning. They also insisted that the Jackson representatives leave the room. A frightened Janet asked for a moment alone with the Jackson investigator. The two then discussed how to tape-record the interview with the DCFS in a manner, the Jackson representative told her, that 'won't be suspicious. You don't have to do nothing,' he told her, according to the tape recording. On the tape, it sounds as if he was some how affixing a microphone to her clothing. 'It's working,' he assured her.

The Santa Barbara County Sheriff's Department has, on file, details of the interview between the Arvizo family and the DCFS. 'Michael is like a father to me,' Gavin told the social workers. 'He's never done anything to me sexually.' Gavin said he 'never slept in bed with Michael.'

Furthermore, Janet said that she was 'always aware of what goes on at Neverland'. She elaborated, 'Michael is like a father to my children. He loves them and I trust my children with him.' She said that Michael was 'kind and misunderstood'. She described him as 'an important part of [her son's] recovery from cancer.' She said that there were times when her children 'would be on Michael's bed, watching TV and eating Smors. But for the allegations that they share a bed, it is no.' She insisted that her children 'were never alone with Jackson . . . there's always someone around.' She concluded that Michael had 'never been anything but wonderful. My children have never felt uncomfortable in his presence. Michael has been a blessing.'

According to the report, Gavin's older sister Daveline was 'teary-eyed' during the interview. 'Michael is so kind and loving,' she said.

Gavin's father, David Arvizo, was interviewed by the DCFS, separately from the others. 'There's no reason to suspect any wrongdoing by Michael,' he said. He added that he, too, attributed his son's recovery to Michael.

Some observers have wondered why Michael had his own representatives at the apartment for the inquiry by the DCFS. According to DCFS standards, Janet Ventura-Arvizo and her children should have been interviewed without anyone present, and tape recordings of their interviews should not have been made by her . . . for Michael Jackson, or even for someone working for him. Of course, the Jackson camp wanted to be there for one simple and obvious reason: they wanted to know what was going to be alleged. If they were able to get away with having someone present to find out what was being said, of course they were going to try to do it. On the tape, Janet insists that Jackson's representatives were there 'per my invitation, per my request'.

Later, after reviewing all evidence available at the time, the Department of Children and Family Services concluded that the case should be closed, that allegations of abuse were 'unfounded'. There was not enough proof in the face of such denials for anyone to continue looking into the matter.

At the same time, the Los Angeles Police Department opened and closed its own investigation quickly, and concurred that there was insufficient evidence to move forward with any action against Michael Jackson.

Then, on 16 April, the Santa Barbara County Sheriff's Department reached its own conclusion. According to records in the Sheriff's Department, 'Based on the interviews with the children and their father, it was determined that the elements of criminal activity were not meant. Therefore, this investigation was classified as a suspected sexual abuse incident report, with no further action required. Case Closed.'

Months later, Santa Barbara District Attorney Tom Sneddon, in his press conference to announce Michael's imminent arrest, minimized the significance of the DCFS report and its findings saying, 'to call that an investigation is a misnomer. It was an interview, plain and simple. And that's all it was.' He also claimed, 'that particular department [DCFS] has a lot of problems.'

It would seem that the District Attorney's office has 'a lot of problems', too, because Tom Sneddon did not mention that the Santa Barbara County Sheriff's Department had actually opened – and *closed* – its investigation, based entirely on the DCFS's findings. Sneddon didn't interview the Arvizo family. Rather, someone from his office merely spoke on the phone to the social worker who visited them, and obtained her notes. The fact that Tom Sneddon then minimized the DCFS's findings in his press conference, though he had relied on them to close an earlier investigation of Michael Jackson, is important information, and it does little to enhance his case that he still hasn't admitted it.

Booze, Naked Women . . . and Michael Jackson?

After the DCFS and Santa Barbara County Sheriff's interviews of the Arvizo family, something happened to change their minds. It's not known yet what transpired, but whatever it was turned them all against Michael Jackson. Suddenly, the family was whispering to others about sexual molestation having occurred, and stories getting back to the Jackson camp were worrisome. However, when Michael heard about them, he didn't seem concerned.

'This could be a problem,' noted someone on his team.

'I'm used to problems,' Michael said, dismissively. 'My focus now is on my new album. I didn't do anything, so this will go away.'

'You mean like Jordie Chandler went away?' he was asked.

Jordie is rarely brought up in his presence. Michael's brown eyes slitted. It was as if he was saying, 'You know better than to mention that name to me.' He drew a deep breath and then exhaled, loudly. 'Look, man, just take care of it,' he said, as he took his leave. 'I don't want to hear another word about it.'

There was nothing to take care of . . . yet. No one knew the details of what was being alleged . . . but, there was a sense that something was about to happen, and it would not be good. 'It was in the air,' said a source in the Jackson camp.

In fact, people who have been in the Jackson camp for years were troubled enough to bring in high-powered attorney Mark Geragos, and a team of investigators, to look into the matter. 'He may want to continue to be naive in the face of danger,' said a person close to Jackson, 'but people who care about him smelled big trouble. They did not want have another Jordie Chandler case on their hands. It was determined that this thing would have to be nipped in the bud, whether MJ [Michael] took it seriously, or not. Michael was told to keep his distance from those people, and he did.'

After Michael's handlers drew a line in the sand between him and the Arvizo family, Janet Ventura-Arvizo made her move: she and one of her attorneys sought out Larry Feldman for advice on how to proceed; Feldman is the same attorney who represented Jordie Chandler against Michael Jackson. In the same conference room in which Feldman sat with Jordie Chandler and his father, Evan, he sat with Michael's new accuser and his mother. After he heard their story, he felt there was more to it than the boy had even alleged – and so he arranged for the boy to be interviewed by psychologist Dr Stan Katz.

After several sessions with the psychologist, the bits and pieces finally came together and the boy started to remember all sorts of things. Dr Katz's notes are part of the material being used against Michael Jackson by the Santa Barbara District Attorney. What the family told him was exactly *opposite* to everything they had ever said before about the pop star to Martin Bashir, Christian Anderson, and the DCFS.

In the records Dr Katz wrote, 'The accuser says he drank alcohol every night and got buzzed . . . whiskey, vodka and Bacardi.' When the youngster – suffering from cancer, don't forget – got headaches from the drinking, 'Michael said, "Keep drinking. It will make it feel better." ' Dr Katz reported that, according to the boy, 'Michael showed him pictures of naked women on the computer.' He said that he once 'saw Michael just standing there, naked for a moment.' He added that Michael told him, 'he had to masturbate, or he'd go crazy'.

Dr Katz further disclosed that Gavin's brother Star said that on a flight from Miami to Los Angeles, he saw Michael lick Gavin's head as the boy slept against Michael's chest. He said that Michael gave them all 'wine, vodka and tequila on numerous occasions'. He also said, according to the doctor, that one of Michael's security guards threatened to 'kill us and our parents if we told about the alcohol'. He said that Michael 'talked a lot about sex', and that he and his brother 'constantly sleep in Michael's room with Michael and his brother in Michael's bed'. He then gave graphic details of two sexual encounters he says he witnessed between Gavin and Michael.

Furthermore, Dr Katz wrote that Gavin's sister Daveline says that Michael gave her wine, as well, and that she witnessed Michael kissing her brother on the cheek, 'hugging him and always rubbing him'.

According to the report, when asked about the DCFS inquiry, the family said that they were 'made' to say that Michael had been a father figure and that nothing sexual had ever happened between him and Gavin. Katz, in his report, wrote that he believed the family had not been forthcoming in the past but was now telling *him* the truth. 'I don't get the feeling the mom is lying about anything, though she may distort', he wrote. 'I really felt the kids were credible.'

However, of Michael Jackson, Dr Katz also wrote in his report, 'He doesn't really qualify as a pedophile. He's just a regressed 10-year-old.'

Exactly as happened in the Chandler case – the mental-health professional, Dr Stan Katz, was compelled by California law to report the details of the recollected sexual abuse to the police. It evolved so quickly, everyone in the Jackson camp was a little stunned by the swiftness of events, even though they suspected there might be trouble ahead. When told about the report to the police, Michael's mouth went agape. 'Huh?' he asked. 'Are you kidding me? Really?' He seemed lost for several heartbeats. 'But . . .' He stammered. 'But . . . I thought . . . *huh?*'

Family Dysfunction

The earlier (and important) denials of sexual abuse aside to Michael Jackson's videographer and also to the DCFS, there are elements of the case against Michael that are still questionable: evidence of dysfunction in the Arvizo family, and what such strange and troubled dynamics may have to do with the charges against the singer, are important to review.

Years ago, in August 1998, the Arvizo family was detained on a shoplifting charge at a J.C. Penney department store in West Covina, California. According to J.C. Penney, the boys – Gavin and Star – were sent out of the store by their father with an armload of clothes, the family was then detained and Janet Ventura-Arvizo started a scuffle with three security officers. The family's side of the story, however, is that the boys were simply modelling clothes for J.C. Penney – odd in that there was no evidence to support this notion – not stealing them.

The shoplifting charges were eventually dropped, but Gavin, Star and their mother filed a lawsuit against J.C. Penney's for $3 million. Janet then charged that, while being detained, she and her sons were 'viciously' beaten by the three security officers, one of whom is a woman.

In more than 200 pages of documents pertaining to the case, a troubling picture of the family matriarch emerges. The psychiatrist hired by J.C. Penney's to evaluate Janet Ventura-Arvizo found her to be 'schizophrenic' and 'delusional'. According to the doctor, 'She felt "sad over being a nobody." With no job . . . a "sad housewife getting fat." ' He reports that she was 'treated with Zoloft'. He wrote, 'her depression may have lingered or worsened.' Of course, that doctor was hired by the department store; his report would not have been used by J.C. Penney had it not been favourable to their case. Janet's own therapist found her to be 'anxious and depressed' after the incident, but not delusional.

Most disturbing about the case, though, is that more than two years after the incident, Janet Ventura-Arvizo added a new charge: she claimed that one of the two male security guards had 'sexually fondled' her breasts and pelvic area 'for up to seven minutes'. It seems odd that so many years passed before she decided to mention the sexual assault. During litigation, the store's psychiatrist asserted that she had rehearsed her sons to back up her 'far-fetched story', and that they had all – mother and sons – suffered 'broken bones' in addition to her sexual assault. 'She just came up with this horror story, and ran with it,' says Tom Griffin, the attorney who represented J.C. Penney in the case. He insists there was no evidence to back up any of the allegations; David Arvizo did not seem to want to be involved in this aspect of the allegations.

Ultimately the department store settled with the family, paying them $137,000 days before the scheduled trial in 2001. 'It was an incident that turned into, in my opinion, a scam to extract money from J.C. Penney,' says Tom Griffin. 'They're going for a home run this time,' he concluded of the family's action with Michael Jackson. 'This is a shake down. Shake down, Part Two.'

Making matters more complex and disturbing, Gavin's parents – who were married as teenagers and divorced in their thirties – have had an acrimonious relationship for years. Janet Ventura-Arvizo filed for divorce in late 2001, about a month after the J.C. Penney settlement. By court order, David Arvizo has not seen his children since 2002 when he pleaded 'no contest' to spousal abuse. A year later, he pleaded 'no contest' to child cruelty. A three-year restraining order was put into place. Since the time of Michael's arrest, David Arvizo has repeatedly petitioned the courts to allow him to see his offspring. Though he insists that the children have been rehearsed by Janet to make statements against him, he has been denied the chance to see them, every legal step along the way.

While the family's troubles are unfortunate, some of their actions do cast a dark shadow over the case against Michael. There seems, at least from appearances, to be a troubling history of exaggeration on Janet Ventura-Arvizo's part, and maybe confabulation, as well – which will be relevant in the trial, say sources in the Los Angeles legal community. 'One wonders, is this a pattern?' asks Karen Russell, a trial attorney in Los Angeles, not involved in the Jackson case. 'What happened with J.C. Penney's, really? Does Mrs Ventura-Arvizo have a habit of not getting what she wants, and then coaching her kids into saying what she wants them to say, and then proceeding legally? These are questions that will, no doubt, be posed at trial.'

Says Dr Robert Butterworth, a New York psychologist, again not associated with the Jackson case, 'There's a possibility for a child to be told something so many times, he is not rehearsing it but, rather, actually believes it. It's possible for a child to become, in a sense, hypnotized by a parent to believe a reality that didn't occur. They go over and over it again, but the facts have been distorted. It's a very troubling phenomenon, very disturbing, and it could be the death knell on this case.'

It could be argued that Michael Jackson, a celebrity with a great deal to lose, should have made a decision to avoid Gavin's family at all costs, if he had known about their history (and he probably did, since he and Janet and Gavin were, apparently, close enough to share confidences). However, the youngster was, and is, quite ill, and perhaps Michael felt he couldn't abandon him under those circumstances.

Also, who knows how many other families in Michael Jackson's life over the years have had problems even more severe that those of his present accuser's? We don't know about them because matters never escalated as they have with the Arvizo family at the centre of the present investigation, but it's likely there've been many similar stories over the years. Without exaggeration, it would be impossible to count the number of disadvantaged families with whom Michael has formed emotional attachments in the last ten, maybe fifteen, years – and equally impossible to fathom the number of boys he has known, befriended and taken into his home and his confidence. There is simply no way to count them, there have been so many. He's fortunate that only two out of what must surely be hundreds have presented a problem for him.

Jesus Juice and Jesus Blood

Jesus Blood. Jesus Juice. Those two descriptions of red and white wine as ascribed to Michael Jackson made headlines in February 2004, as a result of a scathing article about him, by Maureen Orth in *Vanity Fair*. The allegation made by Orth is that Michael gave Gavin Arvizo and another boy wine – Jesus Juice – in Coke cans on a flight from Florida in February 2003. Jackson, though, prefers Jesus Blood. This is a disturbing accusation, obviously, but even more so because two of the charges against Michael have to do with giving a minor 'intoxicating agents' in order to wear him down for sex with him.

Orth's primary source for increasingly lurid stories about Jackson in *Vanity Fair* is his former business adviser Myung-Ho Lee. Lee was Jackson's financial adviser from 1998 to 2001. He sued him for $14 million in 2002, and hasn't stopped talking about him since – even though Jackson settled the suit by giving him money. Lee is the person who told Orth, in another *Vanity Fair* article, that Jackson hired a witch-doctor named Baba to sacrifice dozens of cows in order to put a curse on David Geffen and Steven Spielberg. That's hard to believe . . . even for Michael Jackson.

The wine story, however, is partially true. Michael *does* refer to white wine as 'Jesus Juice' and red wine as 'Jesus Blood'. It's an off-beat joke of his, probably not a very good one, but everyone in his camp knows about it. Also, he *does* drink them both from soda cans. However, Orth reports that the concealment is Michael's way of drinking alcohol without having anyone know that he's doing it. The truth is that he drinks wine out of soda pop cans so that *children* won't see him doing it. 'He's always around kids, and he doesn't want them to see him drinking,' says someone in his camp. 'It's weird, but not criminal.' Also, Jackson has always been afraid that he would be photographed with a glass of wine in his hand, and he thinks that would be inappropriate for his image.

An in-flight passenger profile document that has become part of the public record in litigation between Jackson and XtraJet, the private airline company he once hired, details the pop star's food and beverage preferences and seems to further confirm the wine anecdote. According to the document, dated Sept. 1, 2003: 'White wine in a Diet Coke can' was required 'on <u>every</u> [the word is underlined in the document for emphasis] flight.' In addition, according to the passenger profile document, Michael sometimes drank tequila, gin or Crown Royal on flights.

A strange requirement outlined in the documentation is Michael Jackson's desire for fried chicken from Kentucky Fried Chicken, the American fast-food restaurant, for *every* meal: breakfast, lunch and dinner. Michael demands the so-called 'secret recipe' with 'original chicken breasts, mashed potatoes, corn and biscuits with spray butter'. On short flights, according to the documents, he requests Big

Red gum, mints, cheese and crackers and fruit plates. He will not eat broccoli or 'strong-scented foods'. Prince Michael I and Paris have a stricter diet and are not permitted to eat peanut butter, sugar or chocolate. KFC is part of their regimen when flying, but it must be stripped of all skin. According to the documents, the children 'typically will ask for the same thing their Dad is eating for every meal, but he'll determine what they are allowed to eat, like crackers.' Also, in bold letters next to their menu, it reads 'NO SUGAR!' and 'NO CHICKEN SKIN!' The document says that Paris, in particular, 'is good at cajoling you for sugar'. Moreover, Prince Michael II, a.k.a. Blanket, is always fed by his nanny, Grace Rwamba (who, it is noted, will never eat KFC chicken). The toddler gets the same KFC regimen — 'cut up into pieces' — in addition to crackers, grapes and juice or milk. Finally, the in-flight behaviour of Michael Jackson — a 'non-smoker' — is described as 'very timid . . . but will get out of his seat during takeoff and landing. Be prepared to clean a lot after he deplanes.'

It must be noted, though, that Jackson and Mark Geragos are suing XtraJet, accusing its staff of having secretly video-recorded his flight from Las Vegas to Santa Barbara on the day he was arrested, and then attempting to sell the tape. Documents that surface from XtraJet's side of the litigation have to be, therefore, viewed with at least some scepticism. Also, Richard Matsuura, another youngster Maureen Orth claimed was given wine by Michael when he was twelve, categorically denied the report as soon as the *Vanity Fair* article hit the stands. He says Orth never contacted him before writing the story. His father confirmed that his son was not given any wine by Michael . . . either in a glass, or a soda can.

Stories about Michael that mix truth and fiction — such as the wine in Coke cans anecdote — only serve to confuse people and make them wonder. 'You can't blame people for speculating about odd behavior. In light of charges that he intoxicated a minor in this way, this new information that he actually does drink wine out of soda cans does not look good for him. It has to be a concern to his defense. There are records, and there is also, probably, a stewardess who served Michael wine in this manner. How much of a leap is, then, that this is something Jackson would give to a minor? When you are speaking of this kind of person, when do you cross the line between weird and criminal? That's the question.'

The Time Line

It was an odd morning in the Santa Barbara courthouse on 16 January 2004, the day Michael Jackson was formally arraigned on molestation charges. His parents, Katherine and Joseph, were present for the arraignment to lend their support, as were brothers Jermaine, Tito and Randy. Michael's attorneys showed up without their client. Michael eventually made his entrance with his gorgeous sister, Janet. There were photographers present from around the globe, clicking away as Michael gestured, smiled and shook hands, as if on a red carpet. He looked strong, prepared.

Afterward, much to the thrill of the hundreds – maybe thousands – of fans who came from around the world to demonstrate their support, Michael jumped atop a sports utility vehicle and executed a couple of slight moves – with his cameramen at his side documenting the odd but somehow dazzling moment. He's a man who understands the value of illusion – that being that he's perfectly fine and not broken by recent events – and, also, the importance of simple entertainment. He was giving his fans want they wanted from him. When he's in public, no matter the circumstances – even the most difficult ones – he's on stage. He's also enough of a dreamer to muse that 'one day', the documentation of such an 'historical' day will make one hell of a great film.

After the judge chastised him for being late – as if Michael has ever been on time for anything in his entire life; the judge had better learn to yield to 'Jackson Time' – he humbly pleaded innocent to all the counts against him: seven counts of child molestation and two counts of administering an 'intoxicating agent with intent to commit a felony'. Those who know him well have recalled, privately, that the day of the arraignment was 'the worst of all days for Michael', that he was 'scared out of his wits', and had not had a wink of sleep in any of the nights prior to it. A knot remained tight in his stomach the entire morning, though one would never know it by looking at him. His once agile dancer's body was a mass of aches and pains, the result of stress and anxiety. The back of his neck throbbed. His temples hurt. His vision was blurry, he would later confide. However, he was determined to put on a strong front for the cameras, for the public and, especially, for his fans. He had to rise above. He'd done it countless times before, and he'd do it again.

So, what is the case against Michael Jackson? With the DA Tom Sneddon's evidence still sealed, all of what he has on Michael is still unknown, as of this writing. However, what is known is that the DA believes that Michael abused his victim between 7 February and 10 March 2003 – that is, after the Martin Bashir documentary was broadcast, after Christian Anderson's interview with the Arvizo family, after Michael's TV rebuttal, after he hired Mark Geragos to look into the matter . . . and while the DCFS and the Santa Barbara Sheriff's Department was investigating it.

In essence, what the case against Michael Jackson boils down to, is the following timeline:

6 February 2003 – *Living with Michael Jackson*, the Martin Bashir documentary, is broadcast in the United States.

7 February 2003 – Michael supposedly begins sexually molesting the young boy, Gavin Arvizo, who was seen in the documentary with him.

11 February – Dr Carole Lieberman lodges an official complaint that the relationship seen between Michael and Gavin Arvizo on the Martin Bashir documentary looks suspicious. Others complaints follow.

14 February – The Department of Children and Family Services and the Los Angeles Police Department begin their investigations into the relationship between the star and the boy.

18 February – The Santa Barbara County Sheriff's Department begins its own investigation.

February (date unknown): Christian Anderson conducts an interview with the family for Michael's rebuttal documentary, *The Michael Jackson Interview: The Footage You Were Not Meant to See*.

24 February – The DCFS and LA Police probe ends with conclusions that any allegations are 'unfounded'.

10 March – Michael Jackson supposedly stops molesting Gavin Arvizo.

16 April – The Santa Barbara County Department ends its investigation and closes its case against Michael, saying that the elements of criminal activity had not been meant.

13 June – The Santa Barbara County Sheriff's Department receives a report from Dr Stan Katz in which the family changes its story and alleges that molestation actually *had* taken place, and that Gavin Arvizo (and his brother and sister) were also given intoxicating agents, by Michael. The investigation is re-opened, and the family is (later) interviewed by the Santa Barbara Sheriff's Department.

18 November 2003 – Neverland is raided by the police.

The question remains: Which of the children's stories is to be believed? The one they told documentarians Martin Bashir and Christian Anderson, and also the DCFS, that Michael Jackson was a father-figure who had coddled a cancer victim and his siblings? Or the one they told Larry Feldman and Dr Stan Katz, that paints him as a child-molester who had got them all loaded and had sex with one of them?

In the Arvizo family's defence, their supporters insist that it wasn't until June 2003 – when Janet Ventura-Arvizo took her son to Larry Feldman and then Dr Stan Katz – that Gavin felt he could safely reveal details of his molestation. Perhaps that's true. A victim of sexual abuse often does not want to come forward immediately with details of his ordeal. However, why would all the children change their stories? Why does Star Arvizo suddenly remember witnessing the sexual molestation, but previously hadn't recalled any of those kinds of details, or even hinted at them? Why does he also suddenly remember being given alcohol by Michael? Why does Daveline Arvizo now remember that she was given wine? Even if everyone had been reticent about saying anything critical about Michael and the way he had behaved toward them, did they have to go so far as to, instead, paint a glowing picture of him? If they had all been too frightened or too intimidated to come clean about any of his behaviour, wouldn't they have just not said much at all . . . instead of complimenting Michael Jackson to the point of making him seem like their Saviour? It simply doesn't add up.

In the end, the case against Michael Jackson will hinge on

whatever reasons Gavin, Star, Daveline and Janet Arvizo give as to why they changed their stories, from denials to accusations – and those reasons may not even be known until the trial begins, which will probably not be until early 2005. Were they motivated by money? Did someone else put ideas in their heads? Or did they all finally see the light and decide to tell their *real* story about Michael Jackson? Indeed, the answers to those questions will either send Michael Jackson to prison . . . or set him free.

'Not Debbie too.'

Another surprising development in Michael Jackson's life since the most recent edition of *Michael Jackson – The Magic and the Madness* has been the emergence of his ex-wife and mother of two of his children, Debbie Rowe, in a surprisingly antagonistic manner. Though she has said in the past that she has little interest in the upbringing of the children to whom she gave birth, Prince Michael and Paris, she apparently changed her mind once Michael was arrested.

During the months after Michael's arrest, an alarmed Debbie attempted to contact him to discuss his state of mind. She knows how sensitive he is, and she was concerned about him. However, she had another agenda: she also wanted to discuss the terms of the custody and visitation agreements, especially after learning that the Nation of Islam was involved in Michael's life. She is Jewish – having converted for her first marriage – and was 'extremely, extremely upset', according to a close friend of hers, about Michael's new alignment with the Nation, an organization known to be anti-Semitic.

It could be argued that it makes little sense, at least from a public-relations standpoint, for Michael Jackson to be involved with any organization deemed to be controversial. He has enough problems. However, that said, the Nation of Islam is an easy mark – and there has been a great deal of overheated media coverage of the organization's sudden association with the Jacksons because of its obviously biased cultural positions. In fact, fundamentalist religions usually do lean toward certain biases. For instance, Jerry Falwell and Pat Robertson are both overt in their disdain for Islam and for Muslims. There is open disdain at the top of many religions. Is Catholicism not openly against homosexuals? Fundamentalists of all religions often ignite emotions in people, no matter what the religion: fundamentalist Jews, fundamentalist Christians, fundamentalist Muslims, etc. . . . Debbie has said, privately, that she doesn't want her children around fundamentalists of *any* religion, and especially the Nation of Islam because of its incendiary position against whites and Jews.

Jermaine Jackson is a Muslim, though not a member of the Nation. There are many confounding and contradicting stories about how the Nation became involved in Michael's life, but the simple truth is that the organization contacted him and asked if he wanted their support . . . and he said yes. Michael welcomes all support at this time, and seems happy to have it from any quarter. Is the Nation merely involved in Jackson's security, as he and his handlers have insisted? Or is the group actually managing his business affairs, as strongly rumoured? Is there some kind of religious 'brainwashing' going on? It's doubtful. The Jehovah's Witnesses couldn't tell Michael what to do when was a young adult, and Scientologists couldn't influence him either, when he was with Lisa Marie. It's doubtful the Nation of Islam will be able to tell him what to do.

However, for an artist who has never preached separatism or racism, the Nation's involvement in his life is perplexing. To explain away the surprising association, it's claimed by those presently in his camp that Michael has known Nation leader Louis Farrakhan since he was six years old. 'Excuse me?' remarked a long-time Jackson family associate. 'Were they socializing back in Gary? Did he come by the house for pre-Jackson 5 rehearsals?' Indeed, how did a six-year-old boy who wasn't even famous yet meet Louis Farrakhan in Gary, Indiana? Small world, isn't it?

It is known, though, that twenty years ago, Louis Farrakhan spoke out against Michael and criticized him as a bad example to the world's youth. All has been forgiven, apparently, because Farrakhan is now one of Jackson's supporters. 'We don't believe Michael is guilty,' he said in a recent speech. 'And there are a lot of people that know the mother who is accusing him and the little boy that he helped to heal, and they don't believe Michael is guilty. What happened to the presumption of innocence? See, black people are always guilty until they are proved innocent; white people are innocent until they are proved guilty.'

During this time, Michael Jackson should, it could be argued, only be presented in a way that is credible to critical-thinking people and not just that faction of the public arena – his fans, mostly – who will believe anything they are told as long as it is stated by a famous person, or someone described as 'an official spokesman'. Of course, as soon as Louis Farrakhan made his sweeping and untrue racial generalization in an attempt to play on the basic fears of people of colour, his support of Michael lost all credibility, or as one pundit put it, 'Too bad that after all these years he doesn't know where to draw the line.'

It does seem that the Nation has isolated Michael from those in his circle. Even his family members, such as his own mother, have not had access to him after the generous show of familial support at the arraignment. His videographer, Christian Robinson, has not seen Michael since the day of the arrest, either. He 'absolutely' believes that the Nation of Islam has kept him away from Jackson. At Michael's arraignment, a different videographer was at his side when the star leapt atop an automobile to greet his fans. He says that the Nation's influence is 'hopefully the closest thing to a jail Michael will ever see'.

It's easy to blame the Nation for running interference between Michael Jackson and others, especially lately, but if one traces Michael's history, there has always been some person or some group of people charged with isolating him – and at his own request.

Ten years ago, for instance, when Michael didn't want to be pressured during the Jordie Chandler debacle with the possibility of another Jackson family reunion venture, his attorneys and Elizabeth Taylor were charged with keeping his parents and siblings at bay. Remember Katherine Jackson asking why it was that Elizabeth had access to Michael, but she did not? Years before that, the job fell to Frank Dileo. Everyone in the family complained then that *he* was the one keeping them from Michael. Before that, John Branca was the person certain family members, blamed for preventing them from having free access to Michael. Going all the way back to the late 1970s, Michael's managers Ron Weisner and Freddie DeMann were targeted by Joseph and Katherine as being culprits responsible for ruining their relationship with Michael by not allowing them to speak to him.

In truth, no one has ever kept Michael Jackson from anyone in his family, or from certain staff members, without his explicit request that distance be created between him . . . and 'them'. The representatives from the Nation of Islam may or may not have their own financial or political agenda at hand in their association with Michael. However, to Michael they serve what he feels is a valuable and habitual purpose: they shelter him from those he feels are out to drain him of whatever little joy he has left in life. Maybe his family has all of the best of intentions, and nothing but love for him, these days. However, if Michael doesn't see it that way and if he doesn't act as if he wants them in his life, the notion of their affection and loyalty is moot.

As far as Debbie Rowe is concerned, for her to end up on the outside side of Michael's present circle is a surprising occurrence. The question remains, though, as to whether or not she has a right to an opinion about Michael's children, and the way they are being raised. She and Michael did have a custody and visitation agreement (while she did not have custody, she was allowed a couple of visits a year if she wanted them, an opportunity of which she had not availed herself in the past), but it can be changed at any time, said her attorney, 'with a showing of changed circumstances'. While she gave away custody of her children, she, apparently, did not give away her parental rights. 'She can always go back to the courts and re-petition to change custody,' said one attorney, 'however, no one ever thought she would, but she did – after she could not get a return call from Michael, and after she felt disrespected by him.'

When Michael set a dismissive tone with his ex-wife, his loyalists followed suit and froze her out, as well. Suddenly, no one was returning her phone calls, nor those of her attorney. Whereas just a year earlier, Michael had called upon Debbie to appear in a documentary defending him against the Martin Bashir allegations, now he wanted nothing to do with her. 'Doesn't she know I have enough on my hands?' he asked one associate. 'Why can't she just leave me and my children alone?'

While Michael's associates held a major meeting at the Beverly Hills Hotel in January 2004 to discuss his future, Debbie was in a meeting of her own: at the Ivy in Beverly Hills with two of Michael's former managers, Dieter Weisner and Ronald Konitzer, to discuss her concern over the involvement of the Nation of Islam in Michael's life, and also her options relating to child custody.

A final straw for Debbie came in the week of 16 February 2004 when she heard rumours that Michael had gone back into rehab, this time in Colorado.

In truth, Michael was not in rehab in Colorado, but was being treated there by herbalist Alfredo Bowman for what one source close to him describes as 'not really an addiction but definitely a dependency' on morphine and the prescription-drug Demerol. Michael's use of such drugs might explain his detached and odd demeanour of late, especially during his interview with Ed Bradley for *60 Minutes* during which he seemed physically and mentally lethargic. According to reports, he's been using the medications in order to cope with the stress of the allegations and with chronic insomnia. It's dangerous behaviour, especially considering what happened ten years ago when he became addicted to painkillers during the Jordie Chandler matter and ended up in rehab in England.

Alfredo Bowman maintains an office in Beverly Hills, and another in Honduras. He was treating TLC singer Lisa 'Left Eye' Lopes at his 'USHA Healing Village' when she died in a car accident there, in the spring of 2002. Bowman apparently got into trouble with the New York State attorney general a couple of years ago when that office objected to his claiming to have found cures for AIDS, cancer and leukaemia. On his website Bowman boasts of never having gone to school – 'not even kindergarten'. His website also claims, 'We are proud to inform you that Cosmo Therapy is part of our healing journey realigning with the energy of life which is beyond spirituality. Return to MOTHER!!!'

Debbie tried to obtain information about Michael's so-called 'detox', but, again, was unsuccessful in contacting him, or anyone around him. The walls around Michael and his children were up, and she was on one side, while the Jackson camp was on the other side. She has always said that Michael is not a paedophile; however, according to sources close to her, she is no longer sure what to believe about him – and until she makes up her mind, she wants guardianship of her two children. She's even indicated in court papers filed in Los Angeles that the children are not biologically Michael's, no surprise to his critics who have always been sceptical of the paternity of his children.

In a court order filed on Friday 20 February 2004, Superior Court Judge Carolyn Kuhl approved an agreement reached by the Rowe and Jackson camps to have retired Los Angeles Superior Court Judge Stephen M. Lachs preside over the case. The order said his appointment would continue 'until the conclusion of all matters'.

Judge Lachs works with a centre for alternative dispute resolution that allows parties concerned about their privacy who are involved in civil disputes to hire private judges at a rate of $650 an hour. 'They hire private judges so that everything can be done behind closed doors,' said attorney Dana Cole, an expert in family law who is not involved in this case. However, Lachs has said that much of what occurs in his 'private' court room will still be open to public scrutiny. The private judge's rulings will be as binding as if they were made in a regular family court.

While Michael does not wish for the matter to proceed as it is in the court system, he has had little choice in it. Ironically, the millions he has paid Debbie over the years have made it possible for her to become one of his biggest adversaries, and maybe one of his biggest nightmares. He's going up against a woman who can afford to retain legal counsel as powerful as his own – and using money he has paid her to do it! Michael's signature on the paperwork is big and sprawling, as if he was extremely agitated when he committed it to the document.

Those in his private world say that Debbie Rowe's re-emergence in Michael Jackson's life as an opposing force is as hurtful to him as the allegations of child molestation. In retrospect, Michael handled the matter of Debbie's discontent the way he handles most problems – he tried to avoid it. As has been repeatedly stated by those who know him, he is childlike in many ways, and, it seems, has become more so in this last, traumatizing year – especially when it comes to dealing with unpleasantness.

Like a youngster facing some disagreeable situation, Michael simply could not, or would not, cope with it. He was frightened that Debbie Rowe was positioning herself to pose a serious threat to his family. His hands would shake when he would pick up the telephone to call her. He couldn't follow through, he was so fearful of what it was she wanted from him and how she might impact his relationship with his children, all three of who have given him the greatest joy he has ever known. One of his associates recalled it best: he handed him the phone to call her. 'Do it, Mike. You gotta call her,' he said. Michael looked at him with such an anguished expression, it appeared that he was about to let out a long, desperate scream. But he didn't. Instead, he put the phone down and walked away in tears. 'Not Debbie too,' he said, shaking his in disbelief. 'Not Debbie too.'

Coda

In April 2004, a secret Grand Jury convened in Santa Barbara County to hear from witnesses brought forth by District Attorney Tom Sneddon to testify against Michael Jackson – including his present accuser. The jury then handed down an indictment against the entertainer on molestation charges. The decision means that a majority of the members of the Grand Jury felt enough evidence existed in the case against Jackson to bring it to trial. However, a California Grand Jury is simply a function of the prosecution; the defence does not have the opportunity to present its case, and isn't even present at the proceedings. Therefore, with DA Sneddon vociferously offering everything he has against Michael Jackson – and with no rebuttal or cross-examination of witnesses from Jackson's team – how could the result have been anything but an indictment?

After the indictment, to make matters even more complicated, Michael suddenly dismissed his attorneys, Mark Geragos and Benjamin Brafman. They were replaced by Thomas Mesereau Jr., another well-known criminal defence attorney, who represented actor Robert Blake in his murder case (until they parted company, citing irreconcilable differences). In an interview, Brafman indicated that the decision did not come directly from Michael (though he believes Michael had a hand in it), but rather from 'advisers and family members'. He further added that the parting of ways was 'for reasons we choose not to discuss publicly'. It was reported that Michael's brothers Randy and Jermaine were influential in the matter, as was Leonard Muhammad of the Nation of Islam.

It now seems clear that there are members of Michael's family who have future career plans in mind for him . . . and probably for themselves, as well. They are trying to protect their brother (which is admirable) and, perhaps, their own interests (which is probably not as commendable, but also not particularly surprising, if one reviews family history). Again, one is forced to wonder how much decision-making power Michael has, or even wants, in his present dilemma . . . and how many other key players with mixed agendas may enter stage left and exit stage right before the Jackson show plays before judge and jury.

It is obviously a tragic turn of events if Michael Jackson is being targeted with untrue allegations of child-molestation. At this writing, he is enduring the saddest, most agonizing period of his life. Ironically, prior to this ordeal, he was beginning to rise to the challenge of looking at his world in a new and profound way, trying to come to terms with the ugliness of some of his past. He seemed to be finding a measure of contentment, perhaps for the first time, as he raised his children. He had also just begun to rediscover the joy of music. Finally, the Jordie Chandler matter of a decade ago was beginning to fade from public consciousness. Then, this new *thing* happened, a matter so awful as to lay waste to any personal progress he had made – setting him back years, perhaps making it impossible for him to ever reconcile any of his troubles and to take full responsibility for his choices, indeed his life. However, until he does so, perhaps he is destined to repeat the same mistakes, as if he is the beleaguered star of a horrible, Greek tragedy. In truth, there seems to never be a time when he is free of crisis.

What other famous person has these kinds of problems? Is it that Michael is so different, so unusual, so extraordinary, so . . . *famous* . . . that he is an easy target for one kind of exploitation or another, be it one of the many hundreds of lawsuits filed against him or, now, a second allegation of child molestation? Or, does he somehow bring such madness onto himself by being arrogant, or naive . . . or both? Perhaps he is just one of the unluckiest people ever to be in show-business? You have to feel sorry for the guy.

However, one fact still remains: despite his background – his childhood fame and adult superstardom – at the end of the day it is not reductive of who he is and the challenges he faces to remember that Michael Jackson is only human, no more than the nine-to-five worker trying to support a large family on a meagre wage and no less than the wealthy socialite without a care in the world. Like everyone who draws breath, he is ultimately responsible for making his own decisions. He's a grown man – not a child. He writes his own story, bringing into focus the characters he chooses to have in his world. No one forced Jordie Chandler and his father on him, and no one forced Gavin Arvizo and his mother on him, either. Casting those people to play roles in his life has amounted to some of Michael's biggest mistakes, of that there is little doubt.

It's sad – tragic, even. He's such a privileged person, a man heaped with every blessing of fame, fortune and family. One wonders why there seems no way then, no way at all, for Michael Jackson to lead a good and dignified – and happy – life.

Acknowledgements

Michael Jackson – The Magic and the Madness would not have been possible without the assistance of many individuals.

First acknowledgement must go to my UK literary agent, Miss Dorie Simmonds of The Dorie Simmonds Agency. She's a wonderful representative and a good friend as well; we've done many amazing projects together. Without her, my career would be a very different one – and not nearly as exciting, or fulfilling.

I would also like to thank my editor, Gordon Wise, at Macmillan, whose idea it was to produce an updated edition of the original bestseller, *Michael Jackson – The Magic and the Madness*. Also, thanks to Ingrid Connell, and everyone else at Macmillan who became so invested in this project.

Hillel Black was the editor of the original edition of this work. *Michael Jackson* was our second collaboration; Mr Black also edited *Call Her Miss Ross*. No author could ever hope for a better, more patient person to shepherd a book.

Paula Agronick Reuben has been invaluable to me in so many ways for many years. I was fortunate to have been able to work with her on the original edition of *Michael Jackson*. She is a consummate professional and a close friend.

Private investigator and researcher Cathy Griffin was a vital contributor to this project. I am especially indebted to her for locating sources who had seemingly disappeared from the face of the earth. Ms Griffin also conducted scores of interviews for this work, and I am indebted to her for that as well.

Special thanks to Stephen Gregory, not only for so many years of friendship but also for all of his invaluable input into this book.

He is always there for me, without fail.

I must thank Jonathan Hahn, a fellow journalist, my publicist, and also my good friend. A fellow couldn't ask for a better 'sounding board' than Jonathan. Thanks also to Alysia Garrison for being so vital and important to Jonathan, and also to me.

I thank, as always, Al Kramer, my trusted friend and writing colleague, who has, for years, been there for me.

I must thank Cloe Basiline for all of her work on transcriptions of interviews for the new edition of this work. She spent many hours working under the tightest deadline imaginable to put down every word, accurately. I would also like to thank Stewart Payne who conducted important interviews for me for this updated book. James Burrell also conducted interviews for me in Gary, Indiana. Thanks to him, we were able to track down people who worked with Michael and his brothers in the early days, who have never before been interviewed. I must also thank Thomas DeWitt for all of his work in the United Kingdom on what he calls 'The Jackson Case' – research for this book.

Three others having to do with the research for this book whose kindnesses should not go unacknowledged are Maxwell Taylor, Irene Roberts and Geri Thomas. These researchers typed many of the notes and other minutiae that were unearthed during library research, saving me and others involved with this book so much time and energy. I am indebted to them.

John Passantino provided valuable information about the Victory tour and other aspects of Michael Jackson's career, and Linda DeStefano supplied many videotapes of Jackson and his brothers for research purposes. I thank them both for their assistance, and for years of friendship.

Researcher Julio Vera spent many hours in the Los Angeles Superior Courthouse locating court records so valuable to my research. I thank him for his patience and perseverance.

John Redman also conducted interviews for this book, and I appreciate his assistance.

A number of individuals were helpful in providing information or putting me in touch with prospective interviewees: Janet Charlton, Lydia Encinas, Charles Higham, Steve Ivory, Mark Ingram, Barbara Sternig, Robert Taylor, Patricia Towle and Stephen Viens.

Special thanks to these individuals for their support in tangible and intangible ways on the original edition of this book, including: Cindy Adams, Larry Anderson, Kristopher Antekeier, Sherman Armstrong, Stewart Armstrong, Gil Askey, Virginia August, Vern Austin, Billy Barnes, Glenn Bascome, Jeffrey Beasley, Louis Becker, Gary Berwin, Cindy Birdsong, Stanley Blits, Judith Blum, Wayne Brasler, Len Brimhall, Robert Brimmer, Ralph Brine, Robert Brown, Kenneth and Dolores Bruner and family, Maryann Bryant, the late and so-memorable Walter Burrell, Mark Butler, Tim Burton, Lee Campbell, Geron Canidate, Luis Cansesco, Eddie Carroll, Gordon Carter, Lee Casto, Tony Castro, Kenneth Choi, Herman Cohen, Rob Cohen, Paul Coleman, Michele Connolly, Marvin Corwin, Richard Crane, Ted Culver, Barbara Dalton, Hal Davis, Etterlene DeBarge, David Delsey, David Doolittle, Lamont Dozier, Stewart Drew, David Duarte, Beverly Ecker, Carl Feuerbacher, Mickey Free, Rosetta Frye, Rudy Garza, Rick Gianotos, Louise Gilmore, Sylvester Goodnough, Theresa Gonsalves, Martha Gonsalves, Vivian Greene, Michael Gutierrez, Scott Haeffs, Sharlette Hambrick, Virginia Harris, Max Hart, Mickey Herskowitz, C. David Heymann, Jerome Howard, Mary Ellen Howe, Steve Howell, Willie Hutch, Monty Iceman, A. D. Ingram, Terry Ireland, Johnny Jackson, Sarah Jackson, Susie Jackson, Walter Jackson, Etta James, Joyce Jillson, Edward Jimenez, Val Johns, Richard Tyler Jordan, Gregorio Jove, Patty Kellar, Curtis Kelly, Mark Kelly, David Kelsey, Randall King, Ken Kingsley, Mark Kotler, Dr Robert Kotler, George Lakes, Lance and John (The Hollywood Kids), Randy Lane, Harry Langdon, Joseph Layton, Edward Lewis, Jack Lewis, Michael Lewis, Yolanda Lewis, Dr Carole Lieberman, Harold Long, Leonides Lopez, Peter Lounds, Gregory Matthias, Joyce McCrae, Maryann McCullough, James McField, Phillip Meadows, Charles Montgomery, Byran Moore, Clarence Moore, Lee Moore, Mark Mussari, Susan Myerson, Kenneth Nagle, David Nuell, Barbara Ormsby, Bernard Pancheco, Scherrie Payne, Ross Pendergraft, the late and so-very-missed Derrick Perrault, James Perry, Marcus Phillips, Rhonda Phillips, Stewart Phillips, Andre Pittmon, Jonathan Ptak, John Reitano, Rich Reitano, Deke Richards, Jack Richardson, Lionel Richie, Seth Riggs, David Ritz, Grace Rivera, Danny Romo, Stanley Ross, the late Raymond St Jacques, Ramone Sandoval, Stan Sherman, Joseph

Simon, Liz Smith, James Spada, Reed Sparling, Judy Spiegelman, Gina Sprague, Steven Sprocket, Rick Starr, Nancy Stauffer, Robert Waldron, Vince Waldron, Marjorie Walker, Dan Weaver, Harry Weber, Tim Whitehead, Susan Williams, Edward Willis, Douglas Wilson, Jeffrey Wilson, Reginald Wilson, Rob Yaren and the gifted John Whyman, who took the photo of me and Michael on the book jacket.

I would also like to acknowledge the late but never forgotten former wives of Jackie and Tito Jackson, Enid Jackson and Dee Dee Jackson. They were so helpful to me in the past. Both were wonderful, giving women who left us much too early. They are so missed by their friends and families.

Special thanks to David McGough and DMI for some of the excellent photographs in this book.

I could never do alone what I do with my books, and if I forgot any single person who contributed in any way to the research of this book – particularly those who are employed by my researchers – I am truly sorry. It does take a team of professionals, not just a single author, to tackle a project such as *Michael Jackson*, and I am eternally grateful to all of the players.

I want to thank Jeff Hare for being such a good and trusted friend.

Thanks also to Iake and Alex Eisinmann for so many years of friendship and support.

Thanks to Brian Newman for being such a positive person in my life. What fun we have had over the years!

My colleague Steven Ivory and I have spent many hours talking about Michael Jackson over the years, trying to understand him and his world. I so appreciate his vision, and his friendship, which spans some twenty-five years.

It means the world to me to be blessed with so many good friends, some of whom I would like to acknowledge here, including: Richard Tyler Jordan, Ben Tyler, George Solomon, Jess Cagle, James Pinkston, David Shofner, Paul Adler, Michael Puopolo, Hazel and Rob Kragulac, Lisa Reiner, Andy Skurow, Daniel Coleridge, Randall Friesen, Billy Barnes, Roby Gayle, Sonja Kravchuck, Barbara Ormsby, Rick Starr, John Carlino, David Spiro, Mr and Mrs Adolph Steinlen, David and Frances Snyder, Abby and Maddy Snyder, Maribeth and Don Rothell, Mary Alvarez, Mark Bringelson,

Hope Levy, Tom Lavagnino, David Goldberg, Peter Martocchio; David S.; Anthony Shane, Anne McVey, Bethany Marshall, Bob Weatherford, Jeff Yarbrough, Thoraf Rienow, David Chick, Yvette Jarecki, Dylan and Rydell, Matthew Miles Barasch, Jim Bozora, Ryan Smith and Dr. Jason K. Peters.

My special thanks to Andy Steinlen for the huge role he plays in my life, year after year.

As I have often stated, without a loyal team of representatives an author usually finds himself sitting at home writing books no one reads. Therefore, I thank all of those on 'Team JRT' who masterminded the activities in my office during production of the new edition of *Michael Jackson – The Magic and the Madness*: attorneys Joel Loquvam and James Jimenez; accountants Ken Deakins, Rae Goldreich, Teryna Hanuscin and Harold Stock of CBIZ Southern California, Inc. and also Joe Parisi of Metro Advantage Mortgage. Thanks also to my USA agent, Mitch Douglas, and all of the fine folks at International Creative Management, including Ron Bernstein and Buddy Thomas.

I have always been so blessed to have a family as supportive as mine. My thanks and love go to: Roslyn and Bill Barnett and Jessica and Zachary, Rocco and Rosemarie Taraborrelli and Rocco and Vincent, and Arnold Taraborrelli.

Special thanks to my father, Rocco, and also to my mother, Rose Marie, who has my heart, always.

Source Notes

Much of the material in this book was drawn from personal interviews and conversations with Michael Jackson and the Jackson family over the years, from the 1970s through the 1990s. Among those interviews:

Michael Jackson in May 1972 (New York), June 1973, August 1973, July 1974 (Madison Square Garden, New York), November 1974, October 1977 (New York, for *The Wiz*), August 1978 (Encino), 19 April 1979 (Valley Forge, Pennsylvania);

Michael Jackson on 18 January 1980 (Los Angeles), 18 September 1980 (sound check at the Forum, Los Angeles), 26 September 1980 (backstage at the Forum), October 1980 (Encino, with Janet Jackson), June 1982, April 1983 (Universal Amphitheater, Los Angeles), January 1984 (Shrine Auditorium, Los Angeles), June 1984 (Birmingham, Alabama, with Tito and Jackie), 29 June 1984 (Atlanta, with Jackie), November 1986 (Universal Amphitheater, Los Angeles), 2 March 1988 (rehearsal, Madison Square Garden), 16 January 1989 (sound check, Sports Arena, Los Angeles), 30 January 1989 (rehearsal for American Music Awards, Shrine Auditorium, Los Angeles), 13 November 1989 (rehearsal, *Sammy Davis, Jr., 60th Anniversary* television special, Los Angeles), spring 1991 (Capitol Records 'Record Collectors' Swap Meet');

Michael Jackson on 3 February 1992 (press conference, Radio City Music Hall, New York), 26 August 1993 (from Bangkok), July 1994 (after my appearance on *Good Morning America* to announce his marriage to Lisa Marie Presley), August 1994, September 1995 and 7 February 1998 (with Lisa Marie Presley at the Ivy restaurant in Los Angeles).

Moreover, I drew from interviews with:

The Jacksons – Jackie, Tito, Marlon, Michael, Randy, and parents Joseph and Katherine in February 1975, (Radio City Music Hall, New York), June 1975, July 1975, January 1976, March 1977, April 1977, May 1977, August 1978 and September 1979 (all at Hayvenhurst in Encino), November 1983 (press conference, Tavern on the Green, New York);

Tito, Marlon and Jackie Jackson in July 1974 (Pittsburg, Pennsylvania) and December 1978 (L'Ermitage Hotel in Los Angeles);

Jermaine Jackson in April 1979 (at Motown Records in Los Angeles) and May 1980 (Shrine Auditorium, Los Angeles);

LaToya Jackson and Jack Gordon, December 1993 (Madrid, Spain).

Also useful in my research were two lengthy court documents: Sworn Deposition by Michael Jackson, dated 15 January 1976 and Sworn Declaration of Michael J. Jackson, 20 February 1976. (These declarations became part of case number C139795: *Michael Jackson et al. v. Motown Record Corporation of California et al.*, 30 March 1976.) Text and background from both documents were used throughout the book.

For research purposes, I secured many hundreds of Motown interoffice memos regarding Michael Jackson and The Jackson 5. Because of the confidential nature of these communications, and to protect those former Motown employees who made them available to me, these memos are not enumerated here, though they were vital to my research.

Voluminous Motown press department releases (and also releases from different public relations firms representing Michael Jackson, The Jackson 5, and The Jacksons, as well as individual members) were individually judged as to their validity and value and utilized where appropriate.

As the editor-in-chief of *Soul* magazine (1980) and later its publisher (1981-82), I had access to the complete *Soul* files. *Soul* was one of the first black entertainment publications (*Jet* and *Ebony* were both general interest publications) and, as such, had a close association to Motown. Many of the Motown acts received their only national exposure through *Soul*. A great deal of the material in this book was culled from the extensive *Soul* files (1966-82), including previously confidential notes and memos.

Practically all of the interview sources listed here contributed to more than one subject area of the book, but in most cases they are listed only once.

Wherever practical, I have provided sources within the body of the text. For some of the published works consulted, see the bibliography. The following notes are by no means comprehensive but are intended to give the reader a general overview of my research. Also included are occasional comments of an extraneous but informative nature.

Early Years

I obtained background information on the families of Joseph Jackson and Katherine Scruse from census records dating back to the late eighteen hundreds. I also obtained the birth certificates of Joseph Jackson and Kattie E. Scruse (Katherine Jackson); Martha Bridgett's Affidavit to Amend a Record of Birth, filed on 4 May 1930; as well as Joseph and Katherine Jackson's Certificate of Marriage in Crown Point, Indiana. I compared this and other information to what Katherine Jackson wrote in her memoirs, *The Jacksons – My Family* (St Martin's Press, 1990), and added a substantial amount of information to her account of her and Joseph Jackson's backgrounds.

I also drew from the interview I had with the Jacksons in August 1978.

I interviewed relatives and friends of the Jacksons' family, including Ina Brown (14 September 1989), Johnny Jackson (5 October 1990), Luis Cansesco (3 November 1990), and Terry Ireland (1 December 1990). I drew some information from articles in *Right On!*, *Soul*, and *Rolling Stone* (see bibliography).

My private investigator, Cathy Griffin, contacted Gordon Keith, former owner of Steeltown Records in Gary, Indiana, to obtain an interview. He and Griffin had numerous conversations; background information was culled from a conversation on 16 September 1990. Mr Keith would not consent to an interview with me, however.

I also drew some information, particularly Ben Brown's quotes, from a segment of *P.M. Magazine* about Michael Jackson, which aired in 1984.

Some of the material in these sections is from my 1979 interview with Michael Jackson.

Joe Simon's quote was culled from an interview I conducted with him in 1979. Etta James's comments were extracted from an interview I conducted with Miss James on 12 May 1978. Other quotes are from sources in Gary, Indiana, who requested anonymity.

For the material regarding Berry Gordy and Motown, I drew heavily from research conducted when I wrote the book *Motown – Hot Wax, City Cool and Solid Gold*, published by Doubleday in 1986. I also drew from personal interviews with Melvin Franklin (1977), Smokey Robinson (1980), Diana Ross (1981), Lamont Dozier (1985) and Maurice King (1985).

Richard Arons was contacted for an interview and did speak with Cathy Griffin at his Beverly Hills home for three hours on 12 November 1990. Some of Arons's memories are used here for background purposes. However, he would not consent to an interview with me. Miss Griffin also spoke to Bobby Taylor for two hours on the telephone in October 1990. Some of what Mr Taylor remembered was used here for background purposes.

Motown Years

For much of this material, I drew heavily from a thirty-page Sworn Declaration of Berry Gordy, dated 4 March 1976. The declaration was given under oath during the court battle between The Jackson 5 and Motown. In it, Gordy explained how the group was signed to the label, what his involvement with the act was and how their first records were recorded. He also reconstructed telephone conversations between himself and Joseph Jackson at the time of the group's signing on 26 July 1968, and conversations between himself and other Motown employees regarding his dismay over The Jackson 5's appearances in Las Vegas.

I also drew from a thirty-page Sworn Declaration of Ralph Seltzer, Motown's vice president of corporate affairs, dated 5 March 1976. Seltzer recreated the dialogue, to the best of his memory, between himself and Joseph Jackson on 25 and 26 July 1968, the days of The Jackson 5's audition and then signing to Motown. Seltzer spoke in depth about the Motown recording contract and its terms, his impressions of Joseph Jackson and Jack Richardson, his opinion of the Motown recording contract he had them sign, how Jackson signed the contract without benefit of outside counsel, how he had his sons do the same and how Seltzer executed contracts by other artists at Motown. He also detailed Bobby Taylor's involvement in discovering The Jackson 5 and spoke of the Christmas party at which The Jackson 5 performed and Joseph Jackson's impressions of Gordy Manor. (Regarding that Christmas party, I also drew from my interview with the Jacksons in 1978 and an interview I conducted with Diana Ross in June 1972.)

I also utilized my personal interview with Ralph Seltzer on 6 June 1989, in which he discussed Gordy's aversion to allowing an artist to take a Motown contract home for review purposes.

I culled a good deal of information from the twenty-five-page Sworn Deposition of Suzanne dePasse, Motown's vice president, creative division, dated 4 March 1976. DePasse remembered in vivid detail The Jackson 5's audition for Motown, the recording of certain of their hit records, the early tours, her impressions of Joseph and Katherine Jackson, and the original contract negotiations for The Jackson 5.

I extracted information from the five-page Sworn Statement of Anthony D. Jones, executive assistant to the vice president, creative division, dated 4 March 1976, in which he detailed Motown's marketing campaign for The Jackson 5.

I also gathered facts from the fifteen-page Sworn Statement of Alan D. Croll, attorney for Motown Record Corporation. Interestingly, Croll's statement contradicted Seltzer's claim that Joseph Jackson was not represented by outside counsel: Croll claimed that Jack Richardson acted as counsel for the Jacksons (though Richardson was not an attorney).

I drew from lengthy Sworn Depositions given by Richard Arons, Joseph Jackson's attorney, and Joseph Jackson on 18 November 1975. In his deposition, Joseph Jackson answered questions regarding his antagonistic relationship with Berry Gordy and Ewart Abner.

Most interesting were the Sworn Depositions of each member of The Jackson 5, which were taken on 15 January 1976, including Michael Jackson's. Portions of Michael's twenty-five-page deposition and the lengthy depositions of his brothers were integrated into the information found in other parts of this work.

I acquired copies of the original seven-page Motown contracts, dated 26 July 1968, for each member of the group.

Some of Bobby Taylor's comments to my private investigator, Cathy Griffin, were utilized. I, too, interviewed Bobby in 1995 and again in 1996.

I referred to my interview with Jermaine Jackson in 1980 for some of the details of the meeting at Diana Ross's home in August 1969.

I viewed a videotape of The Jackson 5's performance at the Daisy on 11 August 1969, and used as source material newspaper accounts of the festivities that evening. I also interviewed Paula Dunn on 6 January 1990. Judy Spiegelman's comments were published in *Soul*.

I also obtained copies of the nine-page recording contracts with Motown, dated 11 March 1969, for each member of The Jackson 5.

I procured a copy of the Parent's or Guardian's Guaranty obligating Michael Jackson to perform certain duties as part of his commitment to Motown, dated 11 March 1969.

I also obtained many correspondences between Berry Gordy and The Jackson 5 and Joseph Jackson regarding the Saturday morning cartoon series, the wedding of Jermaine Jackson and Hazel Gordy, the Las Vegas opening and the deterioration of Motown's relationship with The Jackson 5. These were all in the public domain, used as evidence in Motown's suit against The Jackson 5.

I was also able to obtain a complete list of the 469 songs recorded by The Jackson 5 at Motown – including all of those that were not released – as well as the session costs for each tune. I also viewed the entire 16-millimetre black-and-white Motown audition film, now transferred to VHS videotape, for some details.

Motown Hit Years

Much of this material was drawn from two lengthy interviews I conducted with Deke Richards on 22 September and 3 November 1990.

Michael Jackson's comments about Richards were culled from a BBC interview he gave in June 1972. His comments about Diana Ross and early Motown experiences are from my July 1979 interview with him.

As well as obtaining a list of every song recorded by The Jackson 5 at Motown, I also reviewed a computer readout of all of Motown's *exact* sales figures up until December 1990. This computer readout is over ten thousand pages long and includes the album, tape and CD sales of virtually every Motown release from the time of the company's inception. I refer to these figures quite often in this book. I also used this catalogue when I researched *Call Her Miss Ross*.

Berry Gordy's comments about Michael Jackson's living with Diana Ross were culled from the Sworn Declaration of Berry Gordy, dated 4 March 1976.

I reviewed Ralph Seltzer's petition to Superior Court on 29 October 1968 and quoted from the court transcript of the hearing before Judge Lester E. Olson on that day. Also referred to was the Order Approving Minors' Contracts, filed 7 November 1969, and Order Approving Petition for Approval of Amendments to Contracts of Minors, filed 10 September 1970, both in Los Angeles Superior Court.

I interviewed Virginia Harris on 3 September 1990. Susie Jackson was interviewed on 21 September 1990. Two close friends of Katherine Jackson's, who requested anonymity, were also interviewed.

I viewed a videotape of the *Hollywood Palace* segment, 18 October 1969, and interviewed Jack Lewis on 3 March 1990.

I also gathered information from other sources, including interviews with Stan Sherman (19 March 1990), Phillip Meadows (4 April 1990), Gordon Carter (3 June 1990), Susan Williams (5 August 1990) and Eddie Carroll (15 September 1990). I interviewed Willie Hutch in June 1978 in Marina del Ray and drew from that interview. I also have some sources who worked closely with Berry Gordy and who requested anonymity.

I viewed a videotape of The Jackson 5's performance on *The Ed Sullivan Show* on 14 December 1969.

I drew from Suzanne dePasse's interview on *The Pat Sajak Show* on 19 May 1989.

I was fortunate enough to have attended The Jackson 5's first appearance as a Motown attraction at the Philadelphia Convention Center in April 1970. I was not, however, at the airport when they arrived. (That's where even I, a die-hard Motown fan, drew the line.)

I utilized Motown's press release accounts of that day in this chapter.

The information about Gordy and the Osmonds was culled from a conversation with Nancy Leiviska. I also drew from an interview I conducted with Clifton Davis in 1978.

I utilized features on The Jackson 5 in *Right On!*, *Creem*, *Ingenue*, *Time* and *Sepia* magazines (see bibliography).

I viewed a videotape of the television specials *Diana* (18 April 1971) and *Goin' Back to Indiana* (19 September 1971).

In the matter of the property at 4641 Hayvenhurst Avenue, Encino, currently owned by Michael Jackson and LaToya Jackson, I relied on an extensive Property Profile supplied by Fidelity National Title Insurance Company. This profile includes an in-depth and legal description of the property. The profile also contains the original Grant Deed signed by Earle and Elouise Hagen, filed in Los Angeles County, which released the property to Joseph and Katherine Jackson on 25 February 1971; the Deed of Trust from Great Western Savings and Loan Associates, dated 27 April 1971, with details of how Mr and Mrs Jackson arranged to purchase the property with Berry Gordy's assistance; and the Quitclaim Deed signed by Katherine Jackson on 24 June 1987, and filed in Los Angeles County, in which she released her share of equity in the property to her daughter LaToya Jackson.

I also used as source material a Property Profile supplied by World Title Company in which property, sales and tax information were examined.

I interviewed Lionel Richie for a *Soul* cover story on The Commodores in 1981 and drew from that interview.

I drew from the interview I conducted with Tito Jackson, Marlon Jackson and Jackie Jackson in 1978.

The incident between Rhonda Phillips and Jackie Jackson was recreated based on personal interviews with Ms Phillips on 8 March 1990 and 15 March 1990.

Among other sources I consulted were back issues of *Soul* magazine. I also drew from my interviews with Ken Kingsley (14 April 1990), Stewart Drew (3 May 1990), Mark Butler (12 June 1990), Gil Askey (5 March 1984) and Walter Jackson (5 December 1989).

I relied on press reports and eyewitness accounts regarding The Jackson 5's various tours overseas.

I depended on press reports – including those found in *Soul*, the

Los Angeles Times and *Ebony* – as well as eyewitness accounts to write about Jermaine Jackson's wedding to Hazel Gordy. I also reviewed press releases from Motown Records.

I drew from my interviews with Walter Burrell (6 March 1989), Steven Sprocket (24 June 1990), Harry Langdon (16 March 1984), Joyce Jillson (20 February 1990), Hal Davis (5 March 1985) and Susie Jackson. I also drew from an interview I conducted with Marvin Gaye in 1982. Steve Manning's comment about Hazel Gordy was published in *Ebony*.

I obtained background information on The Jackson 5's trip to Africa from press reports. Also, I drew from Cathy Griffin's conversations with Richard Arons. The comments by members of The Jackson 5 about Africa were published in *Soul* magazine.

I viewed a videotape of the *Cher* show on which The Jackson 5 appeared and interviewed one of Cher's assistants for a biography of Cher (St Martin's Press, 1987); the assistant requested anonymity at that time.

Katherine Jackson v. Joseph Jackson (I)

Details of the divorce action brought by Katherine Jackson against Joseph Jackson were culled from the following documents filed in Los Angeles Superior Court, Los Angeles County, all case number 42680:

Petition for Dissolution of Marriage, 9 March 1973.
Certificate of Assignment of Transfer, 10 March 1973.
Financial Declaration, 11 March 1973.
Katherine Jackson's Sworn Declaration, 16 March 1973.

The Final Years at Motown

The background on Sammy Davis, Jr., was culled from information contained in his excellent second autobiography, *The Sammy Davis, Jr., Story – Why Me?* I also drew from my 1978 interview with Michael Jackson and my 1980 interview with Jermaine Jackson. Some of Janet Jackson's comments were published in *Interview*. I also culled information from Vince Aletti's features on The Jackson 5 in the *Village Voice* (see bibliography). Also, I viewed a videotape of The Jackson 5's entire Las Vegas act.

I viewed a videotape of The Jackson 5's performance on *The Bob Hope Show*.

I interviewed Raymond St Jacques in March 1987 and culled comments about *Isomand and Cross* and his relationship with the Jacksons from that interview.

I also interviewed friends of the Jackson family who requested anonymity.

Enid Jackson's memories of her first encounters with Jackie Jackson were culled from interviews conducted with the late Mrs Jackson for this book on 29 October 1990, 7 November 1990 and 19 November 1990. Jackie Jackson's comments about his wedding were meant to be published in *Soul* magazine on 6 December 1974, but most were not. I obtained a transcript of the interview.

Information regarding Jackie Jackson's automobile accident was culled from a report in *Soul* magazine.

Theresa Gonsalves was interviewed on 5 January 1991.

Details of Michael Jackson's meeting with Berry Gordy on 14 May 1975 were culled from the Sworn Declaration of Michael Jackson, 20 February 1976. (The declaration became part of case number C139795: *Michael Jackson et al. v. Motown Record Corporation of California et al.*, 30 March 1976.) I also referred to Michael's account of his meeting with Gordy in his autobiography, *Moonwalk*.

I drew from my interviews with Gil Askey (5 March 1984) for my first book, *Diana*.

I obtained a copy of the Jacksons' original CBS recording contract.

The confrontation between Jermaine and Joseph Jackson was recreated based on my interview with Jermaine Jackson in 1980.

I referred to an interview with Jermaine and Hazel Jackson in *Ebony*. I also referred to Katherine Jackson's autobiography, *The Jacksons – My Family*. I also used as source material reports from *The Hollywood Reporter* and *Variety* (see bibliography).

I referred to my interview with Marlon Jackson in 1978 to recreate the scene at Westbury Music Fair when Jermaine walked out on the group. I was present backstage after the show.

Also I obtained a copy of Berry Gordy's application, dated 30 March 1972, to register The Jackson 5's name as being owned by Motown Records. I obtained a copy of the United States Patent

Office's acceptance of Gordy's request, and documentation that Gordy owned the name exclusively. I obtained the Forms of Patent from the United States Patent Office, numbers 965,808 and 965,809, registering in the name of Motown Record Corporation the logo Jackson 5ive and the name Jackson 5, 'For entertainment services rendered by a vocal group, in class 107, Int. Cl. 41.'

I drew from an interview I conducted with Melvin Franklin in 1977 for *The Black American*.

Again, I referred to the Sworn Declaration of Joseph W. Jackson, 20 February 1976.

I obtained a transcript of the Jacksons' press conference at the Rainbow Grill in Manhattan on 30 June 1975. I also obtained a copy of the 1 July 1975 telegram from Michael Roshkind to Arthur Taylor, president of CBS, informing him that The Jackson 5's name belonged solely to Motown Records. I also interviewed witnesses to the press conference. Vital to my research were Motown memoranda from Tony Jones to Joseph Jackson regarding The Jackson 5's activities at Motown.

I also interviewed Martha Gonsalves (3 June 1990), Edward Lewis (16 July 1990), Michael Lewis (16 September 1990), Susan Myerson (1 October 1990), Harry Weber (5 October 1990), Mark Kelly (15 November 1990) and Lee Casto (2 December 1990). Joyce McCrae was interviewed by Cathy Griffin on 14 October 1990.

The matter of the late Enid Jackson's filing for divorce from Jackie Jackson is documented in papers originally filed in September 1975 in Los Angeles Superior Court, County of Los Angeles, but also included in the 1985 divorce case, file number DI57554.

I obtained a copy of Marlon and Carol Jackson's wedding certificate, dated 16 August 1975. Joseph Jackson's comments about his son's wedding were originally published in *Soul*, January 1976.

The Sworn Deposition by Michael Jackson, dated 15 January 1976, was utilized.

I used as source material an interview with Jermaine Jackson by Cynthia Kirk in *Good Evening*, 29 April 1976.

I viewed videotapes of all episodes of the Jacksons' television series for CBS-TV.

Details of the lawsuit brought by Motown Record Corporation against the Jacksons were culled from the following documents filed in Los Angeles Superior Court, Los Angeles County, all case number C139795:

Michael Jackson et al. v. Motown Record Corporation of California et al., 30 March 1976.

Tariano Jackson, Sigmund Esco Jackson, Marlon Jackson and Michael Jackson, a minor, by Joseph Jackson, his Guardian v. Motown Record Corporation of California, Inc., 11 February 1977.

Ralph Seltzer's Sworn Deposition, 24 March 1976. In this fifty-page deposition, Seltzer recalled Joseph Jackson's original negotiations with Motown regarding his sons' recording contracts. Of Joseph Jackson and the Jacksons, he remembered, 'I do not recall that any of them read the contract prior to signing it.'

Supplemental Declaration of Joseph W. Jackson, 30 March 1976. In this lengthy document, Jackson gave his version of the day he and his boys signed their Motown contracts and described how he felt about Ralph Seltzer and Berry Gordy. He also recreated the telephone conversation with Gordy in which he thought he had successfully renegotiated the contract's original terms.

Sworn Declaration of Joseph W. Jackson, 20 February 1976. Jackson's declaration shed more light on his dealings with Motown, the 'take-it-or-leave-it contracts they made us sign,' the accommodations Motown arranged for them when the group moved from Gary to Los Angeles, how 'neither I or my sons ever read any contracts we signed once we got to Los Angeles,' and his relationship with Johnny Jackson. Most importantly, he reconstructed angry conversations he had with Jermaine regarding Jermaine's decision not to sign with CBS Records. Joseph Jackson's memory of these conversations corroborated Jermaine's in an interview with me on 27 May 1980.

Sworn Declaration of Richard Arons, 20 June 1979. As Joseph Jackson's attorney, Arons was privy to all of Jackson's business dealings, and he described, in this fifteen-page document, how Joseph went about searching for a new label for his sons and how his sons reacted to leaving Motown.

I also reviewed 367 other legal documents and correspondence relating to this case, from which I gleaned details applicable to this book.

Flashback to Early Days on the Road

Tito, Marlon and Jackie Jackson have discussed their father's behaviour in the early days while on the road in a number of interviews. We discussed it in our interview in 1978. Michael wrote about these experiences – though not in a very in-depth manner – in *Moonwalk*. For evaluation purposes, I drew from my interview with Beverly Hills psychiatrist Dr Carole Lieberman on 8 January 1991. Also interviewed: Yolanda Lewis (5 June 1990), James McField (30 October 1990), Gregory Matthias (15 November 1990), Gregorio Joves (1 December 1990), Sarah Jackson (2 May 1990) and Tim Whitehead (18 November 1990). I also drew from interviews with Theresa Gonsalves, Tim Burton and Sylvester Goodnough.

Tatum O'Neal declined to be interviewed for this book. Biographical information about her and her family was culled from accounts published in *Good Housekeeping*, *Ladies' Home Journal* and *Redbook*. The information about Michael and Tatum at the Playboy mansion was culled from an interview with Michael Jackson in *Soul* magazine.

The rumours about Michael Jackson and Clifton Davis were published in many publications. Michael discussed the matter with reporter Steve Ivory for *Soul* (issue of 12 September 1977). I interviewed Clifton Davis in 1978.

Michael and I also discussed rumours of his homosexuality in 1978. His comments about that subject are interspersed through this book.

The Wiz *and* Off the Wall *Years*

I interviewed Rob Cohen, producer of *The Wiz*, on 14 February 1989 and again on 25 April 1989. I also interviewed the film's director, Sidney Lumet, on 22 August 1978.

Other information was drawn from interviews with James McField, Susie Jackson and Theresa Gonsalves. Having written about *The Wiz* in depth in my 1989 book, *Call Her Miss Ross*, I utilized research conducted for that work in this chapter. I attended the press conference for *The Wiz* at Astoria Studios in September 1977, interviewed Michael at that time and drew from an interview I conducted with Diana Ross on 19 October 1981.

I drew from an interview with the Jacksons at their home in Encino in August 1978 and another interview with Michael Jackson in July 1979.

I also culled material from early published accounts of Michael's relationship with Quincy Jones. I interviewed Quincy Jones during a break in the recording of a Brothers Johnson album in 1979, and some of the material regarding *Off the Wall* is culled from that interview.

Cheryl Terrell, Joh'Vonnie Jackson, and Other Subject Matter

I obtained a copy of Joh'Vonnie Jackson's birth certificate, 30 August 1974.

I also obtained property information on Cheryl Terrell's Gardena, California, apartment building from World Title Company. Residents of the apartment house were interviewed on 25 August 1990. Cheryl Terrell spoke to my private investigator, Cathy Griffin, on 29 August 1990, but declined to be formally interviewed for this book.

I obtained the Escrow Instructions from Imperial Escrow Company for the property on 6908 Peach Avenue, Van Nuys, purchased by Joseph Jackson as trustee of the Joh'Vonnie Jackson Trust, 25 January 1981, as well as a Property Profile on 6908 Peach Avenue from World Title Company.

I obtained a copy of the Trust Corporation established for Joh'Vonnie Jackson on 23 February 1981.

I also procured a Property Profile supplied by Fidelity National Title. The profile includes a copy of the Individual Quitclaim Deed signed by Katherine Jackson releasing any of her interest in the property to Joseph Jackson, and the Quitclaim Deed executed on 20 January 1980, and signed by Joseph Jackson, turning the same property over to the Joh'Vonnie Jackson Trust.

Joh'Vonnie Jackson posed for our photographer; the photo appears in this book.

I drew from my and Cathy Griffin's interviews with Marcus

Phillips (3 June 1990), Tim Whitehead and Stanley Ross (1 November 1990) and Jerome Howard.

Paula Reuben interviewed Carol L. Kerster in June 1990.

I also drew from Charles Sanders's story of Jermaine and Hazel Jackson in *Ebony* in August 1981.

Gina Sprague v. Joseph and Katherine Jackson, Randy Jackson and Janet Jackson

Gina Sprague was interviewed for this book on 16, 18 and 21 September 1990.

Susie Jackson was interviewed on 21 September 1990.

I obtained a copy of the police report (DR number 80-749111) filed by Gina Sprague on 16 October 1980.

Other details of Gina Sprague's lawsuit against Joseph Jackson, Katherine Jackson, Randy Jackson and Janet Jackson, a minor, were culled from the following documents filed in Los Angeles Superior Court, Los Angeles County, all file number C383387:

Complaint for Personal Injuries, Assault and Battery, Conspiracy, 21 September 1981.

Sworn Declaration of Gina Sprague, 20 September 1981.

Sworn Declaration of Gina Sprague, 21 September 1981.

Sworn Declaration of Joseph Jackson and Katherine Jackson, 22 September 1981.

Answer to Complaint for Personal Injuries, Assault and Battery, Conspiracy, 5 March 1982.

Notice of Motion for Order Granting Leave to Amend Complaint, 16 November 1982.

Sworn Declaration of Michael S. Fields. Fields was Gina Sprague's attorney.

Amended Complaint, 11 January 1983. This ten-page complaint graphically depicted details of what Sprague alleged happened the day she was attacked.

Fifty-two other court documents relating to the *Sprague v. Jackson* case were also used as source material.

I also obtained legal documents filed by Joyce McCrae, an employee of Joseph Jackson's, on 16 June 1981: Complaint for Declaratory Relief, Partition, Money Due on Demand to Establish

Deed Absolute as Mortgage and Judicial Foreclosure, and *Joseph W. Jackson v. Joyce McCrae*, 16 June 1981, case number C371220. Both were filed in Los Angeles Superior Court, Los Angeles County. Though I decided not to write about this particular suit – which involved a condominium jointly owned by Jackson and McCrae – I utilized the documents to learn more of Jackson's relationship with McCrae and Gina Sprague. In this lawsuit, McCrae claimed, 'I was asked to testify at a hearing held at the Los Angeles City Attorney's office regarding assault charges filed against Joseph Jackson's wife by Ms Gina Sprague. When I informed Joseph Jackson that I had been asked to testify, Joseph Jackson told me that he wanted me to stay out of the matter. I did testify at the hearing on 17 December 1980. I am now informed and believe and allege that my employment was wrongfully terminated by Joseph Jackson in retaliation for the testimony I gave at that hearing regarding his relationship with Gina Sprague . . .'

The Early Eighties

I obtained the Grant Deed filed in Los Angeles County on 20 February 1981, in which Thomas Laughridge and Billie Laughridge granted to Michael Jackson unit nine at 5420 Lindley Avenue, Encino.

I also obtained the Individual Quitclaim Deed filed in Los Angeles County on 26 May 1981, by Michael Jackson, granting 25 per cent of the property to his mother, Katherine Jackson.

I referred to Robert Hilburn's *Los Angeles Times* feature, 'The Jacksons – Hail and Farewell', 13 September 1981.

I also referred to the *Billboard* magazine special on Michael Jackson (21 July 1984) and Steven Demorest's article on Michael Jackson in *Melody Maker* (see bibliography).

The interview I conducted with Michael Jackson through his sister Janet, took place on 3 October 1981, at the Jackson family's home in Encino.

Details of Katherine Jackson's second action to divorce Joseph Jackson were culled from the following documents filed in Los Angeles Superior Court, County of Los Angeles, all case number D076606:

Application for Order and Supporting Declaration of Katherine Jackson, 19 August 1972. This form appears to have been filled out by Mrs Jackson personally. She typed the information used in this book regarding her charge that Joseph Jackson spent 'in excess of $50,000' on 'a young woman' and that he had 'purchased for her parcels of real property from our community funds.'

Katherine Jackson's Request for Dissolution of Marriage, 12 November 1982.

Katherine Jackson's Sworn Declaration, 16 April 1983.

Joseph Jackson's Sworn Declaration, 18 April 1983.

Sworn Declaration of George M. Goffin in support of Motion to Compel Answers to Interrogatories, 8 April 1983. Goffin was one of Katherine Jackson's attorneys.

Notice to Produce Documents, 10 May 1983.

Sworn Declaration of Minda F. Barnes, 15 June 1983. Barnes was another of Mrs Jackson's attorneys. This document details Mrs Jackson's difficulty in obtaining financial information from Joseph Jackson.

A five-page letter from George M. Goffin, Esq., to Arnold Kassot, Esq., dated 20 April 1983, was particularly revealing; from it were culled details of the Jackson family's income and wealth.

A twenty-page declaration of George M. Goffin, 15 June 1983, was vital to the research of this book since it described the manner of the purchases of the Hayvenhurst property, the Peach Street property, the Jackson Street property and the Lindley Avenue property. It also explained Michael Jackson's financial participation in the purchase of Hayvenhurst and the Lindley Avenue condominium.

Exhibit B, Schedule of Community Property Assets, 15 June 1983, was also invaluable to the research of this book in that this exhibit contained a complete list of all of Joseph and Katherine

Jackson's financial assets and liabilities, as well as the dates of all of their acquisitions, and the costs of purchase of all of their properties and Michael Jackson's involvement in those purchases.

The Sworn Declaration of George M. Goffin in Support of Motion for Withdrawal as Attorney of Record, 1 November 1983, detailed Goffin's attempts to continue with the divorce action in the case of *Katherine Jackson v. Joseph Jackson* and Mrs Jackson's unavailability to him. It explained the possible reasons why she had changed her mind about the divorce.

Twenty other documents pertaining to this divorce action were also reviewed.

Some of the late Enid Jackson's comments were culled from an interview conducted with her on 7 November 1990.

Thriller and Victory Tour Years

I obtained a thirty-page Sworn Declaration by Michael Jackson in *Carlin Music Corporation v. Michael Jackson*, case number C347206, 28 February 1983. In it, Michael explained why he was angry not only with his father but also with Ron Weisner and Freddy DeMann. Jackson also explained his publishing goals, his future plans at CBS Records, and John Branca's new involvement in his career. The document is signed by Jackson in huge, scrawling letters.

Mickey Free was interviewed on 7 June 1989.

I also drew from Gerri Hirshey's features on Michael Jackson in *Rolling Stone* (see bibliography).

I referred to Alexander Lowen, *Narcissism: Denial of the True Self* (New York: Macmillan, 1981) and Alice Miller, *Prisoners of Childhood* (translated from German by Ruth Ward, New York: Basic Books, 1981).

I viewed many hours of Steve Howell's extensive video collection of Michael Jackson at home in Encino in order to be able to describe Hayvenhurst. Michael Jackson was upset with Steve Howell when Howell, a former employee, attempted to sell copies of these tapes to the television programme *A Current Affair*. Howell claimed that, as the cameraman, he owned the tapes. Jackson claimed that, as Howell's employer, he (Jackson) was the owner. *A Current Affair* aired some of the footage but decided against further broadcasts.

Steve Howell was interviewed for this book on 28 August, 4 September and 12 September 1990.

I wrote in detail about Suzanne dePasse's efforts to recruit talent for the *Motown 25* special in my book *Call Her Miss Ross*. I drew from some of that research. Michael Jackson also wrote about his meeting with Berry Gordy in his autobiography, *Moonwalk*. I also drew from interviews with James McField (30 October 1990) and Geron 'Casper' Canidate (29 October 1980), Jermaine Jackson (27 May 1980), Larry Anderson (23 October 1990), Joyce McCrae (15 October 1990), Carole Lieberman (8 January 1991) and Randall King (1 September 1989).

I also drew from published reports of the firing of Weisner-DeMann.

I referred to Dave Nussbaum's interview with Michael Jackson published in the *Globe*, 10 April 1984.

John Branca provided some background for the information on the Victory tour as he did for an article in *Rolling Stone* by Michael Goldberg, from which I also culled information. I attended the press conference at the Tavern on the Green on 30 November 1983.

Some of the information about Don King's background was culled from *1984 Current Biography Yearbook*.

Background on Jehovah's Witnesses came from Barbara Grizzuti Harrison's *Visions of Glory: A History and a Memory of Jehovah's Witnesses* (New York: Simon and Schuster, 1978). I also referred to comments by Michael Jackson in the 22 May 1984 issue of *Awake!*

Louise Gilmore was interviewed on 3 August 1990; Seth Riggs was interviewed by my researcher John Redman on 14 October 1990. I also drew from an interview I conducted with Joseph Layton on 23 December 1986, for my book *Carol Burnett – Laughing Till It Hurts* (William Morrow, 1988).

I also referred to Roger Enrico's *The Other Guy Blinked* (New York: Bantam, 1986).

The incident with Michael's glove was described by Bob Giraldi in *The Making of Thriller*. I interviewed witnesses to the accident on 27 January 1984, and referred to newspaper accounts. There were also a number of anonymous sources for information in these sections of the book.

I interviewed James DeBarge in July 1995, after the original edition of this book was published.

Details on Janet Jackson's marriage to James DeBarge and the eventual annulment of that union were culled from the following documents filed in Los Angeles Superior Court, Los Angeles County, all file number 05113:

Petition to Nullify Marriage, filed by Janet Dameta DeBarge, 30 January 1985.

Income and Expense Declaration of Janet Dameta DeBarge, 30 January 1985.

Request to Enter Default, 4 June 1985.

Summons served to James Curtis DeBarge, 10 April 1985.

Amended Petition for Dissolution of Marriage, filed by Janet Dameta DeBarge, 17 July 1985.

Notice of Entry of Judgment, 18 November 1985.

Notice of Annulment and Restoration of Wife's Former Name to Janet Dameta Jackson, 18 November 1985.

Also shedding light on Janet's marriage were details of the lawsuit that resulted from a traffic accident in which Janet and James DeBarge were involved while driving Katherine Jackson's Mercedes-Benz. The suit, brought by Manuel R. Mendez, Carmen Mendez and Barbara Beebe, a minor, against Katherine Jackson, James DeBarge and Janet Jackson, was recorded in the following documents filed in Los Angeles Superior Court, Los Angeles County, all case number C522917:

Complaint – Personal Injury, Property Damage, Wrongful Death, 15 November 1984.

Manuel R. Mendez, Carmen Mendez and Barbara Beebe, a minor, v. Katherine Jackson and Janet Jackson, 8 January 1985.

Manuel R. Mendez, Carmen Mendez and Barbara Beebe, a minor, v. Katherine Jackson, James DeBarge and Janet Jackson, 2 March 1988.

Declaration of Robert J. Davis, 30 January 1989. Davis was the Jackson's attorney. This document illustrated Davis's difficulty in obtaining payment for his work from Katherine Jackson and Janet Jackson, and also demonstrated the way the family tends to deal rather unfairly with attorneys representing them.

Interrogatories to Defendant, Janet Jackson, 28 February 1985.

Janet Jackson discussed her relationship with James DeBarge, her mother and other family members. It is fascinating that most of what Ms Jackson was compelled to reveal here had nothing at all to do with the minor accident in which she was involved.

Post-Victory Tour Years

Louis Farrakhan's comments about Michael Jackson were widely published on 12 April 1983.

The Denise Worrell *Time* magazine story was published on 19 March 1984. I also drew from my interviews with Michael's cousin, Tim Whitehead, and with Steve Howell. I also interviewed Kenneth Nagle (3 January 1989), Harry Weber (3 February 1990), Patty Kellar (15 March 1990), Ted Culver (3 April 1990), David Kelsey (5 May 1990) and Harold Long (19 May 1990). I drew from Cathy Griffin's interview with Joyce McCrae.

John Branca provided some background information on the ATV acquisition on 9 January 1991, just as he had done for Robert Hillburn's analysis of the acquisition in the *Los Angeles Times* on 22 September 1985, which I also utilized as secondary source material. I also drew from published interviews with Paul McCartney (see bibliography).

Bad Years to 1991

Frank Dileo met with my private investigator and researcher Cathy Griffin for three hours at the Sunset Marquis Hotel in Los Angeles on 11 October 1990. Some of the material in this book was culled from that conversation. A meeting was set up between Dileo and myself on 19 October 1990. However, just prior to that date, a *People* magazine article about Dileo was published in which he was critical of Michael Jackson. After receiving an intimidating telephone call from one of Jackson's representatives, Dileo decided not to meet with me.

I then interviewed Frank Dileo in August 1995, after the original edition of this book was published.

Byron Moore and Max Hart were interviewed on 30 August 1990. Mitchell Fink reported on Michael's viewing of *Purple Rain* in the *Los Angeles Herald Examiner* on 5 July 1984.

I utilized J. C. Stevenson's article on Janet Jackson in *Spin* and also referred to Cathy Griffin's interview with Joyce McCrae.

Most of my sources regarding Michael Jackson's publicity stunts – the sprained wrist during the filming of *Captain EO*, the hyperbaric chamber and the Elephant Man's bones – must remain confidential due to the nature of these sources' employment in the record industry. I did refer to 'Michael's Next Thrill: An Oxygen Chamber' in the *Los Angeles Herald Examiner* (17 September 1986), 'Michael Jackson's Bizarre Plan to Live to 150' in the *National Enquirer* (16 September 1986) and 'Michael Jackson Wants Merrick's Bones' by Patricia Freeman in the *Los Angeles Herald Examiner* (30 May 1987). I also referred to a story about Michael's hyperbaric chamber in *Time* (September 1986). Charles Montgomery, who wrote the hyperbaric chamber story, was interviewed in January 1991. Jack Richardson was interviewed on 23 October 1990. The joke about Michael's nose was published in *Playboy* in the December 1987 issue.

A note about 'We Are the World': by January 1991, more than sixty-one million dollars had been raised from the sales of this song to fight hunger in Ethiopia. In addition to record sales, funds also came from the marketing of 'We Are the World' T-shirts, posters, books and videos.

In other unrelated matters, I used as secondary material 'Buckle Debacle' by Bill Steigerwalk in the *Los Angeles Times* (8 November 1987). I also referred to my interview with Jerome Howard in discussing Katherine Jackson's interest in working for Michael Jackson.

In the matter of Michael Jackson's 1988 purchase of Sycamore Ranch, I had a number of anonymous sources, and I also relied on an extensive Property Profile supplied by Continental Lawyers Title Company on 27 September 1990, which includes an in-depth, legal description of the ranch. The profile also includes the Individual Grant Deed filed on 11 April 1988, in which John Branca and Marshall Gelfand, co-trustees under the Trust Agreement dated 11 April 1988, granted the property to Michael Jackson.

Also interviewed: Gary Berwin (16 November 1990), Steven Harris (17 November 1990), Phillip Meadows (22 November 1990), Bernard Pancheco (1 December 1990), Virginia August (3 December 1990), Glenn Bascome (6 December 1990), Patty Kellar (8 December

1990) and Douglas Wilson (10 December 1990). Frank Dileo discussed his feelings about being fired by Michael Jackson in numerous published interviews to promote the film *GoodFellas*. I also referred to Dileo's television appearances to promote the film, including one on *Personalities* on 25 October 1990.

The story about Michael Jackson, the Blarney Stone and AIDS was published in the *Rolling Stone* issue of 6 October 1988.

LaToya Jackson's allegations that Michael had been molested as a child were reprinted in numerous publications and also broadcast on CNN in July 1988. She and I also discussed the matter in 1993, in Spain, after the original edition of this book was published.

In the matter of Lavon Muhammad, aka Billie Jean, I used as source material Muhammad's handwritten Petition for Dissolution of Marriage, 19 January 1988, and the case of *Michael Jackson v. Lavon Muhammad*, 1 February 1987, filed in Los Angeles Superior Court, Los Angeles County, case number 17925. Numerous employees were subpoenaed to testify to Muhammad's harassment of Michael Jackson.

I obtained a copy of Michael Jackson's current contracts with CBS Records. I also had a number of anonymous sources, many of whom are still working for Michael Jackson, who provided the bulk of the information in the last two chapters of the book.

Dr Robert Kotler was interviewed on 4 November 1990.

Donna Burton, Dr Steven Hoefflin's secretary, was contacted on 30 November 1990.

I also referred to the *Handbook of Nonprescription Drugs*, seventh edition, by the American Pharmaceutical Association.

I reviewed the transcript of the Jacksons' appearance on *Donahue*, 10 November 1989, and the transcript of LaToya Jackson's appearance on *Donahue*, 9 February 1989. I also reviewed the transcript of Katherine Jackson's appearance on *Sally Jessy Rafael*, 30 November 1990.

Janet Jackson is the first artist to have seven Top Five singles from one album, her *Janet Jackson's Rhythm Nation 1814*. She signed one of the largest recording contracts in history when she pacted with Virgin Records in March 1991 for an estimated thirty-two million dollars. Some observers feel that Michael may have delayed the finalization of his own 'billion-dollar' contract with CBS (now Sony) until Janet's deal was announced, giving her the chance to hold the record for biggest contract before stepping back in to reclaim it for himself.

Michael Jackson and the Koreans

Regarding the Korean/Moonies incident, I drew from personal interviews with Jerome Howard on 29 October 1990 and Kenneth Choi on 11 January 1990.

I also used as source material the following documents filed in the United States District Court for the Central District of California, all case number CV 90 4906 KN:

Segye Times, Inc., v. Joseph Jackson, Katherine Jackson, Jackson Records Company, Inc., Jackson Family Concerts International, Jerome Howard, Kyu-Sun Choi, Mi Rae Choi, Michael Jackson, Jermaine Jackson, Bill Bray, Ben Brown d/b/a Jackson Marketing & Distributing Company and Does 1 to 100, 17 October 1990.

Bill Bray v. Kenneth Choi, 17 October 1990.

Michael Jackson v. Segye Times, Inc., 17 October 1990.

Sworn Declaration of Michael Jackson, 17 October 1990.

Michael Jackson v. Kenneth Choi, 17 October 1990.

Sworn Declaration of Bill Bray, 17 October 1990.

Answer of Defendant Michael Jackson to First Amended Complaint, 17 October 1990.

Answer of Defendant Bill Bray to First Amended Complaint, 17 October 1990.

Katherine Jackson v. LaToya Jackson Gordon and Jack Gordon

Details of the lawsuit brought by Katherine Jackson against LaToya Jackson were culled from the following documents filed in Los Angeles Superior Court, Los Angeles County, case number NWC55803:

Katherine Jackson v. Jack Gordon; LaToya Jackson aka LaToya Gordon, February 28, 1990.

Notice of Pendency of Action, *Katherine Jackson v. Jack Gordon; LaToya Jackson a/k/a LaToya Gordon*, 2 March 1990.

I interviewed Michael in August 1994, regarding Jordie and Evan Chandler's allegations. Most of the material from that interview was deemed too sensitive at the time and, therefore, went unpublished until now, with the publication of this revised edition of *Michael Jackson: The Magic and the Madness*. Some of it, however, appeared in the following articles I wrote, from which I also drew for the new edition of this book: 'Michael Jackson: "I'd Never Hurt a Child" – World Exclusive: First Interview Since Explosive Charges' by J. Randy Taraborrelli (Michael's Noted Biographer), *Star*, 6 September 1994; 'Save Me, Elizabeth. Save my Life! – World Exclusive' by J. Randy Taraborrelli, *Star*, 13 September 1994; 'Shocking Truth About Michael Jackson Strip-Search Photos – What they Show – World Exclusive' by J. Randy Taraborrelli, *Star*, 20 September 1994.

I attended at least a dozen press conferences relating to the allegations and took advantage of the many opportunities I had to question attorneys Bert Fields and Howard Weitzman and investigator Anthony Pellicano to clear confusing matters in my mind, and then reported my findings on American television broadcasts relating to the case. (Note that the secretly tape-recorded conversations between Evan Chandler and Dave Schwartz were played by Anthony Pellicano during two such press conferences, on 30 August and 1 September 1993. The tapes were also broadcast on the television programme *American Justice*, 21 September 1994.)

Most of my other sources for information regarding the sensitive issue of Jordie Chandler must remain confidential.

In a perfect world, there would be no reason for confidentiality: everyone would be able to speak his mind without fear of repercussions. However, many of those interviewed are high-profile people who still work in the entertainment industry today. Others work in the Los Angeles Department of Children's Services, the Sheriff's Department of Santa Barbara, California, and the Child Abuse Unit of the Los Angeles Police Department. It is not fair to expect these sources to risk their careers and the trust of their clients (if they are in the representation field) so that they can assist me in my work with a book. Other than to set the record straight, these individuals have nothing to gain from offering valuable insight and, in some cases, everything to lose.

The same is true of reporters who work for Associated Press and other news agencies that utilize confidential sources, I make every effort to check the legitimacy and accuracy of any source who requests anonymity. If I do not trust a source, no information from that person is utilized – whether the person requested anonymity or not. Also, I always have more than one source for any information that might be considered controversial.

Whether to use significant information given under a condition of anonymity is always a difficult decision for a writer. However, I feel a strong obligation to my readers to present the facts as best I can, just as I feel an obligation to my sources to protect them should they feel protection is necessary.

From the text, the reader should be able to glean that I have interviewed most of the principals involved in the Jordie Chandler matter over the years, even though they wish not to be acknowledged here.

I also drew from lengthy conversations with Larry Feldman, Michael Freeman, Anthony Pellicano, Diane Dimond, Vinnie Zuffante, Mark Quindoy, Jack Gordon, LaToya Jackson, Ernie Rizzo, Lauren Weis, Gary Spiegel, Robert Wegner, Charles T. Matthews, Tom Sneddon, Harry Benson, Russell Turiak and Susan Crimp.

I also referred to voluminous court records and documents, including complaints, motions and depositions pertaining to '*Jordan Chandler v. Michael Jackson*' Case Number SC026226.

Moreover, I referred to all of the documents pertaining to *Chandler v. Jackson* (ABC and Diane Sawyer and Lisa Marie Presley), Court Case Number SM097360. This was the case filed by Evan Chandler after Michael and Lisa appeared in a television broadcast with Diane Sawyer and proclaimed his innocence.

I also referenced: *Rothman v. Jackson* (Weitzman, Fields, Pellicano), Case Number SC32081; *Morris Williams, Leroy A. Thomas, Donald Starks, Fred Hammond and Aaron White v. Michael Jackson*, Case Number BC093593; *Michael J. Jackson v. Diane Dimond, Stephen Doran, K-ABC Radio and Paramount Pictures Corp.*, Case Number BC 119773 (as well as 'Michael Jackson's Statement Re Lies and Falsehoods' from Howard Weitzman, Esq., 11 January 1995.

I drew from my interviews with Lisa Marie Presley, which first appeared in 'Suspicious Minds – The Troubled Life and Times of a rock 'n' roll Heiress', by J. Randy Taraborrelli, Sunday Magazine (*The Times*), 14 April 1996.

In 1997, as a consequence of the strong reaction to the Sunday Magazine feature, I began researching and writing a book about Lisa Marie Presley, which was to be called *Elvis, Priscilla, Michael and Me*. However, I abandoned plans for the book when my career went into a different direction (with my biography of Frank Sinatra). I conducted a great deal of research for the Lisa Marie biography, some of which appeared in articles I wrote, such as: 'Lisa Marie Presley – *Seule, toujours seule*' by J. Randy Taraborrelli, *Paris Match*, June 1996; 'Lisa Marie, Michael and Debbie' by J. Randy Taraborrelli, *Star*, 25 February 1997; 'Michael and Lisa Marie' by J. Randy Taraborrelli, *Star*, 4 March 1997; 'Millionaire Lisa Marie Presley' by J. Randy Taraborrelli, *Star*, 11 March 1997.

Of course, I also drew from my own interviews with Michael, and stories based on those interviews, such as: 'Michael Insists: 'This Marriage is no Joke'' by J. Randy Taraborrelli, *Star*, 27 September 1994; 'Jackson Insists Kiss was a Thriller' *USA Today*, 13 September 1994; 'Jacko Finally Breaks His Silence' by J. Randy Taraborrelli, *Woman's Day*, September 1995.

On 18 January 1996, I appeared on CNN to announce that Lisa Marie Presley had filed for divorce from Michael Jackson. For that broadcast, I conducted my own, independent research, from which I also relied for this updated book.

I also drew on my article, 'Princess Heartbreak' by J. Randy Taraborrelli, *New Idea*, 28 January 2002.

I also referred to my research for the following articles: 'The Secret Power of Liz Taylor' by J. Randy Taraborrelli, *Woman's Day*, 11 December 2000; 'Taraborrelli Defends Jackson (and Himself!)' by Michelle Cushing, 'King of Pop', the *Official Magazine of MJ News International*, Issue Number 6, 1996; 'Jackson scandal will be History', *New York Post*, 22 June 1994; 'Michael Promises No More Plastic Surgery' by J. Randy Taraborrelli, *Woman's Day*, 25 December 2000; 'Diana Ross and Michael Jackson' by J. Randy Taraborrelli, *Woman's Day*, December 2000.

Regarding Michael's hospital stay in 1995, I reported the story for CNN on 6 December, and did my own independent research for it at that time.

Thanks to Donald Trump, Hugo Alvarez-Perez, Marcel Marceau, Brett Livingston-Stone, Monica Pastelle and Otis Williams of The Temptations.

Of course, I was the reporter at the Polo Lounge in Beverly Hills to whom Elizabeth Taylor said, 'I am not in the business of clarifying rumours,' and then issued the somewhat startling order, 'Now, be gone!'

I also referred to reams of press coverage and TV interviews given by Lisa Marie Presley to publicize her Capitol Records 2003 release, *To Whom it May Concern*, including 'Q and A with Lisa Marie Presley' by Rob Tannenbaum, for *Playboy*, May 2003.

I also referred to the court records relating to Lisa Marie Presley's petition to dissolve her marriage to Michael Jackson (Case Number BD22906).

Michael and Debbie Rowe up to Present Day

For most of these chapters, I drew from my own television reporting on Michael Jackson in the United States and Europe. It would be too lengthy a list for me to detail all of the television programmes I have appeared on having to do with Michael, Lisa Marie Presley and Debbie Rowe since the publication of the first edition of this book; I have made literally hundreds of appearances on shows such as *Today*, *Good Morning America*, *CBS This Morning*, *Prime Time – Live*, *Dateline*, *The Larry King Show*, *CNN Headline News*, and many others, expressing my views about Michael based on my own independent research.

Some of my most recent television appearances relating to Michael Jackson had to do with analyzing his interview with Martin Bashir, on programmes such as: 'Michael Jackson – UnMasked', *Dateline*, NBC, 17 February 2003; 'Michael Jackson,' *Prime Time*, 6 February 2003; *The Many Faces of Michael Jackson – Prime Time Special Edition*, ABC, 17 February 2003; *CBS-This Morning*, 18 February 2003. I also reported on Michael for *Michael Jackson: The E! True Hollywood Story*, June 2003.

I was also a contributor to the highly rated documentary *Michael Jackson's Face*, on Channel 5 in the United Kingdom, the highest-rated original programme ever broadcast on the channel.

I also drew from my research for 'The Secret Michael Jackson'" (three-part series,) by J. Randy Taraborrelli, *Daily Mail*, September 1998.

Thanks also to Gordon Rowe, Steve Shmerier, Marsha Devlin, Tanya Boyd, Mavis McDermott, Mario Pikus and Theodore Miller for their assistance in understanding Michael's marriage to Debbie Rowe.

Library Research

The following institutions were extremely helpful to my research:

American Film Institute Library; Associated Press Office (New York); The Bancroft Library (University of California, Berkeley); The Brand Library Art and Music Center; British Film Institute Library Archives; Born Free Foundation; Boston Herald Archives; The Beverly Hills Library; British Broadcasting Corporation; University of California, Los Angeles; California State Archives (Sacramento); Corbis-Gamma/Liaison; The Glendale Central Public Library; Hayden Library; The Hartford Public Library; The Hollywood Library; The Houghton Library (Harvard University); Hulton Picture Library; Lincoln Center Library of the Performing Arts; Kobal Collection; The Los Angeles Public Library; the *Los Angeles Times*; The Margaret Herrick Library (Academy of Motion Pictures Arts and Sciences); the *Michigan Chronicle*; Museum of Modern Art (The Film Study Center); Museum of the Film; National Archives and the Library of Congress; The Neal Peters Collection; New York City Municipal Archives; New York Public Library; *New York Daily News*; *New York Post*; *New York Times*; Occidental College, (Eagle Rock, California), Philadelphia Free Library (Theater Collection); Philadelphia Public Library; Philadelphia Historical Society; the *Philadelphia Inquirer* and the *Philadelphia Daily News*; Photofest; Princeton University (The William Seymour Theater Collection).

Bibliography

One book I so value and which I would like to single out as wonderful is *Michael Jackson: A Visual Documentary* by Adrian Grant from Omnibus Press, London. It was first published in 1994, and then updated a number of times. If the reader wants to know more about Michael, go to an edition of this terrific book.

For this updated edition of *Michael Jackson – The Magic and the Madness*, I referred to many hundreds of articles having to do with the Michael Jackson molestation investigation and his marriages to Lisa Marie Presley and Debbie Rowe. Space simply does not allow the publication of the lengthy list of these features. One, in particular, that I think deserves special mention is: 'Did Michael Do It?' by Mary Fischer for *GQ*, October 1994.

Also helpful were: 'Not Necessarily the News' by Tom Rosenthal, *Esquire*, January 1995; 'Nightmare at Neverland' by Maureen Orth, January 1994 and 'Prime Time Lies' by Maureen Orth, *Vanity Fair*, September 1995; 'Jackson Files Slander Suits' by Adam Sandler, *Daily Variety*, 13 January 1995; 'Jackson Pays; Case Closed' by Jeffrey Jolson-Colburn, *Hollywood Reporter*, 25 January 1994; 'Priscilla Presley — My Daughter, Myself' by Jim Jerome, *Ladies Home Journal*, August 1996; 'Can He Put Himself Together, Again?' by Tom Maurstad, *Dallas Morning News*, 18 June 1995; 'Is This the End?' by Dana Kennedy, *Entertainment Weekly*, 10 September 1993; 'Michael's World' by Cathleen McGuigan, *Newsweek*, 6 September 1993; 'Who's Bad?' by Richard Corliss, 'Time to Face the Music' by Dana Kennedy, *Entertainment Weekly*, 17 December 1993; 'Inside Michael's World' by Joey Bartolomeo and Jennifer Tung, *US Weekly*, 24 February 2003; 'Michael Jackson –

The Man in the Mirror' by Mary Murphy and Jennifer Graham, *TV Guide*, 10–16 November 2001; 'What Friends Are For' by Karen Schneider, *People*, 2 December 1996; 'Michael Jackson – Losing his Grip' by Maureen Orth, *Vanity Fair*, April 2003; 'Michael Tells Where I Met Lisa Marie and How I Proposed' by Robert E. Johnson, *Ebony*, October 1994; 'Neverland Meets Graceland' by Tom Gliatto, *People*, 1994; 'The King as Pop' by David Friend, *Life*, December 1997; 'A Frank Talk with Priscilla Presley' by Vernon Scott, November 1994; 'Wanna Be Stopping Something' by Tom Sinclair, *Entertainment Weekly*, 21 September 2001.

I also reviewed the PBS *Frontline* documentary, 'Tabloid Truth: the Michael Jackson Scandal', which was broadcast on 15 February 1994, as well as the transcript of CNN's *Larry King Live* discussion of Michael Jackson on 21 February 2003.

Index

J. RANDY TARABORRELLI is the author of eleven books, including the bestsellers *Madonna: An Intimate Biography*, *Once Upon a Time: The Story of Princess Grace, Prince Rainier and their Family*, *Call Her Miss Ross*, *Sinatra: The Man and the Myth* and *Jackie, Ethel, Joan – Women of Camelot*. J. Randy Taraborrelli lives in Los Angeles.